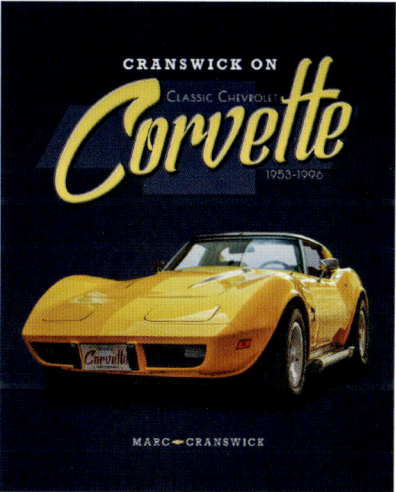

CRANSWICK ON

CLASSIC CHEVROLET

Corvette

1953-1996

MARC CRANSWICK

More by Marc Cranswick:

BMW Classic 5 Series – 1972 to 2003

Cranswick on Camaro – 1967-81

Cranswick on Ford Maverick and Mercury Comet 1970-77

Cranswick on Porsche – A modern interpretation of the Porsche story

Ford Midsize Muscle – Fairlane, Torino & Ranchero

Ford Mustang II & Pinto – 1970 to 1980

The Legend of American Motors – The full history of America's most innovative automaker

Mazda Rotary-engined Cars – From Cosmo 110S to RX-8

MOPAR Muscle - Barracuda, Dart & Valiant 1960-1980

Pontiac Firebird – The Auto-Biography (New 4th Edition)

Volkswagen Type 4: 411 and 412 – The final rear-engined VW cars

www.veloce.co.uk

First published in 2025 by Veloce, an imprint of David and Charles Limited.
Tel +44 (0)1305 260068 / e-mail info@veloce.co.uk / web www.veloce.co.uk.

ISBN: 9781787119086

CRANSWICK ON

Classic Chevrolet

Corvette

1953-1996

MARC CRANSWICK

Contents

Introduction

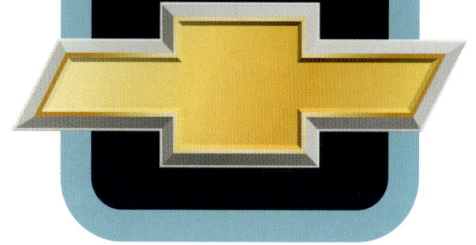

Corvette ⟿ The Talk of The Town

"THE MOST WIDELY discussed car in recent automotive history." That was the caption to the accompanying Chevrolet PR photo of the all new 1953 Corvette, seen here at the golf club.

And the talk of the town it was. You see, Chevrolet publicity had pulled out all the stops. This included arranging for gentleman racer Briggs Cunningham and movie star John 'The Duke' Wayne to be initial owners of the car that would soon be colloquially known as 'The Plastic Fantastic'. Why was Chevrolet, number one

automaker on the planet, dabbling in the mere trifle that was the North American sports car market? GM's styling supremo Harley Earl liked sports cars, so did enthusiasts within GM. So, they gave it the ol' college try.

Earl and Co's plan was an ambitious one: 10,000 sales per annum. That was equal to the entire US sports car market, dominated by the likes of MG and Jaguar. The initial Corvette seemed akin to an American Jag XK120, made softer for mainstream tastes and reliant on existing Chevrolet family car hardware to save costs. No surprises there. What was unexpected, though, was Ford's Thunderbird

V8 two-seater. That gave Harley Earl, Chevrolet's Ed Cole, and soon-to-arrive Zora Arkus-Duntov, the GM brass, mandate to put some fire in the Corvette's belly and make said sports car a serious contender.

Earl, Cole and Duntov's efforts were apparent in 1956, profitable from 1958, and, for what has come to be known as America's only sports car, as the expression goes, the rest is history. Born in the 'Win on Sunday, sell on Monday era', the Corvette's speedy ascension was bolstered by great success in production sports car racing, under the careful guidance of the aforementioned Zora Arkus-Duntov. The Jaguar XK120 and Mercedes Gullwing 300SL were quickly dispatched in this pre AC Cobra time. It left the Corvette with an assured reputation that would be built upon in the decades to come. Such exploits even reached the dragstrip and Le Mans.

The Straight Axle Corvette also arrived at a time when national automotive identities were clear, distinct and understood. However, Chevrolet's Corvette was outward looking from the start, and popularized import car features like 'four on the floor', four-wheel disk brakes, and even handbrakes. British styling inspiration soon gave way to the unique (aquatic) 1963-67 Bill Mitchell-penned 'Mid-Year' Corvettes. Then came a mix of deep sea creatures plus some Ferrari GTO with the Mako Shark II inspired 'Late Model' C3 Corvette, followed by the 1984 C4 Corvette, widely regarded as the best shape Pininfarina never did. All agreed that this downsized Corvette was a fine looking car.

In spite of its exalted position within the GM empire, and becoming a distinct entity and brand in the minds of many, the Plastic Fantastic had to contend with fuel crises, environmentalism, and related domestic legislation, such as the 1970 Muskie Smog Bill, the 1973/74 impact bumper law, 1978's CAFE, etc, like any other passenger car sold in North America. However, the Corvette's underlying honesty, and the efforts of Team Corvette, at first under Chief Engineer Zora Arkus-Duntov, then Dave McLellan, saw it rise to such challenges, and eventually reach new performance heights as the so called 'malaise era' faded away. Corvette ... the Plastic Fantastic ... long may it continue.

Marc Cranswick

Humble Origins – Corvette
1953-55

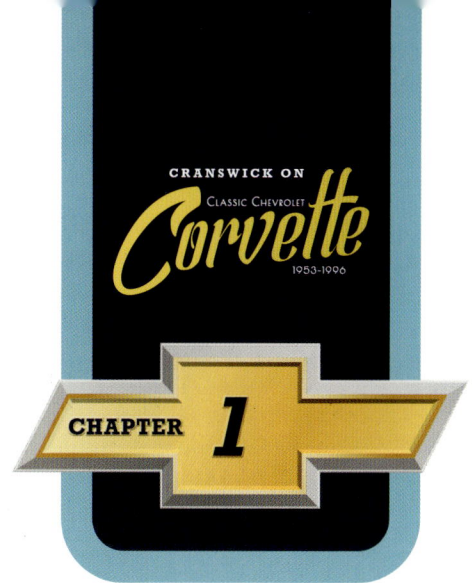

The road to Corvette

CHEVROLET: 'HEARTBEAT OF America'. So says the slogan. However, the 'American as mom's apple pie' brand has a foreign connection, as its name suggests. The company was co-founded by Louis Chevrolet in 1911. Born on Christmas Day in Switzerland, 1878, the son of a clock maker, Louis acquired his mechanical aptitude from his father, and then later, when the family moved to Burgundy, France, the 18-year-old Louis first connected with the automotive world through working at the Paris Mors car company. [1]

Louis also worked at DeDion-Bouton and Fiat while in Europe, before moving to Canada and, subsequently, New York. He made his mark in bicycle racing, and even became a Buick racing driver prior to meeting the founder of General Motors, William Crapo Durant, in 1908. The two men co-founded Chevrolet, with the firm's first automobile, in the form of the in-line six-powered Series C Classic Six, appearing in 1912. However, Louis Chevrolet and Durant's association wasn't a long one.

Louis had his eye on the high end of the market. Cars with a racing pedigree were in vogue at the time – think Stutz Bearcat, Mercer Raceabout and Simplex Speed Car. All were exclusive, expensive, and catered to the high level of interest in motor racing prevalent among well-heeled Americans. In contrast, William Durant felt Chevrolet should go low price and high volume, and it was this latter path that transpired.

The iconic Chevrolet Bow Tie badge was

the SIMPLEX "SPEED CAR"

The Simplex Speed Car (shown), Mercer Raceabout, and Stutz Bearcat all catered to well heeled Americans' interest in sports cars during the early 20th Century. (Courtesy Motor Trend)

introduced in 1913, coinciding with Durant buying out Louis' interest in what was a fast growing company. Indeed, the Chevrolet brand's success aided Durant in retaking control of GM. It was a concern he had once controlled, before getting the bum's rush from financiers in 1910. Upon his departure Louis Chevrolet was moved to say: "I sold you my car, and I sold you my name, but I am not going to sell myself to you." Well, Monsieur Chevrolet was always more at home on the racetrack than in the boardroom. [2]

None of this troubled Durant, however, as Chevrolet and GM went from strength to strength. Chevrolet exceeded one million annual sales for the first time in 1927, ousting Ford from the numero uno position in the US. Henry Ford thought the Model T was all the public would ever want or need. However, in capitalist USA one size didn't fit all, and Chevrolet showed that variety is the spice of life. The Bow Tie brand did this with an ever wider range of sedans, wagons, power top convertibles and trucks. Indeed, the first GM vehicle assembled outside the US was a Chevrolet truck built up from a CKD kit in Copenhagen in January, 1924.

The Roaring Twenties accommodated a boom in domestic sports car racing. Hidemi Aoki is dressed as a '20s flapper. *(Courtesy www.nepoeht.com)*

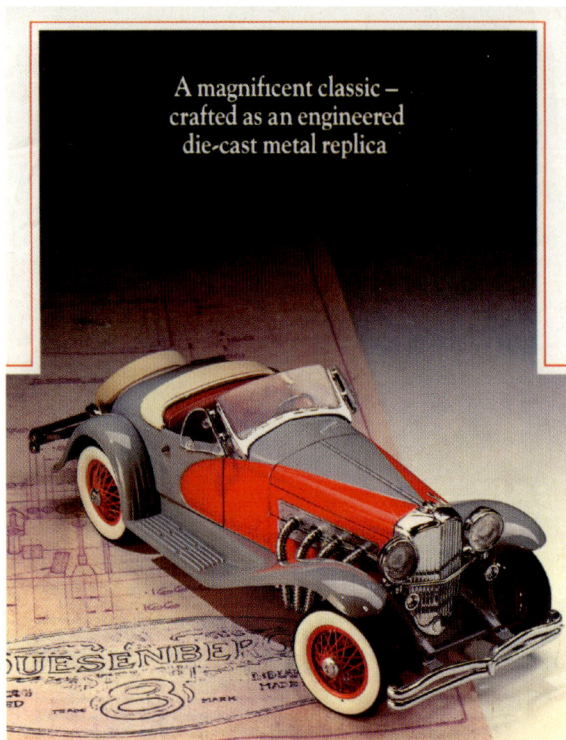

A magnificent classic – crafted as an engineered die-cast metal replica

American sporting machinery soon moved into luxurious ways, as evidenced by this 1930 Duesenberg SSJ. *(Courtesy The Franklin Mint)*

GM's reach quickly extended beyond North America, with the purchase of Adam Opel in 1929, and having Vauxhall and Holden as British and Australian subsidiaries respectively. However, the importance of the home market was always central.

In 1950 Chevrolet delivered a slushbox for the masses, in the form of the two-speed, torque converter-actuated Powerglide. By the close of the 1952 model year, 1.5 million Chevrolets with Powerglides had been purchased. [3]

Once Chevrolet wrestled the number one spot from Ford, most years saw a Chevrolet, Ford and Plymouth 1-2-3 sales ranking, though occasionally Ford outsold the Bow Tie boys. What's more, during the recessionary years, American Motors took third place in the sales race for 1960, 1961 and 1963. Then, when the high performance scene was

firing on all eight pots, Pontiac claimed third place in the sales race in 1969. However, for the most part it was the low-cost three that ruled the roost for the affordable, everyday family car that most buyers chose.

In the early '50s, Chevrolet was facing a sales hiccup, with Ford possessing 'The Right Size Car', and Walter P joining the fray. To cool the sales heat, GM turned to its famous Motorama car show (a vision of the future that raised interest in GM wares) specifically the January 26, 1953 Motorama, held at the Waldorf Astoria Hotel in New York City. [4]

What people saw were four show cars on a rotating stage, one of which was a sports car codenamed EX-122. The question was, what was GM doing by showing an intention to make sports cars? There was no cogent business reason for any member of the Big Three to do so. In 1952 over four million cars were sold in America, but

This 1937 supercharged Cord 812 was a victim of the '30s Great Depression. The Cord showcased unitary construction, a property planned for the 1958 Corvette. *(Courtesy Library of Congress)*

Postwar times saw the diminutive 1949 Crosley Hotshot flying the American sports car and economy car flags. The brand's four-wheel disk brakes set a domestic precedent for the 1965 Corvette. *(Courtesy National Corvette Museum)*

just 11,000 sports cars contributed to that total. [5] Indeed, it was a market where sports car success was measured by modest results. The Datsun Roadster was considered popular with just 60 sold in 1952! The $2950 Sunbeam-Talbot Alpine had done well since its 1953 introduction, with over 1000 units sold in its first year. It was much fancied by sporting car aficionados Stateside. The Porsche 356 was felt to be a strong seller with nearly 500 sales in 1953.

On a larger scale, Jaguar was a name known to most Americans, and a household one among sports car fans. By late 1953 over 10,000 Jaguars were owned in America. One owner was actor Cary Grant, who referred to the XK120 as the "gentleman's mink coat"! Then there was MG.

Starting with the MG TC in 1948, the Octagon brand practically revived amateur sports car racing in the US. Over 20,000 MGs had been sold in America by 1953, and rumors were circulating concerning the MGA's arrival. MG was the sports car sales leader, and in those halcyon, pre-British Leyland days, both Jaguar and MG were known for good finish and quality.

The venerable British Reliant Regal made its US debut in Los Angeles in the early '50s, as the cheapest form of family car motoring. Porsche rival, the Austrian Denzel, was available from US importer Speedcraft Enterprises of Exton, PA. And it was boasted that the Austin-Healey 100 offered tremendous value for money at $2985, serviced from sea to shining sea by the Austin dealership network. However, even the latter paled next to what VWoA (Volkswagen of America) was setting up for the Beetle. Yes, you could buy almost any import in America in 1953, even the Eastern Bloc Skoda. Furthermore, buyers could obtain the same cars through 'hole in the wall' operations, and receive service from shade tree mechanics. [6]

There was no one sports car. They ranged from the very small, underpowered, and relatively inexpensive, through very expensive and exotic grand tourers, and even cars like the Maserati

MG — Britain

ENGINE			
No. Cyls.	4	Weight (curb)	2010 lbs
Bore	2.62-in	Ground clearance	6-in
Stroke	3.54-in	Tire size	5.50 x 15
Displacement	76.28 cu. in	Turning circle	31 ft
Output	57.5 bhp @ 5500 rpm	Electrical system	12 volt
Valves	OHVPR	BODY	
Compression ratio		Type	Roadster
CHASSIS		No. doors	2
Suspension (front)	Ind. coil	Construction	Steel
(rear)	Semi-E	Seating capacity	2
Transmission	Synchro	PERFORMANCE	
No. Speeds	4	Acceleration	(0-60 mph) 16 secs
Brakes	Hydraulic	Maximum speed	90 mph
Wheelbase	94-in	Braking	(from 30 mph) 35 ft
Tread (front)	47¾-in	Gas consumption	(approx.) 28 mpg
(rear)	50-in	PRICE	
Height	52½-in	Delivered US	$3385*
Length (overall)	144¾-in	MANUFACTURER	
Width (overall)	59-in	The MG Car Company Ltd	
		Cowley, Oxford, England	

MODEL TF

*Wire wheels (optional extra) included.

The MG needs no introduction. Beginning with England, there is not a country in the Western world where for the past 20 years it has failed to spark enthusiasm for the sports car movement. The MG backlog of racing and other competition successes is a history in itself, and the influence of this unique small sports car on the revival of US amateur racing was incalculable. Since 1948 (when the post-War TC model began to arrive in any quantities) some 20,000 MG's have been sold in this country. The 1950 TD model—which was a radical departure from the TC and earned the displeasure of sports car purists—actually gained in sales over its predecessor, though hopelessly outclassed in the 1½-litre racing category. Racing enthusiasts account for a very small percentage of

MG buyers, and because of this the later Mark II (with a souped-up engine and a higher axle ratio) was not a signal success. With rumors rampant of an entirely new MG, the announcement of the 1954 TF (and the ZA Magnette) revealed the Nuffield Organization's sober, middle-of-the-road policy. The TF is not radically different in appearance and very little different mechanically. A lowered hood line with curved radiator, restyled dashboard, separate seats, faired-in headlights and optional wire wheels are the main outward changes. The engine develops about three bhp more and embodies the Mark II modifications such as large valves and higher axle ratio. Performance is a shade livelier than that of the TD, with a higher maximum speed.

34

In 1952, 11,000 sports cars were sold in America, out of an industry total of four million units! Most were MGs. *(Courtesy Cornell Publishing)*

JAGUAR XK 120 — Britain

ENGINE			
No. Cyls.	6	Weight (curb)	3000 lbs
Bore	3.25-in	Ground clearance	7½-in
Stroke	4.17-in	Tire size	6.00 x 16
Displacement	210 cu. in	Turning circle	31 ft
Output	160 bhp @ 5200 rpm	Electrical system	12 volt
Valves	20HC	BODY	
Compression ratio	8*	Type	Sports Convertible
CHASSIS		No. doors	2
Suspension (front)	Ind. Tor.-bar	Construction	Steel
(rear)	Semi-E	Seating capacity	2
Transmission	Synchro	PERFORMANCE	
No. Speeds	4	Acceleration	(0-60 mph) 9.5 secs
Brakes	Lockheed hydr; 2L8 front; L6T rear	Maximum speed	125 mph
Wheelbase	102-in	Braking	(from 30 mph) 32 ft
Tread (front)	51-in	Gas consumption	(approx.) 20 mpg
(rear)	50-in	PRICE	
Height	52½-in	Delivered US	$3975
Length (overall)	173½-in	MANUFACTURER	
Width (overall)	62-in	Jaguar Cars Ltd., Coventry, England	

CONVERTIBLE COUPÉ

OTHER MODELS: XK 120 (Roadster): Same specs; 2850 lbs. (Coupé): 2875 lbs. MARK VII (Sedan 4-Dr.): Same specs; 120-in WB; 3696 lbs** XK 120C (Comp. Rdstr): 6 cyl; 220 bhp @ 5800 rpm; 96-in WB; 2072 lbs.

*7.1 comp. ratio optional.

**Borg-Warner automatic transmission optional.

Modified version of all above models except Mark VII and Type C: 190 bhp @ 5800 rpm; optional at $200 extra with Rudge Whitworth wire wheels.

The name Jaguar has today become a household word among sports car enthusiasts, while few even of the general public have not heard of this famous car. Powered by the smoothest double overhead camshaft engine ever built in a remarkably efficient cylinder head, the brainchild of famous designer Harry Westlake), the Jaguar

XK120 showed from the outset that it was capable of performance never even remotely approached before by a production sports car. Starting with a record breaking run at over 132 mph at Jabbeke, Belgium, in 1950, it went on to win innumerable International trials and racing events—including the Le Mans 24-Hour Race in 1951 and again in 1953. The Modified XK120 which appeared in 1952 gave US sales an even greater stimulus, and there are, today, some 10,000 American-owned Jaguars. Other 1953 Jaguar achievements were 16,851 miles in seven days and nights at Montlhery Track by a Modified Coupe which averaged 100.31 mph; a run at 172.4 mph at Jabbeke by a Modified XK120; and a high of over 178 mph on the same road by a prototype competition model. Latest addition is the Convertible—an attractively finished, practical two-seater with the same excellence of detail as the Coupé.

Loosely inspirational concerning the 1953 Corvette, the Jaguar XK120 was dubbed by Cary Grant as, "The gentleman's mink coat". *(Courtesy Cornell Publishing)*

A6GCS. The latter was an $8500 racing car with Formula 2 hardware, and intended for the top Class E of US sports car racing. That said, there was a general sports car sentiment, expressed by John Bentley when describing the desirable 1953 MG Magnette Series ZA sports sedan costing $2695: "For those who like bulk, torque converters and multiple-cylinder engines, it has little to offer." Compactness, lively performance, attractive good looks and fine finish were noted Magnette boons. [7]

By the early '50s America was mostly offering low volume, pricey, V8-powered sporting cars. Sterling Edwards' Edwards Sports V8 was Lincoln-powered, of fiberglass body construction, weighed 2800lb, and was capable of 100mph and 15mpg. The 205-horse five-seater cost $4995, and had limited sales. More capable and expensive was the $10,120 Cunningham C-3, with handbuilt Italian aluminum coachwork and a Cunningham-designed tubular chassis. It did 0-60mph in 8.5 seconds and had a top speed of 121mph. Millionaire sportsman Briggs Cunningham, whose ambition was to win at Le Mans, was selling around two to three dozen of these cars per year. The two/three-seater had 220 horses and weighed 3500lb. Then there was the New York-built, fiberglass-bodied Navajo Sports

Job, with a Ford chassis and optional Mercury V8; it looked like the Jaguar XK120! Once again, they sold in limited numbers.

Competition success and general sporting prowess were respected qualities. Donald Healey in his Austin-Healey 100, did over 142mph on the Bonneville Salt Flats in late 1953. Sunbeam was the first car to reach over 200mph, and the only British car to win the French Grand Prix. The Jaguar XK120 did over 132mph on the Jabekke Highway in Belgium, and Jaguar won Le Mans in 1951 and 1953. The English/American/Italian $6200 Pininfarina-styled Nash-Healey came sixth at Le Mans in 1951, third in 1952 and first in class. However, the high price stymied big sales. There were in fact three Healeys on sale, all associated with Donald Healey. They included the straight-six 3-liter Alvis-engined, aluminum-bodied $6500 Healey.

What's more, the new Triumph TR2 was considered great value for money; enough to revolutionize the affordable sports car market. The steel-bodied 1908lb two-seater with optional overdrive cost $2400, did 0-60mph in 13 seconds, and was capable of 100mph and 24mpg. The earlier Triumph 1800 had not been a US sales winner.

The preceding paragraphs all beg the question: why was GM getting into such unchartered territory?

America's next sports car

THERE WERE ENTHUSIASTS at GM that were wise to the modest, but growing, interest in sporting machinery Stateside. GM's styling boss Harley J Earl was a sports car fan. He started thinking of a two-seater sports car in 1951, with the first mock up completed in 1952. [8] Indeed, the coupe went from clay model to theoretical showroom availability, in just 15 months, but the going wasn't easy.

Harley Earl believed that a sufficient quantity of sports cars could be sold to turn a profit – around 10,000 per annum being the required number. It was a small figure in relation to the size of the auto market, but implied that GM's new bolide would equal the total of all sports cars sold Stateside! In a series of well timed moves, Earl managed to get the approval of top GM brass one by one. Indeed, even

prior to the 1953 Motorama appearance of EX-122, the Corvette was production-approved by Chevrolet Division Chief Tom Keating and GM President Harlow Curtice.

The Corvette moniker has been attributed to Chevrolet PR man and chief shutterbug (photographer) Myron Scott. A Corvette was a highly maneuverable patrol or escort warship, used by the Allies during the tail end of World War II. [9] The car the public saw at the Motorama show was a roadster, with a 55 degree raked windshield, along with fashionable 'Jet Age' styling cues so popular in the optimistic postwar era. To this dream car were added screened in headlamps, common on European racing cars, and a flashy chrome grille. Harley Earl's styling advice to his young charges was always to, "Go all the way and then back off." He admitted that the shark tooth grille was inspired by contemporary Ferraris. [10] Sliding side windows and door handles on the inside were all de rigueur with the contemporary British sports cars that were dominant at the time. The same could be said of the Corvette's general specification.

Rear-wheel drive, a separate chassis, four-wheel drum brakes, straight-six motor and a live axle – such elements were certainly held in common with the Jaguar XK120. And like the sports cars from the British Isles, the Corvette utilized hardware from sensible sedan siblings. Nothing wrong with that, after all MG stood for Morris Garages, where humble origins were no barrier to creating a sports car. For Corvette, this meant 1949 Elliot kingpin-style front suspension, in common with Chevrolet family cars of the day. This family connection was also apparent with the Corvette's powertrain.

The Chevrolet International Six, introduced for the 1929 model year, brought a three-bearing OHV inline-six of 194 cubes/3.2 liters displacement, and 46 gross horsepower. Prior to this model the Chevrolet family car, like the Ford Model T, had been straight-four powered. However, post GM integration, it was decided that the Chevrolet family sedan should have a six-shooter. The motor featured cast iron pistons, at a time when most automakers were going light alloy. Nicknamed the Stovebolt Six, due to the use of the kind of ¼in bolts found on domestic appliances, Chevrolet's sedan motor was a good match for Ford's

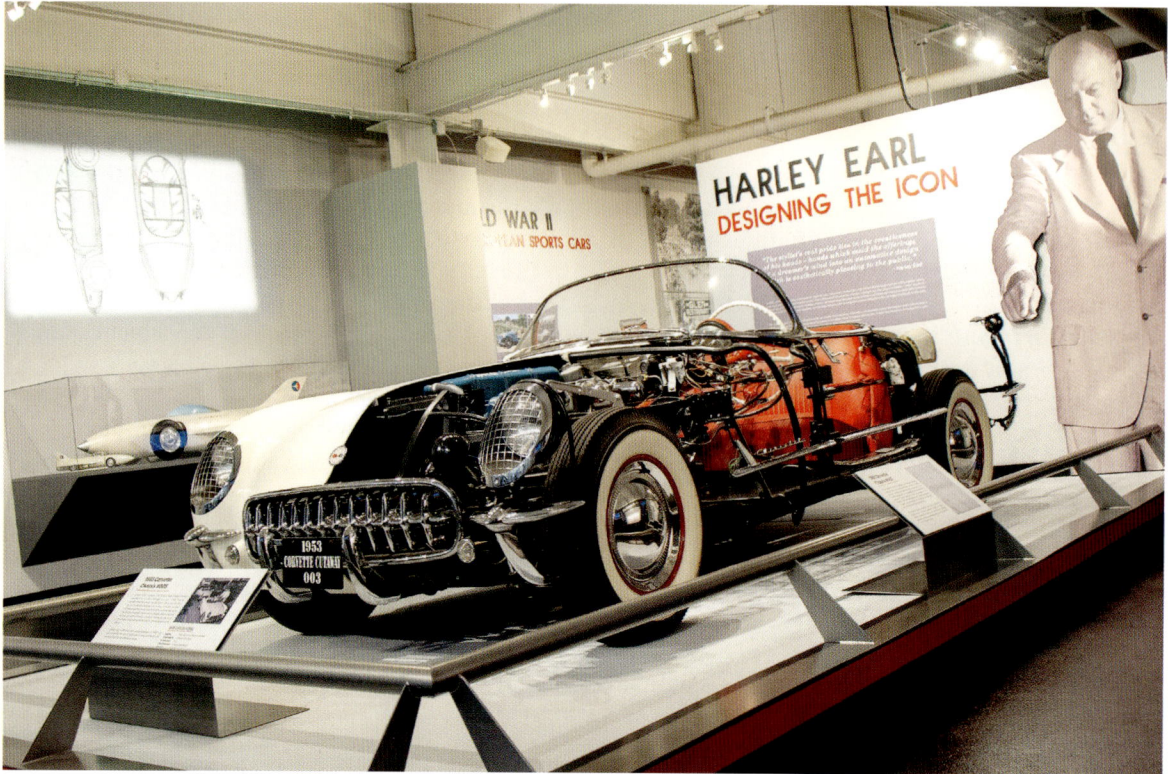

If it wasn't for GM's styling supremo Harley J Earl, the 1953 Corvette would never have existed. Earl liked sports cars, and thought GM could make a success of the concept. *(Courtesy National Corvette Museum)*

hardware, with the whole car suiting the '30s Depression.

In 1937 the Stovebolt Six received a number of upgrades to become the Blue Flame Six. The game had moved on to a four-bearing crankshaft, 85 horses and 235 cubic inches/3.6 liters. [11] However, the cast iron pistons and splash lubrication lived on to 1953. So, in the Chevrolet versus Ford rivalry, the Bow Tie six with overhead valve layout proved stiff competition for the 3.6-liter Ford V8 (the iconic sidevalve Flathead) powering the Model A in those family car wars; and family cars was where it was all at, for now ...

By 1953 the Chevrolet family 235ci six offered 115 or 125 horses, the latter in 7.8:1 comp form at 4000rpm. Either edition could have a three-speed, all synchromesh, manual transmission, or two-speed Powerglide. However, there was a special version of the Blue Flame Six with triple carburetion, just like those fancy Europeans, for

the Corvette. This solid-lifter-six made 150bhp (gross) at 4200rpm. Ford's Flathead replacing 239ci Y block V8 could only muster 130 horse at the same 4200rpm. That said, the Corvette was only available with the two-speed Powerglide slushbox, not Chevrolet's three-speed, nor the four- or even five-speed sticks found on European imports.

The official word was that there was no Chevrolet manual transmission that could handle the Corvette's torque. However, it was also said that the Corvette's single specification enabled Chevrolet to focus on how to make its new sports car properly. This was because of the Corvette's groundbreaking use of a fiberglass body for high volume vehicle production, combined with a superior quality of finish than heretofore seen using this construction medium.

The Corvette's fiberglass body was made up of 54 parts, and saved 835lb versus the Chevrolet family car that normally used the 235 cube Blue

However, the path to Corvette manufacture wasn't so easily solved. Corvette body engineer Ellis James Premo, submitted a paper to the SAE in 1954 concerning the Corvette's body development. It was disclosed that fiberglass was chosen as an expeditious way to get EX-122 ready for the 1953 Motorama show. However, the original intention was to do the body in steel, using Kirksite tooling, to reach 1954's production projection of 10,000 units. Then, two crucial developments occurred. For one, the public was bowled over by the Motorama sports car, and intrigued by its use of fiberglass. No doubt many interested parties hailed from the snowbelt, and appreciated a body that wouldn't rust through. Secondly, the fiberglass industry informed GM, that it was now practical to accomplish large scale production with fiberglass body parts. That said, early Corvette production totals hardly intimated large scale production.

1953's Corvette allocation ran to just 300 hand-built cars, completed in a Flint, Michigan customer delivery garage. A humble origin, and indeed the first few Corvettes had to be literally rolled off the production line, since said line wasn't prepared for grounding to a plastic body; that is, the initial Corvettes wouldn't start! The first 25 Corvettes featured regular Chevrolet Baby Moon passenger car hubcaps due to a parts shortage. The 300 Corvettes were all completed in Polo White with Sportsman Red interior and a black canvas top. The VIN sequence for the 300 made ran from E53F001001 to E53F001300, naturally. All cars rode on 6.70-15s of four-ply construction and whitewall design, wide whites of course. The interior had a flight deck nature worthy of the jet age, including a five grand tach. However, instruments were sited for looks, and weren't immediately in front of the driver.

Side windows were Plexiglass, and your options were limited to two items: Code 101A $91.40 heater, and Code 102A signal seeking Delco AM radio. All 300 cars had the heater, and the set menu nature of this initial 300 unit run alluded to the work in progress nature of America's next sports car.

What was the Corvette, and who was it for? All road cars are a compromise, and Chevrolet GM Tom Keating explained the Corvette's mission statement, "In the Corvette we have built a sports

The '53 Corvette's specification kind of followed British sports car practice. However, its durable drivetrain and boulevard softness were decidedly domestic. *(Courtesy Cornell Publishing)*

Flame I6. Fiberglass also sped the Corvette's path to production, in terms of tooling. Then too, the Corvette sported an extra 25bhp punch. Indeed, whereas the 3625lb Chevrolet Bel Air 235ci I6 could do 87mph, the 2850lb Corvette managed 100mph, and 0-60mph in 14 seconds, along with better gas mileage. These were all conservative factory figures. [12]

The Corvette employed a safety glass windshield, and the rear license plate holder was set back in the trunk and covered by a plastic window that tended to fog up. Solution? Two bags of dessicant were inserted!

Harley J Earl admitted the 1953 Corvette's shark tooth grille was Ferrari inspired. Critics likened the early Corvette's styling to a bathtub! *(Courtesy GM Archives)*

car in the American tradition. It is not a racing car in the accepted sense that a European sports car is a race car. It is intended rather to satisfy the American public's conception of beauty, comfort and convenience, plus performance." [13] Truth be told, Ford's new 1955 Thunderbird two-seater did just that, and more ...

Of course, you have to cruise before you can race. When first announced during the winter of 1952, the Corvette wasn't ready for production. There was a problem involving bonding and joining plastic parts. To overcome this, a new process was effected, stamping out fibrous glass sections covered with a polyester resin. At this point the Corvette was approved for production.

The Corvette's place as an 'American sports car' was alluded to by the roadster's logo, designed by Chevrolet's Robert Bartholomew. It originally incorporated the Stars & Stripes; however, such nationalistic product association is frowned upon in the industry, so the idea was dropped. Instead a circular emblem incorporating a fleur-de-lys on

the left, and checkered flag on the right, proved a fitting tribute to Chevrolet co-founder Louis Chevrolet's Swiss French heritage. Not to mention the Corvette's sporting performance aspirations. [14] Indeed, the Corvette itself seemed to honor Chevrolet's co-founder. It was a sporting car that wasn't inexpensive, and wasn't designed to appeal to everyone. Soon, the Corvette would be seen as America's most European car. Even initially, its 10,000 per annum production target, while big by US sports car standards, was modest compared to most domestic model totals. Yes, this was the high end car of racing pedigree that ol' Louis always wanted Chevrolet to be known for!

In the wide sports car spectrum of 1953, the Corvette seemed a boulevard grand tourer. A role it would successfully commercially settle into by the late '70s. However, in 1953, the Corvette still seemed reasonable value for money, next to quasi rivals.

John Bentley assessed the 1953 Corvette as possessing soft springs and low geared steering,

Model	Body	Motor	Weight (lb)	0-60mph (seconds)	Top speed (mph)	Gearbox	MPG	Price ($)
AC Ace	al2	I6/2L	1700	16	100	4sp	18	3200
Austin Healey 100	al2	I4/2.6L	2156	10	100	4sp	22	2985
Jaguar XK120	steel	I6/3.4L	3000	9.5	125	4sp	20	3975
MG TF	steel	I4	2010	16	90	4sp	28	2335 (included wire wheels)
Porsche 356	steel	F4	1784	11	115	4sp	29	4584
Alfa Romeo 1900	al2	I4/1.9L	2615	11	100	4sp	20+	6100
Ferrari 250 Europa	al2	V12/3L	2450	7	161	5sp	10	13890
Cunningham C-3	al2	V8	3500	8.5	121	2sp	14	10120
Kaiser Darrin	fiberglass	I6/161ci	2100	13.2	100	3spOD	–	3000
Corvette	fiberglass	I6/235ci	2850	14	100	2sp	18	3490

which made for behavior more in keeping with a domestic than an MG, but pick up was judged very good. Then too, damage to the tough plastic panels was described as easy and cheap to repair. Compared to exotic aluminum bodied jobs, it probably was. [15]

The Corvette's bus tires lacked grip, and the stone guarded headlamps were considered rather effeminate. The roadster's powertrain was more durable than that found on European counterparts. However, those triple carbs were hard to keep on song, and even with a high lift cam, the power wasn't forceful. That said, the Corvette was only 10 horses shy of the Jag XK120. You could say the 1953 Corvette was a pleasant cruiser, in search of a market that didn't yet exist in North America. At least, not at the projected 10,000 unit per annum level.

Naturally, GM worked on the image angle, letting the public know that Corvette was worth its attention and cash. To this end, the initial cars were allegedly sold to VIPs. Actor John Wayne and sporting entrepreneur Briggs Cunningham were among recipients of those first 300 1953 Corvettes. Obviously the public's estimation of the new bolide would be higher if they felt the cars were paid for, rather than mere loan vehicles or even gifts. Then again, would GM really charge The Duke, or the man most likely to win Le Mans for America? Then too, Cunningham even had his own line of sports cars. In any case, both Briggs Cunningham and John Wayne returned their Corvettes to GM.

In reality the 1953 Corvette wasn't available to the Chevrolet dealership network, nor the general public. It was a dealer show loan vehicle. Of the 300 1953 Corvettes, only 183 of the roadsters actually left GM. And although the Corvette wasn't intended to be a direct Jag XK120 rival, many sports car aficionados were a trifle miffed that the new Chevrolet wasn't the sporting equal of the much vaunted machine from Browns Lane, Coventry.

Even so, Corvette mystique over the decades has seen a reverence develop for the 1953 Corvette. GM has always liked to show the latest Corvette alongside the original. In 1968, GM's Lonnie Duncan stood with the then new C3 '68 Corvette and a 1953 example for a PR photo. Oftentimes this was 1953 Corvette #004, which was part of the Rinke Chevrolet collection. Rinke Chevrolet rented the roadster out to GM for publicity purposes. In the case of the 1968 Corvette release photo, the 1953 Corvette on hand was most likely car #255, which had been restored in 1967.

In February 1975, *Road & Track*'s editor Ron Wakefield was moved to say that if you stumble upon a 1953 Corvette, buy it, and put your kids through college on the proceeds! In September 1983, the same journal's Paul Van Valkenburgh said, "… there are a lot of people out there who regret not having bought (and kept) one of the first 1953 Corvettes." As a subsequent collector car, this was true. However, back in 1953, it was obvious that Chevrolet had to make improvements to its new two-seater.

Chevrolet has long liked to show the latest Corvette alongside the 1953 original. In this case it was the 1973 edition, as the by now hallowed nameplate turned 20 years old! *(Courtesy GM Archives)*

Home improvement

FOR 1954 MODEL year, Corvette refinements and alterations witnessed new exterior color choices, an alternative interior color scheme and engine upgrades. Out of 3640 1954 Corvettes made, approximately 80% were Polo White, 16% were Pennant Blue with a newly available tan interior, 4% were Sportsman Red, and six Corvettes were black. The Blue Flame Six was uprated to 155 horses, thanks to a revised camshaft profile and dual air filters. Valve covers were altered too. Indeed, in keeping with what would become a Corvette tradition, the alterations kept coming through the model year, with paint bulletins for Metallic Green and Metallic Bronze.

From December 1 1953, Corvette production switched to a renovated Chevrolet truck plant in St Louis, Missouri. GM's sports car would continue to be made at this new location, into 1981. The plant had the capacity to produce over 10,000 Corvettes per year. Sales predictions ran as high as 12,000 units per annum. To entice the public, Chevrolet introduced a new low bait price of $2774. In truth, the real price was $3254.10: in an act common in the domestic auto industry back then and in subsequent years, and not just at GM, essential standard equipment was moved to the options list, for appearances. The sole Powerglide gearbox choice was billed as a $178 option! Windshield wipers and heater were also described as options, when every Corvette did indeed have them.

By the end of 1954, Chevrolet had 1500 unsold Corvettes. A 1954 dealer-installed option Paxton centrifugal supercharger kit certainly redressed any acceleration shortfalls. However, it wasn't a factory

16

option, and the general sports car enthusiast perception was that the Corvette didn't measure up to the Jag XK120 for the money. Various non-functional items, body crudities, and jet age styling touches were all starting to wear thin. That said, faring even worse was the 1954-only Kaiser Darrin, a straight six-powered, fiberglass bodied, separate chassis sports car with sliding doors, styled by Howard Darrin.

Costing three grand, the pricey sports car handled well, but a poor quality fiberglass body, and Kaiser-Jeep's complete move of vehicle production to Argentina as IKA for 1955, spelt the Kaiser Darrin's demise. With a 161-cube Willys motor, it had no chance in FIA Class D (2-3 liter) racing, and as a sports tourer was perceived as no current threat to the European establishment at the price, even with a manual transmission. Just 435 Kaiser Darrins were made. Next to the Kaiser Darrin, the Corvette looked good. However, compared to the sales standing of the 1955 Ford Thunderbird, the Chevrolet left something to be desired.

Commencing as a September 23 1954 debutant, Ford's new two-seater was a mere $2994, and came with a V8 motor standard; a factory supercharged option, your choice of automatic or manual transmission, plus the kind of luxurious, gadget-filled interior that domestic buyers expected at the price. FoMoCo called it a 'personal luxury car', not a sports car. That was Dearborn's gambit. The public agreed with Henry and purchased 53,277 T-Birds during 1955-57, and that ain't chicken feed! The Thunderbird soared even higher, when it gained four seats as a larger, and even more luxurious coupe for 1958. So, the gauntlet was laid down to Chevrolet, and the GM brass gave the green light to continue, and improve what would become 'The Plastic Fantastic'.

Harley Earl had planned improvements, and new ideas for Corvette. There were two concept cars, one was a thin pillar hardtop coupe, and the second a closed fastback coupe … called the Corvair! Indeed, Corvair was the original appellation favored for the Corvette. These concepts, along with general styling changes that encompassed a functional hood scoop, were shelved due to cost and the 1954 Corvette's poor sales. However, now that Henry

Ford was in the sporting car house, GM pride brought action.

Success has many fathers, but failure was a Kaiser Darrin, and so it was with the Corvette. Without Harley Earl the Corvette would never have started, but without two further guys it wouldn't have continued. One key figure putting substance behind the nameplate was the then Chevrolet Chief Engineer, Ed Cole. Cole oversaw the introduction of a modern V8 to the Chevrolet line. The first Bow Tie mobile with a V8 was the 1918 Chevrolet Model D. [16]

The new, modern pushrod overhead valve V8 was 30lb lighter than the Blue Flame Six, and dubbed 'The Mighty Mouse', after the cartoon character. [17] It was also referred to as 'The Hot One' upon its 1955 model year debut. The motor would have a displacement span of 265ci to 400 cubes, and enjoy outputs from 162bhp (gross) to 375 horses (net).

The original plan was to start the new small block V8 at 231ci, or 3.8 liters, but Ed Cole wisely put this up to 265 cubes or 4.3 liters. Luckily for the Corvette, Cole also had the heads reworked for more performance. Weighing around 500lb undressed, the new V8 featured a simple, lightweight ball stud rocker arm design, taken from Pontiac. [18] In addition, there was an innovative diecast intake manifold, that supplied coolant to

1955-57 brought a redesigned 150 series Chevrolet family car, a range topping Bel Air version, and an all new V8 motor. That last crucial item was overseen by Chevrolet Chief Engineer Ed Cole.
(Courtesy GM Archives)

Known as 'The Hot One', Chevrolet's small block V8 ran from 1955 to the 1992 introduction of the LT1 Gen II V8. The Mouse Motor imbued the Bow Tie brand with an enviable V8 reputation. *(Courtesy www.xfireperformance.com)*

Truth in advertising, as the Corvette's single minded sporting nature was outlined. It wasn't a practical six-seater family lead sled. And where else would you find a Chevrolet with a 195 horse 265 cube V8, or triple carb Blue Flame Six? *(Courtesy GM Archives)*

2850 POUNDS OF PLEASURE!

The Corvette is a single-minded car. It is designed for just one thing—to provide maximum driving pleasure. It has no other function—no space, weight or bulk to accommodate six passengers, no concessions to subtract one whit from the savage acceleration of its 195-h.p. V8 engine. Not an ounce of superfluous weight to dull the crisp accuracy of its handling. No unnecessary overhang to mar its fantastic stability through curves.

A Corvette weighs 2850 pounds ... and every pound is dedicated to the proposition that driving is an art and a joy. That's why its body is glass fiber-reinforced plastic, far lighter and quieter than steel. That's why the steering ratio is 16 to 1, lightning-fast response. That's why the special Powerglide transmission has a floor-mounted selector lever for accurate control. And that's why the Corvette was given outrigger rear springs, 11-inch brakes and deep bucket-type seats.

Every quality was designed with the expert driver in mind. But mere description of these qualities can't convey the sum of them all—the sense of absolute command and superlative *control* you feel behind a Corvette's wheel. *That* you have to experience yourself—and that's why we invite you to come in, soon, and try out the *driver's car.*

Drive with care ... EVERYWHERE!

Glass-fiber-reinforced plastic body • 195-h.p. valve-in-head V8 engine or 155-h.p. 6 with triple carburetors • Powerglide automatic transmission • Center-Point steering, 16 to 1 ratio • Form-fitting individual seats • Full instrumentation, with tachometer, oil gauge, and ammeter.

both cylinder heads via a common outlet. There were integral valve guides, and hollow pushrods to lubricate the rocker arms and valve stems. The hollow nature also saved weight! Slipper type auto thermic aluminum three-ring pistons, combined with a circumferential expander for a single oil ring. A pressed steel crankshaft was employed, sufficient for the power at hand, and offering a cost saving. In further detail, individual rocker arms over the valve stem/pushrod, with locknut secured fulcrum ball.

In the Corvette's application, the new Mouse Motor sported a unique specification. There was a more aggressive camshaft profile and single four-barrel carburetion, featuring either of 2218S or 2351S WCFB Carter units. It implied 33 horses more than any other Chevrolet, that is: 195bhp at five grand and 260lb/ft at three grand. So, the now 6500rpm tach was a mite optimistic. From mid '55 MY you could combine this excellent sounding motor, with a close ratio three-speed manual transmission.

Unlike six shooter Corvettes, all V8 roadsters had 12V, not 6V electrics. The latter was common practice on European cars, that didn't have much in the way of accessories to power. The 12V system made for easier cold climate starting. Corvette V8s

also had the convenience of an automatic choke, and the 12V system upgrade facilitated electric in place of vacuum-actuated windshield wipers, plus an associated foot-operated, electric windshield washer set up. The latter a 12 buck option.

An outward sign of the V8 existing underhood, came in the form of an oversize gold 'V', for the front fender Chevrolet logo badge. There was also a broader radiator grille on Corvette V8s. The surcharge for having a V8 was $135, over the six pot Corvette that still continued to be available. However, only seven buyers in 1955 selected a six-cylinder Corvette. Respective option codes and prices were 2934-6 for the straight six $2774 Corvette, and 2934-8 for the $2909 Corvette V8. Both were artificial bait prices, sans mandatory

---

---

equipment. New 1955 Corvette color choices brought Harvest Gold, which replaced Pennant Blue, Gypsy Red and Metallic Corvette Copper. *Road & Track* achieved 0-60mph in 11 seconds, when sampling a Blue Flame Six Corvette in June 1954. This figure improved to 8.7 seconds for its 1955 Corvette V8 test car. Both machines sported Powerglides.

Early 1955 Corvettes retained the six-cylinder frame mounting holes, but later examples had them plugged in. Thinner fiberglass sections allied to smoother bodies also heralded improved quality for the 1955 Corvette, in fit and appearance. This was no low volume kit car! Only 700 1955 Corvettes were built, and 674 were sold. That is, Chevrolet was finally matching demand and supply. It also seemed that the V8 motor caused a mental tide to be turned, in the public's mind concerning the Corvette's worth as a sports car. Zero to sixty in around 8.5 seconds and mid 16s in the ¼ mile were a marked improvement. Plus, a man called Zora Arkus-Duntov was ready, willing and able to take Corvette to the next level.

The apex of the Chevrolet family car 150 series, the '55 Bel Air, was shown with a jet fighter in an ad saying, "Motoramic Chevrolet, stealing the thunder from the high priced cars." This was true for the affordable Caddy, that carried a Caddy and Lincoln-like fuel filler, concealed within the left tailfin! [19] It's also true that the small block V8 was at the heart of Chevrolet's completely redesigned family cars of 1955. However, the Corvette needed more, it needed Zora Arkus-Duntov, who affectionately became known as ZAK.

Zora Arkus-Duntov was a Russian émigré, who utilized his European high-performance car background, to transport the Corvette beyond mere styling and marketing. He had worked at Porsche and Mercedes Benz, prior to joining GM. A 45-year-old Duntov was one of the impressed visitors of the 1953 Motorama car show. He was struck how a mainstream auto giant like GM could show an interest in sports cars. The racer, automotive

Road & Track tested Powerglide equipped 1954 and 1955 Corvettes. It found the switch from Blue Flame Six to Mighty Mouse V8 dropped the 0-60mph time from 11 to 8.7 seconds. *(Courtesy Marc Cranswick)*

designer and engineer, didn't immediately start working on the Corvette when he joined GM. However, ZAK was certainly instrumental in turning the public's perception, concerning America's only volume produced two-seater sports car.

Known for tinkering with the Corvette in his spare time, Duntov wasn't instantly wowed by the substance of that formative C1 or Straight Axle Corvette, as it has become known, "The front end understeered and the rear end oversteered. I put two degrees of positive caster in the front suspension and relocated the rear spring bushing. Then it was fine – very neutral."

The 1955 Corvette coincided with James Dean's second movie, *Rebel Without A Cause*. Unlike Dean, the Corvette wasn't already legendary by 1955. In June 1977's issue of *Road & Track*, the by now retired Corvette Chief Engineer Zora Arkus-Duntov, offered his thoughts upon being reacquainted with a 1955 Corvette with 'three by the knee', for a short test drive, "We've come a long way!" And that's exactly where the Corvette was going.

CRANSWICK ON
CLASSIC CHEVROLET
Corvette
1953-1996

CHAPTER 2

Corvette –
The Rising Star
1956-58

1956 ← Corvette with coves

IT'S OFTENTIMES RECORDED how the Corvette made a rocky start in 1953. *Autocar*'s resident racer Roger Bell said as much, when the journal selected the Chevrolet as being among the World's 100 Greatest Sports Cars in 1999. [20] The troubled start was confirmed by a well known racer with an aviation engineering background, no less than seminal Corvette figure, Zora Arkus-Duntov.

Upon seeing the plastic roadster at the 1953 Motorama show, he wrote to Chevrolet's chief engineer at the time, Ed Cole. Duntov was subsequently hired by GM, and by July 1953 was working on the Corvette. He had his work cut out, for in his words, "It's a big nothing, but we should be able to work it into something." With that aviation background, ZAK certainly made the Corvette fly, but the Bow Tie bolide also needed work in the looks department.

Being somewhat slab sided, critics soon coined the nickname 'The Plastic Bathtub'. Not helped by the predominance of a Polo White exterior as the Corvette's calling card in its formative years. Then there were those jet age styling touches, which also started to generate negative jibes. So, Harley Earl and his staff got working on a major restyle, with Earl taking the proposal to top GM brass for approval mid April 1955. The powers that be were impressed, and immediately gave their blessing. The newly bodied 1956 Corvette sported side coves, unmeshed headlamps and revised French curves. The successful makeover represented the final work of DM Design staff in Detroit. Matters moved to the new GM Technical Center, located in Warren, Michigan.

New accoutrements ran to wind-up glass windows and even a power window option. Door handles were relocated to the exterior, and attention was paid to improving leak resistance of the roadster's soft top, which was now available in beige, white or the existing black. What's more, for an extra $170.60, there was the luxury of a power operated top! Okay, it was partially automated, with a need to manually unlatch and collapse the top. But still, you couldn't get that on an MG, or even a Jag. For $215.20 the hardtop option, another first for Corvette, made for an interior snugger than Jack Benny! The hardtop's style was related to that seen on the 1954 Motorama show.

The 1956 Corvette benefitted from the Motorama show, drawing upon 1955 Motorama mobiles, the Chevrolet Biscayne and the side cove styling of the Cadillac La Salle II, plus Buick Wildcat II. At the time, and since, the 1956-57 Corvette has been judged as an attractive car. Twenty years hence, *Road & Track*'s Ron Wakefield referred to the body as handsome. [21] Inside, new waffle pattern upholstery met the eye, and during the production year a refinement from a recirculating to fresh air heater. For passive safety, seatbelts became a dealer installed option. Fancy radios were the go to gadgets of the 1950s, and for a princely sum of $198.90, a transistorized signal seeking tuner could be factory fitted.

Zora Arkus-Duntov's recollections of the '56 Corvette's mission statement were recorded in the June 1977 issue of *Road & Track*, saying, "… raise the windshield to an acceptable height, provide

This is a 1957 Cascade Green Corvette, with Shoreline Beige side coves. Only 5% of 1957's 6339 Corvettes built were so painted. *(Courtesy Mecum)*

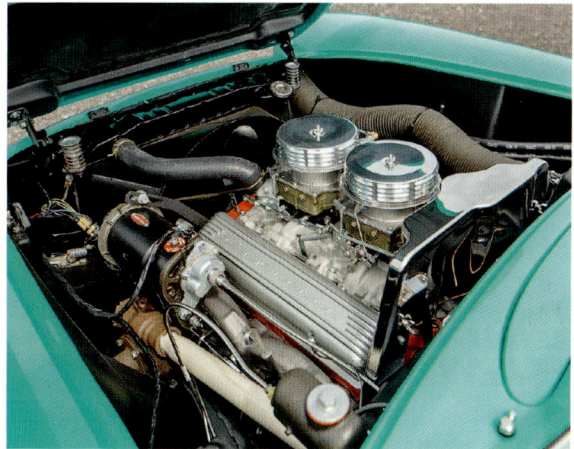

One up from the base 1957 220 horse Corvette 283 4bbl base motor was this optional 245bhp dual quad 283 V8, with 9.5:1 CR. *(Courtesy Mecum)*

roll-up windows and generally civilize the car." Duntov had even developed a handling package for the '56 Corvette, using an early '56 roadster as a test vehicle. There was also a need for more underhood V8 moxie. The late '55 MY Corvette V8 with three-speed manual transmission cut the plastic roadster's 0-100mph time from 41 seconds to 24 seconds. This was about the same as a 1981 BMW 528i five-speed, 1982 Crossfire Corvette or '82 Ford Mustang GT 5.0 four-speed. However, for 1956, power of the Corvette's base 265 cube V8 climbed from 195 to 210 gross ponies at 5200rpm, utilizing a 9.25:1 comp ratio.

Up from the base V8 lay the optional $172.20 dual quad 225bhp 265 V8. The Hot One was living up to its name, and was attracting industry praise for the new V8's efficiency and reliability. Just as Ford's Thunderbird V8 was shared with other Fords, adding glamor to more plebian lines, so too were Corvette powerplants offered as underhood image makers. For example, Corvette valve cover script would greet sportily optioned El Camino owners when lifting the hoods of their car-based pickup trucks. And the 'Hot One' was more than an ad slogan. As *Mechanix Illustrated*'s inimitable Uncle Tom McCahill said, "Chevrolet has come up with a poor man's answer to a hot Ferrari." And "Here's an engine that can wind up tighter than the E string on an East Laplander's mandolin –

well beyond 6000rpm – without blowing up like a pigeon egg in a shotgun barrel." Uncle Tom then proclaimed the '56 Chevrolet to be, "The best performance buy in the world." Indeed, a decade on and specialist manufacturers Iso and Gordon Keeble concurred. They used Chevrolet's small block V8 in their respective Rivoltas and GTs. Such motors were in the Corvette's 300 horse specification. [22]

However, even the optional 265 V8 wasn't enough for Zora Arkus-Duntov. A man whose flat out jaunt across France in his Flathead Ford before WWII, inspired the Ardun cylinder head conversion. Duntov worked with Sydney Allard, and raced an Allard at Le Mans, prior to achieving two consecutive class victories in Porsches, at Club de l'Ouest's La Sarthe circuit. In the win on Sunday, sell on Monday era, the Corvette needed to show its racing prowess. GM approved ZAK's strategy of developing a high lift cam, to get some records and boost the Corvette's image, and therefore sales. To this end, Duntov tested the 'Duntov Cam' in a specially prepared 1956 Corvette on GM's Arizona proving grounds.

Zora Arkus-Duntov was a man on a mission. According to his June 1977 *Road & Track* revelations to John Lamm, "In 1955 only 700 Corvettes were sold and I'll bet a lot of people thought the Corvette was finished, but then came

Starting in 1956, the new side cove styling eliminated jibes that the 1953-55 Corvette resembled a bathtub. Not aided by its oft seen Polo White exterior!
(Courtesy Mecum)

the Daytona Beach run (150mph) and then Sebring, and sales started to climb. Initially, racing was all important for the Corvette."

So it was that GM proffered a factory team of three specially prepared 1956 Corvettes for the February 1956 Speed Week held at Daytona Beach. John Fitch, Betty Skelton and Zora Arkus-Duntov ran the Corvettes at Daytona Beach. It was here that Duntov performed two certified runs of 150.583mph. In so doing he vanquished the Jag XK120 and Mercedes Gullwing, allowing Corvette to become the world's fastest volume-produced production car. All thanks to the Duntov Cam. This item reportedly took the Corvette to 240 horses. It was denoted RPO 449 Special High-Lift Camshaft, with 111 '56 Corvette buyers paying a princely $188.30 for same.

The 1956 Corvette also set a new fastest time at the famous Pikes Peak hillclimb, recording 17 minutes and 24 seconds. [23] Not a glass smooth surface, and even road racing in the '50s took place on stony ground. The Corvette proved equal to the task, even though critics characterized the car's ride as harsh, but controlled. Steering for the 1956 model was three and a half turns lock-to-lock. It was less than the typical family car of the era, which needed five turns between locks for manual steering! However, purists still considered the Corvette to possess too much understeer and brake fade.

In spite of such real or imagined sports car imperfections, the Corvette's Speed Week triumph was followed by success at March 1956's Sebring race. Here, a factory-backed four car team tackled the 12 hour enduro. Two Corvettes registered DNFs, one came 15th, with the remaining Corvette managing ninth outright, which was enough for a Class B win. The Corvette in question utilized a 307 V8 and ZF four-speed gearbox, it was raced by John Fitch and Walter Hansgen. In fact, it was the same car that Zora Arkus-Duntov had used to set the aforementioned production car speed record at Daytona Beach.

On the back of such motorsport achievements, Chevrolet's marketing men had appropriate ads ready, that truthfully claimed that, "Corvette was The Real McCoy!" and, "The 1956 Corvette is proving – in open competition – that it is America's only genuine production sports car." It wasn't mere hokum, and sales rose to 3467 for 1956, with associated base price of $3120. The public was getting the message, as the Corvette started living up to the hype. The three by the knee manual transmission now had closer ratios, a beefier clutch, and the shifter was attached to the transmission housing. There was also a new differential.

1957 ⟿ Fuel injection, four-speed & Positraction

UNDOING THE HISTORICAL legacy of the Corvette debuting with a slushbox, the Powerglide was now optional for the first time at $188.30. Having a stick as standard equipment was only right for a sports car. Plus, in keeping with the Corvette's position as America's only volume-produced sports car, new 1957 developments would underline the Corvette's increasingly accepted legitimacy. Taking a leaf from the book of arch road race rival, the Mercedes 300SL, Chevrolet introduced mechanical fuel injection for '57 MY. It was the GM Rochester Division's Ramjet Fuel Injection. This led to injected versions of the Hot One, gaining the Fuelie sobriquet.

Unlike the 300SL's direct fuel injection, the Ramjet system was indirect, as would become commonplace on modern cars. However, like the MB 300SL, the Chevrolet system was a high pressure, multi injector set up, aimed squarely at high performance. The Chevrolet Fuelie development team consisted of Ed Cole, Harry Barr, John Dolza and Zora Arkus-Duntov. Ed Cole became Chevrolet boss from 1955, Harry Barr was behind the seminal modern V8 design, seen on the 1949 Cadillac.

Fuel injection had been seen on German Messerschmitt fighter planes during WWII. It was also introduced on some West German '50s production cars. The high pressure and temperature environment of the combustion chamber also made Germany's love of direct fuel injection, along with appropriate injector solenoids, technically difficult and expensive. In America fuel injection became a popular power adder in drag racing, as seen with the Hilborn system. However, the idling requirements of a road car implied special provisions, beyond racing requirements.

John Dolza was working on the Rochester Ramjet system from 1955. The set up was a constant flow type, like the Hilborn system, and was adopted in late 1956 by Chevrolet. It involved ram pipes, in a custom cast aluminum housing that resembled a doghouse. Indeed, this 'Doghouse', as it became known, contained its own fuel delivery pump with an integral sump that dealt with bypassed fuel. A pronounced venturi of the air intake produced a strong signal vibration, allowing the constant flow injection to vary the volume of fuel delivered for road car purposes, at a ratio of 40:1. [24] The Rochester system was used for a short time by Oldsmobile and Pontiac. Concerning the latter, it was part of Bunkie Knudsen's successful attempt to rid the Tin Indian brand of its one-time fuddy-duddy image, in favor of a youthful, sporty persona. To that end, there was the Pontiac Bonneville, and the brand's introduction of optional fuel injection for '58 MY. However, its Ramjet iteration was 'low profile', that is, sans Doghouse.

Post WWII, Bosch/West German systems were direct fuel injection, whether it was the diminutive two-cylinder, two-stroke Gutbrod and Goliath, or fancy Mercedes. Maserati and Ferrari also went with direct fuel injection for racing. However, in the GM Ramjet scenario it was indirect injection, with fuel feed by way of the intake valve. GM's plan was

Still with that 1953 Motorama flight deck instrument look, in a period correct waffle seat material beige interior, by Al Knoch Interiors. Note also the standard 'Three by the knee' close ratio manual transmission.
(Courtesy Mecum)

injection for a volume-produced V8 motor. Gutbrod made 14,000 fuel-injected vehicles by mid 1955, but Chevrolet was No 1 in the sales race.

From an image angle, utilizing the publicity of stock car racing, Chevrolet boss and Fuelie team member Ed Cole wanted to make Rochester Ramjet Injection optional on all Chevrolets. Fuel injection seemed the hot ticket item of the time. At 1957's Speed Week on Daytona Beach, the fastest car was once again a Corvette, this time a Fuelie edition. The second fastest car was a Rambler Rebel sedan, with Bendix Electrojector Injection. This fuel injection sensed vacuum intake manifold pressure. That is, the world's first computer controlled fuel injection! Developing fuel injection was challenging.

Zora Arkus-Duntov had been working on his own system since early 1956, but in April that year, at GM's proving grounds, he had an accident testing a prototype Corvette hardtop fitted with experimental disk brakes. Although confined to a body cast for six months, Duntov continued working on Corvette fuel injection. Price, however, proved to be a sales barrier.

Ramjet Fuel Injection was a nearly 500 buck option, and a mere 1503 Chevrolet Fuelie Bel Airs were sold, out of a 47,562 1957 Bel Air total. Fuel injection tended to be for high-end cars, announced as a late '56 MY Rambler Rebel option, and also for 1958 high-performance Chrysler Corp cars. Concerning Bendix Electrojector injection, there were 1500 1957 Rambler Rebels planned, and a mere 300 unit combined Chrysler 300D and DeSoto Adventurer total for 1958. Apart from price, there were technical flies in the ointment.

Chevrolet experienced dirt in the Ramjet system, and overheating injectors. The irony was that GM originally planned to use supercharging as a power adder, but ruled it out on reliability grounds in favor of fuel injection. The Bendix Electrojector system wasn't actually used on the 1957 Rambler Rebels, and was only featured in limited fashion by Chrysler Corp. Once again, injector design and electrical circuitry interference were problems. [25] So it was that Ramjet injection only featured on 1957 Chevrolets, and then only on the Corvette through '65 MY.

The injected Fuelie Corvette 283 V8 allowed Chevrolet to be the first volume-produced domestic car with one horsepower per cubic inch. That is, 283 horses, although this 10.5:1 comp motor was believed to be good for 290bhp. At $484.20, it was a pretty penny for the Fuelie option, and volume production implied only 1040 '57 Fuelie Corvettes. However, it was enough to pass the more limited production Chrysler 300C, released a few months earlier. [26]

The Chevrolet V8 had been bored out ⅛in for 1957, creating the 3.875in bore of the new 283 V8. This resulted in a choice of four optional Corvette 283 V8s: Dual Quad 9.5:1 comp – 245bhp; Fuelie 9.5:1 comp – 250bhp; Dual Quad 10.5:1 comp – 270bhp; and Fuelie 10.5:1 comp – 283bhp. With all Chevrolet Fuelie V8s, the power gains over carburetor equivalents were modest. Some felt that in the Corvette's case the carb version's horsepower ratings were played down, to talk up the Ramjet injection motors. However, horsepower wasn't the Fuelie's only trump card.

Road & Track's August 1957 Fuelie Corvette 283 report, referred to the injected V8 as "an absolute jewel", and the Fuelie's docility was noteworthy. It idled at 900rpm, rock solid and quiet, and would pull from idle in top gear (fourth), smoothly and easily. There was instant throttle response, and a complete character change from the dual

quad Corvette 265 V8. *R&T* had tried that carb Corvette in July 1956, and found it to be quick with 0-60mph in 7.3 seconds, but plagued by flat spots in power delivery. Karl Ludvigsen even relayed the negative sentiment, from a less than diplomatic scribe concerning said dual quad 265 V8, "... a vast improvement (Fuelie 283) over the Chevrolet option of dual 4-bbl carburetors, but then this arrangement is certainly no criterion for comparison with anything." [27]

However, the emphasis was always on high performance, so little wonder that Chevrolet's advertising said, "The Hot One's even hotter," and for the Corvette it played up the "One horsepower per-cubic inch" line. That said, in a world where gasoline was cheaper than water, there were easier ways to generate power. So, turbocharged methods such as the '60s Olds Jetfire and Corvair Monza Turbo, and even the all aluminum BOP 215ci V8, were all superseded by larger cast iron V8s.

From John Dolza's working 1955 Ramjet Injection prototype, to the Fuelie phase out in favor of the big block Chevrolet 396 V8 during 1965 model year, the Bow Tie injected motor lasted a decade. Later Fuelies became intractable, high idle speed, road race engines, as horsepower went way beyond one horsepower per cube. This development exposed the overhead valve V8's Achilles' heel of

The 1956-57 Corvette is a favorite among aficionados, and represented a quantum leap in Corvette ability and style. Harley Earl, Ed Cole and Zora Arkus-Duntov created a masterpiece! *(Courtesy Mecum)*

The glamor of Chevrolet's 1958 lineup: Impala convertible, Bel Air Sport Coupe and 'The dashing Corvette, America's only authentic sports car.' With the Plastic Fantastic featuring 'Safety Plate Glass' and standard seatbelts! *(Courtesy GM Archives)*

excessive valve overlap being necessary to go super high output, with an attendant torque sacrifice, which made the new big block V8s preferable.

Big block adoption seemed great at the time. However, after the fuel crisis and effects of the Muskie Smog Bill, many industry commentators lamented the fact that GM hadn't continued Fuelie development, to achieve performance, economy, civility and lower pollution of smaller, more efficient engines. [28] Europe persevered with fuel injection. Indeed, the Bendix Electrojector system was the genesis for the Bosch D-Jetronic electronic injection of a decade hence. Overseas practice also related to the Corvette's other seminal new 1957 feature, the $188.30 RPO 685 four-speed manual transmission option.

Three by the knee was still standard, and

Powerglide was optional, but as per imported sports car practice, everyone wanted that low second gear. To achieve this, the three-speed Borg Warner manual transmission had its reverse gear moved into the tailshaft housing, to make room for fourth gear's cog. The four-speed had ratios: 2.20 (first), 1.66 (second), 1.31 (third) and direct top 1.00 (fourth). There was also the newly available Positraction limited slip differential, with a choice of differential ratios: 3.70, 4.11 or the 4.56 drag racer special. All ratios were factory fitted at no additional cost, and the Corvette was certainly becoming a serious gentleman's racer. Forget about Cary Grant's Jag XK120 mink coat! It should be noted that four on the floor cost $275, if you started with a carb Corvette.

Another factory option was RPO 684 Heavy Duty Racing Suspension, costing $780.10 and selected by 51 buyers. It contained all the necessary hardware for a track-ready Corvette. However, you could still drive to the race, and back home. No trailer required for this gentleman's racer. RPO 684 got you: HD springs, bigger front swaybar, Positraction, bigger piston dampers, fast manual steering, and finned brake drums.

In more detail, HD front springs were 119lb/in, versus the stock 105lb/in, or a 14% increase in stiffness. HD rear springs raised the stock figure of 115lb/ft to 125lb/ft, which was an 8.7% increase. The front swaybar rose in diameter from 0.6875in to 0.8125in. Plus, the fast steering adapter permitted a steering ratio adjustment from 21.0:1 and 3.7 turns lock-to-lock, to respective figures of 16.3:1 and 2.9 turns. Spicer made the Positraction lsd, the HD brakes had vented backing plates and air scoops, along with Cerametalix brake linings for the duo servo finned Bendix cast iron drum brakes.

Beyond such factory goodies, Zora Arkus-Duntov saw to it that even better hardware was available from parts counters of high-performance oriented Chevrolet dealers; that is, you could build a race car. Such optionality and extensive factory hardware set the Corvette apart from other sporty rides, as did its four-speed. Years before the term became part of the '90s lexicon, the Corvette's four-speed was truly user friendly! That is, a light, easy to modulate clutch, allied to precise knife-

The 1958 Corvette was the first example of the nameplate to turn a profit. However, the critics labeled its styling as excessive. This roadster belonged to GM CEO Dan Akerson. *(Courtesy Barrett-Jackson)*

through-butter shifter action. The latter was how many a Hurst shifter should have been, but wasn't. The Plastic Fantastic's four-speed ease continued, through the introduction of the Chevrolet big block V8, right up to the phasing out of the Muncie manual gearbox during 1979 model year.

Road & Track reported on the Fuelie Corvette four-speed, in its August 1957 issue, with the assistance of enthusiast owner and racer, Andy Porterfield. He was someone that had campaigned Corvette in Palm Springs and Santa Barbara locales. It was back in January 1957 that Chevrolet announced the joint availability of fuel injection and four speed features, concerning Corvette. The magazine witnessed the hardware in Detroit, and sampled a Fuelie Corvette with three by the knee, 3.70 rear axle sans lsd, stock rear springing, and regular issue 6.70-15s.

R&T's four-speed Fuelie Corvette belonged to racer Porterfield. The roadster's four-speed box was fitted just the day prior to the magazine test. The Corvette in question sported a Positraction lsd, 4.11 rear axle, HD rear springs which entailed an extra leaf, and special 6.70-15 footwear. Whereas the three-speed Fuelie Corvette came with radio,

heater and hardtop, the four-speed test car was more primal, no heater or radio, and stock cloth top fitted to every base $3176.32 220 horse Corvette 283 4bbl V8. Indeed, concerning RPO 684's racing orientation, a heater was unavailable.

R&T disclosed that its test three-speed Fuelie machine was $3,909.52, and that the w-i-d-e for the time 15 x 5.5in rims were a separate option (RPO 276). The Fuelie four-speed Corvette started from $4098, came with the C1 Corvette's 102in wheelbase, curb weight of 2880lb and weight distribution of 53.5% front to 46.5% rear. *Road & Track* said Porterfield tested the four-speed Corvette sans speed shifting. That is, he used the clutch. Zero to sixty transpired in first gear, right on the redline with 5.7 seconds! Yowser, Yowser!! It was exactly the same time *R&T* recorded with its 1992 model year Corvette LT1 V8!

Andy Porterfield noted the four-speed's easy short throw, and excellent synchronizer action. No gear graunching here. What's more, the four-speed worked quieter than the gearbox on the three-speed Fuelie Corvette. Porterfield sailed past 7000rpm several times with the three-speed box, necessarily buzzing the box to make up for wide ratio gaps, relative to the four-speed unit. Porterfield said the four-speed allowed him to get the power down more easily. Zero to 100mph with the four-speed roadster was 16.8 seconds, and a 14.3 second ¼-mile at better than 90mph was discovered.

The four-speed's first took one to 60mph at the 6500rpm redline, second and third gears were good for a respective 80mph and 101mph, again at the redline. With 283 horse at 6200rpm and 290lb/ft arriving at 4400rpm, gas mileage was found to be in the 11 to 16mpg range, and top speed was estimated at 132mph in top gear. However, *Road & Track* noted that with the appropriate gearing, the Fuelie Corvette had managed 150mph at both Bonneville and Daytona. Brakes were okay. The duo servo Bendix binders, with Ferodo linings for the all drum set up, were judged good, if not ideal concerning brake fade. However, *R&T* did three stops from over 100mph, no sweat. Power brakes weren't fitted to the four-speed roadster, and the journal felt a brake booster wasn't necessary.

R&T's Fuelie Corvette report was subtitled, "Add fuel injection and get out of the way." It commented, "Even the Anglophiles now readily admit that the Corvette will go." The journal recounted Chevrolet's 1954 statement, that the firm was in the sports car business to stay. Indeed,

success had been achieved in the past couple of years. At 1957's Sebring 12 Hour race, the Corvette garnered a 1-2 result in GT class. This represented 12th and 15th outright respectively. More than that, the 12th placed Corvette was 20 laps clear ... of the top qualifying Mercedes 300SL Gullwing!!

The Plastic Fantastic had finally got the 'All show and no go' monkey off its back. It was certainly the undisputed king of North American production car racing. It seemed the Jag XK120 and MB Gullwing sacred cows had been put out to pasture. Zora Arkus-Duntov told *Road & Track* in June 1977, "The really exciting Corvette was the 1957 model with fuel injection, the four-speed transmission and more handling changes. This car put us on the sports car map."

The Corvette was also on its way to becoming a technology showcase, a halo car for Chevrolet and GM as a whole. It was something Ford never really had at the time, or since. Cars like the Thunderbird and Mustang were never pinnacles of technology. Indeed, quite the contrary concerning the latter, which was always a family car in drag. In addition, the Ford GT40 was too far removed from Ford's regular production cars, both in image and technology flowing to more pedestrian models.

The family Chevrolet could have fuel injection,

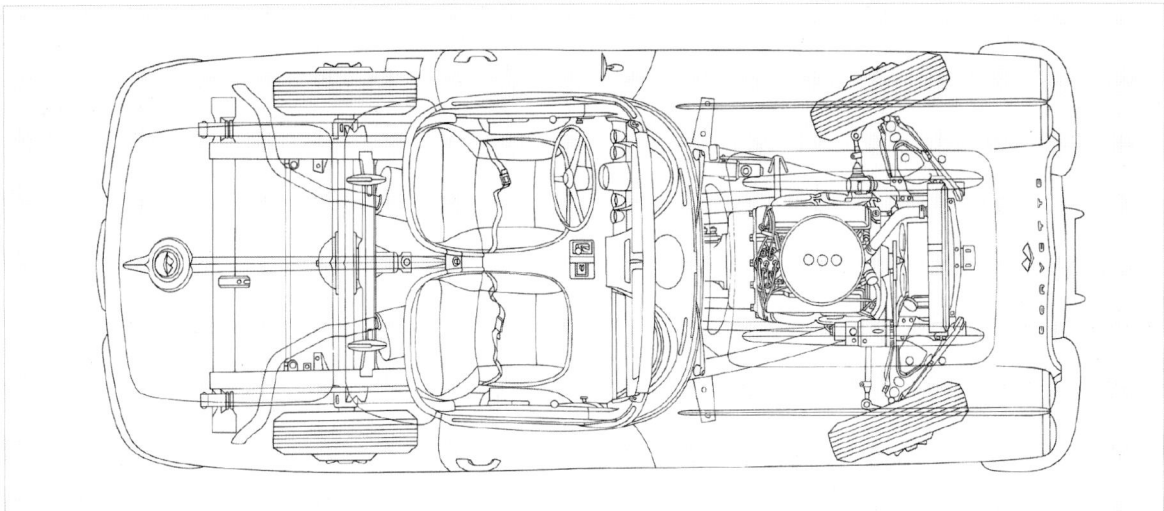

It had been hoped the Corvette would go unibody for 1958. However, as this '58 Corvette illustration shows, the sports car still had body on a frame construction. It would continue to do so, through 1982 model year.
(Courtesy AB Nordbok)

briefly, and a four-speed. In 1957's 12 Hours of Sebring, a Corvette SS special participated, with experimental magnesium body and upgraded racing hardware. It set a new lap record, but had reliability woes. By lap eight, a rear bushing failed and the racer recorded a DNF by lap 23. Even so, the Corvette SS was a vehicle of historic interest. It was presented by Zora Arkus-Duntov to the Indianapolis Motor Speedway on May 29 1967, during the driver's meeting for that year's Indy 500. It was a race paced by no less than the Corvette's, figuratively speaking, little brother, the new '67 Camaro!

1958 – Bigger is better?

THE PUBLIC WERE increasingly warming to the Plastic Fantastic, with sales nearly doubling to 6339 units in 1957 model year. However, the Corvette had yet to turn a profit. This milestone would occur with the 1958 model year, as sales climbed to 9168. Corvette basc pricc also lifted from 1957's $3176.32 to $3591. You got more car with the '58 MY Corvette, but perhaps not always in a desirable sense? There had been great plans for the '58 Corvette. Even as early as 1946, GM executives knew that unitary construction was the profitable, high volume avenue of the future. The new Corvette was in line for such technology.

GM stylists were also looking at two sources for unibody Corvette inspiration. One was the 1956 Oldsmobile Golden Rocket show car. This design was a unibody coupe, with protruding headlamps. The second was the Mercedes Gullwing. Yes, although vanquished in American road racing by the Corvette's turn of speed, the MB Gullwing's image was still golden. Plus, recent events saw image become just as important as racing prowess.

The tragic spectator events of 1955's running of the Le Mans 24 Hour race, and other racing fatalities, cooled manufacturer interest in motorsport activities, lest such corporations face a conservative consumer backlash. So it was, that in 1957 the AMA (American Manufacturers Association) signed an anti racing pact. GM President Harlow Curtice acceded to the viewpoint of the National Safety Council, by signing said pact. Therefore, factory-backed racing efforts gave way

National Geographic's Noel Grove reminisced about '50s cruising mid-western highways on balmy evenings, in the July 1983 issue. Knights in chromium armor racing muscular, deep-throated steeds. Stopping at Sam Slate's two pumper, "A buck's worth Sammy" is all it took for TV's Buz and Tod to cruise Route 66. *(Courtesy National Corvette museum)*

to more arm's length privateer support. However, one could still option a Corvette for road racing. Zora Arkus-Duntov saw to it that such optioning was possible. Plus, even more rarified hardware was at hand via the parts counter. Then too, ZAK and GM execs continued to attend race meets.

Ford ended both its two-seat Thunderbird and supercharged Paxton blower-fitted 312 V8 Y block, at the close of '57 MY. The AMA anti racing pact, and the pursuit of personal car profit through monster four-seater T Bird sales, were only part of the reason for Henry's sporting exodus. No, FoMoCo could see how serious a racing weapon the '57 Fuelie Corvette four-speed was. The two-seater personal car Thunderbird was no match for the Plastic Fantastic on a track.

Even the venerable Mercedes 300SL was off the Corvette's pace. There were powerful sedans in Detroit at the time. The 1957 Studebaker Golden Hawk coupe came with a Packard 275 horse V8. It was re-engined with Studebaker's own 289 V8 and McCulloch blower, for the same power allied to a 100lb weight saving. However, it wasn't a sports car.

True American sporting pursuits were in the Corvette's realm. The 1958 XP-700 prototype provided ideas used on the next generation Corvette, that is, the C2 or Mid-Year cars. However, there was no unibody Corvette for 1958. GM had more pressing matters concerning its use of resources. With the storm clouds of the late '50s recession gathering, the need arose for an economy car to answer rising 1955-57 sales posted by Rambler, VW et al. It gave rise to the Detroit compacts of 1960, which included the new Chevrolet Corvair. Then too, Ford's successful '57 Fairlane family car and even the high-end Edsel implied other fish to fry with standard size vehicles. An all-new Corvette was a lower priority at GM. Chevrolet's Impala made a '58 MY debut, as a limited edition model. It was an avenue for future success, compared to Dearborn's dead-end Edsel. [29] By 1960 the Impala was the nation's No 1 selling car. [30] For GM it was a case of priorities. 1958 saw Corvette sales rise yet again, to 9168, and Chevrolet's two-seater turned a profit for the first time. However, it was still a drop in the bucket for mighty Chevrolet.

So it was that great plans gave way to an extensive exterior and interior Corvette restyle, that focused on that 'Big Dollar Look', while bringing functional improvements. Outside's tale was one of horizontal quad circular lights, within chrome bezels, simulated hood louvers, dummy air intake scoops, phony side cove vents and dual rear chrome suspenders. 1958 marked the year that Harley J Earl retired from the position as GM's styling supremo. Earl's successor Bill Mitchell conceded that stylists tended to ladle on the ol' chrome with a trowel in those days! It wasn't a phenomenon confined to GM. The '58 Ford Fairlane sported quad lamps too, and Chrysler's Virgil Exner even tried reverse tailfins for '61 model year, concerning Dodge!

In a rare act of restraint, the Corvette's previous 13-tooth chrome grille was curtailed to nine teeth. However, other stats were in the ascendant. The 1958 Corvette was bigger, growing 9.2in to 177.2in for length, plus was 2.3in wider at 72.8in. Although diminutive by 21st century standards, the V8-powered Plastic Fantastic dwarfed an MGA, and its increased length made rear radius rods necessary. Corvette weight exceeded 3000lb for the first time, or 200lb over a 1957 Corvette. Indeed, engine for engine, the new Corvette was slightly slower.

When it came to the 1958 edition's interior, Zora Arkus-Duntov presided over functional improvements. Chief upgrade, and essential sports car practice was moving all gauges bar the clock, so instrumentation was directly in front of the

A 1958 Corvette in Britain. The Plastic Fantastic was soon joined by the Chevrolet Impala in overseas production car racing. *(Courtesy IPC Magazines)*

driver. Gone was the 1953-57 Corvette Motorama flight deck. A new 160mph speedo and six grand tach, flanked the steering column. They were complemented by fuel/oil pressure on the left, and coolant temp/ammeter on the right. The latest Corvette possessed a narrower center console, passenger side dashboard grab handle, locking glove compartment between the seats, and first time standard factory fitted seatbelts, of a lapbelt nature.

Among interior niceties were new pebble grain seat fabric, and optional 'Wonder-Bar' signal-seeking radio. Functionally, the '58 Corvette's door cards had night time, arm-level safety reflectors. Bumpers were now attached to the frame, and the earlier nitro cellulose exterior paint was replaced by GM's familiar acrylic lacquer. Ford and Chrysler went for enamel. Naturally you can verify if a car has lacquer, by testing with paint thinners in an inconspicuous location. If color comes off when you rub, it's lacquer. 1958 saw a choice of six Corvette exterior colors.

As for engine selections, it was a case of variations on a 283 V8 theme. Nearly half of buyers saw no reason to go beyond base, which was a 230 horse four-barrel unit. 2436 Corvette patrons went for the $150.65 245bhp RPO 469 dual quad 283 V8, with a mere 978 paying $182.95 for the RPO 469C dual quad 283 V8, which made 270 horse. There was no surcharge between the mild RPO 579 and wild RPO 579D Fuelie 283s. Both options retailed for $484.20, but the wild one possessed a 40bhp advantage. The top Fuelie 283 V8 came with a reported 290bhp and Duntov camshaft, probably more. When combined with the RPO 684 package, one had the means to take on all road racing comers, be they Ferrari, Jaguar or Porsche. There was even a windshield warning label: "This car is not intended for street use." Therefore, forget about a warranty. Positraction, HD brakes, HD suspension and four-speed, this Corvette had it all!

Like the 1958 Ford Thunderbird, the Corvette did well in sales, when many other cars were floundering in the late '50s recession. As would be the case with high-end European imports 20 years hence, specialist and or super luxury cars, tend to survive hard times well. The '58 Corvette's strong sales showed that it was one of those

specialists, not to mention America's only sports car. And you would see one of the 2006 Silver Blue 1958 Corvettes on the silver screen. The movie in question was 1974's disaster flick *Earthquake*. Here, a criminal racing along the streets of Los Angeles in said Corvette was LAPD pursued by George Kennedy's cop character and his partner, in a black and white Plymouth Satellite. (This was just prior to Kennedy playing Bumper in TV's *The Blue Knight*.) The pursuit sees the '58 Corvette display its handling prowess and turn of speed, with the Plymouth struggling to keep up. There was also that nice exhaust note from the pre smog control era, lost in the mists of legislative time. Much to the chagrin of Kennedy's cop, the pursuit had to be curtailed because the perpetrator had dumped the Corvette roadster, and entered the back garden of Zsa Zsa Gabor. In Beverley Hills this practically amounted to hallowed ground. And the '58 Corvette, along with Zsa Zsa Gabor, were certainly part of late '50s glamor … Dahlink!

The 1958 Corvette was, and is, much featured. However, enthusiasts have subsequently expressed a preference for the simpler 1956-57 Corvette's look. In 1975, Ron Wakefield of *Road & Track*, referred to the '58 Corvette as functionally better, but gaudy. [31] In contrast, the 1959 Chevrolet Impala was considered too outlandish at the time, an earthbound spaceship for the Looney Toons Martian, but has gained popularity as a collectible classic over time. Nevertheless, by the late '50s, the Corvette was certainly a car to be seen in.

Popular recording artist Pat Boone did TV ads for Corvette, extolling its sweet handling. At the same time, Dinah Shore sang *See the USA in your Chevrolet*. As No 1 automaker in the sales race, Chevrolet got the biggest names in the entertainment industry to promote its wares. So popular in fact was Pat Boone, that Ford did product placement for its new Ranchero car based pickup truck in the 1957 movie *April Love*, where Boone crooned to Shirley Jones in said pickup, against the idyllic backdrop of the Kentucky bluegrass. Perhaps an omen, concerning the Corvette's future Bowling Green Kentucky plant?

Pat Boone subsequently said that in the seven years he did ads for Chevrolet, he received a new Corvette, and Chevrolet station wagon for his

The Corvette quickly became courted by celebrities like singer Pat Boone and actor Robert Wagner.
The latter's 1958 Snowcrest White four-speed roadster is shown, signed by Wagner.
(Courtesy The Garage Journal)

family, every year! Actor Robert Wagner paid for and liked his 1958 Corvette four-speed so much that he even autographed the roadster's dashboard! An easy vehicle to get enthusiastic about, and in this case a unique one.

Always a Corvette, sometimes a Chevrolet …

LEGEND HAS IT that the iconic Chevrolet Bow Tie logo originated from when GM founder and Chevrolet co-founder, William Durant, ripped off a swatch of hotel wallpaper in Paris, France, 1908. Upon bringing it back to Detroit, its pattern served as inspiration for the aforementioned logo. Or so the story goes. The Corvette, under codename Opel, saw a group of Harley Earl's 'Special Projects' crew work on the icon to be, for which engineer Bob McLean did the general layout. Indeed, the Corvette seems to have always been a 'skunkworks' job. A pet project worked on in a small, secret laboratory, within the giant that was, and to some extent still is, Chevrolet.

Back in 1957, the Chevrolet Bel Air was billed as "sweet, smooth, and sassy." Two and a half inches longer compared to 1956, the 1957 Bel Air convertible sold for $2511, with 47,562 Bel Airs sold that year, within a Chevrolet production total of over 1½ million! Chevrolet's legendary 1957 model, the jewel of the Tri-Year line, reached many folks. So much so, it moved Billie Jo Spears to subsequently sing, "Wish we still had her today … the good love we're living, we owe it to that '57 Chevrolet." [32]

Even the Beach Boys sang about the day that 'daddy took the T-Bird away'. In contrast, the Corvette was beyond such mass market mulling. In 1957, the Plastic Fantastic was earning respect in motorsport, and for its quality hardware. However, it was nowhere near 10,000 units in annual sales, and had yet to turn a profit. A quality car that wasn't for everyone. The same could be said of the Corvette-related Chevrolet Bel Air Nomad.

The Nomad was Harley Earl's Corvette-based dream wagon. A 1954 Motorama star, the stylistic

A 1958 Corvette being pursued in the 1974 movie *Earthquake*. By mid '70s smog controlled standards, any '58 Corvette had a fair turn of speed!
(Courtesy Universal Pictures)

work of Carl Renner, and a 1955 model year debutant. Its Motorama Corvette-inspired roofline was adapted for production Nomads, in just two days! You could have the standard Blue Flame Six, or optional V8, just like the once-upon-a-time Corvette. The Nomad was the priciest Chevrolet, no less. *Motor Trend* called the '57 Nomad, "… one of the year's most beautiful cars." That said, it was a two-door vehicle of limited appeal, with annual sales never breaking 10,000 units. Such commercial performance consigned said Nomad to a 1957 model year demise.

Pickups were an easier sell. The glamorous 1950s Chevrolet 3100 Stepside was more for Mr Mainstream. There was a DeLuxe trim level, 11 exterior color choices, and a V8 option, naturally. It could be the ride of everyman. This all explained the Corvette's niche distinction in the Chevrolet clan, and how, from the secretary at the GM Tech Center to the St Louis, Missouri workers that put the roadster together, and owners of the sports car they made, they all called the car Corvette, not a Chevrolet. A distinction honored by the knowledgeable few … and not that few.

An Accent on Refinement
1959-62

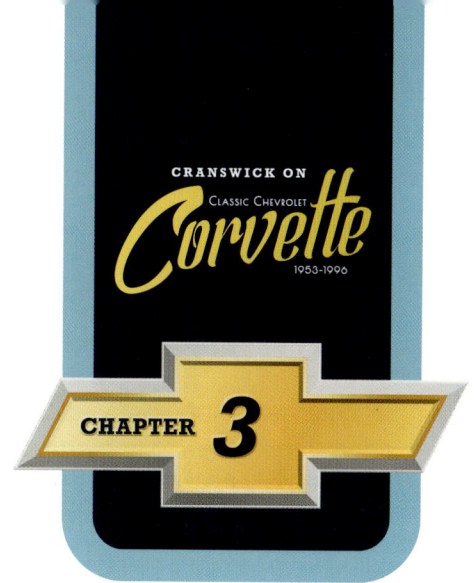

CRANSWICK ON

CLASSIC CHEVROLET

Corvette

1953-1996

CHAPTER **3**

Less is more

HARLEY J EARL gave the Corvette its initial push to fruition. However, being behind America's first volume-produced sports car, in the European idiom, was but one facet of an illustrious career. Earl did the 1927 LaSalle for Cadillac and early concept car that was the 1938 Buick Y-Job. By coincidence the Corvette would assume the inhouse GM designation of Y body. Harley Earl would proceed to pioneer two-tone paint, wraparound windshields, and quad headlights.

Beyond pure design tasks, Earl promoted the use of women stylists in the auto industry, dubbing them 'damsels of design'. More than that, he gave passive safety a helping hand by championing the use of crash test dummies. [33] However, for 1959's Corvette, his successor Bill Mitchell, took a leaf out of Mies van der Rohe's book. It was when commenting on the over ornamentation of 19th century architecture, that van der Rohe coined the expression 'less is more'. To this end, Mitchell set about dechroming the Corvette.

The 1959 Corvette rose to $3875 in price, but no longer featured the rear chrome suspenders of the 1958 edition, nor that car's faux hood louvers. Functional design improvements brought a small storage compartment under the interior passenger grab handle. Door handles and armrests were repositioned, and even the front seats now offered more lateral support. Sunvisors became a first time Corvette option in 1959. Plus, to help deal with strong reflections, dashboard instruments featured concave rather than flat pane glass lenses.

The tachometer was marked with safe zones, and 7000rpm redline. Plus, there was a T-handle transmission lockout for reverse. The T-collar four-speed stick was new for '59 MY. [34]

Trailing radius rods featured, concerning the C1 straight axle Corvette's rear suspension, and the RPO 684 HD brakes and suspension now had even stiffer springs. Under the RPO 686 HD brake package, Delco-Moraine iron sintered linings comprised three pairs of segments riveted to the primary brake shoe, and a thicker set of five pairs for secondary shoes. Although still all drum, Corvette brakes were good brakes. Performance was also more than adequate for the era. *Motor Life*'s September 1959 report on a base 283 V8-powered Corvette, with three by the knee, disclosed 0-60mph in 9.2 seconds and a 103.1mph terminal velocity. The same journal's assessment of a Corvette with RPO 469 dual quad 283 V8 of 245 horses, found the 0-60mph sprint took 7.6 seconds, with top speed at 112mph. *Road & Track*'s January 1959 Corvette test with mild 250bhp Fuelie 283 V8, RPO 579, dropped 0-60mph to 6.9 seconds, and increased top speed to 118.7mph.

It's true that the Corvette was generally slower now, given size and weight gains post 1957, but rising 1959 sales to a 9670 Corvette total, and continued profit, pointed to a roadster of more rounded ability. 1959 witnessed the one year availability of a turquoise soft top, and the first year an all black interior was offered. Therefore, combined with the Tuxedo Black exterior, it was possible for the first time to have a much vaunted, triple black Corvette! In this form, the '59 Corvette

33

truly lived up to that year's ad lines: "From a Different Mold" and "A polished instrument strictly designed for driving pleasure."

Oh heavenly hardware

MOVING INTO 1960 and, once again, the all new, or much revised Corvette had yet to surface. The 1960 Corvette pretty much resembled the 1959 roadster, which in turn was like the '58 Corvette, minus some chrome. However, like a European sporting machine, of which the Corvette was considered closest Stateside, there was more than meets the eye. The top Fuelie 283 V8 motor was still the solid lifter 290 horse RPO 579D unit. Then too, you could choose an hydraulic lifter version, with a mere 250 horse. In both cases one would be purchasing premium gas to quench said 283s' high compression ratio. Now, neither Fuelie could have a Powerglide slushbox. This sole Corvette automatic transmission choice feigned the high rpm torque of the Fuelies.

The changes made to the Corvette were outlined in *Road & Track*'s 'Miscellaneous Ramblings' section, in this case, '1960 Chevrolet Corvette Miscellaneous Ramblings: New Corvette'. The views of Zora Arkus-Duntov were also recounted in this piece. Duntov, now universally seen as Papa Corvette, was enthusiastic concerning the 283 V8's newly optional aluminum heads. Not all discussed developments made it into the '60 Corvette. The V8's higher compression ratio, up from 10.5 to 11.0:1, a larger intake valve size (1.72in to 1.94in), a bigger plenum chamber, nee 'Doghouse', all contributed to the top 1961 Fuelie's 315 wild horses. The absence of valve seal inserts concerning the aluminum heads, saved 5.3lb. The small block V8 now tipped the scales at 480lb, sans flywheel and clutch. In contrast, a VW Beetle's flat four was 160lb, the motor that prompted Chevrolet to come up with a flat six, and Corvair to house it, in the newly important economy car battles of the late '50s to early '60s recession.

Indeed, it was GM's interest in the econo-sector, and the smaller cars it required, that delayed an all new Corvette. The compact Corvair, Chevy II and kingsize compact, or intermediate Chevelle, occupied the minds of GM brass much more than

a niche V8 sports car, selling around 10,000 copies per annum. However, the Corvette continued apace. Hi Po Corvettes with the fabled Duntov cam, tended to overheat, so were recipients of the newly optional aluminum core radiator. This unit was 10% larger in capacity, yet half the weight of current Corvette copper core equivalents. The also newly optional temperature modulated variable speed fan, was also about keeping the Corvette cool. This $21.55 RPO 121 'Thermo Fan', limited fan speed to 3100rpm, and had 2711 takers in '60 MY.

More down to earth Corvette selections commenced with the base 230bhp four-barrel 283 V8, then a RPO 469 $150.65 dual quad 245 horse 283 cube unit, and the $182.95 RPO 469C 270 pony dual quad 283 V8. All three 283s were hydraulic lifter V8s. The top RPO 579D Fuelie 283 V8 cost $484.20. It was frequently backed by the optional four-speed, which retailed for $188.30. Positraction lsd was $43.05, and metallic brake linings cost $26.90. RPO 261 sunshades or sunvisors, were $10.80, and 5276 Corvette patrons optioned 'em in '60 MY. The Corvette heater, still optional and denoted RPO 101, cost $102.25. The Corvette broke the 10,000 unit sales barrier for the first time in 1960, 10,261 to be precise. Of that number, 9808 chilly souls optioned that 101 heater. There would be a similar, near universal uptake rate concerning a/c in 1979.

Notable chassis changes transpired for 1960. The RPO 684 HD brakes and suspension package had been going since 1957, but for 1960 it was discontinued under Zora Arkus-Duntov's direction. This was because, in a move that foresaw Corvette developments in 1984-85, the standard 1960 Corvette was so much improved over its 1959 incarnation, when the latter was fitted with RPO 684. Mirroring European practice, larger front and rear swaybars, with the rear mounted bar placed just in front of the live axle, were combined with softer spring rates. Additionally, Duntov oversaw an increase in rear wheel travel, by one inch, across the Corvette range. The result was that the standard car outperformed the '59 Corvette with $425.05 RPO 684, whose springing had even been stiffened that year! Plus, 1960 Corvettes received nylon belted tires, for the first time. Previously they were cotton ply.

So the stock car came with better ride and handling, but what of RPO 684's associated better brakes? Rest easy, there were 1960's RPO 686 sintered iron lining metallic brakes, costing $26.90, optioned by 920 buyers. Then too, there was the new RPO 687 HD brakes and steering package, costing a princely $333.60, and taken up by only 119 buyers. RPO 687 brought ceramic metallic type brake linings. When 1956 Corvette buyers had their choice between Powerglide and three by the knee, around half went stick shift. Since then, Corvette buyers were increasingly in favor of manual transmission, and only 1766 1960 Corvette buyers out of 10,261, spent the extra $199.10 for Powerglide. However, while stick shifts were increasingly a sporty Corvette thing, the serious hardware options were only bought by a chosen few, who tended to race their Plastic Fantastics. To this end, hi po Corvette mills to be raced had their parts go through a special inspection department. What's more, you couldn't option a Posi rear end with a slushbox. Powerglide Automatic implied a 3.55 diff ratio, but to obtain the 3.70, 4.11 or 4.56 Positraction ratio lsd, you needed a stick shift.

French trip ➔ Le Mans 1960

THIS OPTION DISCRIMINATION didn't worry Briggs Cunningham when he purchased three 1960 290 horse Fuelie Corvettes from Don Allen Chevrolet. They were intended for a team campaign at that year's Le Mans 24 Hour race, and possessed every go fast option that Corvette offered! That is, 290 horse Fuelie V8, four-speed, quick ratio steering in the RPO 687 HD brakes and steering package, Positraction, radio delete and thermo fan. 1960 also witnessed the new RPO 1625 24-gallon fuel tank costing $161.40, and the coming of aluminum heads. Note that big tank cars implied hardtop

Briggs Cunningham brought a three-car Corvette team to 1960's Le Mans 24 Hour race. John Fitch and Bob Grossman drove their #3 car to a class win and eighth overall. *(Courtesy Grossman Motor Car Corp.)*

configuration, since the oversize tank precluded soft top stowage space.

These racing roadsters had all the right stuff. Called 'Cunningham Heads', they helped Briggs Cunningham attain 151mph down the famous Mulsanne Straight. Cast from a high silicon aluminum alloy, they were derived from the 11.0:1 piston and ported heads seen on the swoopy 1957 Sebring Corvette SS prototype racer. The heads were sensitive to overheating-related warping, and had casting problems. It's believed that although discussed in contemporary magazines, the new aluminum heads were never actually available to the public in '60 MY. In any case, although two of the three 1960 Corvettes registered DNFs, the John Fitch and Bob Grossman #3 Corvette did complete those arduous 24 Hours of Le Mans. Their roadster won its class, and came eighth overall. Just like the VW Bug, the sports bug was catching from 1960. The Chevrolet Impala SS 409, with solid lifter 360 horses and iron sintered metallic brake linings, helped Dan Gurney and Graham Hill in European production sport sedan racing. [35]

The 290bhp 1960 Le Mans Briggs Cunningham Corvettes were purchased from Don Allen Chevrolet, with all factory performance option boxes ticked. This included new '60 MY items: aluminum radiator, and thermo radiator fan. *(Courtesy Real Art Replicas)*

The Chevrolet Corvair (seen here), and subsequent Chevy II and Chevelle, were the smaller new family cars that took resources away from a rumored all-new 1959-60 Corvette. (Courtesy GM Archives)

The Impala Sport Coupe played with the Corvette connection, with profile dual chrome pinstriping and Corvette style crossflags, all in the afterburner's tail wake, straddled by the nameplate's iconic chrome impala. Crossflags were also visible on the steering wheel, and the 1960 Impala's seven-motor lineup commenced with the 135bhp Blue Flame Six, a motor the Corvette once used. Round taillights started on Impala, prior to Corvette. The Chevrolet family car's triple-aside lighting was from 1958. [36] It seemed the family Bow Tie brand was warming up for the muscle car era!

It was change for Chevrolet, but a lot of constancy for Corvette between 1957 and 1962. Option prices and power levels were in a holding pattern. The RPO 426 power windows option was the same $59.20 in that era. Ditto power outputs between 1957 and 1960, and power option prices to 1961. Once again in keeping with European practice, the Corvette eschewed the marketing driven, advertising annual power rerating game played by domestics, for now at least. In 1957 it was the optional dual quad pair of RPO 469 245bhp ($150.65) and RPO 469C 270 horse ($182.95). Those

selections were complemented by the mild RPO 579 250bhp, and wild RPO 579 290 horse Fuelie 283 V8s, with different letter suffixes, both retailing at $484.20. Same deal in 1960.

1961-62 The transition Corvettes

NO SURPRISE THAT most chose the wild over the mild Fuelies, for the same price. However, the popularity of the hi po dual quad 270 horse 283 V8 rose as interest in Fuelies declined. The Fuelies were pricey for their horsepower, docile and civilized though they were. For example, in 1958 978 buyers went for the 270bhp dual quad 283 V8, with 1007 selecting the 290 horse Fuelie. By 1960 those respective sales numbers were 2364 and 759. For '61 MY the dual quad motors were still making a respective 245 and 270bhp, and costing $150.65 and $182.95, for the more powerful hydraulic lifter 283 V8. The 270 horse motor also continued as the most popular optional 283 V8, with 2827 buyers going for it. However, the lo po and hi po dual quad 283 V8s, now came with new option codes: RPO 468 and RPO 469 respectively.

The 1961 Corvette Fuelie motors retained their 1957 price level of $484.20, but mild and wild versions were renamed RPO 353 and RPO 354, with 118 and 1462 respective takers. That said, the motors ascended in power, to 275bhp and 315 horse respectively. The mild motor was hydraulic lifter in nature, with the wild 283 maintaining its solid lifter status. Both had 11.0:1 comp, and the latter attained peak power at 6200rpm. All the upgrades promised in *Road & Track*'s 1960

ERNIE SMITH
Denver, Colo.

The restyled 1961-62 Corvette ditched the long standing chrome tooth grille, and incorporated Bill Mitchell's Stingray prototype racer's rear styling. *(Courtesy Ernie Smith & CARtoons)*

Miscellaneous Ramblings report came to pass. For '61 MY the Corvette's chrome tooth grille was gone, replaced with an argent silver, fine wire mesh insert. This was also the last year, that one could option wide whites. Both alterations were a nod to fashion.

The Corvette's front fascia now sported Corvette block letter script, and larger circled crossed flags over said script. Functionally, it was aluminum core radiators across the range, and aluminum case for the Muncie four-speed, which saved 15lb. That Indiana plant-built four-speed was the same $188.30 that it was back in 1957, and 7013 patrons ticked its RPO 685 option box, out of 10,939 1961 Corvette buyers. Base prices from 1957 through 1961, were a respective: $3176.32, $3591, $3875, $3872 and, for 1961, $3934. So, the cost of Corvette life was on a general rise, but you were getting more for the money, and a better car at that!

Other GM spending priorities delayed a truly new Corvette, but 1961's incarnation did have a noticeable restyle. Bill Mitchell, GM's styling supremo until his retirement in 1977, admired aquatic creatures. A development prototype for an all new Corvette, witnessed 1960's Mako Shark I concept. The 1961 Corvette would take elements from this work, plus from the earlier

XP-700 prototype, to give some idea of that Mid-Year delight that was the 1963 Corvette. Mitchell oversaw streamlining of the Corvette's quad lamps into the front fenders, as well as deep sixing the Corvette's tooth grille. However, the ducktail rear styling was the most noticeable aspect, and it carried four round taillights. The latter soon becoming a Corvette calling card. The restyle was also functional, because the Corvette's conventional trunk was now 20% larger. The rear deck had a crease line, and ended in a triple rear bumper effect. Front headlight bezels were now in body color. GM management were satisfied with the Corvette breaking the 10,000 unit sales barrier in 1959, so okayed the 1961 restyle.

Further '61 MY functional improvements, ran to a narrower transmission tunnel, which freed up interior space. There was also a side-mounted coolant expansion tank introduced during the production year. The art of fiberglass manufacturing was improving, and so too was assembly quality at the Corvette's long serving St Louis factory, which had improved assembly techniques. All Corvette buyers now got windshield washers, sunvisors, thermo fan and park brake warning lamp. All at no extra cost. However, the RPO 101 heater remained a $102.25 option. 10,671 out of 10,939 1961 Corvette patrons optioned the heater. Most cars were ordered that way by dealers anyway. And in the final year for RPO 440 two-tone exterior paint, 3368 souls sprung for its $16.15 surcharge. Starting at $19.40 in 1956, RPO 440 became $16.15 for '58 MY, with the option generally garnering one third of buyers. Being a somewhat follower of fashion, the Corvette jettisoned tailfins at the close of '55 MY!

Nearly 90% of 1961 Corvette buyers chose a stick shift, or only 1458 purchasers optioned the RPO 313 Powerglide that cost $199.10. You could get power windows, power top and signal seeking AM radio, but not power brakes, a/c nor power steering. This wasn't the problem it first appeared. It was common for big buck imports, like Mercedes SL and BMW 507 to have dealer-installed aftermarket a/c. Indeed, even the Baby Bird Thunderbird's a/c was a dealer-installed system, resembling the once popular Texan Comfy Kit.

Drum brakes provided a natural assistance

This is the Delmo Johnson/Dave Morgan '62 Fuelie Corvette, which came third in class at the 1962 Sebring 12 Hour race. *(Courtesy Mecum)*

action, lacking with disk brakes. In a car as light as a Straight Axle Corvette, you could get by sans brake booster. What's more, manual brakes could be regulated to the point of lock up, unlike the featherlight 5lb 'stand the car on its nose', of the usual domestic car power brakes. Similarly, classic manual steering was preferable in feel to the insensitive power steering commonly found at the time, especially from Chrysler Corp. And the first generation Corvette was neither over tired nor over burdened by a wide rim.

The Straight Axle Corvette's optional tire was the RPO 290 6.70-15 whitewall, denoted with a 'B' suffix in 1954-55, with a RPO number change to 1832 for 1962. From 1958 to 1962 said tire option cost $31.55. In reality the 6.70-15 whitewall was your only choice between 1953 and 1956, all 3650 1954 Corvettes rode on 'em. Plus, 6.70-15 was your only Corvette tire size from 1953 to 1964. That is, into the Mid-Year Corvette era. From 1957 not all Corvettes were optioned with wide whites, but most were. The standard footwear would have

Texan Chevrolet dealer Delmo Johnson phoned Zora Arkus-Duntov concerning creating this race car. Johnson asked for it to be white, Duntov took care of the rest! *(Courtesy Mecum)*

been a 6.70-15 blackwall, formally listed as 1833 for '62 MY, at $15.70. However, the take up rate of the whitewall 6.70-15 was always high from 1957. For example, 8173 buyers out of a 1959 9670 Corvette total. After all, blackwalls were a social faux pas on any fancy set of wheels. It tended to be the province

This 1962 Big Brake Fuelie Corvette was campaigned in SCCA West Coast production car racing by Tom Mazzola in the '60s. *(Courtesy GT Motor Cars)*

of cop cars with dog bowl hubcaps, and traveling aluminum siding salesmen that sat on the tuck and roll upholstery of fleet strippers!

As for Corvette rims, the stock standard Straight Axle hoop was a 15 x 5in steel unit. Optional from 1957 was RPO 276 costing $15.10, with only 51 out of 6339 '57 Corvette patrons selecting said option. What you got were 15 x 5.5 in steel rims, which became an NCO (No Cost Option) from 1958. Said option retained the RPO 276 name and NCO status through 1962 model year. However, even though free, the option was never popular. Even by 1962 model year, just 561 out of 14,531 '62 Corvette buyers went for the W-I-D-E rims. So the need for power steering, especially given the C1's small block only status, was never pressing. One small change should be noted. For '62 MY, the Corvette's optional whitewall tire became a 'narrow white', in keeping with contemporary fashion.

Corvette did change, but not for the sake of change, and the car's 'all purpose' nature was applauded by *Road & Track*, when said journal sampled the 1961 edition of the Plastic Fantastic. The subtitle was "America's competition-proven sports car revisited". *R&T* noted that at one time the sporty car set (read import crowd) considered the 1955 Corvette V8 quick in a straight line, but wouldn't steer or stop, possessed a boulevard ride, and was derogatively described as having a glass body. Fast forward to 1961, and it was a whole new ball game.

Road & Track acknowledged new bumpers, and exhaust tips placed under the body, rather than through the bumper for style. The modification was judged functional and better looking. There was also more attention paid to the fiberglass molds, evidenced by the sound panel fit and finish. Ride and seat comfort post a 200 mile test stretch, were judged great. Ergonomically, the seats had 3in of fore/aft travel. The Corvette also supplied full instrumentation with fuel gauge, coolant temp, oil pressure, and ammeter gauges. Long before the smog era made driveability an issue, the top Fuelie 283 V8 tested was still docile and tractable.

The 283 V8 motor was rated at 315bhp (gross) at 6200rpm, with 295lb/ft at 4700rpm, using an 11.0:1 CR. *R&T* found the engine very flexible, and capable of pulling smoothly from under 15mph to top speed, sans bucking or hesitation. Some credit was paid to the RPO 675 4.11 Positraction lsd, costing $43.05 and chosen by 6915 1961 Corvette buyers. This was the last year a top Fuelie was tractable. And unlike carb cars, Fuelies didn't starve out in tight turns, or flood in heavy braking. The injected Chevrolet V8 became cantankerous thereafter. Too much valve overlap to get even more power from the by now 327 cube 1962 OHV V8.

For now, the '61 Corvette's problems were a poorly placed console radio, much like European imports, some shifter elbow interference from the body's center fairing, if the driver's seat was set fully back, plus a hazy rear window view if a light color Corvette was at hand. There was a draft with the window down, and some engine and wind noise with the windows up. Steering was accurate, but could have been faster. Back in 1956 the popularity of GM's Motorama shows peaked. Ten million dollars spent drew in two million visitors. [37] In the years since, the rise of television increasingly kept people at home. Motorama shows, with their visions of the future, were now seen as a little corny. *R&T* felt the 1961 Corvette's interior still had a touch of Motorama. By now, this was a criticism. However, the Corvette's four-speed, with 2.20 1st, 1.66 2nd, 1.31 3rd and direct top 4th stayed

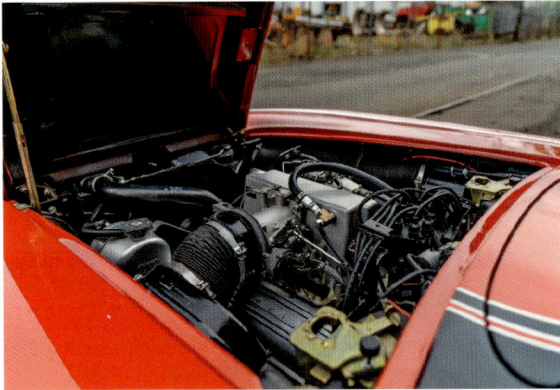

From 1961, Fuelies had bigger Doghouses (intake plenum). Top 1962 RPO 582 Fuelie 327s like on this car were rated at 360 horses. All Fuelie V8s had their high pressure mechanical fuel pump, driven by the distributor. *(Courtesy GT Motor Cars)*

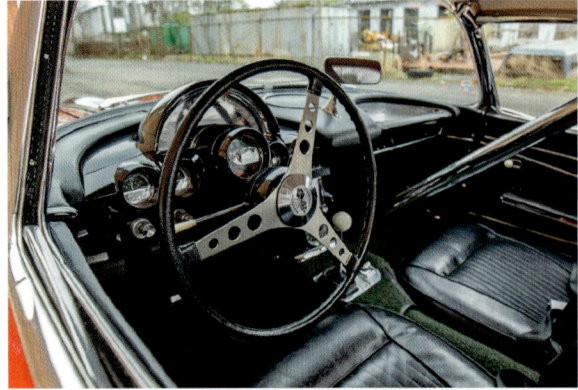

This '62 Corvette has the RPO 488 24 Gallon Fuel Tank (65 cars – $118.40) and RPO 687 HD Brakes and Steering (246 cars - $333.60). *(Courtesy GT Motor Cars)*

beyond reproach; a precise shift pattern action, allied to a smooth and easy clutch. If only all high performance cars were this good.

As for stats, the '61 Fuelie Corvette *R&T* tested, had a 3080lb curb weight, 53/47% front to rear weight distribution, 157in² of brake lining area, the familiar C1 Corvette's 102 in wheelbase, 3.7 turns lock-to-lock, ground clearance of 6.7in, and length/width/height were listed as a respective 178/70.4/52.1in. The roadster hit 58mph in 1st, 77mph in 2nd, 98mph in 3rd, and 128mph in 4th, and was capable of reaching the 283 V8's 6500rpm redline in all gears. Gas mileage was in the 11-17mpg range, 0-60mph was 6.6 seconds, 0-100mph came in 14.5 seconds, with the ¼ mile dispatched in 14.2 seconds at 98mph. However, none of the above intimated the special feeling you got from Corvette driving and ownership. Although the 1961 to 1962 sales rise from 10,939 to a then record 14,531, in spite of an escalating base price from $3934 to $4038, was a clue.

Detail visual changes greeted 1962 Corvette buyers. The chrome cove outline was history, so too the cove contrast color. Former cove chrome side vent accent spears were changed to black aluminum blades. The trunk lid medallion background was black, and newly added ribbed, anodized aluminum rocker panel moldings provided a lengthened, sleeker updated style.

Look carefully at the handily sized conventional trunk and lid. They would be absent until the fifth generation C5 Corvette roadster of 1998! The long standing power top option also ended in 1962. Commencing in 1956, oft called RPO 473, the power operated folding top cost $139.90 between 1957 and 1962, but its popularity declined over the years.

In 1956, 2682 Corvette fans optioned RPO 473 power top, out of 3467 Corvettes sold that model year. By 1962, the renamed RPO 474 was chosen by just 350 Corvette patrons, out of a 14,531 '62 Corvette total. However, four-speed optioning became de rigueur. In 1957 only 664 buyers paid $188.30, for RPO 685 'four-on-da-floor', out of 6339 Corvettes sold that model year. In '62 MY the four speed option carried the same name and price, but was selected by 11,318 buyers from the 14,531 Corvette total that year.

1962 saw the introduction of the famous Chevrolet 327 V8 to Corvette world. With bore and stroke now a respective 4.00 x 3.25in, all base Corvette V8s now had heavier duty bearings, larger ports and bigger camshaft, along with 10.5:1 CR, for 250bhp at 4400rpm. Pay an extra $53.80 for RPO 583, and 3924 buyers did so, and 300 wild horses at five grand landed in your underhood stable! Next up was RPO 396, a four-barrel 327 V8 sporting 340 ponies, with an associated tab of $107.60. 4412 Corvette fanciers took that route. All the above

As part of RPO 687, you got finned brake drums all around. Internal cooling fans at the front were fed by air scoops and front brake mounted deflectors, plus air scoops for the rear brakes. A quick steering adaptor was also included. It was racing courtesy of the factory option sheet! (*Courtesy GT Motor Cars*)

featured 4bbl carburetion, the troublesome Carter dual quad format was gone. However, the top 327 V8 was a Fuelie unit making 360 horse. Now, the one and only Fuelie, it still retailed for $484.20, and 1918 Corvette fans selected RPO 582, to get said powerplant.

The 340 and 360bhp V8s came with the solid lifter Duntov Cam, and 11.25:1 CR. What's more, both were ornery in everyday driving. Due to high rpm power and torque production, Powerglide optioning was limited to the placid 250 and 300 horse mills. And in an ominous sign of pending doom, RPO 242 implied a $5.40 PCV (Positive Crankcase Ventilation) valve. It was for Californian Corvettes, and a harbinger of smog controlled, malaise era high-performance doom, yet to transpire! Fortunately, smog law is of little import in racing, and the Corvette was still perfect for that purpose.

In spite of the AMA's late-50s anti racing pact, support for privateers continued apace from domestic automakers in an arm's length manner. In the Corvette's case matters were relatively easy, given the super hardware on the options sheet.

1961-62 Corvettes had rear styling that mirrored Bill Mitchell's personal proto racer called Stingray. This heralded the tail of the Mid-Year Corvettes, but this Impala-like triple taillight look was something else! (*Courtesy GT Motor Cars*)

They were certainly called upon for the 1960 Briggs Cunningham Le Mans triumph. What's more, Zora Arkus-Duntov had even more under the table, which helped out Delmo Johnson and Dave Morgan with their 1962 Corvette. Texan Delmo Johnson owned the Johnson Chevrolet dealership, and was a successful privateer racer. He had a good friendship with Zora Arkus-Duntov, based on

ZAK's respect for Johnson's racing efforts. That's how Delmo Johnson came by his Ermine White '62 Corvette racer.

Johnson telephoned Duntov and said, "Build me a race car." The only other thing he said was to make it white. So it was, that on January 12 1962, a brand new Ermine White Corvette with black interior, rolled off the St Louis line, replete with the best you could order: 360bhp Fuelie 327 V8, four-speed, 3.36 Positraction lsd, RPO 687 HD brakes and steering etc. Delmo Johnson flew out to St Louis to pick up the new Corvette, but drove back to Dallas to break the machine in. Once back in Dallas, Johnson and his mechanic Bill Goodfellow, carried out race car preparation. That is, engine blueprinting, roll cage fitment, quick fuel fill delivery system, seatbelt, Hurst shifter installation and weight stripping.

Not long after Johnson's return, a magic crate arrived at Johnson Chevrolet. It contained what became known as the 'Sebring Package': 37.5 gallon gas tank, aero headlight covers, louvered hood insert, beefier front swaybar and plexiglass hood deflector. It all contributed to Johnson and Morgan garnering 3rd in class, at 1962's 12 Hours of Sebring, plus the SCCA Southwest Division A-Production Championship for Delmo Johnson.

Corvette glamor

ADMIRED AT THE time, the 1961-62 Corvettes were subsequently judged to have an unharmonious body. *Road & Track* magazine's Ron Wakefield expressed this sentiment in the mid '70s. [38] A comment made in retrospect no doubt, upon becoming familiar with the 1961-62 ducktail, being part of the subsequent Mid-Year Corvettes.

The original C1 1953-62 Corvettes were known for their live axle. They gained the nickname 'Straight Axle' once the IRS Mid-Year replacement became established, as a technical point of generation distinction. However, there was no contemporary criticism concerning the Corvette's live axle usage. Indeed, both Maserati and Jensen persisted with live axles and leaf springs into the '60s and '70s. Alfa Romeo was wary of independent rear suspension, staying with a live axle for their Giulietta and Giulia. They switched to a DeDion rear

suspension for the '70s Alfetta. The DeDion set up was basically a live axle with a flexible joint, and Louis Chevrolet once worked for DeDion-Bouton.

The 1961-62 Corvette's styling is now judged attractively classic, and the revised rear look happened to be practical. On TV show *Iron Resurrection*, when restoring a '62 Fuelie Corvette, Martin Bros Customs' well-sized Mike Z even managed to hide in the trunk! Restoration shop owner Joe Martin and paint expert Shorty also drove said roadster, with room to spare. The later C1 Corvette was a gentleman's racer, in the best sense of that versatile tradition. *Road & Track*'s '61 Corvette, supplied by Harry Mann Chevrolet, was used the following weekend to pace the Riverside Sports Car GP. On test, that Corvette met every braking test, even a panic stop made necessary by a day dreaming driver.

A similar car owned by Alan Lockwood, in race tune, did a 107mph pass at LADS drag strip, in Long Beach California. 1961 axle choices went from 3.36, through 3.55, 3.70, 4.11 and 4.56 even! Horsepower spanned 230bhp to 315 horses. The four-speed synchromesh just couldn't be beat. As for value for money, the Corvette had 'one trick pony' Formula Junior cars licked! You could option the Corvette you wanted, and the Straight Axle cars had rounded ability in terms of their turn of speed, fair ride comfort and luxury options. So much so concerning that last quality, that the Plastic Fantastic was reputed to have stolen some Cadillac sales! Indeed, the later C1 Corvettes seemed to have stumbled upon a niche market demand, for quality, compact, sports/luxury cars. A combination of virtues not fully pursued by Corvette in later times, as the nameplate focused on the sport side of the street.

The concept of a small, luxo sporty car was then taken up by European imports. This was evidenced by the *Popular Mechanics* 'Owners Report: BMW' of July 1975. The subject was discussed by Michael Lamm. One 42-year-old Californian dentist owned a BMW 3.0CS coupe, and had previously owned Cadillacs. Indeed, *R&T*'s editor Ron Wakefield moved from a Corvette to the BMW coupe, as personal transport. A 38-year-old New Jersey executive owned a Chevelle wagon, and chose a BMW 2002tii, saying he would have preferred to

By 1960, the Corvette was stealing sales from Cadillac! The Corvette-based 2003 to 2009 Cadillac XLR
realized the concept of a compact, quality sports luxury car. *(Courtesy Ginger Delvisco)*

Built at the Corvette Bowling Green, Kentucky factory, the Cadillac XLR was the first US car costing over 100 grand. It was in keeping with Louis Chevrolet's high end, exclusive sports car dreams. *(Courtesy Ginger Delvisco)*

buy domestic with a lower price, but Detroit offered no car with such qualities. [39] Although selling in small numbers at this stage, the imports seemed to be getting conquest sales from Cadillac and Lincoln, just as the C1 Corvette had done earlier.

An August 1970 *Road Test* first gen Camaro survey brought up a similar story. Of the 37% of owners that wouldn't buy another Camaro, 28% said they were willing to go import, with mention of Mercedes and Volvo brands. A desire was also expressed for four-wheel disk brakes, economy and moderate operating costs. Certainly a 1961 base engine Corvette, with Powerglide and 3.55 econoaxle, would have been the moderately powered, sound handling and riding, small GT

machine such buyers were searching for post 1962.

Cadillac seemed to realize the concept, with the Corvette-based, but Caddy Northstar V8-powered, XLR of 2003 to 2009. The two-seater was built alongside the Corvette, at Bowling Green Kentucky. However, as per the earlier Allante, sales didn't meet the five to seven thousand per annum prediction. It seemed the big buck imports were too well established to be troubled by this stage.

Beverly Hills collector Bruce Meyer in 1989 with his '62 Corvette, flanked by Clark Gable's Mercedes 300SC and a Ferrari 275 GTB/4. The Straight Axle Corvette has long been a high end collectible. *(Times Newspapers Ltd.)*

However, back in the 1960s, it was Corvette that occupied an enviable sports, luxury image, and astronauts could help!

During the Cold War, NASA's space program and the exploits of its associated astronauts captured the imagination of people around the world. Astronauts were national heroes, so how fortuitous for Chevrolet, when Alan B Shepard turned up to space training in 1959 with a Corvette. It's hard to imagine a more appropriate car for an astronaut! Shepard subsequently became the first American in space, and GM's press release told the story, "On May 5, 1961, Alan B Shepard became the first American to travel into outer space. When he returned to terra firma, Shepard got behind

the wheel of a Chevrolet Corvette." And, "Shortly after Shepard's historic flight, then General Motors Executive Edward N Cole presented the astronaut with a new, white 1962 Corvette. The car had been outfitted by GM designers with a customized space-age interior."

Up to this point, it was almost unknown for giant Chevrolet to make a gift for public relations. Then too, as government employees, astronauts couldn't normally accept gifts. To effect a solution, 1960 Indy 500 champ Jim Rathmann, who owned a Melbourne, Florida Chevrolet/Cadillac dealership, proposed the 'Dollar Car' lease program. An astronaut and his family could lease up to two Chevrolets per year, for one dollar! The cars didn't

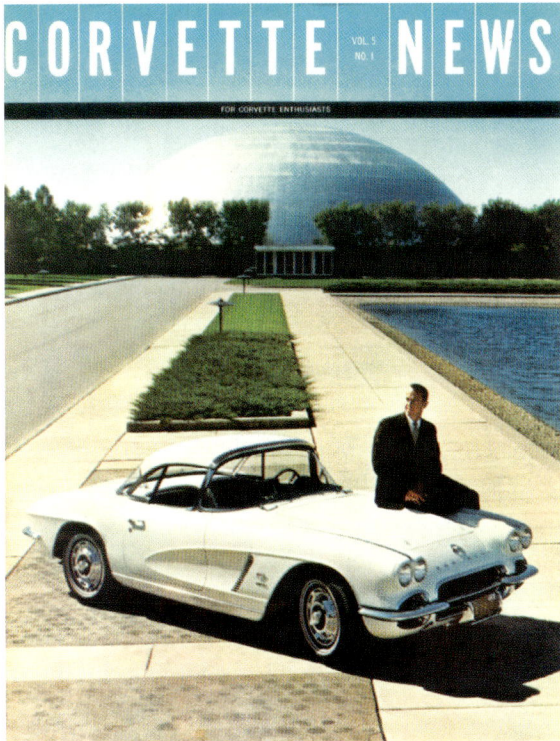

Astronaut Alan B Shepard became the first American to reach outer space, on May 5 1961. GM marked the achievement by giving Shepard this brand spanking new Ermine White 1962 Corvette! *(Courtesy Corvette News)*

At the GM Design Center Corvette presentation to Alan B Shepard were GM Styling boss Bill Mitchell on the left, and Chevrolet GM Ed Cole on the right. Next stop … the Moon! *(Courtesy GM Archives)*

have to be Corvettes, but common practice saw an astronaut get a family type Chevrolet model, complemented with a Corvette as second car. It helped that Rathmann's dealership was located close to the NASA launch site. GM President Ed Cole approved the scheme, and the Dollar Car program continued until 1971.

What next? Following Jackie Gleason's alter ego Ralph Kramden's directive, "To the moon!" The Corvette tried national television. The increasingly successful roadster was showcased on popular 1960-64 CBS show *Route 66*. And it was on *Route 66* that characters Buz Murdock and Tod Stiles got their kicks, every Friday night. Tod was the clean cut college kid, who had been given a new Corvette by his father, the owner of a New York shipping business. Buz worked at said shipping business, and met Tod there while the latter was doing his summer job. Following the death of Tod's father, and failure of the shipping business, the pair set out on the open road, righting wrongs and finding adventure in the Corvette.

Yes, it was product placement, but with the T-Bird becoming more of a mobile lounge with each passing model year, what other car could Buz and Tod use?! If they wished to reach their destination, not a Fiat! *Route 66*'s executive producer Herb Leonard and writer Sterling Silliphant called the show's Corvette – or Corvettes to be precise – the 'third character', so instrumental was the car in the series.

Being a black and white TV show, as all were at the time, a car with a light, neutral color was necessary, so not too much light was reflected. To this end, a Horizon Blue '60 Corvette was pressed into service for the show's pilot and early episodes. This roadster was followed by '61 and '62 Fawn Beige Corvettes, and finally a Saddle Tan '63 Mid-Year Corvette.

As part of product placement, the Corvette was updated with later versions through the show's run. Plus, there was a need to show the Corvette in its best light, using fresh condition examples. The head of production, Sam Manners, said they went through three to four cars each season, "Every 3000 miles, we would turn in the Corvettes on the show and get new ones." George Maharis, who played Buz Murdock, also got a new Corvette, by sleight of hand.

Maharis really dug the Corvette, and wanted one, so he cooked up a plan. Although not owning any car at the time, he told Chevrolet there might be a product promotion conflict of interest, since he would be turning up on set every day in his Ford Thunderbird, a quasi Corvette rival. Maharis prefaced the predicament with a straight face by saying, "We may have a little problem." Chevrolet didn't hesitate in gifting him a new example of the Plastic Fantastic!

Although years before reality TV, all was not what it seemed on *Route 66*. Sometimes Buz and Tod were seen sitting in a Corvair, the little Chevrolet compact. It was felt most viewers wouldn't notice. The Corvair was also used to film the Corvette from behind, as Sam Manners recalled, "That car had the trunk in the front and the engine in the rear. So, we removed the trunk lid, mounted cameras in the trunk, then filmed the scene as we followed the Corvette." *Route 66* was a swell way to celebrate the 68,915 C1 Straight Axle Corvettes made. [40] It was also a great way to introduce the next generation Corvette. The first Mid-Year Corvettes reached dealerships by late September 1962. The opening Season 3, Episode 1 of *Route 66*, featuring the new Corvette, aired one week earlier!

Route 66's commencement coincided with the Corvette breaking the 10,000 per annum sales barrier for the first time. It was a goal hoped for '54 MY! Now a desirable sports car, an increasing number of Corvette patrons would emulate Buz and Tod, in their search for adventure.

Corvette Sting Ray
1963-65

Truly all new

1963 IS REMEMBERED for several historic events, the assassination of President Kennedy, *The Andy Williams Christmas Album* and the all-new Corvette Sting Ray. The last milestone was timely according to Chevrolet, which provided an explanation in a special supplement to the *Corvette News* publication in 1962:

"In the last few years Corvette demand has exceeded supply; so from the standpoint of popularity an entirely new vehicle was not necessary. Nevertheless, we felt that the original design no longer represented our best engineering, so plans for a change were initiated in 1959." [41]

Working under development code XP720, there were cogent reasons to improve upon what subsequently became known as the Straight Axle or C1 Corvette. That Corvette's front end hardware was the kind of stuff used on 1949 Chevrolet sedans. The new second generation Corvette, with Sting Ray suffix, adopted SLA (short long arm) or unequal length A arms, and a more precise steering system, in keeping with Chevrolets since 1955. That is, a spherical balljoint design where the overall steering ratio could be adjusted from 19.6:1 to 17:1, simply by relocating the tie rod ball studs on each steering arm. This would cut turns between locks from 3.4 to just 2.9, if the Sting Ray had manual steering. Yes, the Corvette now offered power steering as a first time option, with its recirculating ball system.

A fair number of British sports cars, the MGB and AC Cobra to name a couple, had rack and

pinion steering. Rack and pinion was more direct versus a recirculating ball setup. However, like Mercedes and BMW, the latter system implied less kickback or road shock for Corvette drivers. The Plastic Fantastic's tire size stayed at 6.70-15, but now the Straight Axle Corvette's optional wider 15 x 5.5in rims became standard. The Corvette's four-wheel 11in drum brakes also became wider for the Mid-Year generation.

Unitary body construction was becoming more commonplace internationally, like with the Corvair. However, the latest Corvette joined the British Triumph Herald in being part of a rarer band of new designs featuring four-wheel independent suspension, allied to a separate chassis. The VW Beetle had IRS and body on platform construction too. The aforementioned Herald was also like the Corvette in having front coils and a frame mounted differential, but unlike the Corvette sported rear coils. The Corvette's rear springing was handled by one transverse multileaf spring, sitting on the differential. Remaining elements of the Corvette's new IRS saw axle halfshafts serve as upper links, to complement lower links and trailing arms. Influence for the Corvette's IRS derived from Zora Arkus-Duntov's racing specials, and the Jag XKE. [42]

The new Mid-Year Corvette only had a front swaybar to this point in time, and four conventional dampers. The latest Corvette had a new frame, plus a number of contemporary touches overseen by Zora Arkus-Duntov. Roll center heights for front and rear suspension were a respective 3.25in and 7.56in. The intention was less body lean, with the outside wheels more upright in cornering. This was

NEW CHEVROLET CORVETTE

The 1963 Corvette: practically the only thing carried over was the nameplate! Note the one-year-only split rear window. Bill Mitchell wanted it, Zora Arkus-Duntov did not. Poor rear visibility was the reason. *(Courtesy GM Archives)*

Chevrolet put the Mid-Year Corvette word out in *Corvette News*. It said the strong selling Straight Axle Corvette no longer represented best sports car practice, with new Corvette planning from 1959. *(Courtesy IPC Magazines)*

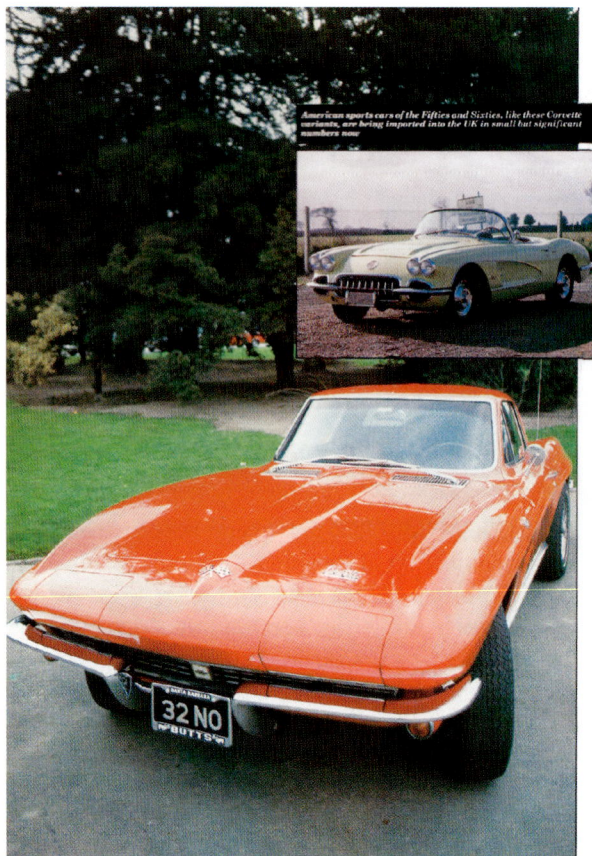

to maximize the tire contact patch with the road surface, and therefore traction, without the use of excessive negative camber.

The Corvette's front suspension members were angled upwards, generating an anti-dive factor of 50% compared to Straight Axle Corvettes. There was also softer springing, and more wheel travel. Given Chevrolet and GM's resources, with every form of road type and surface at the 'Ride and Handling Road' test facility located at GM's proving grounds, you would expect an improvement with the new Corvette.

The Mid-Year Corvette's separate chassis construction suited the high labor content and old school production layout seen at the St Louis, Missouri truck plant, where the Corvette was made. It was the only place the Corvette was made, and it was perhaps no coincidence that the facility would largely see out body-on-frame construction Corvette, before a move to an ultra modern factory, in Bowling Green, Kentucky. The latter location is still used for Corvette production today. As part of chassis changes, versus Straight Axle Corvettes, 80lb was moved rearwards for the C2 Corvette.

Wheelbase was reduced from 102in to 98in. The continued use of the by now fabled small block Chevrolet V8 helped with obtaining the 50/50 front/rear weight distribution, so sought after by automotive designers and sports car aficionados alike, for so many years, to get neutral handling.

Powered by Chevrolet

POWERTRAIN WAS THE sole carry over area, concerning Corvette. Given its excellence in use by low volume British and European sports car specialists, why not?! The starter Corvette motor was a placid 250 horse 327 V8. This was an 'offend no one' powerplant, with hydraulic lifters, mild cam, single point dizzy, but a forged steel crank and premium fuel-hungry 10.5:1 CR, allied to a dual exhaust system. The perfect powerplant for Corvette's sole slushbox of 1953-67, the RPO M35 Powerglide. A unit costing 199 bucks, and selected by just 2621 Plastic Fantastic patrons in 1963, out of a 21,513 Corvette total.

Pay a $53 surcharge, and you could have the most popular engine choice concerning a '63 Corvette, the 300 horse L75 327 V8. 8033 Corvette faithful said yes to L75's bigger 4bbl carb, and larger intake manifold and exhaust valves. The second most popular optional 327 V8 was the 340bhp (gross) L76 unit, costing $107 and chosen by 6978 1963 Corvette buyers. This was the motor, backed by a four-speed, found in the Silver Blue '63 Corvette barn find, on TV show *Dream Car Garage*. According to show host, and Legendary Motor Car Co proprietor Peter Klutt, the coupe was purchased by a New York dentist, then parked once the owner passed away in 1974. The all original car was cleaned, and came back to life after 30 years of storage! Said car still ran on its original tires even, which made Klutt pass on doing a burnout!

Problems with this '63 Corvette? The instrumentation gauge faces needed cleaning, and the embedded windshield radio antenna produced less than stellar reception. However, the coupe was still tightly built and functional. After detailing, it started winning show trophies. Service interval stickers were still visible in the engine compartment. It was all testimony to how well the Corvette was put together at this time, and the durability of Chevrolet powertrain and driveline components. Sadly, this wouldn't hold for the '68 Corvette.

Top motor was still the 360 horse Fuelie 327 V8, now renamed RPO L84, and with a price tag of $430.40. The Fuelie V8 was the least popular engine option, and selected by just 2610 Corvette faithful in 1963. Standard gearbox with the base 327 V8 was a three by the knee stick. However, most went for the wide ratio M20 four-speed, or M21 close ratio four on the floor. Both four-speeds cost $188.30, and indeed this was the four-speed option's price from 1959 to 1965. The optional M35 Powerglide slushbox also held to $199.10 during the same timeframe. Most went four-speed.

Three-speed and Powerglide Corvettes implied a 3.36 differential ratio, with 3.70 supplied on four-speed cars. However, rear end ratio choice from the factory, ranged from the tall two-buck G91 Special Highway Axle of 3.08 to a 4.65 drag racer special.

A very popular option was the G81 Positraction lsd, retailing for $43.05 during 1960 to 1965, and selected by 17,554 Corvette buyers in 1963. Positraction could be had with 3.08, 3.36, 3.55, 3.70, 4.11 and 4.56 differential ratios. Racer or cruiser, the choice was yours!

If you got a Corvette coupe, as opposed to a convertible, then your new bolide could sip from an oversize RPO NO3 36 gallon gas tank. Only 63 buyers sprang for the $202 extra, to get an option that was part of the '62 Corvette's Sebring race package. In contrast 5739 buyers parted with the 236 bones necessary to obtain the convertible related RPO C07 hardtop. Concerning Corvette convertibles, 10,919 roadsters rolled out of the St Louis plant in '63 model year.

The Impala was already America's No 1 selling car. Nova would soon be a standalone nameplate, and Corvair Monza's success would inspire the 64½ Mustang. Chevrolet truly had the competition stung! *(Courtesy GM Archives)*

Styling from the life aquatic

THE MID-YEAR CORVETTE'S almost all new styling was greatly influenced by GM Styling supremo Bill Mitchell's love for creatures of the deep. That is, oceanic inhabitants. Of sharks Mitchell confided, "... they are exciting to look at." [43] Indeed, the second generation Mid-Year C2 Corvette was developed from the 1960 Mako Shark I prototype, once called XP-755. A hint of the new Corvette was intimated by Bill Mitchell's privately created and funded Stingray racer, and the rear end styling of the 1961-62 Corvette that said racer influenced. It could be said the '63 Corvette had the rear end view intended for it. That is, an angular rear resembling the triangular wings of a stingray, blended into an aggressive shark profile.

Many have referred to the Mid-Year Corvette as the most beautifully designed American car of all time. Mitchell considered said Corvette to be his finest design hour. [44] Rearwards, the '63 Corvette also featured a contentious rear split window. While the 1961-67 Corvette's rear boat styling harked back to the roadsters of the thirties, and would be discerned on the 1970-73 Buick Riviera, the Corvette's split rear pane was also a retro touch recalling the Bugatti Atlantique, and Bertone BAT.

The split rear window implied a seminal Corvette development, you could now order a Plastic Fantastic as a coupe, for the first time. The Corvette was no longer limited to being a ragtop roadster. In fact, Zora Arkus-Duntov preferred the coupe bodystyle, "...because to drive fast, you cannot drive in the wind." The new Mid-Year Corvette design saw much happy consensus at GM. However, there were some contentious areas, as relayed by Zora Arkus-Duntov to *Road & Track* in June 1977, "We were all on the same track, styling and engineering. I was, however, dead against the rear window divider bar, but Ed Cole sided with Bill Mitchell, who wanted it. When the 1963 model was out, I took Bill Mitchell for a ride at the proving ground and he admitted, 'Yeah, you were right.'"

The public weren't generally pleased concerning the lack of rear vision, brought by the split window. A one piece rear window was offered as a dealer retrofit, and in fact became standard on the revised 1964 Corvette. Indeed, in the 'nothing older than

NEW CHEVROLET CORVETTE

At one time they were all roadsters, but now Corvette dreams could include a coupe. 1963 selections ran 50/50, with a slight edge to the roadster, which offered a $220 cost saving. *(Courtesy GM Archives)*

A new Corvette, and a new logo. This time incorporating Stars & Stripes colors, although some perceived it as a Tricolor! Apt, given Louis Chevrolet's background! *(Courtesy Marc Cranswick)*

last year's model' era, there was at least one owner of a '63 split window Corvette that had the rear window divider removed, to update the car! Although the split rear window seems to have been the least liked aspect of the then new Mid-Year Corvette, this one year only feature has made the '63 edition sought out by collectors, and valuable.

Signs of the '63 Corvette commanding a premium were already in evidence by the mid '70s. *Road & Track* said the '63 Corvettes in good condition commanded $3500-$4000 at the time, over 20 grand in 2020s money. The 1964 Corvettes were on 2 to 3½ grand, in the same order. The split

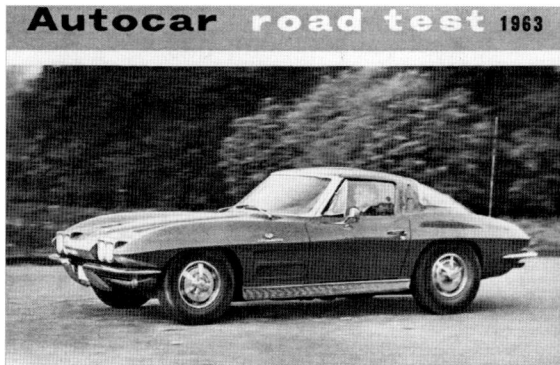

Chevrolet Sting Ray 5,363 c.c.

THE Corvette Sting Ray is a curious mixture of American and European concepts of what a genuine *gran turismo* car should be. The road test version had the hottest of the four optional stages of engine tune available; equipped with fuel injection, this means a gross power output of 360 b.h.p. Making allowances for the power required to drive the various accessories and that absorbed by a reasonably quiet exhaust system and the transmission, it would be fair to assume that 280 b.h.p. is available at the rear wheels—this is real power indeed.

Considering that the car is only a two-seater, the kerb weight is relatively high at 29 cwt. In outline, the shape looks efficient and it must be the overall gearing that restricts the maximum speed to 146.5 m.p.h., compared with 152.3 m.p.h. for the Aston Martin DB4 G.T. Zagato, and 152.7 m.p.h. for the Jaguar E-type fixed-head coupé, each with less powerful engines. The overall impression when reaching this speed was that the acceleration powers were really outstanding. On closer examination, however, it transpires that the Sting Ray will reach 120 m.p.h. from standstill in 8 secs less time than the E-type, but takes 1.4 sec longer than the Aston Martin.

This conflict between impression and fact arises from two causes. First gear is a very high ratio, but second and third are relatively low by British standards. Moreover,

the refinement, particularly in respect of engine and transmission noise, is inferior to that of most of its European competitors and this gives the impression of the car being more powerful than it really is. To the purist, some of the false styling features, such as dummy grilles and air vents in the body, appear unnecessary.

The performance is certainly vivid, but if more attention had been given to such items as tyre adhesion in the wet and wipers that clear the screen effectively above 80 m.p.h., instead of some gimmicks which only attempt to give an impression of engineering thought, the Sting Ray would be a better car.

Chevrolet were the first American manufacturers to produce a genuine sports car in the post-war period, when the Corvette was introduced in 1953. At that time it was a

PRICES	£ s d
Two-seater coupé with Positraction differential, fuel injection, sintered brake linings, four-speed gearbox	
—as tested	2,840 0 0
Purchase Tax	592 4 7
Total (In G.B.)	3,432 4 7

How the Chevrolet Sting Ray compares:

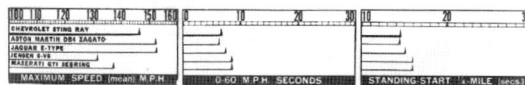

	MAXIMUM SPEED (mean) M.P.H.	0-60 M.P.H. SECONDS	STANDING-START ¼-MILE (secs.)
CHEVROLET STING RAY			
ASTON MARTIN DB4 ZAGATO			
JAGUAR E-TYPE			
MASERATI 3500			
MASERATI 3771 SEBRING			

Autocar found the '63 360 horse Fuelie Corvette four-speed to be sporty, but rorty. The only rival to match its value was the Jaguar XKE, but refinement had a price. *(Courtesy Autocar)*

Corvette received dummy hood grilles. It was felt within GM that rain might enter real grilles and short out the electrics. However, ZAK would have had deflectors to solve that. In any case faux grilles were cheaper than real ones! Well, the split rear pane was deep sixed for '64 MY, but the Mid-Year cars never got functional hood louvers.

The faux grilles went away for '64 MY, although the hood depressions remained. The hood got smoothed out for 1965. The Jag XKE, the Corvette's long time nemesis, also got light in the front end at speed. TV show *Car and Track* tested a revised '68 Jag XKE, with emissionized dual carb 4.2L I6, and dealer fit a/c. Show host Bud Lindemann noted that the test driver had to back off at 135mph, due to front end lift. The Porsche 911 also had its battery relocated within its 'frunk', to deal with the same problem. For 1964 the C pillar vents on the driver's side were made functional, improving ventilation.

The faux knock-off wheel covers were simplified, and the '63 Corvette's ribbed rocker panel trim gave way to a new dress panel with horizontal black dividers. There was also a revised rear deck emblem. 1965 Corvettes saw 1963-64's non functional dual fender speed coves give way to functional, fender triple gills. Plus, inner horizontal grille bars in black were surrounded by a chrome outer grille. Rocker panel trim was altered again, and new six petal faux knock-off wheel trims arrived. The Corvette had skipped the imitation reverse chrome wheel trim fad.

Gadgets galore

THE 1956 CORVETTE had become the first sports car on the planet to offer power windows. With the Mid-Year Corvettes came a number of creature comforts new to the Plastic Fantastic. In another world first, there was $421 RPO C60 factory designed and installed a/c. The first '63 Corvette fitted with said a/c had an October 1962 build date. The car belonged to a GM executive, who returned the coupe for a retrofit. The other 420

window wasn't specifically stated as the reason for the premium. It was merely noted that it was harder to locate a sound condition, unmolested '63 Corvette coupe relative to other Mid-Year Corvettes. [45]

Zora Arkus-Duntov was always concerned with functional Corvette improvement. He ran into conflicts with stylists and product planners at GM on Mid-Year Corvette aerodynamics, and Corvette aspects in general. He subsequently aired his grievances to *Car and Driver*'s Patrick Bedard, in that journal's June 1971 issue. Duntov was around for an interview during 1971 Corvette testing. Concerning the C2 Mid-Year Corvette's general shape, ZAK said it had, "… just enough lift to be a bad airplane." Given his aviation background, he was well informed to make that statement! The C2 Corvette got a little light at the front around 100mph.

Zora Arkus-Duntov wanted functional louvers, to let the air out and reduce lift. Instead, the '63

1963 Corvettes with C60 a/c were built around six months post that initial chilled machine. The second generation Corvette also brought a power brake option, RPO J50 cost 43 bucks and was chosen by 3336 '63 Corvette fans.

Power steering and leather seats were also new to Corvette. They set the two-seater apart concerning optionality. Comforts not even some of the most expensive sporting cars in the world offered, factory direct at least. Concerning option take up rate, 15% of '63 Corvettes had power brakes, and 12% came with power steering. The 1114 that chose RPO 898 genuine leather seats, represented a mere 5% of 1963 Corvette customers. However, only 124 purchasers went with the RPO C48 heater and defroster deletion 'delete option', where you got 100 bucks back for going without what most folks wanted! RPO 941 Sebring Silver exterior paint was an 80 buck option, chosen by 3516 Corvette patrons in 1963. The raucous N11 off-road exhaustsystem (racing only) was 37 bucks, and highlighted the 'no two cars the same' Corvette nature. You wouldn't experience such a wide mix with Aston Martin or MG. Indeed, in 1963-64 the

new Corvette was truly without rival, and the Studebaker Avanti was as close as home grown got.

Sports car world 1964

THE AVANTI WAS the sporting idea of Studebaker's President Sherwood Egbert. Egbert sent a memo with Jag XKE picture to Raymond Loewy, the legendary styling boss at Studebaker, asking if something similar could be cooked up. In very short order, with Avanti making a '63 MY debut like the new Mid-Year Corvette. Being based on the humble live axled Lark compact, the Avanti had a chassis more aligned to the outgoing Straight Axle Corvette. However, its fiberglass body, and 'bottom breather' aero front end, along with V8 wallop, placed the Avanti in the current Corvette's sightline. Indeed, the Avanti's body panels were done by Molded Fiberglass Body of Ashtabula, Ohio. The very same firm that did the body panels for the original 1953 Corvette.

That the Avanti failed to launch a market place challenge to the Corvette was more related to Studebaker's perilous financial state, and related

Internationally judged as stylish and desirable, this 1964 Corvette has the popular options of L75 300 horse 327 V8 and four-speed. *(Courtesy Mecum)*

Model	Engine/HP	Length (in)	Weight (lb)	Price ($)	Gearbox
Buick Riviera	425ci V8/360	208	3950	4394	auto
Chrysler 300K	413ci V8/390	215.3	3965	4043	auto/man
Corvette	327ci V8/375	175.3	2943	4303	auto/man
Ford Thunderbird	390ci V8/300	205.4	4605	4513	auto
Studebaker supercharged Avanti	305ci V8/335	192.4	3365	4445	auto/man
Studebaker supercharged Hawk	305ci V8/305	204	3280	2958	auto/man

Corvette for '64…new smooth ride, improved performance for America's sports car

Both Corvette Sting Ray models are jauntier, sportier than ever for '64. Their aerodynamic styling has been enhanced with a number of things that make news. Ride is one. Variable rate springs, recalibrated shocks give a smoother ride, flatter cornering ability, better road control. In-town driving is quiet because of generous insulation. New wheel covers, hood treatment, ribbed rocker sill moldings for both models. New interior ventilation system, new one-piece rear window on the Sport Coupe. Size remains a sporty 175.3 inches long. And check those great performance teams: 250-hp Corvette V8 with 3-Speed Synchro-Mesh standard. Other optional* engines, 300-hp and the increased-performance 365-hp and 375-hp (Ramjet Fuel Injection) V8's. Also 4-Speed Synchro-Mesh* and Powerglide* transmissions.

CORVETTE STING RAY SPORT COUPE IN SATIN SILVER WITH OPTIONAL CAST ALUMINUM WHEELS*

Corvette Sting Ray Interiors
Bucket seats softly padded with deep foam cushioning. Standard sport equipment: simulated walnut steering wheel rim, new console panel, functional instrumentation. Luxurious deep-twist carpeting, door to door. Two roof styles in Convertible: folding soft top and removable hardtop; or both, with second at modest extra cost. Cast aluminum wheels* with knock-off hubs, shown above. Seven exterior colors. Color-keyed interiors, with genuine leather seat trim* optional.
*Optional at extra cost.

Zora Arkus-Duntov took Bill Mitchell on a drive in a '63 Corvette on GM's proving grounds, and Mitchell agreed with ZAK that the split rear pane had to go, "Yeah, you were right." *(Courtesy GM Archives)*

inability to meet pre-orders with a car of suitable build quality. Beyond this, the Avanti was physically larger than the Mid-Year Corvette, and more of a 2+2 grand tourer. Other possible domestic Corvette rivals were even more grand tourer in guise. They were personal luxury cars of great girth. Indeed, the once svelte two-seater Thunderbird, now sported a passenger reclining seat option, with pull up headrest for '64 MY that *Popular Mechanics* said resembled a barber shop chair! Sports cars such machines were not, nor were they intended to be. [46]

Much like the market of 10 years earlier, when the Corvette started, the imported sports cars or sporting cars consisted of smaller, lighter and nimbler vehicles. These were oftentimes lower powered and slower accelerating. As in the early '50s, the imported sporting field was dominated by the British. The well known Austin-Healey 3000 was considered a powerful, low slung true sports car, and was one of the models imported by English giant BMC. The diminutive Austin-Healey Sprite was popular, and twinned with the MG Midget.

Popular Mechanics said the letters MG were almost shorthand for pleasure driving Stateside. Indeed, the 1947 MG TC was credited as starting the US sports car movement. By 1964 MG offered the Midget, larger MGB and MG 1100 sedan. The last was an Austin related design of front drive nature, felt to handle almost as well as the Midget.

Most popular of English imports was Standard Triumph. Its 1200 and Sports Six (Herald & Vitesse), Spitfire and TR4 sports cars impressed

many. The Rootes Group had its Sunbeam Alpine, which *Popular Mechanics* said was a real sports car. This British sporting machinery made use of rack and pinion steering, along with front disk brakes, which were enjoyed by Studebaker alone, concerning domestic brands. Of course one famous marque offered four-wheel disk brakes as standard: Jaguar. The brand from Browns Lane made imports of great standing in the US. *Popular Mechanics* said that while the Jag wasn't the most expensive import, it was the most glamorous.

Like the Triumph Sports Six and MG 1100, the Jag MkII and Mk10 represented an alien concept for America, that of the sports sedan. Then there was the XKE, a Jag that *Popular Mechanics* called "ultra-rakish". Indeed, in size, weight and performance, the XKE was the closest match for the Corvette, and had even inspired the Avanti! Sure, you could pay more for an Aston Martin, Maserati or Ferrari, but arguably such marques didn't bring any more looks or performance than the Jag XKE or Mid-Year Corvette. Outside the super exotic Italians there were some classy, high-class sporting cars such as Alfa Romeo's 2600 Spider. Mercedes provided what *Popular Mechanics* dubbed the "slick new 230SL". The 230SL had fuel injection, like Corvette. However, both Alfa and Mercedes lacked the Corvette and Jag XKE's turn of speed, and were more grand tourers in nature.

The Porsche 356 came with four-wheel disk brakes as standard, so did the Mercedes 230SL. However, the sub 2000lb, over four grand rear-engine Porsche was more your gentleman's racer, less a grand tourer. It could be driven to a race or rally, then driven home. You could accomplish the same task with a Corvette. That said, with your choice of 75 or 95bhp, from Porsche's 1600 cc (96ci) flat four, the Porsche wasn't for the large engine category of American production sports car racing.

Volvo's 1800 coupe was also more of a durable workhorse than out and out racer. The sturdy Swede's nigh on four grand price brought front disk brakes, and a longevity subsequently proven by Irv Gordon's world record, biggest mileage Volvo 1800. Crankshaft main bearings were sized like those on a Chevrolet small block V8! Also long lived, but slower in operation, was that fashionista favorite the VW Karmann Ghia. That coupe's 40

horse flat four, stylish coachwork, combined with humble, durable Beetle floorpan and mechanicals had their appeal to some. With a price tag just over two grand, weight just under 2000lb, and the same 94.5in wheelbase as most air cooled VWs, the Karmann Ghia was a safe bet.

The Karmann Ghia's separate chassis construction and four-wheel independent suspension, along with all around drum brakes, were common qualities possessed by the Corvette. However, that's where the similarities ended. The VW wasn't noted for its turn of speed. One humorous ad showed a Karmann Ghia liveried with racing number, and the funny caption "You would lose". Unlike the Corvette, the VW was no racer in stock form.

Yes, Corvette rivals were hard to find, but if all else failed you could go Japanese. In 1964 the name Datsun started to surface. *Popular Mechanics* described the Datsun range as conventional, and well put together. Aside from sedan, wagon and pickup truck variants, there was a two-passenger roadster that also utilized the Datsun's 60 horse inline four mill. *Popular Mechanics* called the Datsuns neat little cars. Like the Corvette in 1953, you have to start somewhere!

Imported sports cars

Model	Engine/ HP	Length (in)	Weight (lb)	Price ($)	Gearbox
Austin Healey 3000 MkII	3L I6/136	157.5	2375	3535	4sp OD
Alfa 2600 Spider	2.6L I6/165	177	2688	5295	5sp
Jaguar XKE roadster	3.8L I6/265	175.4	2464	5325	4sp
MGB	1.8L I4/94	153.2	1920	2658	4sp
Porsche 356	1.6L F4/95	158	1990	4178	4sp
Sunbeam Alpine	1.5L I4/87.8	155.3	2211	2595	4sp
Triumph TR4	2.2L I4/105	156	2184	2849	4sp OD (opt)
Volvo 1800	1.8L I4/100	173	2490	3995	4sp
VW Karmann Ghia	1.1L F4/40	163	1808	2295	4sp

A '64 Corvette with, almost, the mostest: 365bhp L76 327 4bbl V8 and four-speed!
(*Courtesy ClassicCars.Com*)

Stats for the starter C2 Mid-Year Corvette 327 roadster, with 'three by the knee', were: 175.1in length, 69.6in width, 48.1in height, 98in wheelbase, 3050lb. The Torque Thrust rims aren't factory issue. *(Courtesy ClassicCars.Com)*

Mid-Year Corvette reception

IT HAD BEEN a long wait for an all new Corvette. Press and public alike warmly received the new 1963 Corvette, with few exceptions. *Car Life* bestowed its 1963 Award for Engineering Excellence on the new second generation Corvette, subsequently known as the Mid-Year or C2 sports cars. *Road & Track* previewed the '63 Corvette at GM's proving grounds in its October 1962 issue. The report immediately noted advances over the Straight Axle C1 Corvette era. The journal repeated its 1960 Corvette assessment, "The Corvette is unmatched for performance per dollar in terms of transportation machines …". However, *R&T* added that the Straight Axle cars could dance like an Apache with a hot foot! Now with IRS, "In a word, the new Sting Ray sticks!" This included dropping the clutch at 5000rpm, in a car with much more compliance than the previous generation. Five inches of ground clearance and an ability to do almost 90mph on GM's S bend were to the good!

The machine *R&T* sampled was a pilot production 360 horse Fuelie 327 Corvette roadster, with 3.70 differential and four-speed, curb weight of 3030lb, riding on 6.70-15s. It was noted that being able to telescope the steering wheel in and out 3in, permitted driving 'Italian-style'. That is, long arm action, even if pedals remained footwell buried, domestic car style, for the usual six-footer. There was a locking glove cubby hole on the new '63 Corvette. *R&T* described this last addition as a "gin bin" to the country club set. Indeed, high-end Corvettes appealed to that Jag loving crowd! The 6in diameter speedo and tach were visibility boons,

and in general the Mid-Year Corvette's functional upgrades and refinements prompted *Road & Track* to refer to the outgoing Straight Axle machine as Corvette's "stone-age form".

Access to luggage space was judged troublesome, but the space itself was relatively well sized. The Corvette was now in its no trunklid era (until 1982). The new car was also swifter, with the 3.70 diff ratioed test '63 Corvette outpacing the '60 Fuelie 283 Corvette with 4.11 rear axle, that *R&T* had tested earlier. At least up to 60mph. Zero to 40mph and zero to sixty were a respective 4.2/6.6 seconds, and 3.4/5.9 seconds for the new machine. However, the old car won out in 0-80mph, 0-100mph and ¼-mile, with respective time sets of 9.6/14.5/14.2 seconds, and 10.2/16.5/14.9 seconds at 95mph for the latest '63 Corvette.

Problems with the latest Corvette? Body resonances, shift linkage buzz, plus poor rear vision, "… all we could see in the rear view mirror was that silly bar splitting the rear window down the middle." Well, perhaps this was the ultimate Anglo-Italo touch?! In *The Gumball Rally*, actor Raul Julia's archetypal Ferrari Daytona Italian racing driver Franco said the first rule of Italian driving was, "What's behind me isn't important!" Whereupon he broke off the Daytona's rear view mirror, and tossed it backwards out of the roadster! A sports car and its owner have their own set of priorities, it would seem. In Franco's case, fast cars and even faster women! Nevertheless, *Road & Track* was sufficiently impressed by the all-new Mid-Year Corvette Sting Ray to say, "… in its nice, shiny new concept it ought to be nearly unbeatable."

R&T found its 3.70 diff, 360 horse test subject could hit the redline in all gears, which implied 65mph in 1st, 85mph in 2nd, 108mph in 3rd, and 142mph in top gear (4th), all at 6500rpm. Regular fuel economy was discovered to be in the 11 to 14mpg range. Britain's oldest car magazine *Autocar*, tried the new C2 Corvette, in split window coupe

Out of 22,229 1964 Corvettes, 7171 buyers paid
the $107 surcharge to option this L76 327 V8.
(Courtesy ClassicCars.Com)

Full instrumentation and 'four-on-da-floor'
were odd in a domestic, but not for Corvette.
The Mid-Year cars were the first Corvettes to feature
optional factory a/c. *(Courtesy ClassicCars.Com)*

form. It had the same 360 horse Fuelie 327 V8/four-speed power team that *R&T* had evaluated. The UK journal found the same refinement resonances as *Road & Track*, namely engine and transmission noise.

Autocar's test car was sportily specified with Positraction lsd (RPO G81), sintered brake linings (RPO J65), four-speed (RPO M21), and L84 360 horse Fuelie 327 V8 mill, for a not insubstantial £3432, 4 shillings and 7 pence. Core, blimey Mary Poppins, that's a pretty penny! However, Jaguar E-type excepted, the Corvette was much cheaper than European opposition of similar speed. Indeed, the Corvette was substantially swifter than the 131.5mph Jensen CV8, which did 0-60mph in 8.1 seconds, and a 16 second flat ¼-mile. The 137mph Maserati GT1 Sebring matched those last two stats, exactly.

The Jag E-type (XKE) was also not as quick with 0-60mph in 7.2 seconds, allied to a 15.2 second ¼-mile. The Corvette recorded respective figures of 6.5 seconds and 14.6 seconds. The only car that was both quicker and faster was 007's Aston Martin, although government employee James Bond could never afford a DB4 GT Zagato. It was *Autocar*'s comparison Chariot of the Gods! The Aston Martin achieved 0-60mph in 6.1 seconds and a 14.5 second ¼-mile, finishing with a 152.3mph top speed. The

Jag just beat out even the Aston Martin's terminal velocity, with 152.7mph. The Corvette could manage a 'mere' 146.5mph in those halcyon pre-emissions days, when cars on both sides of the Atlantic shared the same specification.

The Aston Martin and Jaguar attained their higher top speeds, with less power. *Autocar* wondered if the Corvette's shortfall was due to its relatively high weight of 29cwt, and perhaps aerodynamics? Indeed, the Corvette's beefy body on frame nature, long produced a weight penalty next to unit construction. However, acceleration was a different ball game. The Corvette reached 120mph, 8 seconds before the Jag, and only 1.4 seconds after the DB4 GT Zagato.

Autocar judged the new Corvette as a curious mix of US and European concepts of what a genuine GT car should be. The 360bhp Fuelie 327 V8 on test was stated as the hottest of the four engine choices available, and with 280 horsepower at the rear wheels, "... this is real power indeed." The price of the acknowledged outstanding acceleration was excessive engine and transmission

It could take a while for US exports to reach overseas markets. By the time this 360bhp split window '63 Fuelie Corvette reached Australia, the US '64 edition was already 375 horses strong, and minus the split! *(Courtesy Suttons)*

noise; items that would be addressed on the Mid-Year Corvette, as it matured. However, by now the Fuelie V8 was a rather raucous performer.

When observing the Fuelie Corvette in 1964, *Car Life* magazine mentioned that its test car idled at 1100rpm "with a lope". *Road & Track* retrospectively tried a 1965 Fuelie Corvette in February 1975, finding it to idle roughly at 1300rpm, and bogging down should the throttle be opened wide at 1500rpm. [47] All Fuelies had M21 close ratio four-speeds, but 1st was tall, good for 54mph at the 6200rpm redline, with 4.11 diff ratio. After that, hold on tight because you would be shifting fast, utilizing unbeatable synchronizers and a crisp, light short throw, for 0-60mph in 6.3 seconds, a 14.6 second ¼-mile at 98mph and 0-100mph in 15 seconds flat. The game ended at 127mph, if you buzzed the four-speed to 6500rpm, and could withstand a maximum decibel count of 85dBA! Such stats came from *R&T*'s companion journal at the time, *Car Life*. It was all accompanied by two trash can sized, reverse flow mufflers.

So yes, *Autocar* was right to contend that the Corvette wasn't as refined as European opposition, but in Fuelie form, the Corvette wasn't that kind of car. Not a grand tourer, much more a road racer, for a tight track you might drive to, race on and drive home. Flatbed not required, in the style of Delmo Johnson or Don Yenko. Yes, the wipers lifted at 80mph, but Sir William Lyons of Jaguar and David Brown of Aston Martin didn't have the bean counters and marketing mavens that Zora Arkus-Duntov had to deal with at GM. Somewhat stuffy *Autocar* also skirted the issue of price. In America the Jag XKE was around 25-30% more expensive than the Corvette. The 1963 Corvette started from $4257 for a coupe, with 360 horse Fuelie V8 and CR four-speed as 430 and 188 buck options respectively. That is, a sub 5 grand racer. The 1954 Aston Martin DB2/4 cost $5950. As for a DB4 GT Zagato a decade hence, expect a phone number price tag!

Autocar suggested a calmer version of the Corvette would be more the British buyer's cup of tea. In the comparison field chosen, all cars were straight six powered, except the Jensen, a long time Chrysler V8 and Torqueflite auto devotee. Plus, the 1963 Corvette was the only car in the field to offer factory designed and fitted air conditioning. Albeit limited to hydraulic lifter V8 examples. Mid-Year cars with a/c had two round swivel vents, at the dashboard's ends, along with a high mount dash center grille, for cold a/c air. The system was much more refined than a dealer add on kit, which was what exotic European imports were usually fitted with.

Improving the Mid-Year Corvette

LIKE A VW Bug, or Porsche, the Corvette improved via evolution, seldom revolution. Owners were a first port of call when it came to improving the Mid-Year breed. Redoing panel and trim fit, when rattles surfaced. With the body on frame C1 through C3 Corvette nature, rattles were more quickly encountered on the more stiffly sprung versions, habitually driven hard over rough surfaces. As the Mid-Year Corvette became more established, the factory also got more adept at figuring out how to assemble the C2 Corvette design. The '63 MY C2 debut had been a baptism of fire for St Louis assembly line workers, due to the new Corvette's instant popularity. Sales were 50% up on 1962, with a second shift added to deal with a two month customer wait. Used prices exceeded new Corvette prices. The Corvette was no Edsel!

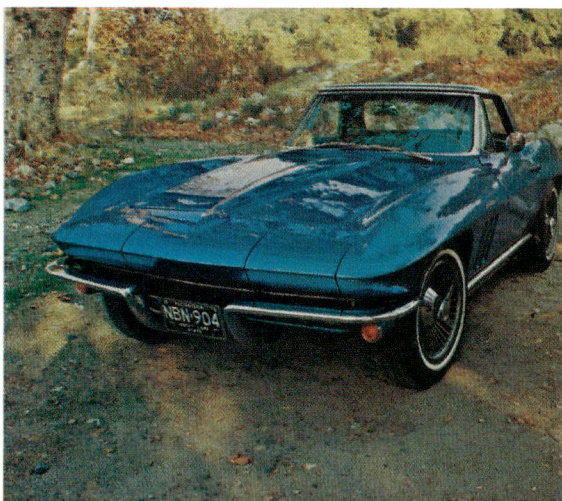

1965 FUEL-INJECTION CORVETTE *High point for the American sports car*

PHOTOS BY JOE RUSZ

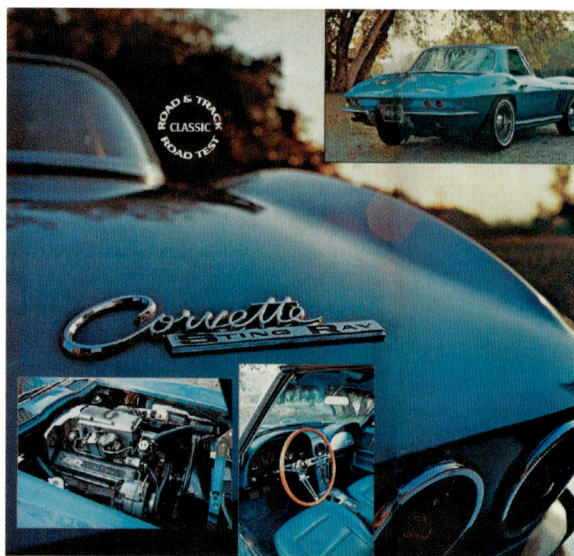

The '65 Fuelie Corvette with IRS and four-wheel disk brakes was the most advanced US car of the time. However, technology had a price, and there's no replacement for displacement!
(Courtesy Road & Track)

THE 1965 FUEL-INJECTION Corvette was the technical high-water mark for the whole Sting Ray series. Until that model year Corvettes still had drum brakes and one had to pay more than $600 extra to get a fancy set of drums and real stopping power. On the other hand, 1965 was the last year for fuel injection; from 1966 on Chevrolet got Corvette power by adding cubic inches. So in the 1965 there was a fortuitous coming-together of technologies and for one year America produced a sports car with fuel injection, all-independent suspension and all-disc brakes.

It seems funny, doesn't it, in the context of 1975 to remember that a leading manufacturer had airflow-controlled continuous-flow fuel injection and dropped it? The Rochester system was just that, and though it was quite different in detail and designed for a lot of power rather than low emissions, it answers the same basic description as the system now used on Volvos and Porsches, for instance, to meet 1975 emission regulations. How times change.

Paul and Mary Jacobson of Mission Viejo, California loaned us their bright blue 1965 FI Corvette for this test. It is a prize, as the photos show: they bought it new and had driven it only 38,363 miles when Mary brought it to us. It looks better than new, thanks to some nice chroming Paul has had done under the hood, and performs like the thoroughbred we all know the injection Corvette to be. Naturally the Jacobsons didn't want the car subjected to our usual battery of performance, braking and handling tests, so most data given here is taken from tests done by R&T and our companion magazine at the time Car Life. But we were allowed to drive the Corvette as much and as fast as we wanted to, and it was indeed a treat to feel the eagerness of an engine that was designed first and foremost to go.

Look at those specifications. A bit over five liters (the good old 327) . . . 11.0:1 compression ratio! . . . 375 bhp @ 6200 ➤

FEBRUARY 1975 **57**

Greeting the 1964 Corvette, *Popular Mechanics* said, "America's nearest thing to an all-out sports car gets better rear vision, smoother ride and optional transistor ignition." [48] That is, Chevrolet itself improved the Plastic Fantastic. No more split rear panic pane, and the front coils and transverse rear spring now had a progressive nature. This allowed the Corvette to ride more softly over small bumps, stiffening up for roll control and major bounces, with dampers tailored to spring changes with a view to reducing the chance of bottoming out. More sound proofing materials were added. There was also greater attention concerning bushings for a quieter shift linkage sans buzz, complemented by a revised shifter boot.

Specifically, the transistor ignition system was RPO K66, and was optioned by only 552 of the 22,229 1964 Corvette buyers, at 75 bucks a pop! The base 250 horse and L75 300bhp 327s carried over, but the hot 11:1 L76 327 and L84 327 Fuelie units rose in power to 365 and 375 horses respectively. The latter increased in price from $430.40 to a hefty 538 bucks between 1963 and 1964. However, its associated four-speed stayed at $188.30. The L76

This '66 Corvette 327 four-speed was made in early 1966 at the long lived St Louis, Missouri truck plant, and delivered to Hanley Dawson Chevrolet, on West Seven Mile Road in Detroit, Michigan. *(Courtesy RK Motors)*

327 gained via a big Holley 4bbl carb, replacing a smaller Carter equivalent. Cam duration also kept valves open longer now. The '64 Fuelie 327 also came with a sportier cam, allied to freer flow head porting and revised valve gear. To take advantage of a four-speed used by other car lines like Chevelle, Corvettes switched from BW T10s in 1963 to Muncie four-speeds for 1964. The economies of scale move brought stronger synchronizers, wider ratios and continued use of a reverse lockout trigger. Only 3.2% of 1964 Corvette buyers went for the base three by the knee. Over 80% chose Positraction.

There were new body and transmission mounts for 1964, and some bodies came from Dow-Smith of Ionia, Michigan. Inside the Corvette's body, the standard color coded plastic steering wheel of 1963 was replaced by the formerly optional faux walnut, N34 woodgrained and plastic steering wheel. RPO N34 had cost 16 bucks, and was chosen by only 130 Corvette devotees in 1963. For 1965, a real $48 N32 teakwood steering wheel was preferable to either of the aforementioned tillers, and was optioned by 2259 of the 23,562 '65 Corvette purchasers.

As for seats, the Corvette faithful had to fit the seat, not the other way around. Mid-Year Corvettes made patrons sit bolt upright, with a fixed backrest. There was only a small adjustment range, courtesy of loosening the seat's mounting bolts, which changed the seat assembly's angle. Not ergonomically ideal. 1964 Corvettes sported chrome door release knobs. One point of distinction between Corvette and imported cars for many years was the speed of power window operation. Domestic cars had truly fast glass, with *Road & Track* wondering if the tight weather seal required for high speed Continental driving was a factor in the slow movement of imports.

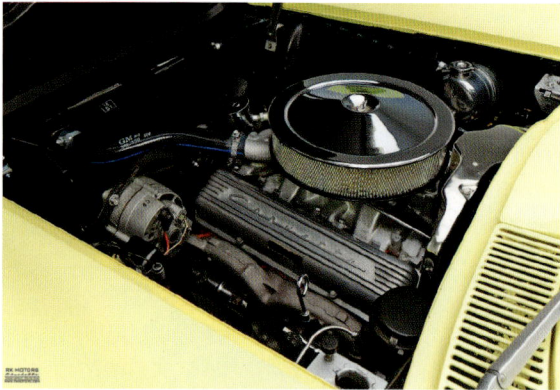

The L79 327 V8 shown was rated at 350bhp (gross).
It cost $104.56 extra, and was selected by 7591
buyers out of a 1966 27,720 Corvette total.
(Courtesy RK Motors)

Mid-Year Corvettes were the first Plastic Fantastics to feature pop up headlamps, and they were actuated via electric motors. The C2 Corvette's soft top was easy to use, but unlike the Straight Axle Corvette, a power top was no longer on the options list. The C2 Corvette's soft top never fitted snugly from the factory, but could fit better with owner fettling. The cover panel was released by a single lever, with two pins dropping into holes of said cover panel. Two latches at the windshield header secured, or unsecured, the soft top barrier between you and Mother Nature. Unfortunately, the $236 RPO C07 auxiliary hardtop was harder to erect, and secure. However, it was optioned by a third of buyers, for a Mid-Year Corvette generation where ragtops always held the upper sales hand, versus coupes. Especially once the initial coupe availability novelty wore off.

The 1964 Corvette provided many more interior color choices concerning the optional leather upholstery. Only Saddle Tan had been available in 1963, but now there was also red, blue or black. Vinyl was standard, and available in the same colors. Then too, it was possible to combine the aforementioned eight possible upholsteries, with silver or white as interior color complements. The Corvette world was your oyster!

Fancy wheels too for 1964-66, in the guise of RPO P48 cast aluminum knock-off wheels, retailing for $322. And you got a full set of five rims, not

the four alloys when aluminum rims returned as a formal 1976-82 option. In that later scenario, the aim was to cut cost. There were 806 takers for the P48 alloys in 1964, with 1116 choosing them in 1965, and a further 1194 sets optioned for '66 MY. As ever, lowering unsprung weight improved handling. And you could see a good looking, handling and accelerating '64 red roadster Corvette in the 1978 movie *Stingray*, even though a 'Sting Ray' was depicted.

Stingray, in this case, was a drive-in pleaser, released in August 1978 by AVCO Embassy. Starring Christopher Mitchum, the plot involved stolen loot and drugs stashed in a '64 Corvette roadster by crooks. Two buddies went dutch on buying said roadster from a St Louis used car lot. They were then chased by the crooks, who sought their plundered largesse. If only they knew that one day that Corvette would be worth more than what they stole!

For 1965 there were numerous changes to the Mid-Year Corvette, some more apparent than others. In detail, flat dial faces replaced plastic cones, and radio surround, along with speaker bezels, were now painted. Door cards featured fully integrated armrests, a European touch, and for the first time on Corvette, there were seatbelt retractors. For improved comfort seat bases were larger and more supportive, and seat backs were in hard plastic backing shells. However, the newly optional RPO N14 side mount exhaust system, set the Plastic Fantastic apart from pretenders. It was $134, functional, factory designed and fitted, but exercise caution … they got hot! Sidepipes were seen on Bill Mitchell's show cars.

Only 759 of the 23,562 1965 Corvettes sold had RPO N14. Given the fake nature of factory and aftermarket side exhausts on other makes, N14 was another Corvette plus point. Then too, there was Corvette braking. Corvette brakes were sound brakes, in the all drum era, and the Mid-Year cars brought improvements. The new J50 power brake option didn't improve braking effectiveness, but did make the task easier. J65 sintered, segmented metallic linings represented what you got in the Straight Axle Corvette era. For '64 MY, the J50 option was integrated into J65, for a reasonable $53. Then there was the J56 special sintered metallic brake package. This cost a hefty $629.50 in 1964, and was chosen by only 29 of the 22,229 1964 Corvette buyers. RPO J56 brought special linings, plus highly finned Al-Fin aluminum brake drums. The latter promised improved heat dissipation, and lower unsprung weight for better handling. You could have J50 and J56 jointly ordered. Positraction and other items were J56 prerequisites.

Al-Fin drums were the high end hardware you would find on late-50s glamor cars like the BMW 507 and Mercedes Gullwing. However, there were developments afoot in the sports car world. Disk brakes, inspired by aviation, were used by Jaguar and adopted by BMW V8s in 1960. These Dunlop disks were also used at the front by the Studebaker Avanti. Here, the disks were made under license by Bendix at a time when the Corvette was still all drum. Even with J56, the Corvette was found wanting in the racing arena; for example, Delmo Johnson and Dave Morgan's '63 Sebring 12 Hour campaign in a 1963 Sting Ray Z06. That said, all was fixed for 1965.

For '65 MY the Corvette adopted four-wheel disk brakes, like AC Cobra, as standard equipment. Huge four-piston calipers gripped 11.75in ventilated disk brakes at each corner. Brake swept area had

This coupe's wide ratio $189.98 RPO M20 Muncie four-speed was the same price as the CR M21 box. Rearwards lay a G81 3.70 Positraction lsd, costing $41.82. *(Courtesy RK Motors)*

increased from 1964's 11in drum-provided 328in^2 to 461in^2. It had two-piece calipers, and a new semi metallic brake pad with slight constant disk contact, to clean said rotor. Beyond federal legal requirements, the Corvette featured a dual master cylinder system with separate fluid reservoirs and front and rear brake circuits.

Testing showed that repeated stops from 100mph were no sweat. GM projected front brake

17,969 '66 Corvette patrons optioned the RPO P92 7.75-15 whitewalls at 31 bucks. However, only 5557 chose the $46.41 T01 7.75-15 two-ply rayon goldwalls shown here. *(Courtesy RK Motors)*

Small block 327 V8 powered Mid-Year Corvettes continued through 1966-67. However, most attention turned to the Mark IV big block 396 and 427 V8 coupes and roadsters. *(Courtesy RK Motors)*

pad wear at 57,000 miles, with twice that for rear pads! In spite of all of the above, you could still choose four-wheel drums on your 1965 Corvette, as a $64.50 RPO J61 delete option, and 316 1965 Corvette buyers did just that! Why wouldn't Corvette patrons join the AC Cobra and Jag XKE's all disk club? There were some teething problems with disks, namely fluid leakage. Enzo Ferrari once said he avoided disk brakes and fuel injection on his cars, because the English had the former and the Germans the latter!

1965 also witnessed greater Corvette firepower. The 350 horse hydraulic lifter L79 327 V8 was a sensible newcomer above the 300bhp L75 327 unit. There also remained the 250bhp 327 V8. 4716 1965 Corvette buyers paid the $107 surcharge for the L79 327 V8, but there were bigger fish to fry. The Fuelie 327 V8 was expensive, and an increasingly cantankerous route to high horsepower. As they say, there's no replacement for displacement. This avenue marked the Corvette's next journey, in a quest for value for money power.

Mid-Year Corvette Big Blocks & Racing

Bigger than *Ben Hur* ➝ The Mark IV motors

THERE WERE BIG things on the way for 1965, literally. The 1965½ Corvette L78 396 V8 involved an engine option that captured the public's imagination ... the Chevrolet Big Block V8! Its headline figure was 425bhp, which was more than the Plastic Fantastic had seen to that point in time. However, it wasn't the first time the motor or engine family had surfaced. That would be the 1963 Daytona 500, when the larger Chevrolet 427 V8 was a mystery racing engine. Then came 1965's Mako Shark II show car preview of the Mid-Year Corvette's replacement. The first full scale mock up featured 'Mark IV 396' as a hood label, and was photographed, even if the model didn't actually have an engine underhood!

The Mark IV family of Chevrolet V8s was designed to replace the fabled but aging 409 V8. The new powerplant would be made at the Tonawanda Chevrolet factory in New York, from mid 1965. The larger 427 V8 was designed first. However, given the AMA anti-racing pact, and a general rule to keep it cool on the street, so as not to raise the ire of uptight Ralph Nader wowser types, the 396 fitted in with GM policy of sub 400 cubes only, outside of fullsize rides. So it was that

The 425 horse Corvette 396 V8 big block made a '65 MY debut alongside the established 375bhp Fuelie Corvette. How are you going to keep 'em down on the farm, once they've seen gay Paris?!
(Courtesy GM Archives)

the Rat Motor, as opposed to Chevrolet's small block Mouse Motor, was first introduced in 396ci form in the Corvette and intermediate Chevelle, to get the ball rolling.

In terms of dimensions the existing 327 V8 was 4 x 3.25in, the 396 V8 increased those measurements to 4.09 x 3.76in, with the Big

Cubic inches, that is. We're ready if you are.

The first-ever production Corvette coupe sported a fastback body with a long hood and a raised windsplit that ran the length of the roof and continued down the back on a pillar that bisected the rear window into right and left halves. The split backlite is usually attributed to Mitchell, who claimed to have been inspired by the 57SC Bugatti 'Atlantique' coupe. The feature actually predated both the C2 Corvette and Bob McLean's Q-Corvette, having been used by Harley Earl on both his Oldsmobile Golden Rocket show car and his own more traditional design studies for the C2 Corvette, some of which had progressed to full-scale models.[9] Earl's inspiration was said to have been an Alfa Romeo Coupe with a body by Scaglione shown at the 1954 Turin Auto Show.

LEFT

22"

FRONT

CHEVROLET CORVETTE C2

TECHNICAL

Curb weight 3,362 lb (1,525 kg)
Length 179.3 in
Wheelbase 98.0 in
427 cu in (7.0 L) L89 Big-Block V8
Torque: 460 lb-ft
Top Speed 130 MPH

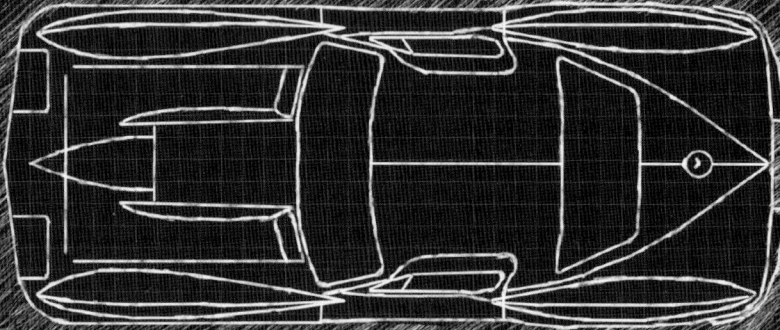

StingRay

TOP

The '65 L78 396 V8 was followed by the '66 L72 427 V8. Both had 425bhp, as part of an insurance dodge. The big block 'Rat' motor added 200lb versus the small block Mouse motor ... but a ton of horsepower!
(Courtesy Brandon Fenty)

Daddy 427 V8 on 4.25 x 3.76in. And whereas a small block V8 was roughly 500lb undressed, the new big block was 200lb heavier. Like most new OHV US V8s coming along since the mid '50s, the recipe was a cast iron head and block, with thinwall construction facilitated by a mold pouring technique that used less material. That is, the latest designs were rigid, while weighing less than their predecessors. The prime 'motorvation' for the Mark IV family? Absolute Power!

One must consider the era the L78 396 V8 was born into. It was one that placed performance as the most desirable, and sole goal. Speaking of the existing Corvette champ, the Fuelie 327 V8, *Road & Track* said, "... it was indeed a treat to feel the eagerness of an engine that was designed first and foremost to go."[49] Then came the big blocks, with the journal adding, "Great throbbing gobs of horsepower and torque, that's what it was all about in those halcyon pre energy-crisis pre-emissions –

crunch days." [50] And it was a uniquely American quality. The automotive equivalent of Melville's *Moby Dick*. Such immense force and power!

There was no need to worry unduly about the big block's likelihood of upsetting the Corvette's weight balance and handling. Like the later Mazda RX7, the Mid-Year Corvette was a front midship design. The motor was positioned close to the firewall, and behind the theoretical axle line. That said, many still feel the finest handling balance belongs to the small block powered Corvettes, and, indeed, after 1974 such a layout would be the Corvette purchaser's sole choice. However, in 1965 the value was clear, you got more with a big block, for less.

The surcharge was $292, to obtain aforementioned 1965½ 425bhp L78 396 V8. That same year, the familiar Fuelie, coded L84 and making 375 horses, retailed for an extra 538 bucks. Holy overdraft Batman! So little surprise that the respective buyer numbers for the two engine options were 2157 and 771. In spite of the L78 396 V8's late 1965 appearance, it quickly gained marketplace traction, and the extra loot brought quality hardware: impact extruded aluminum pistons with chrome rings, solid lifters, oversize four-barrel carb, 11.1:1 CR, bigger oil pump and dual snorkel air cleaner. This was no station wagon motor!

In the early to mid '60s Detroit had experimented with the exotic: aluminum block inline sixes from American Motors and Chrysler Corp. There were also the turbocharged all alloy pair of Corvair flat six and Olds Jetfire 215 V8, with water injection for the latter. However, bigger was simpler, and with gas cheaper than air why worry? The Chevrolet Mark IV big block V8 was an easier and cheaper way to skin a Cougar cat. The 1965½ Corvette L78 396 with four-speed and 3.70 diff ratio spelled low 14s, and near 140mph terminal velocity. *Road & Track/Car Life*'s contemporary Mid-Year Corvette figures tell all.

As indicated by the accompanying table, more was on the way for 1966, and the Corvette's L78 396 V8 was a one year only option. The following year saw a 427 V8, with a decision taken to end high output 327s at the close of '65 MY. So, no solid lifter 4bbl L76 327, nor L84 327 Fuelie for 1966. The

sensible hydraulic lifter L75 and L79 327s were complemented by mild and wild 427 V8s. An extra 181 clams purchased the 390 horse L36 427 V8, an hydraulic lifter 10.25:1 CR motor. L36 427 was practically a family car motor, and yes, you could have a/c with that. Then came the $312 L72 427 V8, a solid lifter Mark IV motor with 11.0:1 comp, larger intake valves, bigger than L36 four-barrel Holley, four-bolt mains, aluminum intake and 460lb/ft, as opposed to the outgoing L78 396's 'mere' 415lb/ft of twist. The respective 427s were optioned by 5116 and 5258 1966 Corvette devotees.

Choosing a L72 427 meant Positraction lsd, close ratio Muncie four-speed, former '65 MY Corvette 396 V8 suspension prerequisites, along with hardware upgrades: stronger shot peened axle halfshafts, U joints, larger capacity radiator, and bigger engine sump. The Corvette 427s continued the 1965½ Corvette 396's 'Bubble Hood'. The 427 V8 was the new belle du jour, before Catherine Deneuve! However, there was some foot shuffling over the L72 427 V8's power rating. Initially it was claimed to make 450 gross bhp, but this was reduced to 425 horse, sans official explanation. So the L72 427 had the same power rating as the outgoing L78 396 V8. This move may have been to pacify the auto insurance industry, whose premiums were already starting to bite. Not to mention road safety advocates, that had royally roasted the poor Corvair.

Ralph Nader's Auto Safety Center mayn't have liked the big block Corvette, but the public did! *Car and Driver*'s L72 427 Corvette stats, with 4.11 diff ratio, ran to 0-60mph in 4.8 seconds, 0-100mph

Mid-Year Model	'63 Fuelie 327 4sp	'64 L75 327 P.glide	'65½ L78 396 4sp	'66 L72 427 4sp	'67 L75 327 4sp
0-60mph (sec)	5.9	8.0	5.7	5.7	7.8
0-100mph (sec)	16.5	20.2	13.4	13.4	23.1
¼-mile (sec)	14.9	15.2	14.1	14.0	16.0
MPG	12.5	14	10.5	12	16
Test date	10/62	3/64	8/65	8/66 Car Life	2/67

The Chevrolet built for two.

It started, that morning, with hints. Work-weary, he says. Kid-frazzled, she says. Who gets the Corvette today? You do. No, you do. Ah, *We do.*

So, Arrangements made, Hamper stocked and stowed in the Corvette. No room for people back there. A

plenty. But you don't compromise so much as an inch when you build America's only true production sports car. Which is why it comes with four-wheel disc brakes, thread-needle steering and fully independent suspension.

Now, he rouses Corvette's Turbo-

Jet V8, the 390-hp version they'd chosen as tractable enough for her and satisfying enough for him.

Then, away. Outside the city unwinds a road as long as the day ahead. A day just for them. In the Chevrolet built for two.

'66 CORVETTE BY **CHEVROLET**

Domestic high performance car ads played up the family car angle to pacify insurance companies and Naderite safety zealots. The ad notes Corvette's eight standard safety feats, including padded dash. *(Courtesy GM Archives)*

in 11.2 seconds and 140mph. With sensible 3.36 highway cruising econoaxle, 0-60mph was 5.4 seconds, with a 12.8 second pass at 112mph. Slower, but at least you were saving gas … as if that mattered in 1966! In truth, it was an inconvenience in terms of having to frequently fill up.

1967 saw a choice of two 327s continue, with the L75 300bhp edition serving as the Corvette's base motor from 1966. However, one now had a choice of not one, nor two 427 V8s, but … FIVE, starting with the family L36 427, followed by the new L68 427 V8 with 400 horse. This motor was basically an L36 427, with triple deuce carburetion, in lieu of the L36's single 4bbl. Both motors were hydraulic lifter jobs, which implied a/c optionability, no sweat! Respective prices and ordering rates for L36 and

L68 427s were \$200/3832 and \$305/2101. However, the most popular Corvette optional engine in 1967 was the \$105 L79 327 V8, with the usual 350 ponies and 6375 takers.

When it came to solid lifter motors, think 427 times three, and they all came with the aforementioned triple deuce carbs. When cruising only the center Holley 2bbl unit was operating, but tromp the loud pedal and the outer two carbs came on song via vacuum actuation. However, sometimes they didn't reliably chime in, which is why the racer crowd favored an aftermarket mechanical linkage kit that one could obtain at most speed shops or specialist performance hardware outlets. First high performance 427 V8 choice in 1967 was the L71 427 V8 costing \$437, and chosen by 3754 '67 Corvette buyers. You got the usual hi po 11.0:1 comp, and 435bhp at 5800rpm, allied to 460lb/ft at four grand, aided by a big valve head.

As a related \$368 option, the L89 aluminum cylinder heads were for the usually all cast iron L71 427. L89 didn't raise the rated horsepower, but did reduce weight. A believed 50lb saving put the 427 at only 60lb over a 327 Mouse Motor. L89 was shorthand for the factory code L89/L71, indicating an L71 427 with aluminum heads. Only 16 1967 Corvette buyers felt the L89 surcharge was worth it. Top of the 1967 Corvette powerplant tree was the L88 427 mill, costing 947 bucks, with only 20 '67 Corvette patrons ticking the option box for what was a competition motor.

The L88 427 came with L89 heads, bigger cam, aluminum intake manifold for a single 4bbl Holley 4150 carb, and suspicious horsepower rating of just 430bhp. The L88's street emissions legality was a gray area. You bought this motor for the expensive, high quality, durable engine internals of a racing engine. Like a forged 5140 alloy steel crankshaft, which was cross drilled and Tuftrided, magnafluxed connecting rods and forged aluminum pistons of 12.5:1 CR. The pricey L88 option made a spring 1967 debut.

Oftentimes, when cars like Corvette L88 427s and Hemi Cudas were magazine tested, the ¼-mile figures didn't seem that hot. That's because the automaker delivered the car in civilized all scenario street form. However, the hardware was present

A 1966 Corvette L72 427 V8 roadster with Muncie four-speed, in code 900 Tuxedo Black.
(Courtesy RK Motors)

to go beyond 600 horse with race tuning. Signs were clear concerning the L88 427's raison d'etre. For one, blanking covers for the radio and console HVAC controls. No optioning of radio or power windows permitted. What's more (or less), you couldn't have that domestic doyen the automatic choke. Chevrolet did offer a manual choke retrofit, however. The Corvette L88 427 was certainly not designed to appeal to the 'set and forget' crowd!

It was said by *Corvette News* that the C48 heater and defroster deletion, chosen by only 35 '67 Corvette buyers, and garnering a 97 buck credit was, "... to cut down on weight and discourage the car's use on the street," not to mention that old street racer trick of racing with the heat on, to cool the motor and make the most power! [51] The L88 427 had no engine shroud, which would normally restrict cooling air through the radiator during high speed driving. Smog controls were conspicuous by their absence – not even a PCV valve. Rather, there was an antiquated road draft tube, that simply vented crankcase vapors into the atmosphere through the driver's side valve cover.

L88 427 powered Corvettes were also supplied with vehicular warnings. Paperwork said, "This unit (L88) operates on Sunoco 260 or equivalent gas of very high octane. Under no circumstances should regular gasoline be used." There was a second warning label inside L88 motorvated Corvettes, "Warning: Vehicle must operate on a fuel having a minimum of 103 research octane and 95 motor octane or engine damage may result." You have been warned!

Corvette and the Mustang

MOTOR TREND'S STEVE Kelly commenced the journal's Shelby GT500 vs Corvette Sting Ray 427 account, with a couple of facts: Firstly, the Corvette started "before the world or Ford Motor Co had ever heard of a car called the Mustang ..." And while Kelly acknowledged the importance of the original straight six Corvette, it was also true that for the past two years the Corvette 427s had been the real image makers, and pre-dated the big block Mustangs. Secondly, the by now accepted billing

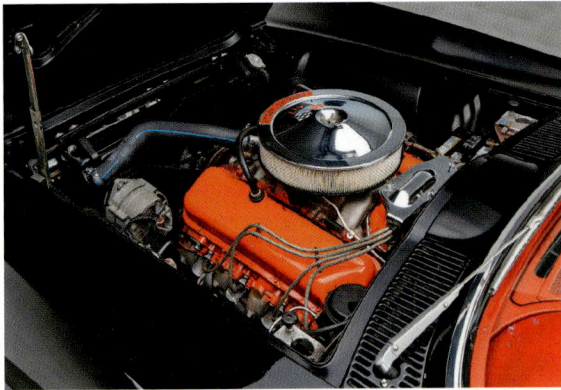

In '66 MY 5258 Corvette buyers ponied up $312 to get this optional L72 427 V8. This particular L72 big block was rated at 425 horse. *(Courtesy RK Motors)*

In a Corvette first, the Mid-Year models were available with an 80 buck RPO 898 leather interior. However, the code 407 Red Vinyl seating, and $199 RPO U69 Delco AM/FM radio are present. The latter chosen by 26,363 patrons, out of 27,720 1966 Corvette buyers. *(Courtesy RK Motors)*

that the Corvette was, "America's only true sports car." [52]

It was also stated that at one time Corvettes possessed luxury and performance in equal measure, with Corvette eating into Cadillac sales. [53] Yes, the luxury was still there, but now allied to a hard ride, at least in big block V8 versions. Unlike regular small block Corvettes, and most sporty domestics, big block Corvettes came with front and rear swaybars. The additional rear bar was as much a chassis stiffener, an extra lateral frame ladder bar to resist the twist of the Mark IV V8, as a handling helper or body roll pacifier. Corvette's 'special front and rear suspension' option, renamed F41 from F40 for '66 MY, cost $36.90, and truly delivered on that heavy duty feel.

GM concern that the Mustang would eat into Corvette sales proved unwarranted. The FoMoCo pony car was less specialized, and derived from a family sedan. Even Carroll Shelby had doubts over Mustang. The suggestion of a Shelbyized Mustang was initially greeted by the Texan, with a response that you can't create a racehorse from a mule. Shelby was also skeptical if a Shelby Mustang would sell. However, once one of his motivated employees was put on the task, the Hertz rental sales connection proved fruitful. That said, cars did return to rental agencies with regular Ford hardware, substituted for Shelby parts!

For 1967 the Shelby Mustang's appeal was expanded beyond the 1965-66 Shelby GT350 racer

focus. Increased sales volume with a more sedate offering that would become even more passive in 1968. *Motor Trend* noted that the purer '67 Corvette 427 roadster gave you more: 0.7 seconds quicker in the ¼-mile, shorter braking distances, and even easier on gas. Better workmanship and more accessible underhood hardware were part of the Corvette's deal. The heavy Shelby GT500 428 V8 motor wasn't the good breathing thoroughbred, that the semi hemi porcupine Corvette L71 427 mill was. Then too, the Shelby Mustang lacked the Corvette's better ergonomics and 'Maserati look' dashboard/instruments, according to *MT*'s Steve Kelly.

Hideaway headlamps, IRS, forward opening hood, a chassis shared with no other Chevrolet, and four-wheel disk brakes possessed by no other domestic. In 1966 only 3% of American cars had disk brakes, forecast to reach 10% in 1967. There was also the possibility of a Federally mandated front disk brake provision for 1969, which didn't happen. [54] Problems with the Corvette? *MT* said that, like the new Camaro, there wasn't enough fender well space for sufficiently big wheels and tires to get the power down, and ward off oversteer. The journal put larger tires on the test roadster, that cured both bugaboos, but introduced fender well fouling on full lock.

The fender wells limited the Corvette to 7.75-15 rayons on 15 x 6in rims. The QB1 Redline nylon tires were a $46.65 option. Indeed, the Corvette's problems were the three Ws, wheel travel, weight and warehouse. The Mid-Year body couldn't accommodate big enough rims, tires nor wheel travel. So, stiff suspension was relied upon to prevent bottoming out. Plus, the Corvette's separate chassis construction made the sports car relatively heavy. The Corvette 427 that *Motor Trend* tested was 3340lb, and the 2+2 Shelby GT500 was 3360lb. This was despite the latter having a heavy 428 V8, and cozy seating for four, along with a conventional trunk.

To maintain structural rigidity, the Corvette needed a beefy frame. That's where the strength was. In contrast the unibody Mustang achieved more rigidity at a relatively lower weight. Then there was the warehouse problem: the Corvette didn't have one. Its abilities to facilitate cargo loading, through external trunk access and commodiousness, suffered post Straight Axle Corvette. The Mid-Year Corvette's possible two-suitcase capacity lay behind it's bucket seats. Even the spare tire awkwardly lay in a panel under the body.

The Shelby's sedan origins made it the more practical of the two, but it was obviously slower. Zero to sixty in 6.2 seconds, 14.52 second ¼-mile at 101.35mph, and 120mph top speed. It all paled next to the Corvette 427's respective figures of 5.5 seconds, 13.8 seconds at 104mph, and 143mph terminal velocity. The Corvette was clearly the superior speed demon, its redline was 1000rpm north of the Shelby's 5500rpm limit. It was straightforward to make the Corvette's Stinger hood scoop functional, and the central rear deck fuel filler, further underlined the Chevrolet's racing credentials. It was pricier than the Shelby Mustang. The Corvette's base price was $4327.50 for a 300 horse ragtop with three by the knee. The Shelby was $4195, but resorted to the chicanery that Corvette tried back in 1954. That is, passing off essentials as options. This time the Shelby Mustang's power brakes, power steering, rollbar and inertia reel shoulder harness, plus fold down rear seat, were a joint $264.77 mandatory package. Shelby American claimed it was standard, probably to undercut the Corvette.

In the end, *Motor Trend*'s Steve Kelly said, "The Corvette is designed as a sports car, and that's what it is. It suffers somewhat as a street machine, but in no way is it reminiscent of early English sports cars with fold-down windshields and side curtains." [55]

RPO P48 Kelsey-Hayes cast aluminum knock-off wheels were a Mid-Year Corvette option during 1964-66. They cost $316 in 1966, and that included a spare fifth rim, unlike post-1975 Corvettes with alloys! *(Courtesy RK Motors)*

The Chevrolet Corvair and Corvette were the only volume produced domestics going with IRS. Like the VW Beetle and Triumph Herald, the Corvette combined IRS with a separate chassis. *(Courtesy RK Motors)*

Racing the Mid-Year Corvette

THE FIVE GRAND Corvette L71 427 V8, probably the most powerful production car in the world, cost around $500 above a realistically priced and optioned Shelby GT500. It seemed worth it, because the extra got one a dedicated sports car, capable of serious speed and happier on track behavior than Mustang. *Motor Trend* considered the Shelby Mustang to be better suited to the road, titling the Corvette, "427 Sting Ray: Reigning King". At the other end of the scale, you could visit a Buick dealership, and buy the new Opel Rallye Coupe (Kadett) captive import. At $2192, the Opel provided the appearance of sport, matt black paint and spotlights. Radials, front disk brakes and an economical inline four, were all standard. Qualities that would become more key entering the '70s. However, going back to the Mid-Year Corvette's '63 MY debut, it had a rival in the AC Cobra.

It seemed the Cobra pulled the same stunt that the Corvette had done in the late '50s concerning Jag XK120s and Mercedes' Gullwing. That is, a lighter car with a big motor will win out. In basic terms AC Cobra 289 with Ford K code Windsor 289 V8 and 271 horse in a 2020lb roadster, versus Corvette 327 with 300bhp and 3030lb. *Road & Track* made the comparison in June 1963, saying it was the Cobra's high 13s and 100mph plus trap speed, against Chevrolet's high 14s and near 100mph trap

speed. *R&T* also said import car fanciers were pleased concerning the Cobra turning the tables on Corvette. Reason being, that the flat cap, jolly good show gang, never saw the Corvette as a 'pure' sports car, whatever that meant exactly?

Aside from the weight penalty, the Corvette also had a greater frontal area of 19.3ft^2, versus the Cobra's 16.6ft^2, even if the Mid-Year Corvette's front end looked slimmer. This implied top speeds for Corvette and Cobra, at a respective 140mph and 150mph. The suspension game favored the Corvette's more modern set up, while the Cobra represented an amalgam of Tojeiro's 1954 AC Ace chassis and Ford V8. That is, the Cobra running a lot of negative camber to keep the outside rear wheel upright during cornering, which messed up take off traction. The Cobra won out with four-wheel disk brakes, which the Corvette would get later.

The story was of a specialized racer, versus a much more refined and practical production sports car. So, it was the faster rack-and-pinion Cobra steering, albeit with more kickback and feedback, versus Corvette's more insulated recirculating ball tiller. This wasn't a car for long trips, although both Cobra and Corvette lacked trunk space. The Cobra's US drivetrain rivalled the Corvette's appeal, having hardware a US dealer network could handle. It sure beat visiting Luigi Chinetti when your Ferrari's prancing horse was off-color! At Riverside's

St. Louis, and another spirited event. Corvette for 1967.

The Arch. A salute to yesterday. A promise for tomorrow. So is another spirit of St. Louis, where it's built–Corvette for 1967. Still America's only true production sports car, the '67 Corvette offers performance from V8s up to 427 cubic inches and blow two-barrel carburetion you can order. Handling from independent rear suspension and four-wheel disc brakes. Comfort with add-ons like air conditioning and power assists. New standard safety features such as the GM-developed energy absorbing steering column, shoulder belt anchors, folding seat back latches, four-way hazard warning flasher. Corvette: magnificently balanced and honed. The spirit of St. Louis revisited.

1967 CORVETTE BY CHEVROLET

The '67 Corvette pictured with the St Louis Arch. The St Louis, Missouri plant that made the Corvette was nearly as iconic. The Corvette was legally safety ready for 1968, whereas the Austin Healey 3000 MkIII wasn't, and ended in '67 MY. *(Courtesy GM Archives)*

2.6-mile course, Dave MacDonald and Ken Miles vanquished the Corvettes, using Cobras. Miles gained five seconds per lap, and both the Corvettes and Ferrari GTOs were outpaced.

Bud Lindemann noted a similar problem, when featuring the Jaguar XKE on TV's *Car and Track* in 1968. It was a very strong performer in acceleration tests, but Lindemann said it was too heavy for its racing class, while at the same time being too fast a car to fully exploit on public roads. That class was large displacement production car racing, or the over 3-liter (182ci) GT category. Only 316 AC Cobra 427s were built at Thames Ditton from 1965 to 1968. There were 2157 1965½ Corvette L78 396s alone, and 216 L88 427-powered Corvettes during 1967-69, issuing from St Louis! Given the high labor content and production style at the Corvette plant, you could say both Cobra and Corvette were hand built. A mere 95 Aston Martin DB4 GTs were produced, but 72,520 Jag XKEs rolled out of Browns Lane. So what's a production car?

In any case, Zora Arkus-Duntov had a couple of Mid-Year Corvette tricks up his sleeve. For one, use the regular Corvette option sheet to skirt around the AMA's anti racing pact. Duntov was always one to guide Corvette customers, and said start with a '63 Fuelie Corvette four-speed with Positraction lsd, that is: L84 Fuelie 327 – $430 + G81 Positraction $43. Then follow the example of 194 1963 Corvette buyers, and tick the $1818.45 Z06 option box (Al-Fin drum power brakes/sintered metallic linings, HD front swaybar, beefier shocks, stiffer springs, dual brake master cylinder and long distance 36.5 gallon gas tank).

You could create a '63 Corvette Z06 327 Fuelie roadster via optioning, but everyone went coupe! Zora Arkus-Duntov had a further Mid-Year Corvette racing plan ... the '63 Corvette Grand Sport. The Grand Sport was ZAK's racer to take on Shelby American's Cobra, using much modified, specialized factory hardware, and a body with half the fiberglass panel thickness to save weight. That is, a 1900lb Corvette 377ci V8 coupe, with 550 horse at 6400rpm, and 500lb/ft arriving at 5200rpm. Duntov planned to build 125 Corvette Grand Sports, offering them to qualified racing customers. Unfortunately, the plan got pre-empted. While the Cobra was British made, and therefore an import, the AMA's anti racing pact still hung over Corvette. It was the ultimate wowser cloud!

Five Corvette Grand Sports were constructed. In the coupe's brief competition history, it did beat the Shelby Cobra; however, the Grand Sport's headlines came to the attention of GM chairman Frederic Donner, who canned the project due to the aforementioned racing ban. Sadly, Zora Arkus-Duntov and his team were ordered to stop Corvette Grand Sport development. This was most unfortunate for Duntov, a racer himself, who was answering the call from across the land for more specialized race craft. One example came from no less than speed shop legend Don Yenko. Yenko was a Corvette racer until, in his own words, "I got tired of looking at the rear bumper of Mark Donohue's

Mustang." Yes, versus Donohue's Shelby GT350, admittedly a tiring daily driver prospect, the off the peg Mid-Year Corvette was too heavy. It pushed Yenko to come up with the Corvair based Yenko Stinger, aimed at the SCCA's D production category.

Another Corvette racer called Delmo Johnson had experience of both the Corvette Z06 and Grand Sport. He had many background similarities with Don Yenko, but also some key differences. Similar in the sense of a family owned Chevrolet dealership since the Depression, and having done duty in the service. For differences Delmo Johnson pulled, as folk from the Lone Star state sometimes say, from Texas rather than Pennsylvania. Johnson and Yenko went on to run their family dealerships, after leaving the service, until the early '80s recession saw their closure, in 1980 and 1982 respectively. However, Yenko served in the air force, Johnson in the army. The most important difference between these two iconic Chevrolet figures was that Delmo Johnson was an accidental racing driver!

Like most fun loving bachelors, Johnson gravitated towards the Corvette. The dealership connection helped, but also the fact that the Corvette occupied its position as America's sole volume produced sports car. Even so, when Delmo Johnson availed himself of a brand new 1959 Corvette, he had no intention to race it, or any vehicle, until a chance encounter in a Playboy Club. There was a sports car emporium in North Dallas,

jointly owned by Jim Hall and Carroll Shelby. Above the showroom was the Playboy Club, that Johnson happened upon one evening. At the club he found several racing drivers, that frequented said club, in a jovial state. They assured Delmo Johnson that their high spirits were solely the product of having participated in a recent motor race. On hearing this news, Johnson decided to try his hand at motor racing.

Delmo Johnson entered and won his first race, which happened to be in Fort Worth, Texas, using his '59 Corvette. He was hooked by the experience, and it proved more than beginner's luck. Johnson was a very talented exponent, and typified the privateer gentleman racer of the era. Delmo Johnson raced both for himself, under the Johnson Chevrolet Co dealership banner, as well as for others, using his cars and those sourced from other parties. He raced Corvettes and other cars in more than one category of motor racing. By 1960 that entailed a Corvette in production class, but also a Jaguar XKSS in C-Modified, and even an ex Jim Hall Elva in Formula Junior. The Jag had its original XK I6 swapped for a Chevrolet V8 while under the stewardship of the original owner, when said I6 blew up! Swapping in a small block V8 for Ferraris, Jags, Mercedes Gullwing and even Elvis' BMW 507, after his ownership of said roadster, was pretty common back in the day. The high cost of a replacement motor, and ready availability of

![The Stinger hood was a one-year-only Mid-Year Corvette option, and only for big blocks like this '67 427 V8 roadster.]

The Stinger hood was a one-year-only Mid-Year Corvette option, and only for big blocks like this '67 427 V8 roadster. *(Courtesy Tony McGrath)*

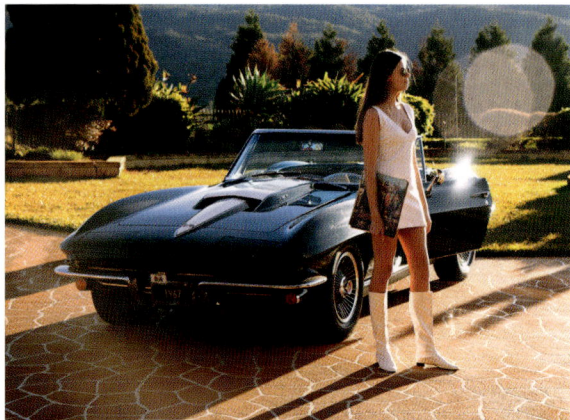

![1967 saw the final Mid-Year C2 Corvettes, which coincided with The Beatles' Sgt Pepper's Lonely Hearts Club Band album!]

1967 saw the final Mid-Year C2 Corvettes, which coincided with The Beatles' *Sgt Pepper's Lonely Hearts Club Band* album! *(Courtesy Tony McGrath)*

the aforementioned V8 made for a popular swap practice. *Road & Track* had said Formula Junior cars could edge out a Straight Axle Corvette on sportiness, but couldn't hold a candle concerning daily driver duty.

Delmo Johnson, and long time co-driver Dave Morgan, successfully continued their association with Corvettes, and Zora Arkus-Duntov, at the March 23 Sebring 12 Hour. It was here, that the pair's '63 Fuelie Corvette Z06 came second in class, behind the Phil Hill, Lew Spencer and Ken Miles Cobra, which equated to 16th outright. However, according to Delmo Johnson, "We'd have done considerably better if we had brakes. Zora gave us some experimental brake shoes that only lasted two hours. By the end of 12 hours, we wore right through the shoes and only had a little T bar left. I told Zora we had no brakes, and he said, 'You have brakes, you're just not pushing hard enough on the pedal!' Ten hours without brakes is a long time."

Johnson's experience with the '63 Corvette Grand Sport was that of tiger taming on four wheels! He raced John Mecom's cars, which included the Grand Sport. Johnson and Mecom referred to the Corvette coupe as the 'Lightweight'. As Johnson said, "At first I wasn't really interested in the Grand Sport. I had driven Mecom's and it was a very fast car in a straight line, but overall they were pretty shitty cars. It wouldn't steer, stop or turn. It was really better suited to a drag strip.

When Jim Morrison sang "Come on, baby, light my fire", he might have been referring to this 1967 Corvette 427 ... but wasn't! *(Courtesy Tony McGrath)*

It was a 200mph car, but by 160mph it was already unpredictable as to where it was going to go." In the old days the racing department of an automaker made a car very fast. It was then up to the team and their drivers to work out how to control it, like with the Porsche 917. However, there's no doubt that if Zora Arkus-Duntov and co were allowed to further develop the Grand Sport, it would have become a more complete racer. Rome and even St Louis' archway weren't built in a day!

With some further irony concerning the Porsche prototype racer, VP of Gulf Oil Grady Davis owned a Corvette Grand Sport. Dick Thompson drove said Grand Sport for Davis, and didn't like the car. Zora Arkus-Duntov then asked Delmo Johnson if he would like to buy the Davis Grand Sport, and Johnson agreed, "... I actually bought the car from GM, which is kind of amusing because GM was afraid of lawsuits and they never claimed to own anything."

1963's Sebring 12 Hour showed how specialized and competitive sports car racing was getting. Ferrari 250 prototypes came first and second, with a Ferrari 330 prototype in third, followed by three Ferrari 250 GTOs, two Jag XKE Lightweights, two Porsche 356B Carrera Abarth GTLs, a Shelby Cobra in 11th and an Austin Healey 3000 was 12th. Under the Johnson Chevrolet Co banner, Delmo Johnson and Dave Morgan's Fuelie Corvette Z06 was the first Sting Ray over the line in 16th with another coming 17th. Then there was the Grady Davis Sting Ray driven by Don Yenko, which finished 25th outright.

The Grady Davis Grand Sport turned out to be the sale of the century, because it cost Chevrolet $86,000, but Delmo Johnson only paid four grand! Johnson and Morgan did race a Grand Sport, at 1964's Sebring 12 Hour, once again under the Johnson Chevrolet Co banner. However, this wasn't Johnson's personal car, more an arm's length Chevrolet association. The 377 cube, 500 horse plus, sub 2000lb racer was the fastest car on the straights. Indeed, faster than the Ferraris that won the race and set the fastest lap. However, handling and mechanical woes produced a poor showing for Johnson and Morgan.

Results of the 1964 Sebring 12 Hour witnessed a Ferrari prototype 1-2-3, then came a Shelby

GM Styling supremo Bill Mitchell considered the Mid-Year Corvette his finest hour.
He ordered an Ermine White '67 427 V8 roadster, with side pipes, for his wife's birthday present.
However, his wife's ride rolled with a Powerglide. *(Courtesy Tony McGrath)*

Daytona Coupe, with Cobra roadsters fifth and sixth. The Hudson/Grant car of Nickey Chevrolet Co was the first Sting Ray to finish, on that March 21, 1964 race date; it was 16th overall. The first Corvette Grand Sport was the 18th placed Penske/Hall machine of dealership Penske McKean Chevrolet Inc. Delmo Johnson and Dave Morgan's Grand Sport, the No 004 Grand Sport built, came 32nd overall. Over 50 years later, Mongoose Motorsports would create a GM license built replica of the No 004 car, liveried as raced by Johnson/Morgan at 1964's Sebring 12 Hour event.

Mongoose Motorsports was an appropriate concern to take on this Grand Sport endeavor, since in nature a Mongoose eats Cobras! Under the replica's period correct exterior lay a Donovan 377ci Chevrolet small block V8, rated at 540 horse, and backed by a Muncie four-speed. A

custom ladder style, tube frame steel chassis had 4in main sections, and C4 Corvette suspension. However, myriad external, cosmetic and hardware touches would lead even a careful observer to think this was indeed the real deal. Authentic body modifications included T3 headlights, hood ventilation, body decals, paper plate, rear window Plexiglas vents, and rear Deltaboat taillights. Then too, the replica rode on 15in Halibrand knock off wheels, wearing vintage style fat Goodyear racing rubber!

Nostalgia on the inside came courtesy of era-correct lightweight buckets trimmed in appropriate material, along with '60s style seatbelts, window lifts, 200mph speedo, oil temp gauges, and the kind of rollbar/Rupert safety harnesses you found back in the day. An original model CB radio was also aboard the replica racecraft. Mechanical

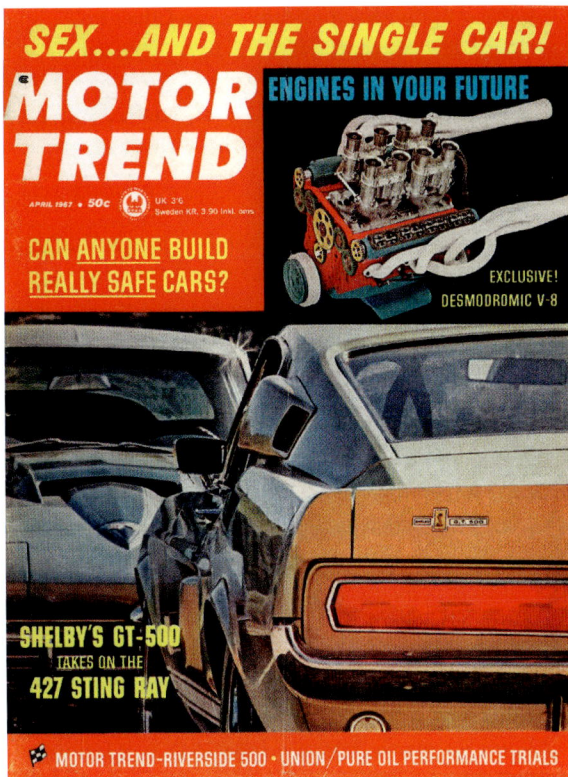

Corvette versus Shelby Mustang. For a number of years it was the great American sports car battle. However, only one machine was a sports car.
(Courtesy Motor Trend)

touches to make this Grand Sport seem like the real McCoy involved a dated Harrison radiator, engine oil cooler, brake booster, tar-top battery, shifter, and shrouded differential oil cooler. With genuine '63 Corvette Grand Sports worth millions a copy, Delmo Johnson's purchase was a steal. What's more, this coupe proved a winner.

Later in 1964, Delmo Johnson and his Grand Sport received a challenge from fellow Chevrolet dealership owner, Jack Ferrill. Ferrill had an AHRA champion Corvette drag racer, and driver Phil Mote. Mote went up against Johnson with his Grand Sport, losing three times straight! Ferrill then instructed Mote to get out of the car, so he could show 'em how it was done, and lost a further two times to Delmo Johnson! Now, understand that Johnson was no pro drag racer, nor was his Grand Sport set up for the 1320ft fandango, but, as he

said, "… I still managed to wax his ass five times.", adding, "My car had 3.55:1 gears and by halfway I had a head of steam, and by the end it was not even close."

Obtaining GM's pink slip for $4000 proved even more fortuitous when Delmo Johnson took his special Corvette to race the November 1964 Carrera Pan Americana in Mexico. On the face of it an ill handling, straight line rocket didn't seem right for this event, but … Johnson enjoyed race leading pace until 12 miles into Vera Cruz, when an oil line broke, causing the differential to weld itself together! His mechanic managed to get a replacement unit from Mexico City, and effected an overnight fix. Johnson wound up coming second in the Carrera Pan Americana. The margin of loss to the winning NASCAR Dodge was under 50 minutes.

Johnson later said that had he known how close he was to the Dodge, he would have upped the pace and stood a good chance of winning the whole ball of wax. However, his Corvette Grand Sport proved to be a casualty of race war. Gasoline was hard to come by on route, making Johnson carry 55 gallons within the car! At each race stop he would add gas, along with an octane booster courtesy of Garland Chemical. Unfortunately the heavy gas load caused the coupe to hit the bumps mighty hard at 190mph. Friction wise, the Grand Sport's frame wore straight through. The car was sold after the race, and as Johnson relayed, "It was a tired old bird at the end of that race." Worn smooth out, and absolutely done, according to Johnson.

However, that wasn't quite the end for Delmo Johnson and the Grand Sport. Come 1965's Sebring 12 Hour race, and Johnson and Morgan were racing the event in a Corvette Grand Sport once again. This time it was Alan Sevadjian's Grand Sport, a #1 coupe under the Ridgeway Racing banner. The weather always tended to be inclement at Sebring, but on March 27 1965, the rain was torrential. There was so much rain, that Delmo Johnson tripped over a submerged trolley jack in the pit area, after exiting the Grand Sport! Johnson had the credo of racing while it was fun, and it was, until now. So, he said to long time endurance race co-driver David Morgan, "My father raised a smarter son than this. I stop as of right now."

The '65 Sebring 12 Hour was won by Hall and

Clean 'Vette front end is product of "hiding" lights. Hood scoop can be opened.

Standard, horizontal back-up light throws excellent beam, distinguishes '67 Sting Ray.

Standard tires resist high-rpm starts by producing slow times and plenty of smoke.

Corvette gauge layout is nothing short of great, as is close-gate 4-speed shifter.

Entry in neat interior is easier than exit. Hand/parking brake is between seats.

of the pilot, but the amp and oil pressure gauges (Shelby additions) are positioned centrally below the radio. It's not hard to see them, but they're not as readable as in the Corvette, nor are they in a direct line of sight with the road.

The really impressive points of the GT 500's insides are its great-feeling wood steering wheel and the integral roll bar with inertia-reel shoulder harnesses. The wheel is one of the most comfortable we've ever had our paws on, with a smooth lacquered finish and genuine "sporty" look. Shoulder harnesses can be cumbersome to attach, and restrict the normal movements of the driver, but not so in the GT 500. They fit around you like suspenders. The inertia retractor in the roll bar allows slow movement, but quickly holds you against any sudden jerk or action. You learn to be leisurely when reaching for the cigarette lighter.

The 'Vette spare is in a panel below the rear underside which, in the rain, may give the Triple A reason to upgrade its rates. There is room for perhaps two suitcases behind the seat.

It takes a while to get used to the stiff-riding Corvette, and the low driver position. Once we became oriented, however, we went along with the "true sports car" claim. The 'Vette is a lot of fun, but discretion must be used in driving around town. It's awful easy to bound past speed limits unknowingly.

Less of an all-out sports car, the GT 500 is more at home on the street than on the track. We received many more comments on the 500's styling than we

MOTOR TREND/APRIL 1967 27

For putting the power down, even the Corvette's best 15 x 6 in rims shod with 7.75-15 rayon tires just weren't enough. Still, the triple deuce 435 horse 427 V8 plus four-speed delivered 0-60mph in 5.5 seconds and a 13.8-second ¼-mile at 104mph. Smokin' in a good way! *(Courtesy Motor Trend)*

Sharp in a Chaparral 2A Chevrolet. Next came the Miles/McLaren GT40, Piper/Maggs Ferrari 250LM, Bondurant and Schlesser in the Shelby Daytona Coupe, two Porsche 904 GTSs, another Daytona Coupe, Ferrari 275 prototype and a couple of Porsche 904s, with a further Daytona Coupe in 13th. The first Corvette Grand Sport over the line was the Wintersteen/Goertz/Diehl coupe, which finished 14th. The first AC Cobra was 19th, but only after a pair of Austin Healeys, a 3000 and Sprite racing as part of the Donald Healey Motor Co team. In 36th position finished a cold, hungry and wet Delmo Johnson and Dave Morgan in their Corvette Grand Sport, for Ridgeway Racing.

As dispiriting as the 1965 Sebring 12 Hour was for Johnson and the Sevadjian Grand Sport, there was a further outing for the coupe with Johnson at the wheel. A few weeks later at Green Valley, Smithfield Texas, Delmo Johnson was a regular race spectator watching Alan Sevadjian's father race the very same Grand Sport ... badly! The poor showing prompted Johnson to alight from

the spectator stands, don Papa Sevadjian's racing helmet and suit, to do the last race of the day. Delmo Johnson won that last race, lapping the 2nd place finisher in the process! He then bid the racing world adieu, having won his first and last races in Texas, with Corvettes.

And if that was the end of one racing avenue, the big block Mid-Year Corvette saw the start of another. Roger Penske retired from racing in 1965 to focus on his Chevrolet dealership. This marked the commencement of his business empire. Penske also launched his racing team, from a modest three bay workshop in Newtown Square, Pennsylvania. The team's first race car wasn't a Camaro, it was a '66 Corvette 427. The machine was the development machine for the pending, fabled L88 427 V8!

So it was, that in January 1966 Dick Guldstrand drove the special Corvette from the St Louis factory, to Roger Penske's race shop. The motor within was an early version of the 1967 RPO L88 427, sent by Zora Arkus-Duntov. Faithful to the formally offered '67 Corvette L88 427, the coupe Guldstrand drove from a chilly St Louis had no heater, necessitating Guldstrand to wrap himself in a furniture blanket for warmth, on route! It was worth it, since in February 1966's inaugural running of the Daytona 24 Hour endurance race, Team Penske's 1966 Corvette 427, with Dick Guldstrand, George Wintersteen and Ben Moore driving, came 12th outright and first in the over 3-liter displacement GT class. However, it almost didn't happen.

Earlier in the 1966 Daytona 24 Hours, the Team Penske Corvette had lost its headlights in a crash. With the rulebook requesting forward facing white lights, the team obliged with duct taped flashlights, affixed to the Corvette's fender tops, much to the chagrin of race marshals! Indeed, the Penske Corvette followed the taillights of a Ferrari prototype, breaking the track class lap record in the process! What's more, the early Corvette L88 427 was the first production car to finish the race. The

Daytona 24 Hours that year witnessed a Ford GT40 1-2-3, followed by Ferrari and Porsche prototypes, then the Penske Corvette. The next over 3-liter GT production car to finish, 2nd in class was a Shelby GT350 Mustang. It was 48 laps behind Roger Penske's Plastic Fantastic coupe. It seemed there was still no replacement for displacement.

In March 1966, the Penske Corvette won the over 5-liter GT production car class, and came ninth overall in the 1966 Sebring 12 Hours. Then too, the Team Penske Corvette represented not only a start for the L88 427 mill, but also the soon familiar Sunoco blue and yellow livery, so closely associated with Roger Penske's racers. Apart from the iconic get up, the '66 Penske Sunoco Corvette sported plastic headlight covers, an original Chevrolet Engineering cowl induction hood, racing gas cap, reinforcement tabs on the windshield and rear backlight, along with door lights to illuminate the coupe's racing number during nocturnal events. Indeed, the Penske Sunoco Corvette was restored by August 2002, under the ownership of Kevin MacKay, to its former original Sunoco livery racing state. In the 1980s this historically significant coupe even rode on 3rd gen Camaro IROC hoops!

The Corvette's position as a GT production class racer was cemented as the '60s wore on. The era of specialized racecraft saw mid-engine prototype machines come to the fore by the late '60s. It was clear to Carroll Shelby that the Cobra couldn't win Le Mans outright, neither could the race refined, but also front-engine Shelby Daytona Coupe. Leave it to the GT40. Indeed, the only time the Mid-Year Corvette appeared at Le Mans was the 1967 edition of the French enduro. The '67 Corvette L88 427 exceeded 170mph on Mulsanne Straight, but conrod failure put an end to that endeavor. In fact, the early L88 427 motors showed a propensity to suffer weak connecting rods, and overheating. However, no such problems were apparent with the legendary '67 Corvette drag racer ... Astoria Chas' KO Motion machine!

Charley 'Chas' Snyder hailed from Astoria,

New York. A young man, like many of his contemporaries, with a great interest in hot cars and drag racing, Charley Snyder lived not far from Joel Rosen's famous Motion Performance speed shop. Snyder already started out with a smokin' hot machine, a brand new Marlboro Maroon '67 Corvette 427 roadster. It was purchased in February 1967. Motion Performance gave this ride their attention, which helped Charley clean up at the local strip, and during late night street racing on Queen's Connecting Highway. However, Motion Performance's upgrading proved too much for the Corvette's stock frame, turning it into a New York pretzel! No problem, in came a new gusset welded frame, plus L88 427 motor, all definitely hardware upgrades.

Unfortunately, the storm clouds of war saw young Charley drafted into the army, concerning

As the Cobra (AC Ace + Ford V8), the Corvette had a challenger in North American large displacement production sports car racing. (Courtesy Cornell Publishing)

the Vietnam conflict. Even so, he continued to race between army duties, with his Ko-Motion Corvette capable of low 11s. Snyder volunteered for the Airborne Rangers, and was sent to Vietnam in the spring of 1968. One month later Charley was killed by a mortar round, he was 20 years old. Joel Rosen and racer John Mahler got permission from Charley's mother Grace to keep racing the Ko-Motion Corvette, with a view to attaining a national record, in honor of the late Charley.

To effect its ambition, Motion Performance made full use of the L88 427's performance potential, balancing and blueprinting the motor, using a stouter bottom end, modified aluminum heads, bigger cam, 850 CFM Holley Double Pumper, Hooker Headers, 4.88 rear gears, Hurst shifter and 10in wide racing slicks!

As a specialist machine, the Corvette got its own drag racing category: AHRA A/Corvette class. Bill Foster raced the Ko-Motion Corvette to an 11.04 second pass at 129mph. The national record book entry read, "In Memory of Astoria Chas". After this feat, John Mahler did a 10.47 second pass at a local track. From this point the Ko-Motion Corvette quietly sat in the garage belonging to Charley's sister. It remained there for 31 years until a local Long Island business man, Glen Spielberg, who was a childhood fan of the Ko-Motion Corvette, purchased the racer on condition that it was kept in its last raced state, never to be restored or modified in any way, shape or form. That was the legend of Astoria Chas' Ko-Motion Corvette!

Owning the Mid-Year Corvette

ROAD & TRACK'S March 1970 Corvette owner survey offered comparative data beyond the mere anecdotal. Especially given such surveys were conducted in the same manner for various makes and models. *R&T*'s survey involved some overlap between the Mid-Year C2 Corvettes of 1963-67 and the first two years of the Late Model C3 Corvettes. Surveyed owners totaled 177, involving 114 Mid-Year Corvettes, and 63 Late Model Corvettes of 1968-69 vintage. Owners hailed mostly from the US and Canada, but some European *R&T* subscribers also participated.

The March 1970 owner survey confirmed many

On March 23 1963, Texans Delmo Johnson (pictured in 2008) and long time co-driver Dave Morgan, finished second in class at the Sebring 12 Hour race, racing this '63 Fuelie Corvette Sting Ray Z06. *(Courtesy Hendrick Heritage Collection)*

beliefs concerning the Plastic Fantastic. That is, it was a durable and reliable car, if not that well put together. In short, the average number of owner survey problem areas, for all cars, was 11. In the pre 1975 era, Mercedes did best with just three problem areas encountered by 5% or more surveyed owners. The Corvette owner survey, covering 1963-69 cars, revealed five problem areas. For comparison, the BMW 1600/2002 registered seven problem areas, with the Jaguar XKE amassing 14 problem areas!

The *R&T* Corvette owner survey also revealed a clear distinction in assembly quality between the C2 Corvettes, and the C3 Corvettes. Beyond question, the Mid-Year models were better assembled. In total, 26% of owners complained about poor workmanship concerning assembly and delivery faults. *R&T* concurred with this finding in light of the experiences of its Corvette owning staff. However, while only 18% of C2 Corvette owners were miffed about poor workmanship, 40% of surveyed C3 Corvette owners complained about the same aspect. Poor workmanship was the Corvette owner's chief dislike.

Road & Track theorized that the sharp distinction between C2 and C3 Corvette quality was due to the St Louis plant having to deal with rising Corvette demand, and working out how to make a much revised design for the C3. In any case, *R&T* offered this assessment, "The worst thing about Corvettes, according to the owners, is the workmanship – or the lack of it". Number two Corvette owner complaint, mentioned by 17% of owners, was the multitude of squeaks and rattles. In this area, the C2 and C3 Corvettes proved equally bad, although overall convertibles were the worst and C2 Corvette coupes the best. *R&T* said with all its strength in the frame, you were always going to get some shake, rattle and roll, compared to unitary construction. The third concern raised by 11% of owners was luggage space, in terms of being too limited or hard to get to. Seven per cent of surveyed owners said the ride was harsh. Final worst feature was ventilation, flagged by 4% of owners, with most criticism directed at the latest C3 Corvette. In this area *R&T* opined that the 427 V8s created heat soak for the interior, a problem compounded by optioning a/c. Choosing a/c on a car, import or domestic, oftentimes restricted the fresh air ventilation system. Although not statistically significant, high insurance premiums and the related greater chance of vehicular theft seemed like part of Corvette life, along with a 'Corvette tax', for Chevrolet parts earmarked for the Plastic Fantastic.

If the above stated the worst features, the good came to mind more easily, and in greater numbers: 61% handling, 60% performance, 28% styling, 26% brakes, 18% reliability/durability. In statistically smaller numbers, owners liked Corvette comfort (powerful heater and defroster), and good gas mileage (small block V8 editions). Why did they buy a Corvette in the first place? 52% said styling, with some 7% singling out the related factor of image. Concerning the latter 'prestige of ownership', the survey revelation: 'girls like it.' Note that a higher percentage of Jaguar XKE owners ticked the styling box.

Second big reason for Corvette purchase, at 44%, was big V8 performance, then came handling (33%), and the readily available parts/service of a US automobile (17%). Engineering was ticked by 14%, like four-wheel disk brakes and IRS, allied to the expected reliability and durability of an American car versus a fragile import tended to by a

Racing under his Johnson Chevrolet dealership banner, Delmo Johnson received experimental brake shoes from Zora Arkus-Duntov; they weren't that effective. As Johnson said, "Ten hours without brakes is a long time." Note the Goodyear Bluestreaks. *(Courtesy Hendrick Heritage Collection)*

shade tree mechanic. Eight per cent said they went Corvette for the rust free body. Under 8% were attracted by power assists and factory a/c being available. You wouldn't get such comfort features on an import.

Overall, the Corvette lived up to owner expectations, except perhaps in servicing. Owners were very critical of the quality of service and repair at authorized dealers. 32% rated dealers as good, the second lowest in *R&T* surveys. 32% said dealers were poor, which was the second worst in such owner surveys. *Road & Track* felt such a specialist car like Corvette wasn't a good match for a high volume, low price, family car Chevrolet. At least one owner agreed, "Although the car costs $5000 they treat you with the same disregard as if you bought a $2000 Chevy II." *R&T* also said one ex GM management executive relayed, "I am compelled to state that dealer service countrywide is abominable, with few exceptions." Complaints in the owner survey mentioned inept mechanics that charged for work not done, with 7% stating the dealer wasn't familiar enough with the Corvette, and that Corvette specific parts could be hard to get.

Indeed, there was an anecdotal story about a Chevrolet dealer mechanic in the mid west that tried a customer's '72 Corvette. He said it was a nice car, then asked what it was?! In many parts of the country, family cars and pickups were a much

The 1963 Corvette Grand Sport was Zora Arkus-Duntov's attempt to create a specialized, race oriented version of the new Mid-Year Corvette, to challenge Carroll Shelby's Cobras. *(Courtesy Mecum)*

more common sight than a Corvette. As mentioned in the August 1970 Road Test, 1st gen Camaro owner survey, the trick was to visit a specialist shop suggested by word of mouth. A great car deserves a knowledgeable expert.

In terms of the five problem areas *R&T*'s owner survey discerned, the biggest concern was instrumentation, with the Corvette's clock singled out as the worst offender. As indeed on TV show *Wheeler Dealers*, Edd China tackled an inoperative timepiece, on a numbers matching '64 Riverside Red L75 Corvette 327 four-speed roadster. In this era, it was a real clock with moving parts, not a compact quartz movement. Second biggest problem for 20% of owners was the cooling system. That is, radiators, hoses and overheating. As per *R&T*'s experience with a '69 Corvette 427 roadster, the alternator belt tended to rub the top radiator hose on '67 Corvettes. One owner of a '67 Corvette with L75 327 V8 used the longer belt from a '62 Corvette (part #3847707) and the top hose from a '65 Corvette 327 (part #383366), as a fix.

The third concern for 15% of owners involved body parts, and this covered everything from fiberglass cracks, through window regulators and more. 13% of owners had trouble with the concealed windshield wiper flap of 1968-69 Corvettes. Once again, *Wheeler Dealers*' Edd China had to deal with a somewhat vandalized

concealed wiper system on the show's Rally Red L79 '68 Corvette 327 four-speed roadster. For all the surveyed years of Corvette, 1963-69, rain leaks affected 15% of owners. Number four most prominent problem involved the Corvette's Holley carbs; 12% of surveyed Corvette owners complained, and 19% of 1966-67 Corvette owners, which represented the start of using such Holley hardware. The fifth, and final, major area of concern was wheel alignment and tire wear. Some cars were out of adjustment on delivery, as new vehicles.

Proving the Corvette's enthusiast buyer base, 29% of surveyed owners participated in rallies, with 18% doing slaloms. Indeed, prospective used Corvette purchasers were wise to look for signs of racing, such as dump tubes and excessive U joint looseness. Concerning that last item, there were six, one on each end of the driveshaft, and one on each end of the axle shaft. And a word to the wise to do a tight turn, while applying and releasing the throttle, to discern any unwanted noises emanating from the oft specified Positraction lsd. Checks for missing noise-suppressing metal shields around the distributor, coil and plug wires, that aided clear radio reception, were advisable. Such shields were oftentimes junked by racers. In a problem encountered with the modern LS V8 of the late '90s and onwards, the Chevrolet V8 has long had an appetite for oil between services, so regular dipstick inspection should be done.

Corvette owners tended to be, and still are, fastidious enthusiasts. *Road & Track* found the cohort to be the most fanatical group going when it came to servicing and looking after their pride and joy. Many owners changed oil and filter more frequently than at the recommended 6000 mile service intervals. So, little surprise that only one *R&T* surveyed Corvette owner mentioned that an engine overhaul had been necessary, due to wear and tear. This was at 45,000 miles, on a hi po Corvette 427 owned in West Germany. Although, there was mention of recurrent mechanical problems on early 427 V8 motors, that were related to valve gear.

Hot cars tend to be run hard and put away wet. However, hi po engine Corvettes brought a lot of valve overlap and low head airflow velocity to the table. This characteristic contributed to poor combustion during low speed driving, and therefore excessive deposits on sparkplugs. So, more frequent sparkplug changes, along with Corvette four-speed clutch changes, were all part of Plastic Fantastic life. Naturally, automatic equipped Corvettes led a more sheltered life.

Four wheel drum and all disk Corvette braking systems were found to be equally long lived, with drum or disk lasting a fair distance. However, the Firestone Wide Ovals of the later 1968-69 C3 Corvettes surveyed didn't provide as much tire life as the rubber fitted to Mid-Year C2 Corvettes. Eleven per cent of surveyed owners had tried radials, reputed to have a longer life than bias ply footwear. A set of radials was found to last around 30,000 miles on cars that were, in general, driven further than some garage toy sports cars. Surveyed C2 Corvettes had an average odometer reading of around 37,000 miles. There were no 1965½ Corvettes in the *R&T* survey. The younger Late Model C3 Corvettes were on 11,000 miles, with 16% of surveyed Corvettes having over 50,000 miles on the clock, one car recording a highest survey odometer reading of 120,000 miles. Have Corvette, will travel!

Owners drove far, but not always hard. *Road & Track* owner surveys found that if a car had more power to start with, owners didn't have to wring

their steed's neck! So, Corvette driving habits were more on the genteel Jaguar and even MG side, compared to Porsche, BMW and Alfa. 44% of Corvette owners drove moderately, and were a group of reasonable affluence, with 62% of owners having other makes in their garage. This was consistent with Camaro owner surveys in other journals. And like Camaro devotees, the Corvette clan were loyal enthusiasts, with some pragmatism and objectivity. This was indicated by *R&T*'s willing to buy another of the same type question, yes/no/undecided. For the various surveyed makes the vital stats were: Corvette 81/15/4, Alfa 94/3/3, Datsun 80/18/2, Jaguar 83/17/0, MG 70/19/11, Porsche 95/4/1, Triumph 67/30/3.

Corvette racing stalwarts Delmo Johnson and Dave Morgan campaigned a Corvette Grand Sport, under Johnson Chevrolet Co auspices, at the 1964 Sebring 12 Hour race. *(Courtesy Mecum)*

Given the Grand Sport's conflict with the AMA anti racing pact, GM chairman Frederic Donner canned the racer's program, after just five cars were built. This was much to Zora Arkus-Duntov's chagrin, as he had planned 125 to be built! *(Courtesy Mecum)*

The data indicated Corvette and Camaro buyers chose their cars because they were good, but were not fanatical in the manner of Alfa, Porsche or, later on, Honda owners. The Jag XKE was a polarizer, as indicated in *Motor Trend*'s later first test of the Jag XJ12. The Jaguar fans were willing to put up with many automotive foibles to enjoy the dignity of the cars from Coventry. By 1970 it seemed the quality problems of British sports cars were causing MG and Triumph prospects to be wary. The Datsun Fairlady roadster was like a Japanese MGB with more quality. This aspect ended up winning conquest sales in the lead up to the all conquering 240Z.

For now, the major reason Corvette owners wouldn't go Corvette again was poor assembly quality, and 17% of Mid-Year Corvette owners said they wouldn't update to the Late Model C3 Corvette, due to the latter's unattractiveness in terms of larger girth and gadgetry, for the most part. That said, one repeat owner confided that he was on his fourth Corvette by 1970, with it still being the only sub ten-grand car that was exciting to drive. So it seemed the positives still outweighed the negatives concerning Corvette, continuing into the latest C3 era. *R&T* said Mid-Year Corvette owner qualms concerning the latest Corvette probably didn't worry Chevrolet, "... as more and more people scramble to buy new Stingrays."

Mid-Year Corvette, on the path to perfection

A LOT OF stuff gets designed for Corvette that's never seen. John Schinella would go on to become Pontiac styling boss, doing the third gen Firebird and Knight Rider KITT exterior. He was working in the '60s Chevrolet camp and, along with George Angersbach, got assigned to Bill Mitchell's Secret Warehouse Studio, where front and mid-engine Corvettes were designed. In John Schinella's own words, "While there, we were also assigned to 'clean-up' the 1963 Corvette for 1965 sales. This was done by eliminating the fake scoops on the hood and rear-quarter panel. Prior to this, we had learned that consumer reaction to the Corvette was poor. They did not care for this fake ornamentation. Corvette buyers have a strong emotional

This GM license built replica of the Johnson/Morgan 1964 Sebring 12 Hour Grand Sport was finished by Mongoose Motorsports early in 2019. Very appropriate, given Mongooses eat Cobras!
(Courtesy Mecum)

relationship to this model. We designed functional front-fender scoops and air extractor vents for the rear-quarter panel, and I personally designed a new wheel cover that reflected an aluminum cast wheel design. When I saw a 1965 Corvette in the dealership, however, the wheel cover looked like a chrome pie plate. Seeing this cut-rate execution of my design got me so enraged that I went straight to Irv Rybicki. Agreeing with me, he contacted Chevrolet to find out what happened. It was discovered that Chevy eliminated the cast wheel cover design and color finish to save money. It was unfortunate that Chevy did not communicate this to the design staff prior to production." [56]

For 1966, those pie plate wheel covers changed to a cherry blossom-like five-petal look, they used to have six contrast outer segments. Then too, cast an eye on the egg crate grille insert, and Corvette Sting Ray driver-side hood script. The latter matched the rear trunk tail script, already present on the passenger side. There were chrome door handles, and no more C pillar vents. This aspect of the fresh air vent system hadn't proved effective, and was another item of exterior visual clutter. Inside, Corvette's bucket seats had more pleats, and the safety aid of head restraints to complement newly introduced shoulder belts.

In spite of various rumors of a new Corvette for 1967, the '66 Corvette witnessed the Mid-Year C2 generation's best sales result, 27,720 units. This was made up of 9958 coupes and 17,162 ragtops, starting from a respective $4295 and $4084. By 1967

This 1966 Team Penske racer was a curtain raiser to the 1967 RPO L88 427 V8. *(Courtesy Hagerty)*

model year it was almost a given, that the Mid-Year C2 Corvette was in swansong mode. Indeed, the pending Late Model C3 Corvette just wasn't ready. Among many 'to do list' items, Zora Arkus-Duntov wanted wind tunnel work to correct aerodynamic problems concerning what would be the Mako Shark II inspired generation. '67 Corvette sales were down to a 22,940 tally. This total comprised of 8504 coupes, with starting sticker $4388, and 14,436 roadsters, which retailed from $4240.

Although it seemed that the Mid-Year Corvette had reached the end of Route 66, many were the detail revisions for its final year. For starters, new rims. Federal safety law said no to knock off hubs, be they faux wheel covers or real alloy rims, no knock offs for '67 MY. The base wheel for the Corvette between 1967 and 1982 was the new Rally rim. It was shared with the new Camaro and Chevelle/El Camino. The Rally style was a 15 x 6in slotted steel rim, with trim ring and chrome center cap. For Corvette it would upsize twice, to 15 x 7in for 1968 and 15 x 8in for 1969. It was judged a visual improvement over the former pie plate knock off wheel covers of 1965-66. Still optional were cast alloys, but 1966's P48 $316 knock offs were replaced with $263 N89 alloys, which had a bolt on chrome cap. Both types were familiar for their numerous raised fins. Such alloys were optioned by 1194 and 720 Corvette patrons, in the respective years.

Functional side fender gill vents, went from three to five gills for '67 MY. The distinctive one year only stinger hood of '67 big block Corvettes was hard to miss, and became a style icon. Corvette designers and insurance companies hoped you wouldn't miss

the Corvette's new, above rear license plate back-up light! As part of the visual simplification road that the Mid-Year Corvette had been traveling, there was less exterior brightwork, and toned down flat finish rocker panel trim, sans ribbing. Door lock buttons were moved forward, with an associated rear attaching screw. In keeping with contemporary fashion, new RPO C08 implied a 52 buck vinyl covering, for the roadster's optional hardtop. 1966 '67 Corvette patrons said yes to that vinyl.

Vinyl on the outside and inside, since from '66 MY a vinyl-covered, foam-backed headliner, replaced the Corvette's earlier fiberboard equivalent. Further interior changes saw no passenger side grab handle above the glovebox. Said handle had been a Corvette mainstay since 1958. Moving from its previous under dash location, the handbrake now resided between the buckets, import car style. The Corvette's upholstery had also been altered for 1967. On the safety front, the new for '67 MY U15 speed warning indicator was a ten buck option to remind one of posted speed limits. It was selected by 2108 Corvette faithful, and would survive on the Plastic Fantastic option list through '69 MY.

Those with a keen eye would notice how '67 Corvettes carried the blue 'GM Mark of Excellence' decal on the back of each door, above the door latch. However, perhaps the best revision for 1967, also something you could see, was improved quality. It seems the '67 Corvettes were the best put together of the Mid-Year cars. They were also the most refined, with an absence of buzz from the four-speed shift linkage. It seemed safe to assume, that the St Louis truck plant workers had got a handle on how to put these beauties together. That was the Corvette's gift to American sports car fans for 1967! It was also Bill Mitchell's gift to his wife Marian!

GM Styling boss Mitchell gave a very special, custom build Ermine White '67 Corvette 427 roadster, with 407 red vinyl interior, to his wife. Mitchell was personally invested with the C2 Corvette, even before day one. The sports car's sea creatures shape having a genesis in a Bahamas trip Mitchell was on, with Larry Shinoda designing the car under his direction. Now for Marian's gift, Mitchell had help from Zora Arkus-Duntov, with the Corvette Chief Engineer taking a hands-on approach to the order. Beyond even this personal service, Marian's '67 Corvette was sourced via the COPO (Central Office Production Order) avenue, more associated with Camaro 427s, but really for anything out of the ordinary.

Starting with a $4240 '67 Corvette roadster, tick the following RPO (Regular Production Order) option boxes: L68 427 400hp V8 ($305), M35 Powerglide automatic ($194), G91 special highway axle (3.08:1 - $2), N40 power steering ($94), J50 power brakes ($42), K66 transistor ignition system ($73), C60 A/C ($412), N36 telescopic steering column ($42), U69 AM-FM radio ($172), A31 power windows ($57), C07 hardtop ($231), A02 soft ray tinted glass windshield ($10), N14 side exhaust ($131), N89 cast aluminum bolt-on wheels ($263), Total: $6268, or, a very pretty penny for the day!

Bill Mitchell was present at the St Louis plant while the Corvette was being built, with it being completed on May 3 1967. The roadster then went to the GM Technical Center in Warren Michigan. Here, Mitchell supervised custom work: red pinstriping from stinger hood to the rear deck, and down to the rear valence, plus door sills in between, red centers for the turbine rims, red for suspension parts and wheel wells even! A couple of pieces of literature help tell this Corvette's tale. For one, the original build order on the gas tank. Under the options selected, it said W Mitchell. Then too, concerning the Chevrolet Memo Book, a note on the cover stated, "Mr Mitchell – special order per Z Duntov." Indeed, through this note book existed Zora Arkus-Duntov's handwriting, with notes on the ordered Corvette, to help guide factory workers with the build.

This April '67 ordered Corvette was loved by Mitchell's wife Marian, who drove it for two years. The ragtop was then sold to neighbor Harry Byrd around 1969, and sold onto another neighbor Richard Brown six months hence. The Corvette accompanied Brown on his Floridian retirement. In 1987 Brown sold the Corvette to Don Newton of Kentucky, with the car subsequently receiving a restoration in 1989. Bill Mitchell's name and address were stated on the warranty booklet, owner's manual and Protect-O-Plate. However, the Corvette's original 427 V8 got blown up sometime during the car's

life. That said, it survived to garner the inaugural Bloomington Gold Historic Award. Marian's Corvette is rolling history of a bygone GM age!

C2 Mid-Year Corvette — A legend in its own time

LOOKED AT IN its own era, and since, the Mid-Year Corvette has perhaps received more praise than any other generation of Corvette, both inside America and around the world. [57] In *Road & Track*'s March 1970 owner survey of the Corvette, it acknowledged that in the historical annuls of the American sports car, the Nash-Healey was forgotten, and the two-seater Thunderbird had become a classic. The Corvette, a Chevrolet stepchild hailing from a St Louis truck plant, had experienced a sales expansion that surprised even the Chevrolet faithful, loyal to the Corvette. Always a lot of car for the money, and in its best form a fine car for driving, the C2 Corvette was described by *R&T* as a moment of glory.

Five years later, the Mid-Year Corvette was the subject of a *R&T* used car survey. The journal's admiration for this generation of Corvette remained undimmed. Two *Road & Track* editors had owned such cars, 1963 and 1964 examples. The latter once belonged to Ron Wakefield, with both cars regarded fondly. Indeed, the February 1975 issue of *Road & Track*'s report was subtitled "Fast, reliable sports cars for the budget-minded enthusiast." *R&T*

The '67 Astoria Chas Ko-Motion Corvette was a drag racing Mid-Year roadster, created by Motion Performance. It was a winner on both street and strip, in Long Island, New York. *(Courtesy Auto World)*

considered the breed, one of good, straight forward sports cars, that improved each year as Chevrolet tidied up the Corvette's styling and engineering.

That the second generation Corvette was the recipient of such fanfare had something to do with it being created in a time when GM and Chevrolet were at their commercial and design zeniths. Plus, safety and pollution law had yet to lay the entire auto industry low, due to over-zealous legislators listening to special interest group fanatics. As a result, in the mid '70s malaise era, the Mid-Year Corvette appeared conspicuously good value. As *Road & Track* said, with careful shopping, a used C2 Corvette could be had for a fraction of a new '75 Corvette's price, and for less than even a brand new four cylinder imported sports car. Second hand, but not second rate according to *R&T*, since the C2 Corvette was, "… up to contemporary standards in ride and noise level, comes close to matching them in handling and probably exceeds them in performance and economy – all for less than $4000." [58]

For less than the price of a new '75 VW Dasher, even the mildest Mid-Year Corvette 327 V8 could outpace a late '70s, early '80s Mercedes 450SL, BMW 6 series, or even one time Chevrolet boss John Z DeLorean's somewhat infamous DeLorean DMC 12. Sadly, it has been many a year since a C2 Corvette has been an affordable used buy, and SoCal Corvette specialist dealer Bob Wingate explained why. By the mid '70s, 50% of all the Corvettes ever made had been stolen, at one time or another in their lives. Of the half remaining, 75% were gone or stripped for valuable Corvette parts, or customized/converted into race cars. The upshot was that only 20% of pre 1968 Corvettes had survived in good, original stock condition. This partly explained the classic Corvette's steady appreciation, as a collectible automobile. The other part being it was simply a desirable sporty car. It was noted in 1975 that Corvette convertibles in California were worth 25% less, compared to the east coast, while imported sports cars were worth 25% more in the Golden State if they were ragtops. [59] It possibly signified the more practical nature of the domestic car buyer versus their import fancying counterpart. Convertibles were once purchased for their cooling effect in hot climes. However, with good factory a/c afoot, ragtop popularity fell. That said, for import fans, the convertible was still part of the sports car mystique.

The Mid-Year Corvette's iconic status has grown over time. Placed in *Autocar* magazine's 100 Greatest Sports Cars, Roger Bell described the 1963-67 Corvette as possessing "Flash Gordon" styling, with the Sting Ray being eye catching both inside and out, with a decent chassis, and superbly finished fiberglass body. In fact, the journal stated that Lotus had never achieved such neat shut lines. The C2 Corvette cockpit was considered roomy, and of restrained opulence. The only criticism was lack of steering feel, but with an overall judgement, "The archetypal American sports car." [60]

The above comments were confirmed in the 2000s TV show *Wheeler Dealers*, when Mike Brewer and Edd China got their hands on a '64 Corvette four-speed roadster. Brewer mentioned the classic American nature of the C2 Corvette, with both agreeing that the car's lightweight and compact dimensions provided a sporting feel, not normally associated with US cars, which were usually judged large and heavy. Indeed, the C2 Corvette's sound suspension even helped its little brother the Corvair overcome Ralph Nader. The rear-engine Corvair's revised rear suspension design was influenced by the C2 Corvette's IRS. It eradicated previous Corvair fears concerning jacking up and sudden oversteer. The Mid-Year Corvette: a car that led by example!

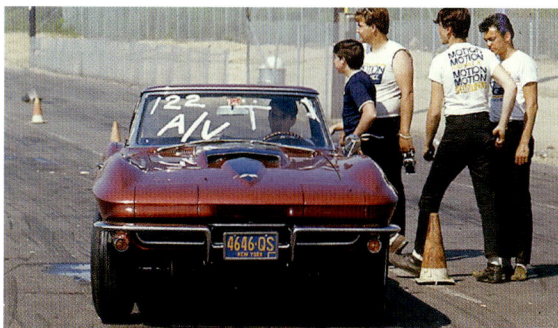

Bill Foster set an AHRA A/Corvette national record of 11.04 seconds at 129mph, in 1968. The L88 427 V8 motor came with the right stuff for racer improvement. Mr Motion Joel Rosen at the wheel! *(Courtesy Motion Performance)*

CHAPTER 6

Makovette
1968-70

From dream car to reality

THERE WAS A competition within GM concerning creating the third generation Corvette. On the one hand you had Zora Arkus-Duntov & Co pushing for mid- and rear-engine designs. Then there was DM Design head honcho Bill Mitchell, and Larry Shinoda with the more conventional, front-engine Mako Shark alternative. Future Pontiac styling boss John Schinella recounted Mitchell's operation: "… I was assigned to Vice President William Mitchell's Secret Warehouse Studio. Under the head of the studio, Larry Shinoda, I was part of the team that worked on the first mid-engine Chevrolet Chaparral racer and Mako Shark II. The Mako Shark II turned out to be the theme car for the 3rd Generation 1968 Corvette. All work in the secret studio was extremely hush hush!"

The Mako Shark II show car was originally dubbed just Mako Shark, with the sequel suffix added once the XP-755 prototype was retroactively renamed Mako Shark I. Mako Shark II started early in 1964, and embodied Bill Mitchell's long standing love for undersea creatures, which was all also instrumental in the design of the Mid-Year C2 Corvette. The Mako Shark II took on the sugar scoop, or question mark roof of the Duntov group's mid-engine Corvette proposals, plus that cohort's vertical back window style. From the start, a targa top and removable back window were in the planning. However, the Mako Shark II also took elements from a prototype called XP-833, aka Pontiac Banshee.

The Banshee project was also moving along

early in 1964, and was Pontiac Chief Engineer John Z DeLorean's sports car proposal. Bill Collins did a flip top roof coupe with Pontiac OHC six, and a 326 V8 ragtop, with powered top. Both prototypes had Muncie four-speeds, with DeLorean planning a 421 HO V8 motor to go with the GM A body chassis parts, 90in wheelbase and Watts-type live axle. Front coil overs, space frame, plus glued and screwed fiberglass panels were all a taste of the 1983 Fiero to come. Of course maverick DeLorean had no permission to do any of this, but that didn't stop him greeting the GM brass with a sales kit pack intro booklet; why not?!

GM management, given the Corvette's long existence, passed on Banshee. However, given John Z's achievements, promoted him to Chief of the Tin Indian division. It also let him have the job of doing the Camaro's kissing cousin, the Firebird, which was probably DeLorean's gambit anyway. Even so, Chevrolet GM Pete Estes instructed the Corvette boys to incorporate the Coke bottle look Banshee's style for the upcoming late model or C3 Corvette. [61] Bill Mitchell's Secret Warehouse Studio designed front- and mid-engine Corvettes, and, come 1965, small scale models of the proposed mid-engine design, incorporating Mark IV big block V8s.

Like John Z DeLorean with his hoped for Banshee 421 HO, Zora Arkus-Duntov always wanted the Corvette to have the very best. In September 1969, *Car and Driver* provided such insight into Duntov's thinking. While the racing world showed the time was right for a lighter mid-engine Corvette, and Duntov did like high revving engines, *C/D* said Papa Corvette couldn't bring himself to do a car

The Corvette C3 was patterned after the Mako Shark II designed by Larry Shinoda. Executed under Bill Mitchell's direction, the Mako II had been initiated in early 1964. Once the mid-engined format was abandoned, the Shinoda/Mitchell car was sent to Chevrolet Styling under David Holls, where Harry Haga's studio adapted it for production on the existing Stingray chassis. The resulting lower half of the car was much like the Mako II, except for the softer contours. The concept car's name was later changed to Manta Ray. The C3 also adopted the 'sugar scoop' roof treatment with vertical back window from the mid-engined concept models designed by the Duntov group. It was intended from the beginning that the rear window and that portion of the roof above the seats to be removable.[5]

LEFT

FRONT

TOP

CHEVROLET CORVETTE C3

TECHNICAL

ENGINE: 427 CU IN (7.0 L) L89 V8
TORQUE 460 LB-FT
TOP SPEED 139 MPH
WHEELBASE 98.0 IN
CURB WEIGHT 3,520 LB
MODEL YEARS 1968-1982
CHIEF ENGINEER ZORA ARKUS-DUNTOV

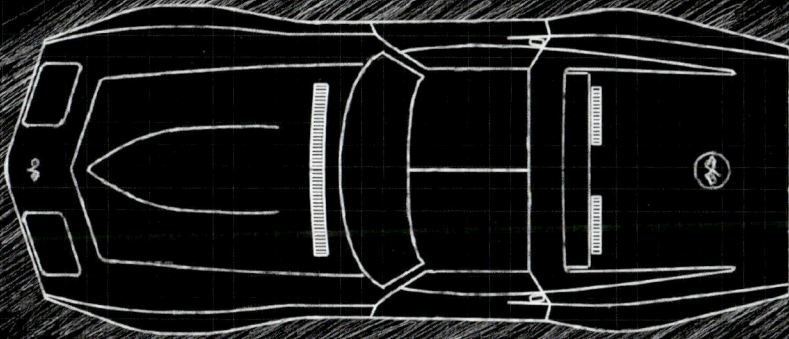

The new C3 or 'Late Model' Corvette was developed by Dave Holls and Hank Haga at Chevrolet Styling Studios. Their basis was the Mako Shark II Bill Mitchell/Larry Shinoda show car proposal. Zora Arkus-Duntov's mid-engine plan had to wait for the C8 Corvette! *(Courtesy Brandon Fenty)*

The Mako Shark II and Late Model Corvette were influenced by John Z DeLorean's XP-833 Pontiac Banshee. *(Courtesy Pontiac Enthusiast)*

without the biggest and most powerful engine in the Chevrolet range. If only to prevent the latest Corvette from getting blown away by a hopped up Chevy II or Chevelle. So, Duntov had consented to the Corvette getting bulkier over time. [62]

As things transpired, Chevrolet's ultimate Mark IV big block 409 replacement V8 family wound up under the hood of the conventional Mako

The new 1968 Corvette brought wider 15 x 7in rims as standard equipment, and many other one-year-only items. *(Courtesy Marc Cranswick)*

This '68 ad used the Mid-Year Corvette's Sting Ray moniker. The 'Stingray' name formally arrived for 1969. T-tops and removable rear window were new to Corvette for 1968. *(Courtesy GM Archives)*

Shark II related Corvette. That is, Bill Mitchell and Larry Shinoda's proposal won out. A mid-engine Corvette needed many unique parts shared with no other Chevrolet, such as a high torque transaxle. Therefore, what had been a relative bargain American sports car would have possibly lost the value for money reputation, and sales, that the Corvette nameplate had garnered over the years.

In a rerun of the events of the late '50s, commercial reality saw the new Corvette remain relatively down to earth, engineering wise. Back then, issues included a recession, rising small car sales, and the importance of the upcoming Corvair, Chevy II and Chevelle compacts/kingsize compact. The result was the C2 Corvette retained a separate chassis and front engine. Now, with the economy on shaky ground again, and rising popularity of imported subcompacts, Chevrolet had higher priorities than a mid-engine Corvette. Industry research had shown a general consumer desire to beat the rising costs of transportation, in terms of purchase price, insurance and running costs. As a

The "convertible" coupe

Look, it's the 1968 Corvette Sting Ray Coupe: sleek, snug, sporty. Look again. Now, with the roof panels off, it's open to the sun, the sky, the air. This "convertible" feature is standard on the new Sting Ray Coupe, as are hidden headlights, concealed wipers, rear-deck spoiler and a cockpit that's impeccably comfortable yet utterly functional. Standard, too: fully independent suspension, four-wheel disc brakes, 300 hp and Corvette's taut, precise sports-car handling. Sting Ray for 1968 at your Chevrolet dealer's.

'68 Corvette by Chevrolet

Removable roof sections stow behind seat, along with the detachable glass rear window. Opened up, Corvette's a "convertible." Buttoned up, it's a coupe. More than ever, it's one-of-a-kind.

result, the high-volume subcompact 1971 Vega, to be built at Lordstown, was a key priority, with fewer resources for a radical Corvette.

It was in late 1964 that Bill Mitchell told Larry Shinoda and his design team to be ready car show wise, for the April 1965 New York International Auto Show. The result was the Secret Warehouse Studio's full scale Mako Shark II mock up, complete with 'Mark IV 396' hood callout, but no actual engine fitted. Pictures were taken in March 1965, with the next step being a functional Mako Shark II with real, honest to goodness 427 V8, and more. More implied wide Firestones filling Can Am fenders, crackle black finish aluminum side pipes, with polished chrome relief fins, exclamation point roofline, duck-tail spoiler and a very special paint job.

The Mako Shark II's exterior featured Firefrost Midnight Blue, with brown highlights. All to invoke thoughts of Bill Mitchell's beloved life aquatic. Yes, you could drive this show car, and eight years prior to the infamous Austin Allegro, the Mako Shark II sported a rectangular steering wheel! The running Mako Shark II 427 was at the Paris Auto Salon, and toured America and Europe during 1965. Other worldly to the eye, but sound business sense led to the Mako Shark II adopting the Mid-Year Corvette chassis, in its journey to being the late model C3 Corvette. There was no time to waste, given the latest Corvette's release had been delayed by all the time and resources devoted to evaluating a mid-engine Corvette. Then again, much had been spent creating the short-lived Mid-Year Corvette. The C2 Corvette had sold well enough, but not so well as to justify the expense of a super exotic Lamborghini Miura rival from St Louis.

It all made Mako Shark II the sensible route, but designers could still dream. That dream was the 1969 Manta Ray show car. Whereas the Mako Shark II was 9in longer than a production Corvette, and powered by an iron block 427 V8, the Manta Ray was even longer and came with the ultimate Mark IV motor, the all aluminum ZL1 427! The Manta Ray was an evolution of the Mako Shark II, and cost three million bucks as a one off design exercise!! It featured body colored Endura bumpers, as an impact bumper precursor to the '73 Corvette. There was a chin spoiler at the front, side pipes in the

The engine line up between 1967 and 1968 was identical, save one difference, a smog pump was added. 1968 ragtop sales dwarfed the coupe tally, 18,630 versus 9936, within the 28,566 Corvette total. *(Courtesy GM Archives)*

middle and a tapered, stretched tail rearwards. The color-matched, deep twist carpeting was present on normal C3 Corvettes.

As for the flow of making Mako Shark II production ready, the transition was from Bill Mitchell's Secret Warehouse Studio, to Chevrolet I Studio, and then Chevrolet II Studio. Chevrolet II Studio's mid 1960s assistant chief designer John Schinella, explained the purpose of the studios, "At this time, the Chevrolet exterior design studio was overflowing with future and production assignments. The chief designer of this studio, Irv Rybicki, felt it was necessary to add a second Exterior and an Interior Chevrolet Studio, and got the okay from Mitchell to do this. Under Irv Rybicki,

A 1968 big block, ragtop Corvette appeared in the 1976 movie *The Gumball Rally*. It broke in two after a big jump! *(Courtesy First Artists)*

Hank Haga, his assistant, was promoted to chief designer of the new Chevrolet II studio."

Subsequently, Mako Shark II was sent to Chevrolet I Studio, now under Dave Holls. The Corvette proposal/show car then traveled to Chevrolet II Studio under Hank Haga, with John Schinella as second in command. Here, the task of productionizing Mako Shark II into the new 1968 C3 Corvette was accomplished. While the sugar scoop roofline and vertical back pane made it through, the production Corvette had softer curves than Mako Shark II. Most importantly, the new Corvette rode on the chassis of the outgoing Mid-Year C2 Corvette. Mako Shark II was adapted to this production reality.

Delayed by the time and resources spent on studying both mid and front-engine Corvette proposals, the C3 Corvette's release was further slowed by aerodynamic problems that Zora Arkus-Duntov wanted addressed, using more wind tunnel work. As Duntov told Patrick Bedard in the June 1971 issue of *Car and Driver*, the stylists had originally wanted a big rear spoiler for the C3 Corvette. However, testing revealed this design generated so much downforce that the car's nose came up, making the steering go spookily light! Duntov was able to get the rear spoiler downsized to its non-functional 1968 duck-tail state.

In June 1970, *Sports Car Graphic* tested a 1970 Corvette LT1 350 against a like engine 70½ Camaro Z28. The journal's aerodynamic results at the customary 100mph benchmark showed front and rear lift readings of 230lb and 55lb concerning

the late model C3 Corvette, with said T-top coupe exhibiting 280lb of drag through the air. Equivalent Z28 readings entailed 325lb, 40lb and 350lb, with the second figure representing downforce, not lift. Both cars were evaluated wearing F60-15 tires, and the drag through the air stats did consider tire drag. Obviously the Corvette was the slipperier of the two machines.

Prior to the July 1967 press preview of the new third generation Corvette, with a Le Mans Blue L68 triple deuce 427 automatic '68 Corvette coupe to hand, Zora Arkus-Duntov added a strip of fiberglass to deepen the front airdam. These actions were done just a few days before the unveiling test drive. Such moves weren't so much to improve aerodynamics as to fix engine overheating. ZAK also cut front valence inlet holes, to further help with radiator cooling. The big block C3 Corvettes had an overheating problem, which Duntov was wise to. The new '68 Corvette lacked a radiator shroud. It would receive one for '69 MY, but that didn't solve the problem.

In the test sessions described in *Car and Driver*'s June 1971 issue, a 454 V8 Corvette with LS5 motor, was run in Nevada at wide open throttle, back when the state had no speed limit. The result was overheating after only a few miles. Zora Arkus-Duntov zeroed in on the culprit, the radiator fan shroud. It was necessary at low speeds, plus when idling in traffic, but the shroud could impede airflow through the radiator during high speed driving. Solution? Duntov had a shroud with flaps, that would open during such

This is a 1968 Corvette L71 427 four-speed. At 435 horse, the highest rated horsepower Corvette you could buy that year. *(Courtesy Cruisin Classics)*

As per the outgoing Mid-Year models, big block Late Model Corvettes were visually differentiated by a raised hood molding. At least until 1973. *(Courtesy Cruisin Classics)*

high speed driving. However, the bean counters didn't want to know. It wasn't a safety issue, so ZAK didn't pursue the matter. Nevertheless, one can imagine an upscale import brand would have okayed Duntov's modification. As things stood, the Corvette's unofficial chief engineer had to deal with the cost and marketing compromises of GM. The overheating issue of Mark IV engine C3 Corvettes was never really addressed. However, Federal smog controls that pacified the Rat Motor's power, helped somewhat.

Engineering ← All in the Chevrolet family

IN SPITE OF a crash program to get the C3 Corvette ready for '67 model year, and its Mid-Year Corvette derived engineering base, the new model wasn't ready in time. Too many things to fix, but it was worth the wait. As ever, the use of existing Chevrolet production line hardware, and labor intensive St Louis separate chassis assembly, helped keep Corvette profitable.

Little surprise that the new Corvette saw the continuation of the C2 predecessor's ladder frame chassis, with five crossmembers, SLA independent front suspension/coils/telescopic shocks, IRS with trailing arms and transverse multileaf spring/frame mounted differential/telescopic shocks, with an additional rear swaybar for big block Corvettes as standard. Your regular small block 1968 Corvette came with a front 0.750in swaybar. For big block editions this bar was upsized to 0.875in, with the additional rear swaybar sized at 0.562in. The extra swaybar served like a sixth crossmember, trying to increase chassis rigidity in the face of 427 V8 torque. 36 buck F41 special front and rear suspension brought a 0.938in front swaybar, and was selected by 1758 of the 28,566 '68 Corvette buyers. F41 was for solid lifter big block Corvettes.

The big change for the latest Corvette was the adoption of bigger 15 x 7in rally rims, with F70-15 tires. 1967's 7.75-15s had no hope putting

The base price Corvette roadster retailed for $4420 in 1968. Then came the options, with 2898 Plastic Fantastic faithful choosing the $437 L71 427 V8, in this coupe. Note the 1968 absence of fender Stingray script. *(Courtesy Cruisin Classics)*

the Corvette's solid lifter 427 V8 power down on the ground. In light of this alteration, Zora Arkus-Duntov wanted to keep the outside rear wheel upright, minimizing camber change and maximizing traction during cornering, while improving steering response. So, ZAK oversaw the rear roll center being lowered 2.85in to 4.71in, and a stiffening of the Corvette's springing, to raise front roll resistance. Front spring rates on small block Corvettes increased from the previous C2 Corvette's 80lb/in^2 to 85lb/in^2, and big block cars were on 92lb/in^2.

Duntov stayed faithful to the linkage type booster, concerning the optional recirculating ball power steering. He felt it gave more feel than the integral-with-gear type seen on other GM cars. Zora Arkus-Duntov favored a slight understeering/neutral Corvette chassis behavior, with a feeling one could make rapid progress, and feed in more power before oversteer set in – which was a given with a semi hemi 427 V8 calling the shots!

The 'Genuine Leather Seats' option cost a mere 79 bucks, but only 2429 Corvette buyers optioned 'em in '68 MY. This coupe has the standard black vinyl. *(Courtesy Cruisin Classics)*

A Corvette sans V8 and four-speed was fast becoming unthinkable. Only 5063 Corvette patrons optioned the excellent three-speed RPO M40 GM THM 400, torque converter slushbox. The two-speed Powerglide ended with the Mid-Year Corvettes. *(Courtesy Cruisin Classics)*

Duntov demonstrated his reasoning at the 1967 July GM press day, held at the auto giant's Milford Proving Grounds. It was an occasion when all Chevrolet model lines were present. Corvair, Chevy II, Chevelle, Impala and of course Corvette. Naturally most journalist interest was directed to the Plastic Fantastic, specifically a Le Mans Blue '68 Corvette L68 427 V8 automatic. A 15 minute spin was permitted, then a short ride with Papa Corvette, Duntov himself!

On the glass smooth Milford Proving Grounds, perfect for the Corvette's nature, ex racer Duntov showed off to *Car Life* magazine, handling on rails at 70-90mph through the bends on neutral throttle, with slight understeer. Backing off the gas was greeted by 'safe as Mom's apple pie' understeer. Corvette steering wasn't domestic car feather light, a common US car failing. Non power Corvette steering involved a 20.2:1 steering ratio, with 3.4 turns lock-to-lock. Optional N40 power steering ($94.80), changed those stats to 17.6:1 and 2.92 turns between locks. 12,364 optioned RPO N40.

"All new all over": that was the ad slogan for the '68 Corvette. [63] In light of the C3 Corvette's engineering similarity to the previous Corvette, the claim was an exaggeration. Many Mid-Year Corvette parts were familiar. Front independent SLA suspension was again Chevrolet sedan sourced, but stiffer. Rear suspension was Corvette specific in IRS design, containing Corvette hub carriers, parallel radius arms and the well known transverse multileaf spring. However, the differential, gears,

plus bearings within were all Chevrolet stuff. At least the Corvette's frame was shared with no other model, although one time Chevrolet boss John Z Delorean did consider making the GM F body and Corvette related.

Zora Arkus-Duntov admitted that the new C3 Corvette body didn't bring significant aerodynamic improvement over the previous Mid-Year shape. It had been hoped the new late model C3 Corvette would have a targa type roof, but body flex made retention of T-tops essential. However, in detail, many were the changes brought by the latest Corvette generation. There was, once again, an underlying 'Birdcage' steel framework under Corvette's fiberglass panels, part visible through a rocker panel inspection door. That said, the fiberglass skin was now bonded to the steel framework, rather than to bonding strips that were in turn riveted to the steel framework, as in Mid-Year C2 Corvette days.

The lower hood clearance on the '68 Corvette, versus the Mid-Year cars, saw three different types of forward opening hood. Compared to the flattish hood of 1968-72 small block C3 Corvettes, big block and LT1 editions sported a raised hood. Plus, the big block's intake manifold was sunk into the 427 V8's lifter valley. However, this wasn't the case with L88 427 powered Corvettes, of which 80 and 116 versions were made respectively in 1968 and 1969, with the price of the engine option rising from $947 to $1032 in this timeframe. The high rise intake of Corvette L88 427s, necessitated a macho 'Bubble Hood', for this NASCAR directed motor with aluminum heads.

The C3 Corvette, represented the first time the nameplate offered T-tops, and a removable back window. The latest Corvette bodystyle also had Chevrolet's new star feature, which was Camaro shared 'Astro Ventilation'. That is, swivel eyeball vents at the dashboard's ends, along with two high mount directable center console vents, with stale air exiting through slots on the rear deck behind the car's backlight. Obviating the need for noise provoking vents panes, stale air moved through the luggage cavity, behind the front buckets. Such front seats were no longer adjustable. Mid-Year Corvettes allowed one to use a screwdriver to loosen seat frame mounting bolts, so as to rock the angle of the seat base slightly, and therefore the backrest angle. New January 1 1968 Federal safety guidelines, which were extensive, put the kibosh on such adjustability. Due to the latest Corvette's lower build height, the now fixed seatback angle tilted back from the Mid-Year Corvette's 25 degrees to 33 degrees. More of a long arm Italian driving style!

Shoulder belts were available on the new Corvette, with anchorage points in the wheel arch area. Indeed, the new collapsible steering column and warning buzzer if the key was left in the ignition with the driver's door ajar were both part of Federal safety law. You got a safety dashboard, sans hostile projections. However, the warning light concerning seatbelt usage could be turned off! In any case, the optional telescopic steering wheel/column with 3in range, coded N36 and costing 42 bucks, was still to hand for 6477 '68 Corvette patrons. Behind the Corvette's bucket seats now lay three secret storage compartments. Behind the driver was the car's battery. Moved out of a crowded engine compartment that was now inhabited by a smog pump (AIR – Air Injection Reaction), moving the battery rearwards also improved weight distribution. The middle rear trap door was lockable, and made up for the '68 Corvette's lack of a glovebox. The third hidden compartment, on the passenger side, housed the jack. The C3 Corvette brought the refinement of an electric rear window defogger. The flat rear glass pane was stored under the rear deck panel, above the luggage area. Straps within the luggage area, could hold down suitcases.

In front of the driver lay full instrumentation, but also a lot of warning lights in an interior, that resembled the pending Boeing 747. Aside from small console gauges, there were warning lights for door ajar, and low fuel, plus a console fiber optic warning light system. Long, clear plastic fiber cords,

Car Life tested all the Corvette 427 big blocks in July 1969, including the L88. Only the L71 powered coupe, with four-speed and 4.11 gears, broke the 14 second ¼-mile barrier (13.943 seconds). *(Courtesy Cruisin Classics)*

Car Life's Corvette L71 427 four-speed, carried a 3560lb curb weight, did 0-60mph in seven seconds flat, 119mph at the 6500rpm redline, and 10.4mpg with an associated range of 200 miles. *(Courtesy Cruisin Classics)*

1969 was essentially a carry over model year for Corvette, albeit with several detail changes. *(Courtesy Corvette Mike)*

Now formally called Corvette Stingray, note the '69 MY fender script addition. The color is code 983 Fathom Green. Caution: Those side pipes could get hot! *(Courtesy Corvette Mike)*

transmitted light from the left taillight, license plate illumination and right taillight, to small callouts behind the shifter. There was a beefed up electrical system, but, unlike the Mid-Year cars, the latest Corvette's pop up headlamps were now vacuum activated.

There was more boost for the power brakes option, from an improved tandem brake booster. The C3 Corvette had a metal vacuum tank, which could leak with age. The Corvette's HVAC control panel also operated using vacuum. Any items not functioning implied a vacuum leak, which if left long enough for several items, could lead to engine damage from running lean, like a burnt exhaust valve. As a short run fix, an under dash knob could keep the headlamps up, even if the lights were off. Then there was the C3 Corvette's concealed windshield wiper set up. This aero and visual aid, had two override knobs located under the dashboard. One raised the wiper's concealing beauty panel, with the second stopping the windshield wipers in any position. Also for passive safety, the windshield header panel was smooth for the optional roadster's hardtop. The soft top had no protruding latches.

Compared to the Mid-Year C2 Corvette, the new late model C3 Corvette was bigger on the outside, but smaller on the inside. Vertical height was down from 49.6in to 47.8in, hence the raked buckets. In addition, the latest Corvette was 7in longer, at 182.1in, but 0.4in narrower at 69.2in. Wheelbase stayed at the C2 Corvette's 98in, but front and rear

track were substantially increased. Front track was up from 56.5in to 58.7in, with rear track raised from 57in to 59.4in, all for improved handling. In its lightest form, a 327 V8 powered roadster with three by the knee and no options, implied a 3210lb two-seater. However, an equivalent Mid-Year Corvette was only 3050lb.

The flush fitting door handles opened the door, potentially, to high performance. The factory spectrum ran from 300 horse 327 V8 and automatic, allied to economy 2.78 rear gears, to a ZL1 427 boasting 500 horses and Muncie Rock Crusher four-speed. The Corvette choice was yours. Certainly the three-speed THM 400 slushbox made the latest Corvette more flexible and refined, compared to the Mid-Year machine's two-speed Powerglide. That said, stick shifts still ruled in Corvette land, with only 5063 '68 Corvette buyers paying the $226 surcharge to go shiftless, in spite of the convenience and marginal, if any, performance loss.

For most folks the hi po choices lay with the 350 horse L79 327 V8 small block, costing $105.35 and chosen by 9440 buyers. Then there was the 435bhp triple deuce L71 427 V8 big block. The former unit was an hydraulic lifter job, the latter solid lifter, with L71 427 cost at $437 and optioned by 2898 Corvette fans in '68 MY. Both units had 11.0:1 CR and were four-speed only. The L79 327 had the oversize valves one would find on a Camaro Z28 302, or a hi po Mopar 340 V8 come to that. That is, 2.02in intake valves, and 1.6in exhaust valves. The L79 327 had a 306 degree sports cam concerning opening duration on both intake and exhaust sides, with 4.472in of valve lift on both sides. Valve overlap was 78 degrees.

For '69 MY the L79 327 became the L46 350 V8, with the same 350 horse. Zora Arkus-Duntov liked this powerplant, because you got 50 more horses for a modest outlay, and could still option a/c, due to the hydraulic lifter nature. Duntov was miffed when bean counters axed the option for '71 MY, feeling the four-speed only and no a/c, 370bhp LT1 350 made the L46 350 redundant. And don't forget the LT1 350 was a princely $447, versus a mere $158 for the outgoing L46 350. What's more, or less, the LT1 350 was only chosen by 1287 Corvette buyers in 1970, compared to 4910 Corvette faithful that went the L46 350 route. ZAK's wisdom was clear.

1968 was the first year the 327 V8 mill met the Rochester Quadrajet. As for the 435 horse 427s, vacuum operation brought the outer two carbs into play, during pedal to the metal action. At 3000-3500rpm a wide open throttle produced enough air velocity through the center carb, to make diaphragms on the outer carbs open. However, not as reliably as a mechanical linkage. The L71/L89 427s had a lumpy, noisy 700-800rpm idle. The 435bhp 427s had 2.190in intake valves, and 1.720in exhaust valves. The camshaft profile had 316 degrees duration on the intake side, 302 degrees on the exhaust side, with 0.5197in of valve lift on both sides, allied to 80 degrees of valve overlap. Due to pending smog law, the enthusiast wouldn't see this kind of street moxie from a regular Corvette powerplant until the late '90s LS V8 era. And even then, not the L71 427's brand of torque. That sucker could really nail your tail in the seat!

As part of engineering changes from C2 to C3 Corvettes, the battery had been relocated to the car's interior, and the by now crossflow radiator's overflow tank was repositioned. The integral header tank was now on the right side of the engine bay. In Mid-Year times it was separate and placed further back in the engine compartment. From 1965, the Delco-Moraine four-wheel disk

The third gen Corvette was criticized for not being as roomy as the Mid-Year cars. So, Zora Arkus-Duntov signed off on new door cards for the '69 edition, to liberate more elbow room.
(Courtesy Corvette Mike)

braking system of the Corvette, had 11.75 x 1.25in vented rotors, with a huge swept area of 461in². It also involved a caliper design where power brakes weren't essential, as they were in most cars with disk brakes and this much girth, lacking the natural assistance of drums.

The '68 Corvette's new U79 AM-FM stereo radio option, retailing for 278 bucks, was selected by 3311 Corvette patrons. It was also the first and last year for the $57 P01 bright metal wheel covers, which were chosen by 8971 Corvette faithful in 1968. The latest Corvette was a harsher riding beast, compared to Mid-Year times. However, Zora Arkus-Duntov felt the extra active safety and control was worth it. For the most part, what ZAK wanted for the Corvette, he got!

Press reaction

WITH THE EXCEPTION of *Car and Driver*'s "too dire to drive" statement concerning quality control, and some import leaning, puritanical sentiment from *Road & Track*, most critics thought the latest incarnation of the Plastic Fantastic was real neat! [64] Quality control snafus aside, even *C/D* enjoyed the new Corvette design, feeling that as a sports car, it was a big car for a big country, and that there was nothing wrong in that, especially concerning expansive grand touring. Just like those T-series MGs of yore being perfect for English narrow

The optional Corvette tiller could tilt and telescope (RPO N37 $84). However, like other domestics, the steering wheel was still too close to the chest for many. *(Courtesy Corvette Mike)*

question! Concerning appearance, *Car Life* said in November 1967 that the new Corvette was endowed with smooth ferocity. Plus, this kamm-tailed, flying buttress wonder, went as well as it looked. So, *Car Life* was correct in titling Chevrolet's latest spiritual flagship 'The Excitement Generator'.

Any qualms concerning quality or space efficiency quickly took a back seat to the Corvette 427's awesome punch! In June 1968, *Car Life* sampled a 435 horse Corvette L71 427 four-speed roadster in code 992 Corvette Bronze, sans a/c, on GM's Milford Proving Grounds, Orange County International Raceway, plus the drag strip. Its conclusion? "… it takes a lot of car to catch this bear." Which was to say this mother could move! Braving the roadster's terrible scuttle shake, that even saw the concealed windshield wiper panel vibrate on rough surfaces, a 3.55 rear end witnessed 0-60mph in 6.5 seconds, 0-100mph in 12.6 seconds, a 13.41 second ¼-mile at 109.5mph, 9-13mpg and 142mph top speed. Barely enough time to drop in, and check the condition of your condition. Hence the statement, "… who needs LSD with something like this to get high on?" No doubt like Jim Morrison and The Doors, if the Corvette could sing, it would have been banned from The Ed Sullivan Show!

In the 'Lucy in the sky with diamonds' era, *Road & Track* was less complimentary concerning the new Plastic Fantastic. In its January 1968 issue, "If there's such a thing as a psychedelic car, the 1968 Corvette is it." That is, in the days of traffic congestion, Chevrolet styling took one on a trip, without even going anywhere. "Far Out!" as Jungle Jim Liberman was wont to say in Funny Car commercials. Fittingly, Jungle Jim was a Corvette fancier, and the drag racing legend was indeed driving his beloved Corvette when he first came upon iconic back-up girl Jungle Pam Hardy.

Road & Track considered the 1968 Corvette to be a funny car, but not in the drag racing sense, more in the gadget, gimmick, gimme a break GM! In this 'ghost of Motoramas past' mobile, *R&T*

Full instrumentation, not idiot lights was a Corvette guarantee. The U69 AM-FM radio was a $172 option, chosen by 33,871 1969 Corvette faithful. *(Courtesy Corvette Mike)*

country lanes, the '68 Corvette fitted its environs like American racer John Fitch's string back driving gloves!

Many journals picked up on the rear profile styling similarity to the '64 Ferrari GTO Berlinetta, not to mention the '67 Camaro's Coke bottle lines, and the Olds Toronado's hidden headlamps. As a dream machine, the latest Corvette was a gee whiz styling tour de force. It outdid the Pantera, a couple of years before that bit of Lincoln-Mercury showroom eye candy even existed. Who needed a mid-engine machine to make a statement? The C3 Corvette's question mark roofline posed the

Wide ratio (M20) or close ratio (M21), optional four-on-da-floor still cost 184 bucks. Three-by-the-knee was still standard, and not popular.
(Courtesy Corvette Mike)

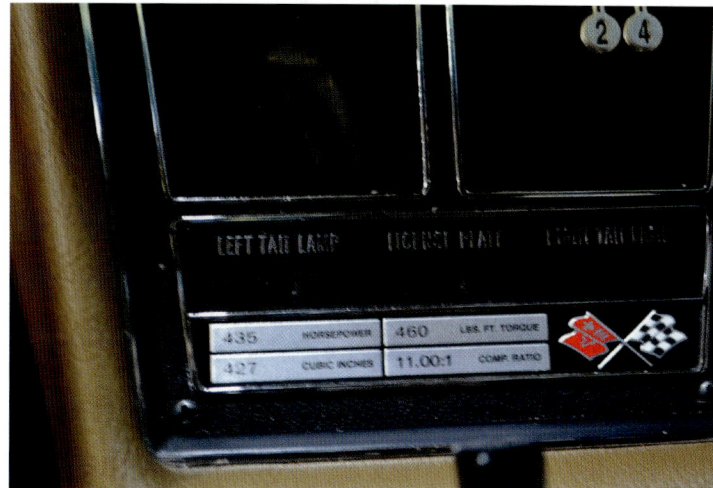

Between 1968 and 1971, Corvette had interior telltales for taillights and license plate illumination, thanks to fiber optics. The Late Model C3 Corvette also started the engine spec callout panel.
(Courtesy Corvette Mike)

wasn't so enamored with the behind the buckets secret compartments, or concealed windshield wipers. The journal, and many others, preferred the much less pretentious Mid-Year Corvette. At the press preview, *Road & Track*'s Ron Wakefield conceded that the '67 Corvette 427 on hand at GM's Milford Proving Grounds behaved like a slippery eel compared to the gripper '68 Corvette L68 427 automatic test car. That said, Wakefield still felt his formerly owned 1964 Corvette stuck much better than either machines.

Britain's *Motor* magazine carried a report on a Belgian tested '68 Corvette L68 427 V8 four-speed, sans power steering, in its August 24 1968 issue. It had this to say, "… one of the most striking performers on the road – you should see the crowds when it stops – the latest in the long line of Corvettes is the best yet." This journal found the newest Corvette to be more refined than the Mid-Year machines of old. Brute power combined with elegance, with said power tamed. Ride comfort was harsher versus European sports cars, but smooth road cornering power proved prodigious. Plus, the test coupe was well equipped with novel features. The fiber optic light monitoring system was appreciated, but the need to make frequent steering corrections, due to the stiff ride on European roads, wasn't liked.

With 1.50in primaries and 1.75in secondaries, 400bhp at 5400rpm and 460lb/ft at 3600rpm, black

streaks were left on Belgian blacktop, with *Motor*'s scribe titling the snapshot of scoot, '*Motor* was here'. The figures were 0-60mph in 6.1 seconds, 14.2 second ¼-mile and 145.7mph top speed, along with 11.8mpg (UK gallon), from a 3.08 diff ratio. Compared to recently tested European rivals, which didn't have a smog pump, the Jag XKE and Aston Martin DB6 edged out the Corvette on top speed. The AC 289 was slightly quicker in acceleration.

The Corvette was the thirstiest, the Porsche 911 the most frugal, and the Mercedes 280SL the slowest. The Jag was second most economical, and only slightly slower in acceleration. However, for all the comparisons, there was no comparison. That was the conclusion of *Autosport*'s David Phipps, in the November 15 1968 issue. He had tried the very same International Blue 1968 Corvette, license plate 3RS02, that UK's *Motor* magazine had sampled, got wheelspin in top gear, tried the coupe on the Spa Francorchamps circuit, and said, "… there is nothing – not even an E-type – which can match the effortless top gear acceleration of a 7-liter Corvette." And added, "My Mini felt awfully sluggish when I got back to London Airport." Phipps judged the Corvette as handsome, but with limited shoulder room in this '68 edition.

For 1969, the Corvette's former base 327 V8 was upsized to 350 cubes, with an eye to tightening smog law. However, this motor is the triple deuce L71 427 big block. *(Courtesy Corvette Mike)*

Unlike the L36 and L68 hydraulic lifter 427s, the L71 427 V8 shown was a solid lifter unit. That implied no RPO C60 factory A/C! *(Courtesy Corvette Mike)*

3RS02 was obtained from GM Continental in Antwerp, Belgium (a central distribution point for US cars sold in Europe). The L68 427 powered Corvette wasn't the fastest of the breed, but slower forms existed. In *Car Life*'s June 1968 'Corvette Duet Chamber Music and Hard Rock' report, the hot Corvette L71 427 roadster was the latter, and a soft Le Mans Blue base 300 horse, automatic coupe with a/c provided the chamber music. The soft coupe rolled some, but was civilized to a fault, with the coupe's body bracing providing more refinement than the ragtop. This coupe was the big distance grand tourer for all surfaces, plus it was fast enough. As fast in fact, Chevrolet Engineering provided ringers excepted, as any factory Corvette made between 1975 and 1979. The stats were: 0-60mph in 8.6 seconds, 0-100mph in 21.3 seconds, 15.82 second ¼-mile at 89.4mph, 128mph top speed and 13-17mpg (US gallons), from a sensible 3.08 final drive ratio. Weight distribution was 50/50, and with a 20 gallon tank, a decent range was on hand.

Whichever Corvette was selected, *Motor Trend*'s Steve Kelly offered this assessment of the '68 Corvette in March 1968, "... one of the world's all-out 'class' vehicles ... " [65] The price was right: $4420 for the roadster, $4663 bought the coupe. Indeed, it would be the last year that the roadster outsold the coupe, 18,630 against 9936 units for the Corvette's '68 MY 28,566 total. The name was Corvette, Chevrolet Corvette, but Sting Ray would return for 1969. A chrome script above the fender

gills, spelt just like Bill Mitchell's Straight Axle Corvette proto racer of yore, that is, 'Stingray'.

The C3 Corvette was a hot car, in more ways than one, especially in big block form. *Road Test* magazine said the Corvette L68 400 automatic at the press preview was a hot place to be, even in mild weather. Journalists all wanted a/c, and *Road Test* blamed the new Corvette's smog pump for higher underhood temps, interior heat soak and toasty fiberglass floorboards. Opinions on the effectiveness of GM's Astro Ventilation, at least on the new Corvette, were mixed. *Road & Track* considered factory a/c, as with other makes and models, to be detrimental to the Corvette's flow-through ventilation. The large-engine Corvettes seemed in good company, because engine related heat soak also gave the a/c system a hard time in the contemporary Ferrari Daytona.

Beyond the interior, big block Corvettes also had a tendency to overheat engine wise. In 1977, *Hot Rod* magazine did a retrospective on the C3 late model Corvette, based on the recollections of an anonymous Chevrolet PR consultant. Said consultant noted a brand new Safari Yellow Corvette L71 427 that overheated within the first 20 miles from a Hollywood Chevrolet dealership. In '68 MY only 5664 and 5063 respective Corvette patrons chose a/c and automatic transmission. So it seemed for now, Corvette buyers were hard livin' four-speed folk, but that would change. The mystery consultant said Zora Arkus-Duntov provided advice on how to deal with overheating big blocks. However, not before *Car and Driver*'s negative experience with a new '68 Corvette 427, involving water leaks, poor starting and overheating. The journal referred to the test's poor quality example, and Mr Consultant was involved in procuring a second test subject for *C/D*. This Corvette L68 427 400 horse coupe saw *Car and Driver* proclaim it "… a brilliant car." Quality control did prove to be a stumbling block with the latest Corvette generation.

Road & Track's March 1970 Corvette Stingray owner survey affirmed anecdotal tales, that the C3 Corvette was giving owners more workmanship related problems than earlier Mid-Year Corvettes. In fact, over twice as many C3 Corvette owners complained, versus earlier Corvettes. In February 1968 *Road Test* said of the latest car's sloppy workmanship, "We just wish they would make 'em a little better." *Car Life* noted high price and lack of luggage provisions compared to European GTs, but the low quality problem irked testers and owners the most. As *Motor Trend*'s Steve Kelly said in March 1968 concerning rough panels and ill fitting sections, "… Corvette assembly line workers are taking time getting used to putting the new model together." [66]

There was a theory that the Corvette's quality control had been put on regular Chevrolet standards for 1968. Then again, Chevrolet had a solid reputation on quality and new model assembly teething problems, while ever rising Corvette popularity and the labor-intensive nature of Corvette assembly at St Louis seemed more likely problem sources. With over 60% of Corvette sales being accounted for by small block versions by the end of 1969, the big block overheating problem didn't affect that many owners, relatively. [67] However, as mentioned in *Consumer Reports (CU)* June 1969 issue's 5 Specialty Cars article, quality control in the American auto industry remained below par. [68]

From the mid '60s, rising production volumes of popular models, cost squeezes by the Big Three on component suppliers, and an increasingly combative UAW (United Auto Workers), all saw to it that the dream car penned on drawing boards and engineered for success diverged from the defect-prone, recall-ridden jalopy foisted onto dealerships

and consumers. In *CU*'s June '69 group test, the Ford Mustang was quality champ with only 18 delivered defects. Maladies such as an engine out of tune, front wheel bearings that were too loose, rumbling heater fan bearings, and unbalanced car wheels that shook Henry's coupe at highway speeds, were all included by FoMoCo at no extra cost!

Although the '68 Corvette seemed caught up, in this general auto industry quality control funk, its problems were different to those commonly

The '69 Corvette is generally more desired than the '68, due to the avoidance of several one-year-only items, and much improved general vehicle quality when new. *(Courtesy Corvette Mike)*

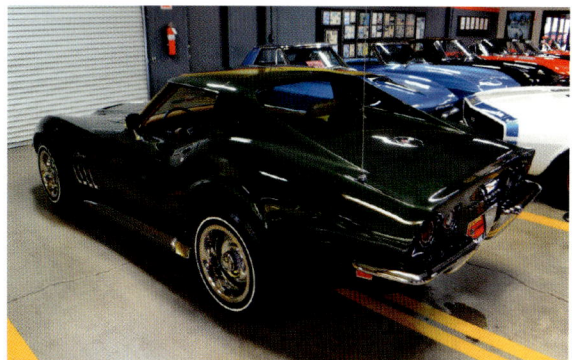

1969 saw over 60% of Corvettes sold with small block 350 V8s. Bodies had a reputation for checking on convex surfaces. *(Courtesy Corvette Mike)*

found in Detroit. As confirmed by *Road & Track*'s Corvette owner survey, the Plastic Fantastic was still a durable, reliable performer, especially in small block form. Its bugaboos majored on poor fit and finish, when other sporty domestics fell down on mechanical woes. *Consumer Reports'* May 1970 Specialty Cars report, which included a Plymouth 'Cuda 340 with: a defective head gasket, where an open air passage sucked in a lot of oil into number eight cylinder; part of the exhaust system collapsed, due to the manufacturing defect of a pipe's joint/broken exhaust support; and sparkplug wires that weren't clipped to said sparkplugs on the left bank. [69] In short, the Corvette's problems were annoying, but other sporty domestics could leave you stranded!

Walk in, America.

GM
MARK OF EXCELLENCE

Why stoop to a wagon you can't walk into.
There are wagons, and there are Chevrolet Walk-in Wagons
with a rear boarding step just the right height. And a roof line slightly on the slant
so you can walk in standing tall.
See if you don't also prefer our enormous third-seat sitting room in back;
our two hundred fifty V8 horsepower up front; and flow-thru Astro Ventilation throughout.
You'll take comfort in a walk-in wagon.
Putting you first, keeps us first.

CHEVROLET

Family cars were Chevrolet's core business. This partly explained why the Late Model C3 Corvette lasted through 1982 model year!
(Courtesy GM Archives)

Did the Corvette have domestic rivals? From *CU*'s 1969 and 1970 specialty car reports, it didn't seem so. In fact, such reports highlighted the Corvette as a distinct breed of domestic sporty car, and that the usual home grown sporty car was oftentimes poor value. Whereas the stock Corvette had fiber optic warning lights, flow-through ventilation, four-wheel disk brakes, forward opening safety hood and IRS, the much vaunted Shelby Mustang, let alone the regular Mustang, had none of these features, not even as options! The domestic specialty car formula ran to a fancily styled hardtop, of family sedan basis, sporting a live axle, with drum brakes all around in standard form.

It has been said Americans don't like buying two-seater cars. AMC's explanation on why it canned its AMX two-seater in 1970 was that showroom visitors requested four seats; hence the 1971 Javelin AMX 2+2. That said, *Consumer Reports* exploded the practicality specialty car myth that Detroit's 2+2s allegedly enjoyed over the Corvette by saying, "... you should consider the specialty car as basically a two-seater." [70] That is, no room at the Mustang Inn!

Then there was the issue of handling. A sporty car should handle: in *Road & Track*'s March 1969 Volvo owners survey, the journal remarked that import buyers expected their purchase to handle. It's commonly said that Corvette is America's only sports car, but, not always mentioned directly, is that Corvette is America's best handling car. The two best handling cars that *Consumer Reports* tested in the '60s were a Mid-Year '66 Corvette 327 with Powerglide, and a subsequent Mercedes Compact sedan. *CU* judged they behaved like a car should. However, that wasn't its experience with the sacred cow specialty cars. The '69½ AMX, '70 'Cuda 340 and '70 Boss Mustang were all demon handlers on smooth roads, but got real squirrely when the going got rough. In the latter scenario *CU* felt the '69 Camaro handled like a bouncing brick!

The Corvette was also at its best on smooth surfaces, but its IRS provided a little more compliance. Plus, its suspension geometry permitted high cornering speeds, outside the skid pad lateral g test. A sporty domestic car needs a four-speed. Here, too, Corvette shone, with a light, precise shifter and easy clutch. *CU*'s Boss Mustang showed what sporty car buyers usually received.

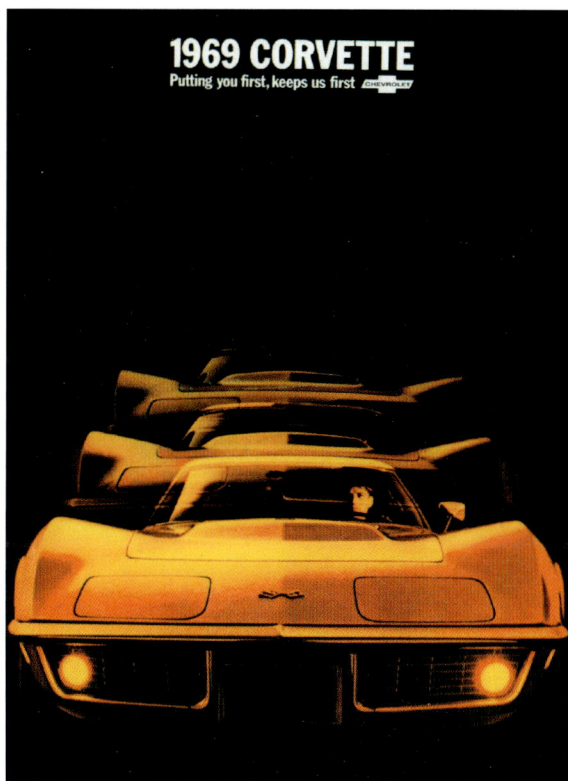

A young GM marketing man confided to *Car and Driver* in 1969 concerning Corvette, "It's a great machine. But it's not a terribly useful device." More akin to a dune buggy than GT/sports car, and hardly practical versus an ordinary car. However, such are the things dreams are made of!
(Courtesy GM Archives)

The fabled 430 horse L88 427 returned to the Corvette option sheet for 1968, but this time with a smog pump!
(Courtesy GM Archives)

The Mustang's Hurst shift linkage equipped four-speed had a rugged, but vague and clumsy action. What's more, *Consumer Reports*' '70 Dodge Challenger SE's leather buckets were hard to tell from vinyl, and hardly had any leather scent.

You paid a premium for a specialty car over its plainer relation. *Consumer Reports* listed the '69½ AMX at $3807, with the '70 Plymouth 'Cuda 340 on $3753 and '70 Boss Mustang costing $3952. The base '70½ Corvette 350 four-speed ragtop was $4849. In *CU*'s opinion, the best specialty cars were the GM machines: '69 Pontiac Grand Prix ($4287) and '70 Chevrolet Monte Carlo ($3950). Both were smaller, lighter and cheaper takes on the personal luxury car, the G/P being an ersatz Eldorado, with

the Monte Carlo as better value for money than a T-Bird. Both GM intermediates were good driving and handling cars. *CU*'s Monte Carlo had almost faultless brakes, and an ability to cope with rough roads. The journal liked the G/P and Monte Carlo saying, "You could do considerably worse and still spend a lot more money." [71]

Outside the environs of the specialty press, and the manufacturer-supplied test cars, *Consumer Reports* found the Pontiac G/P, 'Cuda 340 and Boss 302 all did 16 seconds flat in the ¼-mile, with respective trap speeds of 87mph, 92mph and 93mph. The AMX 390 four-speed, managed a 15.5 second pass at 90mph. A base Corvette with a/c, like the G/P, would split the difference between the first three and AMC. *CU* found G/P 428 gas mileage to be in the 8-15mpg range, the Corvette was in the 13-17mpg ballpark, judging by *Car Life*'s '68 Corvette 327 automatic with a/c.

A really telling stat was that the Chevrolet Monte Carlo sold 2,066,205 copies from 1970 to 1977 with, according to historian Richard Langworth, the longest hood ever bolted to a Chevrolet. In contrast the 250,000th Corvette sold since 1953 was a Riverside Gold Corvette 350 V8 convertible, handed over to George Allen Dyer in Los Angeles. The buyer, hailing from Montebella, California, received his ragtop on November 7 1969 from dealership Harry Mann Chevrolet. The keys were handed over by Peter Mann. Yes, the Corvette never sold in

This is a 1969 Corvette L88 M22 four-speed (Rock Crusher), in Tuxedo Black with 2050 miles!
(Courtesy Legendary Motorcar Company)

L88 427 powered Corvettes were available for three years. 20 were sold in 1967, 80 in 1968 and 116 in 1969. The power dome hood hinted at the $1032 option's presence.
(Courtesy Legendary Motorcar Company)

personal, luxury car numbers, but it wasn't that kind of car. There are specialty cars, and specialist cars. The Corvette belongs to the latter category.

The Plastic Fantastic's true 1968 rivals were two old stagers, contemporaries of the Mid-Year Corvette in fact. Both were tested in red hued four-speed form, by the *Car and Track* TV show, hosted by the inimitable Bud Lindemann. The cars in question were the Studebaker Avanti II and Jaguar XKE. The revived Avanti II was supplied by former Studebaker dealers Nate and Arnold Altman, and Leo Newman. *Car and Track* judged the Avanti II to be superior to the original Avanti. By now the 2+2 came with a Corvette 327 V8, topped by a Paxton blower. Said Chevrolet Mouse Motor dropped 100lb off the front wheels, versus the original Studebaker 289 V8!

Like Corvette 427s, the Avanti II was a bottom breather that overheated in sustained track work. The coupe wore 7.75-15s, like the C2 Corvette, with 0-65mph coming in 6.8 seconds, 50mph achieved through the slalom, and 65mph to zero in 128ft, on average. The Avanti II handled beautifully on track: neutral most of the time, with tail out action when requested by the loud pedal. One man built up the chassis on a seven-day assembly line. Only three Avanti IIs were completed each week, in a bespoke operation. Bud Lindemann said pride of workmanship, including perfect fiberglass panel fit, was a real rarity in 1968 Detroit.

Quality was also the watchword of the Jag XKE, which *Car and Track* tested in 1968. However, it was a pre-emissions/safety '67 MY example, with the real 265bhp 4.2L triple carb DOHC I6. Bud Lindemann declared the XKE a fine touring car,

This '69 Corvette L88 four-speed was originally sold by Wigder Chevrolet of Livingston, New Jersey. The original purchaser left the car at the dealership for a very long time, prior to pick up. It was then trailered home, to be stored as an appreciating asset. *(Courtesy Legendary Motorcar Company)*

with a true racing personality. When you climbed in, Lindemann said you felt you were suddenly surrounded by a Swiss watch, with Jaguar precision and perfection, in an under-promoted car by American standards. Obviously hailing from the era before British Leyland scratched the Big Cat, *C&T* considered this XKE to represent the peak in Browns Lane's history.

Like Corvette and Avanti II, the Jag came with a forward opening hood, but a straight six not a V8, and, according to Bud Lindemann: the wallop of a Missouri mule allied to snob appeal that far exceeded the coupe's price tag. Zero to sixty in 6.2 seconds, a *C&T* record 55mph through the pylon course with hardly any body roll, and 70mph to zero in 169ft. *Motor Trend* discovered its L79 327 and L71 427 Corvettes dropped anchor from 60mph, in a respective 117 and 119ft. Both Corvette and XKE, but not Avanti II, had four-wheel disk brakes. The Jaguar displayed excellent track handling, neutral steering and the ride of a limo. The XKE was summed up by Lindemann as truly a different breed of cat. That said, although the Jag was more readily available than the Avanti II, it was nowhere near as ubiquitous as the Corvette. In any case, when a specialist is required, a warmed over Mustang ain't no substitute!

1969-70

ZORA ARKUS-DUNTOV CONTINUED to wage his battle to create the world's finest sports car, in the face of GM's styling department. The latter had its own ideas according to *Car and Driver*: "... Flash Gordon Thunderbird for the Hugh Hefner school of mass-cult glamor." [72] The forward visibility of an early C3 Corvette styling department proposal was so poor that it contributed to a one year delay in the release of the new Mako Shark II inspired late model Corvette. [73] However, the new C3 Corvette was eventually released, and impressed 1968 Frankfurt Auto Show visitors more so than other GM offerings. With an almost all new Corvette afoot, it might have been expected that 1969 would be merely a carryover year, but not so. The changes were legion, and the model even got a new suffix: Stingray.

Some '69 MY Corvette changes could be seen, but some couldn't. Yes, the 'Stingray' chrome script over the front fender gills, and for 21 bucks the RPO TJ2 front fender louver trim, for said side gills. 11,962 of the 38,762 '69 Corvette buyers ticked TJ2. Then there was the one-year-only RPO N14 side mount exhaust system, costing $147 and selected by 4355 Corvette patrons. N14 replaced the N11

The steep angle at which the M22 Heavy Duty four-speed's gears were cut produced a distinct whining, grinding sound. Hence the M22's nickname of 'Rock Crusher'!
(Courtesy Legendary Motorcar Company)

off-road exhaust system, a former option from 1963. The side pipes had a perforated heat shield, precipitated by the fact Zora Arkus-Duntov's wife burnt her leg sans shield while alighting from the Corvette! More practically, a rear deck luggage rack was a new option. Cast one's eyes lower, and the '69 Corvette revealed a combined backup/taillight, within inboard lamps. 1968's RPO N36 adjustable steering column would telescope, but not tilt. However, the new $84 N37 tilt-telescopic steering column was chosen by 10,325 buyers in 1969. In the Corvette's myriad option selection, this was the final outing for the U15 speed warning indicator, costing 11 bucks and selected by just 3561 '69 Corvette faithful.

Staying outside the '69 Corvette, press in bar release handles originally intended for '68 MY, replaced the earlier conventional door grip and button. The single piece lever now afforded entry to the 1969 Corvette. The Corvette has long been a barometer of auto fashion, and tire choices for 1969 proved no exception. The size, as mandatorily recommended by the owner's manual, was F70-15. However, RPO PT6 implied red stripe tires, PT7 brought white stripe tires and PU9 supplied white letter tires. Respective prices and numbers chosen for the three possibilities were: $31/5210, $31/21,379 and $33/2398. Red stripe rubber used to be the choice of real gone Daddies, but now it was white stripe's turn, and raised white letter (RWL) would dominate, but not just yet. PU9 was new for 1969.

From 1968 to 1969 optional PO1 bright metal wheel covers were replaced by $57 PO2 deluxe wheel covers, and were selected by 8073 '69 Corvette buyers. PO2 resembled the wheelware of Boudicca's chariot! Zora Arkus-Duntov suggested that Corvette buyers stay with the standard rally rims, offering a cost and weight saving. The latter reduced unsprung weight, which improved handling. Further 1969 refinements ran to headlamp washer jets, along with washer jets placed on the windshield wipers. Stepping into 1969 provided a real sense of inner space: one inch more shoulder room to be precise. A tight interior versus the C2 Corvette saw Zora Arkus-Duntov feel the $120,000 retooling cost concerning Corvette's doors to be worth it.

There was also more room for driver thighs, thanks to a steering wheel one inch smaller in diameter, now at 15 inches. The greater popularity of power steering on Corvettes (N40 $105 option for 22,866 buyers) made the leverage of a larger tiller less necessary. Interior niceties encompassed a passenger side double map pocket. There was no glovebox in 1968, so this was an upgrade. The A82 headrests, chosen by only 3197 '68 Corvette faithful, became a mandatory '69 MY delete option ($17.95), although present on each and every 1969 Corvette. The move headed off a January 1 1969 Federal passive safety requirement. In fact, such mandates saw the Corvette's ignition switch move from the dashboard to the steering column, for 1969.

New Corvettes also came with transmission and steering column locks. If you left your keys in the ignition and opened the door, a buzzer was the greeting. Chimes would come later! A behind-the-seats riser panel protected occupants from flying luggage, and there was inertia reel operation for the shoulder part of the two piece seatbelts. This last item was only a requirement for Corvette coupes.

Structurally your C3 Corvette's windshield came with a steel surround. There was also steel reinforcement for rocker panels, door hinge pillars,

The L88 427 option technically wasn't street legal, but in practice followed its RPO (Regular Production Order) nature. However, follow the console 103 RON (Research Octane Number) gas grade warning label, or engine detonation could occur.
(Courtesy Legendary Motorcar Company)

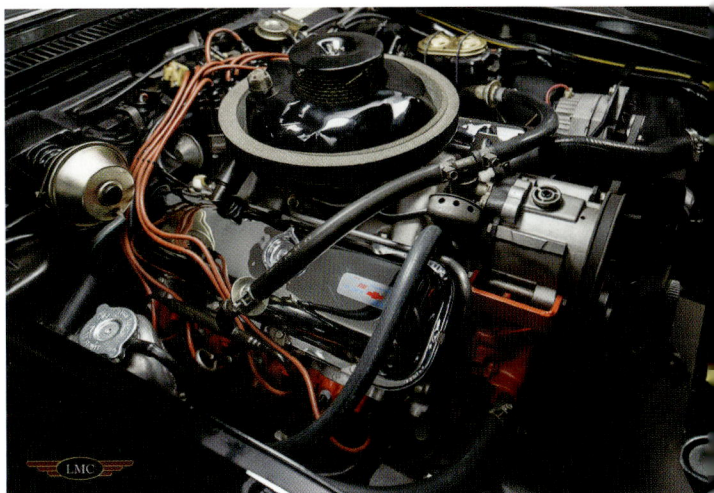

As L88 427 prerequisites, a dealer started with a Corvette possessing: F41 special front and rear suspension, G81 Positraction lsd, and J56 special heavy duty brakes.
(Courtesy Legendary Motorcar Company)

and a lateral steel crossmember tied up the front A pillars. Corvette coupes also had supporting members enclosing the passenger compartment. This was the so-called 'Birdcage' concealed by Corvette's fiberglass panels – panels that were very dent resistant, and warded off salt and corrosive compounds, but did fracture and tear on impact, and had a reputation for checking on convex surfaces. Corvette bodies were somewhat expensive to repair. This led to shortcuts, instead of grounding down surfaces, laying on fresh fiberglass, setting and sanding prior to paint preparation. In any case, the Corvette's frame was stiffened for 1969, which was a good thing in light of new and revised engine options.

The Corvette's base 327 V8 was up-gunned to 350 cubes. Power outputs for the standard and optional small blocks remained at respective 300 and 350bhp ratings. However, the two 350s were now called ZQ3 and L46, rather than the former respective 327 RPO titles of L75 and L79. Acceleration and top speed recorded in journals didn't change much, but the torque benefit was obvious in real world driving. *Car Life* published figures for a four-speed Corvette L46 350 sporting 4.11 gears in July 1969: 0-60mph 6.4 seconds, 0-100mph 16 seconds flat, a 14.55 second pass at 97.93mph. The ZQ3 and L46 350s came with

the same 4bbl carb (1.38 in primaries/2.25 in secondaries, but the latter motor had freer flowing heads, although both were hydraulic lifter jobs. At $131, the L46 350 was the '69 Corvette's most popular optional engine, with 12,846 buyers choosing it. However, just two buyers went for the new, and one year only, ZL1 427. This mill was a monster $4718, or just under a brand new '69 Corvette coupe!!

For 1969, the Corvette went to one inch wider 15 x 8 in rims. This size would hold through to 1982. Combined with 'Corvette Tires', this made for an increasingly harsh ride, but one that Zora Arkus-Duntov felt necessary. For safety in running the Corvette between 80 and 120mph control mattered to Duntov. Weighing up the cost of possible sidewall flex of radials, ol' ZAK stuck with nylon cord construction F70-15s, sourced from several companies. When questioned concerning the use of bias belted rubber in 1969, Duntov responded, "We tried them. You'll notice we're not using them." On a Corvette, suspension matched wheel well clearance, a tach's redline varied with the engine selected. Nothing was by accident, Duntov planned it that way, so you could use that heavy hitter, solid lifter 427 with impunity!

Beyond L88, there was the all aluminum ZL1 427 V8 option. It was an 'off the menu' COPO (Central Office Production Order) $4718 job, fitted to only two 1969 Corvettes! *(Courtesy Legendary Motorcar Company)*

More than any other 427, the ZL1 427 was an iconic engine option, with a racing genesis. An all aluminum motor, the ZL1 weighed 100lb under a L88 427, and was developed with dry sump lubrication by McLaren, for SCCA Can Am purposes. Its output was reputed to be in the 560 to 585bhp range, and centrifugally cast iron sleeves helped its cause. New Zealanders Bruce McLaren and Denny Hulme enjoyed major success in Can Am racing, using the Chevrolet small block V8 in 1967. That same year, Hulme became F1 champ with Brabham. The McLaren team wanted an all aluminum big block V8 for '68 racing season, with Chevrolet Performance Products chief Vince Piggins lobbying to get said motor for 'em. Piggins used McLaren's ultimatum of "No big block and we go to Ford" to make the ZL1 427 a reality. Indeed, the new motor helped McLaren dominate Can Am racing during 1968-71, winning 32 out of 37 races!

Only two '69 Corvette ZL1 427s were produced, and what price for such rarity today? Try $3,140,000!! Yes, that was RM Sotheby's garnered price, achieved by a '69 Monaco Orange Corvette ZL1 roadster in late January 2023 at the Scottsdale Auctions. Even so, the ZL1 427 never achieved a major presence in drag racing, where concern over its aluminum block's thermal properties, produced a preference for the L88 427. In fact, the L88 427 benefitted from the ZL1 427's development, in terms of post 1968 improvements. In 1968 the

L88 427 already had a conrod and bolt ground shrank to spread stretch, with parts shot peened and magnafluxed for strength, and the L88 motor already had durability improvements over its debut '67 MY version.

For 1969 there were beefier connecting rods, and a 7/16 in conrod bolt. Pistons were upgraded, heads redesigned with revised combustion chamber cavity, featuring a stronger oval skirt. Plus, matching the ZL1 427, the '69 L88 427 came with rounder, bigger exhaust ports, as part of the head redesign. One of the 116 '69 Corvette L88 427s was tested by *Hot Rod* magazine in April 1969, and it was an automatic. Yes, solid lifter Corvette 427s could have a slushbox in '69 MY. However, the surcharge and nature of RPO M40 varied compared to other Corvettes.

Normally the '69 Corvette's slushbox was a $221.80 option, but on solid lifter Corvette 427s, the automatic's cost was $290.40. Then too, this special automatic had its valve body, the unit's vacuum-operated brain, adjusted so that shift points occurred later. High friction clutches were built in as well. *Hot Rod*'s '69 Corvette L88 427 was one of the 17 Corvette L88s that year, specified with a slushbox. It also came with 3.36 gears. You could have a 4.56 final drive ratio on request, and *Hot Rod* recommended at least a 4.11 axle, to stop bogging off the line. This sports automatic was set up to shift at 6500rpm.

In *Hot Rod*'s experience, the $1032.15 RPO L88 427 V8 allowed its coupe to fly to a 13.56 second pass at 111.10mph. Average gas mileage was 8.3mpg, using the mandatory premium RON 103 octane leaded fuel that was available in those days. Corvette L88 427s implied: J56 special heavy duty brakes ($384 oversize calipers, riveted linings/ metallic friction surface, anti lock up front/rear valve), F41 special front and rear suspension ($36), K66 transistor ignition system ($81), G81 Positraction lsd ($46). However, Corvette L88 427 meant no power steering, radio, heater or fast glass!

There was no a/c with L88 427, nor a radiator fan shroud that would interfere with air flow to the radiator, during high speed driving. How high a speed? Zora Arkus-Duntov brought a Corvette L88 427 racer to a rented Phoenix track ... and did almost 200mph! A factory order 2.73 axle was

Hot Rod's April '69 issue saw a 1969 Corvette coupe L88 427 automatic, with 3.36 diff ratio, produce a 13.56 second ¼-mile at 111.10mph out of the box. With tuning, quicker was easily possible.
(Courtesy Legendary Motorcar Company)

okay, or special order 2.54 rear gears for super fast running. All L88 427s came with an aluminum intake, 12.0:1 CR and cold air induction prepared air cleaner, in conjunction with an 850 CFM 4150 Holley 4bbl carb, plus ZL2 'bubble hood', a hand selected cam, pistons and conrods, 364 degree duration intake and 357 degrees on the BIG cam's exhaust side, with respective 62-115 degrees intake, 110-74 degrees exhaust for cam timing, with 0.539in lift on intake side/0.560in lift on the exhaust side. The motor was underrated at 430 horse, to keep the Naderites and All State Insurance man down on the farm.

The L88 427 was a serious race motor, tunable to over 600 wild horses. Zora Arkus-Duntov set the motor's prerequisites to keep it out of the hands of the daily driver crowd. After all, a Corvette L88 427 would overheat and oil up its plugs in town. That said, oftentimes the Chevrolet dealership salesmen didn't do the right thing. They let buyers option the works, even if it was against their automotive needs. The sad result was an owner unhappy with their Corvette. *Car Life* provided a case in point: a rental fleet in St Louis, with several Corvette L88s that did overheat! ZAK said Corvette L88 427s were for sport, not bragging. The motor worked well with tuned headers and minimal exhaust muffler

This '69 Corvette coupe L88 427 four-speed has the 16 buck RPO A01 soft ray tinted glass, chosen by 31,270 of the 38,762 1969 Corvette buyers. Sadly, it was the end of the emissions line for the L88 and ZL1 427 V8s.
(Courtesy Legendary Motorcar Company)

restriction. What's more, there was no exterior L88 badge!

Speaking of rare specs, only 230 '69 Corvettes came with 'three by the knee', and 20 with a 4.56 axle. Sometimes dealer sales staff were ordered

David Williams is only 17 but he'd be a good man to have on your side, even if he doesn't know it yet himself.

He graduated from South Mecklenburg High School in Charlotte, North Carolina this summer. He was a 'B' student and an outstanding athlete. Apart from basketball and baseball he was a first-string two-way halfback with enough guts to weave rugs in his spare time.

He is a taciturn boy and serious enough about the future to have turned down two football scholarships to go to Georgia Tech, his father's alma mater, to study industrial management. His Republican father is a $35,000-a-year manufacturer's representative in Charlotte, and he has enough nerve to share a 1969 Corvette (350 cu. in.) with his son.

David Williams will be 18 in October. He is noncommittal about the draft. At high school he only knew of one person who "definitely" smoked pot and in customary southern fashion he addresses people as "Sir".

He cannot afford to regularly buy magazines out of his allowance, and reads communal copies handed around among his friends.

He is a model, mild-mannered American youth, whose only aberration is reading *Car and Driver*.

David Williams: Father's alma mater over football

According to *Car and Driver*, this was one of its typical readers in 1969. At the time, this was also the most popular Corvette, a small block 350 V8 edition.
(Courtesy Car and Driver)

to move customers away from some hardware. According to *Car Life* in July 1969, one sales manager wouldn't order a base Corvette three-speed stick machine, and made sales staff talk customers out of doing so in case the buyer backed out and the dealer got left with an unsellable ride! There wasn't anything wrong with Corvettes with the three-speed stick, but Corvette buyers in general didn't like entry level cars. The four-speed was an iconic feature, also. This almost proved the case with San Diego dealership Guaranty Chevrolet. A Corvette convertible three-speed stick was ordered by the dealer, just to prove they indeed had Corvettes from the $4438 base sticker that automakers like to crow about. The ragtop nearly went unsold, until a San Diego patrolman called Mike Cicchinelli happened by. Cicchinelli had come seeking a '69 Corvette 350 four-speed, and didn't

want a bar of any base Corvette with three by the knee. However, after a test drive, he came to the conclusion the ZQ3 was tractable enough, not to require a four-speed. The patrolman bought said '69 Corvette 350 ragtop with three-speed stick, and saved 1500 bucks in the process! Beware of reputation and general opinions.

You can't argue with the facts, *Car and Driver*'s September '69 report on a Corvette L71 427 four-speed coupe, with 435bhp at 5800rpm and 460lb/ft at four grand, revealed 0-100mph-0 in 23 seconds, with 3.70 gears. The coupe was bereft of a/c, and sported F70-15 red stripe tires, along with 51.5%/48.5% front to rear weight distribution. Zero to sixty came in 5.3 seconds, 0-70mph was 7 seconds, and gas mileage lay in the 9.5 to 14mpg realm. *C/D*'s comparison field was its '68 Corvette 427, Porsche 911S and Jag XKE 4.2L. Respective ¼-mile times and prices were: 14.1/15.1/15.3 seconds, and well under 6k/near 8.5k/just under 6k. The Corvette L68 427 400 horse edition, drank between 10 and 14.5mpg, with Porsche on 19mpg.

C/D's criticisms were the slow acting, concealed windshield wiper panel, gimmicky fiber optic warning lights, console clock in lieu of an oil temp gauge, and the solid lifter 427's thirst for oil. Less opinion driven was the fact the Mid-Year Corvette's transfer to the next owner at no additional cost, five-year/50,000 mile drivetrain warranty, now involved a fee. It was generally the case with domestic cars that such a warranty would pass free of charge. Note that your Mopar Hemi 426 V8 powered car didn't carry a five-year/50,000 mile drivetrain warranty at all.

Road & Track did a 'Four Luxury GTs' comparison in June 1969, featuring a '69 Corvette ZQ3 350 automatic, with power brakes, power steering, power windows, tinted glass, stereo and a/c. 1968 had been the final year of the Corvette's A02 windshield tint alone option. Now, A01 brought full tint. For '69 MY, Corvette engineers backed off the power assistance to the power brakes, which was welcomed by enthusiasts. In *R&T*'s luxo meet, all contenders cost over five grand. It was a princely sum at the time, with Corvette facing off against a Jaguar XKE with a/c and four-speed, Porsche 911T and Mercedes 280SL. The Corvette was obtained from a local dealer, not Chevrolet

Fender grate gills and a smooth hood give this machine away as a 1970 350-powered Corvette coupe. No three-by-the-knee for 1970!
(Courtesy Muscle Cars For Sale Inc)

Engineering, and did 0-60mph in 8.4 seconds, a 16 second flat ¼-mile at 82mph, 0-100mph in 21.1 seconds, along with 14.3mpg. All cars were tested at Orange County International Raceway. However, at the skid pad at Mira Loma California Digitex Corp, equipment put Porsche on 0.782g, and Corvette as runner up with 0.764g.

In this crowd the Corvette was biggest, heaviest, most powerful, fastest, thirstiest and cheapest! The Jag had the best ¼-mile time, and nicest interior scent of fine leather. It was remarked what a diverse automotive field of cars were at hand, versus the usual domestic car stoush. Only the Mercedes had fuel injection on test. Naturally, a car as single minded as Corvette didn't lend itself to consumer guide analysis, as the Porsche did. The Porsche 911T had only one worst category, the Corvette had 27! The Corvette fell down on refinement in terms of noise and ride comfort. However, *R&T* survey data and owner report series confirmed the Corvette's reputation on durability, dependability and resale value. That is, a car that when delivery faults are fixed, would provide a long, reliable service life.

In the dependability of major and minor components, the Corvette was above average with both. Jaguar was below average on both. Mercedes was above average with the former, but average for the latter. Porsche was only average on both. For resale value, Corvette was average, whereas both Jaguar and Mercedes were below average. Only Porsche was above average. As for parts availability, Corvette was above average, the Jag below average, with Mercedes and Porsche just average. Opinion of dealerships witnessed Corvette and Mercedes low, Jaguar very low and Porsche fair. Owner loyalty for Corvette, Jag and Benz was high, Porsche was very high, but so too was its price. The Corvette basically commenced from five grand, but Porsche was six grand!

The results confirmed what *R&T* said in a 1968 Corvette L79 350 four-speed coupe test, that Corvette didn't require much maintenance,

The 1970 model year Corvette was late on the scene, and came with less than expected. That is, no mid-engine format. Total sales for the year were 17,316.
(Courtesy Muscle Cars For Sale Inc)

1970 was the final year before the GM led low compression low lead/no lead, and soon catalytic converter, route to smog control. There was the candy sweet trio of L46, LT1 350s and LS5 454 V8. However, the promised LS7 454 was a no show. The 1970 Muskie Smog Bill graffiti was on the senate wall!
(Courtesy Muscle Cars For Sale Inc)

The 1970 Corvette LT1 350 V8 was a high rpm honey. Originally slated for '69 MY, a shortage of Camaro Z/28 engine parts led to the Corvette LT1's postponement. *(Courtesy Crown Concepts)*

electrics and mechanicals were ultra reliable, and mild editions only required oil/filter and chassis lubrication every 6000 miles, which was considered long at the time. Yes, get the factory glitches fixed under warranty, and the road ahead for Corvette and you was smooth indeed. However, *Road & Track* couldn't resist summary characterizations of the four cars: Corvette was an animal seeking prey, a 5lb axe, not a rapier. The XKE was for cultured swingers, the Benz a real square for doctors and engineers, with the Porsche ending up in the garages of humorless, possession freak technicians. Were such assessments true? Well, an awful lot of doctors used to drive Mercedes-Benz cars …

For *Road & Track*'s March '69 Corvette, 435 horse ragtop, four-speed and 4.11 rear gears, the roadster was pictured outside the Ruth Lewis Warehouse, with a psychedelic era girl mural in the background. The report confirmed the Corvette's mission statement of a stiff tire walled, neutral handling, smooth road demon whose proficiency in said deed, was only surpassed by truly expensive, mid-engine exotica. *R&T* said Corvette was crude, but affordable next to the Ferrari, Lamborghini et al. Corvette's strength was its weakness. According to one of GM's young marketing and advertising types, "It's a great machine. But it's not a terribly useful device." He likened Corvette more to a dune buggy, than a GT or sports car, and plainly impractical next to a Nova. [74]

In spite of all of the above, many folks dug both Corvettes and dune buggies! Plus, some further facts: by the close of 1969, over 7000 enthusiasts were in Corvette clubs. *Corvette News*, published by Chevrolet, had a circulation of 102,000 copies. The Fuelie and now 427 badges were incredibly popular accessories, and Corvette owners still waved at each other, just like back in 1953! Loyal fans, and a

First appearing on the 1969 Chevrolet Canada options list, the 370 horse 1970 Corvette LT1 350 $448 option had a 10bhp advantage over the like powered 1970½ Camaro Z/28 that defied explanation! *(Courtesy Crown Concepts)*

sales survey showed under 25-year-old blue collar guys making less than 10 grand per annum were the most prodigious Corvette buyer cohort in 1969 model year. Second most numerous were the over 50s white collar professionals, earning over $15,000 per year. [75] Through it all, Corvette was no loss leader like the Bugatti Veyron, it paid its way at GM.

You could assert that '69 MY was the peak Corvette year concerning optionability, value for money, and adhering to Zora Arkus-Duntov's sports car ideals. From 1970 onwards, the Corvette became more subject to outside forces, mainly the government and greenies, with some OPEC to come. So it was that 1969 would prove the final outing for the L88 427, ZL1 427, F41 racing suspension and J56 HD brake package. It seemed Big Brother, or general auto buyers, weren't sports fans!

To verify what you have, given the special options of 1968-69, the Corvette's VIN should be

The Corvette's LT1 350 engine option permitted a choice between coupe and ragtop, but automatic transmission, a/c and power steering were off the table. This was the pure Corvette sports car! *(Courtesy Crown Concepts)*

located on the driver side windshield pillar. For a numbers matching car, the aforementioned VIN should match the number on the engine block pad, forward of the passenger side cylinder head. Authentically, the C3 Corvette engine bay should be black.

If you purchased a final model year '69 Chevrolet Corvair, included was a $150 certificate, discounting any other 1969-70 Chevrolet bought. [76] However, this wasn't the reason for the 1969 Corvette's big 38,762 sales total, a record that would last for six years! In fact, there was a May 1969 UAW strike, which caused the '69 MY to be extended a couple of months to meet a backlog of Corvette orders. In 1954 St Louis was making three to six Corvettes per day, and the plant wasn't fully automated. By 1969, 115 Corvettes were rolling out of St Louis each day. That said, a third shift had to be added, to meet the ever rising demand for America's favorite sports car. In the 1968-70 era, quality remained hit and miss, as picked up by independent magazine reports.

The press first got to see the 1970 Corvette in late December 1969 at Riverside International Raceway, and it wasn't the hoped for all new mid-engine dream. Zora Arkus-Duntov was in attendance with the sole press car, and what a car! A 1970 Corvette LS7 454 with 460 gross horses. That said, much was going on behind the scenes. For one, Chevrolet had a new boss. From February 1969 John Z DeLorean, fresh from taking Pontiac to No 3 in the sales race, was Chevrolet GM. Then there were the revised Corvette plans that DeLorean, Ed Cole and GM brass were musing. With demand so handsomely outstripping supply, and yearly stock accounted for by March/April, why give Corvettes away?!

So, base price went up substantially to $4849 and $5192 respectively for Corvette convertible and coupe. Then too, the options list was pruned. No more standalone racing related hardware, nor low production volume, non shared powerplants. That is, the very engines that would be disallowed by the

'70 Corvettes featured buckets with integrated head restraints. However, Plastic Fantastic faithful had to wait for 1978 before Late Model Corvettes got a real glovebox! *(Courtesy Crown Concepts)*

x 95.2mm). Pontiac also went to a 455 V8 for its '70 GTO. However, in the final model year of gross ratings, there was keen interest in Corvette Mouse Motors. The L46 350 was an hydraulic lifter 350 horse device, that could be had with a/c, but all eyes were on the 370bhp, solid lifter LT1 350, that couldn't have a/c. The LT1 350 first appeared on the Canuck Chevrolet options sheet, and was originally slated for a '69 MY American debut. It was basically a 1st gen Camaro Z28 302 with more displacement.

Releasing the LT1 350 in 1969 Corvette would have precipitated a parts shortage for the '69 Camaro Z28's V8. Even though the LT1 350 was formally announced early, and factory shop manuals plus parts listings were prepared ahead of time, the option was cancelled for '69 MY. That said, you could create an LT1 350 from a L46 350 long engine. This was because the L46 and LT1 350s shared heads, and 11.0:1 CR pistons. Some Corvette fans, with the help of dealers, made their own via: part # 384 9346 (camshaft), part # 391 7610 (high rise aluminum intake), and part # 392 3289 (800 CFM Holley 4bbl carb). As per Camaro Z28 302 intake, and other GM aluminum intakes, it was a forging done at the Winters foundry. Well known indeed was Winters' snowflake casting mark, a 'W' surrounded by six snowflakes.

The LT1 350 possessed 1.69in primaries and secondaries, with 0.485in of lift on intake and exhaust sides, of a cam with 346 degrees of duration on both sides, and respective timing of 61-115/109-57. Intake and exhaust valves were oversize Camaro Z28 2.02in intake and 1.6in exhaust. Power rating was 370 horse at six grand, with 380lb/ft at four grand. Although this was the same powerplant, as in the '70½ Camaro Z28, and power and torque figures were produced at the same rpm with equal torque rating, the Corvette had 10 extra horses. This was probably due to model hierarchy. As for the proof in the pudding, *Sport Car Graphic*'s stats concerning both '70 Corvette LT1 350 and '70½ Camaro Z28 four-speeds were shown in the journal's June 1970 issue. Using close ratio M21

1970 Muskie Smog Bill, and the related GM lower compression ratios for 1971, emissions considered. No racing on regular gas. It all implied that Corvette LS7 454 was a no production show. That said, *Sports Car Graphic*'s Paul Van Valkenburgh did test a proto '70 Corvette LS7 454. With a full gas tank, reduced to 18 gallons for '70 MY due to evaporative emissions control, two occupants and luggage, the triple deuce coupe managed a 13.8 second pass at 108mph. Perhaps more importantly, on the test trip from LA to Detroit, the journal declared it had never tested any car that was so secure at speed.

Corvette was still rolling along on its custom nylon cord F70-15s. They did appear too narrow, at a mere 6.2 inches, for the Corvette's 15 x 8in rims of 1969-82, but were rated for a safe continuous 140mph. They represented an acceptable Zora Arkus-Duntov directed compromise concerning cost, road roar and sufficient sidewall strength for big block torque. There were concerns over radials in that last area. Corvette engineers were now using a front spoiler to kill front end lift at 150mph. The Corvette was still a machine planned for all sporting scenarios. Racers could still order an L88 427 long engine through 1970 model year, and even create one from judicious parts counter ordering for years to come!

Getting back to reality, the Corvette fitted in with GM's general plan of larger engines to maintain performance and drivability, in the face of pending tighter smog law, hence the 350 and 454 V8s (101.5

The new for 1970 cheese grater fender gills were reminiscent of same on the long departed Mercedes 300SL Gullwing. They lasted on Corvette through 1972 model year. *(Courtesy Crown Concepts)*

four-speeds, respective Corvette and Camaro Z28 rear gears/curb weights were 4.11/3300lb and 4.10/3580lb. On test the same F60-15 tires were used, producing respective ¼-mile/trap speeds of 14.5 seconds/99.5mph and 14.6 seconds/98.3mph. Corvette was a paint thickness ahead!

As ever, Corvette's four-speed was more user friendly than anything in an F body, or any other domestic for that matter. The Camaro Z28's Hurst shift linkage made no difference, Corvette was King! However, in trial by Duntov, one had to be proven Corvette LT1 350 worthy, beyond the LT1 350's asking price of $447. The 1287 '70 Corvette LT1 350s came sans power steering, automatic transmission or a/c. Sports car heresy all three! The Camaro Z28 could have power steering and automatic, but not the equivalent Corvette. This purest of Corvettes came with the usual non-functional Corvette 1968-72 big block hood, but with an 'LT-1' callout

This '70 Corvette LT1 350 has a close ratio four-speed, and 4.11 lsd diff ratio. So did the LT1 coupe *Car Life* tested in its August 1970 issue. That machine did 0-60mph in 5.7 seconds, a 14.17 second ¼-mile at 102.15mph, allied to a 122mph top speed at 6500rpm, beyond the motor's six grand redline! *(Courtesy Crown Concepts)*

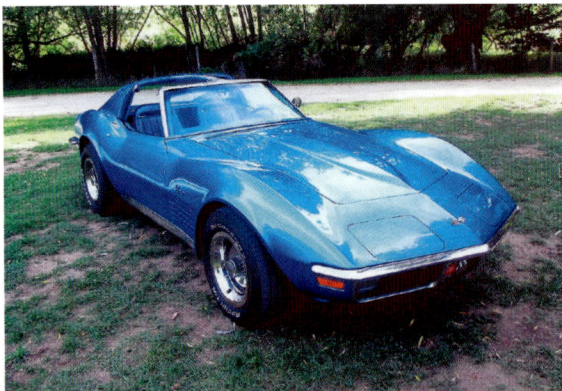

Pictured is a 1970 Mulsanne Blue Corvette
coupe with L46 350 V8 and four-speed.
(Courtesy Shane Burrows)

No MGB, Triumph TR250, nor even Datsun 240Z
was ever this plush! The 411 Blue Vinyl interior
is featured. *(Courtesy Shane Burrows)*

decal. *Car Life* obtained the best stats with the '70 Corvette LT1 350 in August 1970: 14.17 seconds at 102.15mph. Zero to sixty was 5.7 seconds, and terminal velocity of 122mph came from the 4.11 rear gears. And yes, the Corvette permitted heel and toeing by having footwell pedals on the same plane. Not always the case in GM cars, or with other domestics. 50/50 weight distribution bliss, and *Car Life* saw no need for a mid-engine Corvette, nor even the LS7 454. The '70 Corvette LT1 350 was elegant sufficiency, as used to be said.

There was a 454 V8 for '70 MY. Costing 289 bucks, the very tractable 390 horse LS5 454 was selected by 4473 Corvette patrons that year – nearly as popular as the $158 L46 350, chosen by 4910 buyers. The hydraulic lifter LS5 454 torque monster made max power at just 4800rpm, allied to 500lb/ft at 3400rpm! *Road & Track* declared in September 1970 that its '70 Corvette LS5 454 automatic was the most tractable big motor Corvette it had ever tried. Docile perhaps, but with more rumble than the Bronx! Plainly, this was no small block *R&T* said.

10.25:1 CR, bore and stroke a respective 4.25 x 4.00in, and a nearly Caddy like 5600 redline: these were the '70 LS5's figures, but *R&T*'s test subject was somewhat unique. It came from a dealer, not Chevrolet Engineering, so performance figures were more likely to accord with showroom available fare. The coupe belonged to La Hambra, California Corvette specialist Don Steves. His car had a high quality metallic green paint job that

was certainly far superior to anything from St Louis. There was a stereo eight-track tape deck, all the rage at the time, cruise control sourced from a Chevrolet sedan, Nardi steering wheel and American Racing brand alloys sized 15 x 8.5in, shod with metric footprint Michelin X 205-15 radials. With factory a/c optioned, this rig came to a portly 3740lb, or nearly 500lb over a 435 horse '69 Corvette L71 427 four-speed roadster that *R&T* had tested earlier.

Just totting up the factory options, this very special Corvette cost a lot of bread: $6773! This coupe's plush, grand tourer nature, harked back to the days when Corvette took Caddy sales, and perhaps some Plastic Fantastics still did? This test machine was a high end blend of luxury and performance, in a smaller ride than any Caddy, bar the later Cimarron. That said, Michelin Xs were the kind of rubber one would find on a Rolls Royce Silver Ghost, they weren't Michelin's high performance radial. The Michelin X improved the Corvette's steering feel, and reduced road camber following wander of bias belted tires, but lacked grip in acceleration, cornering and braking. Then again, the aluminum rims were half an inch wider than stock. All in all, with Corvette tires, figure a ½-second better than the 0-60mph in seven seconds flat, and 0-100mph in 14 seconds, plus 15 second ¼-mile at 93mph. Very even stats by *Road & Track*, plus a 9mpg reading and associated ... gulp! 162 mile range!

Highway friendly 3.08 rear gears permitted a 144mph top speed, at redline in top. With taller gearing still, the LS5 454 had the muscle to top 150mph. A/C was possible with all 350s bar the LT1, and the ZQ3, L46 and LS5 454 could all have the wide ratio (2.52 1st) M20 four-speed. The LS5 454 came with a single # 704 0204 Rochester 4bbl carb, for easy living. *R&T*'s '69 Corvette roadster showed no brake fade whatsoever, but this weighty LS5 test Corvette had 74% fade during the journal's usual six stop 0.5g deceleration producing brake evaluation. Yes, weight was the culprit, but even heavier was the 454 badge callout street cred – which was bound to succeed the Fuelie and 427 accessories as must have street jewelry! Then there were the changes all '70½ Corvettes came with, like egg-crate grille and side louvers. Parking lights were squarer and placed in the grille's corners. Side marker lights were both better integrated, and visible. Answering the demands of many Corvette owners, wheelarches were more flared to help accommodate larger diameter wheels and tires. The rear saw rectangular exhaust tips, integrated into the lower valance, along with revised taillights. Inside, if optioned, the new 'custom interior' provided leather seats, wall-to-wall carpeting, leather stick shift boot, along with woodgrain trim

for the console and door cards. There was no RPO for the custom interior, but it did cost $158 extra, and 3191 '70 Corvettes were so optioned. All '70 Corvettes came with stainless steel rocker panel trim, along with redesigned seats and seatbelts.

Corvette's head restraints were now built into the seatback, and the inertia reel shoulder portion of the three-point seatbelts fed through the headrest slot at the top of the seatback. This alteration helped free up cargo space. It was also easier to reach the seatback hinge mechanism. The front buckets themselves were redone for more lateral support, with 1in more headroom as a side benefit. On the outside, new Corvettes sat ½in lower. Four-speed was standard, and slushbox was NCO, plus sidepipes were off the menu. AO1 all glass tint was standard, so too Positraction lsd. Standard Positraction implied RPO G81 now referring to the optional rear axle ratio. 2862 '70 Corvette buyers sprung for that 12 buck performance axle ratio.

For the SCCA B production racer, the $968 ZR1 special purpose engine package was built around the new LT1 350 V8. It included HD brakes and suspension, cold air induction, and excluded radio and 'fast glass' (power windows). It's believed 25 people bought this package, aimed at the gentleman racer, in 1970. Trouble was, there weren't as many

Out of 17,316 1970 Corvette buyers, 4910 patrons paid the $158 tab to obtain this 350 horse L46 350 V8. This hydraulic lifter Mouse Motor made an extra 50bhp over base, while permitting the optional $447 C60 factory a/c, chosen by 6659 1970 Corvette faithful. The a/c compressor is present, but the smog pump is not. *(Courtesy Shane Burrows)*

Handsome steel Rally rims started as a new Corvette base wheel choice in 1967 15 x 6 in form, shared with the new Camaro. For '68 MY it was upsized to 15 x 7in, becoming 15 x 8in for 1969. Rally rims remained the standard Corvette wheel, replete with chrome center hubcap and trim rings, through 1982. *(Courtesy Shane Burrows)*

gentleman racers as there used to be. A/C in Corvette was becoming more popular than ever: 6659 optioning C60 a/c at a cost of $447 in '70 MY.

Corvette itself was popular, averaging around 28,000 sales per annum during 1968-70. Not Monte Carlo on every street corner popular, but popular and profitable all the same, even though the economy wasn't that strong. This occurred against a backdrop of more interest in subcompacts, as buyers were counting the pennies. Think 1971 Chevrolet Vega. Meanwhile a six-week strike cost Chevrolet 100,000 sales in 1970, with more to follow. [77]

Things were even a bit jittery for Corvette. Higher prices, fewer options and dealers not willing to take orders for the '70 Corvette LS7 454, even though a '70 Corvette ad did mention the 460 horse permutation as being possible. More than that, GM's PR photo of a blonde babe in a '70 Corvette big block roadster, mailed out on December 2 1969, concerning the February 13 release of the '70½ Corvette, was a trifle odd. On December 5 the press were instructed to destroy the photo, due to interim production changes having been made, so the car was no longer current. A newly issued photo looked the same, but with 'unwanted reflections' removed ...

Dream cars, women & Corvette

EVEN WITH FEWER options, including no LS7 454 mill, the Corvette was still a dream car to many, but a ubiquitous one. To solve that problem, a visit to Baldwin Chevrolet, in Long Island New York, was required. You see, Joel Rosen, of partner concern Motion Performance, had created a custom Corvette. Yes, it didn't have to be a Camaro, it could be a Corvette, and even have that LS7 454 and more! One's dreams could be financed using GMAC (General Motors Acceptance Corporation).

Joel Rosen even snaked an LS7 454 into a Vega, before the Feds got wise, and the 'Smog Nazis' (EPA) put the kibosh on this incredible Vega. Rosen's Motion Performance did offer a 'performance warranty' for his speed shop's Phase III supercars. Supercar was an overused term in pre malaise times, but not with Motion

One of the first cars Joel 'Mr Motion' Rosen ever improved was a 1957 Corvette. After the famous Mid-Year '67 Ko-Motion drag racer, Baldwin-Motion got involved with Late Model C3 Corvettes, like this '69 coupe. *(Courtesy Mecum)*

Performance. It was an ET of 11.5 seconds at 120mph, or better, or your money back! Now that's confidence! Motion Performance's 500 horse plus 1969-71 Phase III Corvette GT with conventional headlights even looked different ... like an XKE meets Ultraman, and more powerful than both combined! Even more far out was Mr Motion's take on Mako Shark II.

Joel Rosen was intrigued, but not limited by GM's famous show car, offering his version as kits or turn key coupes. One example for the show circuit was based on a '70 Corvette coupe with a/c, adding diamond tuft leather interior, unique bubble taillights, one piece flip forward front end, tapered and louvered backlight, Le Mans style gas filler cap, and custom paint job. The price from Baldwin Motion Chevrolet? Try 17 grand. The joy from such an exclusive ride? Priceless! This custom Corvette format, would be seen with later special Corvettes Motion Performance made, prior to the Fed's crackdown on speed shop operations.

For whom was the Corvette dream? Chevrolet statistics concerning 1970 Corvette sales suggested mostly young, single male buyers. To be precise, 93% of 1970 Corvette buyers were men, 26.6 years old on average, 56% were single, 35% professional or managerial, with an average income of $15.5k. It

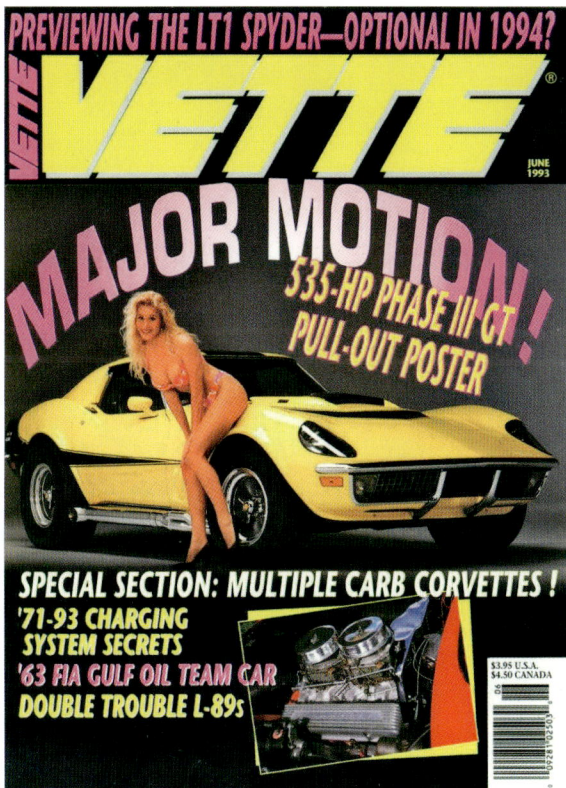

Motion Performance did race cars and custom cars, the Phase III GT Corvette of 1969-71 was certainly custom! *(Courtesy Vette)*

Joel Rosen was inspired by the Mako Shark II show car, and came up with his own even more extreme interpretation in 1970. *(Courtesy Dan Vaughan www.conceptcarz.com)*

was a similar demographic profile as later upscale import brands, like Mercedes, Jaguar and BMW, but younger and not so managerial. It suggests some such younger Corvette owners went to the upscale imports as they got older. However, Corvette buyer loyalty, and repeat ownership, always remained high. Given Corvette owners oftentimes had enough affluence to own more than one car, that other ride might increasingly have become an expensive import as the years went by.

For now, in 1970, 62% of Corvette buyers went coupe, 29.5% chose a slushbox, 38.4% were satisfied with the base ZQ3 350, 28.4% selected the L46 350, 25.8% ordered the lazy LS5 454 (which included the T60 HD battery costing 15 bucks). However, a mere 7.4% went with the high output LT1 350. Of the non motor options, 16.6% bought transistorized ignition, 27.8% went for fast glass, 33.5% chose tilt/tele steering, 38.5% chilled with a/c, which was literally chilly compared to import standards, 68.8% made life easier with power steering, and 98.1% couldn't live sans radio! That said, for the longest time there

seemed one standard feature you got with each and every Corvette ... sex appeal!

Time and time again, seasoned sage scribes of the automotive world asserted that with Corvette, you did get the girl! In May 1970's issue of *Motor Trend*, Chuck Koch declared, "Something about the Corvette seems to induce young females to slip into the passenger's seat at every stoplight." This was followed by Paul Van Valkenburgh of *Sports Car Graphic* in June 1970, when he implored that the Corvette was surely the, "... romance of every aware woman?" Even sober, import leaning *Road & Track*, the buff car magazine closest to Consumer Union's puritanical spirit, asserted in its March 1970 Corvette Stingray owner survey that according to Corvette owners, "girls like it."

In a 1977 *Hot Rod* Special, an anonymous Chevrolet PR consultant, who provided many Chevrolets to West Coast journals for testing, claimed that several Corvettes that passed through his hands had turned many a young lady's head on Sunset Boulevard. Then there was the company that Corvette kept.

117

Don Yenko built and raced the 1968 Corvette L88 427 successfully in the 1968 24 Hours of Daytona, under Sunray-DX sponsorship and livery. *(Courtesy GT Motor Cars)*

At a 1970 Corvette convention of 700 owners in Louisville, Kentucky, no fewer than eight women were present wearing only body paint. The affair was presided over by car doyen David E Davis Jr, one time editor and publisher at *Car and Driver*. Fortunately for their modesty, the women had better paint coverage than contemporary C3 Corvettes rolling off the St Louis line! Objectively, what is to be made of such contentions and conventions? It should be noted that many writers in the car magazine world have PR connections with automakers. For example, Chuck Koch would go on to be VP of product placement firm Vista Group, with president Eric Dahlquist, who helped the Pontiac Firebird become KITT on TV's *Knight Rider*. Marty Schorr was editor of *Cars* magazine, and was involved in the promotion of the wares of speed shop Motion Performance, through Baldwin Chevrolet. That said, Schorr wrote a very fair piece on the '76 Corvette L82 350, in December 1976's issue of *Performance Cars* magazine. Here, he disclosed Chevrolet Engineering's role in improving the test coupe's torque converter.

Before the above claims are dismissed as hopeless PR hokum, consider the recollections of Gale Banks, proprietor of well known marine powerboat engine builder Banks Engineering. In the June 1984 issue of *Car and Driver*, Banks gave his opinion on the importance of '50s hot rod ownership, concerning wooing the fairer sex, "I mean, everybody had a hot rod. If you didn't have a hot rod, girls didn't look at you. We often wondered if their sex organs were not directly connected to their ears, because you know, you'd hit the pipes and they'd all turn around ... " That's science talkin'!

In recent times a classic C3 Corvette 427 was practically serenaded by a group of attractive young women, who pulled up in their ride, and declared the Corvette a cool car. Whereupon, the observation was made that a Prius never engendered such a response. A Jaguar might do, on a one-on-one expensive dinner date encounter. In any case, there seems to be substance to the assertion the Corvette is a social status indicator and symbol of virility, but the author believes more research is needed ...

Production car racing helped establish the Corvette, and it was here the Corvette faced a domestic challenger. Not a Dodge, but the 1968½ AMC AMX. While the two-seater AMX didn't seem like a close showroom rival, more a truncated pony

You could still factory order a racer in 1968. The Yenko Sunray-DX machine involved the 947 buck L88 427, and M22 Rock Crusher four-speed costing $263. The '68 MY ordering of 80 each of such hardware, indicated their joint mandatory option nature. Corvette placed the handbrake lever between the buckets from 1967. *(Courtesy GT Motor Cars)*

Don Yenko waited for a L88 Corvette to race at Daytona. When a factory car failed to arrive in time, Yenko created his own. He converted a new Corvette L71 427, taken from his dealership floor! Note the Tonawanda valve cover decal, indicating the Chevrolet New York factory, where big block Mark IV motors were made. *(Courtesy GT Motor Cars)*

car, it did take the fight right to Corvette's garage, in SCCA B production racing. Indeed, both AMX and Corvette seemed capable of weathering such exalted trackside rivals the AC Cobra, Ferrari and Porsche. The 1969 racing season witnessed a battle royal between AMC's volunteer group of engineers, with electrical laboratory supervisor Dwight Knupp as AMX driver, and semi factory-backed Corvette privateers. Knupp garnered the SCCA Central Divisional Championship with AMX, and was invited to the National runoffs.

At the National Championship decider, held at Daytona in November 1969, Knupp over-revved his AMX 343 V8 when dodging an out of control Corvette! This allowed independent Corvette

campaigner Allan Barker to edge out Knupp, with the pair finishing first and second respectively concerning the National Championship.

At the highest level of motorsport, the Corvette's place continued to be in endurance events. This was typified by Don Yenko and his '68 Sunray-DX L88 Corvette coupe. Iconic Chevrolet figure Yenko wanted to campaign an L88 powered version of the new C3 Corvette at 1968's 24 Hours of Daytona. However, when the factory-ordered Corvette L88 427 failed to materialize in time, Don Yenko just converted a Corvette L71 427 coupe from his Chevrolet dealership floor to L88 427 specification. The usual Corvette L88 427 elements of Holley 850 CFM 4bbl carb and Rock Crusher M22 four-speed were present.

Don Yenko ended up building three Yenko/ Sunray-DX L88 powered Corvettes for 1968's Daytona 24 Hour race, with said coupes coming 1-2-3! The second placed machine was then raced by Yenko at the 12 Hours of Sebring, where it set a GT class lap record, but a subsequent mechanical mishap led to a DNF. Yenko still managed to win the 1968 SCCA Midwest Divisional road racing title in this particular coupe. He was invited to race the machine at 1968's Le Mans, but declined due to a postponed race and sponsorship change. Sunray-DX got bought out by Sunoco, so the above mentioned '68 Corvette L88s ceased to race with the Sunray-DX livery, after the 1968 racing season.

A better known L88 powered late model C3 Corvette was the #57 Rebel Corvette, raced by Dave Heinz during 1969-72. The story started in Florida, with two Tampa businessmen Dave Heinz and Or Costanzo. Heinz owned Dave Heinz Imports, a Jaguar dealership. Costanzo was the new car sales manager for Ferman Chevrolet. Both guys spent weekends racing Corvettes, and Ferman Chevrolet was the medium used by Costanzo to contact GM, and, in turn, Zora Arkus-Duntov. Duntov was

The Yenko Sunray-DX Corvette L88s came 1-2-3 in GT class, at the 1968 24 Hours of Daytona. The #2 coupe went on to set a GT class lap record at the Sebring 12 Hour. Plus, Don Yenko raced the #2 coupe to a '68 SCCA Midwest Divisional Championship title.
(Courtesy GT Motor Cars)

always on the side of successful Corvette privateer racers, and informed Costanzo in mid '68, that his Chevrolet engineers were upgrading the L88 427 for 1969, to make it more race competitive. Lighter, open chamber heads being part of improvements.

ZAK said only four L88 Corvettes would be available early in 1969, and only to Corvette racing teams with Corvette Engineering buyer's key passes. Acting on Duntov's advice, Or Costanzo ordered a '69 Daytona Yellow Corvette hardtop, with black interior, via Ferman Chevrolet. It arrived at the dealership in January 1969, with L88 prerequisites: radio delete, M22 Rock Crusher four-speed, J56 HD brakes, K66 transistorized ignition, F41 HD suspension, MA6 HD clutch and a 'Distance Group' package, stored in the cargo cavity (plexiglass headlight covers, headlight buckets, fender flares, wheel adaptors, Harrison engine oil cooler). Duntov's team also shipped out GM-approved OK Custom headers and sidepipes, along with magnesium American Racing Torque Thrust D

Between 1969 and 1972, Tampa Bay, Florida Jaguar dealer Dave Heinz successfully raced this '69 Corvette L88 427 coupe. Heinz had hoped Heinz Ketchup would be a sponsor, so added #57, but no dice!
(Courtesy Ferman Chevrolet)

In mid '71 racing season, the Dave Heinz Corvette L88 racer became part of Race Enterprises and Development (RED) team. *(Courtesy Goodyear)*

rims, which were installed upon reaching Ferman Chevrolet. It is believed this L88 Corvette was the only car factory optioned and delivered with a dual disk clutch.

The #57 Corvette L88 427 was a veritable race weapon, wielded by Dave Heinz and Or Costanzo during 1969-71 consecutive outings of the Sebring 12 Hours and Daytona 24 Hours endurance races. Dave Heinz even tried to get Heinz Ketchup as a sponsor, hence the #57, but no dice! The coupe won four out of five of the new 1971 IMSA series races. The 'Over 2 Liter Championship' went the #57 Corvette's way, as did the IMSA Drivers' Championship to Dave Heinz. However, in mid '71 racing season, this winning Corvette was sold to Toye English, owner of famed racing outfit Race Enterprises and Development or RED. It was at this time that the #57 Corvette L88 427 took on the Rebel flag livery that it's well known for. The get up was a tongue in cheek response to the John Greenwood Stars & Stripes-liveried 'Spirit Of' Corvette racers.

All the while the #57 signage was retained, but Don Yenko now joined Dave Heinz in driving duties, during the remainder of the 1971 racing season. In the first outing for the #57 Corvette L88 427 Rebel racer, the coupe qualified 26th at the 6 Hours of Watkins Glen, but finished second in class and sixth outright by the time the checkered flag fell. For 1972 racing season, 'Marietta' Bob Johnson partnered Dave Heinz to race the #57 Rebel racer. The car's first '72 season event for Team RED was the 6 Hours of Daytona. Here, Heinz and Johnson won the GT class, beating John Greenwood's Corvette in the process. And it was a case of dueling radials for Corvette!

Before the Daytona 6 Hours, Leo Mehl, Goodyear's worldwide racing director, had asked Team RED to use a set of special, unmarked, experimental racing tires, on the #57 Rebel Corvette. Post class victory, the next day saw a full page *Wall Street Journal* ad, informing of the Rebel Corvette's win on the "first set of Goodyear racing radial tires." Goodyear became the Rebel

The RED Rebel team's Confederate Flag Corvette livery poked fun at contemporary Corvette rival John Greenwood's Stars & Stripes get up. Team RED wasn't just whistling Dixie, it won!
(Courtesy Barrett Jackson)

Corvette's sponsor for the rest of the '72 racing season. It was 'mud in yer eye' for the BF Goodrich shod Greenwood Corvettes, and marked the start of the BFG vs Goodyear tire wars, featuring that latest domestic performance star ... the radial tire! The Rebel Corvette's next race was the Sebring 12 Hours, where it was the second quickest GT car, and 13th fastest outright, in a large field of prototype racers and GT machines. Dave Heinz qualified the Rebel Corvette 10 seconds ahead

of the BFG Corvettes, but was second behind the Rinzler Corvette LS6 454. At the race start, Rinzler led the GT class into turn one, where he immediately crashed into a sandbank! Dave Heinz then took charge, leading for the remainder of the 12 hour event. He finished fourth overall, 50 miles ahead of fifth place, which was Peter Gregg in a Porsche 911. The Rebel Corvette's stats for the Sebring 12 Hours were: 1189 miles of racing in 12 hours, and a 95.776mph average speed for 221 laps,

The '72 6 Hours of Daytona saw the Rebel team win GT class, outdo John Greenwood, and give Goodyear's new racing radial PR kudos.
(Courtesy Barrett Jackson)

in an event where Ferrari 312 prototypes came 1-2, and a Type 33 Alfa Romeo prototype landed third.

Goodyear sent the #57 L88 Rebel Corvette to 1972's Le Mans 24 Hour race. However, it proved ineligible, given many factory parts were no longer present. So, a new car was built for Le Mans, with the Rebel Corvette sold to New York's Alex Davidson at the close of the '72 racing season. After fading out of sight, the Rebel Corvette was restored to '72 Sebring 12 Hours class winning spec, by Corvette Repair Inc of Valley Stream, New York. Authenticity assistance was provided by former Team RED crew member Walt Thurn, with the completed car being the subject of scale model manufacturers like Carousel since the year 2000. The C2 and C3 Corvette's racing prowess was helped by an IRS aimed at handling, rather than ride comfort. The rear of the Corvette didn't steer the car under braking, like other IRS equipped machines. It all helped Corvette remain on its winning path!

The Corvette had also been steadily racing to the Moon, thanks to the Dollar Car program. This enterprise provided Chevrolets to astronauts and their families for a token sum. It was the brainchild of Indy 500 champ Jim Rathmann, with cars provided from his Chevrolet-Cadillac dealership located near to NASA. So far, the astronaut-provided Corvettes, and other Chevrolets, looked stock. However, this was about to change, thanks

to a trio of gold and black '69 Astrovettes. And quite fittingly, given 1969 would see Neil Armstrong as the first person to walk on the Moon. That said, it was the fourth man to walk on the Moon, Alan Bean, who initiated the Astrovette project. Bean and colleagues Richard 'Dick' Gordon, and Charles 'Pete' Conrad were ex-Navy fellows, all interested in Corvettes. Gordon and Conrad went along with Bean's idea, ordering their '69 Corvettes in Riverside Gold too.

Specification wise, the Astrovettes featured L36 427s with 390 horse, wide ratio M20 four-speed, 3.08 rear gears, Positraction lsd, head restraints, PB AM/FM radio, C60 a/c, black vinyl interior, and P02 deluxe wheel covers. More important was the Astrovette's custom get up, with the 'Black Wing' trim from respected industrial and automotive designer Alex Tremulis. Tremulis was commissioned by the astronauts to come up with a standout, custom look. He took inspiration from the world's fastest bike, the '64 Triumph Cyronaut, and the world's fastest car, the Summers Brothers' Goldenrod streamliner. That Goldenrod had even inspired the bike's color scheme.

The Astrovette appearance settled on was Tremulis' third proposal. The crew admired the Black Wing look, and Jim Rathmann added a ¼-in white stripe between the coupe's black and gold paint. To personalize the three Astrovettes, the crew used spacecraft coding system, with red, white and blue rectangular fender plaques, containing their crew title initials: (3) Alan Bean – Blue – LMP (Lunar Module Pilot), (1) Pete Conrad – Red – CDR (Commander), (2) Dick Gordon – White – CMP (Command Module Pilot). In the decade of the Dollar Car program, these were the only cars specially ordered and registered in the lessee's names, eg, Alan Bean's car had a gas tank decal with "Courtesy car delivered to Alan L Bean."

Bean drove his Astrovette around the little island town of Cocoa Beach. As in past years, once the lease was up the cars were returned. Alan Bean's Astrovette wound up at a 1971 GMAC lot closed bid auction, in Austin Texas. It was here that the coupe's long time custodian Danny Reed, had the presence of mind to purchase and preserve this historic piece of both Corvette and NASA history. Reed paid $3230 at the auction, but given Alan

Apollo 12 astronauts (from left to right), Charles 'Pete' Conrad Jr, Richard Francis Gordon Jr, and Alan LaVern Bean, with their nearly identical 1969 Astrovettes. Specified with L36 427, M20 wide ratio four-speed, 3.08 Posi and a/c. *(Courtesy GM Archives)*

Bean's Astrovette is the only survivor of the three special cars done, the coupe is truly invaluable. In the late '90s the Bean Astrovette was reconditioned by Ray Repczynski, of Corvettes by Ray, located in Houston.

This rolling example of history is occasionally displayed at Corvette and NASA related events. For example, the Bean Astrovette was part of the 2019 NASA exhibit at the National Corvette Museum. The "From Gas Station to Space Station' display was part of celebrating the 50th anniversary of Neil Armstrong's "One small step for man, one giant leap for mankind." Have Corvette, will travel! Danny Reed reunited Alan Bean with his Astrovette, and Bean remarked, "He keeps the car real nice – better than when I owned it." Upon leaving NASA in 1981, Alan Bean indulged his artistic passion through painting. The Dollar Car lease program ended in 1971.

Astronauts are one thing, but did anyone get as high as Jimi Hendrix?! The legendary rock guitarist liked the Corvette, and bought a 1968 International Blue Corvette 427 from Blaushild Chevrolet in Cleveland. He purchased the coupe while out car shopping with bassist Noel Redding. Hendrix may not have had a driving license, but

Mostly designed by Alan Bean, with Alex Tremulis doing the 'Black Wings', the color is Riverside Gold, and the P02 deluxe wheel covers and black vinyl interior were common to all three Astrovettes. *(Courtesy NASA)*

Each astronaut placed their space crew title initials within the fender color code panel. For Alan Bean it was LMP (Lunar Module Pilot) in the blue square. Today, only Alan Bean's coupe (shown here) survives.
(Courtesy NASA)

in any case had a reputation of being a rather poor driver. He crashed the '68 Corvette after a Cream concert party. The car was written off, and insurance company payout followed, with Hendrix now buying a Cortez Silver 1969 Corvette 350 with Rally rims. This second Corvette was repainted in silver metal flake, then candy green metallic. The '69 Corvette was purchased at a dealership in California. Guitarist Jeff Beck recalled being driven by Hendrix in the '69 Corvette, while it was green, in New York City. After Hendrix's untimely death,

the '69 Corvette was sold off by the late guitarist's management. The coupe's whereabouts are unknown; you could say it disappeared in a purple haze …

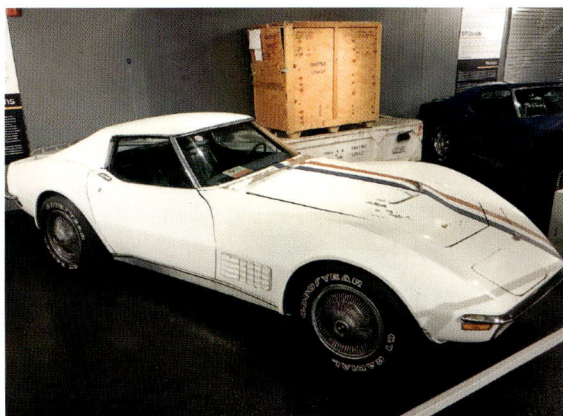

This '70 Astrovette LS5 454, marked the Dollar Car program's final year. In 2019 it was part of a National Corvette Museum display, 'From Gas Station to Space Station', commemorating the 50th anniversary of Neil Armstrong's lunar walk.
(Courtesy National Corvette Museum)

CRANSWICK ON
CLASSIC CHEVROLET
Corvette
1953-1996

CHAPTER **7**

Modified Rapture
1971-74

End of chrome

IN ZORA ARKUS-DUNTOV'S recollections to *Road & Track* in June 1977, he said how busy the St Louis Corvette factory was at the dawn of the '70s, "In 1970, production in the St Louis Corvette plant reached 32,000 and they said no more, that is the utmost capacity." Indeed, due to the late introduction of the '70½ Corvette, the 1971 Corvette was considered by management as a mere continuation, providing a chance to improve on quality within a largely stable design. Over 500 men and women were working each shift at St Louis, and, as intimated by then plant manager Vince Shanks, there was continued pride in building the Corvette. Especially compared to defect-prone, recall-ridden Lordstown Vega! As Shanks said, "When you ask a guy where he works in St Louis, he'll tell you 'Corvette' rather than Chevrolet. Every Corvette he sees on the road is one he's worked on. That's quite an incentive."

The statistics said 21,801 Corvettes were built in 1971 model year, with 14,680 coupes and just 7121 ragtops, priced from a respective $5496 and $5259. Yes, it seemed that T-tops were making the slightly cheaper convertibles somewhat redundant. Plus, Corvettes weren't as affordable as in pre 1970 times. GM pricing was part of the reason for Corvette's profitability, along with high labor content assembly in the old St Louis plant. Plus, continued reliance on the separate chassis design established in 1963. More Corvettes were sold versus 1970, but the total was modest compared to the C3 Corvette's 1968-69 debut. That said,

America's only sports car was still no loss leader. The 1971 AMC AMX was a 2+2, and the Pantera was Italian made, these were facts. *Car and Track*'s Bud Lindemann made an oblique negative reference to the Corvette when testing the revised '71 AMC Javelin SST 401. He noted that although Corvette and Javelin sported Can Am fenders, only the latter was a handler. Oh my, them's fighting words!

In any case, the quality of C3 Corvettes had been improving since the generation's rocky 1968 start. Reduced options helped bring order to production, which for 1971 ran to an easier opening gas filler door and illuminated night time automatic transmission shift quadrant. However, from late 1971 model year, the Corvette fiber optic warning light system was shown the door. Increasingly dismissed as Motorama style hokum, such decontenting permitted the UA6 alarm system ($31) to become standard for '72 MY. Like the rise in assembly quality, a necessary improvement given the Corvette's propensity to get boosted by Light Fingered Larry!

The Corvette had always been a special machine in GM world, and its engines were an important point of distinction, such as the Fuelie 327 and L88 427 V8s from recent times. Zora Arkus-Duntov noted how special engines inspired the Corvette engineers, and were part and parcel of the Chevrolet vs Ford rivalry. Duntov mentioned some planned powerplants to *R&T*'s John Lamm in June 1977: "Single overhead cam 377 (small block), then pushrod hemispherical chamber 377, then 427 hemispherical chamber and 427 single cam." Then too, the Chevrolet high-performance parts

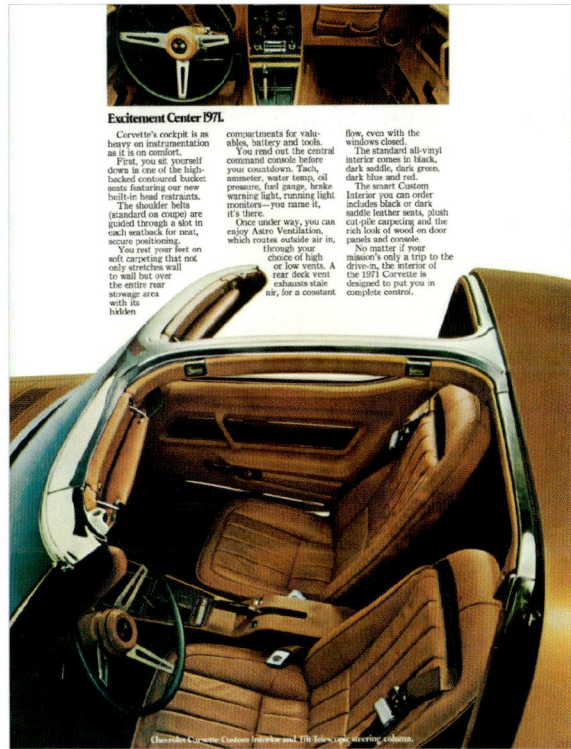

The exterior, custom interior and tele-tilt steering column (N37) all looked familiar.
However, the engine compression ratio drop to drink regular was a key unseen change on the
'71 Corvette. The exterior color shown is 983 Brands Hatch Green, chosen by 3445 '71 Corvette patrons.
(Courtesy GM Archives)

system, the homologated racing stuff available over the counter from some performance oriented Chevrolet dealers. The scheme made sufficient money to satisfy upper management. That said, such hardware wasn't where Chevrolet, GM and the domestics were going.

GM President Ed Cole, an historical Corvette figure, was overseeing a move at GM to tone down engines offered. In line with the 1970 Muskie Smog Bill, GM's new engines, including Corvette mills, would follow an unleaded gas, catalytic converter route. That implied an ability to run on regular to start with. For a low-lead, no-lead future, in came hard valve seats for 1971 and later GM powerplants, plus a compression ratio drop. Pricey, low volume specialized motors didn't fit GM's smog and profit plan. So, say hello to Corvette's new '71 MY base motor, the soon ubiquitous L48 350.

Replacing the high CR 300 horse ZQ3 350, the

new L48 350 had two-bolt mains, cast iron pistons, cast iron crank, 8.5:1 CR, and valve covers in engine block paint. On regular gas it was 270 horse at 4800rpm, with 360lb/ft at a tractable 3200rpm. According to June 1971's *Car and Driver* figures, a sensible Corvette L48 350 automatic, with a/c and 3.08 final drive ratio, produced 0-60mph in 7.1 seconds, 12-15mpg and an estimated top speed of 132mph. All on regular gasoline.

For a hi po 350, your 1971 choice was solely the $483.45 LT1 350. The L46 350 had ended in 1970 model year. The LT1 350 was now rated at 330bhp at 5600rpm, with 360lb/ft arriving at four grand. Compression ratio was down to 9.0:1, but performance seemed little affected. As ever, a four-speed only, non a/c motor, the LT1 350 allowed Corvette to hit sixty in 5.9 seconds and reach 80mph in 9.3 seconds. The ¼-mile was accomplished in a veritable jiffy: 14.3 seconds at

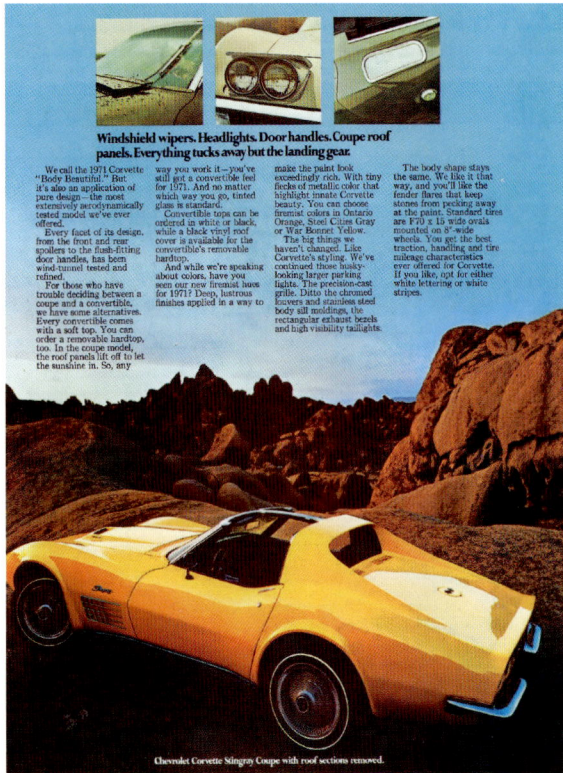

This 1971 Corvette L48 350 roadster was one of only 130 '71 Corvettes specified with the $100 M22 close ratio HD Rock Crusher four-speed. 1971 marked the end of RPO M22, and the start of L48 350 along with the 989 War Bonnet Yellow exterior color. *(Courtesy John Andersen)*

Zora Arkus-Duntov, Corvette's unofficial Chief Engineer since 1953, advised avoiding the P02 deluxe wheel covers shown. It would save the buyer 63 bucks and 28lb, improving handling through less unsprung weight by going with the stock Rally rims. The color is 912 Sunflower Yellow, chosen by 1177 '71 Corvette buyers. *(Courtesy GM Archives)*

98mph. These figures came from the April 1971 issue of *Motor Trend*, which lined up the Corvette against its long-time nemesis, the Jag XKE.

The Jaguar had just been up-gunned to V12 quad carb configuration. With automatic and a/c, the Browns Lane coupe did 0-60mph in 7.2 seconds, 0-80mph in 10.2 seconds, with the ¼-mile dispatched in 14.83 seconds at 96.72mph. Most XKEs had automatic and a/c, and this was fast enough for a genteel gentleman's carriage. Of the two coupes, the Corvette had better sports car credentials, given it involved some sacrifice. What's more, Zora Arkus-Duntov winced at the utterance that the Corvette and Camaro Z28 shared the same motor. You see, Corvette engineers had come up

with the 350 cube version of the 1st gen Camaro Z28 302 first!

Better value seemed provided by that other star motor of 1970, the LS5 454 V8. Like the L48 350, the big block V8 had an 8.5:1 CR, and was assuredly a regular fuel motor. The LS5 box could be ticked for a mere $294.90, and you could have automatic and a/c with that. Indeed, the LS5 454 proved to be 1971's most popular Corvette engine option: 5097 Corvette faithful said yes to it! According to *Car and Driver*'s June '71 data, the '71 Corvette LS5 454 automatic, with a/c, used its 365 gross horses and 3.08 rear gears to sprint to sixty in 5.7 seconds, and do a 14.2-second pass at 100.33mph. Once again, on regular gas, and all you had to do was floor the loud pedal to produce such stats, time and time again. The excellent GM THM 400 slushbox – as used by Rolls Royce, Jaguar and other high class rides – made it all child's play.

1971 fun and games didn't end there, Corvette had one more ace up its sleeve: the 1971½ LS6 454. This low volume, high performance big block came with special internals. The LS6 454 was basically

This Corvette was ordered sans power steering and power brakes! However, it did have Positraction lsd, and factory hardtop (RPO CO7 $274). Fiero buckets, GM Performance ZZ4 350 crate motor, and MSD 6AL Digital Ignition, are mods done. *(Courtesy John Andersen)*

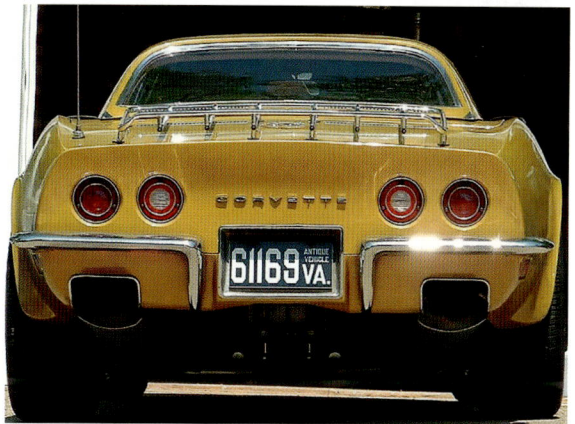

A later composite rear transverse Corvette spring has been retrofitted, along with Van Steel Offset trailing arms and adjustable strut rods. The first owner blew up the original L48 350 in the late '70s. That's two-bolt mains for you! *(Courtesy John Andersen)*

a smog friendly version of the hoped for LS7 454 that never was. It was the kind of V8 management didn't want to know anymore. Honoring the GM compression drop, the LS6 454 had a 9.0:1 CR, and, like the '71 LT1 350, a slight dome to the piston shape. In theory, both such small and big block V8s, and any GM 1971 engine could run on regular. However, in practice, the LT1 350 and LS6 454 needed more, to avoid pinking, or detonation. In truth, GM engineers had only weeks to get GM's 1971 model year engine line up regular-ready.

The new low-lead, no-lead era saw open chamber heads on the small block and big block Chevrolet V8s. There was a perception the small block V8s did relatively worse with such open chamber heads, and that the 454 V8 profited by the move, with better breathing. As for the LS6 454, you got a low rise aluminum intake, 800 CFM Holley single pumper 4bbl carb, dual valve springs, externally balanced crankshaft, alloy steel valves sized 2.19in on the intake side and 1.88in on the exhaust, lashed 0.24in intake and 0.28in exhaust when hot, a big cam with 316 degrees duration intake and 302 degrees duration exhaust, 0.5197in of valve lift on both sides, deck height 0.008in below the block (or 'in the hole' to use racing parlance), forged aluminum TRW pistons with 0.303in dome height for 9.0:1 CR, and lock-in-rod pressed wrist pins, along with 7/16in connecting rod bolts. Horsepower rating was 425bhp, with 6500rpm redline, and engine weight of 604lb. Like the LT1 350, the LS6 454 was a solid lifter job. Heads were aluminum, with connecting rods and crank forged steel. All Mark IV 454s were externally balanced.

Whereas the LS5 454 made 365bhp at 4800rpm and 465lb/ft at 3200rpm, the LS6 454 managed 425bhp at 5600rpm and a mighty 475lb/ft at four grand. Respective redlines were 5600rpm and 6500rpm. In *Car and Driver*'s June 1971 issue, its Corvette LS5 454 automatic achieved a 141mph top speed, based on a two-way average. The journal's

Corvette LS6 454, with M22 Rock Crusher and 3.36 rear end did 0-60mph in 5.3 seconds, a 13.8 second ¼-mile at 104.65mph, burnt premium gas in the 9-14mpg zone, with an observed redline top speed of 152mph.

The factory-delivered Corvette LS6 454 mayn't have seemed much swifter than its LS5 counterpart, but the former had much greater potential, thanks to those high quality engine internals. That big block could be buzzed to 7000rpm without blowing up! No turning valve gear into Cheez Whiz. The LS6 454 was intended for racing, for example, the Rinzler Corvette LS6 454 V8. Double shot peened conrods, tuftrided crank and forged pistons, plus solid lifter format,

The search for the perfect car.

Loren Crites graduated from the University of St. Louis, with a degree in aircraft mechanics, 4 years ago.
In his not-so-spare time, he collects cars, one at a time. Now 25, he has owned nearly 25 automobiles.

"I had a Ford Mach I and I modified the heads a little and changed it over to Champions. It ran real good at the drags.
"When I got the 'Vette, I changed it to Champions, too. It's running real nice now. Trouble is, I drove one of those

little English Lotuses the other day. I sure would like to get my hands on one of them."

CHAMPION
Toledo, Ohio 43601

7 million Chevrolet owners have switched to Champion Spark Plugs.
This has been one of them.

By the time *(1971)* this '68 Corvette 327 was featured in this Champion ad, life was getting a lot more complicated for Corvette, GM and the auto industry than swapping plugs on a Mustang Mach I or Lotus Europa. *(Courtesy Champion)*

transistorized ignition and double disk clutch all spelt high performance. It also caused Zora Arkus-Duntov some regret, in the way of the LS6 454's aluminum heads that saved 55lb, "Maybe for street engine I make mistake – aluminum heads are expensive and that weight doesn't matter on the street."

Duntov knew what the Corvette owner needed, which wasn't always what they wanted. No brake system proportioning valve was utilized on '71 Corvettes, ZAK felt it wasn't required. He didn't think much of mufflers either. According to ZAK, they cost Corvette 50 horses. However, drive-by noise standards of California required mufflers. Such legalities also killed off sidepipes, which were worth 10bhp on Corvette, along with the ZL2 cold air hood. The latter was essential for heat dissipation on Chevrolet's sports car, since the Corvette had the least underhood space of any V8 powered Chevrolet. It was a problem affecting all Mark IV Rat motored Corvettes, to some degree.

That said, cold air induction would return for 1973, and with it, mucho noise!

Zora Arkus-Duntov didn't think you needed the M22 Rock Crusher four-speed to get by on the street. The regular four-speed was plenty good enough, and avoided the straight cut noise inviting teeth of the M22 close ratio four on the floor. The by now fabled Corvette four-speed, with its precise easy shift and light clutch, continued as an unmatched domestic industry standard. Part of that goodness seemed related to a shift linkage, that was frame mounted. That solid connection made for a linkage sans buzz. After all, there were no rubber isolating bushings. The Corvette four-speed's synchronizers were unbeatable, and you could adjust the shifter for an even shorter throw.

In Duntov's opinion, the F41 suspension was also not advisable for daily driver duty, just too harsh. For real racers, not Walter Mitty dreamers. So, group all the track hardware together in one package, to separate the highway cruisers from Don Yenko and Mark Donohue. In 1970 there was such a package, built around the LT1 350, and now there was another. Apart from $1010 ZR1 special purpose LT1 engine package, say hello to the $1747 ZR2 Special Purpose LS6 engine package. It all made for a race-ready Corvette, with ZR1 optioned by eight people, and 12 taking ZR2, the latter for only half the 1971 model year! Zora Arkus-Duntov lamented the fact, that the LS6 454's specialist hardware and high price of $1221 had limited its 1971½ standalone option sales to a mere 188 patrons. However, when things get dedicated, sales shrink to the chosen ones. As a side benefit, any 454 V8 option brought the 15 buck heavy duty battery (RPO T60).

ZR1 and ZR2 implied small and big block, solid lifter motors, respectively, plus: M22 Rock Crusher four-speed, HD power brakes, custom aluminum radiator/metal fan shroud, transistorized ignition, stiffer springs, HD spindle strut shafts, front and rear swaybars the size of baseball bats. That said,

Motor Trend's June 1972 test of a stock '72 Corvette L48 350 four-speed coupe produced 0-60mph in 8.5 seconds and a 15.2 second ¼-mile at 83mph. This '72 Corvette L48 350 ain't stock! *(Courtesy Steven D Francis)*

the ZR1 cars didn't always have the rear swaybar. Forget about deluxe wheel covers, AM/FM radio etc. This stuff was for the track. Such single-mindedness was exemplified by the Corvette LS6 454's 0.9375in front swaybar and 0.5625in rear swaybar, the former being ex F41. Your standard Corvette 350 came with just a 0.75in front swaybar! With curb weight just under 3500lb, the Corvette LS6 454 four-speed was no Lotus Europa, nor MG Midget, and unlike those cars you could have a slushbox. However, the LS6 454 did represent the last special Corvette motor, until the 1989 Corvette ZR1. Little wonder *Car Craft* titled its August 1971 report "Goodbye Forever LS-6."

Corvette caught in the SAE net of horsepower

WITH THE PONY car market cooling, higher insurance premiums and general inflation, sales of Detroit's extraordinary powered and decorated 2+2s were hit. The Big Three and little AMC hoped junior pocket rockets would save the value-added day – cars like the compact AMC Hornet S/C 360, Dodge Demon and Plymouth Duster 340s, Ford Maverick Grabber/Mercury Comet GT 302s, and the Chevrolet Nova SS 350. Only 7016 Nova SS 350s were sold in '71 MY, marking that Nova version's demise. A Nova SS 454 had been planned. Growing

Compared to the stock '72 smogger 200bhp L48 350 with 300lb/ft, this blown LS V8 supplies well over double the horses! This potent powerplant is connected to a TKO 600 five-speed stick shift. *(Courtesy Steven D Francis)*

The custom dashboard of this '72 Corvette features Dakota Digital gauges, Vintage Air a/c and a removed map pocket. Unlike the stock C60 a/c, the Vintage Air C3 Corvette system fits completely within the cabin, and involves some welding of the firewall. *(Courtesy Steven D Francis)*

Fiero seats with custom covers give more lateral support than stock buckets. Custom door cards with C2 Corvette chrome handles complement the C3 interior. Custom floor mats and a seven-speaker Pioneer sound system are further personal touches. *(Courtesy Steven D Francis)*

interest in smaller subcompacts was catered to by GM with the '71 Chevrolet Vega, which resembled a mini 2nd gen Camaro. That sport compact coupe didn't seem long for this world. [78]

The 174-day strike at the Lordstown, Ohio plant in 1972 nearly ended the GM F body. In the final reckoning, 1100 part completed Camaros that couldn't meet 1973 bumper laws were either sent to vocational colleges, or simply junked. Chevrolet sold 2,151,076 vehicles in 1972, but only 68,656 Camaros. Many in management didn't think the F body was worth it. In contrast 27,004 1972 Corvettes were sold, split between 20,496 coupes and 6508 ragtops. Their respective starting prices were $5533 and $5296. This tally was a substantial increase over 1971's showing. The Plastic Fantastic was still popular and profitable. After December 1971, it even became slightly cheaper, given the repeal of a Federal excise tax. And whereas the important Chevrolet Nova's production was moved from Norwood to safeguard the model from the UAW, the Corvette seemed happy enough in St Louis.

The '72 Corvette looked much the same, and this would be the final year the two-seater sports car sported chrome bumpers at both ends. It was also the end for the infamous disappearing wipers. Zora Arkus-Duntov liked them, from a streamlining, aerodynamic perspective, but did concede there were times when drivers needed wiper action, right now! 1972 also marked the end of code 989 War Bonnet Yellow paint, and the only year for code 924 Pewter Silver, with 2550 and 1372 '72 Corvette patrons selecting such respective hues. Much more popular than either exterior was the new AV3 three-point seatbelt option, 17,693 '72 Corvette buyers ticked that RPO. The Corvette continued to roll on its domestic auto industry specific, nylon cord bias belted F70-15 tires, with the white letter PU9 option increasingly more popular than the PT7 white stripe edition since the 1970 model year.

All 1972 Corvettes came with a standard alarm system. This was activated by turning a key cylinder located above the Corvette's chrome tailscript letters, whereupon the alarm would sound (horn honking), if an attempt was made to pry open either door or hood of the locked sports car. Softer shocks were another standard feature. Such new, welded piston shock absorbers, had valving that

made good on the promise of better ride comfort, according to *Road Test*'s May 1972 report. Note that the big block Corvettes, post 1970, featured the former F41 front swaybar diameter of 0.94in, rather than the one time stock Mark IV engine Corvette diameter of 0.875in. The big block 0.562in rear bar remained constant. However, it did seem to move Corvette further towards European car practice of softer damping, and more reliance on swaybars for roll control.

Detail changes for the '72 Corvette saw blue interior instrument/control lighting, not green, plus the adoption of international symbols for control knobs. 1972 would also mark the demise of the Corvette's 1968-72 F70-15 tires, Firestones on small block cars, Goodyear for Mark IV machines. The industry and racing now revolved around radials, and that was Corvette's next move. In spite of the insurance industry/Naderite-placating switch to net horsepower ratings, there were no changes to the Corvette's engine line up in substance, bar the sad omission of the LS6 454. So, the L48 350's 200bhp rating was equivalent to 1971's 270 gross bhp rating, and engineers even played around with the engine speeds at which power and torque outputs were given, to further cloud the fact no real change had occurred.

In *Motor Trend*'s April 1971 issue, a 330 horse Corvette LT1 350 did a 14.3 second ¼-mile, and *Road Test*'s May '72 evaluation of a 1972 255 SAE net horse Corvette LT1 350 also produced a 14.3 second ¼-mile. *Road Test* also tried the latest Corvette LS5 454 automatic, with 3.08 rear gears. This coupe's 14.1 second ¼-mile would have been normal even in the pre 1971 era. The big block Corvette with 270 horse at four grand and 390lb/ft at only 3200rpm, proved more frugal than the L48 and LT1 350 cars that *Road Test* tried, with respective gas mileages of 14mpg, 10.5mpg and 13mpg.

The Corvette's L48 350 base V8, had already assumed its position as the most popular Corvette choice. *Road Test*'s Corvette L48 350 coupe, came with the standard M20 wide ratio four-speed, and single dry disk clutch. The Corvette LT1 350 came with the optional close ratio M21 four-speed, and dual disk HD clutch. Sales optioning saw 3913 Corvette faithful pay $294 for the LS5 454, but only

The C3 Corvette luggage area's usual three secret compartments (left to right: tire iron/oddments cubby/battery) with fiberglass buckets. All lighting is now by LED, with the cargo lamp relocated, and the secret compartments illuminated when open! *(Courtesy Steven D Francis)*

1741 souls went with the solid lifter $483 hi po LT1 350. 240 of those Corvette LT1 350s came with factory C60 a/c, costing $464. Late '72 Corvettes and Camaro Z28s, with the LT1 350 V8, could now have a/c. That used to be a solid lifter no-no, but now it seemed a lead in to the hi po hydraulic lifter L82 350 of 1973-80.

Although relatively ubiquitous in America, the Corvette was a rare sight overseas. St Louis was always flat out keeping up with domestic demand. There was no commercial need to supply export markets, especially when GM's overseas subsidiaries had sporty cars, finely attuned to the needs of such markets. Therefore, Corvettes were the proverbial forbidden fruit, obtained outside America using specialty importers. Such importers put their end on, and with the usual import duty figured in, that made Corvettes an expensive curiosity in the rest of the world. Something for the guy with everything, who wanted something novel. In the UK, Corvette LS5 454s were the only port of call, listed at a princely £4875. That said, plebian 350 powered editions could be special ordered. The Corvette was also available in another right-hand drive market, Japan. Here, 18 1972 Corvettes were sold at around $17,000, much more than the five to six grand back home! [79] In these right-hand drive countries, few bothered converting from left-hand drive.

Restrictive trade practices meant something, given America's relative open door policy to trade, and the changing shares of the US auto market held by domestic and Japanese entities. In 1973, relative shares were a respective 84.7% versus 6.5%. By 1982, those figures became a respective 72.2% against 22.6%, on the eve of the C3 Corvette's demise. [80] The Corvette didn't have a Japanese rival in 1972, but did so when the C3 Corvette's successor was about to be launched. However, all this was a decade away. For now, Corvette was the standard bearer of appeal on four wheels in America.

Corvette – love unlimited

SURVEY STATISTICS AND press assessment attested to the popularity of the Plastic Fantastic. During 1966 to 1970, *Car and Driver* readers had consistently chosen the Corvette as the best all-round car in the world. Over 80% of Corvette owners surveyed said they would buy another Corvette. Then too, trade in data at the time of the '72 Corvette, placed Corvette repeat ownership at over 90%! More than that, *Car Craft* concluded its August 1971 farewell to the '71½ Corvette LS6 454, by saying, "The Corvette has got to be the world's greatest ego trip as far as American cars are concerned, especially with the 454 emblem. And rightly so."

In 1972, the Corvette LS6 454 was no more! Even the humble Corvette LS5 454 was unavailable in that hot car mecca, and the Corvette's second biggest market after Michigan – California! California had just decided to monitor oxides of nitrogen, and although the '72 Corvette LS5 454 could pass the Golden State's stricter law, Chevrolet passed on certifying the LS5 454 in that state, due to cost. In theory you could buy a '72 Corvette LS5 454 out of state, then bring it into California and have it re-licensed. At least you could back then. Although the big block Corvette still had force akin to the guns of Navarone, even the base Corvette would serve you well. *Autocar*'s Ray Hutton discovered just how well, on a rushed 1000 mile trip from Detroit to Watkins Glen and back to Detroit! The jaunt was all part of covering the 1971 US Formula One Grand Prix.

Chassis upgrades involve Borgeson steering, updated springs/Bilstein sport shocks, and Drag Vette six-link rear suspension. The custom exhaust, with crossover pipe and Flowmaster mufflers, provides a resonant note.
(Courtesy Steven D Francis)

Braking and cooling have been improved with hydro-boost brake booster, all stainless steel brake lines and stainless steel sleeved calipers with O-rings, drilled and slotted rotors, custom radiator, and dual electric fans!
(Courtesy Steven D Francis)

Hutton's test machine, featured in the December 23 1971 issue of *Autocar*, was a Corvette L48 350 automatic roadster, unusually with a/c. Carrying an extra 100lb, and 20 horses less underhood, this was the kind of car most Corvette buyers would purchase during 1975 to 1981. For starters, it made one feel like a celebrity. Upon reaching Watkins Glen, a little girl asked for Hutton's autograph! The journalist assumed the little girl must have reasoned that any guy turning up to the US Grand Prix in a Corvette must have been a gentleman of note. Even though there were many Corvettes around the racing paddock, the reverence in which the Corvette was held, led one to such a conclusion. Fortunately, the Corvette's glamor was backed up by substance on test.

Compared to the hi po '63 Fuelie Corvette *Autocar* had previously tried, this '72 Corvette L48 350 roadster was a no fuss, no muss transport express. Judged similar in size to a XKE, the Corvette featured excellent fiberglass finish, and well done neat black vinyl interior (code no 400) to complement the code 989 War Bonnet Yellow exterior. And the convertible top was a snap to use, "... one of the best we have experienced" said Hutton. The functional front fender vents did contribute to a hot interior, so the factory a/c was welcomed. *Autocar*'s Hutton estimated the Corvette's performance as 0-60mph in 9 seconds, with a 120mph top speed. It was an expectation realized by *Road Test*'s May 1972 report on a similar machine. This Corvette article yielded 0-60mph in 8.9 seconds, and estimated top speed of 115mph, for this mildest of 1972 Corvettes.

It was more than adequate go for any given situation on a public road. What's more, *Autocar* found equally smooth up and down changes from the Corvette's automatic transmission. There was also a useful kickdown facility, for safe overtaking, up to 85mph. Hutton judged the power steering good, with an unboosted feel outside parking chores. Indeed, handling and roadholding were great on smooth roads, the best of any standard American car, allied to excellent brakes. Problems concerned the Corvette's trademark jittery nature on imperfect surfaces, and Firestone Wide Ovals that would nibble road ridges and markings. Radials could do better, but the Corvette's bias ply

F70-15s were an affordable compromise choice of 140mph domestic tire with sidewalls stiff enough to withstand a 454 V8's torque.

In conclusion, *Autocar*'s Hutton said the Corvette's all-around performance gave it "... an honest claim to be a real sports car." In addition, a prediction this car could be a future classic. And in fact, in a June 1985 retrospective article on 1968-77 Corvettes, *Road & Track*'s Peter Bohr noted that 1968-72 Corvettes were already becoming collectible, even though at this stage convertibles were no more valuable than coupes. However, back in 1972, concern existed over the C3 Corvette's future, due to Federal smog and safety law, skyrocketing insurance premiums, not to mention a mid-engine Corvette that, if rumors were to be believed, was 'ready to go'. Ray Hutton mentioned these points, plus additional sports car gossip centered around a new two-seater based on the Vega. Pending impact bumper law was also aired, as a Corvette appearance concern. Of course, what eventuated was the mini GT machine known as the Chevrolet Monza 2+2, that was Vega related, but with said Monza lacking the hoped-for GM rotary engine. The mid-engine Corvette was also a no show, but the C3 Late Model Corvette would return.

Bumpers impact Corvette

THE 1973 CORVETTE was particularly special. It represented the last major reworking of the Corvette, overseen by the sports car's spiritual father, Zora Arkus-Duntov. They were alterations largely dictated by federal law, and contemporary driver tastes; however, the result in Duntov's mind, and that of the press, was the best Corvette yet for real world driving. *Car and Driver* concurred, after putting four '73 Corvettes through their paces. *Road & Track*, which initially regarded the Late Model Corvette as a psychedelic gimmick mobile, conceded that the 1973 Corvette was, "... one of the best Corvettes we've ever driven." Optioned properly, a pleasant and rewarding drive – not that hard to do, given there were fewer options now.

Appearance was the first thing to notice with the '73 Corvette. Chiefly, its rubber front bumper, allied to the usual chrome rear bumper. It was due to Federal Safety Standard (FSS) 215, which was

This 1972 ad let folks know about the Corvette's integrated compliance with federal smog and safety dictates, or reassurance features. *(Courtesy GM Archives)*

motivated by insurance companies that wanted to collect premiums, but not pay out anything when someone had a parking lot snafu. So, the insurance industry leant on the government to force front bumpers to be able to withstand 5mph impacts, and rear bumpers 2½mph impacts, sans damage to safety related car items. Somehow, that implied things like a/c condensers. As a carrot, the insurance companies gave lower premiums to 'bumper ready' cars. However, after a little while, the result was higher premiums, fewer payouts and uglier bumpers for most.

GM cars had a better handle on impact bumpers than most. Pontiac's Endura nose section was bash resistant, and, concerning Corvette, there were studies done of New York taxis fitted with special bumpers as a pre trial. On '73 Corvette, the earlier separate cast vent grille/chrome bumper complex was replaced by a flexible, molded urethane cover, over steel bumper bar and two ductile steel draw bolts. On 5mph impacts, both the bumper and bolts

would have to be replaced, but that was all. It was a compromise solution, considering the extra weight, added Corvette length, repair cost and law. To have something needing no replacement parts would have made Corvette longer, heavier and probably as ugly as many new cars coming along. As it was, length increased marginally to 184.7in, and visually the Plastic Fantastic still turned heads, in a good way.

New Corvette front fender moldings made for new, cleaner, side vent apertures. What you couldn't see were the new federally mandated side door guard beams. Such bars ran from the door hinges to the locking plates, and tied up the Corvette's underlying birdcage steel frame structure. More rigidity, less shake, rattle and roll, thank you very much! Also invisible were new style body to chassis mounts, and sound deadening material virtually from nose to tail. The Corvette body was no longer rigidly mounted to a steel frame.

1973 Corvettes sported rubber body mounts encased within a steel sleeve, the idea being to permit vertical shock absorption, while resisting lateral twisting forces. Ford had gone back to separate chassis construction on its '72 MY intermediate sized cars. In 1974's episode of *Car and Track*, host Bud Lindemann remarked on the great amount of body movement on rubber mounts, when the show's test '74 Mercury Cougar XR7 made its way through the pylon course. Hence the '73 Corvette's steel sleeves. The Corvette went to flexible chassis mounts for 1973, because that was the year Corvette finally switched to radial tires. Something the domestic auto industry had been tardy in doing. With radials came a need for more compliance in the chassis. Previously, bias ply tire construction had been a shock absorbing element.

Zora Arkus-Duntov, and top GM management, had been anti radials, since such tires tended to be noisy, increase braking distances, and reduce cornering power. However, ZAK and others

Complementing the LT1 350 option, this 1972 Corvette LS5 454 four-speed coupe represented the other Corvette high performance avenue in '72 MY. *(Courtesy RK Motors)*

acknowledged radial tire advantages, such as increased tire life, improved straight line stability, and superior wet weather grip. The dilemma didn't exist for European cars, because they had usually been designed for radials from the late '50s. However, given the current Corvette's chassis dated back to 1963, it and other US cars had to be adapted to radial tires. Plus, economically, US tire makers no longer wanted to do special tires just for Corvette.

The Pantera, Corvette's contemporary nemesis, had Goodyear Arriva bias belted rubber, sized C60

front and H60 rearwards. They were custom-made for Lincoln-Mercury's mid-engine captive import. However, that quasi Italo-American V8 hybrid was about to get back on the boat for Italy, for the close of '74 MY. Thinking of getting an affordable, domestic made, steel belted radial tire for the foreseeable future, Corvette and other GM sporty rides went to GR70-15s. For less exalted machinery, that oftentimes implied GM related Uniroyal tires. For Corvette, it was Firestone or Goodyear. The switch dropped the Corvette's tire speed rating from 140mph to 120mph for 1973, and lateral grip

The 221lb weight penalty over the base L48 350 V8 was compensated by SAE net figures of 270bhp at four grand and 390lb/ft at 3200rpm. More than enough to smoke the F70-15s out of the hole, onto a low 14s ¼-mile! *(Courtesy RK Motors)*

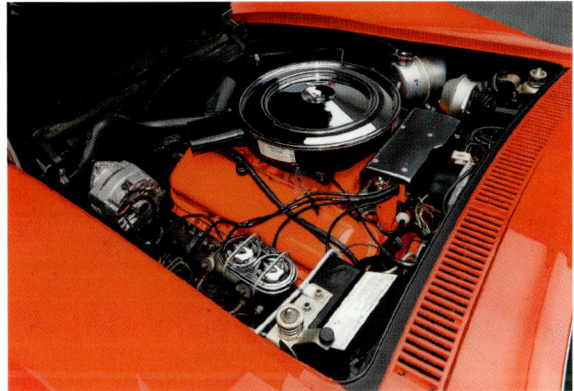

wasn't what it was. Zora Arkus-Duntov wasn't happy, but desirable Michelin XWX radials were too pricy and noisy. Duntov was a realist. Henry Ford II, and the Ford family in general, were initially anti Michelin, due to the French connection alone!

When it came to PR photos of the '73 Corvette, or magazine tests, the latest Corvette rode on handsome 15 x 8in aluminum wheels, produced by Californian concern American Racing Equipment, with casting number 329381, and recessed center area lugnuts, painted black. Their style was nearly identical to those alloys seen on the 1970 New York Auto Show star mid-engine Corvette XP-882 prototype. However, the '73 Corvette had eight slots, not the prototype's 10 slots. On '73 Corvette, such aluminum rims brought a 35lb weight saving, counteracting the nameplate's 100lb '73 MY increase. They were also a boon for handling, given the reduced unsprung weight.

When it came to reality, the 175 buck RPO YJ8 aluminum wheels didn't eventuate, beyond four '73 Corvettes sold. The official reason was rim porosity. Component supplier American Racing Equipment had difficulty meeting Chevrolet's quality requirement. Apparently 800 sets were made, with the majority recalled due to that porosity problem. Based on '60s Mid-Year Corvette experience Zora Arkus-Duntov was confident such alloys would be resistant to salt used on winter roads, but the porosity was something else. Wait for 1976 model year for such optional YJ8 alloys to resurface. By then it was a set of four aluminum rims, with a steel spare to save cost, in inflationary times.

Contrary to contemporary fashion, white stripe tires got the RPO upper hand, in 1973 Corvette land. The cheaper $32 QRM GR70-15 white stripe steel belted tires outsold the QRZ GR70-15 white letter steel belted tires, costing 45 bucks extra. It was 19,903 '73 Corvette customers versus 4541 buyers for such respective tire choices. The reason being that white letter radials were only available from mid '73 model year.

The exterior color is 973 Mille Miglia Red, chosen by 2478 Corvette buyers in 1972. Inside it was a tale of code 400 Black Vinyl. A base '72 Corvette coupe came in at $5533 base sticker. *(Courtesy RK Motors)*

The '73 Corvette was also a quieter place to be, with more attention paid to sound deadening material. There was an underhood pad, thicker carpeting, and heavier mats for under the dashboard, console and rear quarter areas. An asphalt-based spray type insulation was applied to the Corvette's floor, and most other interior panel surfaces. So the '73 Corvette ads that claimed a 40% noise reduction were probably true.

Based on *Car and Driver*'s experiences, a 1971 Corvette LT1 350 four-speed registered 81 decibels at a 70mph cruise, versus 79dBA for a comparable '73 Corvette L82 350. The new Corvette LS4 454 automatic, with 3.08 rear gears, led the way with a mere 77 decibels. This was all true, unless one tromped the gas pedal, then all bets were off! It

This numbers-matching '72 Corvette LS5 454's Muncie M21 HD close ratio four-speed came with a dual disc clutch, with the gearbox made on March 7 1972. The coupe was completed at St Louis on May 16 1972. The first two VIN entries '1Z', indicate Chevrolet and Corvette respectively. *(Courtesy RK Motors)*

Since the '72 MY switch to net power ratings, only the engine size/torque/comp ratio appeared on the console plaque. *(Courtesy RK Motors)*

was because '73 Corvettes came with cowl cold air induction that, according to Zora Arkus-Duntov, was worth a whole second in zero to sixty action for a base '73 Corvette L48 350. Along the lines of the earlier ZL2 cold air hood option, there was a high pressure area at the base of the windshield, causing air to shoot forward. On the '73 Corvette, your motor was inhaling warm underhood air to get the engine off choke sooner for smog. However, put your foot to the floor, and a solenoid operated valve, in a leading edge hoodscoop, admitted cold air at the windshield's base.

According to *Road & Track*, its '71 Corvette LT1 350 registered 94dBA at wide open throttle, in 1st gear. However, its '73 Corvette L82 350 four-speed managed a full, even 100dBA, and

that's frightening! Suffice it to say, as a high performance machine, the Corvette was still trying in increasingly somber times. And the Corvette still had concealed wipers, but courtesy of a simpler, lighter trench and diecast aluminum flap at the windshield's base. The problematic powered flap of the 1968-72 era had been deep-sixed, along with its troublesome mechanical nature, and slow operation. A '73 Corvette saved 10lb in this area!

Zora Arkus-Duntov exerted an influence on the Corvette rarely seen in the modern world. He decided if you needed something, or not. In his view, you didn't need a removable back window on Corvette. The 1973 Corvette had a fixed backlight because, as Duntov said, "We know what is best for them." He then elucidated, "At 140mph, with the roof panels off and the side windows up, the air in the cockpit is still. The wind goes right over the top. Remove the rear window and you get a buffeting backdraft."

ZAK also wielded his Corvette will over the sports car's performance specification. Previously you had to jump through hoops to obtain the Corvette's F41 sports suspension, since it was very firm and track suited. In 1970-72, F41 was part of the ZR1 and ZR2 special purpose engine packages. For 1972, that implied only the $1010 RPO ZR1 ensemble, taken up by a mere 20 Corvette buyers. However, for 1973 RPO ZR1 gave way to the Z07 off-road suspension and brake package. The latter cost $369, and was optioned by 45 '73 Corvette devotees. Because the 1973 Corvette was a softer, more compliant beast, the Plastic Fantastic's HD suspension was more readily available, with a little sacrifice.

RPO Z07 implied one of the Corvette's hi po motors, the L82 350 or LS4 454, close ratio M21 four-speed, and no a/c! In return for the loot and standard sweat, one received a track-oriented brake vacuum booster, stiffer calipers and more securely retained front brake pads, with all four

By 1972, the Corvette's 1968-72 era F70-15s were bias belted. Normally, however, small block cars rode on Firestones, with big block cars on Goodyears. This coupe's optional Delco AM/FM radio (RPO U69) was chosen by 19,480 '72 Corvette buyers, and cost $178. *(Courtesy RK Motors)*

brake pads being made of more fade resistant material. That was the stopping part of Z07, the F41 HD suspension components brought a bigger front swaybar, stiffer springs, with front and rear springing stiffer by a respective 70% and 55%, and high control shock absorbers, permitting roll rates of 82% up at the back and 41% frontwards, to generate reduced understeer.

Back to reality, the average Corvette was becoming more GT cruiser. Of the 30,464 1973

Corvettes sold, 17,927 came with the M40 GM THM 400 automatic NCO. The M21 four-speed was also a NCO. 21,578 Corvette buyers went for the 452 buck C60 a/c, with 14,024 splashing out $83 for A31 power windows, not to mention 27,872 buying the N40 power steering at $113, and 17,949 going for the 82 buck N37 tilt-telescopic steering column. Plus, if you optioned all the creature features, your Corvette's weight would increase, along with your monthly payments. Proving that Corvette

141

Like this '72 Corvette ad said, you got a lot of functional equipment standard with Corvette. Other stock domestic sporty cars tended to be all hat and no cattle. *(Courtesy GM Archives)*

20,496 1972 Corvette coupes, versus 6508 convertibles, showed T-tops provided enough fresh air for most. Only 3593 folks paid 63 bucks for the P02 deluxe wheel covers shown. *(Courtesy GM Archives)*

was still a fine tuned machine, speedo and tach needles moved in unison, in top gear! The Corvette engineers also arranged for two special engine options in 1973.

Beyond the base L48 350, 250 bones afforded one the LS4 454 Mark IV big block V8 underhood, and now all Corvettes had the same hood. The motor in question was the new replacement for the departed LS5 454. The LS4 had 8.25:1 CR, and 275bhp at 4400rpm, plus a huge 395lb/ft at only 2800rpm. Redline was a limbo low 5500rpm. Like the outgoing LS5 454, the new LS4 454 had a single Rochester Q-jet carb, but five more horses. That said, the final manifestation of the Mark IV big blocks wasn't as quick as the LS5 454 motorvated Corvettes. It was a case of high 14s, not low 14s in the 1320ft sprint. The LS4 454's tractable nature, saw it favored by Zora Arkus-Duntov and Team

Corvette engineers over the 350 V8s, on the basis of bountiful torque.

Revealing the LS4 454's flat torque curve, *Car and Driver*'s December 1973 test report showed little or no discernible difference in specifying manual or automatic transmission. 0-40mph, 0-60mph and 0-80mph took the same number of seconds, a respective trio of 3.5, 6.4 and 10 seconds flat. Given the tall 2.20 ratio 1st of the close ratio Muncie four-speed, and 3.55 rear end, manual transmission didn't worry the GM THM 400 slushbox. In 0-100mph, the manual transmission Corvette was one whole second tardier, at 17 seconds, but marginally beat out the slushbox Corvette in the ¼-mile, with a 14.6 second pass at 95.7mph, versus 14.7 seconds at 97.2mph. The four-speed coupe did 122mph at redline in top, *C/D* estimated 135mph for the Corvette LS4 454 automatic.

C/D's Corvette 454 with automatic was a loaded, luxo leviathan. It had a/c, Tilt-Tele wheel, fast glass and much more, so weighed 3742lb, against the 3585lb lithe Corvette LS4 454 four-speed sampled. Price of the no shift Corvette, which included the 'custom interior', ran to $7097.50, not cheap! That said, your alternative was the pricier L82 350 powered version, with RPO L82 asking $299 extra, for only 250 ponies. The L82 350 was like an hydraulic lifter version of the earlier LT1 350, which meant you could have a/c. The new L82 350 was five horses down on the 1972 255bhp LT1 350, but still contained forged pistons, forged crankshaft, big valve heads, four-bolt mains and duals. And as with the LT1 350, the Corvette and 1973-74 Camaro Z28 shared the L82 350 V8. However, the former carried five more horses on paper, befitting its exalted Bow Tie position.

Yes, the Camaro Z28 LT1 350 could have an automatic, whereas the equivalent engined Corvette could not. Now, the L82 350 powered Corvettes and Camaro Z28s could both enjoy shiftless driving. Although an hydraulic lifter motor, the L82 350 had a similar character to the previous LT1 350. That is, it needed to be revved, and needed a tight rear end ratio, in this case 3.70. With max power arriving at 5200rpm, and 285lb/ft at four grand, the L82 350 was pokey. The THM 400 automatic was your friend, by the torque amplifying nature of the torque converter it masked a low end gap, exacerbated by the CR M21 four-speed. Earlier, you could order rear gears tighter than 3.70, but for now, *C/D*'s '73 Corvette L82 350 four-speed with a/c and 3.70 final drive ratio, with curb weight of 3540lb, did a 15.1 second ¼-mile at 95.4mph.

Respecting the redline saw *Car and Driver* reach 117mph in its '73 Corvette L82 350 four-speed. However, the L82 350's quality internals promised a 7000rpm potential like the LT1 350, except the hydraulic lifter nature brought up the dreaded issue of valve float. Nevertheless, the L82 350 was exotic on the inside and outside. The L48 350 had engine paint on its valve covers, whereas the L82 350 sported chrome ribbed covers, which get retrofitted to a lot of L48 350s, because they look good.

In June 1985, *Road & Track*'s Peter Bohr reviewed the 1973-77 Corvette era, saying the cars represented refined daily cruisers. The change of pace was also identified in the journal's June 1973 issue, where a Corvette L82 350 four-speed was mistakenly referred to as being LT1 350 powered. Its comparison field was as follows:

Federal law made the 1973 Corvette feature front 5mph and rear 2½mph bumpers. On the fun front, cold air induction was standard on all '73 Corvettes. *(Courtesy Elizabeth Cranswick)*

Regardless of the Firestone or Goodyear GR70-15s fitted (Firestone in this case), domestic sourced radials were compromising Corvette's performance, in braking and lateral grip. *R&T*'s experience confirmed Zora Arkus-Duntov's test of the latest Corvette on the GM skid pad. Here, Corvette's lateral g reading fell from 0.85g, to around where *R&T* wound up. However, wet pavement adhesion tests displayed an improvement with radials. Ride comfort also benefitted. The 1973 Corvette also lived up to GM's Numero Uno position when it came to smog tuning drivability.

A leaner Rochester Q-jet, retarded ignition timing, and smog pump, together produced a Corvette that was as easy to drive as in past years. *R&T* acknowledged the smog pump's help. Similarly, *Road Test*'s Chuck Koch noted in June 1973 that his test Corvette LS4 454 four-speed showed no signs of dieseling, or running on, which was a common problem at the time. On the negative side, GM's lap and shoulder belts were still separate, although the latter portion did work on an inertia reel. GM's nut on the retractable shoulder

Model	Price ($)	0-60mph	¼-mile (secs)	Lateral g	dBA 70mph	mpg	80-0mph (ft)	Brake fade %
'73 Corvette L82 350 4sp	5635	7.2	15.5	0.726	78	14.5	314	40
Datsun 240Z	4500	Approx 8.7	17.1	0.723	N/A	21	287	10
Porsche 911E Targa	10,025	6.6	15.4	0.732	78	18.6	273	0
DeTomaso Pantera	9995	7.6	15.6	0.816	80	10.5	256	25

Corvette started as a roadster, but by the time of the '73 MY car shown, only 4943 chose a ragtop out of 30,464 Corvettes sold. It was the final year for chrome rear bumpers, and the P02 Deluxe Wheel Cover option, chosen by just 1739 '73 Corvette buyers. *(Courtesy National Corvette Museum)*

belt buckle tended to damage the Corvette's sill plate.

$5398.50 got one a '73 Corvette convertible with wide ratio four-speed, attached to the 190 horse L48 350. $5561.50 took things to T-tops. In total, 30,464 1973 Corvettes were sold, although VINs went to 34464, the 4000 serial numbers between 24001 and 28000 were not used. The family Impala continued its reign as the nation's best selling car: over 10 million sold, with more than 14 years as a sales leader. Sporty domestic interest was moving away from pony cars to the Monte Carlo type of personal intermediate machine. Meanwhile, the Japanese were overtaking VW and its Beetle in

the subcompact wars, but no matter. Corvette continued as many people's dream car, and America's only sports car.

The last year of leaded

THERE WERE FOUR visual signs to look for concerning the '74 Corvette. One of which was invisible. Most apparent was the federally mandated 5mph impact rear bumper, directed by FSS 208. As per the front of the car, Corvette and other '74 MY cars had to be able to withstand a 5mph rear whack, sans damage to safety related items. So the insurance folk were happy. This

Zora Arkus-Duntov considered the 1973 Corvette to be the best Corvette yet. *Car and Driver* and *Road & Track* magazines agreed. Definite engineering improvements made the Corvette better in real world driving. *(Courtesy GM Archives)*

QRZ GR70-15 white letter steel belted radials were promised for mid-'73 MY. The YJ8 alloy rims only made it onto four cars! So, most '73 Corvettes had the QRM GR70-15 white stripe steel belted radials, covering Rally rims, as shown. *(Courtesy GM Archives)*

involved a vertically split, urethane end cap, concealing an aluminum bumper bar. Having the mold in two halves was due to a manufacturing limitation that would be overcome for 1975 model year. The vertical split is a way to tell your Corvette is a 1974 edition! There was also a wide spaced Corvette tailscript.

While still perusing the rear, one would also notice that the Corvette's tailpipes no longer exited through the rear valence panel: they now alighted from beneath. Finally, the key lock arming the Corvette's standard alarm system was moved from the rear deck, to the driver's side front fender. Then came the change you couldn't see: no optional wheels or wheel covers in 1974 model year! The YJ8 alloys promised for '73 MY were listed as a 1974 model year RPO early on, but never came.

Plus, with no decorative wheel covers, it all implied 15 x 8in Rally rims and trim rings, center chrome cap and GR70-15s were all she wrote! Zora Arkus-Duntov favored this choice, on cost and weight saving grounds anyway.

Further concealed refinements involved a more durable THM 400 automatic coded M40 (a NCO selected by 25,146 Corvette fans), a more efficient radiator in low speed driving, magnets for the power steering pump to attract debris, and exhaust resonators for improved sound. Power steering (RPO N41 – $117) was chosen by 35,944 '74 Corvette patrons, or virtually everyone! Like an import, Corvette focused on substance, rather than year to year style changes. *Motor Trend*'s September 1973 Corvette vs Pantera Flat-Out American Classic proved Corvette's true grit. Conducted at Ontario Motor Speedway, with Zora Arkus-Duntov present in his own Corvette coupe, the exercise showed how fast America's best were in 1973-74.

It was a qualified 'were', because MT's Jim Brokaw exaggerated the Pantera's 'Americanness', by calling the Italian import a 'Ford Pantera' – the automotive equivalent to a naturalized Mario Andretti! Actions speak louder than words, and Alejandro DeTomaso would part ways with Henry Ford at the close of 1974 model year, although the Argentinian would retain Ford V8 power for said mid-engine Pantera. Naturally, the Corvette would still officially be with the North American buyer for 1975 model year, and always proved more affordable and reliable than that Pantera. Elvis shot his car for a reason!

For now, at Ontario Motor Speedway, a 1973 Pantera and Corvette managed a respective 129.68mph and 126.76mph. However, Duntov pushed the latter to 129.87mph, upholding Bow Tie honor! Timing equipment was by Chrondek, and the 1973 Corvette was a code 976 Mille Miglia Red LS4 454 V8 automatic with stock 3.08 rear gears, running on Firestone steel radials, sized the usual GR70-15 with white stripe decoration. Rims on this Corvette, and code 922 Medium Blue prototype 1973/74 Corvette on hand, Duntov's own car, were the promised YJ8 alloys. Rumors were abound concerning the two-seater Vega-related Chevrolet sports car, which turned out to be the '75 Monza. However, whether it was this machine, or the 'here today, rust tomorrow' all-steel Pantera, Corvette was a practical production reality. Unlike the Pantera, you could fit in a Corvette, even if you had the audacity to be over 5ft 10in! There was also the issue of torque: the Pantera didn't have any.

On paper the Pantera's Cleveland 351 V8 made 266 horse at 5400rpm and 301lb/ft at 3600rpm. The LS4 Corvette had 275bhp at 4400rpm and 395lb/ft at 2800rpm in 1973. Hence the respective 4.22 versus 3.08 rear gears in the MT encounter. However, as *Hot Rod* discovered in June 1973, the Cleveland cam was dead below 2500rpm. Pantera's 3580lb played Corvette's 3560lb. So, Pantera by Ghia, as *Hot Rod* called it, was pricey and heavy. The import's driving character, with five-speed only ZF transaxle, made it spiritually closer to Corvettes with the L82 350 and four-speed. Yes, the Pantera was half the price of comparable Italian mid-engine exotica, you could obtain this captive import from Lincoln-Mercury, and, being mid-engine, the Pantera could generate 0.85g in cornering. However, the Corvette had that much grip on ye olde bias belted rubber, and even with LS4 454 mill, it was only 60% of the Pantera's price. Of course, the Pantera was never a commercial threat to the Corvette. What's more, in 1973 a Corvette designer was moved to say, "No matter how much we stumble, no matter how many mistakes we might

Like the contemporary VW Super Beetle, so many were the C3 Corvette's evolutionary changes that they were starting to show! Witness the vertically split urethane, rear 5mph bumper end cap.
(Courtesy GM Archives)

make, we just can't seem to help the Pantera."

On test at Ontario Motor Speedway, Zora Arkus-Duntov's blue hued '73/74 Corvette prototype was a wild card. *Motor Trend* editor Eric Dahlquist took the machine to 141.06mph. This Corvette proto was a 1974 coupe, dressed in 1973-style, chrome rear bumper, fiberglass. It was LS4 powered, but rode on Firestone 6.20/11.30-15s, with raised white letters (RWL) on what was really sports racing rubber. Also hiding under the fiberglass was Duntov's new for '74 MY RPO FE7 Gymkhana suspension. FE7 only cost seven bucks, and was fitted to 1905 '74 Corvettes. The suspension pack was aimed at the autocrosser, and tried to put the sports car back in Corvette, after the inevitable annual weight gains brought by federal safety mandates. FE7's genesis, came from Corvette's former F41 HD suspension,

THE INTERIOR

If the outside of Corvette is exciting, the inside is fabulous. There are warm courtesy lights when you open either door. Lavish color-keyed deep-twist carpeting. Rich textured vinyl seat trim. And the seats themselves . . . deep-pleated and saddle-stitched for that special Corvette look and feeling . . . with deep foam for comfort . . . contoured for the support you want on long trips. They're even canted at the edges to keep you firmly positioned behind the wheel, during hard cornering.

Tipping either seat back forward gives you access to the carpeted and surprisingly roomy luggage space. Two under-the-floor compartments (one lighted and lockable) provide concealed storage for cameras and other valuables. A third gives access to the battery.

Two people, going anywhere, never had it so good.

INSTRUMENTS & CONTROLS

The real soul of the Corvette interior comes on when you start up and settle back.

Everything you want to see is right in view. Tachometer and speedometer-trip odometer are over the steering column, big and prominent. Your auxiliary instruments (fuel, temperature, sweep-second-hand clock, oil pressure and ammeter, plus seat belt, door ajar and headlight door warning lights) are just to the right, over the console. This year, we also widened the rearview mirror to a full 10 inches to give you a broader view astern.

Corvette controls are practically an extension of your arms and legs. The sports-type wheel is well forward for superb steering control. The center console puts the shift selector right under your palm (with the hand brake directly behind). Heater-ventilation controls, lighter and ashtray are right at your fingertips. Even the brake and accelerator are positioned so you can do a crisp and credible heel-and-toe downshift.

You might say your Corvette interior is as personal and as practical as a pair of driving gloves.

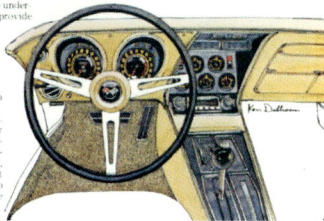

Corvette coupes had three point seatbelts,
but roadsters still came with lap belts in 1974.
That year, Federally mandated Interlock was the
bane of many a motorist, until mid model year.
(Courtesy GM Archives)

which itself arose from the '63 Corvette's gentleman racer Z06 package.

Yes, Corvette didn't forget about the gentleman racer. F41 was still incorporated within the $400 Z07 off-road suspension and brake package that had been introduced in 1973, and was optioned by 47 1974 Corvette purchasers. The 1973 Corvette's tires were only rated at 120mph, and ZAK was pushing the '73 Corvette at nigh on 130mph. DANGER! That said, in the wake of the 1973/74 fuel crisis, and ensuing 55mph national speed limit, top speed was fast becoming academic. You could say OPEC's decision to quadruple oil prices overnight, bringing the fuel crisis, was in response to Western support for Israel in the 1973 Yom Kippur War. However, there was also the failure of OPEC and 17 Western oil companies to reach agreement on oil price increases. The oil producers weren't going to sell off their resources cheaply anymore. The sports car world was adversely affected by outside events. Corvette, Jensen, etc, needed petroleum distillate.

By Christmas 2018, under the Trump administration, America became a net oil exporter. However, back when OPEC cut production in 1973/74, America and many other countries were oil dependent, leading to an immediate worsening in their trade balance. So in came gas lines, rationing and blanket speed limits. Even 50mph on the West German autobahn! America introduced a 55mph national speed limit. However, while other countries dropped their temporary speed limits, once the price of oil stabilized, America kept its speed limit. Apart from saving gas, it also seemed to save lives. That said, many were displeased.

The state of Nevada used to be limitless, but agreed to the 55mph limit so the state could keep receiving federal highway assistance funds. In 1975 a disgruntled owner of a 1974 Lotus Europa Special, another two-seater fiberglass sports car, wrote to *Road & Track*. The Lotus owner noted you weren't likely to get a speeding ticket out in the desert. He had driven from Vegas to Zion and back on a Sunday, at a constant 90mph, averaging 32mpg. He felt if someone drove an 11mpg behemoth, they should drive 55mph, but perhaps in light of his thrifty Lotus, he might be permitted to go 75mph? [81]

The gas crunch seemed to contribute to buyers missing out on a great Corvette option, the $250 RPO LS4 454 V8. In 1973, 4412 buyers went LS4 454's way. 5710 plumped for the pricier $299 L82 350. In 1974, option prices remained the same, but respective sales were 3494 and 6690. Even before the fuel crisis, there was a perception that all big motors were thirsty. Insurance and inflation were also swaying buyers towards small block V8s. What's more, the LS4 454 wasn't California smog legal, and the Golden State was a key Corvette market. There was also the idea of a lighter engine bringing better handling, via improved weight distribution.

The fuel economy theory wasn't always justified. In February 1974, *Road Test*'s John Ethridge said gas mileage was 'even-Steven' between a '74 Corvette LS4 454 and its L82 350 counterpart,

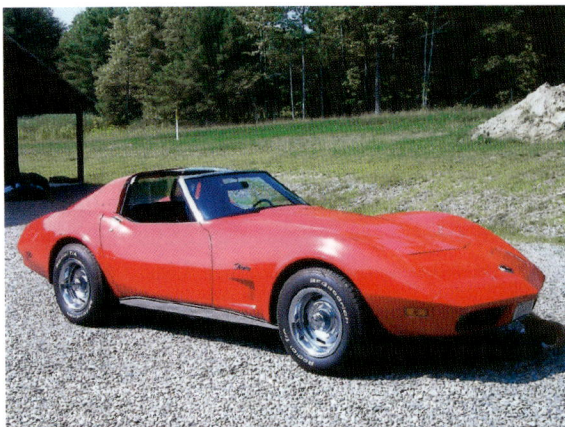

You are looking at the most popular '74 Corvette: an automatic L48 350 motorvated coupe, with raised white letter radials! *(Courtesy Robert Spinello)*

The 974 Medium Red shown joined the existing 976 Mille Miglia Red as your rouge range for '74 MY. The 5mph rear urethane end cap quickly became accepted in Corvette land. *(Courtesy Robert Spinello)*

comparing four-speeds with their respective 3.08 and 3.55 rear gears. Independent testing backed up this claim, with the easier going LS4 454 being more frugal in real world driving. More so than even the L48 350, which most Corvette buyers settled on. By the time *Road Test*'s report went to press, Chevrolet had already announced that there would be no big block for 1975. So, not even a last chance to get a Corvette with Rat Motor Mark IV V8 swayed the public! The LS4 454 flunked its 1975 smog test. Chevrolet could have got it to pass, but weren't going to the trouble nor the expense of a re-test, concerning the EPA's 50,000 mile smog certification process. This implied that Corvette would fall into line with fellow domestics and imports. Fewer powertrain choices, since each carried a certification cost. In any case, the LS4 454 was one helluva good buy, and the great unwashed didn't even realize it.

One important person did know, Zora Arkus-Duntov! In June 1977, he revealed to *Road & Track* that although he had affection towards past Fuelie Corvettes, his present partner in crime was a '74 Corvette LS4 454 automatic coupe, with 2.72 rear gears, or as ZAK put it, "… it's a very nice touring car." The fact the 1974 Corvette LS4 454 came with 3.08 rear gears, and five fewer horses versus 1973, and that increasingly popular L48 350 with five more horses for '74 MY, was of little concern to those in the know.

The crowd-pleasing L48 350 made 195bhp at 4400rpm and 275lb/ft at 2800rpm. In a word, it was tractable. This powerplant plus THM 400 slushbox implied a 3.08 diff ratio, 3.36 if the stock four-speed was accepted. Corvettes with L82 350 came with a steeper 3.55 ratio. In theory, 1974 LS4 454 implied just the 3.08 axle ratio. It was stated in press releases that power brakes would be standard on the '74 Corvette, but 33,306 '74 Corvette patrons ponied up the 46 buck surcharge for J50 power brakes, out of 37,502 Corvettes sold that model year. A mini logic sequence computer, or early harbinger of Orwell's *1984* Big Brother, wouldn't permit your new car to start, unless a particular order was followed when buckling up. The Interlock device proved unreliable and politically unpopular, so was dropped during 1974 model year.

Still America's only sports car

MOST ENTHUSIAST AND magazine interest, seemed concerned with Corvette's optional L82 350 V8. So, that's what *Road & Track* evaluated in its ragtop group test, featured in the journal's 1975 'Five Open Exotics' article, published in that year's *Sports & GT Cars* annual. It was a combined $64,012 of four-wheeled hedonism, including: $6869 Corvette convertible L82 350 four-speed, $15,225 Ferrari Dino GTS, $8475 Jaguar XKE V12 ragtop,

In the C3 Corvette ragtop's penultimate year, this 1974 roadster added $250 LS4 454 and $467 C60 a/c to the convertible's $5765 base sticker. *(Courtesy Smoky Mountain Traders)*

$15,450 Mercedes 450SL and $10,800 Porsche 911 Targa Sportomatic. *R&T* had done a similar evaluation in June 1969, with two differences: the Ferrari was absent, and all equivalent models had roofs in 1969.

Wise was the person that bought the Dino over the Benz back then, concerning future collector value. Beyond that, the *R&T* report showed that as in previous years, the Corvette was the sole US representative in the true sports car field, and that there were still advantages in going domestic. In design, Corvette and Dino showed two different ways to do a separate chassis. The former with ladder frame construction, combined with

unstressed fiberglass panels, the latter employing a tubular steel frame, and stressed steel panels. Indeed, the new Citroën CX utilized a separate chassis, made up of front and rear subframes, two longeron members and 16 flexible attachment points. The current *Road & Track* article had remarked that the Corvette and Jag needed 6000 mile chassis lubrication, but Ferrari called for a chassis lube every 3000 miles!

Drivability was a GM and Corvette forte, showing a 'designed for American smog and safety law' approach. The L82 350 pulled strongly to the 6500rpm redline, and displayed tractability along with no surge or stumbling. That said, in the

The Corvette's light, easy shifting Muncie four-speed was welcome, the federally mandated, seatbelt enforcing Interlock, less so.
(Courtesy Smoky Mountain Traders)

February 1974 issue of *Road Test*, John Ethridge noticed that the L82 350 fitted to the journal's '74 four-speed Corvette coupe, had an idle that jumped 300rpm in fourth. TCS (Transmission Controlled Spark) implied no spark advance in the lower gears. However, as per other domestics, wide open throttle acceleration should have been unaffected, in theory.

The Dino had some difficulty starting in 30°F New England weather, plus a smog pump related backfire or two, post shut down. However, those were the Dino's only smog gear issues. In spite of Porsche flat sixes, and Porsches as a rule, being okay on low octane juice and being smog compliant, the 911 on test was a cantankerous cold starter.

The Jag had lost some punch, nine horses, since its US V12 debut, falling from 9 to 7.8:1 CR. While the 250 horse Corvette mill was 50 state legal in 1974, the Mercedes 450SL was 10 horses down in the Golden State. In terms of impact bumpers, Corvette and Porsche were handsome. However, Daimler-Benz used diving boards. Mercedes said with only 12% of its production going to America, the ugly result would have to be the sum of its meagre efforts. This was in spite of *Road & Track* styling analysis, showing more attractive proposals for the MB W116 S class sedan. The Ferrari was pretty, but was, in truth, a 1973 car legally. All remaining test examples were '74 MY machines. The Dino's 308 GT4 replacement would have Italian diving boards!

As ever, the Jag XKE was sterling value for money, but also as ever, the Corvette undercut the British roadster. Respective option prices, Corvette versus Ferrari, also placed the Chevrolet sports car in the affordable camp. Observing power windows, a/c and leather interior for Corvette vs Dino, involved: $86, $467 and $145 vs $270, $770 and $450. However, although one would expect Corvette fast glass and a/c to be more effective, Maranello cowhide was probably superior. And, although not all Chevrolet dealers were willing or able, to deal with the Corvette, GM's Plastic Fantastic certainly beat out the high class European import crowd when it came to service network coverage. Indeed, dealers for imports were concentrated in the major sales areas, located on the East and West coasts.

Quality and reliability weren't always the same thing, and could be surprising. As Peter Klutt, host of TV's *Dream Car Garage,* said when trying a similar Dino V6, the Ferrari wasn't your fragile Italian. It was pricy to fix, but mechanicals were durable, as was construction. In *R&T*'s 1975 report, the Dino was even more bodily solid than the Mercedes! The latter exhibited some creaks on the bumpy Lime Rock test track, sans hardtop. As for the test's Corvette roadster, solidity was much better on the Corvette coupe. What's more, the

The chrome valve covers and 390 horse air cleaner decal hail from the 1970 high comp LS5 454 V8. The LS4 454 mill put out 270 net horses in 1974. This roadster was rare, in coming with factory air – a/c that is! *(Courtesy Smoky Mountain Traders)*

journal said steer clear of the Gymkhana option, if you wished to retain your fillings!

John Ethridge's February '74 *Road Test* report, echoed *R&T*'s sentiment. He said *Road Test*'s coupe leaked not a drop when run through an automatic car wash. T-top panel sealing surfaces were liberally coated with silicone grease. The journal urged Corvette coupe owners to re-apply such grease annually. As for *R&T*'s Corvette ragtop, quality control wasn't good. The doors didn't fit right, panel gaps were wide, and the convertible's rear deck cover panel kept popping open. The Benz was almost incredibly well put together. That said, *R&T* had doubts that Mercedes cars were as reliable as they once were. This sentiment was confirmed by the journal's owner surveys. There were three problem areas in its 1970 survey of the Pagoda roof SL, but nine problem areas were revealed in its August 1977 Mercedes 450 series survey. The Porsche 911

Sportomatic wasn't that well constructed, and neither was the Jag.

In true British Leyland tradition, the XKE's passenger seat fell out and hood latches were loose. As for reliability, *Road & Track* made the understatement of the century concerning Jaguar's record, "… as everyone must know by now, [it] is not enviable." Based on *R&T* surveys, the Jaguar gave owners a lot more problems than average. Porsche and Ferrari were better, and Mercedes much better than average. When it came to the open top aspect, the Dino sealed well, but had a loud engine. The Jaguar sealed poorly, but had a quiet engine. The

This numbers-matching '74 Corvette 454 four-speed convertible was a 15 second flat machine in the ¼-mile. The Rally rims and trim rings were your only choice in 1974 Corvette land. *(Courtesy Smoky Mountain Traders)*

Mercedes hardtop sealed better than most sedans, and the 911 was a class act too. However, regardless of hard or soft top, the Corvette sealed poorly, had a lot of wind noise, and a loud motor.

Corvette and Benz soft tops were easy to use, beautifully designed, and lived under a hinged panel. The Jag's top was just a little harder to use. It was a two man job, to get the hardtop on either the Benz or Corvette. The latter's hardtop was secured by bolts at five locations. An easier task accomplished with ratchet/sockets than wrenches, but no walk in the park either way. When it came to acceleration and speed, the former favored the Corvette, the latter was the domain of the Ferrari and Jag. In truth, the Corvette was geared for acceleration, all three cars were equally swift. They also relied on carburetion, with respective single Rochester Q-jet, triple Weber 40 DCNs and quad Zenith-Stromberg 175 CD2SEs. The fuel injected West Germans were slower; the Mercedes much slower. Porsche went mechanical Bosch K-jet, and Benz electronic Bosch D-jet.

Handling honors went to the Dino, Benz came second and Porsche third. Underlining admiration for the mid-engine format, the Ferrari was in the 0.85g skid pad league, where the Corvette used to live on bias ply rubber. Now, Corvette was with the other conventional cars, in the 0.75g vicinity. The Plastic Fantastic was still the consummate smooth road handler, and was only second to the Dino in slalom speed. *Road & Track* felt that with so much L82 350 power on tap, the roadster's quick steering was welcome to correct oversteer. However, such steering lacked feel. Last in handling was the poor Jag. The XKE displayed understeer, slow, light steering sans feel. Then too, although smog equipment had diluted the V12 motor, there was still some torque steer!

Corvette was braking champ. It produced the shortest stops, no locking, and the inclusion of a brake proportioning valve for '74 MY was a boon. 60-0mph in 129ft, 80-0mph in 247ft, the Corvette was the only test car with an excellent *R&T* braking rating. Like Corvette, the Dino's seatback angle was fixed, but the Italian's ergonomics seemed better. In conclusion, *Road & Track* found two very expensive and outstanding sports cars in the Ferrari and Porsche, an exemplary and obscenely expensive luxo tourer with the MB 450SL, and a good value domestic (Corvette). The Corvette could be optioned for sport or touring, but from Browns Lane, "… an obsolete British job with an excellent engine." The Corvette and Jag had been compared in America since the former's inception. Comparisons became even closer when the XKE

Road & Track – Five Exotic Opens – 1975

Model	Top speed (mph)	0-60mph (secs)	¼-mile @mph	0-100mph (secs)	Interior noise (dBA)	mpg
Corvette L82 350 4sp conv. (3.70 fd)	124	7.4	15.8 @ 92.5	18.5	83	13.5
Dino GTS	141	8	16.2 @ 87	22	83	15.5
Jag XKE V12 Roadster	138	8	16.2 @ 89	21.2	80	12
MB 450SL	124	10.2	17.7 @ 81.5	28.7	80	14.5
Porsche 911 Targa Sportomatic	127	8.5	16.4 @ 84	24	77	15.5

drove into view. However, Coventry's V12 would now be placed in the new XJS. With the arrival of this all new coupe, the press comparisons between Corvette and Jaguar seemed at an end.

For now, *R&T* repeated its viewpoint from the abovementioned June 1969 group comparison: Corvette was big on the outside, small on the inside, heavy (3490lb vs Jag 3450lb vs MB 450SL 3590lb!) fast and, "... least sophisticated of the five cars, favoring brute force when finesse would do nicely." However, not when it came to shifting, here *R&T* praised the Corvette's Muncie four-speed as light shifting, and one of the best. It was a long recognized asset. In contrast, the Dino's shift was mid-engine car awkward, and the XKE four-speed brought a heavy clutch and stiff shifter, which proved cumbersome in traffic. The Dino V6 provided the closest thing to racing sounds, while *R&T* found the Jag V12 lacking in the typical Italian melodic V12 engine note. There was still a desire in the mid '70s for that exotic car experience, but could you still get it?

Fuel crisis, inflation and smog law resembled the typical doomsday scenario. In 1975, Al Cosentino, of Italian performance parts importer FAZA, penned an open letter ad in enthusiast magazines, that Lancia Beta Cars were coming to America, and FAZA would make them better, "When and if the time comes and you have to give up your exotic GT car because it is 'bad on gas mileage', don't sulk – test drive the Lancia Beta cars." Cosentino suggested high-end import owners of Ferrari, Maserati, Lamborghini, BMW, Mercedes, Porsche, and Jaguar would find their desired qualities in the frugal Lancia Beta. Al Cosentino was pictured with a Merak and Beta coupe to reinforce his message. Straight Axle Corvette iconic racer Bob Grossman, felt there was no need to leave the prancing bull to downsize. Grossman Motor Car Corp was distributor for Lamborghini and Maserati in New York. Bob Grossman opined in his ad, "I didn't think Lamborghini could build a better all-around car than the Miura." Then, Grossman offered forth the 1975 Urraco GT V8, and claimed it was superior

Zora Arkus-Duntov also had a '74 Corvette LS4 454 with optional luggage rack. However, Duntov's ride came with T-tops, slushbox and 2.72 rear end. Not the ragtop, four-speed and standard LS4 454 issue 3.08 axle of this numbers-matching roadster. *(Courtesy Smoky Mountain Traders)*

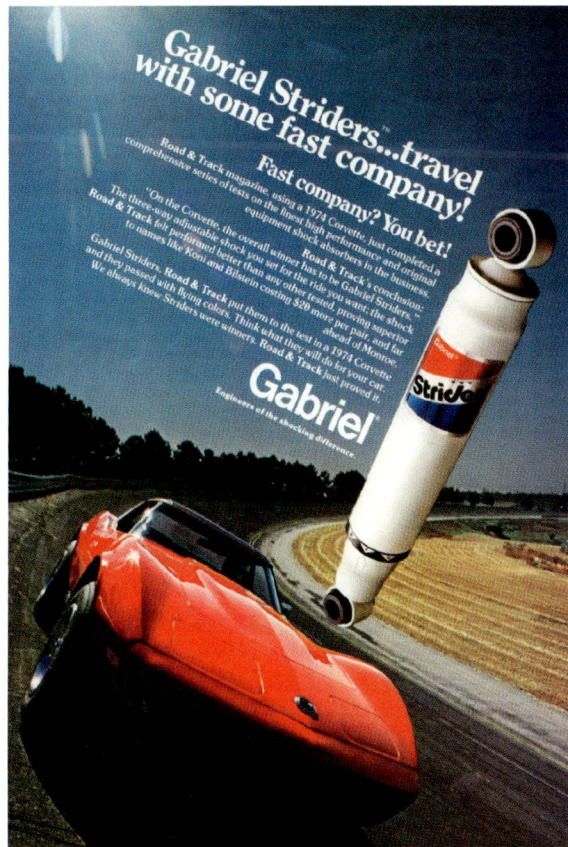

Using a '74 Corvette as test subject, *Road & Track* found three-way adjustable Gabriel Striders beat out Koni, Bilstein and Monroe shocks for ride and handling! *(Courtesy Gabriel)*

to the Miura in terms of quietness, comfort and gas mileage. A relative statement if ever there was one! And it seemed Volvo had the Countach soundly beaten as well.

The Baltimore police were trialing Volvo 164E cop cars, in terms of improved durability, maneuverability and economy, versus the usual domestic fullsize Ford, Chevrolet or Plymouth cruisers. In this sensible, brave new world, it seemed that federal roll-over testing could make open cars illegal soon. Indeed, the new Maserati Merak, Lamborghini Urraco and Dino 308 GT4, along with the Jag XJS, were all hardtops at first. Given such developments, *Road Test*'s John Ethridge said in February 1974, "Perhaps the most remarkable thing about this remarkable car (1974 Corvette coupe L82 350 four-speed) with a long and colorful history is this: You can still buy it. For that, all who appreciate such cars ought to be thankful." *Road & Track* was thankful for the 1974 Corvette. It used a Corvette coupe to test the ride and handling worth of various shock absorbers, before coming to the conclusion that out of Koni, Bilstein and Monroe, Gabriel Striders were tops. When it came to high performance, the journal didn't use a Civic CVCC as a test subject!

Goodbye Zora & Opel GT

EVEN IF THE public didn't appreciate the big block V8 anymore, they did value Corvette. Sales of Chevrolet's sports car rose from 1973's 30,464 to 37,502 in 1974. Almost an all time record. The buying was happening even with inflation. A standard Corvette broke the six grand barrier in 1974. Coupes now started from $6001.50, with ragtops continuing their Corvette entry level point at $5765.50. As always with Corvette, you paid less for a convertible, because you got less. Unibody convertibles saw strengthening work done in rocker panel areas, and around the A pillars, to compensate for the rigidity loss of no roof. With pre-1984 Corvettes, strength and rigidity rested in the ladder frame, common to both Corvette coupe and roadster. So a Corvette ragtop furnished a discount for the absent roof!

Sadly, there were no discounts overseas, where Corvettes were premium priced, rare exotics,

sold by small scale specialists drawing stock from Belgium. For Europe, sporty US cars met that continent's requirements of smaller vehicles that handled well. In 1974 that implied a GM selection of Camaro Z28 automatic for £3420, with the Camaro Z28 LT, Chevrolet Monte Carlo and Pontiac Firebird Formula, all retailing for £3540. The Firebird Trans Am raised the stakes to £3680, with the Corvette Stingray 454 automatic on £4150, or $9628! Given the M40 automatic was a NCO, and the LS4 454 a mere 250 buck option, that was one helluva mark up!

Fitting in with the low volume, sports/luxury ambit of US cars sold in Europe, it was natural to prefer models in one loaded spec, no strippers please, we're British! The Camaro Z28 and Monte Carlo were supplied with the same export 402 V8/ THM 400 powertrain, and both Pontiacs came with the L75 455 V8. No catalytic converters, because Europe/UK wouldn't get unleaded gas until the late '80s. So, smog was out the window ... literally! And if the Corvette seemed expensive next to the £3199 asked for a 1974 Jaguar E-type V12 roadster with four-speed, well, everyone in Britain already had one of those!

Back home, 1973 Corvette sales were strong, in an automotive sales year that happened to be very buoyant. In 1974, Corvette sales were even better, even though most car sales had fallen off the proverbial cliff, post fuel crisis. In the first half of 1974, recessionary auto sales were 24% lower. All size classes were in freefall, especially fullsize six-seater family fare that cost the most to buy and feed. Fullsize sales were around 50% down, but even small, frugal players like the Chevrolet Vega and Ford Pinto slowed by a respective 13% and 25%. Chevrolet Nova and Ford Maverick were down a respective 13% and 21%. The headlong hurl into small cars hadn't happened to the extent predicted, because the general move to smaller vehicles, due to an increasing preference for handier sized and more affordable cars, had been happening even prior to the gas crunch. Compacts were on 18-23% of the market mix, subcompacts and intermediates were steady, and imports had even fallen from 15% to 14% market share, versus 1973. Smog and safety law were fueling auto inflation. Current compacts were equal in price to 1970/71 big cars! [82]

The 1969-73 Opel GT combined C3 Corvette looks with Triumph GT6 size, price and scat. And you could get one at Buick dealers! *(Courtesy Stellanatis)*

As in earlier times, such economic concerns didn't trouble Corvette, as Zora Arkus-Duntov said, "Then came the energy crunch and we were forced to let people go from our plants in St Louis. But the Corvette was not affected by the oil crisis, and that plant tried to find work for the furloughed employees. With the same facility and same floor space, we ended up eventually producing 44,000 Corvettes." At one more car made per hour, Corvette demand was finally satiated, sans order book backlog. Once again, no need to worry about exports, or a right-hand drive version, when the Plastic Fantastic was so popular at home.

It seemed Zora Arkus-Duntov had achieved his objective, of transforming the 1953 Corvette into a sporting car of substance. As of January 1 1975, 61-year-old Duntov, or ZAK as he was affectionately nicknamed, retired from the post of Corvette Chief Engineer. As he relayed to *Road & Track*'s John Lamm in June 1977, the word that came to his mind was 'struggle' concerning the Corvette, with "whoever came to have an opinion different than mine." It was a constant fight at GM to get his vision

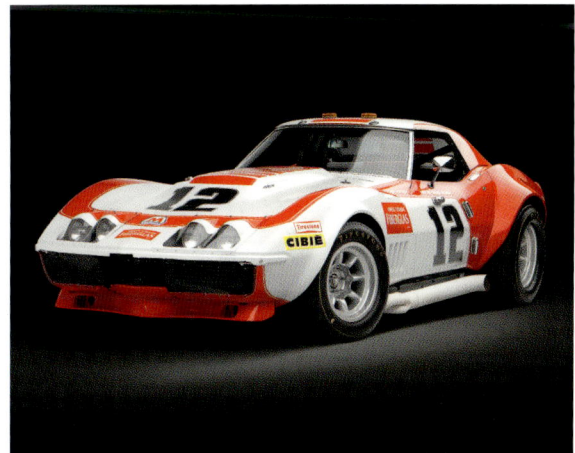

The Owens Corning #12 Corvette was a 1968 L88 427 V8 powered coupe with M22 Rock Crusher four-speed. *(Courtesy Owens Corning)*

of the Corvette done his way, the right way, in his opinion. There is no doubt that Duntov stamped his authority on the Corvette, in a manner that would never be repeated.

Raced under Tony DeLorenzo's Troy Promotions Inc, the #12 Owens Corning Corvette was successful in the hands of mechanical engineer Jerry Thompson. *(Courtesy Owens Corning)*

Shown in its 1971 racing season Daytona 24 Hours livery, the #12 Owens Corning Corvette came 4th overall in this event, garnering a GT class win in the process. *(Courtesy Owens Corning)*

His successor was 38-year-old Dave McLellan, who admitted subsequently that his Corvette influence wasn't immediate. That is, by the time he came on the scene, the 1975-77 Corvettes were largely a done deal. So, Duntov's work carried on, in a very real, practical sense.

Running alongside the C3 Corvette, during 1969-73 was a captive import that looked very much like a scaled down Mako Shark Late Model Corvette, the Opel GT. It was Buick that had long been handling the importation, sale and service of products produced by GM's West German subsidiary. Opel was the second best selling import, after VW, until Toyota happened upon the scene. [83] Opel usually made sensible transport with US styling resemblance similar to the wares of parent GM. The Opel GT started as a one-off concept car, that appeared at the 1965 Frankfurt Auto Show. Therefore, a show car contemporary of Mako Shark II! The reception was positive, and the result a sports car in the nature of British machines MG and Triumph. That is, the utilization of humble sedan mechanicals to create a modestly priced and powered two-seater. In this case, the sedate basis was the Opel Kadett.

Items a C3 Corvette owner would recognize, apart from general shape, were the oversize round speedo and tach, behind the seats trunk cavity, and front independent SLA type suspension. However, the Opel GT was a steel bodied unitary construction car, with rack and pinion steering and a live axle. Being an Opel, the GT's Cam-In-Head inline four had drivability problems, even in such early smog times. A further difference from Corvette was the fact the Opel GT was no handler. The Kadett underpinnings let it down. That said, it had a respectable turn of speed, with mid 17s in the ¼-mile, certainly in the Fiat 124 and Triumph TR250 ballpark. Then too, the Opel was well made. With Opel being so busy in those days, 90% of exported Opel GTs were assembled in Antwerp, Belgium. The body and interior were courtesy of Brissonneau et Lotz of France.

The Opel GT was a $3500 captive import, at a time when a '69 Corvette 350 was in the five grand zone. Maxwell Smart drove a bronze-colored Opel GT, in the final 1969/70 season of TV's *Get Smart*. By the close of '73 MY, 103,373 Opel GTs had been produced. 60% were exported to America, and with 5mph front and rear impact bumper law pending, the Opel GT was yet another sporting import that called it a day at the end of 1973. Like the Mako Shark era Corvette, the Opel GT is a fondly recalled collectible. A bronze example, like that driven by Agent 86 Maxwell Smart, was apparent in the showroom of Charlton Heston's 1971 movie *The Omega Man*. The Opel GT seemed to emulate the real world experience of the C3 Corvette, in attracting admiring glances from the fairer sex.

This 1971 Motion Performance modified C3 Corvette was the final Phase III GT coupe that Joel Rosen's speed shop built. *(Courtesy Vette)*

Corvette on the small screen

THE IMPACT BUMPER Corvette, in code 910 Classic White, featured on popular Channel NBC shows in the mid '70s. In *The Magician*, Bill Bixby played playboy philanthropist illusionist Tony Blake. Like other contemporary crusader shows of the '60s and '70s, Blake solved crimes and helped the helpless, aided by a cool V8-powered set of wheels! In this case it was mostly a '74 Corvette coupe, with saddle brown interior, and custom license plate 'SPIRIT'. However, the show's pilot episode, and the regular 1973-74 season episodes' opening credits, featured a 1973 model.

Up to mid season, the Corvette complemented Blake's mobile home, a Boeing 720 jetliner, called 'The Spirit'. It was certainly in keeping with the glamorous jet set lifestyle, popular with viewers on both the small and big screens, during such times. Blake's Corvette even featured a car phone, the ultimate in 1970s high living!

A white '74 Corvette coupe 350 was also on show in season 1 of Angie Dickenson's hit TV show *Police Woman*. Episode 17, titled 'No Place to Hide', carried a police pursuit scene where two bad guys were in the white Corvette. The Plastic Fantastic's still impressive acceleration and handling were in evidence. As expected, this 1974 coupe featured steel Rally rims, chrome center caps and trim rings: the only choice going that year. The episode aired January 31 1975. It seemed the Corvette had survived the Ford Thunderbird, Studebaker

Avanti, AMC AMX, not to mention the fuel crisis, 55mph national speed limit, skyrocketing insurance premiums, and impact bumpers. However, what about smog law?

Smog story

IN 1971, BUD Lindemann had this to say on TV's *Car and Track*, "The love affair between men and cars is an old story, and the reasons for it are many. Probably the strongest is the thrill a true car lover feels from the power, agility and responsiveness of a truly fine automobile." He added, "We in America are at a time when concern for safety and environment are threatening much of what makes men love cars."

Lindemann's sentiment, shared by a good number of the public, was part motivated by the

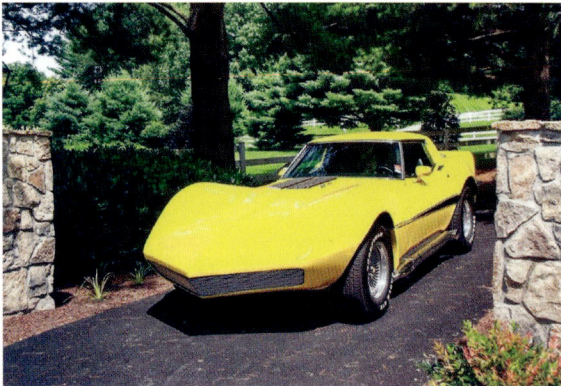

Motion Performance continued doing special Corvettes through the early '70s, like this 1972 Moray Eel. *(Courtesy Barrett-Jackson)*

Naderization of the auto landscape, post Chevrolet Corvair. Indeed, in 1971 lawyer Ralph Nader and his Washington DC Center for Auto Safety wrecking crew were hard at work, trying to remove the VW Beetle and Bus from the nation's roads. The other side of this ledger from hell, had something to do with a piece of proposed legislation hailing from 1970, colloquially known as the Muskie Smog Bill. In the wake of recent notable environmental events, President Richard Milhouse Nixon spent an inordinate amount of time in his 1970 State of the Union address, discussing the environment. Something had to be done via strict laws, and the automobile, which had provided so much economic prosperity and freedom in the post WWII era was now branded, "… our worst polluter of the air."

Nixon's speech was quite a diatribe for someone that heretofore had been pre-occupied with stamping out communism, and the prosecution of the related Vietnam War. Indeed, he subsequently said he didn't wish to see Chile turn communist on his doorstep. However, the 1972 election was looming, and Democrat presidential rival Edmund Muskie was the architect of the 1970 Clean Air Act (Muskie Smog Bill), which sought to cut hydrocarbons and nitrogen oxides by over 50% by 1975. Nixon's address to the nation amounted to the President stealing Muskie's thunder, and he signed the Clean Air Act into effect on December 31 1970.

As part of the Muskie Smog Bill came the newly created EPA (Environmental Protection Agency), to fix the environment. The EPA implied powers falling into the hands of a bunch of Los Angeles engineers and regulators, to give effect to the legislation. More than this, Republican President Nixon gave to fellow Republican Californian governor, Ronald Reagan, the Californian Waiver. The waiver recognized the Golden State's special topography and climatic conditions, allowing the state to set its own smog law. State regulatory body CARB (California Air Resources Board) had a key figure in Steve Albu, who set emissions standards

Fiberglass bodies made for easier custom jobs on Corvettes. Joel Rosen's flip open front ends and tapered tails were a Motion Performance signature style. *(Courtesy Barrett-Jackson)*

Joel Rosen managed to fit the hi po big block LS7 454 into many of his cars, including the Super Vega! Hamstrung by smog law and public safety issues, GM didn't carry out respective plans to have the LS6 and LS7 454s as Camaro and Corvette options. *(Courtesy Barrett-Jackson)*

for the Golden State for many years. Concerning the abovementioned legislative developments, Albu admitted, "I was kind of astonished at the power that I had." Indeed, it set in motion a process whereby California has been trying to use its great commercial market value, to strongarm automakers, and all the cars they make, to their standard.

In the short run, this led to the most lethargic and lamest cars being sent to California. More fortunate folks received vehicles tuned to 49 state specification. In June 1973, *Road Test*'s perplexed and bewildered scribe Chuck Koch, tried the latter, a '73 Corvette 454 four-speed coupe sans a/c. In traveling the wide open spaces, along the famous Route 66, he questioned the presence of the low compression ratio, air pump and EGR, bestowed upon his deep throated steed by bureaucrats in the smog bowl of downtown LA and "... unnecessarily strict smog laws." In Koch's opinion they turned this 15 second flat ¼-mile Corvette 454 into a sexy boulevard cruiser, albeit one that was still "... fast for this day of government intervention." If you visited one of the 6140 Chevrolet dealerships nationwide, a coupe like Koch's would cost $6788.50. A pretty penny, contributed to by the cost of incorporating federal smog and safety law. With some irony Chuck Koch had picked up the test Corvette from Zora Arkus-Duntov in Detroit, for a drive to Los Angeles via Route 66. The beginning of the end indeed.

In spite of automakers attempting to work with the by now infamous EPA, said body declared some Fords, Chryslers, Oldsmobiles and VWs weren't smog legal in June 1973. What's more, the EPA threatened a 1.4 million vehicle recall. GM wasn't impressed with the EPA, and blasted the government body's claims, saying that its cars were clean, and that the EPA's testing capacity was too small, and inaccurate. [84] Given the actions of garage tinkerers arbitrarily setting pollution limits,

The diamond tuft interior of Motion Performance Corvettes was in keeping with contemporary custom car fashion. *(Courtesy Barrett-Jackson)*

you can kind of understand GM's umbrage. In truth, GM's Bob Stempel was on the case.

Robert C Stempel was most certainly a car guy. He joined GM in 1958 at the age of 25. As a design engineer at Oldsmobile, he was a key figure in developing the original Oldsmobile Toronado. Stempel enjoyed attending car races, motorsport events and working on his cars, which over the years included a 1974 Corvette. He was assistant chief engineer at Oldsmobile in 1972, and in 1973 GM boss Ed Cole put Stempel in charge of overseeing pollution controls. That is, getting GM smog ready for 1975, in light of the Muskie Smog Bill. Bob Stempel didn't invent the catalytic converter, but he was a significant force behind getting GM cars to use this emissions strategy, and therefore the entire auto industry in general. For

At a time when a '72 Corvette commenced from $5296 (convertible), the Motion Performance Moray Eel was around the 20 grand mark! *(Courtesy Barrett-Jackson)*

his trouble, colleagues nicknamed him 'Captain Catalyst'!

For a while, GM wasn't fully committed to catalytic converters. The corporation first shied away from them, and then, in the words of CU (Consumers Union) embraced the filter device with passion akin to teenage romance! There were other pollution control methods around, most notably Honda's CVCC device of segmented combustion chamber, with a small rich portion igniting a larger lean part. CVCC met 1975 smog law, sans hang on devices, and was even successfully tested on a Chevrolet 350 V8. However, the specter of even stricter smog law loomed. In the meantime, CARB was persecuting Californian motorists with a

vengeance. The state body wished to oversee the retro fitment of nitrogen oxide fighting pollution control equipment, of which six devices had been approved by 1974, to 3.5 million 1966-70 cars. The penalty for non compliance was no license! It invited over-charging at smog test centers, with an early ambitious plan to retrofit over three million kits in under a year.

Authorities could have let old cars go to the junkyard, and concentrate on new vehicles. Sadly, common sense was in critical short supply in government. Federally, Congress wished to use public money, to pay NASA to develop clean, quiet and economical engines to fix the nation's problems. It was a classic case of Washington overreach. [85]

The 1973 Motion Performance Manta Ray GT represented a custom Corvette swansong for Joel Rosen. The speed shop's XKE/Euro style headlamps featured. *(Courtesy Mecum)*

As *Car and Track* examined the 1971 Olds 442 455 W30 four-speed convertible, it was clear the high performance car was in peril. This machine represented, "A car that has just about everything car lovers love," according to host Bud Lindemann, who added that convertibles provided that great feeling of freedom. Lindemann noted the Olds ability to scoot from 0-70mph in 7.3 seconds, and move through the pylon course like a ballerina, not to mention completing a superb J-turn! He reasoned that HD suspension wouldn't be legislated out of existence, because it didn't affect smog. Indeed, as power sank during the ensuing malaise era, an increased emphasis was placed on handling, a Corvette forte.

In keeping with tradition, Lindemann made no comment concerning the Old's gas mileage, but concluded, "… there was so much to like in the 442. And we're going to miss what progress takes from it." *Car and Track* also tried a '71 Ford Torino Cobra Jet 429, and if that coupe didn't come with the weight of every creature feature in Christendom, plus tires that did a great impersonation of mill ends by modern standards, would have got to

sixty a whole lot faster than the 7 seconds flat that actually transpired. Fast forward to August 1975, and Joe Oldham of *Cars* sampled one of the sole survivors of the big inch brigade, the 1975½ Trans Am 455 HO four-speed. Ol' Chubbs had his racing helmet on, but 0-60mph was still only 9.8 seconds, and smog control drivability quirks were legion. If only motors could still run properly from cold, and didn't have power delivery flat spots when warm. The real kicker was that this coupe couldn't even pass smog in California. That sports fans, is what the government called progress!

Corvette ➥ Still on track for success

THE CORVETTE CONTINUED to be a force in production car racing, albeit with earlier versions of the C3 Corvette, aided by hot hardware from the pre-1971 era. Perhaps the most successful machine in its category of racing was the Owens Corning 1968 Corvette L88 427 #12 coupe, associated with Tony DeLorenzo and Jerry Thompson. Tony DeLorenzo, son of GM executive John DeLorenzo,

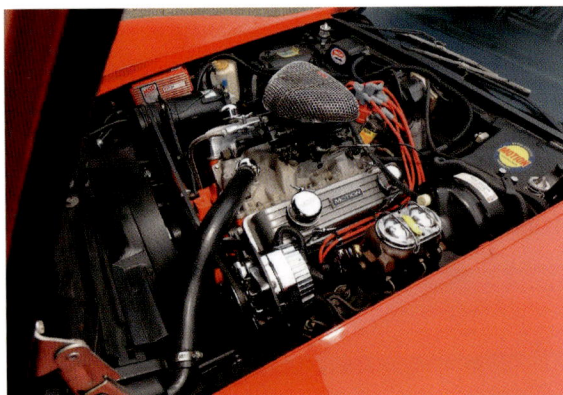

Of the three '73 Manta Rays built, two were based on Corvette LS4 454 four-speeds. However, this sole surviving Manta Ray GT started as a Corvette L48 350 automatic coupe. It was restored with a dyno proven 425 horse 350 V8, built by Joel Rosen! *(Courtesy Mecum)*

This coupe's original small block V8/slushbox cruiser power team is probably the reason this '73 Manta Ray outlived its big block siblings. *(Courtesy Mecum)*

possessed degrees in business administration and public relations. He set up Troy Promotions Inc, and nabbed Owens Corning as a key sponsor for his fledgling privateer team, an important acquisition. Jerry Thompson was a noted mechanical engineer, and raced the Owens Corning #12 Corvette, which expectedly utilized the well known M22 'Rock Crusher' four-speed. In 1968, this #12 coupe driven by Thompson, secured second place in the SCCA National A Production class Run-Offs, held at Riverside, California. Just as well smog law doesn't apply to track activities!

In 1969 racing season, the Owens Corning #12 Corvette garnered a GT class victory in the Daytona 24 Hours, followed by a second in GT class at the Sebring 12 Hours. That year, Thompson secured the National A Production Championship, and the Owens Corning team added a #11 Corvette L88 427 four-speed for Tony DeLorenzo. 1970 saw the #12 coupe notch up another GT class win, in the Daytona 24 Hours. This achievement entailed sixth outright, amidst Porsche and Ferrari dominance. The same year, Jerry Thompson got second in the SCCA's National A Production Run-Offs, with the #12 Corvette coupe.

Come 1971 racing season, and the Owens Corning #12 Corvette amassed 11 SCCA and FIA national race victories, including fourth place

outright at 1971's Daytona 24 Hours, being one of that year's two class wins in FIA events. At one point, the Owens Corning #12 Corvette dominated SCCA A Production, with 22 consecutive wins! The Corvette had continued its success story, in endurance events. Tony DeLorenzo felt that the only sports car close in handling was the Ferrari Daytona. For 1972 racing season, the Owens Corning Corvette had a new owner, Jerry Hansen. Hansen continued the coupe's tradition, by winning the 1972 SCCA A Production Championship.

The #12 Corvette coupe went on to the Trans Am and IMSA series, racing under Dick Bauer, finishing SCCA and IMSA exploits in 1989. The #12 Corvette coupe was eventually restored back to its 1971 Daytona 24 Hours campaign state, with an original L88 427 V8, sporting an estimated 685bhp. Tony DeLorenzo continued to campaign Corvettes, and with the 1973 Budd Company Corvette he achieved a GT class pole position at the 1973 Daytona 24 Hours. Bob Johnson and Dave Heinz managed fourth overall, in their #57 Rebel Corvette at the 1972 Daytona 24 Hours. This was the last time the event was run on the old circuit.

In the February 1975 issue of *Road & Track*, Mike Knepper described the climactic spectacle of the SCCA's annual A Production Run-Offs, featuring the thundering, lumbering Corvettes. In 1974, the A Production Championship went to Corvette racer J Marshall Robbins, with second place garnered by Lou D'Amico. Bill Jobe was B Production champ,

This '73 Manta Ray GT has been signed by Joel 'Mr Motion' Rosen and Corvette Chief Engineer Dave McLellan! *(Courtesy Mecum)*

also in a Corvette. It only went to prove, that in GT class production car racing, nothing succeeded like Corvette! [86]

Apart from race cars, enthusiast dreams are also fueled by customized cars. Here, Joel Rosen of Motion Performance created some very special Corvettes. It was in 1966 that Brooklyn-raised Rosen, along with business partner and editor of *Cars* magazine Marty Schorr, set up shop next to Baldwin Chevrolet, located in Long Island, New York. Ordered through the dealership, super hot Baldwin Motion Novas, Camaros, Chevelles and Corvettes could come with a ¼-mile ET guarantee! Special looks and high performance were frequently found on the cars Motion Performance made, and Marty Schorr promoted 'em!

1971 proved to be the final year, for a Motion Performance created Corvette Phase III GT. However, Joel Rosen continued the style of his work, exhibited by his 1970 custom take on the Mako Shark II show car. Evidence of this was the 1972 Moray Eel, with one piece flip open front end, tapered rear fascia, Le Mans style gas cap and diamond tuft interior, along with demarcation line paint job that accentuated the rear fascia and tail. The sky was the limit, concerning a hot big block, or small block, whatever you wanted, Joel Rosen could deliver. However, the Corvette path for the drag racer, street racer and hot rodder, seemed to end with the 1973 Manta Ray GT.

Three turn-key Manta Rays were built by Motion Performance, and as with Joel Rosen's earlier work, the fiberglass Corvette body provided tremendous customization potential. This included Rosen's familiar European XKE-like integrated headlamps, and boat tail rear meeting ducktail spoiler that echoed Bill Mitchell and Larry Shinoda's 1965 Mako Shark II concept. The three Manta Ray cars included two LS4 454 four-speed coupes, and one L48 350-powered coupe, with slushbox. Perhaps unsurprisingly, only the meek small block coupe survived, power corrupts!

By the late '80s the surviving Mouse Motored coupe was owned by a body shop proprietor, who

The wheels at Motion Performance, and sales via Baldwin Chevrolet, continued until the EPA put the kibosh on engine mods by speed shops, in the early '70s. *(Courtesy Mecum)*

didn't realize the coupe's historical worth. In poor shape, the Manta Ray survivor was saved by the body shop owner having a chance encounter with Joel Rosen at a car show. So commenced a faithful restoration, featuring a period correct 425 horse 350 V8, that Joel Rosen helped build himself! The original engine was lost in the mists of time. Not to worry, the endeavor was dyno proven and sported an Edelbrock intake, MSD ignition, headers and duals, as well as the THM 400 and power brakes the '73 coupe was originally specified with.

There was a letter of authenticity from Joel Rosen, stating the coupe was built by Motion Performance. Then too, the car's console was signed by Joel Rosen, and the Corvette's second Chief Engineer Dave McLellan signed on the

This '73 Motion Performance Manta Ray GT sold for $100,000 in 2016, and its collector value is rising!
(Courtesy Mecum)

T-top, next to Rosen's name. This '73 Motion Performance Manta Ray GT is rolling history, blessed by Bow Tie royalty! Back in the day, all the good things came to an end, thanks to the EPA. Joel Rosen got the LS7 454 into his cars, whereas Chevrolet did not, due to smog and public safety issues etc. The 1974 Baldwin Motion Super Vega LS7 454 was a red flag to an EPA bull, that weaponized the DOJ (Dept Of Justice) to stop Baldwin Motion in its tire tracks!

Under smog law, the government could slap a ten grand fine on a speed shop, or Joe Q Public, each and every time a piece of pollution control equipment was removed from an automobile. For a spell, Baldwin Motion got around the problem by exporting its cars, or just marking them on invoices 'For Off Road Use Only.' However, with the fuel crisis, recession, insurance premiums, and a related public cooling off on fast cars, Baldwin Motion, and almost everyone else, left the speed shop scene. By 1974, the original Mustang morphed into the Mustang II subcompact. By the close of '74 MY, Mopar Marvels the Barracuda and Challenger were gone, so too AMC Javelin, Camaro Z28 and Super Duty Trans Am. Not forgetting Pantera, Jag XKE and Ferrari Daytona, along with the Saab Sonnett III! That said, the Corvette would return for 1975, and its popularity was on the up!

From Flying Buttress to Fastback

1975-79

INTRODUCING A MORE EFFICIENT CORVETTE.

That's it on the right, the 1975 Corvette. It has something no Corvette has ever had before: The Chevrolet Efficiency System.

Efficiency System? We're talking about a series of significant engineering improvements working together to help lower the cost of operating your Corvette while, at the same time, improving engine performance. No small accomplishment.

System components include High Energy Ignition, catalytic converter, Early Fuel Evaporation, outside air carburetion and steel-belted radial ply tires.

High Energy Ignition. With High Energy Ignition, there are no breaker points, there is no ignition condenser. More important, the solid-state circuitry, plus a special High Energy Ignition coil, provides a hotter spark than conventional ignition systems do. Advantages: reliable firing and starting, especially in cold or wet weather, plus longer life

for spark plugs. (Recommended replacement is now up to 22,500 miles.) Tune-ups, as we've known them, will be simpler and further apart.

Catalytic converter. As you probably know, a catalytic converter is part of the exhaust system on every 1975 Corvette. Essentially, it involves a core of porous pellets coated with platinum and palladium which helps complete the oxidation of carbon monoxides and hydrocarbons. Using unleaded gas, the 1975 Corvette should emit the cleanest exhaust

Catalytic Converter

of any Corvette ever. And with the converter on the job, the factory can now tune your Corvette more toward smooth, responsive, efficient performance. Incidentally, GM's catalytic converter development program included 1,000 vehicles, going over 20,000,000 miles.

Early Fuel Evaporation. Early Fuel Evaporation is designed to reduce the possibility of chugging and stalling when you first start up. EFE uses exhaust gases in a more sophisticated way to warm the incoming fuel-air mixture so you can be on your way sooner, and more smoothly. With EFE, the automatic choke cuts out faster, which should help save you gas on short runs in cold weather.

Outside air carburetion. Air trapped under the hood of a running automobile is hot stuff. Outside air is cooler and denser. We have found that, after warm-up, the use of a carburetor induction system that puts outside air in the fuel-air mix contributes to improved performance. Consequently, both Corvette engines employ outside air induction.

The roll of radials. Corvette's Efficiency System extends right to the road and those special GR70-15 steel-belted radial ply tires. Above and beyond the handling and durability characteristics offered by steel-belted radials, they roll with less resistance. The result is a slight but real contribution to improved fuel economy.

Extended service intervals. We mentioned earlier that you'll have no points or ignition condenser to replace, and your spark plugs should now last up to 22,500 miles. The 1975 Corvette will also go longer between recommended oil changes, oil filter changes, chassis lubrications, transmission fluid changes. Example: We now recommend oil change and chassis lube every six months or 7,500 miles. Last year it was four months or 6,000 miles.

Free catalog. The 1975 Corvette is described in detail in the 1975 Corvette catalog which is available free at any Chevrolet dealership. We invite you to go in and pick one up, and if your dealer has a Corvette in stock—ask him for a test drive.

Chevrolet

The 1975 Corvette employed cold air induction, electronic ignition, a catalytic converter, exhaust gas heat to get off choke sooner, and radials. The aim was to cut smog and boost gas mileage. However, versus older, less encumbered Corvettes, was it really efficient? (Courtesy GM archives)

1975 — A more efficient Corvette?

A 1974 CORVETTE ad proudly stated that *Car and Driver* readers had yet again voted the Plastic Fantastic as the 'Best All-Around Car.' Perhaps that's because the Corvette had long been Detroit's most honest car? With other sporty domestics making great use of the advertising angle, Chevrolet's two-seater sports car was like a good vanilla ice cream. There were no fancy nuts, syrups or flavors to conceal an ordinary base. For years that substance was guarded by Zora Arkus-Duntov. However, the Corvette's long time Chief Engineer, although only officially holding that desk plaque from 1968, was no longer in charge of America's

That light, dent-resistant fiberglass body on a rugged frame, rear-drive, front V8, and four-wheel disk brakes were all familiar. In 1975, Corvette was still Detroit's only sports car, and probably its most honest car. In the words of Flip Wilson, "What you see is what you get!" (Courtesy National Corvette Museum)

165

By 1975, the Plastic Fantastic was rolling solely on small block V8 power, for the first time since the first half of '65 MY. The sidepipes aren't stock. *(Courtesy Dean Green)*

only sports car. No sir, that position from January 1 1975, belonged to David Ramsay McLellan.

McLellan was previously a staff engineer under Duntov. He joined GM in 1969, and during 1973/74 matriculated at MIT's Sloan School of Management, where he garnered a Masters degree. Legendary GM boss Alfred P Sloan Jr once said, "The perpetuation of leadership is sometimes more difficult than attainment of that leadership in the first place." The Sloan School was a fitting connection, because that leadership task now rested with Dave McLellan, only the second Corvette Chief Engineer in history. It was his job to preserve the Corvette's position as America's premier, and oftentimes only, sports car.

During 1974-76, the Corvette seemed to have a North American challenger, of sorts, in the Canadian Bricklin SV1 sports car.

The Bricklin seemed to embody elements of the past, such as the gullwing doors of the Mercedes 300SL. However, there was also the promise of the future. An early, socially responsible DeLorean DMC12, if you will. The Bricklin SV1 was the brainchild of Canadian entrepreneur Malcolm Bricklin, creating a Pantera with a conscience! The SV1 (Safety Vehicle One) had a choice of five safety 'day-glow' colors, pedestrian friendly nose-cone, no interior cigar lighter or ashtray, to avoid fire risk, and, from 1975, no manual transmission! Like the DeLorean DMC12, the days of the over-powered sports car, from a social angle, seemed over. Malcolm Bricklin felt the automatic-only nature was a safety boon, because you kept both hands on the steering wheel. However, that development may have been due to powertrain supply problems.

Just as Corvette drew upon some humble Bow Tie hardware, the Bricklin made use of American Motors' Kenosha stuff! It was a case of AMC Hornet suspension and brakes, Pacer dashboard and console. Most interestingly, apart from bonded acrylic fiberglass body panels and troublesome electro-pneumatic gullwing doors, the 1974 Bricklin came with a potent AMC 360 4bbl V8, making 220

Even with the optional $82 N37 Tilt-Telescope steering column, *Car and Driver's* Don Sherman felt the '75 Corvette's steering wheel was still too close to the chest. It was a domestic car trait. This coupe has the '77 optional sports wheel. *(Courtesy Dean Green)*

net horses, plus a possible four-speed. The car drove well, and had promise. In the May 1975 issue of *Car and Driver*, Don Sherman's report was titled, 'America's Best Sports Car: Bricklin or Corvette?' It was noted that women fell hopelessly in love with the Bricklin SV1, from two lanes away! By now the Bricklin was exclusively powered by a FoMoCo Cleveland 351 2bbl V8. It made 175 horses net, and was connected to an automatic transmission. At 16.6 seconds in the ¼-mile, it yielded half a second to the Corvette on test, but that wasn't the Bricklin's problem.

The SV1 project had been commercially ill conceived. Even though a comparable Corvette

With 38,465 '75 MY sales, the Mako Shark II related Corvette wasn't quite as popular as the movie *Jaws*. However, it was decidedly more likeable than a mechanical shark … more reliable too! *(Courtesy Dean Green)*

was only 70% of the Bricklin's price, money was lost on each Bricklin SV1 made. Indeed, the total 1974-76 SV1 production run ran to just 2854 units. It was a figure dwarfed by the Corvette's respective 1974, 1975 and 1976 totals of 37,502, 38,465 and 46,558, the last model year total finally beating the Corvette's previous extended '69 MY record. In the world of premium priced cars, you wouldn't think there was a gas crunch, nor recession. It seemed entrepreneurs out East bought Bricklin SV1s to sell on the West Coast for over 10 grand. Exclusivity

has always had a price. More Corvettes had always been sought than produced, so, by March 1, dealers already experienced all stock being taken up. They charged a grand over list, as a rationing measure!

Car and Driver's Don Sherman felt the Bricklin was a genuine Corvette challenger in a number of areas. However, like early Corvettes, the Bricklin experienced quality shortfalls, compromised material finish, and some engineering crudity. Then there was Canadian politics. In the potential sports car battle royale between St Louis and New

CRANSWICK ON *Classic Chevrolet Corvette*

Brunswick, Premier Richard Hatfield loomed large. Hatfield had bankrolled Bricklin to secure his re-election. Indeed, the 'Bricklin Election' and entire SV1 project offered parallels with the subsequent DeLorean debacle. If only they made a movie about Malcolm and his Bricklin, eh!

So, it seemed the Corvette's premier sports car position, and popularity, were assured through the troubled mid '70s. In fact, Corvette market research had shown 60% of Plastic Fantastic owners to trade in their steeds for a ritzy personal car like a Monte Carlo, Grand Prix or even a Mercury Cougar. As with pony cars, GM research showed

buyers weren't necessarily loyal to the same brand. For 1975, the Corvette had a series of small, but significant alterations. Visually, there were dual black bumperettes, front and rear. Not exactly in the style of Cadillac Dagmars of Eldorados old, but functional in the context of federal 5mph impact bumper law. Then too, manufacturing advancements saw the Corvette's rear fascia end cap become a one-piece urethane molding. No longer the '74 MY vertically split affair.

Except for $35 QRM GR70-15 WS SB tires, versus $48 QRZ GR70-15 WL SB tires, options chosen by a respective 5233 and 30,407 '75 Corvette faithful,

Now with 5mph impact bumpers at both ends, the post 1973 Corvette was 185.2in long, or 10in longer than the C2 and C4 Corvettes! *(Courtesy Dean Green)*

The color is code 56 Bright Yellow, chosen by 2883 1975 Corvette buyers. *(Courtesy Dean Green)*

your Corvette wheel, tire and size choice were set. No options, and the familiar Rally rims continued. On the inside you might have noticed three new items: headlights on warning buzzer (a proposed federal mandate), km/h markings within the speedo, and an unleaded gas only warning for the gas gauge. Yes, the '75 Corvette succumbed to GM policy of adopting a pellet type catalytic converter, and therefore an unleaded gas only diet. It was all part of meeting the much tighter 1975 emissions law.

In an act of Corvette heresy, duals were off the menu! It was a case of exhaust manifold meets Y pipe, one cat, a pair of mufflers then tailpipes. Duals were planned, but couldn't meet smog law, making the single cat a last minute reality. There were initial hopes for the same three motor line up as 1974. However, Corvette nearly ended up with just the base L48 350! The LS4 454 failed smog, and only a handful of '75 Corvette LS4 454s were built. With much struggle, the L82 350 returned as a mid-1975 model year option. Even later in California, and only with an automatic transmission. It would be the final curtain call for the L82 350 in the Golden State. Another smog law casualty.

The SAE net figures of the 1975 L48 350 were a mere 165bhp at 3800rpm, and 255lb/ft on the familiar 8.5:1 CR. The L82 350, when it came, improved those respective readings to 205bhp at 4800rpm, maintaining the 255lb of twist at 3600rpm on the also previously seen 9.0:1 CR. So, as ever, there was a tractability penalty, for choosing hi po over lo po 350 V8. In the background were the now expected TCS (Transmission Controlled Spark) and EGR (Exhaust Gas Recirculation) that made GM powerplants smog legal, but also maintained sound drivability when all else were falling by the roadside. For 1975, there were some new initials to learn, HEI or High Energy Ignition.

HEI was GM's electronic, transistorized ignition. No points, no problems and less servicing work. According to GM, sparkplug changes were now extended from 6000 miles to 22,500 miles! And "... significantly lengthened engine oil and filter change intervals." The newfangled HEI distributor, implied

In 1975, the Corvette was still America's only volume produced, two-seater sports car! *(Courtesy Dean Green)*

an electronic tach drive. That is, the new distributor received an electrical signal, translated into a dashboard rpm reading. GM and Chevrolet were setting up a motor that drank less, and therefore polluted less. Gasoline was supplied by a new race car style, internal rubber bladder type of gas tank. It was safer and more environmentally friendly. Gas fumes didn't escape, nor did air enter or potentially get trapped within the tank.

The 1975 Corvette was also the last chance to experience air that the government hoped was getting cleaner, for a couple of reasons. It was the final model year for GM's Astro Ventilation flow-through-cabin system, shared by Corvette, Camaro and Firebird since 1968. So don't look for rear deck vent slots near the base of the backlight, come 1976. 1975 was also the last year a factory

IT LETS YOU INDULGE YOURSELF WHILE STILL BEING SENSIBLE.

Until now, if you wanted to indulge your desire for luxuriousness in an automobile, you might have expected to sacrifice efficiency.
This year, you can have both improved efficiency and luxuriousness in the same automobile: Caprice Classic for 1975.

Lots of luxuriousness.
Caprice Classic transports six adults smoothly and comfortably. And handsomely: the new Caprice grille, taillight assembly and rear window treatment more than meet the most demanding ideas of luxuriousness. So does the deep, cut-pile carpeting which extends up the lower door panels and the available 50/50 reclining front seat. Indulge.

Quiet elegance.
Caprice rides as

elegantly as it looks. It's particularly quiet on the road, with its radial-tuned suspension and built-in Quiet Sound Insulation to get you from place to place smoothly and quietly. Indulge.

New efficiencies.
Caprice Classic for '75 is a more sensible automobile than ever. The new standard engine is a 350-2 V8, replacing last year's 400-2. And the combination of this new smaller V8 and Chevrolet's new Efficiency System lets Caprice go substantially farther on a gallon of gasoline, based on Environmental Protection Agency City Driving Tests. Caprice also goes farther between recommended oil changes and tune-ups and lets you operate a truly luxurious automobile without being out of step with the times. Sensible.

There are no Caprice sort-of-classics.
Other car companies are currently offering lesser versions of their traditional top models. But there is only one uppermost Chevrolet. Caprice Classic is uppermost in quality, in luxuriousness and in quiet elegance. And for 1975, Caprice Classic is uppermost in overall operating economy compared to Caprice models of recent years. We think that for '75, Caprice offers you the best of two worlds in allowing you to indulge yourself . . . while still being sensible.

CHEVROLET MAKES SENSE FOR AMERICA

As shown by this '75 Caprice Classic, smaller engines (2bbl 350 from 2bbl 400 small block V8), were a first step in cutting smog, and boosting economy. Late '70s downsizing and an '80s switch to front drive, would follow. *(Courtesy GM Archives)*

Corvette convertible was possible, until 1986. Proposed federal roll-over safety tests put the kibosh on the ragtop, and caused an industry-wide freeze on convertible development. To beat the planned ban, one 72-year-old Nebraskan fellow purchased not one, but six 1976 Cadillac Eldorados, [87] acknowledging the passing of a great American institution. The act of purchasing two or more examples of the same car is somewhat of an American collector car tradition, concerning domestic automobiles. That is, buy one to drive, and store one or more as an appreciating asset. It's a phenomenon that certainly covers Corvette. However, even properly stored 0-mile collector examples would need substantial recommissioning work to make such cars safe to drive again.

If you wanted to buy one or more Corvettes in 1975, the convertible started from $6550.10, and the coupe from $6810.10. It would be the last time a Corvette convertible would cost less than its

coupe counterpart. Only 4629 Corvette devotees chose the roadster version in 1975, out of 38,465 Corvettes sold. The coming of good HVAC, longer hairstyles, worsening air quality in city areas, and general buyer desire for more insulated comfort, all conspired to reduce ragtop popularity over the years, and not just with Corvettes. In 1975 form, the Corvette's dimensions were 185.2in length, 69in width and 57.2in for height. Front track was 58.7in, rear track was 59.5in and ground clearance 4.3in. A 37ft turning circle, came from a 2.9 turn lock-to-lock, recirculating ball steering setup. The gas tank was 18 gallons, and curb weight was 3540lb for a 1975½ Corvette L82 350 four-speed coupe, sans a/c.

For all the stats, the 1975 Corvette seemed much like the one you could have got in 1968. No bad thing in the minds of many. However, the '68 Corvette shared its chassis with the C2 1963 Corvette, which was an all new design. Critics recognized that the Late Model Corvette was bigger on the outside, but smaller on the inside than the much loved Mid-Year Corvette. With the 1975 Ferrari 308 GT4, Lamborghini Urraco and Maserati Merak newly arriving Stateside, as cutting edge proponents of mid-engine technology, the buff mags were starting to get a bit antsy, concerning when the truly all new Corvette would debut. In February 1975, *Road & Track* brought up how Chevrolet itself, via the 1962 *Corvette News* publication, said that although the Straight Axle Corvette was doing good business, it no longer represented up-to-date, best Chevrolet engineering practice, so a new car was necessary. *R&T* felt the same scenario was playing out in 1975, "The same situation applies today and it's still unknown just when the next all-new Corvette will appear, but that's another story." [88]

In May 1975, *Car and Driver*'s Don Sherman noted that the Corvette L48 350 automatic was only a little quicker than a Mazda RX3. *C/D* gas mileage was 15mpg, even with the 12 buck 2.73 highway axle option. *R&T* discovered the RX3 could achieve

One of the final model year 1975 4629 Corvette ragtops. This roadster was specified with the popular base L48 350, and NCO automatic. (*Courtesy Legendary Motors*)

18mpg, thirsty rotary and all! However, public perception concerning rotary Wankel thirst saw Mazda USA sales fall off a cliff, post fuel crisis. In contrast, Corvette was doing very nicely in sales. It seemed Corvette patrons were content with their chariot, although ordering patterns had evolved since the late '50s. 28,745, 31,914, 35,482, 28,473 and 37,591 Corvette fans optioned the respective $93 A31 power windows, $490 C60 a/c, $50 J50 power brakes, NCO M40 THM 400 autobox and $129 N41 power steering.

So, in some ways Corvette was moving from Sun Records to Las Vegas Elvis, but the tune was still familiar. FE7 Gymkhana suspension was a seven buck Zora Arkus-Duntov legacy, selected by 3194 1975 Corvette buyers. Plus, the decidedly more rock, than rock and roll, Z07 off road suspension and brake package was taken by just 144 '75 Corvette buyers, at $400 a pop! It made the Corvette more track ready than any other 1975 vehicle, import or domestic. The most popular

The '75 Corvette sported dual front and rear rubber bumperettes, but no duals! Adding to the heresy was an unleaded gas necessity brought by a catalytic converter. Horsepower of the base L48 350 fell 30bhp for 1975, to 165bhp. Hardly the seat of power! (*Courtesy Legendary Motors*)

Since 1963, Corvette convertibles were a cheaper alternative. When the Corvette roadster returned for 1986, the switch from a separate chassis to beefed up Uniframe made the ragtop pricier than the coupe. *(Courtesy Legendary Motors)*

Longer hairstyles and better HVAC had seen a general industry move away from convertibles since the mid '60s. Regardless of proposed federal rollover safety tests, the public just weren't buying ragtops. *(Courtesy Legendary Motors)*

Corvette color in 1975 was code 10 Classic White. 8007 people went for that shade. Code 13 Silver came second, with 4710 Corvettes so painted.

There were two new upholstery choices in 1974, code 14 Silver and code 60 Light Neutral. Such choices continued for 1975, with Light Neutral still the only Corvette interior shade unavailable in leather. Now for 1975, interior color codes carried a 'V' suffix for vinyl, and '2' for cowhide. And yes, you could even tow with your Corvette! Towing up to 2000lb was okay, with a Chevrolet trailer hitch, featuring 200lb tongue weight (Part #994532 –

dealer installed accessory). More than that, GM was in compliance with state and federal law towing requirements, with tests at its Milford Proving Ground showing up to 4000lb was possible! Is there anything a Corvette can't do?! To achieve this seemingly Sisyphean task, Chevrolet recommended one specify a Corvette with HD radiator, RPO V0-1, F40 HD suspension, and UA1 HD battery. You also needed an aftermarket equalizing or platform hitch. Then it was a case of wagons roll!

1976 Corvette – Practical dream car

IN 1974, THE Honda Civic was the EPA gas mileage leader. Come 1975 and VW was advertising its Scirocco as 'The Hot One', borrowing Chevrolet's small block V8 slogan from the '50s! VW gave 0-50mph as 7.5 seconds, while extolling the virtues of front drive and rack and pinion steering, or rack and peanut steering as Homer Simpson mistakenly called it! The Scirocco's EPA figures were an impressive 24-25mpg city and 35-44mpg hwy. According to the June '76 issue of *Road Test*, a '76 Corvette L82 350 automatic with 3.36 gears, did 0-60mph in a scant 7.4 seconds, even though it merely had rear drive and recirculating ball steering. *Road Test* was impressed by the Corvette's new found frugality ... 16.2mpg! However, front wheel drive was gaining traction, and it signaled modernity. Also in 1976, *Autoweek*'s scribe suggested that the vast majority of drivers would do just fine and dandy with either a diminutive Honda Civic or Accord.

The Corvette, contrary to appearances, hadn't been standing still. 1976 saw several detail refinements that curried favor with the Plastic Fantastic's core buyer. And 1976 model year sales set an all time Rocky Mountain high record of 46,558 units! It seemed Chevrolet still knew its buyers, and the Corvette was coupe only by now. With standard T-tops, there seemed little need for

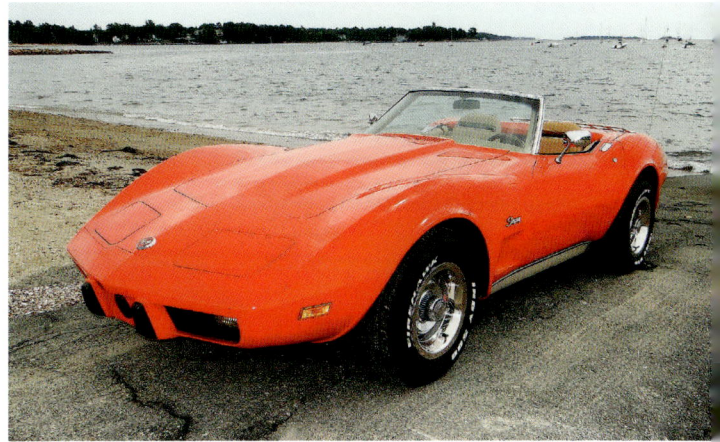

Some feel the C3 Corvette's C07 Auxiliary Hardtop option made the interior a little claustrophobic. Rare was the ragtop that came with Corvette's optional C60 a/c, costing $490 in 1975. Fresh air fiends had other ideas! *(Courtesy Legendary Motors)*

a ragtop. The '76 Corvette had moved from having the former C50 rear window defroster, costing $46 and chosen by 13,760 patrons in 1975, to the new C49 rear window defogger. Although possessing a steeper 78 buck surcharge, 24,960 Corvette fans optioned C49. They appreciated the refinement of embedded heated elements for the backlight, rather than recirculated hot air. C49 was even more necessary now that Astro Ventilation had gone.

The 1976 Corvette deep sixed the nameplate's 1973-75 cowl induction, although the intake grille remained through '76 MY. The official word was that owners complained of a whistling noise from said cowl induction. The system introduced loud wide open throttle acceleration that troubled Californian drive-by noise standards. This was a more likely explanation for cowl induction's absence. In its place was an air duct, forward of the radiator support, that tapped some of the outside air that usually fed the radiator exclusively. Moving rearwards, the '76 Corvette initially carried over the 1975 model's one piece end cap and Corvette tail script style. However, during 1976 calendar year, the Corvette tail script switched from large font lettering, which filled the space between the taillights, to smaller recessed script.

If you had an extra $299 to spare, a 1976 Corvette could have RPO YJ8 aluminum alloy rims, finally! Sized the Corvette's usual 15 x 8in, RPO YJ8 was originally promised for 1973. Now you got a set of four alloys, plus a conventional steel spare to save on cost. The rims were made by Kelsey-Hayes in Mexico, but it seemed most Corvette patrons were okay with the standard steel Rally rims. Only 6253 Corvette buyers optioned YJ8 in 1976, even though they were a critical hit. Marty Schorr, former *Cars* magazine editor, was complimentary towards the Corvette's new alloys, in the December 1976 issue of *High Performance Cars*. He said Corvette was still a head turner, even after eight years in its current guise, but was sporting fewer options in such Bicentennial days.

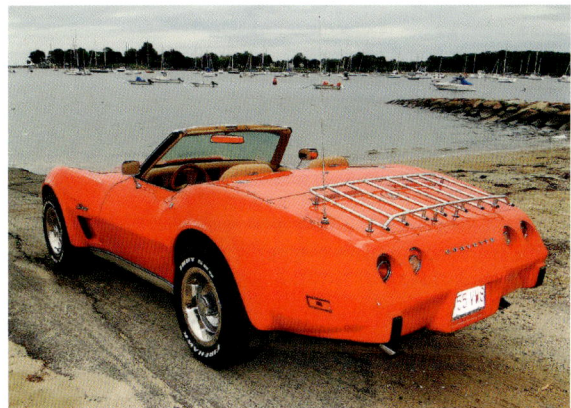

This '75 Corvette convertible has code 76 Mille Miglia Red. It was the last year for this shade. 3355 Corvette fanciers chose Mille Miglia Red in 1975. The interior is code 65V Medium Saddle Vinyl. *(Courtesy Legendary Motors)*

If people didn't buy an option, that was the reason to discontinue it. That happened with QRM GR70-15 white stripe SB tires, which ended in 1976. Even though a mere 37 bucks, versus the now much more fashionable QRZ GR70-15 white letter SB tires costing $51, only 3992 buyers were persuaded to go RPO QRM, a huge 39,923 ticked RPO QRZ! GM had been recommending just 20psi for tire pressure since radials came on the Corvette scene as part of compensating for the harsher riding radials. The lower pressure did aid ride comfort, compared to the Corvette's stiff riding, hard rock reputation; however, low pressures combined with the semi flexible body

173

No duals in 1975, and large font Corvette
script filled the space between taillights.
(Courtesy Legendary Motors)

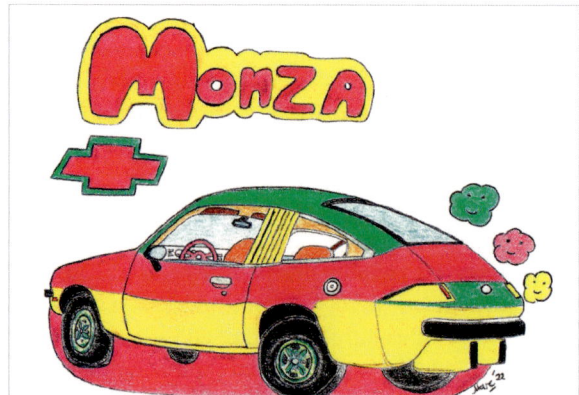

If you couldn't stretch to a Corvette, well, there was
the Monza. And if you lived in a high altitude area,
a 4bbl 350 V8 similar to Corvette's unit could
be optioned. *(Courtesy Marc Cranswick)*

mounts, impact bumpers and weight gains post 1972, implied that the Corvette's handling wasn't as single minded as it once was. To make matters worse, ride height was raised for '76 MY, bringing Corvette into bumper height compliance with other domestics. There was a federal mandate to stop submarining during collisions.

Road Test wasn't so complimentary concerning the Corvette's latest handling. In June 1976 the journal said the Corvette now had an untidy transition to oversteer. That said, Marty Schorr was kinder to Corvette in the December 1976 issue of *High Performance Cars*. He said that while the Corvette wasn't the crisp handler that an Alfa Romeo or BMW was, the Plastic Fantastic could still get one out of a tight spot. The softer touch may even have been preferable over imperfect surfaces, where the Corvette had a reputation for being jittery, bringing frequent steering corrections with stiffly sprung predecessors. Okay, but the tough of tush could still option $35 FE7 Gymkhana suspension, and 5368 '76 Corvette fanciers did just that; even though FE7 wasn't the seven buck bargain it was in 1975, its popularity was rising. That may have been aided by the track focused Z07 off road suspension and brake package being discontinued at the close of '75 MY.

There was rising interest in handling, and cars that handled, but that didn't mean folks were racing more. In *Road & Track* owner surveys, for VW Dasher and Audi Fox in February 1976, only 5% did slaloms, fewer rallied and only one raced out of 194 surveyed owners. In *Road & Track*'s March 1979 BMW 530i owner survey, just 5% did slaloms and rallies. In the former survey, 98% of owners purchased their rides for daily transportation. For 1976, only 5720 Corvette buyers went with the somewhat pricy $481 L82 350. For most, the L48 350 was enough, and the buff mags were in agreement with that choice. The ideal compromise of performance, tractability and economy, allied to zero surcharge. Then too, 36,625 said yes to the slushbox, the NCO RPO M40, that was a fine transmission. In conclusion, the current game was real world driving. The Corvette was fast becoming a 'Cowboy Cruiser'.

To improve Corvette refinement, via better structural rigidity, changes were made during 1976. There was a switch to steel panels instead of fiberglass in the floor area. These steel panels were now welded to the pillar support panel, and bonded to the Corvette's rear fiberglass section, which had a molded in closing panel. There was even more use of sound deadening material. The Corvette's passenger area had been previously poorly shielded from the heat of the Corvette's dual exhaust system, which had returned for '76 MY. However,

Corvette Coupe

By 1976's Bicentennial, the Corvette was almost as much of an American institution as Thanksgiving or Groundhog Day! *(Courtesy GM Archives)*

some folks in the snowbelt liked those fiberglass footwell panels, it kept 'em toasty!

It's believed the Corvette's formerly optional power brakes (J50), and power steering (N41), were standard by mid '76 MY. Indeed, all 46,558 1976 Corvettes seemed to have been specified with the 59 buck power brakes. Plus, the 46,385 coupes with $151 N41 represented a near universal take up rate. There was even more power to control, with the L48 350 now making 180 horse at four grand, the optional L82 350 was re-rated to 210bhp at 5200rpm. The term re-rating was used, because the engine speeds at which the peak outputs were measured were higher for 1976. The L82 350's 255lb/ft arriving at 3600rpm went unchanged, the L48 and L82 350s also kept their previous compression ratios: a respective 8.5 and 9.0:1. Redline for the latter was 5600rpm.

There was also a phasing out in Corvette land of the beefy THM 400 automatic. With contemporary smog motors, the smaller, lighter THM 350 would do just fine. You could get 3.55 rear gears, but that was oftentimes limited to high altitude areas. According to *High Performance Cars*' Marty

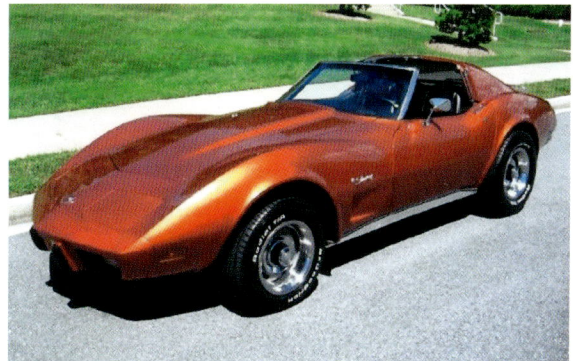

Coupe only by 1976, and starting from $7604.85. The color is code 69 Dark Brown, selected by 4447 Corvette fans in that year. *(Courtesy Flemings Ultimate Garage)*

Schorr, the area restriction was strictly enforced. Helping to pare down the pounds, GM's Delco Freedom Battery, saved 13lb. On the outside, code 37 Mahogany was a new hue possibility. Plus, the evocatively named Mille Miglia Red was no more. 1976 would prove to be the final outing of the Stingray sobriquet with Corvette. Stingray had been

175

Cold air hood induction was off the table for '76 MY, but the associated hood entry aperture was still present. *High Performance Cars'* Marty Schorr got 0-60mph in 6.9 seconds, and a 14.96 second ¼-mile at 92mph. There was some help from a tricked out torque converter, courtesy of Chevrolet Engineering, with the journal's test '76 Corvette L82 350 automatic. *(Courtesy Flemings Ultimate Garage)*

a front fender script. Inside, a silver interior was off the menu, but code 112 white leather and 15V white vinyl were new interior choices.

Corvette fans weren't over-enamored with the Vega GT four-spoked steering wheel, on prestige grounds. Simply too low rent for the 1976 Corvette! According to *Road Test* magazine in June 1976, the journal had received outraged magazine mail, to the effect that Corvette owners were displeased with the model's year to year constancy. That said, like the VW Beetle, the Corvette didn't go unchanged. Worthwhile improvements had arrived in a constant flow since 1953. What's more, the flat out state of Corvette's St Louis factory

There were a few '75 Corvette LS4 454s built, but by 1976 you had a single engine option: $481 210 horse L82 350. A mere 5720 Corvette patrons took the L82 350 route in 1976. Ribbed decorative valve covers, set the L82 350 apart from the 180 horse L48 350, underhood. *(Courtesy Flemings Ultimate Garage)*

home, suggested there was no real problem. In fact, Chevrolet management in 1976 came to the conclusion that with sales so strong, laissez faire was the best approach, and there was no real need for an all new Corvette.

Road Test felt otherwise in June 1976. It considered the Corvette too big, heavy and pricy at over 10 grand fully equipped. Quality was judged no better than a lowly Vega, and ergonomic woes like trouble reaching controls when belted, close steering wheel, and non-reclining seats still grated. As a counter point, long time Corvette racer John Greenwood was complimentary towards the 1976 Corvette. *Road & Track* was carrying out one of its road and race comparisons in March 1976. Greenwood was on hand, for show and tell concerning the stock '76 Corvette and his Spirit of Sebring '76 IMSA Corvette racing car. Both machines were tried at Daytona, and it was the first time John Greenwood had driven a stock Corvette on a racetrack. He was impressed with the regular Corvette, stating, "The car is very neutral." Like a race car it moved from understeer to neutral, when pouring on the power.

Greenwood found the brakes surprisingly good, with only a bit of fading. Throttle oversteer was available and controllable. The steering got a tad light on Daytona's banking at 130mph, but there was no wander. The Firestone GR70-15s rolled over on their sidewalls a little, according to Greenwood. This was unlike his racer's Goodyear Blue Streaks. Of course, Greenwood was in the BF Goodrich camp, back in the Goodyear vs BF Goodrich Tire Wars. That said, the stock Corvette at hand was predictable, had good grip and displayed no sudden breakaway. That regular 1976 Corvette coupe was a code 70 Orange Flame painted Corvette, with close ratio M21 four-speed, high altitude 3.55 axle, power steering, power brakes, and the Corvette's long promised YJ8 alloys. The Gymkhana suspension pack was also present.

YJ8 alloys were a new official '76 MY Corvette option. Just 6253 buyers took the $299 YJ8 alloys. Most of the 46,558 '76 Corvette buyers stuck with the standard Rally rims shown. *(Courtesy Flemings Ultimate Garage)*

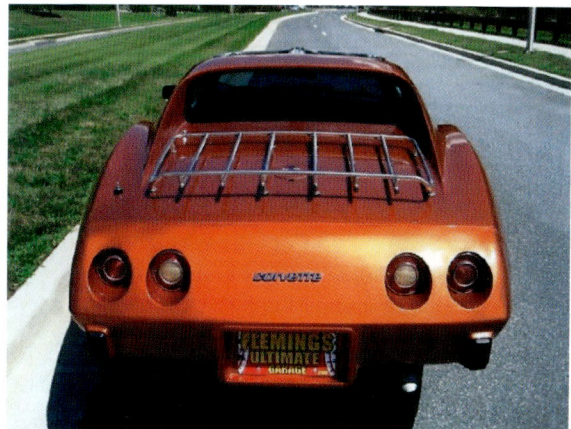

This was the sight that most import and domestic sporty car buyers would see in 1976! Such observers might have noticed Corvette's smaller and recessed '76 tailscript, versus '75 MY. *(Courtesy Flemings Ultimate Garage)*

The standard Corvette that John Greenwood tried was timed for 0-60mph in 8.1 seconds, 0-100mph in 23.6 seconds, with the ¼-mile in 16.5 seconds at 87mph. The coupe stopped from 60mph in 160ft, and showed 33% brake fade after *R&T*'s usual six-stop test. The first 0.5 deceleration stop needed 30lb of brake pedal pressure. 75dBA was registered at 70mph, with 84 decibels at wide open throttle, in first gear. 62dBA was registered at idle, for Greenwood's IMSA racer the same stat was 112dBA! John Greenwood lapped the Daytona circuit in 2min 36.2 seconds in the stock '76 Corvette at an average speed of 88.6mph. Chevrolet's prescribed high speed tire pressures of 26psi front, and 36psi rear, were observed. In contrast, Greenwood's Daytona pole time in his racer was 1min 52.05 seconds, at an average speed of 123.4mph!

Whereas many sporty cars were better on the road than track, the Corvette was the other way around. The stock '76 Corvette's performance figures represented as fast as anyone was going in 1976, without spending insane import money on a Porsche 930, or something equally exotic. The Corvette was never really designed to rack up the points, in a *Consumer Reports* type of assessment. In contrast, the German Corvette (aka Porsche 928) could do just that. That's why Zuffenhausen

won the 1978 European Car of the Year title with the Porsche 928 – doing things regular family cars could do! In June 1976, *Road Test* claimed the current Corvette was a "ubiquitous drive-in transvestite." The journal claimed that with ever rising sales, more cool blondes were buying Corvettes, leading to the situation of the Corvette being macho on the outside, but having a woman within! The previous year, *The Rocky Horror Show* movie had been released, and according to *Road Test*, it seemed if Frank N' Furter drove a car, it would be a Corvette! It seems you can't pick your family, nor sometimes even your friends ... On the current state of affairs, *Road Test* concluded concerning a somewhat stagnant Corvette, "... the Corvette deserves a better legacy than drive-ins and vacuous blondes."

Getting ready for 1977, Chevrolet seemed unperturbed by media observations. The Bow Tie brand released a print ad with code 56 Corvette Bright Yellow coupe, rolling stock Rally rims, and the title: "The role of the dream car in an age of reality." Indeed, at a time when the four cylinder econobox was on the rise, and GM was releasing its downsized, fullsize family cars, the Plastic Fantastic continued its billing, "Corvette, America's only true production sports car." In spite of claimed demographic developments in Corvette buyer

177

patterns, Corvette's '77 ad stated "And there are just two seats. One for you, one for her. – Corvette. Not just a car, an inspiration. Sweet Dreams."

1977 – End of the flying buttress!

IN THE DECEMBER 1976 issue of *High Performance Cars*, Marty Schorr said Corvette was still America's No 1 four-wheel status symbol and head turner. That same month came *Motor Trend*'s article by Tony Swan on the new 1977 Corvette, subtitled, "The name's the same, but the dream is changing." Swan recounted his youthful dream, shared by many contemporaries, of being a young Corvette devotee in 1958, eagerly awaiting the latest issue of *Hot Rod*. A fantasy Zora Arkus-Duntov handed him the keys to a tricked up Corvette, with all the goodies. Now, in late 1976, the dream was becoming reality, with a very early build, code 83 Corvette Dark Red resplendent 1977 Corvette. It was a new color for 1977, one of nine new Corvette colors in fact, with only code 10 Classic White a carryover from 1976. Then too, Swan was getting his test car, from the recently appointed Corvette Chief Engineer, Dave McLellan, accompanied by McLellan's top lieutenant Jim 'Jingles' Ingle.

For a Corvette fan, this was all from the horse's mouth, as it were, with Tony Swan about to take the Corvette Dark Red coupe on a 3500 mile jaunt from the GM Proving Grounds in Milford Michigan to *Motor Trend*'s HQ in LA, where formal test figures would be obtained. A cross country jaunt – quite normal for a Corvette; however, it was now a different Corvette, because, as Swan said, "... the brute horsepower that Duntov once envisioned for the Corvette hasn't much place in the 55mph world of the safety Nazis." As a counter point, Dave McLellan reminded Swan, "It's still the fastest car made in America." *MT*'s figures were a 16.6 second ¼-mile at 82mph, and 0-60mph in 8.8 seconds for the L82 350 powered automatic coupe, with 3.55 gears and a/c, were similar to those obtained by the like-engined *Road & Track* 1976 Corvette four-speed, driven by John Greenwood. Compared to the 20 second flat ¼-mile, of a 305 powered downsized fullsize Chevrolet Caprice V8, the Corvette was still swift, but yes, the dream was changing.

The Corvette was now a more refined GT cruiser,

CORVETTE & SUPER CORVETTE

John Greenwood helps us test a stock Corvette and his 221-mph race car

A code 70 Orange Flame '76 Corvette with four-speed, L82 350, FE7 Gymkhana suspension, 3.55 high altitude axle, YJ8 alloys. Racer John Greenwood was impressed with *Road & Track*'s test coupe. *(Courtesy Road & Track)*

and as for scat, Dave McLellan went on record saying, "We're concentrating hard on just trying to keep our performance where it was in 1975 through all the tightening emissions regulations that are coming." Concerning how the Corvette dream was evolving, McLellan made a personal comment, that he was worried over the Corvette's move to boulevard GT status. However, the Corvette crew were still honing the latest Plastic Fantastic to meet public demand for this kind of Cowboy Cruiser.

Never lose sight of the fact, that Team Corvette was still made up of enthusiasts with, as Bill Mitchell would say, gasoline in their veins. The perennial skunkworks project that was Corvette, happened out of a collection of engineering garages or offices, at GM's Milford Proving Ground. To be precise, several joined mobile homes. It was an arrangement that would persist through to the Late Model C3 Corvette's demise, at the end of 1982 model year. Plus, the Corvette crew were no strangers to handling, nor imperfect backroad surfaces. Dave McLellan and Jim Ingle discussed Tony Swan's route back to LA, describing on maps obscure roads in South Indiana, and Northern Kentucky, where they had tested the Corvette.

Like *Road & Track*'s March 1976 Corvette and Super
Corvette report, this roadgoing '76 Corvette has
the L82 350, M21 four-speed and 3.55 gears, plus
YJ8 alloys. This coupe now has a modified 355 V8,
with L82 internals and replacement four-bolt mains
block. The small block makes a dyno proven 357
rear wheel horsepower! *(Courtesy Mike Ploughman)*

Reference was made to the towns of Napolean
and Ballstown where, as McLellan relayed, one
could get airborne on occasion and experience
decreasing radius turns. The Corvette Chief
Engineer considered the roads out West to be not
as challenging. So it seemed, as in Zora Arkus-
Duntov times, the Corvette was still set up for
control, rather than Cadillac or Citroën style
comfort. As ever, the ride/handling compromise
is a personal one. On his drive back to the City
of Angels, *MT*'s Tony Swan discovered some
hydroplaning in Arizona, but enjoyed excellent dry
road handling and braking, feeling the ride comfort
compromise to be okay, given the Corvette's
benefits. Corvette power steering was aces, very
quick and possessing great feel, with just 2.9 turns
lock-to-lock.

Swan had other observations concerning the
Corvette, and fellow road users. Over the 3500 mile
jaunt, body creaks and groans accumulated quickly.
Footwells remained Corvette cramped, and in spite
of '77 MY alterations, console and steering wheel
clearance were still tight. Gas pedal engagement
was awkward, and the new cruise control wasn't as
easy to use as Ford's equivalent. It succumbed to
speed creep. Although the footwell floor was now
steel, engine and transmission heat soak could still
be felt. Corvette fresh air ventilation was improved,

Canuck Corvette fans needed to take one long,
last look at this '76 Corvette's optional L82 350.
From 1977, only the base L48 350 would be
available in the Great White North, due to smog law.
This motor now has Air Flow Research 195 Street
Eliminator aluminum heads, Weiand 7530 single
plane aluminum intake, Holley 750 Street HP double
pumper 4bbl carb with mechanical secondaries,
K&N air filter, Howard's Cams hydraulic roller
cam and Keith Black hypereutectic pistons.
(Courtesy Mike Ploughman)

The exterior shade in code 33 Dark Green, chosen by
2038 '76 Corvette fanciers. The sidepipes ain't stock.
Indeed, sidepipes had been absent from the Corvette
option sheet since 1969. Further mods run to 4.11
gears, and MSD 6530 programmable ignition module,
with MAF sensor. *(Courtesy Mike Ploughman)*

but C60 a/c was still a wise option. 45,249 Corvette
faithful did pony up the additional 553 clams for
a/c, out of 49,213 1977 Corvettes sold.

As for the L82 350 on test, it sounded great when
McLellan and Jingles handed the Corvette to Tony
Swan. However, like the early LS V8s of the future,

BUILD STICKER

Build Sticker created at
Davies Corvette Parts & Accessories
www.corvetteparts.com

MAKE CHEVROLET   MODEL 1YZ37 1976 CORVETTE COUPE - V8

VEHICLE IDENTIFICATION NUMBER 1Z37X65419891   FINAL ASSEMBLY POINT ST. LOUIS, MISSOURI

DELIVERED TO: MIKE PLOUGHMAN
               HAMMONDS PLAINS NS

THE FOLLOWING ITEMS ARE STANDARD ON THIS MODEL AT NO EXTRA CHARGE	SUGGESTED RETAIL PRICE OF THIS MODEL INCLUDING PREPARATION	7,604.85
	Suggested Retail Price for Options and Accessories installed on this Vehicle	

• 350-4 V8 ENGINE	A31 POWER WINDOWS	107.00
	C49 ELECTRO-CLEAR REAR DEFOGGER	78.00
• HIGH ENERGY IGNITION SYSTEM	C60 FOUR-SEASON AIR CONDITIONING	523.00
	FE7 GYMKHANA SUSPENSION	35.00
• POSITRACTION REAR AXLE	J50 POWER BRAKES	59.00
	L82 SPECIAL 350-4 BBL V-8 ENGINE	481.00
	M21 FOUR SPEED MANUAL TRANSMISSION	0.00
• 4-WHEEL DISC BRAKE SYSTEM	N37 TILT-TELESCOPIC STEERING WHEEL	95.00
	N41 POWER STEERING	151.00
• TAPERED HIGH-BACK BUCKET SEATS	QRZ GR70-15/B S/B RADIAL W/LETTERED	51.00
	U58 AM/FM STEREO RADIO	281.00
• FULL INSTRUMENTATION	UA1 HEAVY DUTY BATTERY	16.00
	UF1 MAP LIGHT	10.00
• TINTED GLASS	YJ8 ALUMINUM WHEELS	299.00
	322 BLUE-GREEN LEATHER BUCKET	164.00
• ANTI-THEFT AUDIO ALARM SYSTEM	33L DARK GREEN	0.00
• 4-WHEEL INDEPENDENT SUSPENSION SYSTEM		
• STEEL-BELTED RADIAL PLY TIRES		
• FREEDOM BATTERY		
• ENGINE COOLANT RECOVERY SYSTEM		

	Installed Options and Accessories Subtotal	2,350.00
	Destination Charge	0.00
	TOTAL AMOUNT	9,954.85

In no way should this document be considered authentic or original documentation for any vehicle. Prices of Vehicle & Manufacturer's options are original published retail prices at the time of manufacture.

Fully equipped, the 10 grand Corvette was considered expensive by the US press. However, considering the hardware, it was still well priced, and undercut imports like the BMW 530i by a couple of grand or more. *(Courtesy Mike Ploughman)*

there was oil drinking. Sump capacity was five quarts, and they were all used up on the way back to LA! Tony Swan judged the 16.6mpg to be so-so. The Corvette people, just like the Mazda RX3 folks, had been working to boost gas mileage, but Dave McLellan and staff said fuel economy wasn't a high priority for Corvette customers. It was more so for the rotary crowd, explaining their falling sales. The test L82 350 bogged down at high altitude. Even though GM led the way on smog drivability, it seemed the humble carb was on the way out for the smog, economy and performance trio.

There were small visual changes with the '77 Corvette, and Tony Swan got more waves from owners of older Corvettes than from drivers of more recent C3 Corvettes. Then too, in Kentucky and Indiana there was some negative behavior. They didn't call it road rage in those days, but the Corvette's ubiquity in such areas seemed to breed contempt. This was perhaps another reason a rising number were turning to the lower profile import marques of Alfa Romeo, BMW, Mercedes and Porsche. Tony Swan said the Corvette was still

the great American dream machine, but was now for grown ups. Indeed, the Corvette and GM's other sporty chariots were much improved in several areas but one, power. Yes, the one thing missing in such rides, which earlier incarnations had, was a really banging engine. And you can blame OPEC and the smog Nazis for its absence. That said, Dave McLellan was proud of the many changes wrought on the 1977 Corvette.

The Corvette design staff were under Chevrolet Studio Chief Jerry Palmer, and the mood revolved around a more low key look. Black windshield moldings, made for a thinner look to the Corvette's windshield pillars, and the front fender Stingray script was absent. The Plastic Fantastic's familiar crossed flags now graced the front fenders, Corvette nose, and gas filler door. Nine new exterior colors for 1977 added a fresh touch. However, the carryover code 10 Classic White was still the most popular, with 9408 coupes so painted. Code 19 Black came second with 6070 Corvettes. But only one, yes one, 1977 Corvette was purchased in code 41 Corvette Chartreuse!

The new D35 sport mirrors cost 36 bucks, and featured on 20,206 1977 Corvettes. Apart from style, D35 implied a remote driver side cable control, for mirror pane adjustment. The convex surface came with a printed notice on the passenger side, warning of the Corvette's traditional blindspot. GM had planned 'Moon Roof' style tinted glass T-tops for 1977. However, the proposed option had to be cancelled due to a manufacturer dispute, that led to GM doing its own design for the feature's formal 1978 model year introduction. In any case, the '77 Corvette's optional RPO V54 luggage and roof panel rack ($73) was designed to safely hold T-top panels. This freed up the Corvette's luggage cavity.

The 1977 Corvette brought standard leather seating. However, as a NCO you could have cloth inserts to stop one sliding around. Such leather and cloth ensembles were denoted with the 'C' code suffix, pure leather with the familiar '2'. For the

The interior is code 322 Blue-Green Leather ($164), the four-speed was the NCO close ratio Muncie. One advantage of the much maligned Vega GT tiller was its ability to be color keyed! (Courtesy Mike Ploughman)

Getting down to detail, a Hurst Competition Plus shifter works a DFX clutch, with Center Force billet steel 31# flywheel handling the horsepower. The Howard's Cams 280 degree duration unit has 0.560in of lift, on both intake and exhaust sides. (*Courtesy Mike Ploughman*)

first time, the Corvette was without vinyl seating. Speaking of leather, forget about the Vega GT sports steering wheel, there was now an optional three-spoke leather clad tiller. This was only if you didn't go for the desirable N37 tilt-telescopic steering column, which went with the '76 MY Vega GT wheel.

The Corvette's former door card woodgrain, switched to a satin black finish. Plus, if $22 were expended on the new B32 color keyed floor mats, and 36,763 Corvette buyers did, a selection of four colors would replace the standard black rubber mats. As part of a console area redesign, auxiliary gauges now lived in pods. Concerning the Corvette's ever rising plushness, *Car and Driver*'s Patrick Bedard was moved to say in March 1977 that the Plastic Fantastic's price and interior quality were on the rise. There was even a visual change underhood, and engine paint color change from the usual Chevrolet orange to blue, which occurred during August 23 to September in 1976, at GM's Flint, Michigan engine plant.

The motoring media had long criticized the Corvette's ergonomics. To make amends, the '77 Corvette had a steering column 2in shorter. For tall North American drivers, domestic cars had long had the steering wheel close and the pedals far, so Corvette was now more European style. The four-speeds shift lever was one inch taller for 1977. So,

you no longer banged your elbow on the handbrake when going for second! Not a problem for domestic family cars that rarely had a four-speed, and never a European style handbrake! Domestics also put the high beam dipswitch in the footwell, and generally steered clear of column stalk functions. Dashboard buttons and knobs were normal. The Corvette went European style for 1977 with Smart Switch. That is, a left side steering column stalk, controlling wash/wipe, directional and high beam action.

For 1977, the Corvette indulged domestic taste with the long loved gadget of cruise control. Formally, it was RPO K30 speed control, costing 88 bucks, with 29,161 '77 Corvette faithful ticking that box. K30 implied an on/off lever switch, placed ahead of Smart Switch. Both stalks were not quite ideally located. You had to remove your left hand from the steering wheel. Was Smart Switch too smart? Possibly too many features on one stalk? In any case, America's only sports car still lacked a glovebox! Even so, the dashboard and console area had been reworked. The long standing thumbwheel HVAC controls gave way to the kind of slider lever,

181

1976 Corvette sales beat out the Plastic Fantastic's previous record set in 1969. It seemed that despite industry critics who predicted the demise of sporty V8s, the Corvette would be around a while yet. *(Courtesy Mike Ploughman)*

An absence of Stingray badging, and a shorter steering column distinguished the latest '77 Corvette in the age of reality. *(Courtesy GM Archives)*

control panel one would recognize on GM F body and G body cars. $116 A31 fast glass switches were moved from the handbrake housing, to just behind the shifter. A volt meter replaced the former console ammeter, and Corvette got a new low fuel warning light.

Corvette's steering column lock also changed from back drive linkage style to a simpler key release lever. However, a major motivation for the Corvette's interior redesign concerned in-car audio entertainment. Domestic cars had long had larger apertures than the European DIN mount, but to accommodate GM's latest, wide and physically large audio range, Corvette needed some finagling. Forget about an aftermarket 8-track player you might find in a Ferrari Daytona, or Rolls Royce even – Corvette's GM Delco hardware was specially designed, factory-fitted, and it looked real neat! 1977 Corvette set a new world standard for in car audio, factory-fitted gadgetry.

There was the chance of a four element communications and entertainment center: AM/FM stereo radio, Citizens Band radio/console CB microphone and 8-track player. Official word was that all elements would be functional from January 1977, that is, available. Complimenting this ensemble was a black antennae, with coupe body color matching tip! All eyes, and ears were on the new RPO UM2 AM-FM stereo radio with 8-track, and 24,603 '77 Corvette buyers paid the sizable $414 for the privilege. The factory CB radio issue, common to many contemporary domestics, was indicative of a craze sweeping the nation from the mid '70s, and immortalized in the 1977 movie *Smokey and the Bandit*, starring Burt Reynolds.

Soon, everyone got a handle, and joined trucker folk listening to CB chatter, while traversing endless miles of gray flannel interstate. It was invaluable to stave off 55mph boredom. It was surely no coincidence that Corvette got cruise control and factory CB radio at this hour. And, if you wanted to push things beyond double nickel, and avoid four-wheel gumball machines, Kojaks with Kodaks, or Bears in the air, well, you had better have your ears on good buddy. Do you copy and receive? That's a big 10-4!

To help Corvette travel, 1977 saw standard swiveling sun visors to block out side glare, a

As sensible as '70s domestic driving got, the new downsized '77 Caprice featured a new economy oriented small block 305 V8. GM made a lot of $$$ from its downsized fullsize family cars.
(Courtesy GM Archives)

What do you get when you cross AMT, George Barris and Farrah Fawcett? The 1/25 scale AMT Farrah's Foxy Vette, naturally! *(Courtesy Round One)*

passenger coat hook, and easier cargo cavity access with a revised top molding. If all this and the V54 luggage rack weren't enough, don't get mad, go nomad. No, not the classic contemporary wagon of the Straight Axle Corvette era, rather the RPO ZN1 trailer package costing $83, and the help of U-Haul. To keep an eye on what one might be towing, '77 Corvettes had a rubber-mounted Donnelley rear view mirror on the windshield. It had been roof mounted, and more prone to vibration in previous years. When parked, the Corvette's factory alarm system was handy, since as ever, Corvette and its parts were a thief magnet. From 1977 you would arm the system via the left door lock button.

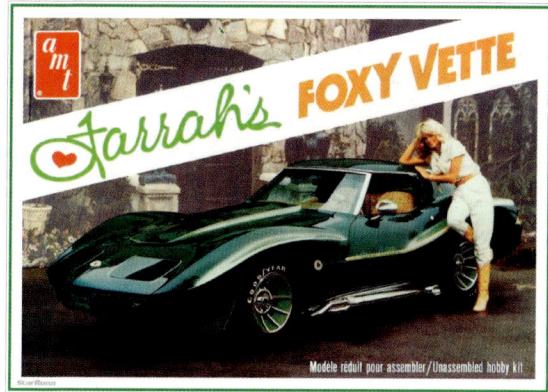

Those Corvette people really did seem to think of everything. Corvette was the sports car where stuff was designed in, not just tacked on. In earlier times that meant high performance hardware, now it was creature comforts. Indeed, 40,872 1977 Corvette buyers paid 22 bucks for the ZX2 'Convenience Group'. Of Corvette's rationalized options list, pure performance items were just: L82 350 V8, close ratio M21 four-speed (NCO), Gymkhana suspension, alloy rims and G95 optional rear axle ratio, permitted 3.70 on the happy high, and 2.73 rear axle on the sleepy side of the street. Canada was now limited to the L48 350, due to smog law. Regardless of the environment, 1977 was the final year for Corvette receiving the THM 400 automatic, and then only on L82 350 coupes. From 1978-81 it would be just the THM 350. If you wanted a THM 400, try the Jag XJS! 1977 Corvettes also lacked the old cold air induction hood entry point.

J50 power brakes were a technical option, but all '77 Corvettes had them. Plus, N41 power steering was virtually standard, just 173 Corvette coupes lacked this power assist. Through all the changes, the one mostly constant was how and where the Corvette was constructed. The venue, from December 1953 was the old St Louis truck plant, that by the late '70s had 1000 employees, made up to ten Corvettes per hour, and also assembled Impalas and upscale Caprices. With much in common with the English Morgan, the Corvette had separate chassis construction, and was, by

The 1978 Corvette was planned to be a hatchback. However, this intention had to wait until the 1982 Corvette Collector Edition. In the meantime, there was C&C's 1978 conversion. *(Courtesy C&C Concepts)*

modern standards, handbuilt. There was virtually no automation, and plant workers didn't allow the work-in-progress Corvette to move to the next work station until the previous sub assembly workers were happy.

The Corvette's still hefty ladder type chassis was done in a separate part of the St Louis factory. Suspension, exhaust system and gas tank were installed on an upside down chassis, which was then turned over for powertrain fitment. The by-now famous Corvette birdcage body sub structure was worked on in yet another part of the plant. The birdcage was dipped in caustic solution, dried and then painted black. The Corvette body panels had bonding agent applied between seams and flanges, via cone shaped cake icers. Proud joints were then ground/sanded away. Heavily padded lifts grasped the Corvette's fiberglass body by its Can Am style fender wells, to lower said body upon the frame.

The 15in rim's five nuts went on in one maneuver, with each car then test run on rollers, with a front end alignment performed at this stage. Corvette completion then entailed interior fitment, which included seating components, followed by headlamp alignment, and careful overall inspection. The finished 1977 Corvette then made its way to the storage yard, where it awaited shipment. Note that while in said yard, Corvettes could get rained, snowed or even hailed on! Just as well fiberglass is very dent resistant. While Corvette plant workers were a proud group, the Corvette's hand assembled nature, construction type, high demand, antiquated nature of the St Louis plant that had trouble meeting such high demand, all implied that the finished Corvette oftentimes fell short of the fit and finish one would expect on a vehicle of its price and market position.

A case in point was enthusiast 1977 Corvette owner Jerry Whitman. Whitman's code 52 Corvette Yellow coupe (a hue chosen by just 71 buyers that year, while 1942 went for code 56 Corvette Bright Yellow) was so poorly finished, it required an immediate repaint. Of course, like most Corvette fans, and Jag lovers come to that, such outrageous fortune would be stomached to an extent that the typical Honda Civic or Toyota Celica buyer would never bear. In truth, Corvettes weren't as well made as in pre-1968 times. Then too, countering the assertion of *Road Test* magazine from June 1976, Jerry Whitman and the vast majority of Corvette owners were still male bachelors. Don't believe everything you read!

This 1978 Corvette coupe is called Brownie Bear, and features Corvette's most popular power team of 1975-80: L48 350 & THM 350 automatic. A spreader bar has been added. Exterior color is code 89 Corvette Dark Brown, selected by 1991 '78 Corvette fans. *(Courtesy Charlie Kersch)*

Corvette at the movies

BY THE MID to late '70s, cars in movies and car movies were increasingly in vogue. Perversely, interest in the genre rose as horsepower and performance fell with tightening smog law and gas mileage CAFE targets. A very popular sporty car, you would expect to see a Corvette on the silver screen. Yes, but sometimes it wasn't even a real Corvette! Such was the case in producer Roger Corman's low budget, cult film *Death Race 2000* from 1975, directed by Paul Bartel. Lead character in this dystopian horsepower fest was 'The Monster', played by David Carradine. His ride was called Frankenstein's Monster. Although it looked like a modified Late Model C3 Corvette, it wasn't. It was indeed a custom job, utilizing a '65 Corvair floorpan, Corvair flat six under a dummy engine

cover and automatic transmission. All cars in *Death Race 2000* were built by Dick Dean.

A real Corvette, a new '76 code 13 Silver Corvette L48 350 automatic coupe, with Rally rims and RWL rubber to be precise, was the eventual winner in Roger Corman's New World Pictures 1976 flick *Cannonball*, also directed by Paul Bartel. Like *Death Race 2000*, Sylvester Stallone appeared, but was uncredited in *Cannonball*. The movie depicts Brock Yates' (*Car and Driver*'s one-time Editor in Chief), illegal Cannonball Baker Sea-To-Shining Sea Memorial Trophy Dash. This movie slightly preceded the better known 1976 film *The Gumball Rally*, and later still Burt Reynolds/Hal Needham *Cannonball Run* movies. Such acts of social disobedience, and the movies that depicted such wanton acts were a protest against the 55mph national speed limit, introduced to improve

185

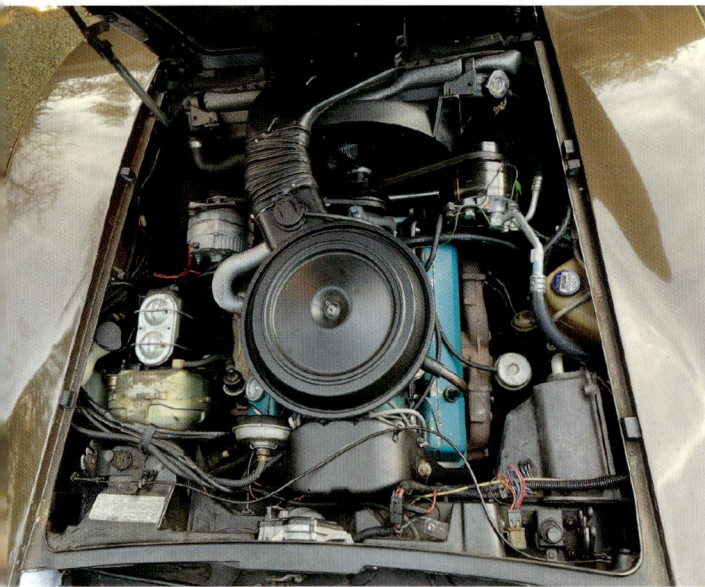

For 1978, the ultra reliable and torque rich L48 350 gained five horses to reach 185bhp SAE net. Its sound is enhanced on this coupe by Magnaflow mufflers.
(Courtesy Charlie Kersch)

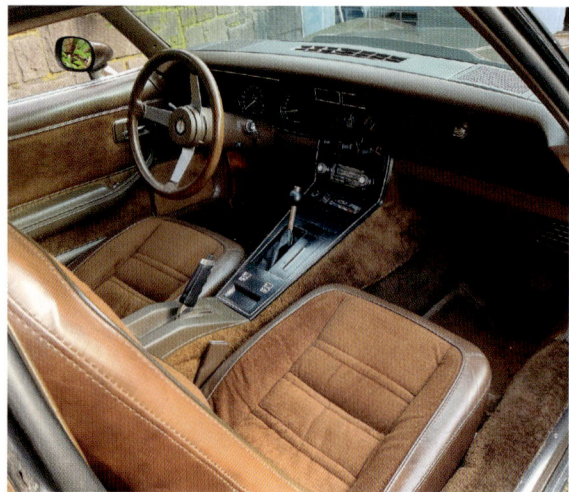

A glovebox and molded armrests were 1978 Corvette refinements. If a L82 350 was underhood, a special THM 350 with low inertia, high stall speed (2400rpm) torque converter was fitted. Interior code shown is 69C Dark Brown Cloth. Earth tones were very much in vogue during the late '70s.
(Courtesy Charlie Kersch)

America's balance of payments in the wake of the first OPEC fuel crisis, and retained for road safety purposes.

1976's *Cannonball* featured a plethora of future classic cars, like the aforementioned Corvette, plus yellow '73 Pantera, two identically liveried '70½ Trans Am Ram Air III 400s, a Dodge Charger, Chevrolet Blazer, Lincoln Continental, '69 Mustang 427, plus souped up van and stock van. The Corvette's real life foe, Pantera, was driven by German ace Wolfe Messer, and blown up in an act of sabotage. The Corvette was driven by a young, good Samaritan, sweetheart surfer couple. Indeed, the girlfriend had purloined her daddy's new Corvette for the LA to NY road race. The stock Corvette featured made some powerful noises, and did a few strong take offs en route. The only mechanical malady was a broken fanbelt. This was patched up at a gas station with adhesive tape. The station attendant said that otherwise, the Corvette would have to sit while the part was ordered in.

The boss of the Modern Motors racer team, eventually bestowed a contract upon David Carradine's racer character, Coy Cannonball

Buckman. The boss drove a BMW 2002, and this sedan, along with the Pantera, were the only imports featured. It was a sign of how things were. According to the data from the Motor Vehicle Manufacturers Association and Wards Communication Inc, 1970, 1973 and 1976 saw the domestic share of the auto market running at a respective 84.8%, 84.7% and 85.2%. It declined thereafter, as Japanese imports became more assertive.

In the road race movie *The Gumball Rally* of 1976, a new code 56 Bright Yellow Corvette coupe with YJ8 alloys was briefly shown. It was surrounded by coffin nose AMC Matador cop cars, given the Corvette was an apprehended racer! However, not all Late Model C3 Corvettes shown in contemporary movies were new. Also in *The Gumball Rally* was a '68 big block cream colored Corvette roadster, with custom flared fenders for its oversize rims and tires. This Corvette got airborne, and broke in two upon landing! Also in 1976 came Clint Eastwood's third Dirty Harry movie, *The Enforcer*. Here, opening scenes showed a '69 code 984 Daytona Yellow small block Corvette roadster,

In the background is Brownie Bear, in the foreground another '78 Corvette L48 350 automatic called …
Yellow Beastie! *(Courtesy Charlie Kersch)*

driven by a racing Romeo trying to pick up a hot blonde chick in denim cut offs. She shined him on, being part of a violent activist group, wishing to lure utility workers that would be happening along soon.

1978 saw the release of movie *Corvette Summer*, literally a vehicle for Mark Hamill in his first flick post *Star Wars*. Hamill played car crazy Californian teen Kenny Dantley, who spots and rescues a wrecked 1973 Corvette from a junkyard for a shop class project. Transformed into right-hand drive, the customized coupe is soon stolen from the streets of Van Nuys, thanks to the inattention of Danny Bonaduce's character. Dantley then tracks down the purloined Plastic Fantastic to Vegas. While on the casino strip, he teams up with trainee hooker Vanessa (Annie Potts). Sincere car and Corvette lover Kenny informs Vanessa of the Corvette's qualities. Vanessa is impressed that someone so young is in possession of the status symbol that was, and still is, Corvette.

Kevin Dantley's Corvette description almost went without saying. That is, the Corvette was America's only sports car, and a man's car at that,

For most of the 46,776 1978 Corvettes, the L48 350 and THM 350 slushbox got the job done. This coupe has xenon headlights, wired directly to the alternator. *(Courtesy Charlie Kersch)*

although sometimes girls bought one, but just to get noticed. The last point of view was circulating at the time. *Road Test* magazine in June 1976 went a step further, asserting such ladies were trawling for a mate! In substance, the automatic Corvette L82 350 *Road Test* tried got 70/100, with the top scoring Saab EMS and Porsche 930 reaching 79 points out of 100 overall. So, the Plastic Fantastic was still a solid performer, but perhaps not the fire breather of young Dantley's dreams. In truth, both the character and Corvette characterized in the movie were more appropriate to the legendary Astoria Chas and his 1967 Corvette big block, than 1977's teenager with the latest Corvette model.

Two 1973 Corvettes were built for MGM by Korke's Kustom Studios: a main machine and back up coupe. For a spell, the original mold

was displayed at the Corvette Americana Hall of Fame, in Cooperstown NY, and became part of the National Corvette Museum's collection. The two movie cars survived, with the main and back up cars moving to Australia and New Zealand respectively! As a custom car, the *Corvette Summer* creation was representative of customization of the era that horsepower forgot, making up for malaise with overtly extrovert style. It possibly lacked the taste, imagination and whimsy of Ed Roth, Von Dutch or George Barris in the '60s. However, as a late '70s high school shop project, it was believable. *Corvette Summer* was profitable. Some of the movie's success was attributable to the Corvette's popularity, and the high esteem the nameplate has long been held in, malaise era notwithstanding.

You got to see a 1977 Corvette in code 13 Silver

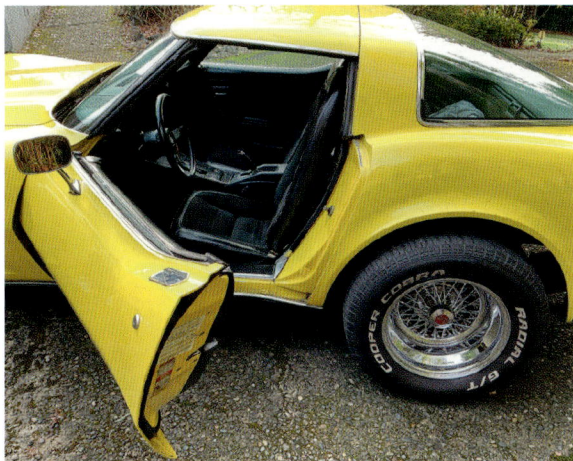

Modifications include real wire wheels, Wilwood brakes and a 2in lowering job. Dual-mount composite spring, shorter coil springs and spreader bar, help handling. *(Courtesy Charlie Kersch)*

The redesigned Corvette dashboard, had a hooded instrument binnacle, and steering wheel like '70s arcade game racing simulator cabinets. The Lancia Scorpion and BMW 320i also adopted this fashionable Atari Gran Trak 10 look! *(Courtesy Charlie Kersch)*

with code 722 Red leather interior, and L48 350 automatic powertrain, in the 1979 sci-fi/horror film *The Dark*. William Devane's writer character Ray Warner owned the silver Corvette. He was tracking down a mysterious creature that killed his daughter, and others. He was aided by TV personality Zoe Owens, played by Cathy Lee Crosby. The Corvette coupe had a CB radio, and a newly released product of the time, a Bearcat 210 radio scanner. This drive-in pleaser was produced by *American Bandstand* host Dick Clark, with further music tie in, given *Billboard 100* presenter Casey Kasem played a pathologist!

A modified 1977 Corvette also featured in the 1986 Charlie Sheen movie *The Wraith*, where it was street raced by Nick Cassevetes' bad guy character. However, for real 24-carat glamor, you had to leave it to America's leading car customizer George Barris, and a custom Corvette he did for *Charlie's Angels*' star Farrah Fawcett, that is: Farrah's Foxy Vette! Barris became a household name, creating iconic TV machines like the Batmobile, Munster Koach and the Green Hornet's Black Beauty, not forgetting the demonic coupe shown in the 1977 James Brolin film, *The Car*.

Farrah's Foxy Vette, one of Barris' lesser known projects, was a celebrity and model kit tie in deal. A free custom car would go to a famous person,

with Barris retaining the rights to make a second car for the show circuit, as well as marketing rights for scale model kit manufacture. Following Farrah's Foxy Vette, came the Travolta Fever Firebird. Indeed, Barris did a couple of wide body Firebirds. One was pictured with *Playboy* Playmate of the year, Dorothy Stratten, which appeared in the 1979 Steve Martin comedy *The Jerk*. John Travolta's Firebird even had a *Midnight Cowboy* theme interior, with kits produced by Revell.

Farrah's Foxy Vette was available in a 1978 ¹⁄₂₅ scale model kit, made by AMT. The box art graphic 'Farrah' mimicked Farrah Fawcett's signature style, oftentimes seen on posters and merchandise. In Farrah Fawcett and John Travolta, George Barris certainly had the most famous celebrities of the late '70s. Farrah's Foxy Vette was a green car, influenced by John Greenwood's road race conversions. The Monza rear end cap seems to have irked many, like the Corvette's '76 Vega GT steering wheel. Too low rent for a Corvette, but it did look good! The coupe's pictured hood bulge suggested a big block 454 V8 underhood, but a real life survivor example has displayed pinstriping, a 350 V8 and four-speed.

A replacement, later design 350 crate motor resides, but looks like the L48 350 original. This V8 exhales through Tri-Y headers. *(Courtesy Charlie Kersch)*

An aluminum radiator, with dual electric fans, keeps Yellow Beastie cool. Wrapping the engine bay-located a/c evaporator box with insulating material improves a/c effectiveness. *(Courtesy Charlie Kersch)*

Inside, you'd find a car phone, TV and lots of shagpile carpet, all expected in the '70s. With Farrah Fawcett pictured inside, it was probably the ultimate man cave! In any case, the AMT kit was based on AMT's 1969-77 Corvette kit. The Eckler Corvette and Farrah's Foxy Vette came out post 1977, but featured the 1968-77 flying buttress look. A rare kit in the present, indicating it wasn't a hot seller back in the day. As for the real life Farrah's Foxy Vette, an automotive unicorn if ever there was!

1978 ⇒ Fastback special editions

IN THE GLORY days of the Motor City, one in six US worker's incomes were tied to the auto sector. The 1978 movie *Blue Collar* revealed a Goodyear electronic billboard, informing highway drivers of Detroit's rising 1977 vehicle product tally. The Corvette reached a milestone in 1977, the half millionth Plastic Fantastic dream car produced no less! The coupe in question alighted off the St Louis line on Friday March 11 1977. The Corvette was a code 10 Classic White edition, with red interior, a/c, tilt-tele wheel, automatic transmission, rear window defogger, cruise control, alloys, sports mirrors, Gymkhana handling pack and RWL tires.

The 500,000th Corvette provided a small historical tie in with the original 1953 Polo White

only Corvette roadster that started it all. The special 1977 example had serial number 1Z37X75426583, and was delivered to Bernie Hunt Chevrolet of Mt Clemens, Michigan, but first some PR work! That is, taking said coupe off the line, cleaning it up, placing a No 500,000 decal across the windshield, and then sending it back down the line on Monday March 14, with the official press release time of completion, shutter bugs on hand, being Tuesday March 15 at 2.01pm.

The Corvette had long been a milestone car, and a car of milestones for Chevrolet, GM, and the auto industry. It happened again for 1978, when a fastback Corvette returned to St Louis for the first time since 1967 model year. To be precise, a compound curve rear window, bonded around the fiberglass body's base edges, using Thyokol. Indeed, 1978 pilot examples #001-006 went to Chevrolet Engineering, #007 was destined for the well known Rinke Chevrolet collection. However, it could have been even more. Plans were made for a rear hatchback, with this layout's accessibility benefits and attendant sunshade draw cover. However, in the final analysis, Corvette Chief Engineer Dave McLellan decided not to complicate the 1978 Corvette. That year you could get a hatchback conversion from Cars & Concepts. Failing that, bide your time for the Late Model

Yellow Beastie announces its presence with a dual exhaust system. High flow cats feature, and an oxygen sensor is linked to a dashboard fuel/air mixture gauge. *(Courtesy Charlie Kersch)*

Corvette's swansong that was the 1982 Collector Edition Corvette!

In October 1977, *Car and Driver* exclaimed, "At last, the fast is back!" Falling in, and out of, love with the nation's only sports car, 1975-78 seemed to be a time when both *C/D* and *Road & Track* liked the Corvette, but before and after was a different matter. For now, the fastback was Steve McQueen cool, even if the extra rearward weight made handling more tail happy. That said, there was more to the 1978 Corvette than a fastback. Indeed, this was the first Corvette that Zora Arkus-Duntov's successor, Dave McLellan, truly influenced. The small evolutionary refinements added up.

The glass moonroof T-top panels arrived for '78 MY, coded RPO CC1, and separately optioned by 972 buyers, at a cost of $349. The legal dispute with the planned '77 MY supplier was past, and GM went its own way. Acknowledging the fact that by the end of 1977 the Corvette was one of the most stolen cars around, the coupe's glass T-tops came with a key lock. Then too, the Corvette's T-tops were tamper wired into the Corvette's alarm system for 1978. The biggest change to the Corvette's interior for 1978 was the return of a conventional glovebox, for the first time since the Corvette's Mid-Year era.

The Corvette's dashboard was modernized, with a one piece, fully padded molding. It featured a front mount instrument cluster. Said cluster had a new speedo and tach layout, and the whole assembly promised easier service access. Ergonomically, the wiper/washer selector was moved back to the dashboard. However, the dipped beam facility remained on the column stalk. Single

1978 saw the Corvette pace the Indianapolis 500, for the first time! Naturally, there was a pace car replica, called Limited Edition Corvette Pace Car. *(Courtesy GM Archives)*

inertia reel seatbelts implied no more belt guides. Plus, the new style '78 Corvette door cards featured screw on armrests, not the molded variety seen on Plastic Fantastics since 1965. There were also integral door pulls. One might also have been sitting more comfortably in 1978, given Corvette's adoption of Chevrolet's new thin-shell bucket seat design. It promised greater lumbar support.

Engineering wise, the Corvette also promised more comfort, allied to improved range. There was still a domestic perception that radials rode harsher. Given the '78 Corvette availability of 60 series tires, Aramid belt construction made for a smoother ride. However, this new $216 RPO QBS P225/60R15 WL SBR tire, necessitated factory fender trimming to fit. 18,296 Corvette faithful chose QBS in 1978, but 26,203 optioned the $51 QGR P225/70R15 WL SBR tires. Either way, Corvette was now rolling on a metric sized footprint – goodbye GR70-15s!

Anyone irked by Corvette's relatively frequent

6502 Limited Edition Corvette Pace Cars were sold, with a 1978 price of $13,656. However, many paid way over list! The original plan involved 300 two-tone silver/redstriped coupes, to match the '53 Corvette total, plus Goodyear tires with 'CORVETTE' RWL script. *(Courtesy RK Motors)*

The L82 350 motor had a dual snorkel air intake for
'78 MY, and 220bhp. L82 350s featured decorative,
ribbed valve covers. *(Courtesy RK Motors)*

need to be refilled with gas, would be heartened
that the Corvette's smallish tank rose in size from
1977's 17 gallons, to 24 gallons for 1978. What's
more, an internal molded plastic liner within the
tank's steel shell implied greater tank corrosion
resistance and safety. However, the downside of the
larger tank was a smaller space saver spare. The
Corvette had long featured thoughtful alterations to
an existing design, rather than change for the sake
of change. The domestic auto industry was known
for the latter. If GM had applied such thinking
to its other lines, it may have coped with import
competition more easily. Then again, the Corvette
owner wasn't the typical domestic car buyer.

It was a sign of the times that Corvette's
performance changes for 1978 were a mere
footnote to that model year's revisions, even
though they represented the first increases after
two years of constancy. The ever popular L48 350,
and increasingly popular L82 350, were now rated
at a respective 195bhp and 220bhp. They were a
respective five and ten horse improvement, over
1977 levels. Perhaps Chevrolet was following
Woolworths' one time pricing policy?! In any
event, the L82 350 now sported a dual snorkel
air intake, allied to larger exhaust/tailpipes and
lower restriction mufflers. In a coupe weighing
around 3600lb, objectively these were modest
increases, but in the Love Boat/disco/CAFE era,
they were welcome nonetheless. *Car and Driver*
proclaimed the 1978 Corvette L82 350 four-speed
to be the fastest American production car, with
certainty, even if Pontiac fans might have added
equal fastest, citing the 1978 Pontiac Firebird Trans
Am W72 400 four-speed. By some incredible state
of happenstance, both Corvette and Trans Am
possessed 220 SAE net horses.

The M21 close ratio four-speed was still a
Corvette NCO, but could only be enjoyed with L82
350 and 3.70 gears. It was a set menu performance
trinity. That said, you could order a '78 Corvette
L82 350 with wide ratio M20 four-speed, the
Corvette's standard gearbox, and 3.70 rear gears,
of the sensible 3.36 axle. If a 1978 Corvette L48

The 1978 Corvette Pace Car received a silver leather
interior, a year before the 1979 10th Anniversary
Trans Am! Note the red L82 350 hood badge.
(Courtesy RK Motors)

350 four-speed was your bag, settle for that 3.36
axle. Corvette L82 350 with slushbox now had
a low inertia, high stall speed (2400rpm) torque
converter. *High Performance Cars'* Marty Schorr
had driven just such a car, saying in the December
1976 issue that Chevrolet Engineering had
been working on a tricked up torque converter.
Corvettes with automatic transmission came with
3.55 gears, but a taller 3.08 rear end applied to
Californian and or high altitude Corvette L48 350
automatics. In such locales, the L48 350 was rated
at 175bhp, thanks to the purity of the Golden State.
Fortunately, as *Car and Track's* Bud Lindemann
predicted in 1971, HD suspension would continue
unabated, since it had no bearing on smog. The
familiar Corvette package was RPO FE7 Gymkhana
suspension. It consisted of HD shocks, higher ratio
springing, thicker than stock front swaybar, and an

GM Styling boss Bill Mitchell's final influence, prior to his 1977 retirement, included the '78 Corvette Indy Pace Car's interior. Full silver leather, or leather/gray cloth and gray carpeting. Chevrolet's more supportive 'Thin Shell Buckets', were originally for 1979. *(Courtesy RK Motors)*

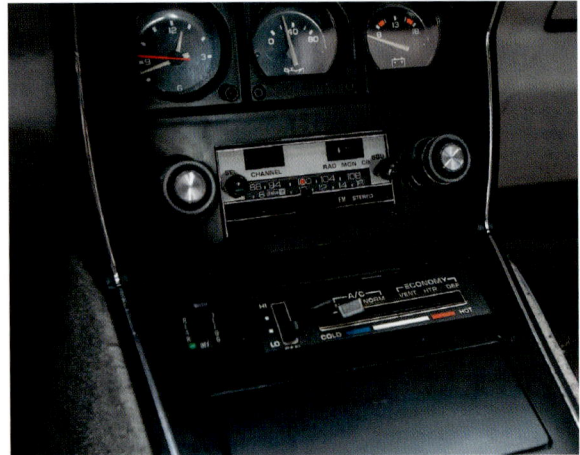

Introduced during 1977, UP6 AM-FM stereo radio and CB was a formal 1978 option, costing 638 clams. CB couldn't be combined with 8-track, nor subsequent compact cassette decks. Pace Cars came with either radio/8-track or radio/CB. *(Courtesy RK Motors)*

added rear swaybar. In the stagflationary trend of the OPEC/malaise era, FE7 rose from seven bucks in 1974 to $41 by 1978!

Concerning ordering preferences, 12,590 and 12,739 respective 1978 Corvette buyers chose FEY and L82 350. L82 350's popularity was definitely on the up: 5720 buyers in 1976, 6148 Corvette fans optioning same in '77 MY. The L82 350's 1978 price tag was $525. 12,187 1978 Corvette buyers went for the new $120 AU3 power door locks, a feature now expected on any pricy automobile. There was no factory compact cassette player in 1978 Corvette land, but the AM-FM stereo radio with CB, costing $638, now carried the UP6 option code, 7138 '78 Corvette buyers went for it. U75 power antenna was now formally listed, along with the new U81 dual rear speakers. Costing an identical 49 bucks, and selected by a respective 23,069 and 12, 340 Corvette faithful in 1978.

In-car audio, comfort, and appearance were all of increasing importance to buyers. 38,614 '78 Corvette devotees went for the MX1 NCO automatic transmission, 37,638 chose C60 a/c ($605). YJ8 alloys, now $340, were gaining in popularity: 6253

buyers in 1976, 12,646 Corvette patrons in 1977, and now 28,008 wanted YJ8 alloys in 1978! With the base L48 350 sufficient for nearly ¾ of the 46,776 1978 Corvette buyers, a lower total than in 1977, the latest Corvette seemed to offer an alternative to the Mercedes SL range. Neither Corvette nor Mercedes SL were the racers they were back in the late '50s; more well padded GT cruisers, but still two-seaters all the same. At a mere $9351.89, the Corvette's starting price was far lower than that of the Benz, and its performance noticeably higher. Naturally Corvette and Mercedes buyer groups were completely different. Corvette fans were unlikely to consider the Beverly Hills golf cart, that was the MB SL. They also weren't into the Porsche 928, much to Ferry Porsche's chagrin. However, they were open to the idea of a special edition, or two.

Chevrolet celebrated the Corvette's 10th and 15th anniversaries, with new Corvettes. The 20th anniversary of Corvette was marked by the adoption of radial tires, and promise of YJ8 alloys. By now, times had become tight for GM and the Corvette, with foreign competition, a desire for small cars, and another fuel crisis looming. Lack of resources, and the Corvette's now iconic status, brought the special edition commemorative model. In this respect the B2Z Silver Anniversary paint package, costing $399, was an early industry foray, into appearance models. In effect, add on another $380, because special badging, YJ8 alloys, and D35 sport mirrors were mandatory. It helped that GM's Bill Mitchell, the corporation's styling supremo who retired in 1977, had silver as his favorite color.

Chevrolet wanted to celebrate the Plastic Fantastic's Silver Jubilee. Not using the regular code 13 Silver exterior, the Silver Anniversary paint package employed code 13/07 Silver Anniversary paint, over a gray lower body part, a pinstripe separated the two zones. It was the first two-tone Corvette since 1961, and was attractive enough to lure 15,283 Corvette prospects. Fewer, 6502 to be precise, chose 1978's other Corvette appearance model. And this one really was a model in its own right, not a package: RPO 1YZ87/78 Limited Edition Corvette Pace Car, costing $13,656. The regular Corvette base coupe was RPO 1YZ87. Unlike regular appearance deals, the 1978 Limited Edition Corvette Pace Car had a special VIN, with a '9' as the 8th digit, instead of the usual '4'. That is, you couldn't make your own Pace Car just by ordering dealership options, neither could dealers themselves! So, several dealers price gouged, to the tune of up to twice the price of a regular Corvette coupe … ouch!

Never standing still, the Corvette replaced its ammeter with a volt meter, and gained a new low fuel warning lamp from '77 MY. *(Courtesy RK Motors)*

What was the Corvette Pace Car pacing? The Indy 500 no less, the first time the Corvette had done so. What's more, the Pace Car was stock, except for two rear body apertures for mounting flagpoles. Even in the malaise era, a stock Corvette had enough street moxie to pace the great race, and meet the performance requirements of the

The 1978 Corvette had enough punch to pace the Indy 500 sans modification. The Pace Car's livery was chosen because it photographed well in b/w magazine pages and print ads, which were still commonly b/w at the time. *(Courtesy RK Motors)*

The Silver Anniversary Corvette.

25 years of men, machines, and memories.

It stands alone today as it has since the summer of 1953, a truly unique and finely machined two-seater, America's only true production sports car.

The legend lives on and improves, as legends do, with the passage of time.

The Silver Anniversary Corvette. Twenty-five years in the making, and we've enjoyed every minute of it.

And now, if you will, please join us in a round of applause for the Corvette founding fathers, that spirited corps of doers and dreamers who created the legend, brought it to life, and kept it there.

Also for the countless men and women who've had a hand in building and refining Corvettes over the years. For everyone who has ever owned a Corvette, driven one, loved one. Or dreamed about owning one someday.

Which, we'd imagine, includes just about everybody.

SEE WHAT'S NEW TODAY IN A CHEVROLET.

Chevrolet

By 1978, the Corvette was getting self referential, in terms of the Silver Anniversary Corvette. Baby, you've come a long way! *(Courtesy GM Archives)*

Indianapolis Motor Speedway. The 1979 Foxstang did not, which was why Jack Roush did a tricked out 302 Windsor V8 for the '79 Ford Mustang Cobra Pace Car.

As for appearance, all 1YZ87/78 replicas came with the new glass T-tops (CC1), alloys (YJ8), defogger (C49), a/c (C60), sport mirrors (D35), tilt-tele steering column (N37), HD battery (UA1), and AM-FM stereo tuner with either 8-track (UM2) or CB radio (UP6), plus power door locks (AU3) and regalia decals. The decorative decals could be installed by the dealer, at customer discretion, and consisted of Indianapolis Speedway winged logo placed on the rear fenders, and large door emblems saying, "Official Pace Car, 62nd Annual Indianapolis 500 Mile Race, May 28, 1978." All '78 Corvettes carried Silver Anniversary exterior badging.

The 1978 Limited Edition Corvette Pace Car, had

a black over silver exterior, with bright red pinstripe as a demarcation line between the two colors. Spoilers were kind of functional. The coupe's exterior color scheme was chosen because many magazines and ads were still in black and white. Inside the Corvette's winner's circle, Bill Mitchell had left his mark again. A full leather interior (code 152), or silver leather/gray cloth (code 15C), and complementary gray carpet. It was the sporty and plush '78 Corvette that buyers wanted. Those cloth inserts kept a determined racer in place during spirited cornering that the Plastic Fantastic was still more than capable of. There were initial plans for 2500 replicas, that is, 100 for each year of Corvette life. However, the game moved onto a 6200 total, or one for each Chevrolet dealership. It was certainly a showroom magnet, or Chevette bait!

1979 – A Corvette record!

IN 1979'S APRIL issue of *Road & Track*, there lay yet another sports car comparison report, this time titled "Four Automatic Sports & GT Cars". Previous *R&T* comparisons that included Corvette were done in 1969 and 1975. This time around the field included two Japanese cars, reflecting the Land of the Rising Sun now sending sports cars, not just econoboxes, to America's shores. The Corvette's long time nemesis, Jag XKE, was gone, so too the Porsche 911. The subject of the report was combining sports with luxury. Mention was made of the lush and convenience of a Cadillac, in a trim sporty machine. It harked back to the late '50s, when some believed lavishly optioned Straight Axle Corvettes actually stole some Cadillac sales. It seems such demand never went away.

Going on median price, the over 30 grand Porsche 928 was ruled out, simply too pricy. At under $7000, the Triumph TR7 was too cheap. The ex Buick V8 powered TR8 would fit, but wasn't available yet. Test price placed the Mazda RX7 at $9455, the Corvette L48 350 automatic on $12,505, the Datsun 280ZX was $12,682, with the Porsche 924 a supreme $17,790! All test subjects had a/c and automatic transmission. In keeping with the times, such cars weren't strippers. Three had sunroofs, and two had cruise control. The Porsche 924's 911 sourced leather buckets spoke of restrained

The B2Z Silver Anniversary paint appearance pack cost $399, and was selected by 15,283 1978 Corvette buyers. *(Courtesy Restore A Muscle Car)*

sporty opulence – a hard to express quality, that was appealing to more and more buyers. High performance wasn't as foremost in people's minds as it used to be. The Corvette still delivered excellent value for money, but the side pipes and multiple engine options were history, and not missed. The L48 350 V8 was the crowd pleaser, especially with a THM 350 automatic attached. Most Corvette buyers were happy with this set menu way of life.

With its fat tires and extrovert bodystyle, luxurious nature and instant V8 throttle response, even in 1979, the Corvette seemed evergreen in such younger company. That said, *R&T* highlighted areas where an all new Corvette would help.

Outward vision and driving position were found wanting. The Corvette's power steering also caught testers out, with its quick then slow dance steps. You never knew just how much lock to wind on. *Motor Week*'s John Davis owned a '78 Corvette, and said he never quite got used to GM's variable ratio power steering. As ever, Corvette's separate chassis construction lacked rigidity. A rough ride, and skittish behavior on imperfect road surfaces were expected.

The Corvette won the categories of best gearbox, heating and ventilation, and only came second to the Mazda on engine. Just as the Triumph TR8 had a GM engine connection, the Mazda rotary powerplant was the one that got away

Cynics might have said that the Corvette started offering appearance packs because the nameplate had nothing new … but damn it looked good! *(Courtesy Restore A Muscle Car)*

GM Styling supremo Bill Mitchell liked silver, it was his favorite color. Hence the Silver Anniversary Corvette's silver over gray exterior, separated by a pinstripe. *(Courtesy Restore A Muscle Car)*

for GM, Corvette and the '75 Chevrolet Monza! The '78 test Corvette scored number one rating for lateral grip (0.798g), with joint top for slalom speed (59.3mph) with the Mazda RX7. The RX7 had taken Japan's top sports car position from the now Vegas Elvis Datsun 280ZX. At 12mpg, the Corvette was the worst on gas mileage, the Porsche topped as expected with 19mpg. The Corvette stopped shortest from 60mph, at 142ft, Porsche came second on 150ft. Both were Porsche traditional areas. The Corvette and Porsche had the same weight distribution, 48/52% front to rear. The Corvette and RX7 were both considered front midship designs, given the rearward placement of their front engines. However, the RX7's weight distribution was 53/47% front to rear. The Porsche won handling and brakes, but like the Corvette had an average of 25lb of brake pedal pressure, and zero fade. Whereas Corvette never did well in such *Consumer Reports* style evaluations, the increasingly sedan-like Datsun did. Comfy, well made and rattle free the Datsun was, but sporty it was not, and testers didn't care for the 280ZX that much. It wasn't quick in a straight line, nor round corners, had vague steering, from a steering wheel more at home in a Cedric! The Datsun inline six was breathless, and the brakes were over boosted and faded too much. And yet, the Datsun 280ZX

was a sales winner! As the saying goes, the dogs loved the dog food.

The likeable Mazda RX7 won over the *R&T* testers, and like Corvette, easily commanded way over list at dealerships. The Plastic Fantastic came last in six categories. The points tally saw: Datsun 1 Mazda 2, Porsche 3, and Corvette 4. That said, sales results put Corvette numero uno. Yes, 1979 model year saw Corvette set an all time sales record, that has never been beaten: 53,807 coupes! They must have been doing something right, and as Chevrolet GM Robert Lund said in March 1977, St Louis was still very busy, "The St Louis plant is operating two nine-hour shifts daily and working overtime two Saturdays a month just to meet sales demand. Current demand is running more than 29% ahead of last year."

The Corvette turned out longer lived in its third incarnation, and more popular, than GM expected in the late '60s. The Late Model C3 Corvette maintained the nameplate's profitability and popularity in the face of the ever rising import wave, many of which were younger in design. With such success, don't rock the boat. Corvette's '79 MY improvements were subtle and evolutionary. For the first time, the base coupe broke the 10 grand barrier ($10,220.23), but more standard equipment was included, like an AM-FM radio.

As with the '78 Corvette Pace Car, the Silver Anniversary Corvette benefitted from general '78 Corvette refinements. This included T-tops being tied into the Corvette's standard alarm system. Plus, a windshield wiper/washer control that returned to the dashboard. *(Courtesy Restore A Muscle Car)*

From May 7 1979, Tilt-Tele tiller, a/c and fast glass became standard too. Nearly 80% of '78 Corvettes had been ordered just like that. The Corvette's latest high back buckets, looked like those from the '78 Corvette Indy Pace Car. They had more side bolstering and a higher fold point, to allow easier cargo cavity access. In keeping with NHTSA testing, the seat backs resisted falling forward, if the Corvette was rear ended. For ergonomics, the '79 Corvette's buckets had one more inch of seat track travel. Plastics in the seat frame structure saved 12lb per seat. 1979 model year also saw the phasing in of more effective tungsten halogen headlights. The fuel filler pipe made accidental fill ups with leaded gas less likely. Plus chrome trim gave way to black moldings, concerning the rear window and roof panel. On the Corvette's nose and sides, the Silver Anniversary commemorative emblems of 1978 gave way to cross flag equivalents. Manual and automatic Corvettes now shared the same firmer shock valving, and the Corvette's ignition cylinder lock, had more shielding to ward off grand theft auto.

When the '79 Corvette's ignition key was turned, there was a more authoritative exhaust note. The Corvette had gone to an open flow muffler design. It was claimed to be worth five more horses. Then too, the humble 1979 L48 350 now included the dual snorkel intake, first seen on the '78 Corvette L82 350. So, power was up for 1979. The L48 350 powered almost 80% of '79 Corvettes, and was on 195bhp SAE net. The optional L82 350 rose five horses to 225bhp. To help with scat, automatic Corvettes now featured 3.55 gears, not the previous 3.08 axle. Options saw a new illuminated, passenger side sun visor vanity mirror, and $272 ZQ2 power windows and door lock package went to 28,465 '79 Corvette patrons.

Convenience was increasingly where Corvette life lay. Only 4062 buyers went with the renamed MM4 (was M21) NCO CR four-speed, against 41,454

Now at 220 ponies, equal to the Trans Am W72 400, this Silver Anniversary Corvette's optional L82 350 added $525 to repayments. *(Courtesy Restore A Muscle Car)*

Corvette faithful preferring to go shiftless (that is, with the NCO MX1 automatic, formerly known as M40). It became RPO MX1 for '78 MY. Then there was the newly at hand, UN3 AM-FM stereo radio with cassette player, costing $234. The existing UM2 8-track cartridge deck equivalent was $228. Respective buyer optioning for the two sets went to 12,110, versus 21,435 in 1979 model year, but that would change as compact cassette popularity increased. However, don't think the Corvette had gone completely marshmallow like. Performance hardware still existed.

Hallowed hardware ran to D80 front and rear

In addition to the Silver Anniversary Corvette's $399 B2Z paint job, $40 D35 sport mirrors and $340 YJ8 alloys were mandatory options. *(Courtesy Restore A Muscle Car)*

1968 1977 CHEVROLET CORVETTE STINGRAY

HIGH PERFORMANCE   USA

The Corvette, with returning fastback, stayed visually constant during 1978-79. The fastback's extra weight contributed to oversteer. *(Courtesy Autopresse/Edito-Service SA)*

spoilers, costing $265. These items had been seen on the '78 Corvette Indy Pace Car, and were functional enough to gain a half mpg in gas mileage. The CC1 moonroof T-top panels were also from the '78 Pace Car package, and cost $365. Both options were chosen by a respective 6853 and 14,480 Corvette buyers, in '79 MY. For the hard riders (12,321), there was the 49 buck FE7 Gymkhana suspension pack, with 2164 '79 Corvette fans choosing the separate option $33 F51 HD shocks. The NCO close ratio four-speed (MM4) transmission and N90 (formerly YJ8) alloys costing $380 were certainly functional too.

And a word on color optioning: the most popular 1979 Corvette exterior color was code 19 Black, selected by 10,465 Plastic Fantastic fans. Black had been re-introduced to the Corvette for 1977, having last been seen as code 900 Tuxedo Black in 1969. It was a color that had gained in popularity since its re-introduction. In general for sporty cars, it seemed black trim was replacing chrome, but could anything replace the Corvette? If you had the cash there was no substitute, not even a Porsche! However, if your budget didn't stretch to a Corvette, but you admired the C3 Corvette shape, rust free fiberglass body, sturdy mechanicals, and desired better gas mileage, why not build your own? Yes, build your own, with a Bradley GT!

Even post Opel GT, there was Bradley GT, and it too was German powered. Bradley Automotive offered you a VW Bug based sports car, in kit or turn key forms. The Bradley GT even had rudimentary gullwing doors, and mere covers for the headlamps, so technically they weren't pop ups! There was a Corvette connection, beyond the looks. The Bradley GT utilized a Mid-Year Corvette windshield, and was fancy enough to attract celebrity patrons like Barry Goldwater, Liberace and tennis player Andrea Jaeger. The more sophisticated Bradley GT II had fully functional gullwing doors and electric pop up headlamps. However, fraudulent business practices finally put paid to the Minnesota business concern, and financial woes didn't help. Matters wound up in 1981. Around the same time, John Z DeLorean's DMC12 suffered a similar fate, for the same reasons. Successfully making a sports car wasn't easy. It's worth noting that at this recessionary hour, the Corvette was still a strong selling, profit making concern.

Of the Corvette's many upgrades over the years, practicality was an area of limited improvement. Well, that's what the GM F body was there for, right?! That said, there were attempts inside and outside GM to make Corvette more family friendly. During the Mid-Year Corvette's development, Ed Cole made a 1961 proposal to Bill Mitchell, concerning a Corvette 2+2. Not unlike the Jaguar XKE 2+2. Mitchell handed the job to Larry Shinoda & Co at GM Styling. Clay modeling went to an actual car with XP-796 prototype designation.

Chevrolet celebrated the 1979 Corvette dream car with help from a poster by artist Ken Dallison. *(Courtesy GM Archives)*

There was a 6in wheelbase stretch, and other re-engineering. In came longer doors and door glass, stretched internal door hardware, reworking of the roof cutouts, longer split window panes, fold down rear seats, and strengthening of the rear frame pick up area. That last engineering alteration was incorporated and retained on all 1963-82 Corvettes.

Ed Cole may have been thinking of the Thunderbird's four-seater sales explosion post 1957, so why not Corvette? Subsequent DM Design director Chuck Jordan, said everyone at GM Styling thought the Corvette 2+2 looked awkward. Then too, there was GM President Jack Gordon's negative experience with XP-796. Gordon was curious if an adult could really fit in that '+2' compartment. Ed Cole assured him it was possible, whereupon Jack Gordon inserted himself into said rear compartment, only to find himself trapped! The

201

Corvette hit an all time high in 1979, with no fewer than 53,807 Plastic Fantastics sold that year!
(Courtesy Muscle Cars For Sale Inc)

20,066 1979 Corvettes came with the standard steel Rally rims, and this was one of 'em!
(Courtesy Muscle Cars For Sale Inc)

fold down rear seats wouldn't fold, necessitating union mechanics to unbolt the Corvette's front seat, to free Gordon. Once out, Jack Gordon wasn't a big fan of the Corvette 2+2 concept, contributing to the project getting canned.

Ed Cole kept the Corvette 2+2 idea going for a while, perhaps in light of the 1964½ Mustang's success. It was a Ford that GM management thought might steal Corvette sales, but this belief proved to be unfounded, and XP-796 was subsequently junked. All that would remain were a few GM Styling Studio photos. That said, the idea of a four place Corvette never really disappeared. 15 years hence, the concept of a four-door, four-seat Corvette, seemed ready for a Lazarus like return. This time Corvette's practical route came by way of an outside concern. California Custom Coach (CCC) was well known in the '80s, for its Excalibur challenging Auburn replicas. Concerning a Corvette four-door, CCC cooked up the 'America'. This project entailed 30in being added to the Corvette's frame, just aft of the front seats.

Since the Corvette's stock frame was pretty beefy, the conversion presented few problems. There was no need to add a crossmember. The Corvette's long doors, which aided cargo cavity access, were a boon too. Stock windows and Chevrolet Malibu door handles helped out, and Bow Tie dealers participated with CCC. That is, you could order your America from a local participating dealer, and pick it up like any Corvette. According to *Road & Track* in February 1979, The America

drove well, with minimal frame flex. CCC was thinking of 20 Americas created per month, and even worked out a 2+2 version, a mere 6-8in longer than a stock Corvette.

CCC did try to make its four-door and 2+2 Corvettes look right and balanced, but a four-door and or stretched sports car is never an easy task. Similar attempts were made with the air cooled Porsche 911, and in modern times, with that firm's Panamera. They were roomier, but somewhat odd looking. A two- or four-door sedan is one thing, but a stretched sports car quite another, and it seems most prefer stock in this regard.

Ringers 'r' us

1975-79 COULD BE the only time in Corvette history that specially prepared Corvettes were submitted to magazines for testing, beyond just basic tune up prep. From 1956 to 1970, Corvettes didn't really need any help in the acceleration or top speed departments, and were easily ahead of European opposition in the former area, at any price. Indeed, once the big block Corvette arrived in the mid '60s, if you wanted to travel faster, strap a Saturn V rocket to your person, and have at it! The Mark IV Corvettes were some of the fastest cars on the planet, when correctly optioned. Ferrari, Lamborghini, Maserati, et al notwithstanding.

Matters became tempered a tad, with the 1971 compression ratio drop, brought by stricter smog law and a transition to unleaded gas. No catalytic

25 years on the Chevrolet small block V8 was still a winner! It's shown here in base 195 horse L48 350 1979 form. That year, the optional L82 350 was rated 225bhp strong. The L82 350 cost $565, and was optioned by 14,516 Corvette fans.
(Courtesy Muscle Cars For Sale Inc)

converters yet during 1971-74, but the Corvette and others were gradually getting slower, post 13 second stock 1971½ Corvette LS6 454. By 1974 you could say a Corvette LS4 454 was high 14s, with an L82 350 powered Plastic Fantastic in the mid 15s. It didn't really matter, as a road handler the Corvette was still just about tops domestically, certainly the only machine marrying IRS with four-wheel disk brakes. Corvette sales were on the rise, and the Plastic Fantastic could still see off a Pantera. Plus, GM had other concerns like smog and safety law, import competition and the price of a gallon of gas.

The game changer was the 1975 model year, that gave effect to the 1970 Muskie Smog Bill. No Zora Arkus-Duntov, no big blocks and the arrival of a catalytic converter ... oh my! The Corvette looked much the same, and was essentially the same car first released in 1968, which pleased some, but not others that wanted something radically new. That aside, smog law meant that for the first time, there now existed a gulf between how fast people thought the Corvette was, and how fast it really was. How to fix the problem? Ringers, that's how! This had been done with muscle and pony cars in the '60s, most notably by Pontiac ad man Jim Wangers and dealer/speed shop Royal Pontiac with the GTO.

Dave Wallace of *Hot Rod* magazine has also written that, in the '70s, Petersen Publishing, with some financial support from the Big Three, tested prepared cars, hoping to generate a popular spin for the latest versions of well known nameplates, during the malaise era. The result for Corvette was that independent testing sometimes produced better results for post 1974 Corvettes than the

41,454 '79 Corvette faithful went with the RPO MX1 zombie shift. From '77 MY, if you didn't spring for the optional sports three-spoker, this color-matched Vega GT tiller was what you got.
(Courtesy Muscle Cars For Sale Inc)

lighter, more powerful, less smog restricted C3 machines of earlier times. Older examples that had high compression ratios, ran premium High Test leaded gas and lacked a cat!

All the below Corvettes had 350 cube small block V8s. The '82 Firebird Trans Am had a 305 V8, but the same horsepower as the '75 Corvette L48 350, and weighed 300lb less. So, the '75 Corvette and '82 Trans Am, which both had automatic and a/c, should have had similar acceleration. Especially since the Trans Am had a more performance axle ratio.

Car and Driver's May 1975 report was one of

Model	Motor/HP/CR	Weight (lb)	0-60mph (secs)	¼-mile/trap speed (secs/mph)	Top speed/ axle ratio (mph)	Automatic & a/c	Issue
1969 Corvette	ZQ3/300/10.3	3405	8.4	16.12/84.46	126/3.08	Yes	Car Life July '69
1975 Corvette	L48/165/8.5	3690	7.7	16.1/87.4	129/2.73	Yes	C&D May '75
1978 Corvette	???/???/???	3655	6.6	15.6/91	115/3.55	Yes	R&T April '79
1982 Trans Am	LU5/165/9.5	3385	9.2	17/80.5	106/3.23	Yes	R&T Sept '82

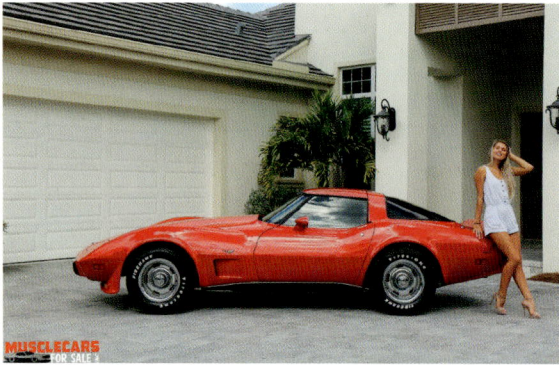

The '79 Corvette's vital stats were: 185.2in length, 69in width, 48in height and 3600lb. Team Corvette was formally working on the downsized C4 1984 Corvette from 1978. *(Courtesy Muscle Cars For Sale Inc)*

This Late Model C3 Corvette is graced with the optional RPO D80 $265 front and rear spoilers. They appeared on 6853 '79 Corvettes, and originated from the '78 Corvette Indy 500 Pace Car. Such spoilers cut drag 15%, with a ½mpg improvement in gas mileage overall. *(Courtesy Muscle Cars For Sale Inc)*

the few times a '75 Corvette was evaluated, and seemed oddly fast given the specification. *Road & Track*'s April 1979 automatic sports car quartet comparison was worthy of an Agatha Christie mystery. It involved a 1978 Corvette with THM 350, and a Californian spec 350 V8, and very strong performance for a Corvette of the era. Being California, the L82 350 was off the menu, but *R&T* provided 1978 49-state L82 350 engine specs in the report's data panel. The article picture showed an L48 350 with plain valve covers. *R&T*'s description of the Corvette's test V8 sounded more like a warmed over L48 350 than a high rpm L82 350. The journal remarked on the strong low end, detonation on regular gas, running out of breath at five grand and topping out at 115mph. The test 924, RX7 and 280ZX, also could do no better than 115mph.

The Corvette's 0-60mph in 6.6 seconds, and mid 15s in the ¼-mile, with engine pinking, seemed like an L48 350 with shaved heads, re-jetted Quadrajet, and advanced timing. Indeed, more often than not, test subjects came from Chevrolet Engineering, rather than dealer direct, and other domestic automakers did the same. GM's other high profile performance car, the Pontiac Firebird Trans Am, also seemed to benefit from the submission of prepared cars. On first acquaintance in April 1977, *Car and Driver* found a '77 Trans Am W72 400 four-speed, with 3.23 axle, capable of a 16.9 second ¼-mile at 82mph. *C/D* got 17 seconds flat

from a BMW 530i four-speed in July 1975. This all corresponded to the 16.5 second ¼-mile at 87mph, recorded by *Road & Track* in March 1976, concerning the '76 Corvette L82 350 four-speed with 3.55 gears that John Greenwood had tried at Daytona. However, come 1977-78, and you would find test reports for both Corvette and Trans Am, with mid six-second 0-60 times, and low 15s in the ¼-mile.

Just as there was a need to maintain the Corvette's high performance image, GM didn't want the Trans Am looking stone slow in the wake of *Smokey and the Bandit*. In Corvette's case, the slower times seem to accord with the big effect that 1975's tighter smog law had. Basically, the L48 350 and L82 350 were mostly the same internally during 1975-80. The L82 350 retained its 9.0:1 CR, although the L48 350 dropped from 8.5 to 8.2:1. Taken by itself, the L82 350 saved a ½-second in the ¼-mile. The performance option brought around 30 more horses, but sacrificed 30lb/ft in torque. And, as the '80s C4 Corvette L98 350 proved, torque matters.

Beyond relatively minor intake and exhaust revisions, and different rpm points to take peak power and torque, the Corvette's 350 V8s were in a 1975-80 holding pattern. As Corvette Chief Engineer Dave McLellan told *Motor Trend*'s Tony Swan in the December 1976 issue, Team Corvette was busy

The OPEC fuel crises threatened V8s. Here in Bahrain, a local enjoyed a Little Chev VW dune buggy, with Chevrolet V8, on the eve of the 1979-80 gas crunch! *(Courtesy National Geographic)*

just trying to stop Corvette backsliding from its 1975 performance level, in the face of stricter smog law, for the next few years. *Motor Week*'s John Davis discovered his '78 Corvette did an 18 second ¼-mile, at MW's Maryland, Ohio 75-80 Dragway. In March 1975, *Road Test* found a Pontiac Firebird Trans Am 400 automatic, did a 17.99 second ¼-mile. It was a loaded coupe with highway axle, that was pretty sleepy. Fortunately, Corvette lost 200lb for 1980. There was an absence of prepared Corvettes during 1980-82, as Chevrolet got busy getting the new C4 Corvette ready for the world. Plus, GM was focused on foreign competition, gas mileage and smog law.

In spite of press criticism concerning its weight and size, the '79 Corvette was more popular than ever. However, the revised '80 Corvette would make concessions to CAFE and smog. *(Courtesy Autotrader)*

The New Old Corvette
1980-82

Dream with DKM

IN 1979, *CAR Craft*'s associate editor Neil Britt described the Corvette as a blissful anachronism within Big Three conformity. True, you got shake, rattle and roll through hard turns, with the driver hanging on in an uncomfortable excuse of a bucket seat. However, the Corvette was still top domestic dog in handling, speed, sleekness and ego. Praise, according to Britt, came from tall, thinly clad blondes, who gave you more than mere side glances if you drove a Corvette. *Car Craft* said it was all worth the poor gas mileage.

If you thought all of the above was good, then be prepared for the '79 DKM Corvette L-82S. The 'S' suffix indicated the ultra sports versions of the Porsche 911, and so too here. Dennis and Kyle Mecham's Phoenix, Arizona, DKM Inc speed shop was normally associated with improved Trans Ams, aka Macho T/As, and now uprated one's Corvette L82 350 four-speed. On the outside D80 spoilers were apparent, so too code 19 Black paint, L-82S door callout decals, and subtle pinstriping. There were also mean, black center rims. On the inside was a console plaque, and beyond such visuals, a lot of substance for an appreciable surcharge over stock. First an uprated L82 350. Back in 1971, amid the GM compression ratio smog drop, Chevrolet engineers admitted how much their 350s were leaned out for emissions control. This included the Corvette and Camaro Z28's LT1 350s. With help from HO Racing metering kits, it was time to unlean the 350 V8. The Hawthorne, Californian firm did kits for both Mouse and Rat Chevrolet

V8s, plus the motor mods on the DKM Corvette L-82S. Changes were made to 4bbl primary jet size, metering rods, power valve oiling, secondary metering rods, vacuum break assembly and secondary pullover accelerator discharge.

A distributor advance curve kit, saw revised weights and springs, a larger centrifugal advance bushing, plus new vacuum diaphragm, for more spark advance at idle and part throttle. Recall the nullifying effect of GM's smog law aiding and abetting TCS (Transmission Controlled Spark), killing advance outside WOT (wide open throttle) in the lower gears. Hooker Headers improved exhaling, as did dual cats in place of the stock mufflers. They fitted well under the fiberglass body's seating hollows. Stock saw Corvettes use one cat, to appease accountants and the EPA.

The DKM Corvette L-82S was more vocal, outside and in, thanks to a 100 watt Fosgate amplifier, and Concorde AM/FM cassette deck. Controls for the Fosgate unit replaced the Corvette's usual four-speed console shift map. So, you would now have to remember that reverse was out left and up! Indeed, there was now a Hurst shift linkage for the BW T10 four-speed stick shift, and even a five-speed was possible! 1979 was the final outing for the close ratio four-speed Corvette option. The five-speed was also a close ratio box, not an OPEC/Jimmy Carter/CAFE pacifying overdrive five-speed, but with a real one-to-one direct top! Who made this goodness? Like Hooker Headers and Hurst, it was another household name ... Doug Nash! Nash, a noted drag racer in 1963-67, moved into prototype engine work and

This is the second of only two DKM Corvette L-82S coupes ever made. It was the car used in DKM Inc's brochure for the model. An uprated L82 350 featured. *(Courtesy Barn Finds.com)*

To the right of the shifter is the DKM Corvette L-82S 100 watt Fosgate amplifier controls. The #2 DKM Corvette shown had a Doug Nash 4+1 Quick Change stick shift. That's code 722 Corvette Red Leather, a NCO. *(Courtesy Barn Finds.com)*

modifying transmissions from 1971. For racing he came up with a 4+1 quick change five-speed manual transmission, and subsequently did a street equivalent. Both versions had an aluminum split case, and, at 95lb, they weighed 3lb more than the BW Super T10 that you would find in many a sporty GM car. The reason for the heft was the Doug Nash box ability to handle a lot of torque.

In common with the one time Corvette optionable M22 Rock Crusher four-speed, the Doug Nash 4+1 five-speed had the first four gears cut at a 20 degree helix angle, versus the 25 degrees of a normal gearbox. This was the reason for the Rock Crusher's noisy, but tough nature. For the street 4+1 five-speed, Doug Nash planned to make the gearbox more user friendly, with fourth gear cut at a 25 degree angle. In keeping with its competition background, the Doug Nash 4+1 involved a notchier, higher effort shift than your regular BW Super T10 four-speed. However, it did have shorter throws.

There was no dogleg pattern with the Doug Nash five-speed, first through to fourth were within the 'H', and fifth right and up, with reverse below it. Naturally, the first four ratios were shorter, compared to a normal Corvette M21 four-speed, and the oft found 3.70 Corvette M21 differential ratio was changed to a more highway amenable 3.08 ratio. Not only did the taller ratio make fifth happy on the highway, but more differential pinion teeth gave the effectively overdrive fifth an easier,

longer life with less strain. Doug Nash Equipment and Engineering Corp of Franklin, Tennessee charged $995 for its street five-speed, and $1100 for the racing version, by late 1978. If your '79 Corvette had the five-speed, a '4+1 five-speed' badge lived above the Corvette's usual cross flag fender logo.

Four-speed or five-speed, the DKM Corvette L-82S possessed a bigger shifter ball, versus a stock Corvette four-speed. The improved coupe also had a more determined suspension. Polyurethane took the place of normal Corvette rubber bushings. Konis now lived at all four corners, and DKM took off the rear swaybar that you would normally find on a Corvette by this stage. Dennis Mecham's reasoning was that there was less chance of oversteer in high speed cornering, the Corvette's expected forte. That said, *Car Craft* felt this modification made the Corvette too loose for spirited highway driving. In any case, even a stock Corvette was hardly a Citroën DS in ride comfort. In other words, DKM's Corvette was for the committed.

A DKM creation, be it Macho T/A, Camaro or Corvette, was hopefully 49-state legal. This was achieved by sleight of hand. The DKM edition was technically not a new vehicle. It started out from a new car dealer, then transferred to the speed shop side of operations. So, the mods weren't done on a new car … technically. The fruits of such labor were tested at Orange County International Raceway (OCIR), by *Car Craft*.

For the stock code 52 Corvette Yellow '79 L82 350 four-speed coupe, the best ¼-mile and trap speed were 15.2 seconds and 93.36mph, but not at the same time! The latter figure corresponded with a 15.25 second ¼-mile. With the DKM coupe, dropping the clutch on the third pass proved a charm. From a 3500rpm start, a 14.69 second ¼-mile was associated with a 99.44mph trap speed. However, *Car Craft* felt DKM's price premium, could only be justified in the minds of an ardent Corvette few.

Using movie censor ratings, *Car Craft* had the stock Corvette down as a 'R', but the DKM Corvette L-82S was a definite 'X'. The ratings weren't entirely car related, and recalled the popular Commodore's hit song from 1978 *X-Rated Movie*. As for the standard Corvette on Van Nuys boulevard, well, "… young ladies were the most ardent of the stock Corvette's admirers." Then, *Car Craft*'s Neil Britt described the reaction to DKM's Corvette L-82S coupe, "… the ladies' nervous systems instantly turned to jello." It was in response to the DKM Corvette's loud pipes, and was reminiscent of engine builder Gale Banks' '50s *Hot Rod* recollections. Hit the pipes and the girls turn around. Banks' cohorts speculated their sex organs were connected to their ears!

Banks was a California native, and *Car Craft* attributed some of this Valley wantonness to the SoCal lifestyle, some to high or distilled spirits. Britt elucidated *Car Craft*'s experience with the DKM machine, "Some were prompted to approach us with a reckless abandon atypical of their status. Others merely asked for rides." And this with *Car Craft* Tech Editor Baechtel and Associate Editor Britt aboard. It seemed more like the allure of a Corvette or two, than any desire for a sugar daddy! From personal experience, the C3 Corvette does seem to bring a positive reaction from the fairer sex, and sometimes an unsolicited comment that the Corvette is their favorite car. Such adulation and praise seems more related to the Corvette's style, and the excitement the sports car generates,

In 1979, *Car Craft* got a 14.69 second ¼-mile at 99.44mph from its four-speed DKM Corvette L-82S. This was ultra speedy for the time. *(Courtesy Barn Finds.com)*

than the status or price associated with a big buck import. Indeed, *Road & Track*'s August 1977 Mercedes 450 series owners survey, revealed that a young Philly student, who had a MB 450SE, said his ride created the expectation of expensive dinner dates. That is, we won't be stopping by Arby's or Chuck E Cheese!

Neil Britt reached this conclusion in *Car Craft*'s 1979 Fraternal Twins Corvette encounter, after all "… what chances for action does a guy have when he's driving a 1965 Rambler American? Even if the front seat does recline!" Of course, *Car and Driver*'s well known one time editor David E Davis Jr, once wrote the January '79 *C/D* article "Paris By Trans Am". Here, he asserted that American Motors' reclining seats for sleeping, had confronted conservative folk in the heartland, and turned the Big Three off reclining seats, which even by 1979, GM's sporty cars did not have, Corvette sadly included.

Big and low buck imports had reclining seats as standard, and it was a shame domestic buyers weren't so ready to drop big $$$ on special versions of home grown machines as readily as gray market import customers. DKM Inc only made two DKM Corvette L-82S coupes, that's all she wrote. A sales brochure was done, featuring the #2 car, which had the Doug Nash 4+1 Quick Change five-speed stick, but no dice. It was the same story concerning enhanced Camaro Z28s that DKM planned with Don Chapman Chevrolet of Tempe.

Hot Rod's Dave Wallace said the proto Camaro Macho Z, which the journal reported on in September 1978, could really haul ale versus the tepid ringers the Big Three usually drove to Petersen Publishing's door in this era. Even so, although DKM planned 200 '79 Macho Zs, only seven were built, and only a few Camaro Z29s and Z29Rs from Berlinetta bases. Don Yenko's 1981 Camaro Turbo Z followed a similar fate. It had long been difficult to sell premium price sporty domestics, from the modest AMC AMX two-seater, to the glacial Shelby Mustang, and the slower than molasses in an ice age '69 COPO Camaro ZL1 427. Brand had something to do with it. DKM Inc had much greater commercial success with its extrovert Macho T/A. It was the more rarefied Pontiac brand, and Acura was a good guise for upscale Hondas. Charge what the market will bear, and here the stock 1980 Corvette hit a home run!

The lightness of being Corvette!

THE STARTING PRICE for a 1980 Corvette was $13,140.24, but it didn't stay at that level. The second world fuel crisis and ensuing inflation saw base price jump four times during the model year, reaching $14,345.24! The overnight doubling of world oil prices by OPEC was related to the Iranian Revolution, and the West's support of the Shah of Iran's regime. It precipitated troubled times for the world's auto industry. Porsche made its first loss ever in 1980, but Corvette weathered the economic storm with aplomb, as in past times. While the 40,614 total of 1980 Corvettes was down on 1979's stellar result, it was still a very impressive total for such times. What's more, such sales were achieved with a model that started in 1968, with a basic chassis that hailed from 1963! Although the latest Corvette seemed little changed, many were the changes made under the skin, and to the skin itself! The central 1980 Corvette goal was a more efficient Corvette, and the goal was realized.

As with other automakers during the fuel crises, steps were taken to reduce weight and improve

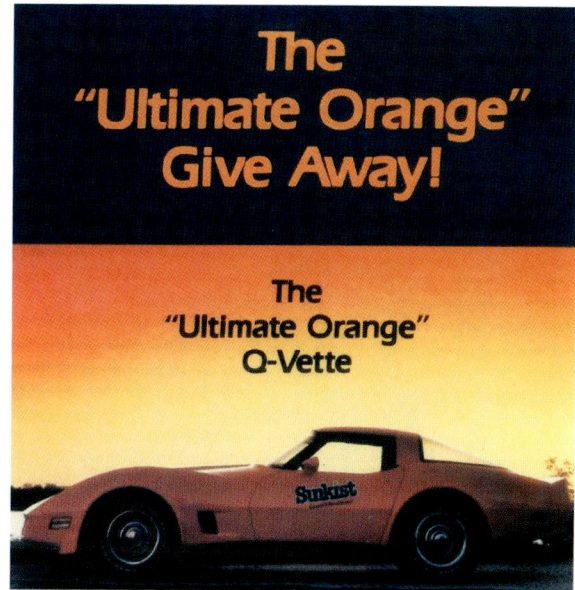

Chevrolet banished orange peel from the 1980 Corvette, or tried to, by molding urethane to body panels forward of the firewall, plus the roof. *(Courtesy Sunkist)*

aerodynamics. Thinner fiberglass, more plastic usage, as well as aluminum, along with lower density roof panels, a thinner hood and outer door skins. More plastic was used for interior trim and sub assemblies, for example, bucket seat construction. Aluminum now featured for the differential housing, front frame crossmember, and the intake manifold of both the L48 and L82 350 V8s. Formerly, only the latter motor used alloy. Plus, no more front fender cross flag badging, and exterior chrome trim was reduced. All automakers were doing these tricks and more.

For 1980 model year, the Corvette's cross flags logo was elongated. The result was a 200lb plus weight reduction. It put the 1980 Corvette in line with the 1968 edition. This was in spite of federal impact bumpers, door bars etc. On the aerodynamic side, a lower hood profile line, raked back front grille and integrated spoilers cleaned up drag and looks. The D80 front and rear spoilers looked tacked on, versus the integrated front and rear spoiler/bumper complexes of 1980-82. The new look was a popular modernizing update, nicknamed the Darth Vader nose on black cars. Urethane was now molded into

This is a numbers-matching 1980 Corvette L82 350 automatic. A lower hood profile for '80 MY meant the L82 callout badge now lived on the front fenders, no longer on the hood. *(Courtesy Flemings Ultimate Garage)*

the Corvette's body panels, forward of the firewall, and the roof. The move improved fiberglass finish, and brought an aerodynamic benefit.

Initial aero improvements lowered the Corvette's drag factor from 0.503 to 0.443. Before, wind tunnel work was more concerned with a car's handling, how it behaved in crosswinds. Now, reduced drag and lower weight were key to boosting gas mileage. With CAFE tightening its grip on the auto fleet, Corvette's revisions were timely. Reducing the auto fleet gas mileage average, and avoiding the gas guzzler tax, became a national pass time. Less fuel usage was also linked to reduced tailpipe emissions. You burn less, therefore you pollute less. With more exacting 1980 smog law, the new '80 Corvette was a car of its time. It was a time for civic responsibility, and there was a need for net oil importing America to improve its balance of payments. The new federally mandated 85mph speedo, had the national 55mph speed limit marked in the yellow km/h

color, helping the nation stay in the black!

The Corvette remained in the black, even with the plethora of standard equipment. The one time optional A31 power windows, C60 A/C and N37 tilt-tele steering column, were no longer on the option sheet, the trio now came standard. With options, AU3 power door locks cost $140 and 32,692 buyers chose 'em. Their buttons were relocated for 1980. K30 cruise control cost $123, and was optioned by 30,821 Corvette fans. The HD crowd stayed approximately constant, with around one quarter (9907) selecting $55 FE7 Gymkhana suspension, and 1695 the 35 buck F51 HD shocks, 34,128 wanted Corvette $407 alloys, and 26,208 paid $62 to obtain raised white letters with the QGB 225/70-15 radials, but 13,140 serious Plastic Fantastic fans went for the $426 new size QXH 255/60-15s, which were also RWL SBR in nature. The latter were Goodyear Eagle GTs, and with 8in wide RPO N90s, this was the Bigfoot of domestic cars! Then too, steering got zappier for 1980. Turns between locks went down from 2.9 to 2.6.

That's factory code 592 Doeskin Leather upholstery. Except for early in '80 MY, most 1980 Corvette L82 350s, and most '80 Corvettes for that matter (34,838 coupes), had the NCO MX1 THM 350 slushbox. *(Courtesy Flemings Ultimate Garage)*

When it came to in-car audio, compact cassette had gone from half the popularity of 8-track to nearly even. $168 UN3 radio/cassette (15,148 chosen) versus $155 UM2 AM-FM stereo radio/8-track (15,708). Okay, some people were buying Leif Garrett and Andy Gibb on compact cassette in those days! CB radio seemed on the decline, with $391 UP6 AM-FM stereo radio/CB radio placed in only 2434 '80 Corvettes. Nearly half the 1979 figure and only 201 folks went the UL5 radio delete route, to get $126 credit. 36,650 Corvette buyers optioned the $52 U81 dual rear speakers. 1980 Corvettes could have a new ribbed pattern cloth for seat inserts with 'C' suffix interior opening. 722 Red Leather continued from a 1977 start, and like code 192 Black Leather, implied no cloth inset equivalent.

Convenience seemed to be getting an upper hand in Corvette land, as with all cars. There was a driver side sun visor side shield to block glare, and a new 'Convenience Group' had everything bar an American Express card, that you wouldn't want to leave home without! Timer delay on dome/courtesy lights, headlights on warning buzzer, low fuel warning light, intermittent speed wipers, and passenger illuminated sun visor. What's more, or less, the behind the buckets cubby compartment count, went from three to two. That is, the passenger side and central cubbies that used to house jack/tire iron and oddments respectively,

became one big locker. The behind the driver battery compartment continued.

Outside were new front side, cornering lights, revised taillights, and, in between, functional front fender vents to expel underhood heat. That last item was previously seen on Corvettes in 1972. On 796 1980 Corvettes, a $105 ZN1 trailer package was factory fitted, but what powertrains and rear axles would '80 Corvette owners be U-Hauling with? By the greatest margin it would be a 49-state L48 350, teamed with a THM 350 (RPO MX1). You paid nothing extra to get this ensemble. The motor was rated five horses lower for 1980, 190bhp at 4400rpm, and 280lb/ft at a low 2400rpm. You also paid nothing over list to get a four-speed, the RPO MM4 or BW Super T10. However, your sole four-speed 1980 choice was a wide ratio box that a mere 5726 Corvette fans selected, in a sports car that was once overwhelmingly stick shift in nature.

Stray outside the stock standard 49-state base L48 350, and you would either be richer or poorer, in a financial sense. Yes, the L48 350 had trouble meeting 1980 Golden State smog law, and the L82 350 left that state at the close of '75 MY. So, Californian Corvettes now came with the single combination of 180 horse LG4 305 V8, and THM 350 slushbox. 3221 1980 Corvettes were sold in California. For such a performance sacrifice, these 'lucky' souls received a 50 buck credit from Chevrolet. The Jimmy Carter coupon choice actually brought a 5bhp improvement over the '79 Californian Corvette L48 350 V8. You also got an emissions approach that would be applied to all 1981 Corvettes: three-way cat, EGR, Computer Command Control ECU (CCC) governing fuel/air mixture/ignition timing, exhaust oxygen sensor in a closed loop architecture. In English, a 17 second flat ¼-mile, but hey, that gave more time for whitened teeth to be admired in SoCal!

Your 1980 axle choice was also a set menu: 3.07. This included the 49-state L82 350 four-speed combo. Said L82 350 gained five horses for 1980, to an even 230bhp. L82 350 was never cheap, and now retailed for $595, in what would be the powerplant's final model year. Sales of L82 350 had slumped to 5069, for the Corvette unique powerplant. For a ½-second saving in the ¼-mile, most felt it just wasn't worth the expense. Early in

'80 MY, some Corvette L82 350s were built with a four-speed. However, most L82 350 powered 1980 Corvette coupes carried the zombie shift THM 350. There had been some four-speed evolution over the Corvette years. Up to 1980 it was the respective close ratio and wide ratio selections of M21 and M20. However, changes were made as horsepower and torque went south due to smog law:

	Up to 1975		1975-79		1980-81
	CR M21	WR M20	CR M21	WR M20	WR MM4
1st	2.20	2.52	2.43	2.64	2.88
2nd	1.64	1.88	1.61	1.75	1.91
3rd	1.27	1.46	1.23	1.34	1.33
4th	1.00	1.00	1.00	1.00	1.00

In '79 MY, 8-track topped compact cassette in Corvette ordering 2 to 1. In 1980 it was even-steven: UM2 $155 radio/8-track 15,708 cars versus UN3 $168 radio/cassette 15,148 coupes. The UP6 CB option halved to 2434 '80 Corvettes! *(Courtesy Flemings Ultimate Garage)*

Basically, the four-speed was given more of a stump puller first and second, as the Corvette 350 V8s lost punch and vehicle weight went up. However, now the Corvette had come back from Weight Watchers, with some improved stats. *Road & Track* tested a 1980 Corvette L48 350 four-speed, in its Sports & GT Cars 1980 annual: 0-60mph in 7.7 seconds, 0-100mph in 22.2 seconds, 16 second flat ¼-mile at 86.5mph. All with an ability to hit the 5200rpm redline in all gears (130mph in top), and 14.5mpg overall for the 3345lb coupe. Genuine figures, no ringers, Chevrolet was too busy developing the next Corvette to get into those shenanigans. In the malaise era depths of 1980-82, the revived Corvette appeared more than capable of taking on all comers, as *R&T*'s contemporary stats showed:

The Japanese contingent came in at under 10 grand each, the exotic Europeans over 20 grand. The Corvette was half the price of a Porsche 911SC and was, as ever, in a unique market position. America's only sports car, with exotic car performance for reasonable money, no change there. Independent testing placed the Corvette L82 350 V8's 0-60mph time at 7.1 seconds. Quality and reliability? Same story again, the Corvette was a mechanically reliable car, with assembly problems related to its handbuilt nature. *Road & Track*'s owner surveys continued the Corvette credo, it wouldn't leave you stranded, but oftentimes might annoy you. Since 1975, *Road & Track* had included a second 'reliability problem area', things that would leave you stranded. The 1980 average was 11/6, and Corvette scored 13/2, which implied

	Corvette L48 350 four-speed	Datsun 280ZX	Toyota Celica Supra	Ferrari 308 GTSi	Porsche 911SC	BMW 528i	Jaguar XJS Auto
0-60mph (sec)	7.7	9.2	10.2	7.9	6.7	8.2	8.6
¼-mile (sec) @ mph	16 @ 86.5	17.2 @ 82	18 @ 79	16.1 @ 88	15.3 @ 91	16.7 @ 86	16.7 @ 90
60-0ft (mph)	130	160	145	154	140	158	166
Skid pad (g)	0.790	0.76	0.726	0.810	0.798	0.737	0.726
Slalom (mph)	61.2	56.5	59.8	60.6	59.7	57.2	52.7
mpg	14.5	22	20	11.5	18.5	22	11.5

The L82 350's power rose to 230bhp for '80 MY. Price for the option increased 30 bucks to $595, but sales plummeted to nearly a third the 1979 level, at 5069 Corvettes. It was the end of the road for L82 350. *(Courtesy Flemings Ultimate Garage)*

Over the Rochester 4bbl Q-jet is an air cleaner signed by the Corvette's first and second Chief Engineers: Zora Arkus-Duntov and Dave Ramsus McLellan. Corvette royalty no less! *(Courtesy Flemings Ultimate Garage)*

average reliability. At this time, the high priced Europeans and affordable Japanese scored best, the British and Italians the worst. BMW 530i 6/0, with 68% of BMW and Mazda rotary owners rating dealer service good or excellent. 94% of Honda Civic owners said they would buy Honda again. However, only 57% of Fiat X1/9 owners said they would trade in on another Fiat (Fix It Again Tony)! The Triumph TR4, Rover 2000TC, Fiat 850, along with the Ford Mustang, were in *Road & Track* surveys where only 70% of owners would stay with the brand. What's more, when *Car and Driver* tested the new Series 3 Jag XJ6, they needed four cars to get one set of performance figures! And the Porsche 911? *R&T*'s December 1980 issue Porsche 911 owner survey, saw a score of 11/4. Not appreciably different to the Corvette, even though the Porsche was a much more expensive car. That said, in light of poor panel fit, and a hood latch that malfunctioned on one side of *R&T*'s 1980 test Corvette, the journal requested world standard quality from Chevrolet.

For some thoughts on the 1980 Corvette, refer to *CAR* magazine's Ian Fraser, who owned a 1980 Corvette, liked Corvettes and was a fan of them even prior to owning the '80 Corvette. In the May 1989 issue of the journal, he said the integrated spoiler introduced on the '80 Corvette made driveways and kerbs a challenge, with regard to avoiding damage. Speaking in general, Fraser said,

"Corvettes rattle on bad roads; it's just the way they are, and can be traced, I suspect, to chassis that are too flexible."

Obviously a separate chassis vehicle is never going to match the rigidity of a unitary construction machine. In this area, the Corvette's flexible body mounts post-1972 did it no favors. Fraser also said Corvettes suit automatic transmission, and from 1980 this may have been even truer. Once known for its precise, easy to shift stick, matched to a relatively light clutch, the Corvette seemed to lose this tradition post-1979. Come 1980, the Corvette's tall, narrow H shift pattern, allied to vague, long throws and awkward first, seemed no better than the four-speed in a GM F body.

Indeed, *Motor Week* described the '82 Camaro Z28's four-speed, in identical terms. Don't blame the BW Super T10, the Corvette L82 350 had been using that transmission for some time. The newly stiff shift on Corvettes seemed more like standardized parts for shift pattern and linkage, being used on the Y body (Corvette) and GM F bodies (Camaro & Firebird). With a lower four-speed take up rate than ever on Corvette, it made economic sense to share parts between the three sporty models. So, automatic transmission meant no time lost on a quick change, and a smooth change guaranteed, thanks to the THM 350. It made the slushbox the ... err automatic choice!

1981 – Bowling Green, Kentucky and the plastic spring

OVER 1979-80, THE Chevrolet Corvette wasn't just America's only sports car, it was America's fastest car! According to GM's official figures, the top Camaro Z28 was good for 120mph, the Trans Am W72 400 and Corvette L48 350 managed 130mph, and the Corvette L82 350 could attain 135mph. However, the truly big news for 1981 concerned where the Corvette was made, rather than detail model specifics. Yes, we soon wouldn't be seeing you in St Louis, Louis!

The St Louis truck plant, had been completed in 1920. At the time of the Corvette's initial garage like assembly in Flint, Michigan, which ceased on December 24 1953, St Louis seemed like a good home for the Plastic Fantastic. Skilled tradesmen and laborers were available, and Chevrolet's general manufacturing manager Edward Kelley, proclaimed St Louis to be a sound central location for shipping. So it was, that on December 28 1953, Corvette assembly took up at this location, but over time a number of problems arose.

For one, St Louis eventually lacked both size and capacity to deal with the ever more popular Corvette. It didn't help that Corvettes weren't all that the factory produced. Then there was labor unrest, with worsening relations between workers and management in the Mississippi River region. Thirdly, there was an environmental problem looming. By 1979, rumors circulated that St Louis had trouble meeting federal EPA air quality standards.

Rumors of the move of Corvette production surfaced as early as 1973. At this time GM denied the rumors, with GM VP Robert F Mayill moved to write to a Missouri congressman, saying there was no plan to close Corvette's St Louis home, and that any rumors were without foundation. However, on the quiet, two St Louis plant managers traveled to Bowling Green, Kentucky in 1978, looking for a suitable plant location, and found one. What the gentlemen discovered was a former air

The color is code 47 Dark Brown Metallic, chosen by 2300 Corvette fans in 1980. That year, the front fender vents became functional for the first time since 1972! *(Courtesy Flemings Ultimate Garage)*

conditioning plant. To be precise, it was a 550,000ft² ex Chrysler Corp, Fedders Corp & Air Temp concern. On March 26 1979, GM made a formal announcement regarding Corvette's new domicile. As part of the production relocation, the ex a/c plant would be expanded to 1 million sqft, and have state of the art equipment installed.

Even though the new facility would be highly automated, most of the 900 St Louis plant workers moved to the new Bowling Green, Kentucky facility. A factory with a modern paint shop, higher quality and the ability to do more durable enamel paint finishes, including a new clear coat finishing process. In a two month window, '81 Corvettes were built at the two plants, simultaneously! This was because the Bowling Green plant started June 1 1981, with St Louis building its final Plastic Fantastic on August 1 1981. Of course, St Louis stayed with the traditional GM choice of lacquer, whereas Bowling Green moved to enamel exteriors.

The plant transition wasn't a completely happy one. A Chevrolet dealership service manager spoke of his experiences with a number of Corvettes, and a few new '82 Chevrolet Celebrities that the dealership received in 1981. The Corvettes all hailed from the St Louis plant, and all had a problem of one kind or another. One exhibited white smoke on start up, another had been obviously 'keyed' on its hood, prior to clear coating. Yet another Corvette displayed a rattling noise from its four-speed on PDI. It transpired a bunch of roller bearing balls were floating around in the case. This was even though the roller bearings the four-speed was supposed to have, were present and correctly located. It seemed that some St Louis workers weren't happy about losing their jobs, and had resorted to industrial sabotage. As for the Celebrities, they were unsaleable in their delivered state. It looked like they were painted with a roller! If all this didn't drive customers to Toyota, Datsun and Mazda, nothing would.

In a 1981 Corvette ad, Corvette's Chief Engineer Dave McLellan said, "We critique Corvette with the same engineering objectivity we'd use to evaluate a military aircraft: What is Corvette's mission? How well does it carry out its mission?" To keep Corvette flying high, 1981 witnessed a number of engineering, cosmetic and option

At 16,914 miles, this Corvette is claimed to be the lowest mileage '80 Corvette on the planet! For 1980 fast glass (A31), a/c (C60), and tilt/tele steering column (N37) were all included standard in Corvette's $13,140.24 base price.
(Courtesy Flemings Ultimate Garage)

adjustments, to help the established 1968 Late Model C3 Corvette stay relevant to the marketplace. Underhood, 1981 Corvettes had one engine alone, the L81 350 V8, and it was 50-state legal. The L81 350 made 190bhp at 4200rpm, and 280lb/ft at an amazingly low 1600rpm. The latter a Corvette small block V8 tractability record. One might notice magnesium valve covers, which were lighter and more attractive than the L48 350's engine painted equivalents. Indeed, the L81 350 looked like the now departed L82 350. On the inside, it was the same 1980 L48 350's 8.2:1 CR. However, L81 350 made more power versus the '79 California spec L48 350, and the same torque, all at lower rpm. The secret was high technology.

The L81 350 was basically a L48 350 V8, with all the outer hardware/software of the 1980 Californian Corvette LG4 305 V8, bolted on. It was all in aid of meeting stricter smog and CAFE standards of 1981, with improved drivability. The secret was electronic control unit (ECU) management of the Rochester Quadrajet 4bbl carb, and more sophisticated emissions controls. Beyond 1975's HEI transistorized ignition, there was GM's subsequent Electronic Spark Control (ESC). ESC advanced timing to the point of detonation, without actually reaching it. Then too, there was an electronic tie in concerning torque converter lock up, to maximize economy.

This is a 1981 Corvette L81 350 four-speed. The sidepipes aren't stock. Given the post-1979 Corvette weight cuts, this coupe weighs under 3400lb.
(Courtesy Cruisin Classics Inc)

Two notable changes in 1981 Corvette land: the 50 state L81 350 was your only motor, and a plastic composite fiberglass rear transverse, non HD suspension spring for Corvette automatics.
(Courtesy Cruisin Classics Inc)

Long story short, it all came under the marketing banner of Computer Command Control or CCC.

The starting point for the L81 350 V8's carburetion was the same basic Quadrajet four-barrel that the Corvette's 327 V8 met in 1968. That is, a carb with a primaries side and secondaries side. For each half of the carb there was a float bowl on the outside, then metering plates/fuel jets, followed by the barrels. Each float bowl chamber had its own fuel line, there was a vacuum hose, and the carburetor had four mounting bolts. The number on the side of the jets indicated bore size. Regarding float bowl chambers, an accelerator/ lever/pump was on the outside, with a diaphragm inside. Going heavy on the loud pedal, saw more fuel pumped in, with a rising float in the bowl chamber eventually shutting off fuel with a valve, avoiding flooding the carburetor.

With the electronic Q-jet, an electronic solenoid was connected to a narrow band oxygen sensor. The sensor observed the air/fuel mix, adjusting the pulse width of the solenoid, to achieve optimal emissions and performance. Fuel supply was set, in parallel with the Q-jet's primary metering circuit. The electronic Q-jet adjusted the air fuel mixture ten times per second. Inputs came from sensors monitoring throttle position, coolant temperature, and air pressure at the intake manifold. That is, manifold absolute pressure (MAP).

Times had also moved on from GM's initial two-way pellet catalytic converter, that could get gummed up pretty badly and was powerless to control nitrogen oxide, which the state of California was very interested in, as well as hydrocarbons and carbon monoxide. To control oxides of nitrogen, you needed a three-way cat. Now that such more advanced catalytic converters were available, Honda's CVCC, and the thermal reactors used by BMW, Mazda, Mercedes and Porsche, fell by the wayside. BMW adopted a three-way cat for '79 MY, Porsche followed on its 928 for 1980. Porsche rigged up the V8's air pump, to inject air directly into the 1000F cat's oxidation chamber, rather than introduce back pressure by pumping into the usual exhaust ports. BMW didn't need an air pump. For 1981, Corvette went three-way cat, plus the usual air injection and EGR. Using a cat made unleaded gas mandatory, and the three-way cat required precise control of the fuel mixture, at the stoichiometric 14.7:1 ratio. This necessitated an exhaust oxygen sensor, with an electronic link to the fuel mix managing ECU, so that the 14.7 parts air to one fuel was maintained. Hence Corvette's 50-state adoption of an electronic Q-jet for '81 MY.

The GM ESC system was most prominent publicly on the 1978 Buick Turbo Regal and 1980 Pontiac Turbo Trans Am; exact boost enrichment and avoiding detonation were especially crucial on turbo cars. On 1981 Corvettes, their ESC under CCC, locked up the THM 350 in second and third gears, to maximize gas mileage. Headers were also great for efficiency, and present on the L81 350 V8. However, the whole game was let down by super tall axle ratios, necessitated by CAFE. Like the Corvette's 1981 engine choice, the axle selection was simple: four-speed = 2.72. automatic = 2.87. There was a G92 performance axle ratio, costing 20 bucks, and chosen by 2400 '81 Corvette devotees. This performance axle allowed 1981 Corvette four-speed fans, to get the 2.87 axle ratio! A step in the right direction, but not enough.

Based on *Road & Track*'s experience with 1980 and 1981 Corvette four-speeds, with respective axle ratios of 3.07 and 2.72, the taller axle saw ¼-mile performance and associated trap speed worsen from 16 seconds flat at 86.5mph, to 17 seconds flat at 82mph ... ho hum. What's more, or less, 0-100mph increased from 22.2 seconds to 27.5 seconds, and the 1981 Corvette four-speed could no longer hit redline in top gear! Therefore, top speed fell on *R&T* figures, from 130mph to 124mph, the latter corresponding to 4400rpm. And the reward for the snooze axle? Compared to the lively '79 Corvette L82 350 four-speed with 3.70 axle that *Road & Track* tried, overall gas mileage improved from 15mpg, to 16mpg. Not really worth it.

Corvette Chief Engineer Dave McLellan said super gas mileage wasn't a high priority with Corvette buyers. In recent times, McLellan's top lieutenant Jim Jingles Ingle, who worked on Corvette powertrains of the era, couldn't recall what axle ratio RPO G92 got in 1981. Interest in madcap performance wasn't at its zenith in 1981. Team Corvette was putting its efforts towards getting the new C4 Corvette ready. For 1981, the work at hand involved cosmetic and comfort refinements, and at least, thanks to the smart L81 350, you could get a Corvette with four-speed in California again. The tall axle ratios worked against 1981 performance helpers like the more efficient 350 V8 and plastic rear spring. Yes, 1981 Corvettes with automatic transmission, and standard suspension, received a composite fiberglass rear transverse spring.

When you consider only 5757 '81 Corvettes had the MM4 NCO four-speed, 7803 buyers paid $57 for

FE7 Gymkhana suspension, and only 1128 went the $37 F51 HD shock route. Yes, most 1981 Corvettes came with the plastic rear spring, and this implied no rear swaybar. The percentage of Corvette buyers going for HD suspension, declined a little versus 1980. Therefore, more folks took advantage of the 36lb weight saving that the composite fiberglass rear spring brought. The unit weighed a mere 8lb, with the conventional steel spring coming in at 44lb. However, there were some trade offs to consider. Most Mid-Year C2 and Late Model C3 Corvettes came with 196lb rear transverse steel springs, increasing to 260lb/in^2 during 1978-80. A steel spring may lose 40% of its initial stiffness over a 20 year timeframe. In contrast, a plastic spring loses no stiffness, remaining at its original spec for its entire life. However, whereas a steel spring will never break, a plastic spring just might.

If a plastic spring gets hit by a stray object, at just the right point, like a thrown up road rock, it could break or delaminate immediately, game over! Then too, the plastic spring would also worsen the C3 Corvette fastback's tail biased weight distribution – in the sense that the fastback added weight back there, whereas the plastic spring sitting low and behind the axle, took weight away. On the other hand, with its fiberglass transverse spring, and 2.87 axle, a stock '81 Corvette automatic coupe was the best form to scoot off the line. Especially when you factor in the torque amplifying effect of the torque converter style THM 350, working with the L81 350's peak 280lb/ft. Of course, it would have been better with 1980's 3.07 axle. The 1981 Camaro Z28 LM1 350 could have a 3.08 axle, so why not the mighty Corvette? Calculating GM's fleet mileage average for CAFE was somewhat like walking a tightrope sans safety net. Gas mileage was king, and 'gas guzzler tax' was the new bad language.

On the plus side, an '81 Corvette four-speed with 2.72 axle, implied just 2000rpm at 60mph, or even less at the 55mph national highway limit. This meant the latest Corvette was a great place to enjoy the Plastic Fantastic's expanded audio range. 1981 was the first time Corvette could enjoy a radio/tape deck ... with Citizens Band radio! That is, UM4 AM-FM stereo with 8-track (8262 cars optioned at $386), or UM5 AM-FM stereo with 8-track/CB (792 cars optioned at $712). Then came UM6 AM-FM

stereo with compact cassette (22,892 cars optioned at $423), or UN5 AM-FM stereo with compact cassette/CB (2349 cars optioned at $750). Then too, there was plain U58 AM-FM stereo radio, which 5145 '81 Corvettes had for a 95 buck surcharge. The Corvette was the only sports car in the world, factory fittable with radio tape deck and CB radio simultaneously. However, there was no doubt the popularity of CB radio was on the decline. So too the 8-track player.

What good is fine music, or highway chatter, if one isn't seated comfortably? Well, in 1981, Corvette fans had their best chance yet, with the first time availability of a reclining driver's seat. It happened to offer six-way power adjustment, American style. It was all a first for Corvette. The option in question was RPO A42 power driver seat, selected on 29,200 '81 Corvettes, at a cost of $183. The six-way power seat, a long time domestic car staple, also arrived on the Mercedes S class for the first time in '81 MY. So yes, the 1980 Corvette and Mercedes S class, although not cheap cars, were limited to manual front seats. In another Corvette first, 1981 saw the first time option of power side reversing mirrors. Once again, not a new option in the car world by any means, but a Corvette first nevertheless with $117 RPO DG7 electric sport mirrors, and 13,567 buyers thought DG7 was worth it. As for the Corvette itself, the starting list price was now $16,258.52. Some considered that a bargain, but some in the automotive press weren't so sure. Regardless, it was hard to disagree that the Corvette's new RPO D84 two-tone paint option, made a great visual impact.

5352 '81 Corvette buyers paid $399 for the two-tone paint, returning for the first time since the

Straight Axle Corvette era, concerning a regular Corvette. There were four possible combinations: codes 33/38 Silver over Dark Blue, 33/39 Silver over Charcoal, 50/74 Beige over Dark Bronze and 80/98 Autumn Red over Dark Claret. *Road & Track* said it didn't much care for any of the combinations. Kentucky Governor John Brown drove the first Corvette off the new Bowling Green line. Most '81 Corvettes made at Bowling Green had D84 two-tone paint. Of trivialities, the '81 Corvette now had a quartz clock and digital display radio tuner, standard. Of more importance was the new Bowling Green plant's ability to knock out 15 new Corvettes per hour, St Louis was flat out at 10! Finally, Corvette supply could meet demand for the Bow Tie brand's Plastic Fantastic.

That was the Corvette's story of gradual development. Always a leader in quality fiberglass finish for a mass production car. The low density panels used from 1980 represented a composite lighter than the pre-1980 mixture. That is, tiny low density glass beads within fiberglass, that displaced heavy resin with light glass. The 1980 Californian Corvette LG4 305 automatic's stainless steel tubular headers were lighter and freer flowing than Corvette's usual cast iron exhaust manifold. Proof of the freer flowing headers came from the fact that 1980 Californian Corvettes with the LG4 305 were rated 30 horses higher than Golden State GM F bodies, using the same powerplant. It was 180bhp against 150 horses, seen in one's 5-liter V8 1980 Camaro Z28, Firebird Formula or Trans Am. Such headers were applied at the 50-state level in 1981, concerning L81 350.

The low density panels, stainless steel headers, plastic transverse spring, etc, allowed the 1981 Corvette automatic to be 274lb, or over 7% lighter, than an equivalent 1979 model, according to GM statistics. Corvettes had long put a lot of rubber on the road. *Road Test* magazine always gave Camaro

Z28s and Firebird Trans Ams 100/100 for tire reserve, concerning their GR70-15 gumballs on 15 x 7in rims. The Corvette went one better with 15 x 8in rims! Now in 1980/81, the Corvette's footprint was bigger again with the QXH RWL SBR P255/60-15s, costing $492 in 1981, and chosen by 18,004 '81 Corvette devotees. In the May 1980 issue of *Car and Driver*, Don Sherman was complimentary towards the Corvette's optional 255 section Goodyear Eagle GT rubber. He said they permitted high lateral grip, along with a gradual breakaway of the tail, highlighting the Corvette's neutral behavior on smooth surfaces.

From 1968 onwards, Corvettes had some pretty good wheels and tires. *Motor Week*'s chief mechanic Pat Goss said as much, on the eve of the C4 Corvette's release. To that point in time, Goss had owned no fewer than 43 Corvettes. So, he seemed eminently qualified to comment on the detrimental effect that oversize tires on an offset rim would have on a C3 Corvette. Strut rod bushings could get destroyed. Stub axle bearings got stressed, and would run dry. Eventually, the axle end would seize and break off. Even sans modification, it was wise preventative maintenance to grease and pack stub axle bearings every 30,000 miles. Oversize tires on offset rims, also put stress on the differential. Under continual stress, the entire end facing could crack and break off. Transverse rear Corvette springs would lose their stiffness faster, and 1981-82 Corvette automatics with composite plastic rear springs could suffer immediate delamination and spring breakage! Why fit oversize tires on an offset rim? Sometimes it was just as much about image, as it was about improving traction.

Corvette – The image maker

MORE WOMEN IN your Late Model C3 Corvette, said *Road Test* magazine in June 1976. Not as passenger-seated girlfriends, but as driver-seated Corvette owners. *Road Test* and the movie *Corvette Summer* asserted that the ladies were trying to attract a fella. However, this could equally have been where women's lib met the Plastic Fantastic! That is, lady car enthusiasts appreciating a responsive, powerful steed, and that seemed the case in the TV show *Lobo*.

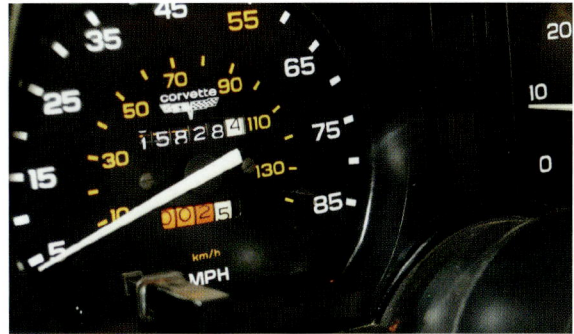
This was Jimmy Carter reminding you to drive 55, to save gas and lives. Concerning gas mileage, Corvette's 1981 2.72 snooze axle for stick shift coupes had CAFE written all over it! *(Courtesy Cruisin Classics Inc)*

Road & Track considered headroom and legroom to be good. However, like ye olde Jag XKE, the footwells were narrow. 1981 was the final year for a Corvette four-speed, established 1957. *(Courtesy Cruisin Classics Inc)*

The 1980-81 season of NBC TV show *Lobo* was a follow up to the 1979-80 series *The Misadventures of Sheriff Lobo*, itself a spin off from trucker TV show *BJ and the Bear*. Indeed, the later C3 Corvettes were much a part of this law man, CB radio, trucker *Smokey and the Bandit* era. In *Lobo*, the corrupt, schemer sheriff and his offsiders Birdy and Perkins moved from Orly County, Georgia, to the big smoke of Atlanta. In *Lobo*, female detectives Peaches and Brandy used a black C3 Corvette. The coupe was owned and driven by Brandy, played by Tara Buckman, who went on to partner Adrienne Barbeau in team Lamborghini, for the 1981 movie *The Cannonball Run*, starring Burt Reynolds. Yes, you couldn't travel very far from the Bandit in those days! However, the 1981 movie *Polyester* had different stars, Tab Hunter and a code 10 White '80 Corvette L48 350 automatic.

You could say Tab Hunter was a matinee idol, from the Corvette's Straight Axle era. *Polyester* was a New Line Cinema feature film, with Hunter playing Elmer Fishpaw, the polyester jacket clad adult movie theater owner. His wife was played by drag queen Divine. She worried about her family's upper middle class, social suburban standing in Baltimore, Maryland, given her glue sniffing son and freely associating daughter. *Polyester* came with cinema gimmick 'Odorama', a scratch and sniff card that drew one into the cinema experience. For example, when the appropriate number flashed on the screen, as Elmer Fishpaw alighted from his Corvette, you could enjoy the scent of genuine Corvette leather, by scratching the displayed number, and inhaling from the card.

Polyester was a comedy, but the automotive press was questioning the contemporary Corvette's seriousness, and the legitimacy of Detroit's business practices and products in general. In the May 1980 assessment of the latest Corvette, Patrick Bedard made the observation that whereas in 1970 a Corvette would have had its hood open, while being tuned for street racing, today the Plastic Fantastic was more likely to be driven to the country club, by a middle aged man wearing white shoes and matching white belt. Indeed, thoughts of Rodney Dangerfield's character from the 1980 movie *Caddyshack*, immediately come to mind. In that film the car in question was a 1963 Rolls Royce Silver Cloud III convertible, whose red exterior matched its owner's pants! And like Dangerfield's oft spoken catchphrase, the Corvette wasn't getting any respect, although criticisms from press and public alike, seemed churlish, given the automotive realities of 1981.

For *Road & Track*, the Corvette's ubiquity was "harshing their mellow", when it came to enjoying America's only sports car. The Corvette's spirit didn't appeal to the critics, in their view, the Corvette's technical merits were outweighed by the cons. The journal wondered if it might enjoy the coupe's unique sporting properties more, if there weren't quite so many Corvettes on the

It's the one-year-only L81 350, complete with CCC (Computer Command Control) ECU, magnesium valve covers and 190 horses! Tubular headers and electronic Q-jet helped deliver 280lb/ft at a mere 1600rpm! *(Courtesy Cruisin Classics Inc)*

road. Just not exotic enough. It seems a prophet is never appreciated in his home town. It's true, that like the Jeep Grand Cherokee, the Corvette was now a country club, suburban status symbol. Neither rigs were cheap. Plus, when you sell over 40,000 cars per annum, your client base is going to widen beyond just enthusiasts, and or racers. *R&T* held this view of the 1980 Corvette, "America's only sports car: showbiz through & through. The sort of car, we've got to admit, that turns young men's heads and causes young ladies to smile as you motor by. Its own reward perhaps?" Their red exterior, white interior with silvered CC1 moonroof T-top panels test coupe, certainly made the Corvette no wallflower. However, it was an image not to *R&T*'s tastes.

Car and Driver's 1980 close encounter of the Corvette kind was subtitled by Patrick Bedard as, "America's only sports car, but that doesn't excuse everything." *C/D*'s Rich Ceppos was lying in wait with the journal's familiar Devil's advocate counterpoint, "Another year, another Corvette." Along with, "... I'll welcome its successor with open arms." The summary of *C/D*'s trio Bedard, Sherman & Ceppos was Corvette: likeable old warhorse, but needs much improvement. The journal attributed GM and Chevrolet's apathy towards self improvement as greatly related to the Corvette's continually high sales numbers. If it ain't broke, don't fix it, but it acknowledged that a tightening CAFE and automaker desire to avoid the

At 40,606 1981 model year sales, Corvette's 40,614 1980 tally was almost repeated. This 1981 coupe was one of 5757 Corvettes with RPO MM4 BW Super T10 four-speed stick shift. *(Courtesy Cruisin Classics Inc)*

5352 '81 Corvette buyers took the newly available $399 D84 two-tone paint. Four combinations were possible, and this is code 33/39 Silver over Charcoal. '81 Corvettes were built in St Louis with traditional GM lacquer. The Bowling Green, Kentucky plant used enamel for Corvette exterior paint. *(Courtesy Cruisin Classics Inc)*

gas guzzler tax would bring Corvette changes in the near future. For now, it was just a more refined version of your favorite perennial. That said, *C/D*'s account sold short the continual grace under pressure of Dave McLellan and Team Corvette, as well as ignoring some commercial realities.

The Corvette folks wanted to keep real duals going past 1974, and have dual cats, but cost and smog dictated otherwise. Even though *C/D* felt the Corvette's V8 Mouse Motor was indistinguishable from units in lesser Chevrolets, like Monte Carlos, Monzas and El Caminos, the chance to have a four-barrel V8 in the early '80s was reason enough to celebrate! Tightening CAFE and an industry wide move to front drive I4 and V6 vehicles meant that, outside of trucks, it was getting harder to find a V8. Plus, respected European opposition was struggling for sales.

In 1980, Porsche made its first ever loss. Porsche President Dr Ernst Fuhrmann and the Zuffenhausen volk had recently hoped that their Corvette clone, the 928, would sell in big numbers, and replace the 911. Neither thing happened. So much so, that Porsche denied those were ever goals of the respected, but not greatly liked, 928. By 1981 the Porsche 928 was selling around 5000 units per annum, or less than half its planned figure. The Jag XJS was hardly selling at all, a mere 1000 coupes worldwide in 1980. Industrial action by the UAW's British brethren, and a post fuel crisis fall in V12 demand, saw the XJS coupe go on

a short hiatus in 1981. As for John Z DeLorean's dream, the former Chevrolet boss didn't quite reach reality. It seemed his DMC12 did its best work in fiction. The Mercedes SL and BMW 6 series had no sales problems, but they weren't sports cars, nor did they sell at Corvette volume. It all left the Plastic Fantastic in its usual unique, and profitable, position.

However, directly and indirectly, the automotive press continued its anti-Detroit tirade. In November 1979, *Car and Driver* lauded the Porsche 924 Turbo, two-tone paint and all! Larry Griffin noticed, "Heads turn and eyes appreciate, but people in Corvettes catch a glimpse and their eyes dart away." Griffin speculated on Porsche licensing an American company to build a 924 Turbo to help with CAFE and, "... thin the bilious ranks of the disagreeable and thirsty plastic mastodons." He then warned against a poorly assembled 924 Turbo copy, while *C/D*'s Rich Ceppos likened the 924 Turbo to Bruce Jenner ... The commonly held belief at the time was that Detroit made gaudy, inefficient and badly built machines. *Road & Track* in March 1977, even used the Mazda RX4 sedan as a proxy whipping boy, for the Big Three's ills.

R&T had once admired the Mazda RX4 sedan, putting the model in its 10 Best 1975 list but, "Now it's like an American car that didn't grow up." The Mazda was the only Japanese car in a field of eight sports sedans, the other seven were from Europe. *R&T* and *C/D* were both much in favor of the European contingent. There was some irony in that the Corvette was once seen as America's most European car. After all, it had a floor shift, handbrake and independent rear suspension. Along with excellent four-wheel disk brakes, the Corvette still stood alone in Detroit. Although a base 1981 Corvette was over 16 grand, a Porsche 928 was nearly $39k! Then too, the Porsche's new handling pack, called Competition Package, cost $1100 versus the Corvette's 57 buck FE7 Gymkhana deal. True, the 928's Competition Package ran to more than just springs and shocks, but the 928's electrically adjustable driver's bucket seat was $660, against a mere $183 for the Corvette's RPO A42 equivalent. Perhaps the US automotive press was the new Marie Antoinette? If they lack bread, let them eat cake indeed.

1982 → Requiem for a heavyweight

CHEVROLET ENGINEERING WAS working on a special Corvette during 1979-80. They utilized the latest automotive phenomenon … turbocharging! Get around smog and CAFE by making a small engine behave like a big one, only on demand. The prototype Turbo Corvette, complete with 'Turbo' door decal, used many existing elements from GM world: L82 350, L48 350 cam, modified stock cast iron L48 350 intake, adapted digital Caddy Seville injection, Turbo Regal knock sensor ESC (Electronic Spark Control), pre 1980 Corvette 3.55 diff ratio, FE7 Gymkhana suspension, THM 350 automatic and Garrett Ai Research T3 turbo compressor, with integral wastegate. Chevrolet Engineering placed the throttle blade controlling incoming air, upstream of the turbo to reduce lag. The familiar optional Goodyear Eagle GT P255/60R-15s (RPO QXH), wrapped non Chevrolet 15 x 8½in turbine alloys. The Turbo Corvette coupe got into the 13s, using 7lb of boost.

There were no plans to produce the Turbo Corvette, leaving a choice between the Datsun 280ZX Turbo or gray market BMW 745i to get blown! That said, fuel injection and the aforementioned prototype's interior décor (door card and seat shading), did find their way onto the

1982 Corvette. And yes, in spite of media carping, the Late Model C3 Corvette was still with us, for yet another model year. However, this 15th appearance, would be its last, sadly. The formal announcement of a brand new 1983 Corvette had finally come down from on high, Mount General Motors. If anyone was in doubt, the Corvette's second special edition model of all time, the 1982 Corvette Collector Edition Hatchback, yes hatchback, was a self evident bookmark, to the most commercially successful Corvette generation, and longest running, of all time.

For 1982, the Corvette got a new powertrain, and indeed the coupe was a test bed for the new, concerning the relatively new Bowling Green plant, new manufacturing machinery, and standardized assembly procedures. What's more, of the same, Corvette Chief Engineer Dave McLellan said they wanted to go partial production on the plastic rear spring one more time, before going exclusively composite with the new Corvette. That is, your standard non HD suspension Corvette coupe relied on that plastic transverse rear spring, first seen in '81 model year. As McLellan said of the 1982 Corvette, "It's a harbinger of things to come. For the 1982 model is more than just the last of a generation, it's stage one of a two-stage production. We're doing the power team this year. Next year, we add complete new styling and other innovations."

With all this talk of what was coming, little wonder that sales of the final Mako Shark II derived Plastic Fantastic fell noticeably. The 25,407 1982 Corvettes sold only beat out the truncated 1970½ Corvette, which managed 17,316 units. Some blame for the sales drop has been laid at the feet of the Corvette's price, for a domestic. There was also the slow economy, and the Late Model C3 Corvette's aging state. However, such factors didn't stop the C3 Corvette vaulting to over 40,000 sales in 1980 and 1981! No, many Corvette devotees were putting off their expenditure until the promised 1983 Corvette roared into view. Unbeknownst to them, they had a wait on their hands.

The power team Dave McLellan spoke of involved the new L83 350 V8 Mouse Motor, connected to a GM THM 700R4 automatic transmission. No stick shift for '82 MY. It was the

Now in 1982 model year with a new Corvette color: code 99 Dark Claret. This hue was selected on just 853 of the 25,407 '82 Corvettes. It was the Late Model C3 Corvette's final model year. *(Courtesy XFirePerformance.com)*

first time that happened since 1955! The official word was that the cost of emissions certification, meant Chevrolet was going to hold off on a stick shift until the new Corvette arrived. The L83 350/THM 700R4 was an exclusive combo concerning the '82 Corvette. Underhood, the decorative ribbed rocker covers as seen on L81 and L82 350 V8s. However, the L83 350's fuel injection was something else. To be precise, Cross Fire Injection meant two throttle body injector solenoid units mounted on the intake manifold cover (flat mounting plateau), supplying air/fuel mixture through the tuned runners of the intake manifold to the cylinders on the opposite side of the V8. So, each bank of the V8 was supplied by single point injection.

The theory of long intake runners, or tubes, to boost power and torque wasn't new. Back in 1960, the Dodge Dart Phoenix D-500 option, implied a Super Red Ram 361 Ram Induction V8: a forerunner of later fuel injection, but with widely spaced carburetors, with long pipes in between. A partial vacuum effect happened when the intake valve opened, helping to fill the combustion chamber. In 1960 and 1982 the theory worked. Power was now 200bhp at 4200rpm, with 285lb/ft at 2800rpm, both stats were improvements on the outgoing L81 350, which in turn bettered the L48 350 V8. Compared to L48 and L81 350s, the new L83 350 had a higher 9.0:1 compression ratio, rather than 8.2:1. There were now also handbuilt, tubular titanium headers, and sportier cams with higher

223

The '82 Corvette opened the door to a new, and single, Corvette power team: L83 350 & THM 700R4 four-speed automatic. *(Courtesy XFirePerformance.com)*

Chevrolet said emissions certification costs ruled out a stick shift for 1982 Corvettes. The Bow Tie Boys were going to wait for the next Corvette to introduce a manual transmission. This coupe has a built up THM 700R4 unit. *(Courtesy XFirePerformance.com)*

lift and slightly more overlap. The big cams were possible due to the added torque brought by fuel injection. It was also oft mentioned, that the L83 350 possessed flawless drivability. In contrast, the June 1982 issue of *Road & Track* report on the carb fed '82 Camaro Z28 and Ford Mustang GT 5.0 four-speeds, revealed engines that wanted to stall a few times, after a cold start. The Ford more so. Indeed, the journal also sampled an '82 Camaro Z28 with LU5 305, a Cross Fire injected version of the smaller Chevrolet 5-liter V8, and noted the automatic only iteration felt much more powerful and responsive, than its LG4 305 carb counterpart. Sophisticated electronics, and revised emissions control equipment, were part of Cross Fire Injection's powerplay.

Inputs came from sensors for engine speed, throttle position, coolant temp, MAP (Manifold Absolute Pressure) and an exhaust oxygen sensor. The Cross Fire system was a more advanced setup than 1980-81's CCC. Now the air fuel mixture was adjusted 80 times per second. Tied into the ECU's ambit was the Electronic Spark Control, and also when the automatic transmission's torque converter locked up. The ECU observed both vehicle speed and engine speed/load, to work out when to lock up the torque converter. This was

only done if the L83 350 V8 was up to operating temperature. Emissions controls like air injection and EGR were also looked at by the ECU. Indeed, the '82 Corvette featured a revised emissions control approach. Apart from 1981's charcoal air filter element being replaced by a paper filter, the latest Corvette had a smaller, lighter, but still single, monolith catalytic converter.

Exhaust gases were piped directly into the cat to get the unit working faster and more efficiently. Post cat, the exhaust gases went into dual low restriction mufflers to maintain the expected Corvette rumble. What's more, true fresh air induction was back for the first time since 1975. A solenoid actuated, hood mounted fresh air door opened up when you floored the gas pedal! Something not seen before was an in-tank fuel pump, replacing the previous mechanical pump. The Corvette was a long time GM technical leader and test bed. The Cross Fire type electronic Throttle Body Injection (TBI), would soon feature on countless GM trucks and passenger vehicles. For example, the 2.5-liter Iron Duke inline four, fitted to the 1984 Pontiac Fiero.

The Corvette's four wheel disk brakes and IRS soon became commonplace on virtually all cars. However, there was a long held suspicion

1982 was the first time the Corvette had been without a manual transmission since the 1955 Corvette's sole Powerglide choice. It also marked the return of fuel injection for the first time since 1965. This stroker L83 383, has 7747 ECU, EBL Flash II, Renegade intake & DUI Dizzy. *(Courtesy XFirePerformance.com)*

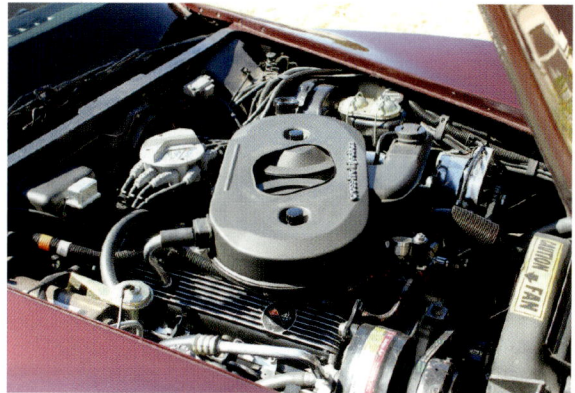

concerning computer controlled fuel injection. In February 1971, *Road & Track* noted how flawlessly the Bosch D-jetronic injection helped its test VW 411 behave. However, the journal worried that if the ECU 'black box' (actually silver) gave out, then what? Ten years later, in the November 1981 issue of *R&T*, Joe Rusz had Dave McLellan on the spot concerning the '82 Corvette's ECU. McLellan assured Rusz that the Corvette's Cross Fire Injection possessed a 'limp home' mode, soon commonplace on modern cars. Beyond that, he joked they had another back up system, "We call it our walk-home mode."

Somehow, the public and mechanics seemed more willing to place their faith in a carburetor, with all its complexity and many moving parts subject to wear and dirt, than the witchcraft of fuel injection. At least at this hour. The '82 Corvette's four-speed electronically controlled overdrive automatic, would soon also become normal on '80s and '90s cars – indeed, two model years prior to BMW's usage of the ZF 4HP22, in North America. In the '82 Corvette's case, the THM 700R4 was a THM 350, with an overdrive fourth (0.70) added. The torque converter would lock up in second, third, and fourth under the right conditions. The only diff ratio for 1982 was 1981's 'performance axle' 2.87. Concerning CAFE, that's all she wrote. To aid scat off the line, first was now a shorter 3.06 ratio.

Next to all the 1982 powertrain developments, other '82 Corvette amendments seemed modest. A quartz console clock, with the word 'QUARTZ' printed large on the clock's face, and some alterations concerning option ordering. A new code 99 Dark Claret exterior color, formerly only available in two-tone, and no UM5 AM-FM stereo with 8-track and CB package. To have it all, you needed a compact cassette deck. That is, UN5's AM-FM stereo/compact cassette/CB radio, costing $755 for 1987 '82 Corvette buyers. To obtain an 8-track player, try UM4 AM-FM stereo/8-track, costing

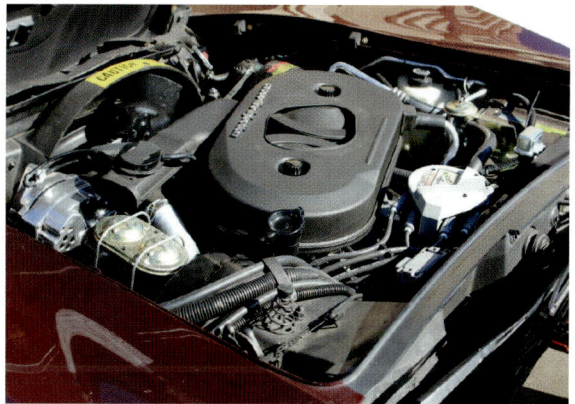

2.13in throttle body injectors (#90), AFR 195 heads, Bullet HR cam, 1.6 Ultra Pro roller rockers, 10.5:1 Wiseco pistons, FSI I-beam conrods, forged crank, 3200rpm stall speed Yank torque converter, custom tune by XFire Performance and R/SL Tuning, plus Hedman, Hooker Max-Flows, all equals really righteous 12-second passes! *(Courtesy XFirePerformance.com)*

$386. However, a mere 923 '82 Corvette fans took that 8-track path, whereas 20,355 buyers payed $423 for UM6's AM-FM stereo/compact cassette. In short, 8-track was yesterday's hit.

1982 also witnessed several goodbyes in Corvette world, the end of many familiar elements. It was the end for T-tops, and the 70 profile tire. Both features had been going since the C3 Corvette commenced in '68 MY. Your standard 1982 Corvette, rarely seen, rolled on SBR P225/70-15 blackwalls, covering 15 x 8in Rally rims. The same steel rims and trim rings, plus chrome center cap, that Zora Arkus-Duntov used to recommend over heavier and pricier wheel covers. 5932 '82 Corvette folk, paid 80 bucks to get the aforementioned tire size in RWL, using RPO QGR. However, the popularity of the pricy $542 QXH RWL SBR P255/60-15s got strong for 1982, with 19,070 optioning same. With the ever rising interest in handling, QXH was now judged worth it.

1982 Corvette Collector Edition

TO REDUCE UNSPRUNG weight, and further enhance handling and visuals, 16,844 '82 Corvettes had the $458 RPO N90 alloy wheels. These 15 x 8in eight-slot alloys had been seen on and off from 1973. 1982 was their final outing, and so too FE7 Gymkhana suspension, beloved by the autocross crowd and introduced under Zora Arkus-Duntov for '74 MY. Only 5457 '82 Corvettes had RPO FE7, even though it cost only 61 bucks. In contrast, 22,585 Corvette faithful optioned the $197 AG9 power driver seat, with 23,936 buyers selecting the $155 AU3 power door locks. More signs of that Cowboy Cruiser than Circuit Crusher in 1982. But for the ultimate in appearance, you couldn't drive past RPO 1YY07's Corvette Collector Edition Hatchback: $22,537 – 6759 '82 Corvette Collector Edition Hatchbacks. It was the first Plastic Fantastic to break the 20 grand barrier! Once one overcame sticker shock, then came the realization that RPO 1YY07 was one HE Double Hockey Sticks of a deal!

As Dave McLellan said, the Corvette Collector Edition represented, "... a unique combination of color, equipment and innovation (resulting in) one of the most comprehensive packages ever offered to the Corvette buyer." The visual impact came from: code 59 Silver Beige Metallic exterior, unique to the '82 Corvette Collector Edition, graduated shadow contrast striping for hood, fenders and

You couldn't get a 3.31 rear axle or heim joint strut rods on a stock '82 Corvette, but this coupe ain't stock! *(Courtesy XFirePerformance.com)*

With official word that 1982 would be the C3 Corvette's final model year, with the long awaited new Corvette coming soon, sales of the Mako Shark II inspired Corvette finally slowed, as Corvette fans saved up for the all new model. *(Courtesy XFirePerformance.com)*

doors, bronze tint T-tops, cloisonné Corvette Collector Edition emblems around the Corvette's cross flags logo on hood, tail and steering wheel, color matched silver leather seats and door cards, 15 x 8in turbine rims shod with QXH RWL SBR P255/60-15 tires, and hatchback cargo access.

The '82 Corvette Collector Edition was the only factory Corvette sold to this point in time with the practicality of a hatchback. A long overdue addition, but as Bogi demonstrated on TV show *All Girls Garage*, the stock hatch clamps were on the weak side. They were unable to exert enough pressure in the closed hatch position to seal the hatch glass to the underlying body aperture's rubber strip. The show featured the installation of beefier, custom hatch clamps. The Collector Edition's rims looked a lot like the one-year-only '67 N89 cast aluminum bolt-on wheels, but were much wider. On the inside the Collector Edition had a steering wheel with color matched, hand sewn leather wrap, which covered the horn cap. Upscale color matched luxury carpeting was part of the wall-to-wall deal.

The only high performance aspect of the '82 Corvette Collector Edition was its QXH 255 section, 60 profile rubber. For luxury, a key facet of Corvette life by now, the AG9 power driver seat and UN5 GM Delco AM-FM stereo with compact cassette/CB were part of the Collector Edition spec. Vehicle id plates prevented Collector Edition cloning, like the '78 Limited Edition Corvette Pace Car. Indeed, having a numbered console plaque with the owner's name was a personalized touch hard to pass up. You were now literally part of Corvette history! As a complete visual statement, the Collector Edition showed the creativity in appearance packages that was a one time hallmark of the Big Four automakers. Sadly, it went into decline during the minimalist, monochrome sleeper look of the 1980s.

The '82 Corvette Collector Edition had a '0' 6th digit in its special VIN. Would there be price gouging, as per the '78 Corvette Pace Car? Not

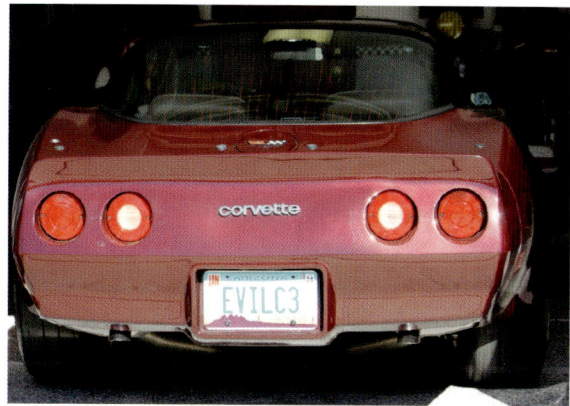

Those are Mickey Thompson ET Street RDR tires. With this modified '82 Cross Fire Corvette capable of 12s in the ¼-mile, by golly you need 'em! *(Courtesy XFirePerformance.com)*

according to Dave McLellan, the new Bowling Green, Kentucky Corvette plant could produce as many '82 Corvette Collector Editions as the market desired. So, no insane mark up due to limited supply. The Collector Edition came with Corvette HD suspension, implying a rear swaybar and steel transverse, multileaf spring. RPO UN5 in-car audio came with four speakers, featuring front to rear balance control, and U75 Power Antenna, a $60 value. As had been seen on Corvettes since 1977, with factory CB radio, one received a Velcro-backed microphone stuck to the console. Even though the Collector Edition didn't have faux wood interior trim, as seen on other '82 Corvettes, *Road & Track* still considered the final C3 Corvettes as possessing an interior with a hint of Las Vegas boutique!

Cross Fire injection Corvette performance

AT LEAST ONE wasn't taking a gamble, with traditional Chevrolet small block V8 reliability, but the THM 700R4 did cause some concerns. The electronic to mechanical interface, for locked torque converter engagement, seemed to introduce a few snafus. In its November 1982 'Chevrolet Corvette Last Word, Third Chapter' look at the '82 Corvette, *Road & Track* said a GM mechanic had informed them of several '82 Corvettes with problematic THM 700R4s. They didn't shift as they should have, were rough in action etc. *R&T* had to go through three test cars to get one set of good figures. It seemed the L83 350 V8 oftentimes got blamed for problems that were actually related to the automatic transmission. However, when everything worked, like any exotic, the results were worth it.

In a preview article for the '82 Corvette, *R&T*'s Joe Rusz discussed the Corvette with Dave McLellan, as well as with development engineers Rick Darling, Richard Johnson and Vince Wagner. Team Corvette were working on the '82 Corvette, but also the very important all new Corvette. The Corvette folks asked Rusz what came to mind when he heard the term Cross Fire? Both Rusz and Team Corvette agreed that Cross Fire inferred induction induced ignition interference. However, Chevrolet test marketing said the Cross Fire moniker seemed well enough received. In any case, Rick Darling said Chrysler Corp used 'Ram' in its nomenclature, with some irony given Chrysler's long intake runner usage from 20 years earlier. Trying an '82 Corvette Collector Edition, at GM's Milford Proving Ground, Joe Rusz got 0-60mph in 7.5 seconds. Dave McLellan said using GM test equipment, and corrections for speedometer lag, brought the expectation of low sevens.

As was the case with previews for the 1972 Ford Gran Torino 351 Cobra Jet, and Porsche 924 Turbo, it seemed that final smog calibrations resulted in a slower car than previews would have led one to believe. That said, the 1982 Corvette Cross Fire Injection V8 was a rapid machine for the time and place. Although 1975 has commonly been regarded as high performance ground zero for the malaise era, that year should be 1982. Government smog and CAFE law were overwhelming automakers and their technology. 1982 saw sporty cars advertised with 0-50mph times, to look good. Ford did so in brochures, for its Mustang Cobra Turbo 2.3L. BMW introduced its economy focused '82 528e. Mercedes' only V8 in North America was the 3.8-liter all alloy unit. Cadillac was using its 4.1-liter all alloy V8, the Porsche 930 was gone, and you couldn't get a Jag XJ12 anymore!

This is a 1982 Corvette Collector Edition Hatchback. The hue is code 59 Silver Beige Metallic, a Collector Edition exclusive! Weight distribution with driver was 50/50, according to *Road & Track* in November 1982. *(Courtesy Smoky Mountain Traders)*

After the 1978 Corvette Indy Pace Car, the '82 Corvette Collector Edition Hatchback, RPO 1YY07 was only the second special edition Corvette appearance package, with 6759 built. *(Courtesy Smoky Mountain Traders)*

With the C3 Corvette at an end, and the new '82 GM F body and Mustang GT 5.0 starting, it seemed many had forgotten about the Plastic Fantastic! *Motor Week* tried the all new '82 Camaro Z28 four-speed LG4 305, and Mustang GT 5.0, at Charlestown, West Virginia's Southern Summit Point Raceway, in early April 1982 saying, "These are the real McCoy. The first high performance sporty cars to come riding out of Detroit since 1973." The Camaro Z28 was defeated by the Mustang in a straight line, but had a clear upper hand over the race track, lapping 2.1 seconds quicker, with an average speed 1.22mph higher. *MW*'s John Davis proclaimed the Camaro Z28 as the nation's best handling car, but what about Corvette?

The 1982 Corvette Cross Fire Injection coupe, in Collector Edition form, was tested by *Motor Week*. The automatic only coupe did a 16 second flat ¼-mile, at Maryland Ohio's 75-80 Dragway. Trap speed was 84mph. At Summit Point Raceway, *MW* got a 15.93 second at 85mph ET, from the four-speed only '82 Mustang GT 5.0. Okay, that was one test, and *MW* echoed the comment of many that those Ford TRX/Michelin wheels and tires didn't offer the best off the line traction or braking, but the Corvette Cross Fire seemed to have a slight, consistent edge on the Mustang GT 5.0 in acceleration and top speed, as *Road & Track*'s import versus domestic figures reveal:

Model	Datsun 280ZX Turbo Auto	Porsche 944 5sp	Corvette Cross Fire Auto	Camaro Z28 LG4 4sp	Mustang GT 5.0 4 sp
Base Price	$17,299	$18,450	$18,290	$9700	$8965
0-60 mph (sec)	7.4	8.3	7.9	9.7	8.0
¼-mile secs	15.6	16.3	16.1	17.5	16.3
@mph	@ 88	@ 84.5	@ 84.5	@ 80	@ 84
Lateral g	0.754	0.818	0.826	0.821	0.736
Test date	7/81	5/82	11/82	6/82	6/82

According to *R&T*, the Mustang GT 5.0 took 25 seconds flat to hit 100mph. However, it timed the '82 Corvette Cross Fire at 24.8 seconds, even with

the Corvette's sole 2.87 snooze axle. So, the '82 Corvette was slightly quicker, but greatly faster. *R&T* said the Foxstang could reach a top speed of 118mph in third or fourth. The Corvette did 125mph in third and fourth, also. At five grand, the Corvette was 200rpm off redline in third, and with only 3500rpm at 125mph in fourth, the '82 Corvette Cross Fire was a latter day Nevada road burner. If only that state still lacked speed limits!

The Porsche 944, on an August 1983 re-test, also reached 125mph exactly. As the above stats show, the new '82 Porsche 944 and Corvette Cross Fire were close in a number of areas. As ever, North American sports car conversation still revolved around Corvette and Porsche. These days the Porsche also came with standard a/c. The 944's Pasha checkered cloth upholstery matched the Corvette's cross flags emblem, even if the remaining 924 dashboard looked decidedly 'Vega low rent' next to the Corvette's aircraft themed cockpit interior. However, there were some things to note. North American Porsche + Audi dealerships were price gouging mightily with the new 944. In a fashion similar to the '78 Corvette Indy Pace Car. Plus, such stealerships were reluctant to order in a basic 944. Therefore, the Zuffenhausen coupe's base price was strictly theoretical.

Road & Track's Porsche 944 recorded 22mpg overall, and 21.5mpg with the '82 Corvette Cross Fire Automatic. It was a substantial improvement over the 14.5mpg and 16mpg the journal had achieved with the Plastic Fantastic in 1980 and 1981, with four-speed sticks. In fact, 22mpg was *R&T*'s overall gas mileage figure for the non turbo Datsun 280ZX. As for the very speedy 280ZX Turbo, fuel economy dipped to 16.5mpg. The Datsun 280ZX Turbo was an enticing performance bargain. A well built Corvette alternative, that also had T-tops and a slushbox. With each passing year, the Datsun Z car seemed more Corvette like, and less like a Jag XKE. However, the Japanese car's chassis and interior also seemed more sedan like than ever.

In terms of speed, the '82 Corvette Cross Fire could claim to be the fastest car in America, and perhaps still the best handling. Although the Camaro Z28 was hardly under tired, with 215/65-15s on a 15 x 7in rim, even the stock Corvette offered wider rims with a bigger footprint tire. The '82

As with any '82 Corvette, your sole power team was L83 350 & THM 700R4 automatic. The air cleaner design was a one-year-only fitment, and shared with LU5 305 CFI powered GM F bodies.
(Courtesy Smoky Mountain Traders)

The '82 Corvette scooted to sixty, one whole second faster than the US spec Ferrari Mondial. The real V8 power was at Bowling Green, Kentucky, not Maranello, sorry Enzo!
(Courtesy Smoky Mountain Traders)

Corvette Collector Edition *Motor Week* tried, even more so. Given the '82 Camaro Z28 and '82 Corvette Cross Fire weighed about the same (3400lb), and the latter had more power, and put more rubber on the road, it seems likely that in skilled hands, the Corvette would have lapped Summit Point Raceway, quicker than the Camaro Z28. It very well mayn't have been as neat around the track, the Camaro Z28 was most tidy in its behavior, but the 1982 Corvette Cross Fire with 255/60-15 radials on 15 x 8in alloys would have probably done the job quicker.

In *R&T*'s June 1982 Camaro Z28 Vs Mustang GT 5.0 match up, the journal aired the view that the Camaro Z28's track competence made them judge the coupe's well located and tamed live axle better than IRS for track control. Similarly, *Motor Week*'s lane change swerve test seemed to show the latest GM F body as nicely neutral, compared to the twitchy '82 Corvette Collector Edition. That said, *MW* track compared the 1983½ Camaro Z28 with high output 175bhp L69 305 V8 against the Porsche 928S at Summit Point Raceway. Even though the Camaro Z28 lapped quicker, it got ragged on the limit. Sudden oversteer was the finale. So, it

seemed the neat display of the '82 Camaro Z28, came from a chassis not being challenged by the meek 145bhp LG4 305 V8.

In 1982 at least, the Corvette could still claim the domestic high performance crown, but what of the L83 Cross Fire Injection 350 V8? Critics would note the Cross Fire motor's intake had limited port size, plus the rough sand casted finish inside the intake's pipes. Large peaks due to casting seams also impeded breathing. However, by 1982 standards, objective testing has shown that the Corvette still matched or bettered its opposition. Then too, some point to the low profile of the Cross Fire Injection's intake manifold, necessary to clear the Corvette's low hood, as impeding flow. To compensate for the lack of high riser nature, a richer fuel mixture was introduced to maintain performance. That said, the Corvette Cross Fire was 50% more economical versus *Road & Track*'s 1980 Corvette four-speed. What's more, the *Road & Track* tested '82 Corvette Cross Fire nearly matched the 22mpg, that the same journal achieved with the 1979 BMW 528i four-speed, Datsun 280ZX and Porsche 944. That is, a world class field of stick shift cars. And don't forget, such improved fuel economy over the 1980 *R&T* Corvette four-speed test was achieved with a slightly quicker ¼-mile time, and no trace of cold start stumble, nor over carburetion displayed by the otherwise well mannered '80 Corvette.

That's a code 132 Silver Gray Leather interior, enjoyed by the '82 Corvette Collector Edition. With a shorter steering column from '77 MY, and AG9 power driver seat from 1981, the C3 Corvette had ergonomically improved since a 1968 start.
(*Courtesy Smoky Mountain Traders*)

More performance for a Corvette Cross Fire is provided by the aftermarket Renegade intake. This better breathing intake replaces the stock CFI intake, and originally came from company DCS, now called XFirePerformance.com. The Renegade intake has produced an independently verified 0.7 second reduction in ¼-mile time, while keeping stock Corvette smog equipment. The Renegade intake was the subject of quality control problems when a different sub contractor was employed to handle the casting process. However, quality has now returned, and you can still order the Renegade unit from Summit Racing online. Naturally, the Renegade intake is applicable to all sporty GM Cross Fire Injection cars, implying Camaro Z28 and Firebird Trans Am of the 1982-84 timeframe. Additional modifications, like adjusting the fuel pressure regulator, oversize injector solenoids, and ECU fuel map recalibration, can further enhance the Renegade intake's high performance contribution. Indeed, making the Cross Fire Intake perform like the late '60s Camaro Z28 intake it resembles! Some owners of Cross Fire Injection cars have followed the Renegade intake's principle, by using a Dremel tool to hollow out a stock CFI intake manifold. However, this needs to be done with great care, lest too much material is removed – just like trashing a cylinder head that has been ported and polished incorrectly.

Motor Week farewells the C3 Corvette

WITH MUCH HUMOR, *Motor Week*'s host John Davis turned up to 1982's show, wearing a black armband! He quickly took off said armband, saying there was no need of it because, "You see ol' King Corvette still has a lot of life left. And anyway old Corvettes never die, or sometimes they do get redesigned." The Corvette had been around for many a year by now, while others had come and gone. For example, Davis added, "… and after Corvette, we've got a new star making its debut from France. The new Fuego sports coupe, it's quite a car!" *MW* gave the Fuego Turbo a glowing review. However, in modern times Davis has conceded that the Fuego has become the best looking car broken down by the side of the road! Oh dear, it's Dauphine revisited!

In the meantime, John Davis said, "Coming soon to your local Chevy dealer, the all new from ground up 1983 Vette. The first redesign since 1968." But first, a letter from a Mr Joe Rhinehart of Dayton, Ohio, requesting *MW* to test the '82 Corvette Collector Edition. *MW* and John Davis were happy to oblige, "So here it is Joe, a last look at the car that has stolen so many American hearts and pocket books." It's true that most car enthusiasts had owned, or still owned, a Corvette. From Zora Arkus-Duntov, to GM brass like Bob Stempel, to *MW*'s John Davis and chief mechanic Pat Goss, singer Pat Boon, and the list goes on. For *Motor Week*'s 1982 Corvette Collector Edition report, John Davis had his own 1978 code 72 Corvette Red coupe, displayed on the Maryland grass, alongside the test '82 Corvette Collector Edition coupe.

Corvettes, and all cars, had risen greatly in price through the stagflationary 1970s, so Davis put this to the audience, "The question then has to be, is this car, America's only true sports car, that much changed in four years to be worth double the price?" He did concede that many formerly optional items had become Corvette standard issue. However, when it came to performance, the latest Corvette seemed to leave Davis' '78 Corvette coupe in the dust! Verified on the Maryland 75-80 Dragway, the '82 Corvette test coupe managed the 40-55mph passing maneuver in 3.2 seconds, the 500ft on ramp sprint in eight seconds flat at 70mph, with a 16 second flat ¼-mile clocking at 84mph. John Davis confided his '78 Corvette took 18 seconds flat for the ¼-mile! The latest Corvette also managed 0-60mph in eight seconds flat. Davis said, "This car is very quick", and added with all the four and six cylinder cars *MW* had tested of late, it was easy to forget what a full range engine was like. It was noted that the Corvette had recently lost 200lb. With economy, the EPA rated the '82 Corvette Cross Fire at 19mpg city and 26mpg highway. *MW* achieved 19mpg overall, with the show stating that for a high performance car, the Corvette's Cross Fire motor permitted easy service access. This was except for sparkplugs, that were only accessible from underneath. As for the variable ratio GM power steering, John Davis still wasn't used to it. He put the system's heavier steering feel in 1982 as being related to the wider 255 section radials. Concerning emergency maneuvers: 30-0mph in 30ft, averaging 103ft from 55mph, with only occasional front locking. The semi-metallic brake pads worked better, with some heat in them. The emergency lane swerve test showed less twitch than that displayed by older Corvettes. However, a light rear end still implied a more abrupt change to oversteer, than a GM F body. That said, Corvette still managed a better showing than the '83 Porsche 911 Cabrio *Motor Week* tried. The West German car missed its intended lane altogether! Cars that can change direction quickly don't always go where you want them too!

Davis judged the Corvette Collector Edition's silver leather seats as supportive and comfy, with the power seat and tilt/tele wheel bringing proper seating for all drivers. John Davis felt all Corvettes should have the Collector Edition's hatchback facility, and many agreed, given the easier cargo access it afforded. Plus, the post 1979 Corvette look of integrated spoilers front and rear, allied to Collector Edition get up, made for a handsome winner in *MW*'s opinion. Still, in spite of the Corvette's dream car status, Davis said, "Despite

The Corvette Collector Edition Hatchback format allowed easy access to the coupe's 10.4ft³ (295 liters) worth of cargo area. However, relatively weak hatch hinges invite water ingress, and therefore damaged carpet and trim. *(Courtesy Smoky Mountain Traders)*

whatever GM tells us, this car is really a Chevrolet in shark's clothing. That means available service in almost every small town from coast to coast. Something no import sports car can claim." True, although some Chevrolet dealers were more attuned to handling the Corvette in terms of stocking parts and mechanic ability than others.

John Davis concluded that the latest 1982 Corvette Collector Edition wasn't worth double what his '78 coupe cost new, at least not to him. The long running nature of familiar car models did make for sound resale value. That is, John Davis' '78 Corvette coupe was still worth 80% of its new car price. Then there was Corvette's undoubted lust factor. Passers by did drool over the *MW* '82 Corvette test coupe, proving, "... that when it comes to the original four-wheeled American dream, price may never be an object". Would that dream survive in today's car world? With stricter smog and safety laws, and the fuel crises, it seemed everyone would soon be driving a front drive, transversely engined, inline four hatchback econobox, designed by international committee.

Qualities like the Jaguar XKE with its 13-piece hood, and the Corvette's foibles, or character if you will, were alien to the World Car Concept. *All Girls Garage* TV show fixed up a 1963 split window, Fuelie Corvette four-speed, and '82 Corvette Collector Edition Hatchback. Automotive bookends, to one and the same separate chassis. With all the body mods the Corvette had experienced

since 1963, *Road & Track* described driving the
1982 Corvette Cross Fire, as a car akin to, "… a
go kart under a home coming float." That is, the
bulk went away during driving. Radials, semi
flexible body mounts, impact bumpers, a returning
fastback etc. Yes, the Mid-Year Corvette chassis
had been adapted over the years. The Corvette's
stiffly sprung racer ways seemed at odds with
contemporary soft riding handlers, which offered a
lot of grip. However, that wasn't the Corvette's style.

Road & Track's Joe Rusz tested the '82 Corvette
at and around GM's Milford Proving Grounds. The
Corvette handled, but with somewhat overboosted
steering, not as sensitive as it should have been.
It was in keeping with Corvette tradition, and
as ever, it was a heavy car that moved with the
road surface. Not as badly as in pre radial tire
days though. Corvette development engineer Rick
Darling promised that the new Corvette would
be different, "The 1983 Corvette will not be like
that. You'll see." At the same time, Dave McLellan
said Corvette buyers still demanded V8 power.
With GM's '80s fleet going front drive, V6 and
unibody, would newer Corvettes still be able to
raid the GM parts shelf, for assorted hardware and
powerplants?

A hint of the upcoming Corvette came in the
form of the downsized 1982 GM F body. Critics
were heartened by the new F body, and hoped
Corvette would follow this move to a smaller,
lighter, more cleanly styled sporting car, with
tighter body quality. That said, *Road & Track*'s
final November '82 observation of the outgoing
Corvette acknowledged that the Plastic Fantastic
had a particular flavor, and appeal, plus, "… the
automotive world would lose a great deal if the
Corvette were to become too much like other
automobiles." Familiarity breeds contempt indeed.

John Greenwood's Corvette world

IF THERE IS one person more closely identified
with the C3 Corvette (apart from Zora Arkus-
Duntov) than anyone else, it would have to be John
Greenwood. The race cars that Greenwood built
and raced, and the road cars he sold, were more
than memorable. John Greenwood campaigned the
Corvette at a time when SCCA and IMSA racing

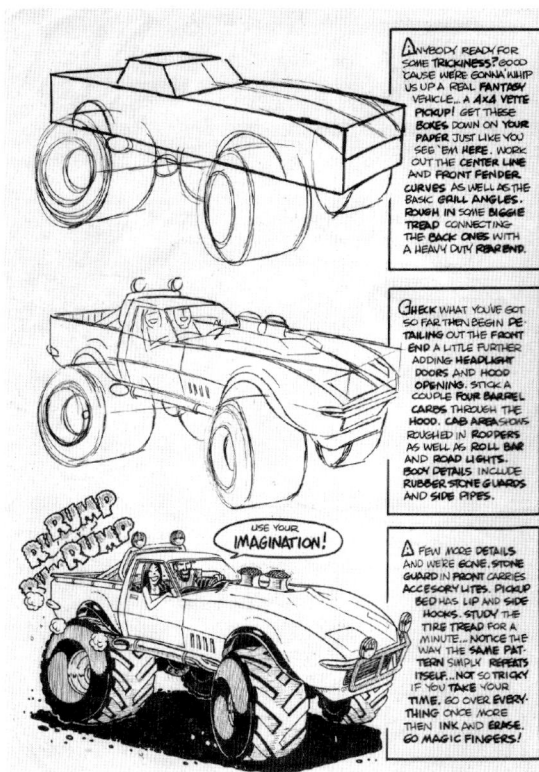

The Late Model C3 Corvette of 1968-82 was the
longest running Corvette, best selling and best
known globally. Imagine that! *(Courtesy CARtoons)*

became increasingly dominated by imports. Foreign
brands entered SCCA's big car ranks in 1973. Early
on, such governing bodies made rules to keep the
dominant Corvette at bay, but now it was the other
way around! And of course, the informal factory/
automaker backing of the late '50s to early '60s was
largely absent. Increasingly, privateers like John
Greenwood were on a one man crusade.

Greenwood started building and racing
Corvettes in 1969, winning the SCCA A Production
Championship in both 1970 and 1971. Such success
attracted the eyes and sponsorship of BF Goodrich.
Greenwood racers were a high profile exponent for
BF Goodrich, during the early '70s radial Tire Wars,
between said tire company and rival Goodyear.
Each camp talked up their contribution to the hot
automotive topic of the day, the domestic made
radial tire. During Greenwood's BF Goodrich
sponsorship run of 1972-73, his Corvette racers on

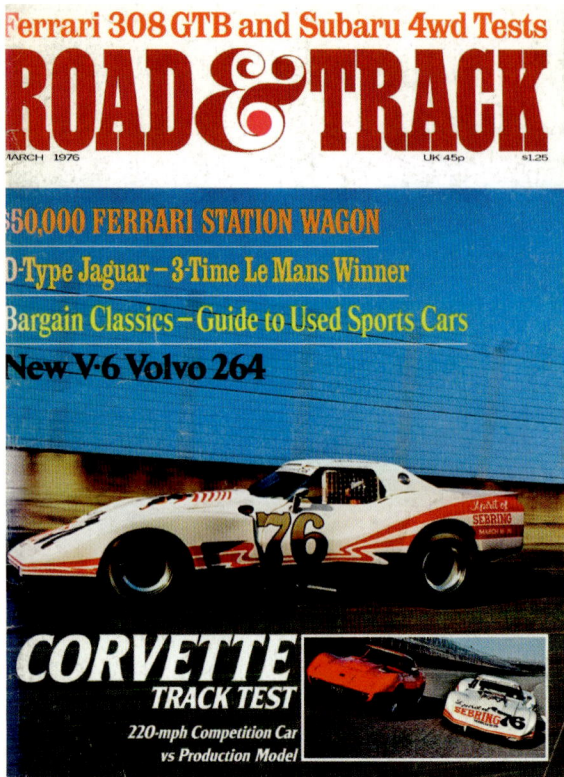

Ferrari 308 GTB and Subaru 4wd Tests
ROAD & TRACK
MARCH 1976 UK 45p $1.25
$50,000 FERRARI STATION WAGON
D-Type Jaguar – 3-Time Le Mans Winner
Bargain Classics – Guide to Used Sports Cars
New V-6 Volvo 264
CORVETTE TRACK TEST
220-mph Competition Car vs Production Model

John Greenwood successfully raced patriotically liveried wide body Corvettes from 1974. The racers had input from Zora Arkus-Duntov, GM stylists and engineers, in an IMSA era increasingly dominated by imports. *(Courtesy Road & Track)*

street radials beat out many an adversary using race rubber. Indeed, at 1972's 24 Hours of Le Mans, Greenwood qualified fastest in GT class on road tires. Sadly, engine problems meant no class win.

Post BF Goodrich sponsorship came the Greenwood wide body Corvettes, dubbed Batmobiles by the American auto press. These fender flared racers, that somewhat resembled hovercraft, had much behind the scenes input from GM. Zora Arkus-Duntov, aka Papa Corvette, was no stranger to helping a determined privateer, and explore new concepts to improve the Corvette racing breed. ZAK got the GM stylists to help, with Jerry Palmer and Randy Wittine on aerodynamics. Bob Riley assisted with the Greenwood racer's chassis. The result was a coupe, with tube-type roll cage for stiffening, a body dropped around the frame producing a low nose, and car to road sucking ground effects. Greenwood's custom coil over rear suspension, retained one transverse leaf spring from the stock Corvette, to stay legal. Making its debut at Road Atlanta in 1974,

Greenwood's Corvette beat Bobby Allison's big block Camaro by 20 seconds, in the 10-lap race. The unique looking Corvette coupe, would go on to win its IMSA championship class in 1974, as well as the 1974 Daytona finale.

The patriotically liveried 1975-76 Spirit of Sebring Greenwood Corvette racers had coil over suspension front and rear. In fact, John Greenwood's Troy, Michigan outfit had built two full chassis cars, with a third for spare parts. Now on Goodyear Blue Streak racing rubber, and Sterling alloys, Milt Minter took the Greenwood Corvette to victory at Talladega in 1974. However, it was Greenwood who piloted the #002 chassis coupe to victory in the '74 Daytona finale. That said, Corvette coupe #001 was the faster of the two chassis cars. 1975 had been a year of engine reliability problems. The Chevrolet all alloy big block V8, with Greenwood cross ram intake and Kinsler mechanical fuel injection was in the 700 horse ballpark. However, time limitations implied that the racers were never fully sorted out in 1974.

The Greenwood Corvette still managed to win three 1975 SCCA Trans Am races in a row, and take the class championship again in 1975. Coupe chassis #001 won the 1975 Daytona finale, with John Greenwood at the wheel. Greenwood took pole, forcing Al Unser in the Horst Kwech built Chevrolet Monza into second place on the grid. In the end, it was a walkover victory for Greenwood in his Spirit of Sebring '75 IMSA Corvette, over the second place Brian Redman in the BMW CSL coupe, also dubbed Batmobile back home in Europe! The Greenwood Corvette was heavier, but more powerful than the BMW CSLs, Porsche RSRs and Monzas. The Greenwood Corvette certainly inspired the others to adopt body flares and an open wheel well style.

John Greenwood bought in the Corvette's stock production frame from Chevrolet, then strengthened and modified same. What helped with the Daytona finales was the fact that several

The rulebook required some stock Corvette hardware items to be retained. That said, the links between Greenwood's Spirit of Sebring '76 racer and the normal '76 Corvette were tenuous. *(Courtesy Road & Track)*

years earlier, Chevrolet had developed a Daytona suspension package, when Corvettes started racing on the Daytona banking. Greenwood said the stock Corvette's front camber curve was very good, but the stock rear suspension produced too much squat and toe change during acceleration and braking. Front control arms and attachment points were stock, to accommodate the rulebook, but then came the mods! The racer used Teflon bushings, and steering geometry was set for zero bump steer, the V8 motor was moved 1½in to the right, and nearly 1ft back. Definitely a front midship configuration! Greenwood's custom IRS had unequal length A arms (SLA), plus coils.

By the time of the Spirit of Sebring '76 racer, an aluminum block ZL1 454 V8 was overbored 0.060in to 467 cubes, to make 700bhp at 6800rpm and 620lb/ft at four grand. The custom fuel injection entailed a Greenwood cross ram magnesium intake, bottom placed fuel cooler, and Lucas fuel injection hardware. Chevrolet pistons, valves, valve springs and heads, went into a big block with Chevrolet crankshaft reworked by company Moldex. The V8 motor was connected to ye olde M22 'Rock Crusher' four-speed. With a 2.73 diff ratio and 28in tall rear tires, 221mph was the result at 7000rpm! The racer's ZL1 V8 and M22 four-speed used to be optional on your regular pre-1970 and pre-1972 Corvettes, respectively.

Stopping the whole affair were Hurst-Airheart brakes, featuring drilled rotors. Greenwood's 1976 season racer had a fiberglass front that could be replaced sans disconnecting the radiator, unlike in 1975. While the stock Corvette was no slouch by 1976 standards, the Greenwood racer generated 1.2g on the skid pad, and reached 100mph from rest in 9.8 seconds, not 23.6 seconds! For 1976, Greenwood switched to a more subtle rear spoiler, versus the previous oversize ducktail. The new item generated 1000lb of downforce at 200mph, but with greatly reduced drag. Price? For a stock '76 Corvette: $7605 base sticker, but the Greenwood racer was 35 grand!

As the Spirit of Le Mans '76, IMSA racer John Greenwood and teammate Bernard Darniche lasted five hours. Their coupe got sidelined by fuel tank woes. Back in 1974, Greenwood's wide body Corvette set a record down the Mulsanne Straight, 211mph! [89] It was acknowledged that when they worked the Greenwood racers were formidable racecraft. John Greenwood's #001 chassis car was featured on and in *Road & Track* magazine. The coupe wound up with actor/racer Paul Newman for a spell. John Greenwood Sales of Elmwood Troy, Michigan, would sell you a race car copy, sans motor, for 20 grand.

Assorted bodies, engine parts, suspension parts, even the complete Greenwood IRS, were available to purchase. Then there were the road cars built by Greenwood International from 1975 to 1982. Five bodystyles, most with serialized ID plates: 32 Greenwood GT/Sebring GT, one Sportwagon, three Turbo GTs, five Daytonas and two GTOs. The total came to 43 cars, and like Enzo Ferrari, the plan was to finance racing by selling such road cars. The

Unlike many race car conversions, Greenwood doesn't start with a street car which is then torn down to the bare chassis. Rather he buys a production Corvette frame, gussets it for strength and crash protection and modifies it to accept the engine which is relocated approximately 1½ in. to the right and back almost 1 ft.

Modifications to the front suspension are surprisingly few. The front suspension including control arms and attachment points is purely production. According to Greenwood, the production Corvette front camber curve is very good and although the race car is considerably lower than production the only thing changed (besides the expected switch to teflon bushings) is the steering geometry to achieve zero bump steer. The rear suspension is an all-new independent design featuring unequal-length upper and lower A-arms and coil springs in place of the production Corvette's transverse leaf spring. The production rear suspension has two big drawbacks for racing, Greenwood says: it results in a tremendous amount of squat and toe change during acceleration and braking. With Greenwood's design, the swing-arm length is considerably longer which means he not only has the ability to adjust to zero toe change but also can dial in 50–75 percent anti-squat.

A high-speed banked track like Daytona obviously calls for a different chassis setup than the more usual road courses the IMSA cars run on. On a track such as Riverside or Laguna Seca the ideal setup is one where the car handles equally well ➡

PHOTO BY CHUCK SCHMIDT

At the 1975 IMSA Daytona finale, the American Batmobile vanquished the European Batmobile when John Greenwood, in his Spirit of Sebring '75 Corvette, easily beat Brian Redman's BMW CSL into second place! *(Courtesy Road & Track)*

most popular Greenwood Corvette GT/Sebring GT resembled a narrow Greenwood racer, and was built from a 1975-77 Corvette basis.

Concerning Greenwood Corvette GT/Sebring GT, look out for the round aluminum Greenwood logo on B pillars, custom plastic rim center caps attached via machine screws with script 'Greenwood GT', hand painted 'John Greenwood GT' script on the rear spoiler/pinstriping, grafted on wide fenders/spoilers, with engine block and body in the same color. Rims were 10in wide American Racing Vector 10 spoke design, shod with BF Goodrich Radial T/As, like John Greenwood used to race on before 1974. Suspension was a custom tune, given selected stiffer springs, bigger swaybars and adjustable Gabriel shocks that could lower the Corvette's center of gravity. Changes to the steering box, and needle ball bearing idler arm, improved steering response over stock.

Greenwood didn't touch the stock interior unless requested to by clients. Similarly, some owners wanted ported and polished heads for their 350 V8. The Greenwood GT/Sebring GT were repainted in the Corvette's stock color, but to a much higher standard than anything rolling out of St Louis. The price for such special attention, coming from the foremost Corvette production sports car racer? Double stock base sticker, or 16 grand! Not much for an import, but a tremendous amount for a Plastic Fantastic! The Greenwood GT made its debut on July 10 1975, and was the culmination of much discussion between John Greenwood, via telephone calls, Skokie, Illinois Chevrolet dealer Mancuso Chevrolet, and racer Rick Mancuso. Mancuso ordered 15 Greenwood GTs, with a solitary ragtop done for Mancuso. This 1975 roadster, the end for C3 Corvette convertible production, had a white exterior, red interior, black soft top and black hardtop, along with a four-speed. Rick Mancuso bought in base cars, with top quality and the incorporation of racing know how – and John Greenwood knew how! After 30 cars, a joint venture for the manufacture of parts and vehicle assembly was established with first ACI (American Custom Industries) of Toledo, Ohio. Then, from 1980 model year, Eckler's of Titusville, Florida entered the scene.

The genesis for the Greenwood Sportwagon was a 'Panelwagon' kit offered from the Ralph Eckler catalog, concerning 1968-73 Corvettes. This wagon conversion was designed by Chuck Miller. John Greenwood's version reworked this original, for the impact bumper Corvette era of 1974-82. The redesign was performed by Norm Bogiel and Charlie Selix, making use of rear hatch glass, hinges and struts from the humble Ford Pinto!

The prototype Greenwood Sportwagon was a converted version of a 1975 white Corvette L48 350 automatic coupe, owned by John Greenwood's then girlfriend Sharon Vaden. The car was subsequently repainted metallic brown, and was shown by Greenwood at the SEMA show in this new hue. Many Sportwagon orders were received. The metallic brown Greenwood Sportwagon proto was also featured in many magazines, including *Playboy*. Indeed, such publicity and orders, allowed John Greenwood to negotiate with ACI and Eckler's. The latter concern made the various kits, parts, and did complete car assembly, when John and Burt Greenwood moved from Ohio to Florida. Parts, kits or complete cars could be ordered from Greenwood Automotive, ACI or Eckler's. Molds of the original Greenwood Sportwagon were taken to create kits. Some Corvette Turbo Sportwagons were created, also.

The Greenwood Sportwagon, like John Greenwood's racers and modern cars, had windows glued into place sans moldings. There were five hood vents, and a passenger side non-functional NACA duct, which became functional on later Turbo GTs. Staying with visuals, 8in wide Dayton knock off wire wheels wearing BFG. Radial T/As were present, along with Greenwood logo etched into the lower left corner of the rear glass, concerning Sportwagon kits. As with Greenwood's other post 1976 cars, Corvette D35 sport mirrors were in evidence.

With Sportwagon engineering, there was a reinforced flat rear load floor, custom rubber lined 22-gallon fuel cell, and space saver. The original prototype carried no smog controls, nor spare tire carrier, but did have custom duals around said fuel cell. Subsequent safety issues saw the stock Corvette gas tank return; a pity because it ate into cargo space. Jac Pac air shocks allowed rear ride height to be adjusted, via a dashboard knob on the proto. Sportwagon provided the practicality of a

John Greenwood partnered Bernard Darniche at 1976's Le Mans 24 Hour race. Unfortunately, the coupe shown registered a DNF. In 1974, Greenwood set a record in his wide body Corvette down Mulsanne Straight: 211mph. 4mpg in race trim, take that tree huggers! *(Courtesy Goodyear)*

family hauler allied to Corvette sporty nature in the one machine: Greenwood Sportwagon!

Bodywork, suspension and tires were one thing, but given stricter pollution laws, speed shops were now wary of touching the motor, and could be EPA fined for removing smog equipment from new cars. So, like automakers, performance specialists resorted to turbo kits, oftentimes of a bolt-on nature. Then and now, turbo systems promised great power gains, while involving low fuel usage and pollution, by being off boost for the majority of the EPA's test cycle, hence the Greenwood Corvette Turbo GT! This post-1976 project involved consultation between Zora Arkus-Duntov and John Greenwood. GM itself was working on a blown Corvette, curious to see if a turbocharged Corvette could work, and how it would be received by the public.

In fact, the prototype Greenwood Turbo GT wasn't even turbocharged! It was a fastback

automatic coupe concept car, featuring more radical aero bodywork. As such, this coupe had two-tone silver over gray exterior, like Greenwood's #77 Batmobile wide body racer, not to mention the factory '78 Silver Anniversary Corvette. The Greenwood Turbo GT proto went on tour, with BF Goodrich picking it up for magazine promotion of its Radial T/A tire. In the process, many orders and interest were generated for the Greenwood Turbo GT, Sebring GT and Greenwood company cashflow. That last facet having the greatest priority at this time.

As for the Greenwood Turbo GT, three 1978 coupes were constructed from brand new Corvettes, all supplied by Mancuso Chevrolet of Chicago, Illinois. The turbo system employed was a performance-oriented, blow-through affair, with pressurized carburetor. Many turbo carb V8 affairs of the day took the cheaper, easier suck-through route, where air and gasoline pass through the turbocharger. Greenwood Turbo GT #1 was an L82 350 machine, but the other two had L48 350s. The L48 350 was judged as preferable, given its lower compression ratio, that was better able to avoid detonation with 7psi of boost. Turbo kits of the day didn't usually involve lower compression pistons, or even employ intercoolers for that matter. It was bolt-on or bust baby! As some insurance you got water injection, like on a '60s Olds Jetfire V8, courtesy of windshield washer reservoir sourced H2O. Even so, with the low octane juice of the late '70s, detonation was still a concern.

In other respects, John Greenwood put together a quality turbo 350 V8. A Garrett T04 turbo on a custom cast iron exhaust manifold, mounted on the right side, wastegate, aluminum crossover pipe for heat dissipation, sealed to a modified, pressurized Holley 650 CFM carb, supplied by two electric pumps. The motor backed onto a worked THM 350 slushbox. Expect 0-60mph in six seconds flat, and maybe 49-state legality. To harness the power, a trick suspension: rear Koni coil overs, HD swaybars, rear Greenwood custom five link SLA resembling a '97 C5 Corvette's apparatus. There was a need for a fiberglass rear floor, with the Greenwood rear suspension effective in reducing dive and squat, plus permitting softer rear springs, for better ride comfort.

The custom Greenwood rear suspension required a longer than stock parking brake cable, and associated hoses. Unlike other Greenwood projects, there was no opening rear hatch on the Turbo GT. However, there were two small speedo lights, showing water injection operation, and said system's low fluid level. The dashboard had a neatly integrated boost gauge, and an ashtray door plaque that carried the coupe's serial number. Front fender and rear deck Turbo callouts signified high performance to observers. Two Greenwood Turbo GTs were black, with a red interior. The third coupe was burgundy with saffron interior. The burgundy car spent much of its life in New York.

Greenwood contracted assembler ACI made very similar blown Corvettes, called American Turbo. Such cars were made after the Greenwood Turbo GT stopped production. Therefore, there were no Greenwood Turbo GTs built in 1979. A few ACI American Turbos were sold as Greenwood Turbo GTs. However, such coupes were replicas, not the real thing. John Greenwood continued forced induction Corvette work with the Greenwood Daytona Turbo. This time around, a suck-through turbo set up, from Turbo International, permitted the Corvette's stock Quadrajet carb to be utilized, concerning road cars. It was enough, because the Daytona Turbo's true purpose was bodywork. This coupe had the most radical exterior of any Greenwood machine. It represented John Greenwood pushing the envelope, concerning vague IMSA rules.

The Greenwood Daytona Turbo had far out extended fenders, joined by very wide sills, and it was all functional! For racing the wild bodywork aided both engine and brake cooling. Plus, made for improved aerodynamics. Whereas previous Greenwood road cars were derived from racers, here the road car was transformed into a racer! Hence John Greenwood's desire to have as much racing hardware on the road-going Daytona Turbo as possible. That is, a Greenwood five link rear suspension, set up on two of the five coupes built, BBS 8in wide front and 10in wide rear rims, and Kevlar brake cooling fans. The first Greenwood Daytona Turbo was built from a 1980 Corvette, via Tico & Rene Racing. Race Daytona Turbos had an aluminum ZL1 big block from yesteryear, because Uncle Sam wasn't on your case trackside. Styling reaction to the Greenwood Daytona Turbo was mixed. However, there was enough interest for John Greenwood to sign a body panel deal with Eckler's.

Greenwood made five Daytona Turbos, with four based on 1981 Corvettes. All street coupes had C&C's (Cars & Concepts) rear opening glass hatchback conversion kit. Only one turbo car had a stick shift, this being a Greenwood Corvette GTO, to be precise. Rick Mancuso also happened to be a Ferrari dealer, and sold two red Greenwood Daytona Turbos. Greenwood, now Florida based, sold the other two red machines, and solitary Sunoco Blue coupe. The first Daytona Turbo that Mancuso offloaded, sans John Greenwood's custom five link rear suspension, went on to spend its days in the National Corvette Museum. Indeed, it was donated by the car's second owner, a Beverly Hills dentist. Greenwood's price range was 37 to 53 grand, at a time when a Mercedes 380SEL was

45 large! After Greenwood's five Daytona Turbos, Eckler's did its own kits, and even some complete cars. In fact, Eckler's did its own body conversions, in addition to Greenwood's 43 road cars of 1975-82. Eckler's Can Am Corvette was one example, and its CR-II series with rectangular headlights, triple taillights and functional hatchback was another.

The final Greenwood Daytona Turbo made had experimental fixed rectangular headlights, which were faired in on three sides, with a plexiglass cover. This coupe also had a new style hood, with raised center section, and vents on the side of said raised section. There were also revised brake cooling fans, featuring flat vanes on the BBS rims. For this Daytona Turbo, there was hand painted Greenwood script on the B pillar, rear wing, front airdam and running boards, carrying the callout 'Greenwood Daytona'. The altered hood and brake coolers made their appearance on the final Greenwood C3 Corvette evolution: Greenwood Corvette GTO. A change to IMSA rules brought the more restrained and likeable styling of the new GTO. These GTOs were 1982 built machines, utilizing a 1981 Corvette base coupe.

For the GTO, John and Burt Greenwood redid the Corvette hood with vacuum assist cold air induction, rather than the usual NACA ducts. The exit point was now the windshield base. IMSA rulebook changes saw the Daytona Turbo's long tail give way to a stubby rear spoiler, and the GTO's flat brake cooling vanes probably influenced the same on the '84 C4 Corvette. Tico & Rene Racing replaced its race car's Daytona Turbo body with a GTO equivalent, concerning the #13 IMSA racer. It could attain over 200mph! In racing, a big block Chevrolet V8 with Greenwood cross ram fuel injection would be employed. For the two black street GTOs built, the Daytona Turbo's Turbo International draw-through system and C&C opening hatchback were present, so too the expected Greenwood suspension mods.

Both the #001 '81 Daytona Turbo and second GTO constructed had four-speeds, the only Greenwood C3 Corvette Turbos to do so. Normally you could order a turn key car, or parts, from John Greenwood International. Plus, Greenwood never had his Corvette bodystyle designs patented. This implied some company knock-offs. That said, the Greenwood GTO's body wasn't copied. The rear bumper had 'Greenwood' script recessed into it, not forgetting 'Greenwood/GTO' rocker panel lettering. Only John Greenwood's firm made GTO body parts, with both the street GTOs sold by Rick Mancuso's Lake Forest Sports Cars, Chicago dealership. John Greenwood would return with the C4 Corvette!

Greenwood American Custom Industries, 5035 Alexis Road, Sylvania, Ohio 43560, USA

Nach einer Pause ist der ehemalige Rennfahrer John Greenwood wieder dabei, Corvettes umzubauen. Grundsätzlich beschäftigt sich die Firma mit Corvettes — Repa-

ratur, Wartung, Tuning, Fahrwerks- und Karosseriemodifikationen. Darüber hinaus bietet Greenwood auch vier mehr oder weniger festgelegte Modelle an: ein auf dem älteren

(bis 1977) Corvette-Coupé basierendes Heckklappen-Coupé mit Kotflügelverbreiterungen usw. Der GT ist auch ein Coupé, mit noch breiterer Karosserie. Mit dem Sportwagen

hat Greenwood einen Sportkombi aus dem Corvette gemacht, und der Greenwood Turbo ist eine Version mit turbogeladenem 5,7 Liter-V8. Preise auf Anfrage.

Greenwood Corvette Sportwagon

Greenwood Corvette Turbo

For cars, kits and parts, Greenwood switched contracts from ACI (American Custom Industries) to Eckler's for '80 model year, in its move from Ohio to Florida. *(Courtesy Vereinigte Motor-Verlage)*

The New 1984 Corvette

Evolution not revolution

THE 1984 CORVETTE, or rather the 1983 Corvette as the media referred to the crucial new model for a long time, was an advanced evolutionary development of the existing Corvette theme. The new C4 Corvette was the Corvette that Zora Arkus-Duntov's successor as Corvette Chief Engineer, Dave McLellan, truly made his mark with. McLellan was working with most of Duntov's engineering crew from the great, pre-legislation days. Experiments had been made with a smaller version of the mid-engine, Four-Rotor Wankel Corvette, using the Chevrolet Citation V6. However, such prototypes lacked both

the performance, and image, associated with the Corvette's brute force style.

Irv Rybicki had taken over from Bill Mitchell, as GM Styling head honcho, post Mitchell's 1977 retirement. That said, it was Chevrolet Studio styling boss Jerry Palmer that was lead designer of the new Corvette. Palmer had done the Four Rotor Corvette, and the task at hand was an aerodynamically clean Corvette, especially given gas mileage really mattered now. Indeed, the previous Mid-Year and Late Model Corvettes weren't as aerodynamic as they appeared. By late 1977 it was decided that the new Corvette would keep its traditional V8 front-engine, rear drive layout.

By mid to late 1978, Corvette sketches showed a T-top sports car, with clamshell hood. 1979 clay models followed. It was all evidence that the 'All New Corvette' would be evolutionary, not revolutionary. Indeed, by the close of 1979, barring minor front and rear styling revisions, the general look of the latest Plastic Fantastic was locked up. 1980 saw fullsize clay models that adhered to design goals of more interior space, allied to trimmer weight and exterior dimensions, along with a lower build height and more ground clearance. As for weight, the new Corvette was 200lb lighter than a comparable 1982 Corvette, with two swaybars and the L83 350/THM 700R4 power

Out of 43 pilot test cars built, this is the sole surviving 1983 Corvette! The others got junked. Note the 15in alloys with Goodyear Eagle GTs. This was going to be the new C4 Corvette's standard wheel/tire spec. *(Courtesy National Corvette Museum)*

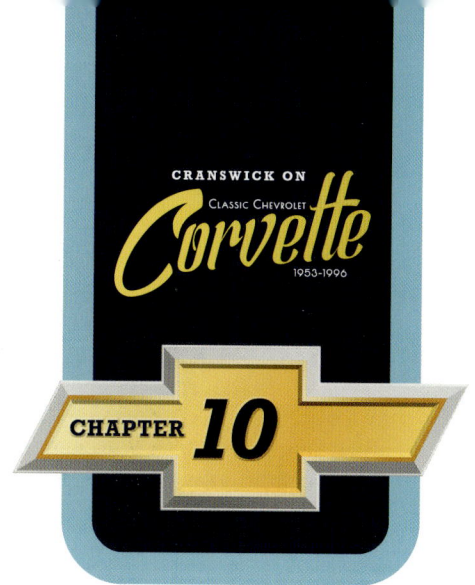

241

team. Yes, the C4 Corvette was 500lb lighter than the outgoing C3 Corvette, as was suspected by the press, if one compared the new machine against a loaded automatic Corvette from the 1975-79 era. That is, the new '84 Corvette weighed around 3250lb, even though Ron Wakefield in *Road & Track*'s 'Sports & GT Cars' 1983 annual mentioned a prediction of 3050lb. This was about what the '63 C2 Corvette roadster had weighed, and by 1982/83 in a post downsized, OPEC wary world, even 3050lb wasn't considered light!

The Straight Axle Corvette's body weighed 350lb, the next Mid-Year Corvette was on 300lb for its fiberglass equivalent, with 50lb worth of aluminum parts. The latest C4 Corvette had a 250lb fiberglass body and utilized 350lb of cast and forged aluminum parts for the vehicle. There was also 20lb of high-strength glass and epoxy components. The 1984 Corvette featured aluminum for its front A arm suspension, single piston finned calipers, rear differential and carrier, axle half shafts, driveshaft if an automatic car was at hand, radiator, water pump, rims, intake manifold etc. The 1984 model year designer air cleaner and V8 rocker covers were made of magnesium alloy.

A whole new chassis

THE GM F body had moved from part to full unibody for '82 MY. Like the Mercedes 190, the latest Camaro and Firebird used some high-strength steel in their construction. Unitary construction made for a lighter, more rigid structure than the separate chassis style used previously. In a downsized, post fuel crisis world high-strength steel maintained strength, while allowing less steel to be used. Saving weight, this strategy helped avoid the now dreaded gas guzzler tax, linked to a tightening CAFE standard. The EPA's City/Highway MPG ratings now became crucial in car advertising copy, just like the old advertised horsepower ratings used to be. The C4 Corvette abandoned the Plastic Fantastic's long used body on frame construction. In its place came the somewhat unorthodox 'Uniframe' that married the best of unibody and separate chassis worlds, creating what resembled a cut down unibody for the passenger compartment. The

latest Corvette made use of high-strength steel also.

In yet another break from tradition, the '84 Corvette's central unit steel structure had bonded on fiberglass panels, in and around the passenger compartment, with fiberglass nose and tail bolted on at the car's extremities. The Uniframe possessed a high-strength steel rear rail, and the same material for the passenger compartment's roof bow, along with the entire front rail assembly, all high-strength steel. Apart from a more rigid structure, the Corvette's Uniframe promised better passive safety or crash protection than earlier Corvettes. One now effectively sat within a roll cage. What's more, you could drive around in the new Corvette, sans body panels, while sitting within the Uniframe cage! All the weight saving aluminum for suspension meant lower unsprung weight. This was an advantage for handling.

Handling was a particular goal for the '84 Corvette, its forged aluminum suspension parts were based on aviation technology, with steering knuckle and SLA control arms being of such alloy construction, in common with expensive racing machines. Front spindles were offset half an inch rearward, for improved handling response and better directional stability. The latest Corvette's more pronounced front midship design, no big blocks this time around, permitted a more compact and precise feeling rack and pinion steering system. The rack and pinion steering was bolted to the front of the Uniframe, a Corvette first. Integral power assist featured.

With the single drivebelt accessory system, Chevrolet felt it had solved the squeakiness commonly associated with such contemporary serpentine belt set ups. Aluminum wheel carriers were at each corner. The previous Corvette had front SLA suspension too, but the new C4 Corvette came with an all new five-link IRS. There were twin trailing arms, plus upper and lower lateral arms. The trailing arms governed fore and aft movement, the rear steering arm action handling roll and deflection steer. This time around, plastic monoleaf transverse springs featured at both ends of the Corvette. Such springing weighed in at half that of conventional equivalents, according to Chevrolet's C4 Corvette engineering video. A 25mm front swaybar was beefy,

A tradition continued with the Corvette still America's only sports car.
Now in downsized '84 model year, 96in wheelbase form. *(Courtesy GM Archives)*

to say the least. The new Corvette didn't promise French style ride and handling!

Corvette's steering, especially with the Z51 performance package, was greatly reminiscent of Citroën DS power steering. Gentle, not abrupt, steering corrections were called for. Indeed, the Z51 steering ratio brought a mere 1.9 turns lock-to-lock! Z51 implied asymmetric 9.5in wide rear rims, higher ratio Positraction differential, engine oil cooler, HD Bilstein shocks (later in the production year), bigger swaybars and Eagle VR50 rubber. Normal '84 Corvettes came with larger, standard alloy rims, versus C3 Corvette days. No more stock steel rims, but vaned unidirectional 16 x 8.5in alloys. The vanes scooped in cooling air for the Corvette's oversize disk brake rotors.

The Goodyear Eagle VR50 tire was a joint Chevrolet and Goodyear development effort for the new C4 Corvette. It represented the best aspects of the respected Goodyear Eagle GT tire, allied to Formula One rain tire influenced tread design. There were claimed joint properties of 40,000 mile tread life, and sustained cruisability of 130mph plus: a world first!

As per front-engine Porsches, the new Corvette's powertrain was unified with the differential, for structural rigidity. In the case of automatic C4 Corvettes, an open running, aluminum driveshaft beam, rather than Zuffenhausen's torque tube encased propshaft running in bearings. In its engineering video, Chevrolet discussed the need to avoid compliance, or flexing, in a sports car. So driver input and the Corvette's responses weren't adulterated by extraneous compliance. It explained the C4 Corvette's beefy, high side sills, and sturdy transmission tunnel, but not totally. In the absence of the Corvette's traditional separate chassis, ladder frame crossmembers, the C4's strengthened sills and transmission tunnel were essential, given the absence of T-tops.

Why no T-tops, that mainstay of contemporary North American sporty car life? The reason was that Chevrolet GM Lloyd Reuss said the Corvette should eschew T-tops in favor of a Targa top, for style. Porsche had long been a Targa top proponent, with its 911 and 914. Observing the new code 72 Bright Red '84 Corvette that *Motor Week*'s John Davis sat in, on the very green grass of the Corvette's recently new Bowling Green, Kentucky home, it was hard to argue against Reuss' decision. Resplendent with those silver finish 16in vaned alloys, the Corvette looked a million bucks, or certainly more than the '84 Corvette's RPO 1YY07 $21,800 base coupe sticker price. The downside was that despite Chevrolet engineers' supplementary sill strengthening work, the new C4 Corvette would have been stiffer still, with the originally planned T-tops. And that missing rigidity was desirable, with the $600 Z51 performance handling package chosen by 25,995 Corvette faithful in the C4 Corvette's first model year.

Z51 implied, at least as the model year progressed, FG3 Delco-Bilstein shocks ($189), G92 performance axle ratio ($22), KC4 engine oil cooler ($158) and QZD P255/50-VR16 tires ($561). So, one got quite a deal by ordering Z51! It implied a track ready Corvette, like yesteryear's 1966-69 Corvette F41 package. On a GM test track, a 1984 Corvette with Z51 achieved 0.95g on the skid pad. That is, the design goal of breaking the 0.9g lateral grip barrier with a production car was honored. It lent credence to the Chevrolet engineers' assertion that the new Plastic Fantastic was the best handling production car in the world. For smooth racetracks, it really was. The uninitiated could, and did, step into a new Corvette automatic, and set their best lap times on certain tracks, outdoing sports car rivals. It was the point and squirt, neutral sports car of video game dreams!

The look of sport

FROM A STYLISTIC and practical perspective, the new Corvette had to look sleek, and was. Versus the outgoing Corvette, the latest C4 iteration dropped the co-efficient of drag from 0.440 to 0.340. All the

The almost all new '84 Corvette was around 10in shorter in length, 2in less tall, 200lb lighter, but 2in wider than the outgoing '82 Corvette. *(Courtesy RK Motors)*

more impressive, when you consider the fact that compared to Europe's nose down method of measuring Cd, GM was using the nose up attitude. Then too, the '84 Corvette and '82 GM F body finally answered Detroit's problem of how to achieve a sleeker, import car look while incorporating relatively bulky US powertrain hardware. The '82 Firebird and '84 Corvette were certainly as sleek as anything rolling out of Pininfarina's studio. On Corvette, that implied a rakish 64.5 degree windshield. The L83 350 V8's low profile intake and halogen pop-up headlamps, that rotated 167 degrees, also certainly helped. Concerning that last item, the Corvette had returned to using electric motors, for the first time since Mid-Year Corvette days. That is, no more vacuum assistance for pop-up headlamp actuation. If the pop-ups are stuck in the closed position, a manual override mechanism down at the bottom or nearby, as on most cars with such headlamps, allows such lamps to be slowly wound up into the upright position. A relay box concerning the pop-up headlamps is located on the inside of the front driver side fender, secured by two bolts. If disconnected, or not working, the box can prevent the headlamps popping up, even if the lights are on.

A conservative path was taken with the C4 Corvette's styling, so as not to alienate existing Corvette fans. Therefore, pop-up headlamps continued, as did the Corvette's by now trademark four circular taillights. The C3 Corvette's Coke bottle profile swage line wasn't as pronounced this time around. The new Corvette aimed for more interior space, so the previous profile look was only faintly discernible. No body seams were exposed on any panel, and the mid body mold seam was concealed by a single black rubstrip, circling the new coupe. The Corvette had pioneered the big wheel, short overhang look back in the 1968-72 era. The kammtail had helped in that regard. This big wheel, short overhang nature wasn't as apparent, once federal impact bumper law added to vehicular length.

In 1982-84, the Porsche 944 took over the 'big wheels pushed to the corners' mantle, capturing the public's imagination with flared fenders that greatly influenced the second generation Mazda RX7. The 1984 Corvette reclaimed this look for Chevrolet. The kammtail was back, and those, large for the

times, 16in vaned rims were striking. However, the original C4 1983 Corvette plan revolved around standard 15in alloys, shod with 65 profile Goodyear Eagle GT tires. Indeed, just like the top '82 Camaro Z28s and Firebird Trans Ams. This choice would probably have reduced criticism, concerning the '84 Corvette's stiff ride. The sole surviving 1983 Corvette, with 15in rims and Eagle GT rubber, can be seen at the National Corvette Museum. Said 15in rims, changed the whole look of the Corvette. It looked less dramatic, and, dare it be said, more Nissan 300ZX like. The '83 Corvette with 15in rims can also be seen in GM's engineering video for the C4 Corvette. While the 1984 Corvette received very favorable reviews worldwide concerning its appearance, there were some folks that said the new car looked a touch bland, with sides that were too upright. However, this was a minority viewpoint, aired in the light of the dramatic Mako Shark inspired C3 Corvette being on the streets for so many years.

The 1984 C4 Corvette had dimensions of: 176.5in length, 71in width, and 46.7in height on a 96in wheelbase. 1982 Corvette stats were a respective: 185.3in/69in/48.4in on a 98in wheelbase. Trunk space was up from 10.4ft³, to 11.6ft³. What's more, the new Corvette, like the '82 GM F body, came with a standard hatchback. You popped open the rear hatch via a button on the inside of the driver's door, near the latch mechanism. The latest Corvette also maintained the tradition of a racing style, centrally placed rear deck fuel filler. This time, under the fuel flap lay a cradle in the recessed area to place the fuel cap while filling up.

Enter the '84 Corvette

THE '84 CORVETTE'S high sill was the enemy of skirt wearing ladies with high heels. Comfort was found within, although the feeling was like sitting in a bathtub, not unlike the Porsche 928 experience. However, matters were also similar to the narrow, long footwells of the Jag XKE. At least good legroom was provided. Outward visibility was streets ahead of the Porsche and Jaguar, if the latter was a fixed head coupe. The new Corvette also brought a European-style ergonomic arrangement of steering wheel to hands, and pedals to feet. No longer the domestic practice of close steering wheel and distant pedals, although post-1976 Corvettes had been much better. The new Corvette was a nice compromise between traditional Detroit style, and racing ape Italian as per Alfa Romeo Giulia 105 series coupe! That said, Corvette's side to side interior space seemed abbreviated for a 71in wide car.

Dominant in the new '84 Corvette were dashboard, console and instruments. A contemporary energy absorbing black plastic, Darth Vader type molding, with GM Delco LCD (Liquid Crystal Display) of multi colored nature, that polarized popular opinion between, "Tokyo at night" and something to watch and stave off boredom while traversing never ending gray flannel interstate at 55mph. In the video game era, many delighted in the cutting edge display. Although without being critical of same, *Motor Week*'s John Davis jokingly said, "Whatever happened to needles and dials?!" The information provided, and technology behind the display were impressive. High end domestic and Japanese cars post-1979 complied with this new display vogue. However, such displays had to be read, rather than merely glanced at, as with traditional dials. Plus, during the day, sunlight was your display enemy.

Electronic speedo was on the left, tach graph on the right, and, around a fuel bar, four smaller displays of twofold nature, that were toggle selected: oil pressure/oil temp, coolant temp/volts, range/trip distance, instant mpg/average mpg. Off switches between settings allowed resets on both sides, and one could switch between English and metric, depending on preference. Leaving nothing to chance, the LCD display was computer checked on the assembly line. GM's engineering video showed CRT terminals at the Bowling Green plant completed in 1980, with a dot matrix 'OK' printout, dated 1/12/83. And very well such checks were performed, because the instrument unit was beyond 'ol shade tree mechanic Clem!

Removing a faulty display for a swap to a working used unit, the common method for repair, was straightforward enough. The cosmetic fairing was overcome by undoing four securing bolts, one located at each top corner, with two either side of the steering column. With the unit's back panel removed, the non electronic odometer with traditional flip numbers should be transferred to the working instrument display unit, to maintain vehicle mileage honesty. Swapping the odometer was a fiddly, delicate task. Now, with the passing of decades, being long beyond warranty replacement units, and finding working used units also difficult, actually repairing an existing display has become more common. Companies like Battee are known specialists, in repair and refurbishment of C4 Corvette instrument displays.

For starters, the instrument display's polarizing screen film, can get sun damaged and require replacement. A photocell at the top left reads interior brightness of your Corvette, adjusting display brightness accordingly. The four illumination bulbs factory fitted can, and do, generate a lot of heat, damaging instrument cluster plastic. Modern xenon bulbs run cooler, and are a common retrofit. To access the display's internals, there are five screws on the back of the case, with the '84 C4 Corvette featuring an additional screw on the side. The cluster's top circuit board, is a logic board, with the 12 pin internal power connector proving troublesome.

There were some specification changes and integration during 1984-89, concerning the Corvette's instrument display. Leaking capacitors are indicated by burn marks, and a 5 volt power output supports the instrument display's processor and ROM etc. The bottom display driver board

This coupe's color scheme was code 18 Medium Gray Metallic, with code 152 Medium Gray Leather interior. The '84 Corvette's base bucket was leather trimmed. The optional multi adjustable super seat had cloth inserts. *(Courtesy RK Motors)*

affords photocell and bulb access. The odometer's three securing screws are 7/32in sized. Display unit bulbs can be removed using fingers, or pliers if necessary, to clean connectors. LCD displays would feature on most modern cars one day. As ever, the Corvette afforded a view into an exciting, if complex, future!

As with '82 GM F bodies, the '84 Corvette had no glovebox. One had to use the console locker between the seats. As with the outgoing Corvette, there were two large, deep storage compartments in the luggage area. Observing the Corvette's passenger side dashboard, a large crash pad with Corvette script inlaid was very prominent. This protrusion was originally meant to house an airbag, part of a supplementary restraint system, broached as compulsory under the Reagan administration, that never came to pass. *Motor Week*'s John Davis said, "Look for that bulge to be replaced by some form of storage compartment before too long." Don't hold your breath! Windshield wiper/washer controls were inlaid within the driver's door card molding. As said by *Fast Lane* magazine in July 1984, it was a handy ergonomic move. The Corvette's long standing 'clap-hands' wipers, carried over to the C4 Corvette. Their ability to park out of sight, concealed between hood leading edge and windshield base, was appreciated. However, watch out on a street parked Corvette, when it snows. Buried wipers can result!

The '84 Corvette's Doug Nash 4+3 electronic overdrive stick shift, present here, was originally slated as a mid summer '83 option, but was delayed until December 1983.
(Courtesy RK Motors)

The Corvette eschewed token 2+2 seating, staying with the more realistic two-seater nature. The '+2' part on a Porsche 911 or Ferrari Mondial was for kids under eight years old. As Butzi Porsche said, give a man a seat, and he expects to sit in it. Then too, the Porsche 911 and Enzo's Mondial lacked hatchback practicality. *Motor Week*'s John Davis, when testing the '82 Corvette Collector Edition Hatchback, said all Corvettes should have the hatch. Now they did, along with more power!

Go & whoa!

THE COMING OF pollution laws and the energy crisis posed the question to engineers everywhere. How do you create a powerful, clean and economical motor? Automakers had struggled dealing with the EPA, OPEC and CAFE, witness plummeting performance from thirsty engines through the '70s. Retarded spark, lower compression ratios, and leaner fuel mixtures, along with EGR, smog pumps and catalytic converters were all enemies of the auto enthusiast. The Corvette, as a GM tech test bed and dream car of the future, had courted various powerplant concepts, even the Wankel rotary unit, and now possibly, Smokey Yunick's Hot Vapor or Adiabatic engine.

Smokey Yunick, proprietor of 'The best damn garage in town', racing rulebook guru and industry consultant extraordinaire, had been involved with the creation of The Hot One, Chevrolet's Mouse Motor small block V8. That jewel of a powerplant, had been a big part of the Plastic Fantastic weathering the nameplate's rocky early commercial start. Could Smokey Yunick come through again for GM and the Corvette? Early signs were good, a two-cylinder 78 cube 150 horse engine, that could deliver 60mpg in a test Plymouth Horizon. Yunick was a *Popular Science* correspondent, and had a section in the journal that answered car owner's fix it questions. "Smokey's Amazing 150-hp Two-cylinder Engine" story was in the April 1983 issue of *Popular Science*, and again in November 1983 ("Smokey's Engine").

By late 1985, Smokey Yunick said there had been a great deal of interest in the Hot Vapor concept. A presentation was made to the SAE, and the motor had even passed smog at manufacturer's labs. Yunick was in consultation with seven US manufacturers for gas and diesel applications, including GM. A retrofit camshaft kit by Crane Cams was even in the works. [90] Smokey Yunick had been pictured with a specially converted white Pontiac Fiero, fitted with an Adiabatic Iron Duke. *Hot Rod* tested this Corvette two-seater mid-engine rival. It was 250 horses from a 2.5-liter inline four, with special cam, that delivered 50mpg and 0-60mph in six seconds!

The principle was a three stage, pre-combustion method of fully vaporizing gas, to deliver it into a combustible state, sans detonation. Coolant heat was used near the carb or throttle body injector unit, followed by an exhaust gases surrounded turbo mixer, that got the air/fuel mix to 285°F, forcing the expanded mixture into an exhaust gas wrapped intake manifold, that took the temperature to 440°F, prior to the 1600°F of the combustion chamber. How exactly detonation was avoided earlier on was Smokey's secret. The various stages had different patent owners on an engine concept where the patent expired in March 2002. The engine concept had come close to going into production at GM. However, it seemed that like with Wankel rotaries, high oxides of nitrogen (NOx), put an emissions kibosh on the project. The test motor was present in Smokey's shop R&D area in February 1988, at the time of his big auction.

The 1984 Corvette didn't have an Adiabatic engine, nor rotary powerplant like quasi rival the Mazda RX7. No, the '84 Corvette used a revised version of 1982's L83 350 V8. Essentially a carryover from the '82 model year, including the 9.0:1 CR, but there were some alterations. Most apparent was the new designer air cleaner, and revised rocker covers, both in magnesium alloy, a new cold air induction system that was molded into each side of the hood. There was a re-rating of the L83 350 to 205bhp at 4300rpm and 290lb/ft at 2800rpm. Once again, Cross Fire Injection, or two times GM Rochester division TBI, and computer controlled electronic ignition. The output increases over 1982 were attributed to revised stainless steel headers. Lifting the clamshell hood, the largest single piece of fiberglass molding on a volume production car, to that point in time, recalled the Jag XKE. It was all on show, including the forged alloy front suspension hardware. As part of underhood beautification, GM got Delco division to change its usual patriotic red, white and blue livery to silver and black, for consistency.

Connected to the L83 350 V8 were two gearbox choices: THM 700R4 four-speed automatic or Doug Nash four+three-speed stick shift. The first gearbox was the 1982 Corvette's only gearbox choice. It had a high stall torque converter, and, as ever, was a revised THM 350 with 0.70 overdrive top gear. Once again, the OBC would sense light throttle and lock up the torque converter in second, third, and fourth, to minimize traditional torque converter fluid losses, via a solid mechanical linkage between V8 flywheel and automatic clutch. As in 1982, the differential ratio was 2.87. However, Corvette tradition mandated a four-speed. You couldn't get one in 1982, but now you could, almost. Slated as a mid summer 1983 NCO, RPO MM4 actually came in December 1983, and was called Doug Nash 4+3.

Doug Nash was a well known specialist in the world of high performance, racing manual transmissions. However, the '84 Corvette's stick shift was something else. It was the familiar Borg Warner Super T10 four-speed, which took regular gear oil, with an auxiliary overdrive unit bolted onto the back. This piggyback unit was stamped Franklyn Tennessee, Doug Nash's home. The auxiliary unit was a simple automatic transmission, containing two gears, a one to one ratio, and the overdrive ratio. The oil pan of this piggyback device said to use ATF (Automatic Transmission Fluid) only. Such units are oftentimes forgotten about when it comes to maintenance. You need to change their fluid, otherwise they can, and do, seize up!

With the Doug Nash 4+3 box, the OBC observes engine speed and throttle position. On a light load and throttle, the driver would be placed into overdrive automatically in second, third and fourth. You then got a kickdown effect by flooring the gas pedal, whereby the overdrive was disconnected, going from second + OD, third + OD, and fourth + OD, back to second , third and fourth directly. There was no first + OD, because that was effectively second gear, so no Doug Nash 4+4, which would probably have confused the off-road fraternity at any rate! You could toggle switch off the OD function, which returned the driver to a normal BW

The GM Delco LCD instrument cluster featured 14 separate instrument readouts, imperial or metric, updated 16 times per second! EPA gas mileage figures were: 16mpg city/28mpg highway.
(Courtesy RK Motors)

Super T10 four-speed. However, *Motor Week*'s John Davis said that was for export coupes only, so as not to fall foul of CAFE and the gas guzzler tax.

'80s export GM F bodies and Corvettes came with paddle type side mirrors, a slow selling third gen Firebird option, which is probably why GM tried to offload the item for export! Exported GM cars going to Europe and the UK, from the mid '70s to the late '80s, didn't have catalytic converters. This was because in this era, unleaded gas wasn't available in Europe. So, to get around the special filler flap permitting only the smaller nozzle of an unleaded pump, such export cars had a plastic tube insert to keep said flap open, and permit leaded gas to be pumped in via a larger diameter leaded gas nozzle.

The official word from GM Europe's Antwerp HQ in Brussels was to fill up with leaded Super or premium, so said the factory service department. However, in the UK, three star leaded gas, or 91 RON, seemed to be used on post-1970 GM F bodies and Corvettes – that is, as of the 1971 model year compression ratio drop. How much could dropping a cat yield? Although involving the earlier pellet type catalytic converter, Pontiac guru Nunzi Romano, of Nunzi's Automotive in Brooklyn, demonstrated in Super Stock magazine, how removing the cat from a '77 Firebird Trans Am W72 400 automatic improved the ¼-mile ET by 0.5 seconds, and increased trap speed by 1.5mph.

To stop the '84 Corvette, Chevrolet retained the nameplate's four-wheel disk brake rotors, now 4 x 11.5in in size. However, hardware was now sourced from outside the GM family, for the first time. GM went to Australian firm Girloc, and to Japan for semi-metallic brake pads. The Girloc system was dubbed 'Slimline', and consisted of low aero drag, aluminum single piston finned calipers. Anti lock brakes weren't available yet, but combined with the 255mm footprint of the Goodyear VR50 Eagles, and at least 8.5in wide rims, such conventional brakes really let the Corvette drop anchor!

Building the '84 Corvette

IN 1982 THE Corvette's base price was $18,290, for the '84 Corvette it was $21,800. Still a bargain, but the Corvette was ascending in sophistication, as well as the company it kept. The DeLorean DMC 12 was history, except on the silver screen, so Corvette challengers were now the Mercedes SL, BMW 6 series, Porsche 911/928/944, Jag XJS and Cadillac Allante. The common denominator in the big buck crowd was classy quality, not an easily defined facet. Most Corvette powertrain items carried a 36/36 warranty, but quality in this rarefied world went beyond mere mechanical durability.

For starters, Corvette's recently new Bowling Green, Kentucky plant was state of the art concerning vehicle manufacture. You couldn't say that about St Louis! With the '84 Corvette, the Plastic Fantastic had the benefit of line technicians with an average of over 14 years job experience, and 120 hours training concerning Corvette assembly. The pace of Corvette manufacture wasn't hurried by GM standards. The Bowling Green plant was working on a projection of 25,000 to 37,000 Corvettes produced in 1984 model year. There was an allowance of 40 hours per car, one coming off the line every four minutes, or four times slower than your typical Impala, Rabbit or Datsun shooting off the line!

To create the equivalent of the C3 Corvette's Birdcage, the C4 Corvette's Uniframe was constructed by an automated two stage, robot welding machine performing computer controlled welds. Special fixtures checked Uniframe geometry, against a fullsize blueprint, for correct alignments.

The Uniframe was composed of two sided galvanized steel, with the robot welder resembling a garage. Here, 140 initial welds of an over 1200 total were done. Bowling Green employees dubbed the robot welder 'Pac Man', after the popular contemporary video game character. In addition, six other American-made robot welders were utilized, with some called Speedy, Blinky and Clyde! Once again, after the ghosts that pursued Pac Man in his maze world. Such additional robot welders were made by US company Cincinnati Milacron, and did 120 inches worth of MIG welding, with such welding work still overseen by humans. The new C4 Corvette was certainly a car of its time, both technically and culturally.

The Uniframe was dipped in anti rust solution, and, while on the car track, the Corvette's six reinforced fiberglass panels were attached. Indeed, as a car to avoid corrosion, the Corvette was better protected than ever. On top and underneath, salt or other corrosive snowbelt material was only likely to make contact with plastic of some kind. With random frame checks, the current assembly went on to the body line, and clean room for 14 hours. Environmentally friendly solvents were part of a new paint chemistry, and new two stage base coat/clear coat process. The exterior carried two coats of primer, two coats of color enamel, not old style GM lacquer, and two coats of clear. A 250 degree oven was employed. At first, all C4 Corvette paint application was done by people, but, before the model year was out, some robots were brought on the line. Masking prevented under panel paint from marring the exterior finish. Any problem panels were completely sanded down, and repainted.

In keeping with modern vehicle assembly, different tasks were assigned to specific work stations for sub assemblies, like suspension. The Uniframe and sub assemblies were readied for the Corvette's L83 350 V8, which came from another plant. Air conditioning and smog controls were added, with electronic and electrical circuits of the Cross Fire Injection checked. The '84 Corvette was the first car in the world with transverse plastic springs, at both ends, created by a mechanical bender. Computer controlled wrenches were used for the front SLA aluminum suspension's control arms, and disk brakes. CRT computer terminals

The '84 Corvette had a slightly reworked L83 350 V8, still with 9.0:1 CR, but re-rated to 205bhp at 4300rpm and 290lb/ft at 2800rpm. There were also magnesium designer air cleaner and valve covers, plus a new style cold air induction. Four V8 rubberized isolation mounts boosted refinement. *(Courtesy RK Motors)*

followed the assembly process, storing information for future problem solving, parts inventory and eventual computerized wheel alignment, for each Corvette made! The LCD dash display sub assembly was pre-checked, with buyer-specified in-car audio fitted after dashboard installation.

There could be as many as 17 wiring harnesses in a 1984 Corvette. The next stage was body and trim line where all glass was installed by hand, with the body sealed for a heavy duty water leak test. That is, a four minute, 1000 gallon H2O deluge, with an inspector inside each car. This was one of two leak tests. A custom hydraulic corvair then married the body to the chassis. An overhead plaque on the assembly line marked the union, showing two bunnies kissing, with the words, "Together Forever". The completed Corvette met another assembly line plaque, this time showing Heckle and Jeckle crossing the finish line in a Polo White '53 Corvette, with checkered flag in hand! A symbolic Corvette start to finish indeed!

Each and every Corvette made its way to a toe-in pit for a check at 35mph simulated speed. A plaque with a crocodile on a scooter, marked the toe-in test. A 60mph rolling road test involved checks for interior noise, brake proportioning, and drivetrain evaluation. Random Corvettes off the line were subject to a quality control audit, with a quality plaque heralding this stage. The quality audit was highly competitive among assembly plants, with then Corvette plant manager Joe Delario overseeing the audit, and employee involvement that helped with problem solving. Morale at Bowling Green, Kentucky, with the new '84 Corvette, was high indeed. As *Motor Week*'s John Davis said, the plant's 1300 workers were heroes of the Corvette story, achieving big strides concerning built in quality. Their enthusiasm was displayed by an employee-designed circular material pad. It depicted the new Corvette in profile, Bowling Green, Kentucky factory lawn, and a checkered flag!

The emphasis on quality control seemed to yield results. *Road & Track*'s August 1983 group test, with a production example of the new '84 Corvette, brought the following praise, "Overall, the state of interior and exterior finish was higher than any we have seen on a Corvette." It was a necessary result, given the Corvette's upscale import company, and the reality that domestic build quality during 1968-83 was very poor. Miami's *WTVJ* anchor Bob Mayer showed the quality shortfall in his car reports from the mid '70s. This included the first public test, of GM's crucial downsized Nova compact replacement, the Chevrolet Citation. This new front drive GM X car ran poorly on test, and made ominous noises. An early Ford Foxstang suffered complete electrical system failure, and an AMC Spirit's key instrumentation was non-functional for much of the time Bob Mayer had the test car. Plus, a downsized Chrysler Cordoba ran off the road, during the *WTVJ* show's slalom test. Its power steering pump was defeated by rapid direction changes. *Consumer Reports* also had a very bad quality experience, with a 1980 Dodge Aspen.

The C3 Corvette had improved from its very shaky 1968 start, and by 1978-82 it was one of the better made domestic cars, especially with the 1981 move to Bowling Green, Kentucky, from the old St Louis plant. The GM F body was also better built, aided by full unitary construction from 1982, and greater model parts interchangeability between Camaro and Firebird cousins. Up from 25%, to 65%, in the transition from second to third gen F body. Morale at Norwood, Ohio seemed up as well. Although UAW workers were still naturally used at the GM plant, employee discounts on the new

Camaro Z28 and Trans Am, etc, seemed to foster goodwill. Ditto with non union Nissan workers, at the greenfield Smyrna, Tennessee factory, concerning easy terms on the 300ZX coupe. As for the new Corvette, around 650 cars were in a finished state at any given time, kept outside in the holding yard, locked away prior to shipment. They would be on their way to dealerships within 72 hours of vehicle completion.

'84 Corvette ➼ your options

AS AMERICA'S PREMIER performance machine, interest focused on the Corvette's special stuff, the go fast goodies, as it were. As in 1981-82, you had but one engine choice, in this case the returning L83 350 V8, with CFI. For performance fiends, there was a four-speed from December 1983, the NCO MM4 Doug Nash 4+3 box, optioned by 6443 patrons, and a Corvette exclusive. From summer 1983, officially at any rate, the FG3 Delco-Bilstein shocks, chosen by 3729 buyers at $189, and part of the Z51 package eventually. The G92 performance axle ratio, costing 22 bucks, was only selected by a mere 410 buyers as a separate option, it would also be in the Z51 pack, and implied a 3.07 ratio at first, and 3.31 from February 1984. The KC4 engine oil cooler was $158, and chosen by 4295 '84 Corvette fans. The QZD P255/50-16 Eagle VRs/9.5in wide rear rims cost $561, and you got them too with Z51. The VO1 HD radiator was 57 bucks, and selected by 12,008 buyers of '84 Corvettes. Of course, the headline Z51 Performance Handling Package was 600 bucks, and 25,995 buyers took the bait!

The CC3 removable transparent targa roof panel cost $595 to 15,767 Corvette fans, and 8755 went for the $428 D84 two-tone paint, in choices of code 16/18 Silver/Medium Gray, 20/23 Light Blue/Medium Blue and 63/66 Light Bronze/Dark Bronze. That was the cosmetic stuff. The most popular color in 1984 was code 72 Bright Red (12,942 cars), the least popular was code 20 Light Blue Metallic (1196 coupes). AG9 power driver seat, AU3 power door locks, K34 cruise control and Z6A rear window/side window defogger were all practically optioned by everyone, but didn't come standard. If one chose RPO UL5 radio delete, and 104 1984 Corvette buyers did, a $331 credit was yours. You did get an AM-FM stereo radio as standard, and very few (178 parties) went for UN8 $215 AM-FM stereo, CB radio. However, a very high percentage paid $895 for the optional (43,607 coupes) UU8 Delco-Bose stereo system.

In truth, you didn't need to tick any option boxes on the new Corvette. It came fully equipped with all essentials. The regular automatic transmission proved just as quick, if not quicker in the 1984-88 era than the NCO stick shift. Similarly, the standard suspension of the '84 Corvette, provided an optimal ride/handling compromise. With cars in general getting firmer post-1984, owners in modern times have found the stock '84 Corvette to ride okay, contrary to popular teeth rattler opinion. If you were track day inclined, then the Z51 package made sense. Just as in pre-1970 F41 Corvette days, that was indeed what the suspension was created for. Just add gas and go!

The Corvette's TV ad, showing a code 16 Bright Silver Metallic coupe, would have got buyers interested not only in the first new Corvette since 1968, but said car's innovative features and options. As the voice over song declared, "You've never seen anything like this before." The first computer activated manual transmission, LCD display with 14 separate instrument readouts in English or metric, updated 16 times per second. Reference was also

Hatchback was standard on the new '84 Corvette, and compared to the '82 Corvette Collector Edition cargo capacity was boosted from 10.4ft³ to 11.6ft³. This coupe has the UU8 Delco-Bose $895 audio option, with an amplifier in each speaker.
(Courtesy RK Motors)

made to the Delco Bose stereo option. The clincher was, "... the most advanced production car on the planet is now called Corvette. Chevrolet is taking charge."

In light of the C4 Corvette's technical qualities, it was certainly the most advanced car globally at this price; definitely the most advanced American production car, and, at 64 degrees, possessing the most steeply raked windshield of any US automobile to that point in time. One would be hard pressed to find, or even order, a base car at a competitive price. Dealers loved options, and were unwilling oftentimes to order a plain vanilla Corvette. In the case of the '84 Corvette, prospects were price gouged concerning early serial numbered '84 Corvettes, exploiting the collector car angle. However, there was absolutely no chance of obtaining an '83 Corvette. They existed at one point, but apart from a unicorn living in the National Corvette Museum, the answer for the public was, and is, a flat no.

Whatever happened to the '83 Corvette?

43 PROTOTYPE STAGE '83 Corvettes were built, subsequently re-serialized as 1984 Corvettes, and 42 of such cars were junked. Not one '83 Corvette was ever sold to the public. Of the official cars, the first 70 '84 Corvettes were retained by GM for engineering and development work. The new C4 Corvette was launched very late in the 1983 model year, March 1983. Robert Stempel, Chevrolet's boss at the time, and future GM CEO, gave the order to release the new Corvette coupe as an early '84 model year machine. After all, the L83 350 was already smog legal at 50-state level for '84 MY. The original intention was a genuine 1983 model year debut, but there was a lot of work to be done. Aside from previous Chevrolet boss Lloyd Reuss' decision to make the new Corvette have a Targa top, there were several bugs to be ironed out, and much going on behind the scenes.

The EPA and CAFE were constant headaches. The engineers took it easy with the L83 350 Cross Fire Injection motor. More power could have been made, as the aftermarket Renegade intake attests, but the greater fuel and air also equaled more gas and smog. The Cross Fire Injection 305 V8 was a Californian no show during 1982 model year. However, the L83 350 CFI V8 did feature in Californian 1982 Corvettes. This was because if engineers made the smaller CFI V8 smog legal in California in 1982, it would have become thirstier, and attracted the gas guzzler tax for the Camaro and Firebirds it was fitted to. GM and other automakers avoided the gas guzzler tax like the plague at this time, and the Corvette did dodge said tax. This wasn't easy, and arriving at the right smog calibration with acceptable economy and drivability took time.

Getting a heavy, stick shift car to be driven smoothly enough to pass the hydrocarbon part of the stricter smog law was challenging. So, the '84 Corvette started out as an automatic only model. The Doug Nash 4+3 stick shift did arrive, but why no five-speed like in the latest '83 Camaro, Firebird, Mustang and AMC Spirit? The reason was torque. The light shifting Borg Warner T5 manual transmission, seen from 1982, couldn't handle a 350 V8. As a result, the Corvette stuck with essentially a fancy BW Super T10, through '88 MY.

If you pleased the EPA on smog, you could fall foul with CAFE, and this was where aerodynamics helped. In the '80s, Ford VP Donald Kopka said how lowering drag allowed Ford to quickly, and economically, play CAFE catch up to GM, without incurring the heavy downsizing cost to improve gas mileage. The '84 Corvette was the first Plastic Fantastic without a front grille. That is, the C4 Corvette was a bottom breather. The front spoiler valence now housed halogen fog lights and driving lights, inspired by the Porsche 928, and other Europeans of the day. Being a bottom breather, made this the first Corvette with a factory engine oil cooler option. Indeed, RPO KC4 engine oil cooler would become standard during 1984 model year.

The downsized third gen Firebird, had a bottom breather, no grille set up, with the optional aero package fitted to the 1983 Daytona 500 pace car Trans Am. This W62 aero package, became a formal Firebird option in 1984. It became somewhat associated with overheating, when combined with the hi po L69 305 4bbl V8 option. So, there was much for Team Corvette to consider in the area of smog, gas mileage and durability. Not everything

was ready straight away. Rome wasn't built in a day, and like the Porsche 911, the Corvette was always a work in progress. Indeed, Corvette Chief Engineer Dave McLellan, followed what Chevrolet engineer Jack Turner said about the 1977 Camaro Z28 project. We're not done yet, watch this space for improvements. Similarly, McLellan said the 1984 Corvette brought all new bodywork, brakes and chassis, next year watch out for powertrain work!

Before the '84 Corvette's 17-month life was over, and the L98 TPI 5.7-liter V8 could surface, upgrades were effected. Those Delco-Bilstein shocks, to calm down the Z51 package from summer 1983. A change to fasteners concerning the power mirrors, so they held position post door closing. Engine oil cooler (KC4) and transparent acrylic roof panel (CC3) were introduced before 1983 was out. December 1983 witnessed cast iron and rubber dampers, for the Corvette's differential aluminum subframe mount, reducing rear axle gear noise to the body. The Doug Nash 4+3 arrived the same month, with the cut of teeth on ring and pinion gears altered in February 1984 and the 3.31 rear axle arriving as a performance option.

By March of 1984, a brace was added to the Corvette's alternator bracket, and iron material brake rotors squealed less, thanks to honing rather than cutting. As of April 1984, the C4 Corvette's

All C4 Corvettes had a Uniframe with aluminum backbone. This '84 Corvette coupe with Doug Nash 4+3 stick shift has a 3.07 axle, plus Z51 Performance Handling Package, and just 2355 miles!
(Courtesy RK Motors)

door hinge bushing material changed from brass to sintered iron, and a lightweight locking nut improved wheel balance. At the same time pointed ends were incorporated for the Targa top's securing bolts, which made for easier fitment. Also concerning the Targa top, anti rattle bumpers made said panel's trunk storage more refined.

Refinement was certainly the name of the Corvette game. When the Corvette was being assessed in *Car and Driver*'s May 1984 "Best-Handling American Car" report, it was remarked that this latest Corvette did better on squeaks and rattles than earlier C4 Corvette coupes tried. Chevrolet attributed the improvement to many changes in material specifications and Corvette assembly procedures. When you talk the talk about being a world class car, you have to walk the walk. That involved quality and handling. Concerning the latter, Corvette Chief Engineer Dave McLellan wanted the new C4 Corvette to be the best handling sports car in the world. A double wishbone front suspension, five-link IRS and Goodyear's 50 series Eagle VRs certainly made the latest Corvette more track effective than previous ones. One thing that didn't change for a long time was the C4 Corvette's so-called 'Breadloaf'. That is, the passenger side dashboard molding with Corvette script inlaid, intended to house an airbag. The Reagan administration's passive restraint system proposed law didn't eventuate. Washington begrudgingly cut domestic automakers some slack, given current and future burdens concerning smog, economy and safety laws, in an auto market where imported cars, especially those from Japan, were making major inroads.

Just the facts Ma'am ➤ performance data

DRAGNET'S JOE FRIDAY would have liked the '84 Corvette. Based on performance data, the latest model was honestly up to speed. As a 1983 model year car, the C4 Corvette had the measure of its exalted competitors, as the opposite *Road & Track* test data proves. However, these weren't easy times for GM. The need to get the Corvette ready amid legislative hurdles and foreign competition that made projects like the GM J car a top priority, meant that the new Corvette just missed out on

being the quickest accelerating and fastest on top speed, production car sold in North America – excepting gray market Countachs, BB 512is, BMW M1s and Porsche 930s. Indeed, the 930 was last formally available in 1979 model year, and wouldn't return to North America until 1986!

Before the new Corvette could reach showrooms, Ferrari released its four-valve 308 GTBi Quattrovalvole, and Porsche its 928S. These two megabuck imports edged out the delayed C4 Corvette. Indeed, Corvette, Ferrari and Porsche had respective base prices of $21,800, $53,745 and 43 grand! The 1984 3.2-liter Porsche 911 Carrera was also a swifter machine than either the outgoing 3-liter 911SC or '84 Corvette, but was once again a lot more money than anything rolling out of Bowling Green, Kentucky.

Road & Track data

Model	'84 Corvette Automatic	Ferrari 308 GTSi 2 valve	Porsche 911SC (3-liter)	Ferrari 308 GTBi QV	Porsche 928S five-speed
0-60 mph (sec)	7.0	7.9	6.7	6.8	7.0
¼-mile secs	15.3	16.1	15.3	15.2	15.4
@mph	87.5	88	91	91.5	92
60-0mph (ft)	144	154	140	153	156
Skidpad (g)	0.842	0.810	0.798	0.811	0.818
Slalom (mph)	61.4	60.6	59.7	60.9	58.4
mpg	15.5	11.5	18.5	16	18.5

SOME POINTS TO note, the Corvette was the only car above with an automatic transmission, the rest had five-speed stick shifts. Although Corvette, Ferrari 308 GTBi QV and Porsche 928S top speeds were a respective 139mph, 142mph and 146mph, *R&T* had tested the 928S a month earlier, in its July 1983 issue, and got 136mph on a shorter test area. The above Corvette, Ferrari 308 QV and Porsche 928S figures were gleaned from Willow Springs Raceway. The '84 Corvette blew away all comers with 0-30mph in just 2.2 seconds, underlying the torquey nature of the Chevrolet L83 350 V8. *Road &*

Chevrolet claimed the '84 Corvette automatic, with optional 3.31 performance axle *(February '84 arrival)*, could do 0-60mph in 6.8 seconds. The '84 Corvette was the quickest, and fastest, US production car of the day. Take that Foxstang! (Courtesy GM Archives)

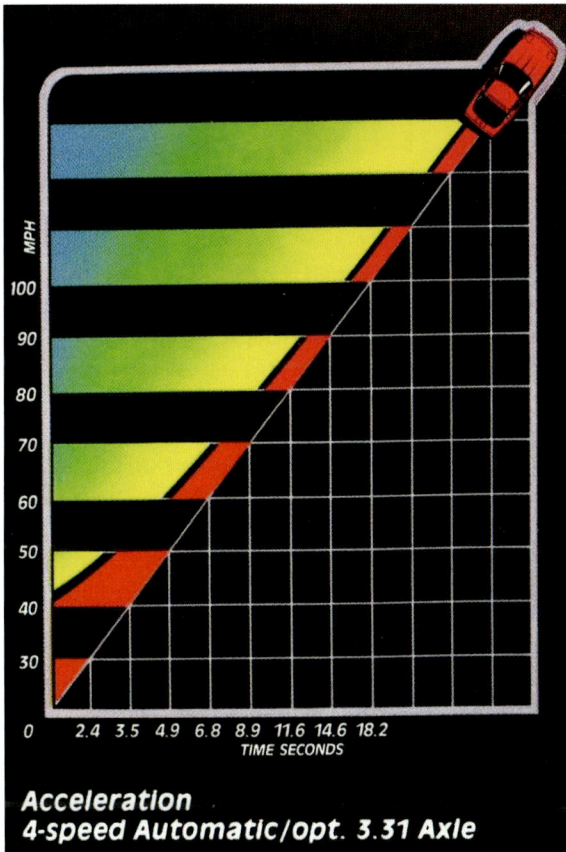

**Acceleration
4-speed Automatic/opt. 3.31 Axle**

mind if not on price. Trackside, the Corvette was an easier car to drive than either. The Ferrari's five-speed needed quite a bit of warming up, before Maranello let one access all five gears. Although the Porsche 911 was much improved, the pendulum of rear weight bias played on the mind. Should the 911's high rear grip limit be exceeded, the consequences were troubling.

Was the new Corvette a fast car? Ringers aside, Corvettes hadn't been this speedy since the demise of the big block '74 Corvette 454. What's more, UK magazine *Autocar* showed that an '84 Corvette could mix it with European exotica that didn't carry smog equipment.

Autocar (UK) test figures

Model	Top speed (mph)	0-60mph (sec)	50-70mph (sec)	mpg	Test date
'84 Corvette Auto	142	6.6	4.0	16.7	4/14/84
Ferrari Mondial QV 3.2	143	6.8	3.7	16.8	6/25/86
Lotus Esprit Turbo	138	6.1	3.1	17.6	12/19/84
Maserati Merak	143	7.7	5.0	17.9	2/28/81
Lamborghini Jalpa 3500 V8	144	6.2	3.8	15.9	11/5/86

AS EXPECTED, THE only car above with automatic transmission was the Corvette. You couldn't even get an automatic with the others as an option. That said, there was an automatic car that matched the '84 Corvette automatic's August '83 *Road & Track* 7.0 second 0-60mph and 15.3 second ¼-mile times … the 2002 Acura 3.2TL Type-S! *R&T* figures for the Acura showed it took 18 years for the average sports sedan to achieve what the Corvette did in 1983[1] [(91)] The Corvette had long been one of those performance benchmark cars. Its track prowess

Track found the $19,485 Porsche 944 only reached 125mph, but was gas mileage champ on 21.5mpg, and won out 60mph to zero in 141ft. However, the Corvette beat out everyone in 80mph to zero, recording only 250ft. The '84 Corvette was also victor on the skid pad.

With the latest C4 Corvette there was much talk of world class performance, handling and Porsches, of one kind or another. Porsche was viewed as the sports car gold standard. It was commonly felt that the Porsche 924/944 represented Zuffenhausen's best handlers. *R&T*'s August '83 group test featured a non Z51 '84 Corvette, with QZD P255/50-16 Eagle VRs, and 9.5in wide rear rim package, and a Porsche 944 five-speed. Only the Corvette and Porsche 944 achieved an 'excellent' overall brake rating from *Road & Track*. The two coupes also had the joint highest slalom speed, of 61.4mph. Corvette's natural nemeses of the time were the Ferrari 308 series and Porsche 911, in the public's was also legendary, the archetypal gentleman's racer. Here, the '84 Corvette maintained tradition, as *Fast Lane* Magazine said in July 1984 concerning balance and grip, "When we first tried a Corvette, on Goodyear's table-smooth test circuit in Luxembourg, both felt sensational. GM were right, the graphs said it all. Here was a car that could out-corner the best of the opposition, generating the sort of lateral g normally associated only with slick-shod racers."

Fast Lane added that on a public road you could use full throttle, on a second gear corner, and even with 290lb/ft on tap the tail stayed put. Oversteer was hard to provoke, even in the wet, and easily tamed when it arose. *Road & Track* concurred in its August 1983 group test, saying that on Willow Springs Raceway, the Corvette's grip made fast driving a piece of cake, on the fast, smooth track. Plus, out of the Corvette, Ferrari 308 GTBi QV, Porsche 928 and 944, it was the Corvette that at least one tester achieved his fastest, and most consistent lap times with. Indeed, the new '84 Corvette seemed ideal for the new SCCA category of Showroom Stock GT Class cars. *Road & Track* tried eligible sports cars concerning this new category: '84 Corvette, Mustang GT 5.0, Camaro Z28, Porsche 944, Trans Am, RX-7 and Daytona Turbo Z, plus Nissan 300ZX. Out of this field, it was the Corvette that was the fastest at Willow Springs, and acceleration champ. The big, soft and over equipped 300ZX won braking, and was second fastest around Willow Springs.

The '84 Corvette subscribed to the old school view that a car in control shouldn't break traction at any of its four corners. The civility of the new Corvette's performance was displayed by *Motor* (UK) magazine's test figures, for its Belgium tested 1968 and 1984 Corvettes:

Motor (UK) test figures

THE '68 CORVETTE 427 four-speed had a 3.08 axle, and no a/c. The cabin also suffered from heat soak supplied by the big block Rat Motor. Pollution controls were limited to a smog pump. The '84 Corvette had a/c, automatic, 2.87 snooze axle and more comprehensive pollution controls. The younger coupe achieved a lot from the little 350 Cross-Fire-Injection Mouse Motor, and went a heck of a lot further on a gallon of gas. With the optional 3.31 axle, the '84 Corvette was a high 14s car, and could still reach 140mph, albeit with more rpm registered on the early C4 Corvette LCD bar graph tach. Plus, it could do all of the above on low octane juice. Its older big block bro would be pinking to high heaven on regular!

Even so, when it came to GTP racers in the IMSA series, a more specialized machine was required. After years of arm's length racing support, GM was now more directly involved with motorsport. The Buick March used a single turbo version of the Buick V6, allied to a chassis courtesy of Britain's March Engineering. Similarly, for the 1985 racing season, GM turned to the UK company Lola for chassis aid, and the creation of the Chevrolet (Corvette) Lola. [92]

When it came to challenging the Porsche 928S five-speed, on the track, *Motor Week* also passed on using the '84 Corvette. The TV show went with the '83½ Camaro Z28 L69 305 five-speed instead. It was late April, and 65°F in the West Virginia Hills, as Chevrolet's $13,600 Camaro Z28 (considered the Corvette's little brother since the American Zee car came out in 1967) took on Zuffenhausen's 43 grand heavyweight. In truth, the Porsche was only 40lb heavier. The result at Summit Point Raceway was Chevrolet 1, Porsche 0. The Camaro Z28 lapped

Model	Engine (cc)	Top speed (mph)	BHP	lb/ft	0-60mph (sec)	30-50mph top gear/ kickdown (sec)	50-70mph top gear/ kickdown (sec)	MPG	Test date
'68 Corvette L68 427 4sp	6996	145.7	400	460	6.1	4.9	4.5	11.8	8/24/68
'84 Corvette Automatic	5730	139.2	205	290	7.0	2.9	3.7	17.5	3/31/84

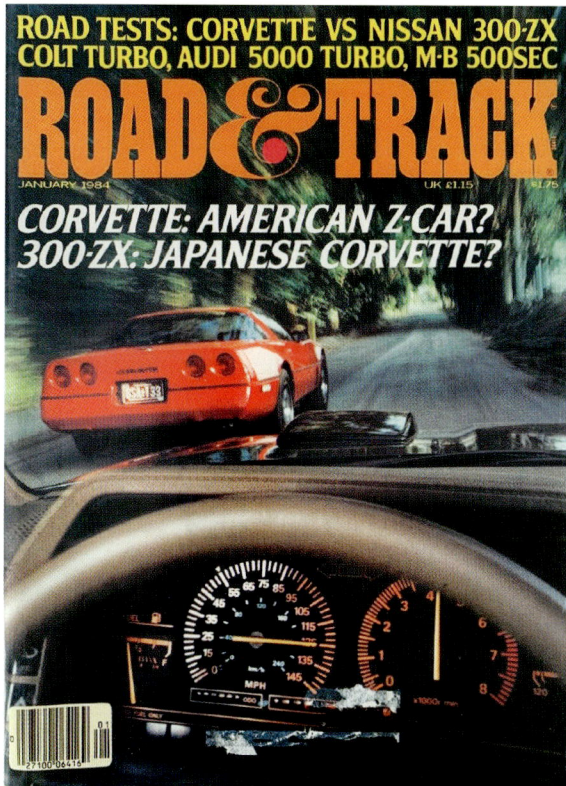

In spite of similarities, the '84 Corvette had a subjective style edge, and objective performance advantage over the Nissan 300ZX Turbo. *(Courtesy Road & Track)*

measurement and subjective feel. With the third gen F body, Camaro Z28 had gone "go kart zeal", and *Motor Week* did note the Zee's bone rattling ride when facing off the Chevrolet against the Porsche 928S. The Porsche rolled in cornering, the Camaro did not. However, the '84 Corvette with Z51 trumped all for roller skate, minimal compliance 'handling'. The Corvette, in *Car and Driver*'s opinion, was a 'numbers car', and true enough GM had aimed for 0.95g lateral g from said coupe. With the Camaro Z28 and Porsche 944 shortlisted as the best of the domestic and import handlers, *C/D* faced 'em off, with the 944 triumphing due to its lithe balance. However, if lateral skid pad grip and lap times were your bag, the Plastic Chevrolet was still Fantastic. Just the facts ma'am.

Meet the press

THE '84 CORVETTE'S introduction had been a long one. The automotive press had been invited to try the new Corvette, as engineering prototypes living at GM's Milford Proving Ground, from December 1982. The coupe's official release was March 1983. *Car and Driver* carried a Corvette article in March 1983, penned by the inimitable Brock Yates, the journal's one time editor at large, founding force behind the real life 'Cannonball Run' and numerous other automotive related activities. Yates dismissed the outgoing Corvette, the Mako Shark inspired Late Model C3 Corvette as, "... a rolling cult object rooted in the ethos and technology of another automotive era." He even added the description, "phallic silliness" to a generation of Corvette that was undeniably effective in road and race, not to mention the nameplate's all time commercial zenith of 1979 sales. Towards the incoming C4 Corvette, Brock Yates said, "... the new Corvette is a truly stout automobile ... a true-born, world-class sports car loaded with technical sophistication."

Indeed, a Uniframe chassis of galvanized steel with alloy girders, plastic panels bolted and bonded to a kind of space frame, front double wishbone

the circuit in 1.38:30 at an average lap speed of 73.25mph. The Porsche recorded one minute and 40 seconds, with an average lap speed of 72mph. Yes, the Camaro Z28 did throw off fanbelts like discarded hula hoops, the coupe was delivered with the wrong fanbelt, there was also sudden oversteer and brake fade if a corner was entered too fast, but damn it all, a win is a win! What's more, or perhaps less, a victory at a much lower price.

It seemed that Chevrolet was enjoying a Reagan renaissance, after a Carter crisis. New GM CEO Roger Smith matched the bullish market and buoyant times, fearing not federal anti monopolistic court action, as he strove for corporate gold. Don't be bashful about being No 1! Chevrolet was number one, according to *Car and Driver*, at least when it came to the best handling domestic car. However, once again the champ was Camaro Z28, not '84 Corvette! The '84 Corvette was perceived as being too stiff. It was in May 1984 that *C/D*'s "Best-Handling American Car" report said the Camaro Z28 was tops, based on a mix of objective suspensión, fixed length driveshaft that served as a locator, Girloc vented disk brakes, semi metallic brake pads, dual transverse glassfiber reinforced epoxy resin springs, five-link IRS, fuel injected V8, 13.0:1 1.9 turn rack and pinion steering (rack and peanut according to Homer Simpson!), vaned asymmetric 8.5 and 9.5in wide 16in aluminum rims, Goodyear Eagle VR50 F1 inspired Z51 pack Gatorbacks, LCD instrumentation. The GM PR blurb claimed, "most exotic package ever offered." In any case, it was an impressive, and timely replacement, for the 15-year-old C3 Corvette. The official GM word was that the new Corvette would be marketed as an '84 model year vehicle, for 18 months.

Naturally, *Car and Driver* allowed Team Corvette to get its viewpoint across. Channeling the former Zora Arkus-Duntov, in a way, was Freerk Schaafsma, nicknamed Fred. Schaafsma was an engineer hailing from the Netherlands. He provided the imported sports car influence that Duntov used to bring to the Corvette party. Still working from the temporary collection of trailer offices at GM's Milford Proving Ground, the home of Team Corvette, Schaafsma laid out the '84 Corvette spiel to *Car and Driver* thusly, "I'll take all comers. You bring what you want." Them's fighting words, indeed!

The Corvette folks said they benchmarked the new Plastic Fantastic against the Porsche 928, with Schaafsma saying, "When we compared our car against the Porsche, I can tell you there were a lot of good feelings at Chevrolet." This was perhaps not surprising. The Porsche 928 available in North America was a rather tame animal. It retained the original 8.5:1 CR4.5-liter V8, even after all 928s got a compression ratio hike in Europe to 10.0:1, for 1980. Automatic North American 928s got somewhat plebian Dunlop SP Sport 215/60 VR-15s, rather than Pirelli P7s, plus a super snooze 2.75 axle! So, one had a soft grand tourer that hit 60mph in eight seconds flat and, eventually, reached 130mph. The suspension tune also suited the easy going nature of the 928's Monterey Peninsula, cocktail crowd clientele.

Road & Track said the Corvette targeted the Ferrari 308 GTBi and Porsche's 928. In fact, the '84 Corvette's 205bhp power rating was exactly the same as the 308 GTBi two-valver's output. *R&T* suspected the Corvette's real sales rival was the

Heroes of the small screen, NBC's *The A-Team*. The show featured a '79 GMC Vandura and '84 Corvette with matching red stripes! (*Courtesy www.spencer1984.com*)

similarly priced and very popular, Porsche 944. Putting all that to one side, Corvette Chief Engineer Dave McLellan said the Plastic Fantastic was like power boats or ultra light planes, something beyond basic needs, "Like them, the Corvette goes beyond serious transportation. This is a sports car, and we wanted it for one simple mission – to go fast." As for that LCD display digital dashboard, McLellan confided, "We were having a little fun with the instrument panel." Holy Atari Batman!

Well, the Corvette's Doug Nash 4+3 stick shift was as difficult to use as the Ferrari's shift and Porsche's dogleg manual transmission. And like the Porsche 928, most Corvette buyers went with the automatic. There was some contention over the C4 Corvette's weight. Critics said it should have been lighter. However, it was around 400lb lighter, than the Porsche 928 automatic, and the same weight as the Ferrari 308 GTBi. On the skid pad, the '84 Corvette set a new record at *Car and Driver*, 0.90g. The journal was trying a code 20 Light Blue Metallic '84 Corvette with Doug Nash 4+3 box, and Z51 pack. A stick shift '84 Corvette wouldn't be available until Christmas 1983. However, *C/D* still felt the coupe was representative enough, concerning showroom fare, to disclose stats.

Car and Driver gleaned 0-60mph in 6.7 seconds, with a 15.2 second ¼-mile at 90mph, and attained

140mph. *C/D*'s previous best skid pad figure was a 0.82g, achieved by the Porsche 928, Ferrari 308 GTBi and 1980 Turbo Trans Am WS6. The '84 Corvette's 173ft 70-0mph stopping distance also improved upon the 928's 180ft showing. That said, the Porsche 930 still held *Car and Driver*'s ultimate record of 165ft, although the 930 had been absent from the North American market for some years. For now, the '84 Corvette ruled, and *C/D* judged the coupe's underhood magnesium castings and black enamel a stylistic triumph.

Road & Track had also sampled an engineering prototype, in March 1983. In August that year, the new Corvette was in the journal's Ferrari 308 GTBi vs Porsche 928 vs Porsche 944 group encounter. *R&T* judged the latest Corvette to be a substantial improvement over its predecessor, in performance, handling and quality. Perhaps most importantly, it was still a Corvette in spirit, "For all of its new-found chassis sophistication, the Corvette hasn't lost any of its old kick-and-rumble personality." *R&T* added, "... instant torquey acceleration ..." and said you had to concentrate hard in the Porsche 928S with its awkward dogleg five-speed, to outlap the Corvette at Willow Springs Raceway. What's more, the Corvette possessed the only V8 motor on test that actually sounded like a V8! *Road & Track* had feared the Corvette's nature might be lost, in a post fuel crisis,

Mr T's GMC G series van look has been attributed to legendary car customizer George Barris. It's believed only one '84 Corvette was used during *The A-Team*'s 1983-87 run. *(Courtesy www.spencer1984.com)*

pollution controlled world, rushing headlong into the future of the one size fits all World Car. However, the C4 Corvette allayed such concerns, "The best thing about the Corvette is putting down your right foot and throwing great big clouds of Corvette dust on all the other traffic." After all, the Corvette had never been a shrinking violet!

The new Corvette's handling proved a major bone rattler of contention. It was a battle of control versus comfort for automotive testers during 1983-84. *Motor Week*'s host John Davis drove a Z51 pack equipped engineering prototype at high banked Riverside (California). He felt surprising security, even at full throttle. The Corvette's 1.9 turns between locks suited the racer nature of the '84 Corvette. Davis disclosed that the Corvette felt crafted to the driver and, "Makes you feel that telekinetic steering might just be possible." In the show's lane swerve test, the old C3 Corvette's oversteer twitchiness was absent. John Davis said almost anyone with more confidence than sense could drive the '84 Corvette, "The new car is definitely more handler than most owners will be drivers." So, Corvette patrons would just have to take it on faith that they had the world's best handling production car.

Britain's *Fast Lane* echoed such comments in July 1984, saying the C4 Corvette just squatted, pointed and clung on in response to tiny steering inputs. Steering that while being heavily weighted, still lacked feel. Even so, it was the best gripping, sharpest-responding, flattest-cornering smooth-road car you could get. Then came the big but, such ability was allied to a Dr Jeckyll and Mr Hyde nature. That latter nature implied the worst ride comfort that *Fast Lane* had encountered in recent years.

There were a number of reasons why the '84 Corvette brought this reaction, and why it was set up this way. For starters, most magazines want to try, and are given, the ultimate version of any car. In this case, that implied an '84 Corvette with Z51 (Performance Handling Package) or QZD Gatorback tire and wheel set. The latter included with Z51. Plus, export Corvettes, just like the modern C8 Corvette, included Z51. The reasoning was probably: European buyers like handling, so give 'em handling! The standard '84 Corvette was the one most people would really have preferred.

That's certainly what *Motor Week*'s John Davis said, when *MW* tested its code 53 Gold Metallic '84 Corvette automatic with Z51. Of course, with modern cars getting stiffer over time, the '84 Corvette is increasingly perceived as normal. At least one UK person has described the export spec '84 Corvette automatic with Z51, with yellow Bilsteins clearly visible, as even being comfortable!

North American thinking has commonly perceived sporty cars as being two-door jobs with stiffly sprung suspension. Indeed, in *Car and Driver*'s July '84 "The Best-Handling Imported Car Is ..." *C/D* said the one true quality of a Lotus, and therefore a sports car, is handling. So, the magazine was pretty miffed when the Lotus engineer on hand explained that ride comfort was very important in Europe. As a result, the Lotus Esprit's rear trailing arm suspension bushes were soft. *C/D* testers didn't like this at all, saying, "... if you can't drive hard in a Lotus, what's it good for?" Well, be careful what you wish for!

As ever, Dave McLellan and his team drove Corvettes, not just at GM's Milford Proving Ground, but on back roads out East. They knew America wasn't solely composed of glass smooth straight interstate. However, the Corvette was America's only sports car, and if you took one to a track, it had better perform. Otherwise Victor Kayam might have asked for his money back?! Yes, the Corvette wasn't a Remington electric shaver, but it also probably wasn't the only car a guy or gal owned, if owner surveys have taught us anything. So, let the Corvette be the specialist that it is, and if you don't drive on a track regularly, avoid RPO Z51. On a related note, the Corvette has never been adept to consumer magazine type analysis. In contrast, the Porsche 928 was, explaining why it won the 1978 'European Car of The Year' title, the only sports car to do so in a competition aimed at mundane family transportation.

Therefore, *Road & Track*'s August '83 group test had Porsche 944 and 928 a respective first and second on 482 and 481 points. Ferrari 308 GTBi QV was third on 451 points, leaving Corvette last on 420 points. In performance categories Corvette won 0-30mph (2.2 seconds), 80-0mph (250ft), lateral g force (0.842g) with joint top on slalom speed (61.4mph), shared with the Porsche 944. Being a GM car, it was no surprise that the Corvette won the HVAC category. It was also equal first with the 944 on seats. However, the Corvette's wide seat back was better suited to the broader shouldered North American owner. The Porsche 944 seemed to only fit slimmer Formula One stars! And, like the 944, the Corvette was the recipient of one of *R&T*'s rare excellent brake ratings.

R&T judged the Corvette's power, cornering, handling balance and scat as tops. Ride comfort, indecisive automatic shifting, overdone instruments and body rattles were negatives. Britain's *Fast Lane* picked up on the GM THM 700R4's odd behavior for a US slushbox. That is, jerky shifts and thumped changes. The hunting between ratios and slip and grab nature seemed related to electronic calibration of the essentially computer controlled THM 350 with overdrive 0.70 fourth.

The Uniframe wasn't as rigid as a conventional unibody, like the Porsche. As *Fast Lane* magazine said, US C4 Corvette launch euphoria was followed by some qualifications. As *Road & Track* said, the new Corvette was excellent, among the world's best, but lost several small battles of degree against the Porsches 928 and 944, plus Ferrari 308 GTBi QV. Two of those three cars cost a lot more. The Porsche 944 was arguably the best balanced, and most fun to drive car that Zuffenhausen didn't make. The big buck 928 was respected, but not well liked. The Ferrari was the sexily desirable racer, as expected.

Road & Track's January 1984 comparison between the '84 Corvette and Nissan 300ZX Turbo had America's favorite on 538 points, against the Nissan's 630 point tally. That said, the Doug Nash 4+3 equipped Plastic Fantastic outgripped the 300ZX Turbo: 0.88g Vs 0.795g, and was judged better handling. The Nissan was also marginally slower in acceleration and top speed, in most independent testing. More than that, like the Porsches, the Nissan was more sedan than racer. The Datsun/Nissan Zee car had been in transition from Samurai to Cedric, with each generation post 240Z. So much so, that in March 1984 *Road & Track* said of the 300ZX, that compared to the original Mazda RX7, "... the sports car element has been well and truly lost."

Those were harsh words for a coupe that was increasingly a Corvette commercial market rival.

The New 1984 Corvette

The A-Team Corvette belonged to Templeton 'Faceman' Peck, although it was occasionally driven by Hannibal and Murdock. Mr T was only ever a passenger in the coupe! It was driven one time by recurrent character Tawnia Baker. (Courtesy www.spencer1984.com)

In February 1984, *Car and Driver* said that if not for the 300ZX's excellent engine, it was a total disappointment, "... a snore to look at," with worse directional stability than the '84 Corvette. Of the Nissan's electronic three-way shocks, 'F' was too firm and 'S' too sloppy. Overall, *C/D* felt the Porsche 944 was a better car for two grand more, and the Toyota Supra was a better sporting coupe, for a couple of grand under the 300ZX Turbo!

'84 Corvette ➡ Value for $$$ champ!

THE '84 CORVETTE'S appeal was plain to see. Starting with a glassfiber skin that *Fast Lane* called "... beautifully finished, tactile in quality," the Corvette had been the gold standard in great finish fiberglass exteriors. Tradition was also maintained by the hint of Ferrari Pininfarina style. In the Mako Shark C3 Corvette era, it was a rear fender similarity to the Ferrari 250 GTO. Now it was more Ferrari 308 GTB. Then too, paddle type exterior reversing side mirrors on export Corvettes, and GM F bodies resembled Maranello parts too! Under the skin, the Corvette was still the value for money, rorty racer, it had been since getting V8 power in 1955.

What's more, the '84 Corvette may well be the best value Corvette of all time! Earlier Straight Axle, Mid-Year and Late Model Corvettes have a classic aura, and are now all seen as rising value collectibles. They hail from an era when foreign competition at Corvette sales volume didn't exist. However, the C4 Corvette is developing its own classic vibe, thanks to nostalgia for the power dressing, big shoulder pads and hair 1980s. That said, the durability of C4 Corvettes, and their big sales numbers, mean they may never reach the lofty collector values of their predecessors, at least outside special edition or ZR-1 versions. The '84 Corvette is in an even more unique position within C4 Corvette world. Given rapidly improving post malaise era technology, subsequent C4 and later

generation Corvettes are faster and have more tech toys, so buyers go for them.

The '84 Corvette can outperform many an earlier Corvette, and its value for money nature was on show in TV's *Wheeler Dealers* Season 4 episode. Hosts Mike Brewer and Edd China bought and fixed up a code 23 Medium Blue Metallic '84 Corvette automatic, on a budget. Edd China said of the coupe, "I've had a fantastic time driving this beast back to the workshop. Its got an awesome engine. It's just pure Americana." On Britain's poorly surfaced secondary roads, Mike Brewer experienced twitchiness and oversteer. However, reaction to the '84 Corvette was very positive. It was praise unaffected by the coupe's ubiquity in America, or the home market negative perception, concerning the Cross Fire Injection 350 V8. Quite the contrary, Brewer was impressed by the powerful sounding appellation of Cross Fire Injection! As *Wheeler Dealers* discovered, the '84 Corvette was an enjoyable, entry level point into the exciting world of Corvettes. In real world driving, the '84 Corvette goes way better than its modest 205bhp power rating would have you believe. Then too, ride comfort isn't the deal breaker that many claim, although Brewer did find the high sill difficult to get over.

C4 Corvette on the small and big screens, 1983-87

WITH THE NEW C4 Corvette's popularity, handling ability, and still great amount of vehicle stuntwork in TV and movies, it's little wonder that the latest

Plastic Fantastic soon became a fixture in living rooms and cinemas around the world, and from this, toy shops! In the 1983-87 era, the early C4 Corvette's round taillights and vaned alloys were a common sight on real life streets and in entertainment land. In several popular TV shows it had a prominent action role either in one episode, or an entire series. In the Series 3 Episode 17 (Diced Steele) of detective show *Remington Steele* on NBC, Steele and Laura's Vegas rental was a code 72 Bright Red '84 Corvette on Nevada plates.

More involved for the C4 Corvette was the code 16 Bright Silver Metallic '84 Corvette, driven by Scarecrow in ABC's *Scarecrow and Mrs King* (1983-87). In this series, Lee Stetson (Scarecrow) was a secret agent who teamed up with housewife Mrs King (Kate Jackson). Scarecrow originally drove a '63 silver Porsche 356 ragtop, which got wrecked in the show's plot, and voila … in came Corvette! Actor Bruce Boxleitner who played Scarecrow, said it was just as well, because the Porsche was always breaking down during filming.

Boxleitner loved the C4 Corvette. The show's plot inferred the same silver Corvette being used, but in fact '84, '85 and eventually an '86 Corvette served production. Aside from Tuned Port Injection script replacing Cross Fire Injection on the front fender body seam line, you couldn't tell an '84 from an '85 Corvette, unless the '85 Corvette's wider standard 9.5in front rims were discerned on close inspection. The '86 Corvette had silver, rather than black wheel centers. Once again, very hard to spot in a car chase. A ¹⁄₄₃ scale diecast model of Scarecrow's Corvette was produced.

A silver Tuned Port Injection '86 Corvette also featured prominently, in the Series 1 fourth episode of CBS TV detective show *Jake and the Fatman*. Detective Jake Styles normally drove a silver Porsche 911 Carrera convertible and then, unfortunately, a Foxstang. However, in this particular episode, Jake was apprehending a car thief trying to sell the silver Corvette. Pretending to be a car buyer, Jake was asked if he knew how to drive a stick? The silver coupe then scooted around LA's streets, displaying the Corvette's neutral, glued to the road handling to good effect. However, if you're talkin' TV, there was one '80s show you couldn't drive past: *The A-Team*!

NBC's popular show ran from 1983 to 1987, and featured two visually complimentary GM vehicles: 1979 GMC Vandura & 1984 C4 Corvette automatic. The Vandura, with visual get up attributed to car customizer extraordinaire George Barris, sporting a red stripe over a black exterior, with the Corvette having a matching red stripe over a code 10 White exterior, plus code 742 Carmine Leather interior. The Vandura was part of the GMC G series. The show's Vandura had a 350 V8 and slushbox activated via column shift, but in '79 MY one could have optioned a 454 V8. The Corvette was straight L83 350/THM 700R4. Of course the Vandura belonged to BA Barrachus (Mr T), and the Corvette to Templeton 'Faceman' Peck (Dirk Benedict). The Vandura rolled on 15in red American Racing turbine rims, the Corvette relied on stock 16in vaned alloys.

Being a two-seater somewhat limited the Corvette's usage in the show. Apart from Faceman, Colonel Hannibal and Murdock occasionally drove the Corvette. Plus, in one episode (Series 2, Episode 16, 'Say it with Bullets'), recurrent character Tawnia Baker (Marla Heasley) borrowed Faceman's Corvette to race Monte Markham's corrupt army officer Mason Harnett. BA Barrachus only ever rode in the Corvette's passenger seat. It's believed only one Corvette was used for the show's entire run. However, some accounts indicate that sometimes

The A-Team Corvette came up for sale in 2011, with 19,165 miles, and a signature on the gas filler door, by the show's creator Stephen J Cannell! The Corvette color combination was code 10 White exterior, with code 742 Carmine Leather interior. *(Courtesy www.spencer1984.com)*

on location a white Corvette was hired, and the red stripe applied.

In 2011, what is considered the only Corvette used in *The A-Team* came up for sale. It was in very sound condition, with 19,165 miles on the odometer, still retaining its original powertrain. *The A-Team* show creator Stephen J Cannell, had signed the gas filler door. There was a hole for a camera mount, on the passenger door. There were also two blank shells discovered in the coupe. One was from a 9mm, and the other from a 0.223 caliber handgun. By coincidence, UK brothers Liam and Jerome Brett created a faithful replica of *The A-Team*'s Vandura, using an '82 G series combined with the '84 Corvette's L83 350/THM 700R4 powertrain. As soldiers of fortune, on the run from authorities, was it wise to drive around in such conspicuous vehicles?! You have to suspend belief in such cases.

From TV to the silver screen, the '84 Corvette was much featured in the 1984 flick *Cannonball Run II*. The original *Cannonball Run* movie of 1981 was a Burt Reynolds & Co smash hit. Dean Martin and Sammy Davis Jr drove a red '79 Ferrari 308 GTS, dressed as Catholic priests! Martin played scotch loving ex F1 star Jamie Blake, with Sammy Davis Jr as gambler friend Morris Fenderbaum. Perhaps given Martin's reputation, he was a whiskey priest?! In any case, come *Cannonball Run II*, and the pair were dressed as uniformed cops, racing a red '84 Corvette. There's that Ferrari to Corvette connection again. Shirley MacLaine was also around, and Frank Sinatra too, in what would be the final outing for The Rat Pack.

When Ol' Blue Eyes' Daytona Turbo passed Blake & Fenderbaum's Corvette, you had to suspend belief again, but maybe The Chairman of the Board was running more boost than stock? As a friend of Lee Iacocca, Frank Sinatra did Chrysler Corp ads, had some product merchandise involvement, and seemed to always be driving some Pentastar product, on both small and big screens. In real life, Sammy Davis Jr owned a red '84 Corvette, and Johnny Carson had a white coupe. In *Cannonball Run II*, a silver '84 Corvette was getting its L83 350 checked pre-race. Yes, the '84 Corvette had certainly matched high media with commercial profile, in superior fashion to the DeLorean DMC 12, that John Z tried to promote with celebrity amigos.

In 1985's film *What Comes Around*, Jerry Reed starred in a light hearted, semi-autobiographical telling of his Country & Western career, playing the fictitious singer Joe Hawkins. Hawkins' younger brother Tom, a racer/mechanic, owned a silver '84 Corvette. Come 1987, and the Corvette could be seen in the Walt Disney ABC network TV movie *Double Agent*, starring Michael McKean, with a dual role as veterinarian, standing in for his secret agent twin brother. McKean drove a modified C4 TPI Corvette that was given the James Bond gadget treatment. Art imitated real life, given all those Porsche 944 vs Corvette magazine references, *Double Agent* saw McKean's Corvette jousting with a black Porsche 924 driven by an enemy female agent. Naturally, the Corvette won! And a Corvette in the real James Bond film too. In 1985's *A View to A Kill*, James Bond got a lift from a friendly Russian lady agent, driving a silver '84 Corvette!

All of the above marked the new C4 Corvette out as a special and desirable set of wheels, and the Holiday Inn hotel chain agreed. At the Holiday Inn World HQ, located in Memphis, Tennessee, an '84 Corvette was part of the HQ's auto fleet during the mid to late '80s. It was mostly laid on for visiting company executives, from out of town. That is, something special for them to drive around in. The Holiday Inn HQ facilities manager made sure said Corvette was washed, gassed and ready for any VIPs, prior to their visit. A couple of hours were set aside for such vehicle preparation. It was a task that the facilities manager rarely shared with subordinates!

1985 ➡ Improving the new Corvette

MOTOR WEEK **TOOK** a long hard, soup to nuts, look at the '84 Corvette, with host John Davis concluding, "We think the 1984 Corvette was well worth waiting for." He added, that despite some minor flaws, the new C4 Corvette represented the best performance car combination overall, regardless of origin or price. That was quite an assertion. However, when one considers how the '84 Corvette wasn't much pricier than many mediocre sporty cars, but a great deal cheaper than classy imports of similar speed, then it seemed the

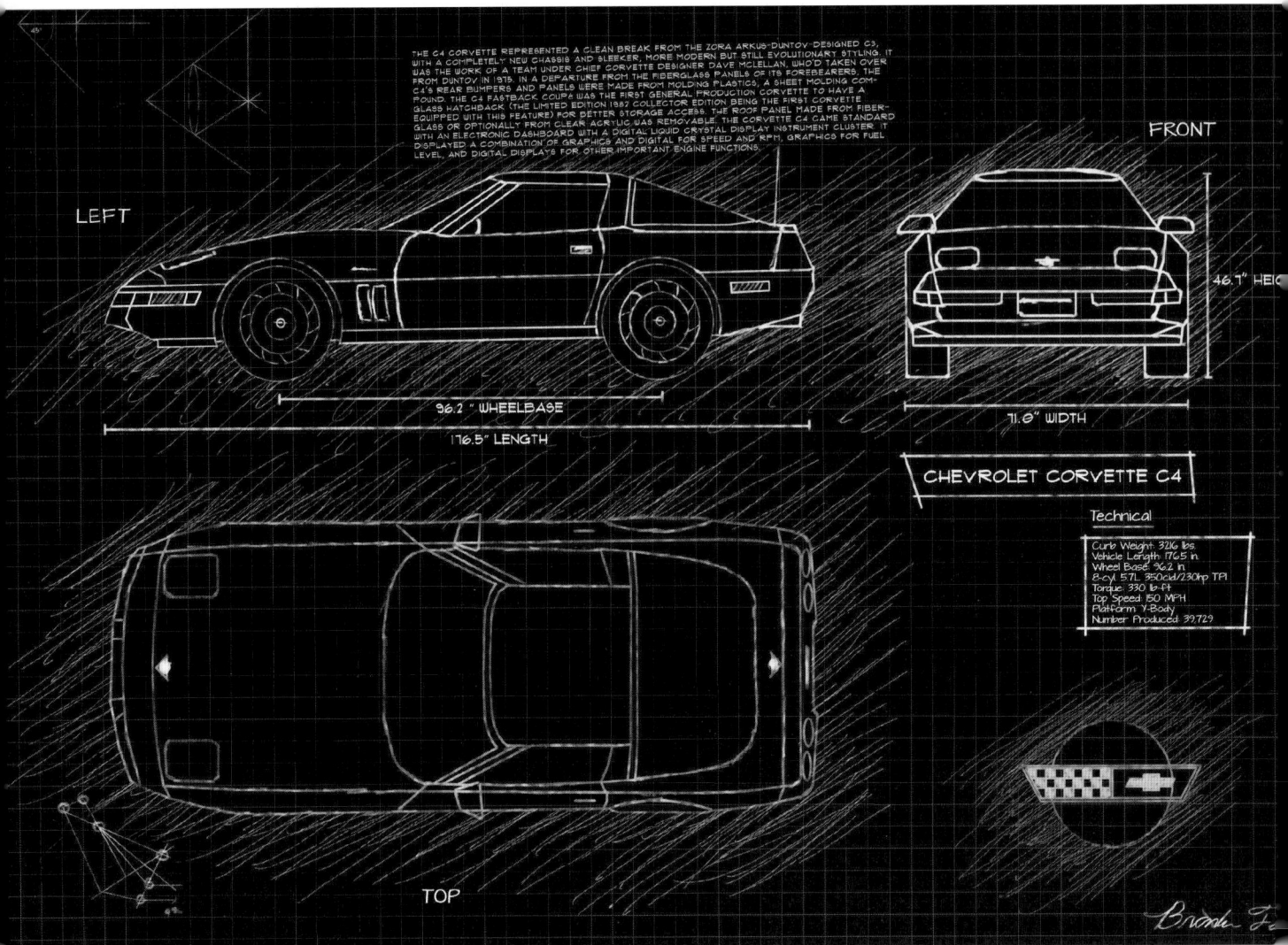

THE C4 CORVETTE REPRESENTED A CLEAN BREAK FROM THE ZORA ARKUS-DUNTOV-DESIGNED C3, WITH A COMPLETELY NEW CHASSIS AND SLEEKER, MORE MODERN BUT STILL EVOLUTIONARY STYLING. IT WAS THE WORK OF A TEAM UNDER CHIEF CORVETTE DESIGNER DAVE MCLELLAN, WHO'D TAKEN OVER FROM DUNTOV IN 1975. IN A DEPARTURE FROM THE FIBERGLASS PANELS OF ITS FOREBEARERS, THE C4'S REAR BUMPERS AND PANELS WERE MADE FROM MOLDING PLASTICS, A SHEET MOLDING COMPOUND. THE C4 FASTBACK COUPE WAS THE FIRST GENERAL PRODUCTION CORVETTE TO HAVE A GLASS HATCHBACK (THE LIMITED EDITION 1982 COLLECTOR EDITION BEING THE FIRST CORVETTE EQUIPPED WITH THIS FEATURE) FOR BETTER STORAGE ACCESS. THE ROOF PANEL MADE FROM FIBERGLASS OR OPTIONALLY FROM CLEAR ACRYLIC, WAS REMOVABLE. THE CORVETTE C4 CAME STANDARD WITH AN ELECTRONIC DASHBOARD WITH A DIGITAL LIQUID CRYSTAL DISPLAY INSTRUMENT CLUSTER. IT DISPLAYED A COMBINATION OF GRAPHICS AND DIGITAL FOR SPEED AND RPM, GRAPHICS FOR FUEL LEVEL, AND DIGITAL DISPLAYS FOR OTHER IMPORTANT ENGINE FUNCTIONS.

The 1985 Corvette L98 350 with Tuned Port Injection (TPI) was the blueprint for the '80s American sports car!
(Courtesy Brandon Fenty)

new Plastic Fantastic was on the right track, and not too shabby on most roads either.

Car and Driver's Csaba Csere said that *C/D*'s staff weren't blind to the new Corvette's problems. The good about the '84 Corvette, in *C/D*'s collective view, were: styling, high tech suspension parts, much improved interior accommodation, flexible/powerful V8 engine (L83 350), race track handling, Chevrolet's near clean sheet design. However, on the negative side of the ledger: C3 Corvette squeaks and rattles persisted, twitchy chassis, THM 700R4

automatic never in the right gear, harsh ride. In December 1984, *Road & Track* repeated its praise for the landmark '84 Corvette versus the body on frame, V8 front-engine, rear drive C3 Corvette of old, "... a careful application of high technology converted this simplistic layout into a state-of-the-art sports car."

Road & Track also acknowledged that the C4 Corvette could be improved upon. This journal had done a comparison report with the Nissan 300ZX Turbo in January 1984. Living with the two

SPECIAL ENGINEERING FEATURES

Much of the excitement in the Corvette relates directly to the many design and engineering features apparent throughout the car. Chevrolet believes a high-performance machine should also be a car its owner can live with comfortably and rely upon.

We offer an automatic 4-speed transmission with overdrive, as standard equipment.

Or, if you prefer, there's a 4-speed manual transmission with automatic overdrive on its top three gears, exclusive to Corvette. It's an option, but at no additional cost. Engineered with a hydraulically operated clutch at the front and a computer-controlled overdrive at the rear.

The basic feature of the hydraulic clutch is that it reduces shock-loading along the driveline during maximum acceleration from a standing start, and it also introduces damping similar to a shock absorber during quick shifts. The computer blocks out the overdrive during high-performance acceleration.

When the overdrive system is operating, a message is illuminated in the center of the dash panel. If you want total command of the manual transmission operation, there's an overdrive 'On/Off' switch on the center console.

The engineering of the Corvette goes far beyond transmissions that think, however. There's an induction system supplying air to the engine by a duct leading to a louvered plenum-type air cleaner behind the front facia. And stainless steel headers lead to an exhaust system that is carefully engineered to fit the undercarriage configuration, yet maintains the high-flow characteristics of the traditional Corvette dual exhaust.

There's more. The parking brake is located to the driver's left, which helps to reduce driveshaft tunnel width. For easy access to the cockpit, the handle retracts to the floor after the brake has been set. Little things. The glass is flush for better aerodynamics. From the coin holder in the console to the fully accessible fuse box location, the Corvette emphasizes convenience and serviceability.

Inspect the one-piece roof panel. Note how securely it fits. A specially designed new ratchet wrench is supplied for its removal. The top may be stored within the car and there's still room enough for a two-suiter in the luggage area. Even the top tool fits into a special retainer compartment.

The theft deterrent system has been specifically designed for Corvette. (Perhaps that information is more properly left for your perusal of the Owner's Manual.)

The list of innovative and practical design features is far longer than on most cars: halogen fog lamps, a designed-in body side molding to help prevent unsightly paint chips and scratches, a fuel tank access lid which provides a recessed area in which to set the removed gas cap so that paint isn't marred and hidden halogen headlamps that rotate open from a sealed compartment which shields them from under-car road spray.

The interior is ergonomically designed for optimal comfort, luxury, and driver control. Driving purists will appreciate all that, just getting in. Open the door, step over the beaming structure into the pilot's seat. A seat and belt system holds you in position, with upholstery support that molds and conforms to the contour of your body—like the fit of a good ski boot.

All this and more is precisely why Corvette is respected as so much more than the kind of road machine that it is. The 1985 Corvette is a designer's car, an engineer's car and, most important, an owner's car.

Integral halogen fog lamps operate independently of headlamps.

40

Advanced anti-theft system is standard.

Four-speed manual transmission features electronic overdrive in top three gears.

Removable transparent roof panel stores securely.

Powerful electric motors rotate the headlamps.

41

It may have looked the same as in 1984 but, with a new multi-point injected V8, softer suspension tune and revised LCD display, there was even more substance behind the Corvette's comely 1985 form.
(Courtesy GM Archives)

cars saw some of the awe for the Corvette rub off. For example, the 0.880g skid pad figure was incredible, but the cost to comfort to achieve it was less welcome. Improvements were done to the '84 Corvette, through its extended 1984 model year. For 1985 model year, this process of improvement continued apace on what appeared, at first glance, to be an identical coupe! You can't see suspension settings, and whether it was standard or Z51, the '85 Corvette rode softer.

Concerning a standard issue Corvette, the '85 coupe had front spring stiffness reduced 26%, and by 25% concerning rear springing. You could now option the FG3 Delco-Bilstein shocks, on the standard car. 9333 '85 Corvette buyers did just that, at a 189 buck surcharge. All 1985 Corvettes came with 9.5in wide vaned alloys, at each Corvette corner. These were combined with softer compound 16in Goodyear Eagle VR50 tires. The changes seemed to cure tracking wander, and standard Corvettes now even understeered a little, which was no bad thing. The 1985 RPO Z51 pack, came with standard '84 Corvette front spring rates, revalved shocks and bigger swaybars front and rear. As in Europe, softer springs and more reliance on the swaybars, to curb roll. John Heinricy had replaced Fred Schaafsma as head of Corvette development. Heinricy confessed there was only a limited time to recalibrate the suspension, so he and his staff focused on real world road driving when revalving the shocks.

The L83 350 had been judged powerful in '84 MY. It could make more power, as modifiers and the Renegade intake have shown, but not without a gas mileage and pollution penalty. On the '85 Corvette's front fender body seam, Cross Fire Injection script had given way to the words Tuned Port Injection (TPI). Under that C4 Corvette clamshell hood, the outside script change implied the new L98 350 V8. It was yet another evolutionary refinement, of Chevrolet's long standing small block V8, established 1955. The new stats were 230 horse at four grand, and 330lb/ft at 3200rpm. Just as important as the increases over the outgoing L83 350 was the fact the '85 Corvette still avoided the gas guzzler tax.

Fuel economy and pollution went hand in hand. That is, you drink less, you smog less. So, the new TPI system also applied to GM F body coupes with a 305 V8, and automatic transmission, for '85 MY. The Corvette now made more power for a given amount of gasoline and pollution. The indirect, multipoint electronic TPI set up was a Bosch-Rochester affair. Cold air induction fed a long plenum chamber, supplied by eight 21 x 1.5in curled under runners. A hot wire mass-air flow sensor (MAF) was employed, with the intake involving a dual plate throttle body, at the front of the aforementioned cast aluminum intake plenum. The long standing principle was of eight columns of air, stacked just above each intake port. The air columns pulsated, and were rammed in when the intake port opened.

Motor Week's John Davis likened TPI to turbocharging, sans the complexity. Like turbocharging, fuel injected engines are noted for more torque, and unlike turbocharging but like supercharging, TPI implied more bottom end pulling power. The heart of the TPI system was Bosch L-Jetronic computer controlled fuel injection. L-jet was a follow up to Bosch D-jet, which itself was inspired by the Bendix Electrojector system fitted to some Ramblers and Chrysler Corp cars in the late 1950s. Bosch D-jet observed intake manifold pressure, L-jet the amount of air aspirated. The latter started with a vanemeter box with moveable flap, and was seen on some imported cars from the mid '70s. In May 1977, *Car and Driver* carried a sidebar article called "Bosch L-Jetronic: Fuel Injection of the Future," noting the set up was currently only on the BMW 530i/630CSi, Datsun 810/280Z and VW Beetle.

L-jet could accept a Bosch Lambda Sond exhaust oxygen sensor, necessary for a three-way catalytic

The color was code 53 Gold Metallic, and you were golden with your new '85 Corvette. *Road & Track* said in December 1984, "Considering the improvements, it's a better deal in 1985 than it was in 1984." *(Courtesy GM Archives)*

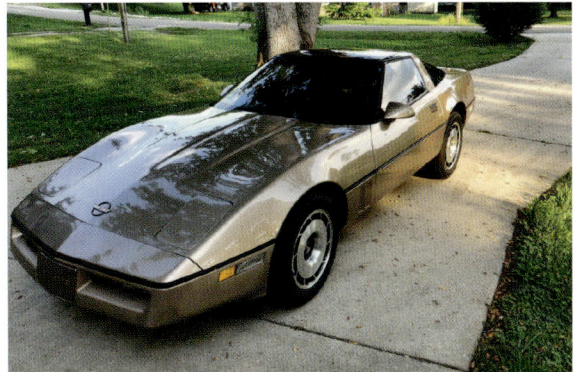

This is a 1985 Corvette L98 350, with NCO Doug Nash 4+3 stick shift. 9576 Corvette patrons signed up for manual labor with RPO MM4 in 1985. *(Courtesy Brandon Fenty)*

converter that could deal with oxides of nitrogen by keeping the air/fuel mixture at the efficient stoichiometric ratio of 14.5 parts air to one fuel. In the mid '80s, L-jet would be seen on Corvettes, and the Toyota Supra. Cross Fire Injection had also used a vanemeter, but TPI employed a hot wire air flow sensor. This Bosch component allowed air mass to be measured directly. A MAF sensor compared the electrical power needed to maintain the heated wire's temperature against a calibration map. The hot wire was less restrictive than a vanemeter. What's more, the TPI ECU had an electronically programmable, read only memory chip, or EPROM. This took GM's sporty cars into the power chip era. The swapable chip, 32k to start with, 128k from 1986 and 256k from 1990, had burned-in calibration maps for fuel flow, fuel cut off and ignition timing.

For 1990, GM switched to speed density TPI. Here, air density was more accurately measured from intake air temperature, rather than using the aforementioned hot wire. That is, MAF gave way to a MAP (Manifold Absolute Pressure) sensor. 1992 would be the final model year for TPI at GM. The tech upgrades implied a more responsive, powerful, while thriftier and cleaner, 350 V8. The TBI to TPI move was aided by the 1985 Corvette V8 having a higher compression ratio, now 9.5:1 from the L83 350's 9.0:1. What kind of gains came from the L83 350 to L98 350 move? Using *Road & Track* figures for automatic transmission equipped Corvettes, 0-60mph dropped from 7.0 to 6.2 seconds, with a ¼-mile improvement from 15.3 to 14.6 seconds. Team Corvette's John Heinricy said top speed was a mite over 150mph, so figure a 10mph gain over the 1984 Corvette. The three aforementioned performance parameters involve a continuous, sustained application of power. That is, not the short bursts seen in real world driving. So, little surprise that *Car and Driver*'s Csaba Csere, when trying 1985 Corvette prototypes at Firebird Raceway in Phoenix Arizona, said the L98 TPI 350's advantage over the L83 TBI 350 was

Corvette's LCD instrument display involved larger, brighter visuals with less color for '85 MY. It's a popular retrofit on '84 Corvettes. The C4 Corvette LCD display adds to this generation's '80s vibe, and is beloved by many. *(Courtesy Brandon Fenty)*

The Doug Nash 4+3 stick shift was supposed to have its 'on-off' console rocker switch become a shifter mounted button for '85 MY, but the changeover was tardy. *(Courtesy Brandon Fenty)*

The '85 Corvette sat 0.75in closer to terra firma versus 1984. It was enough to lower the coupe's drag factor from 0.340 to 0.330; another part of evading the gas guzzler tax. *(Courtesy Brandon Fenty)*

more noticeable on a track than in road driving. However, Csere said the L98 350 still choked by five grand. That is, the Corvette's 350 V8 was still biased towards torque and real world scat!

Corvette gearbox choices remained the THM 700R4 four-speed automatic, seen in 1982-84. However, for 1985 there were electronic recalibrations concerning shifting, and when torque converter lock up occurred. Shifting was smoother now, with reduced gearbox ratio hunting. You could also now shift between D-2-1 positions, sans detent button engagement. The NCO Doug Nash 4+3 stick shift was also to hand, with its electronics refined so that overdrive wouldn't engage so readily. Plus, the previous console rocker switch, which turned the Doug Nash 4+3's OD on or off, became a button on the shifter. That said, *Motor Week* disclosed that its February '85 built Corvette, still had the console toggle. On a related note, Chevrolet increased the size of the differential's ring gear from 7.9in to 8.5in for '85 MY. The Doug Nash box had long implied

a near half-second penalty in both 0-60mph and ¼-mile times, versus the Corvette's automatic. Even so, stalwart Corvette engineer Jim 'Jingles' Ingle demonstrated that speed shifting would enable a Corvette with Doug Nash stick shift to out accelerate its slushbox counterpart.

Road & Track didn't recommend changing gear sans clutch, even if the ring gear was now beefier. Only prudence would prevent a stranded Corvette, and a walk back home! As before, your Corvette's automatic ratios were 3.06/1.63/1.00/0.70. The Doug Nash 4+3 box brought ratios: 2.88 (first) 1.91 (second) 1.28 (second+OD) 1.33 (third) 0.89 (third+OD) 1.00 (fourth) 0.67 (fourth+OD). Given the '85 Corvette's extra torque, and, with a view to maximize gas mileage to dodge the gas guzzler tax, the stock axle ratio was made taller, from 2.87 to 2.72. However, the 3.31 G92 performance axle was still an option. Corvette dimensions for 1985 were still 176.5in length/71in width and 46.7in height. Definitely not a GT40! Weight for *Road & Track*'s

December '84 tested Corvette L98 350 4+3 speed was 3280lb. The '85 Corvette was officially 0.75in lower, which reduced the drag coefficient from 0.340 to 0.330.

Lower drag spelt better gas mileage, but even so, rumors abounded concerning the C4 Corvette's early demise. In August 1985, *Popular Science*'s Jim Dunne mentioned the possibility of an all new Corvette for 1988 model year. Speculation was of Emtech of England, helping with the engineering development of a 2500lb, mid-engine Corvette V6 two-seater, which retained rear wheel drive. Emtech helped to do the hot selling to that point in time, mid-engine Pontiac Fiero two-seater. Dunne explained why this might happen, "Today's 3200-pound Corvette is too heavy to deliver outstanding performance along with fuel economy that beats the federal government's gas-guzzler limit." [93]

It didn't happen of course, but there was a counterpoint movement to the Detroit wide 'econobox mantra' that once predicted that soon everyone would be driving a four-cylinder, front drive hatchback. In 1983 Lee Iacocca said that in a sea of K cars, Chrysler's old school rear drive, V8 M car, happened to be the corporation's best seller. [94] By 1984, the nation's top selling passenger car was the Olds Cutlass, a member of the rear drive, oftentimes V8 powered, downsized separate chassis G body, that GM introduced for 1978 and would continue through '87 MY. Then too, in 1985 Ford said it would be retaining its rear drive, separate chassis Panther platform, which had arrived for 1979. It was FoMoCo's belated downsized response to GM's smaller big cars of 1977, which were built on the B body platform. Rear drive and V8 power was still selling, it seemed Big Three buyers still fancied the traditional route. However, a Ford insider said plans could change tomorrow, depending on gas prices.

As it turned out, econoboxes and gas prices were on the decline. The Reagan administration saw no need to hold to the original CAFE aim of 27.5mpg

Road & Track tested an '85 Corvette L98 350 Doug Nash 4+3-speed in December 1984. Zero to sixty happened in 6.6 seconds, with a 15 second flat ¼-mile at 91mph. Top speed for the 3280lb coupe was estimated at 149mph. *(Courtesy Brandon Fenty)*

The big Corvette news for 1985, and for the GM F body, was Tuned Port Injection or TPI. For Corvette it meant 230bhp at four grand, and 330lb/ft at 3200rpm. *(Courtesy Brandon Fenty)*

What looked like a ninth injector on early TPI L98 350 and LB9 305 V8s was a cold start valve for choke action. This L98 350, would be Corvette's only factory fit engine during 1985-89, and standard engine during 1990-91. *(Courtesy Brandon Fenty)*

for 1985. So, the C4 Corvette and high performance renaissance matched the improving '80s economy. The Corvette was always a combination of traditional and modern simultaneously. It retained its V8 rear drive credo, plus a larger, brighter and clearer LCD display with less color, for 1985. All part of the many small improvements seen from Corvette since 1953. 1985's not so minutiae, included stiffer sun visor frames, and more tinting for the Targa panel. The multi adjustable super seat from Lear-Siegler was now available in full cowhide! Concerning the serious business of driving, the '85 Corvette featured more fade resistant brake pads, one more degree of steering caster (now four degrees), bigger plastic master cylinder and more powerful brake servo action. More aluminum engine parts and ABS were still under development. In short, the '85 Corvette was well suited to the SCCA's new Showroom Stock GT category. That included a revised RPO V08 HD cooling system for the Z51 package.

Limited options

BY 1985 STANDARDS, especially imported car selections, the $24,403 '85 Corvette got one from A to B quicker than many could believe, even with an Alpine switchback in between! A lot of options, AG9 power driver seat, AU3 power door locks, K34

cruise control and Z6A rear window/side mirror defogger, adding a respective $215, $170, $185 and $160, were fitted to most of the 39,729 '85 Corvettes sold. 35,998 buyers couldn't do without the optional $895 UU8 Delco-Bose stereo either. Therefore, the latest Corvette was really a 26 grand automobile. Although very capable, that was pricy for a domestic. However, Corvette still provided the world's most advanced four-speed as a NCO, and other serious hardware befitting the hallowed nameplate.

FG3 Delco-Bilstein shocks were $189, chosen by 9333 '85 Corvette buyers, 5477 paid 22 bucks for the G92 performance axle ratio (3.31). 17,539 buyers ticked RPO V08 HD cooling at $225, with 14,802 going for the $470 Z51 Performance Handling Package, which included V08. Over half of '84 Corvette folk tried the Z51 route, but a much lower number and percentage went with the option in 1985. The standard '85 Corvette suspension was already excellent. Stories of Z51's hard living nature were also already abound.

On the cosmetic side, D84 two-tone paint ran you $428, for 6033 1985 Corvette buyers. Color combinations were: code 13/18 Silver/Gray, 20/23 Light Blue/Medium Blue and 63/66 Light Bronze/ Dark Bronze. There was something to be said for combining the Corvette's long standing white

At the Monrovia Maryland 75-80 Dragway, *Motor Week*'s 1985 Corvette automatic did " … an incredible … " 13.9 second pass at 95mph, according to host John Davis. *(Courtesy Brandon Fenty)*

exterior with red leather interior. For 1985, that would be a respective code 40 White exterior, and code 742 Carmine Leather. The latter was the only interior color available in leather alone. Otherwise, one had a choice of standard seat with cloth insert, sport seat with cloth insert or leather, in colors: code 12 Graphite, code 15 Medium Gray, code 28 Medium Blue, code 62 Saddle, or code 65 Bronze. Respective material suffix for cloth/sport seat cloth/ leather were C/V/2.

As for tunes, only 172 buyers undertook the UL5 radio delete and the $256 credit which followed. A mere 16 Corvette faithful paid $215 for RPO UN8 AM-FM stereo/CB radio. 1985 was the final year, that one could obtain Citizen's Band radio in a Corvette. At one time, even the Caddy Seville, carried a factory CB option. So too, the AMC Eagle Kammback! Unfortunately, the Smokey and The Bandit/trucker CB handle craze had passed. So too, the era of an extensive Corvette options list.

It seemed the '85 Corvette already had the right stuff as standard. Exterior color was now your main choice, and like in 1984, Bright Red was most popular, with 10,424 coupes so hued. Black and then white followed as the next popular Corvette colors in 1985.

Stunning performance & quality snafus

IN LATE 1984, *Road & Track*'s John Lamm penned a piece on Europe's pending 1990 smog law, in light of America's post-1975 experience. From initial fears of forest fires courtesy of hot cats, and sulphur filled streets for the same reason, came the modern miracle monolith honeycomb interior, three-way catalytic converter, exhaust oxygen sensor and corrective signal back to the ECU. The result was an '85 US spec 16-valve Saab Turbo, only 10% weaker than its European spec counterpart. Lamm said a colleague commented that cats were now considered as much as light bulbs! Concluding, John Lamm mentioned the German Black Forest,

Los Angeles' pine forests and noted, "It's a matter of priorities," in an article that could have been construed as a tree hugger call to arms! [95] Lamm failed to mention the long decade of suffering whereupon early smog controlled V8s with pellet cats and carbs performed weaker, thirstier and less reliably than their pre-1975 counterparts. Plus, being wedded to unleaded gas could make filling up expensive, and/or troublesome. This was certainly so during the 1979/80 gas crunch. It would have been handy at that time to have been able to fill up with leaded regular during the gas shortages. However, 1984 and 1985 Corvettes were at the forefront of driving out of the malaise era.

Press praise for the '85 Corvette was plentiful. *Road & Track* titled its December 1984 report "1985 Chevrolet Corvette Smoother, faster and better than ever." Adding, "An improved ride and more power elevate its world-class status," and concluding with, "Considering the improvements, it's a better deal in 1985 than it was in 1984." The performance, and its manner, really socked it to *R&T*, who even found something good to say about the awkward, long

The '85 Corvette's 39,729 coupe total was lower than the 1984 Corvette's tally.
However, the '84 Corvette ran for nearly 18 months! *(Courtesy Brandon Fenty)*

throw Doug Nash 4+3 stick shift. Wind up to five grand in second gear, let off the gas and, "Zounds, the sound is magnificent." [96] The '85 Corvette's 230bhp matched the US spec Ferrari 308 GTBi Quattrovalvole, and *R&T*'s 0-60mph and ¼-mile figures for the '85 Corvette and Porsche 911 Carrera 3.2-liter, tested in February 1984, were identical. That is, a respective 6.2 and 14.6 seconds.

Base prices for Porsche and Corvette were a respective $31,950 and $24,403. Both were much lower than the 55 grand Pantera GTS. However, the by now 14 second flat Pantera was a gray market special, with toxic Cleveland 351 V8. The *R&T* '85 Corvette tested showed an identical 0.880g skid pad result, but the latest Corvette's 61.8mph slalom speed was nearly 1.5mph slower than *R&T*'s '84 Corvette with comparable Z51 pack and Doug Nash 4+3 box. That said, echoing other reports, *Road & Track* said, "From a handling standpoint the Corvette is so responsive that you can practically will it to go where you want." [97]

Car and Driver joined in the 1985 Corvette love fest, with one staffer entering the following logbook statement: "This car makes you want to drive fast. District court, here we come!" [98] Look to handling, engine torque, rumbly exhaust and a pop top two-seater, nowhere else could one find such performance and personality for under 40 grand. It was enough to put Corvette in *C/D*'s 'Ten Best Cars' list in 1984, 1985 and 1986! *C/D*'s figures for its 3272lb '85 Corvette automatic were top flight too. Zero to sixty in 5.6 seconds, 0-100mph in 15.7 seconds, a 14.1 second ¼-mile at 97mph, 70-0mph in 188ft, 0.84g on the skid pad and 151mph top speed! What's more, the Corvette gripped the road like Velcro, and improved that skid pad reading to 0.87g on a re-test of the same car at 30,000 miles, with softer compound Goodyear Gatorbacks. Stopping distance fell to 166ft, but acceleration times were slightly slower, and top speed was also a little lower.

With the limited number of options, you might have thought one '85 Corvette was much like

another? Yes and no, as *Motor Week* proved in 1985 with its comparison of two 1985 Corvettes, or, in host John Davis' words, "Our unmatched pair of America's premier sports car." Specifically, one '85 code 81 Bright Red automatic Corvette with standard suspension, weighing 3300lb, and another '85 Corvette with Doug Nash 4+3 stick shift, Z51 pack and code 13 Silver Metallic exterior. Contrary to expectations, the stick shift coupe was 35lb heavier. At Monrovia Marylands' 75-80 Dragway, both coupes let it all hang out on the 1320ft dash. On take off, the silver coupe's low first gear and L98 350 torque spelt wheelspin, but the manual transmission Corvette still got an edge out of the hole.

By the first third of the drag strip, the red coupe's front bumper was level with the silver coupe's door. However, from there on in, the long throws of the Doug Nash 4+3 box, versus the slushbox coupe's loose torque converter working with all that V8 torque, saw both Corvettes even steven by two thirds of the track. In the end, the red coupe ran out the winner with, "an incredible" 13.9 second

¼-mile at 95mph, while the stick shift silver job managed a 14.2 second pass at 93mph. Those low elapsed times and trap speeds highlighted the L98 350's big torque but limited top end. That is, it reached a given speed mighty quick!

MW found both '85 Corvettes to ride much more comfortably than their 1984 counterparts. Even the Z51 equipped silver coupe was fine on the roughest roads. In extreme racing and track conditions, the Z51 coupe was more composed. No axle tramp in braking, and no momentary loss of grip when encountering rough spots on the track. In fact, in six stops from 55mph the automatic and stick shift Corvettes managed an average of 103ft and 100ft respectively. They represented some of the shortest stops that *MW* had recorded. That said, the Z51 coupe's 1.9 turns lock-to-lock steering was almost too quick. This Corvette was less forgiving on bumpy turns in real world driving. Then too, although this silver coupe was a hoot to drive, the clutch did get tiresome in stop and go city traffic.

Motor Week's conclusion was that unless you were going to track run your Corvette regularly, or were some super sport purist, the standard automatic transmission red coupe was the way to go, "And whether you pick the standard suspension or Z51, manual or automatic, you're in for one heck of a ride!" *MW*'s John Davis was clearly more impressed with the 1985 Corvette than the 1984 iteration. It seemed the entire automotive press were in agreement, plus a Z51 equipped '85 Corvette was more neutral than a Swiss mountain dog! However, no car is perfect, and *Car and Driver*'s 30,000 mile long term test of an '85 Corvette, showed that unbridled passion must sometimes be tempered by reality.

Car and Driver's Rich Ceppos made the pilgrimage to Bowling Green, Kentucky. His mission was to pick up *C/D*'s long term test coupe: code 66 Dark Bronze Metallic '85 Corvette automatic license plate 342EPD. Said Corvette arrived at *Car and Driver* on January 11 1985, whereupon it delighted and troubled *C/D* staff, although on balance the joy was greater than the sorrow, even if the report's subtitle read, "A 30,000-mile trial culminates in a hung jury." For starters, the 1985 Corvette seemed higher quality, due to the softer suspension it rattled less. However, as *C/D*'s long term test car

logbook showed, the body groans and squeaks still increased with mileage. That said, let it be noted that when *Motor Week* tried the '84 Corvette, most of the 74 decibels at 55mph, came from exhaust rumble. There was no wind racket around the Targa top.

Car and Driver discovered with age and mileage, too much stuff went wrong with this '85 Corvette. More so than you would expect from a car of this price. At 19,511 miles, a rough running V8 required a replacement coil and ignition module, the door locks were stiff, a window leaked, there was a loose seat cushion and the heater was on the fritz. Fortunately, *C/D* got the Corvette to 25,000 miles, prior to warranty expiration. Therefore, the above mentioned foibles were fixed gratis. That said, under the magazine's watch the test Corvette made six unscheduled dealership visits to get stuff rectified. This prompted *C/D*'s Arthur St Antoine to write, "A car that costs nearly $30,000 shouldn't burden its owner with the problems out test car had." [99]

Road & Track had a similar experience with the '84 Corvette versus the Nissan 300ZX Turbo. However, you had to weigh up the Corvette's characterful enjoyment against the Nissan's quality with blandness. Oftentimes, the problems with enthusiast cars, the fragility of the Mazda FD RX7, unreliability of the Jag XJS, and annoyance of Corvette, are more than compensated for by fun that you never could have got from a Toyota Camry. As *C/D*'s Arthur St Antoine said, in deciding to buy a Corvette, "We wish you the best of luck in your own soul searching."

Concerning *Car and Driver*'s long term report, located in one storage bin of the test coupe was found wedged several old GM repair orders, with the test coupe's VIN. It seemed this Corvette had been checked out several times, and repaired at GM's Milford Proving Ground. It had a transmission swap, and had accrued at least 250 miles on the odometer, prior to *C/D* getting the car. *Car and Driver* always requests a factory fresh car for its long term tests. Not the usual "prepared car" of brief tests. There was no response from Chevrolet on the matter. Had the torque converter been tricked up? This had happened, and been revealed by Marty Schorr, concerning a '76 Corvette L82 350 automatic, sampled by *High Performance Cars* in December

1976. *Car and Driver* still regarded its long term test '85 Corvette as typical of the breed. That said, the episode suggests late '70s ringers could have given an overly favorable performance impression.

GM for '86

MOTOR WEEK WAS greatly impressed by the nearly all new C4 Corvette, with host John Davis concluding, "You have to say that if it's representative of Detroit's advanced thinking for its more pedestrian models, then the future looks good for the American auto industry." And a need for improvement, in the face of foreign competition, was very necessary. Examples of market misses weren't hard to find. For one, the Cadillac version of the GM J car, called Cimarron. Aimed at the Audi 4000 and BMW 320i, the littlest Caddy wasn't ready on release, but did improve. Similarly, the Chevrolet Citation, and its GM X car siblings were quality deficient on debut. However, waiting lists arose, especially for V6 editions. It was because families desired the fuel and space efficient front drive family cars of the '80s, right now!

The quality and reputation of GM's X cars did get better, but the model family concluded badly. There was public outrage concerning the X car's propensity to lock rear brakes. 1985 was the final model year for the GM X car. Although the Buick Skylark nameplate lived on, the Citation and other X car reminders were quietly consigned to history. (100) Many car enthusiasts were thinking back fondly, to those good ol' V8, rear drive days, and found them, in the GM G body Olds Cutlass. That said, even here *Motor Week*'s 1984 Olds 307 V8 edition of the nation's most popular passenger car nameplate displayed misaligned trim and badges that fell off!

GM's very new luxury sedans for 1986 were more than hopeful. Fullsize, front drive, bigger on the inside, smaller on the outside, and up to 700lb lighter than outgoing models. Four wheel independent suspension, unibody construction, and four door styling reminiscent of the Volvo 700 series. The Olds Toronado had been front drive since its 1965 debut, but for the first time there was no V8. Sole choice being the Buick injected 3.8-liter V6, or GM family engine in '80s parlance. The old

divisional distinctions were being played down for powerplants. Only Cadillac was permitted to retain its own V8 design in this crowd, the all alloy 4.1-liter job. Drag coefficient was 0.34, and there was an emphasis on handling.

Olds chief engineer Ted Louckes said the optional third level suspension gave the Toronado handling equal to a Porsche 928, Mercedes 380SL or BMW 633CSi. Buick chief engineer Dave Sharpe, said the Riviera's top suspension was in the 0.84-0.85g skid pad range. Almost as good as Corvette, and better than a Porsche 928. High class import benchmarking was in evidence. Corvette too was an example of an ultimate level of ability. It seemed that where the Plastic Fantastic had gone, other GM cars would follow. Indeed, the Cadillac switched from TBI to Bosch sequential TPI. What's more, GM's new Toronado, Riviera, Le Sabre, Eldorado and Seville clan, featured a single transverse plastic leaf spring, for the rear suspension. Imitation is the sincerest form of flattery, concerning something the Corvette had shown to work from 1981. (101)

The Pontiac nameplate would join this high tech ensemble in 1987. Buick CRT displays, and the latest Olds Toronado's digital instrumentation also seemed to take the C4 Corvette's lead. So too GM's push for international performance with its latest sedans featuring compact front springs for a low hood line, sourced from Hoesch of West Germany. However, some of GM's sourcing was raising the ire of regulators, Big Four compatriots, and the UAW. The act was backdoor importing. GM had a big stake in Suzuki and Isuzu, bringing in the respective Chevrolet Sprint and Spectrum, that weren't really Chevrolets. However, they allowed GM to make money selling small cars in America without incurring the low profit margin, if any, of making such subcompacts using UAW labor.

There was a 1.85 million unit import quota agreed between America and Japan, for 1981 to 1985. GM worked its influence with the Reagan administration to lift such limits. To circumvent the problem, GM got into a deal with Daewoo, one day to become GM of Korea, to build a version of the Opel Kadett. Opel would rework the small sedan slightly for the US market, creating the Pontiac Le Mans. Pontiac would handle a very mild restyle, federal safety and smog compliance. America had no quota restrictions with South Korea, and Daewoo's labor cost was only a sixth of that of the UAW. So good times for one and all! The Korean Le Mans was a stopgap measure while GM developed the technology to make small car production economically viable Stateside with its Saturn program. A program delayed by cost blowouts. [102]

Japanese companies were also anxious to get around quota limits by making cars in America. So, GM paired with Toyota, creating New United Motor Manufacturing Inc. Its job was to build the Chevrolet Nova in California. Not the Nova of old, but a Toyota Corolla! Similar tie ups between Chrysler Corp and Mitsubishi with Diamond Star Motors, and Ford/Mazda with the Probe/MX6 in Flint Rock, Michigan. Even Renault was making its Renault 9 at Kenosha, courtesy of AMC. The result was the AMC/Renault Alliance. [103]

Mirroring the experience of British Leyland, putting together a Honda in the early '80s under license for the Triumph Acclaim, the Japanese origin Chevrolet Nova had the lowest warranty claims of any GM car. It was believed Japanese engineers had designed such cars so they were easier to assemble. Using US labor, and a good percentage of local parts, quality was still high. The C4 Corvette was no low ball subcompact. The Corvette nameplate had been profitable since 1958. However, its constructional nature always challenged build quality.

Even the Corvette's current Uniframe wasn't the pure unit construction found on most cars. However, the Corvette wasn't most cars, and it seemed that car design by the mid '80s was walking away from the World Car concept. Toyota Corolla aside, automakers seemed less interested in putting a vast amount of design money into a one size fits all vehicle, like the GM X and J cars. There was a rising belief that more specialized designs, to meet national tastes, were the way to go. What's more, smaller specialist automakers could survive, with the predicted future of a few mega producers now not so likely, at this hour anyway. Jaguar, BMW, Volvo and Saab, had been doing very well, Saab exceptionally so during 1983 and 1984. Indeed, it was thought that Europe's lead in technology and design was necessary to stave off Japanese competition. Like Saab, the Corvette was a long time niche player, aimed at

enthusiasts. For 1986, the Plastic Fantastic's familiar evolutionary tale continued. [104]

Corvette for '86

SO OFTEN, THE press makes feature announcements for the next model year that eventually come late, or not at all. Not so concerning the 1986 Corvette. In 1985, when *Motor Week* observed two different '85 Corvettes, John Davis mentioned what was in store for the '86 Corvette. For starters, a sneak look at a white prototype, with a small light bar, integrated into the top of the Corvette's hatchback door. The feature was a federally mandated measure. It looked designed in on Corvette, and tacked on when it came to imports. *MW*'s illustration of a white '86 Corvette, with an in-motion flash of red light bar looked attractive.

Other promises that came to pass for the 1986 Corvette were a convertible body and ABS (anti lock brakes). The former feature had been absent since 1975, and the latter Bosch ABS II system was a Corvette first. Although computer controlled anti lock rear brakes were seen on the 1970 Lincoln Continental Mk III. With fears of federal rollover tests receding, domestic and imported ragtops soon returned, after years of Targa and T-tops. However, this time around a Corvette roadster was pricier than its coupe counterpart. In the old days of separate chassis Corvettes, the ragtop was cheaper, because you literally got less car! Part of the body was missing. In the absence of a traditional frame, the C4 Corvette's Uniframe had to be beefed up in places, to regain coupe structural rigidity.

The 1986 RPO 1YY07 Corvette Sport Coupe, to give the model its full billing, started from $27,027, but the RPO 1YY67 Corvette convertible was $32,032. The two variants had respective totals of 27,794 coupes sold, and 7315 ragtops. It made for a 1986 Corvette grand total of 35,109. That was pretty much the same sales rate as the 18 month long '84 Corvette. For the convertible conversion, Team Corvette went to the much respected ASC (American Sunroof Corporation). ASC had also done the Foxstang's ragtop, ditto the Porsche 944. With the Corvette, a reinforced frame crossmember now lived in front of the V8 motor. There were also

In an unprecedented move, Chevrolet honored top Corvette selling dealer, New Jersey's
Malcolm Konner, with a commemorative C4 Corvette in 1986! *(Courtesy Mecum)*

larger X braces tying door hinge pillars to the rear chassis torque boxes. There was also a crossbeam to said torque boxes. K braces were now larger, and connected the under engine member to the Uniframe rails. The cowl was beefed up, same for the steering column area and mounts. There was a dashboard mounted beam connected to the front torque boxes, plus a steel rider behind the Corvette's seats for a double walled structure. A presentation boot covered the convertible's top when stowed, and the federal central rear brake light was relocated to the center of the rear bumper fascia molding. The weight increase over a Corvette coupe was just 50 pounds!

You couldn't have Z51 with an '86 Corvette convertible. Too much shake, rattle and roll otherwise. However, the new Corvette convertible was still fast enough to pace the 1986 Indianapolis 500, with no less than Chuck Yeager at the wheel! Although the 1986 Corvette couldn't break the sound barrier, like Yeager's Bell X-1 jet, the standard Corvette powertrain was more than capable of meeting Indianapolis Motor Speedway's requirements. Pace car changes were modest: strobe lights, five-point racing harness for both buckets, and onboard fire suppression system.

Pace cars at the 1986 Indy 500 were code 35 Yellow. However, the Corvette convertible pace car that you could buy could have been any color. A door decal package was included with the 7315 RPO 1YY67 Corvette convertibles sold. Modesty permitting, the Chevrolet dealership could affix said decals. That said, there was no special 1986 Corvette Convertible Indy 500 Pace Car model, as such, not beyond the aforementioned RPO 1YY67 ragtop designation. All 1986 Corvette convertibles were deemed Indy Pace Car replicas. However, 1986 did have a standalone, special Corvette model package.

Back in those halcyon Corvette glory days of the '60s and '70s, one specialist Corvette dealer stood out from the madding crowd: Malcolm Konner. Konner's Chevrolet dealership in Paramus, New Jersey focused on selling Corvettes, and sold more Corvettes than any other Chevrolet dealership in the nation! Such commercial success went hand in hand with Malcolm Konner building up a number of close personal relationships with Bow Tie brass over the years. Konner passed away in 1983. His family asked GM if a special Corvette could be made, honoring Malcolm Konner's life. This had never been done before, so Konner's family were pleasantly surprised when GM said yes!

Konner had a close relationship with top GM brass through the '60s and '70s. The commemorative edition Corvette bearing Konner's name carried RPO code 4001ZA. There was a 500 buck surcharge for the 50 coupes involved. *(Courtesy Mecum)*

RPO 4001ZA implied the 'Malcolm Konner Special Edition Paint Package', costing $500 over Corvette base list (RPO 1YY07 = $27,027), and concerned 50 coupes. This collectible coupe involved a Silver Beige Metallic (code 59) over Black (code 41), two-tone interior, plus code 122 Graphite Leather interior. Of the 50 special coupes, 30 had automatic transmission, 20 came with the Doug Nash 4+3 stick shift. Ten manual transmission cars had the Z51 package, and a like number of automatic 1986 Corvette Malcolm Konner Special Edition Paint coupes were so specified with Z51. One of the lesser known Corvette collectibles, but an appreciating asset nevertheless. Special badging bearing Malcolm Konner's name was also in evidence.

As had been the case since 1981 model year, the Corvette implied a single engine choice for 1986. That said, L98 350 was upgraded during the model year. Early '86 Corvettes came with the same all cast iron, OHV small block L98 350 seen in 1985. However, soon this 230bhp unit was revised into 235bhp form with aluminum heads, with larger intake ports and sintered metal valve seats. Mid '86 MY saw such aluminum heads become thicker castings to combat a cracking problem that had surfaced around the attachment bosses. This revised 235bhp 350, had centrally placed, copper core sparkplugs.

The now more powerful L98 350, had to face stricter federal smog law for 1986. This entailed triple catalytic converters! CAFE guidelines, and a perpetual desire to skirt the gas guzzler tax, saw

a new upshift economy dashboard light, on both stick shift and slushbox '86 Corvettes! Buyers considered this idiot light unnecessary. There were also warning lights for low coolant, and operation of the Corvette's newly offered and standard, Bosch ABS brakes. To aid straight line stability at speed, steering caster was raised from 3.8 to 6 degrees. Indeed, back in the early '70s, Chevrolet engineers had been inspired by the handling of their general manager's Mercedes, and gave the Monte Carlo's steering lots of caster, to mimic the West German Merc's high speed stability.

To further help with controlling Corvette, the dashboard's LCD display was re-angled, and the standard Corvette tire size was upped from 235/VR50-16, to 245VR50-16s. However, the Z51's 255 section rubber remained. The C4 Corvette's vaned alloys continued, but with raised hub emblems possessing a bright brushed finish, in place of 1984-85's black centers.

In terms of more frequent fill ups, the automatic Corvette had its gas tank size reduced by two gallons. However, other parameters showed the '86 Corvette to offer more, and be more desirable. For example, it was the first time alloy heads were standard since 1969's C3 Corvette L88/L89/ZL1 427. All of this has prompted commentators to say what tremendous value the '86 Corvette represented, as a classic collector car. IRS, TPI, alloy heads, four-wheel ABS disk brakes etc. Some of which were retrofitted, via the aftermarket, to old Chevelles and the like, at great expense. They were standard on Corvette! Then too, it seemed the C4 Corvette's ubiquity and durability would keep market values low for a while yet.

Back in 1986, the Corvette seemed more coveted than ever, and that implied the Corvette's long standing achilles heel: vehicle theft. The 1984-85 Corvette experienced a 7% theft rate. Team Corvette had a solution for '86 MY, called VATS (Vehicle Anti Theft System), with a pass-key, all standard. The set up had a small metal pellet, with a specific electrical resistance in the ignition key, read by a concealed electronic decoder. Should a nefarious individual try to purloin one's Corvette, VATS would shut down the starter relay and fuel pump for two minutes. It was enough to cut the Corvette's theft rate to under 1% in 1986. For the '87 Corvettes, theft percentage fell further, to almost zero. VATS invited lower insurance premiums in the short run. In the long run, VATS could develop electrical gremlins, stopping a Corvette from starting. The result is owners disabling the system.

As with any modern car, Corvette complexity was increasing, while options declined. Performance options of interest included RPO B4P. This brought a 75 buck radiator boost fan, chosen by 8216 1986 Corvette faithful. FG3 Delco-Bilstein shocks, KC4 engine oil cooler, NCO MM4 four-speed, VO1 HD radiator, Z51 pack and G92 performance axle ratio were the usual options. For that last item, 22 bucks supplied a 3.07 axle to 4879 buyers, flirting with CAFE to get more action off the line!

The Corvette had long offered comfort and convenience features. For '86 MY this implied RPO C68 climate control a/c, and B4Z Custom Feature Package. For both appearance and function, there were now three new fresh air options. Apart from ragtop, RPO 2CL dual removable roof panels, costing $895, and chosen by 6242 buyers. At $595, respective RPOs 245 and 645 brought blue or bronze tint Targa panels. The blue tint was much more popular than bronze, 12,021 buyers versus 7819 coupes with bronze tint. $428 D84 two-tone paint for Corvette coupe provided four choices outside the Malcolm Konner Commemorative Edition Corvette, but there were a mere 3897 takers in 1986.

For exterior colors, Bright Red (code 81) was still tops in C4 Corvette land, with 9466 '86 Corvettes so painted. Second most popular was code 74 Dark Red Metallic, followed by former respective second and third placements, black and white. Concerning interior, red still implied leather only, and was coded 732. It wasn't called Carmine anymore, simply Red Leather. However, of key concern with a performance car, is the level of said performance. *Autocar* magazine could see an improvement, compared to the 1984 Corvette Z51 equipped automatic it had tried earlier in Belgium. That '84 coupe was judged fast and frugal, but with a harsh ride that upset handling and stability on imperfect surfaces. Steering was judged too quick and lacking in feel. Overall refinement was poor, but luggage space was judged generous. Similarly, *Autocar* considered the Nissan 300ZX Turbo to be

Malcolm Konner special paint meant code 59 Silver Beige over code 41 Black. 20 coupes had the Doug Nash 4+3 stick shift. Ten Doug Nash 4+3 shifted coupes had Z51, and so did ten automatic Corvettes. *(Courtesy Mecum)*

rough but quick, but neither as quick, nor as fast as the '84 Corvette. Once again, overall refinement was lacking.

With the '86 Corvette, *Autocar* found an improved coupe, which it tested with the Doug Nash 4+3 stick shift and Z51 pack, in its November 13 1985 issue. The latest assessment was, "European ability from the US bruiser." [105] A Bright Red '86 Corvette made *Autocar*'s cover, with a 150mph headline, which was verified on test. Indeed, the Corvette had increased its performance margin over the Nissan 300ZX Turbo, while almost matching the fastest cars Europe had to offer, from past and present. Namely, the Ferrari Testarossa's predecessor, the Berlinetta Boxer 512, as well as a toxic Pantera from the very early days. The current Porsche 911 Carrera 3.2 and BMW M635CSi, in full European spec, were of equal performance. For such testing, the Corvette was running 'open loop'. That is, not seeing oxygen sensors or cats, for the Corvette was in European export guise, sans cats.

Since the Europe/UK region didn't have unleaded gas readily available until 1990, GM's post-1974 cat equipped cars went without the fancy filter when exported. *Autocar*'s test weight for their Doug Nash 4+3 equipped Corvette was only 3173lb. This was helped by the new aluminum heads, claimed to cut 125lb versus the L98 350's previous cast iron equivalents. With soft alloy heads, it pays to put anti seize lubricant around the sparkplugs, because they can become stuck with heat and time. Compared to the '84 Corvette that *Autocar* tried in its April 14 1984 issue, the '86 Corvette was 0.6 seconds quicker to sixty, 0.6 seconds quicker from 50 to 70mph, 9mph faster on top speed, and 0.9mpg (UK gallon) more frugal. In fact, the latest Corvette had the exact same overall gas mileage as the Lotus Esprit Turbo that *Autocar* had featured in its December 19 1984 issue. You could say the 1986 Corvette was well up to speed!

Autocar performance data 1972-89

Model	Top speed (mph)	0-60mph (sec)	50-70mph (sec)	mpg	Test date
Ferrari BB512	163	6.2	3.1	15.7	05/06/78
DeTomaso Pantera	159	6.2	3.5	13.0	12/14/72
'86 Corvette L98 DN 4+3	151	6.0	3.4	17.6	11/13/85
Porsche 911 Carrera 3.2L	150	5.4	3.6	22.2	12/24/83
BMW M635CSi	150	6.0	9.3 (5th)	20.6	01/18/89

'80s family cars

BY THE CLOSE of 1986, over 110 million Chevrolets had been built since the company started 75 years earlier. [106] The firm had taken the populist path of everyday cars, directed by William Durant,

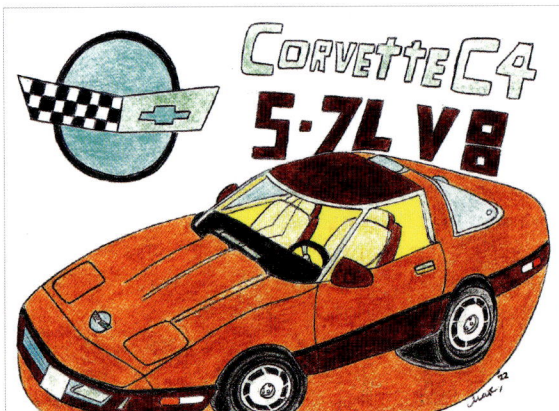

rather than the specialist, exclusive dream of Louis Chevrolet. The daily driver selection from Chevrolet, encompassed the subcompact GM J car called Cavalier, and the current best seller known as the Celebrity. The latter was a range of sedans, coupes and wagons, in the 2690 to 2855lb weight range, powered by the Iron Duke I4 and Citation V6, measuring 185in/69in/54in, for respective length, width and height. The Cavalier and Celebrity were part of GM's post fuel crisis, downsized, front drive, non V8 move for the '80s and beyond. The dream had changed, but the badge was still the same.

Of course, the earlier GM X car heralded this volume transition. As an early '88 MY replacement, for what *Road & Track*'s John Lamm described as the, "not very lamented" Citation X-car, the new Chevrolet Corsica sedan and Beretta coupe had a drag coefficient of 0.329 and forecast sales of 400,000 units for 1988 model year. The Corsica/Beretta would be sized midway between the Cavalier and Celebrity, and also utilized the familiar Iron Duke I4 (half of Pontiac's departed V8) and aforementioned Citation V6. Sadly, in this new efficient reality, the concept of a small, rear drive, V8 powered family car, ye olde Nova, was off the table! That said, the Beretta would have styling from the same folks, that did the still sexy Camaro and Corvette. That is, Chevrolet II Studio. As ever, that Corvette connection was marketing gold.

Traditionalists weren't ignored by GM, there was still the Cadillac Brougham. As described by Cadillac, "The Brougham retains its distinction in 1987 as the longest, tallest, heaviest production car built in America." Still with rear drive, and cast iron 307 V8, unlike the front drive Fleetwood D'Elegance, which had Cadillac's own 4.1-liter all alloy, injected V8. Indeed, sales of the Caddy Brougham were 40% up during 1986, while the rest of Cadillac's range was in decline. [107] And for the first time since 1981, one could option a Chevrolet 350 V8, in a GM F body! Corvette was sharing again!

The 1986 Corvette received aluminum heads. It was the first time Corvette got this feature standard since the 1969 C3 Corvette L88/L89/ZL1 427s! Corvette's 1986 total was 35,109 cars. That figure included 7315 units of the returning Corvette convertible. *(Courtesy Marc Cranswick)*

The long arm of GM Design

IN THE MIDST of old and new, GM was still the biggest automaker in the world, with vast resources. GM Research had 900 college graduates, half with PhDs, two hundred had Masters degrees, and 15% of the department's work was pure research. Subject matter encompassed bio mechanics of passenger protection, impacts of products and processes on the environment, metallurgy physics and analytical chemistry. What's more, even at this time, creating and producing smaller rare earth material magnets for starter motors and hi fi speakers. Machine tools and robotics were also studied. The latter was of particular interest to GM CEO Roger Smith, in dealing with the UAW! [108]

In computer research, the fruits of GM's labor were Autocolor and Fluid Dynamics Group. The former allowing a design to be created on screen, adjusting color and highlights as required, with a computational time of 11 hours to generate a complete car. The term 'virtual' hadn't entered the public's lexicon yet. Autocolor was for presentation purposes only. Fluid Dynamics Group enabled aerodynamic body development on screen, without a wind tunnel. Such abilities were relevant, because the press perceived that Ford had the upper hand in vehicle aerodynamics, with GM being behind the curve. Given the low drag achievements of Ford and Audi, high tech that resonated with the critics and public alike, BMW too was criticized for retaining boxy shapes, in what was fast becoming a 1980s aero culture war. GM fired back at critics, using the new Chevrolet Corsica/Beretta's press release, saying it was designed in a studio "where it's an article of faith that in matters of aerodynamics and family sedans, the jelly bean can be improved upon."

The use of Autocolor and Fluid Dynamics Group sped up design tasks, allowing ideas to be tested prior to physical studies. It was a benefit in reducing the labor cost advantage that import brand challengers from Japan and Korea enjoyed. The extent of GM's research was shown by some of the wacky concepts emanating from GM's European Design Center, located in Russelsheim, West Germany. The branch included American GM

Not as fast as the Bell X-1 that Chuck Yeager used to break the sound barrier, but fast enough to pace the 1986 Indy 500! All '86 Corvette ragtops were designated Indianapolis Pace Car replicas. The convertibles came with a door decal pack, but weren't all code 35 Yellow! *(Courtesy GM Archives)*

designers Charles Taylor and Frank Saucedo. An Electro electric bicycle, and vertical jogging Telecar were thought up, both aimed at reducing urban congestion. The latter became a treadmill when it ran out of battery power! Then there was a short wheelbase, three-wheel open sports car, not to mention a wearable transport suit. On the big side of things, a literal land yacht – that is, an aircraft carrier with wheels! This vision of the future, the year 2000, had a resort, helicopter pad and swimming pool. A sort of moveable Vegas, lacking only Ol' Blue Eyes, Elvis and Liberace! [109] Wayne Cherry was head of GM Europe's Design Center at this time.

Of more pressing concern going into 1987, was a need to replace the aging rear drive Chevrolet Chevette/Pontiac T-1000. Such diminutive econoboxes, along with the original Caddy Seville, had been GM's opening mid '70s salvo, in the Big Three Downsizing War. Backdoor imports like Chevrolet Sprint (Suzuki), Spectrum (Isuzu), Pontiac Le Mans (Opel/Daewoo), and joint US manufacturing partnership of the Chevrolet Nova (Toyota), would have to suffice until the Saturn program made good on its promise, of a profitable, small GM car, made in America. The Corvette was both profitable and made in America, and there were good reasons to look at its 1987 edition.

For 1987, the Corvette convertible became optionable
with $150 C68 climate control a/c for the first time.
All regular '87 Corvettes received a boost to
240bhp, thanks to roller hydraulic valve lifters.
(Courtesy GM Archives)

Tick the RPO B2K option box, and you got this ...
the 1987 Corvette Callaway Twin Turbo! Reeves
Callaway got initial notoriety for designing and
making a bolt-on turbo kit for the late '70s BMW 320i,
sold by Miller and Norburn. *(Courtesy Hemmings)*

Corvette for '87

THOSE WITH A very keen eye would notice that
the C4 Corvette's vaned alloys had subtly altered
since 1984/85. From black caps and radial slots,
to 1986's silver caps and black slots, with both
caps and slots in Argent Gray for 1987. Underhood
refinements also existed that weren't always visible.
Roller valve lifters kicked the L98 350 to 240 horse,
and the revised small block V8's rocker arm covers
had raised rails to prevent oil leaks. Invisible good
was also apparent in the $470 Z52 Sport Handling
Package, for stick shift '87 Corvettes alone. It was
a softer Z51 pack, that was press praised for being
just right. There were the usual four 16 x 9.5in
alloys, combined with a solid and thicker than
stock, front swaybar, new gas charged shocks,
quick ratio steering, and all but one of the C4
Corvette convertible's chassis stiffeners. Standard
Corvette spring rates and bushings were retained.

The Z51 Performance Handling Package, costing
$795, continued as a coupe RPO. Its much stiffer
springs, lower control arm bushings, and solid
non link type rear swaybar, all spelt track day hero.
At $325, the '87 Corvette's new low tire pressure
indicator system was pricy, but could detect
drops in tire pressure of just 1lb/in^2. A miniature
radio transmitter was placed in each wheel,
with a counter weight to handle wheel balance.
A dashboard warning light informed of pending
doom, but not always. There were false alarms, and
the option didn't make it into '88 MY. However, it
did return in modified form for 1989, with greater

success. A thicker radiator core, second electric
cooling fan, and finned power steering cooler were
'87 MY Corvette upgrades of worthwhile racer
nature. So too, the comfort of climate control a/c,
now for Corvette ragtops as well!

The Corvette's official 1987 model year billing
was, 'America's fastest production car'. *Motor
Trend* proved an '87 Corvette convertible was
capable of 0-60mph in 6.3 seconds, with a 15.11
second ¼-mile at 93.8mph. *Autocar*'s stats, for an
'86 stick shift coupe, saw a 14.8 second ¼-mile.
Conservative times, though fast enough for this
era and price; but what price? The '87 Corvette
coupe started from $27,999, with the convertible
requiring $33,172. For the first time since the 1981
Turbo Trans Am, the fastest car GM made, fastest
accelerating at any rate, wasn't a Corvette. No, in
1987 that accolade went to the revered 1987 Buick
Grand National. It was a story that started with the
'76 Buick Century Turbo, which paced that year's
Indy 500, pre-dating the 1978 Buick Turbo Regal.
The 1987 Grand National was the ultimate G body.
A final outing for the rear drive, midsize separate
chassis platform, combined with the ultimate
intercooled and turbocharged version of Buick's
231 V6. However, be prepared to baby those rear
drum brakes!

Reeves Callaway had a distinguished apprenticeship with Autodynamics Corporation and Bob Sharp Racing. After celebrated turbo kits for BMWs and Alfa GTV6s, he successfully turned to Corvettes with this monstrous 345 horse 465lb/ft twin turbo L98 350 V8! *(Courtesy Hemmings)*

If having your 240 horse '87 Corvette bested, by a 245bhp GNX was too much to take, there was an option. Tick RPO B2K, costing $19,995, and the Corvette now commanded 345 horses, allied to 465lb/ft. Holy horsepower Batman, what debauchery did RPO B2K entail? Being a scientist, Batman carefully explained to Robin that such a horsepower trip came courtesy of forced induction, like that Buick GNX. The Corvette got the Callaway Twin-Turbo trick. A normal Corvette was sent from Bowling Green, Kentucky to Callaway Engineering in Old Lyme Connecticut, for modification. Reeves Callaway designed and made a twin turbo kit, for the Corvette's L98 350. Now America's only sports car could reach 177.9mph! 184 1987 Corvettes were so converted, and the '87 Corvette Callaway Twin-Turbo could be ordered from participating dealers.

At this price, and with so few cars, Corvette was moving in very exclusive circles. Proving Corvette's ascension into the realms of the ultra exotic, observe the figures gleaned by *Motor Trend* concerning 1987 examples of the Ferrari Testarossa ($87k, 177.24mph), Lamborghini Countach ($116k, 160.27mph), Porsche 928S4 ($59k, 166.94mph), and Lotus Esprit Turbo ($55k, 145.79mph). The report on Europe's fastest was in the January 1987 issue of *Motor Trend*. Top speeds were recorded at the Transportation Research Center (TRC) in central Ohio. Even with RPO B2K, a Corvette was still a shade under 50 grand, and possibly more reliable than Italian exotica, for as *Motor Trend*'s Ron Grable said, the Testarossa failed to start. It was in Bellefontaine, Ohio that two pretty young L&K coffee shop waitresses push-started Maranello's finest at 1.00 am on a Saturday morning. Fiat had owned Ferrari for several years by this stage. It seemed that Turin had imbued the expensive Red Head, with a touch of 'Fix It Again Tony'! Then too, late 1986 had seen a recall of every Ferrari Mondial built up to early 1985. Apparently, in extreme conditions, the Mondial's rear hubs could fail.

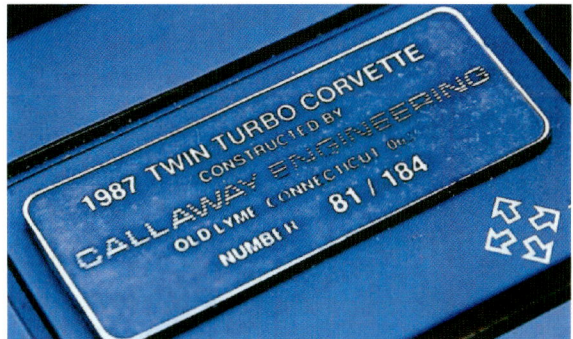

Tick RPO B2K, and an '87 Corvette went from the Bowling Green, Kentucky Corvette plant to Callaway Engineering's Old Lyme, Connecticut operation. Here the engine enhancement was done for just $19,995! *(Courtesy Hemmings)*

Ferrari test engineers in Italy made the discovery, but not to worry, dealers offered free replacement hubs of new design.

Of the '87 Corvette's other options, the convertible could now have RPO DL8 twin remote heated mirrors, costing 35 bucks and bought by 6840 '87 Corvette ragtop fanciers. In the monochromatic '80s, Corvette's $428 D84 two-tone paint for coupes, had slumped to just 1361 takers. The successful softer Z52 handling pack, had really taken sales from Z51, or 12,662 cars Z52 optioned against only 1596 1987 Corvettes with Z51. Bright Red was still top color choice, for 8285 Corvettes, followed by Dark Red Metallic (5578 cars). At 16, 1982 and 1987 offered the biggest Corvette color pallet to that point in time. In 1987 it was even possible to order a Corvette from Bowling Green,

Only 184 '87 MY Corvettes had the B2K Callaway Twin Turbo trick. Top speed was 177.9mph, and 0-60mph could be accomplished in top gear with a floored gas pedal. Callaway's Sledgehammer Corvette managed 254.76mph! *(Courtesy Hemmings)*

Kentucky, sans motor! One for the racers, looking to put their own custom job in a Plastic Fantastic. They would have tossed out the L98 350 anyway!

Commercial considerations

1987 CORVETTE SALES ran to 30,632, encompassing 20,007 coupes and 10,625 convertibles. This represented a reduction of 4523 sales versus 1986. The US, and therefore world, economy wasn't that hot. This was indicated by the 1986 slump in the world price of oil, an essential input in manufacturing and daily life. However, as in past times, the Corvette and upscale Europeans weathered the commercial storm. In general, domestic automakers and some large Europeans, like Renault and Fiat, were in trouble. GM posted big third quarter losses, and had a bloated inventory of 1 million cars going into 1987 model year. The giant was offering 2.9% finance to move stock by late August 1986. A common sentiment among car sales folk was that there just wasn't the money around that there used to be.

Corvette, BMW, Volvo and Saab were profitable niche players. Saab was selling 45,000 cars per annum Stateside, with a dealership sign saying '7.9% on all '86 Saabs'. [110] The US baby boomer yuppie, doctor or lawyer involved a household earning at least 100 grand per year. Basically, they wanted 'His

& Hers' Saab 900 convertibles, on their journey to materialistic suburban nirvana. Now, the Corvette was never really part of the camembert and white wine set. It's unlikely that upscale imports were taking Corvette sales. That said, a couple of Japanese sports cars might have made an impression.

With falling gas prices there was a renaissance of the sporty car market, covering everything from Golf GTis and Renault Alliance GTAs, through 5.7-liter GM F bodies, to uber pricy Porsche 911 Turbos and 928S4s. Concerning Corvette sales, the new to America Mazda RX7 Turbo, and revised Nissan 300ZX Turbo were key, particularly the latter. The Nissan 300ZX had been viewed as a middling performer by the press, but American sales continued at the 280ZX level, and even increased. Then the new FC Mazda RX7 and Toyota Supra, forced a Nissan sales reality check. It precipitated a reworked, more muscular 300ZX for '87 MY. The new iteration was well received in America, and might have poached a few Corvette sales. [111]

On to 1988

GM HAD ACQUIRED a controlling interest in Lotus, from mid-1986. This would lead to a couple of high profile projects for the 1990s, on both sides of the Atlantic. They were the Corvette ZR-1, and the reborn, front-drive Lotus Elan. The former the fastest, most sophisticated Corvette production package, ever! The latter, reputed to be the best handling front-wheel-drive car that the world had ever seen. Claims are always up for debate, but beyond question was a little Lotus assistance with hotting up the venerable Corvette's L98 350 V8 for '88 MY. That is, Lotus' former technical director led the team to improve the Corvette's V8, with freer breathing heads and reprofiled cam. The result, with freer flowing mufflers too, was 245bhp. However, the extra five horses were coupe only, with the 3.07 axle, represented by the RPO G92 Performance Axle Ratio.

The throatier mufflers were deemed too loud for a Corvette ragtop. So, the convertible made do with '87 MY mufflers, 2.59 snooze axle, and 240 horses. That said, all motor and no chassis maketh not an import crusher, so the 1988 Corvette featured discernible upgrades in suspension, brakes, wheels

Tick the RPO Z01 box, pay $4795 plus the base coupe's $29,489, and you could get this: the 1988 35th Anniversary Corvette! *(Courtesy Cars & Bids)*

and tires. The Corvette underlined its billing as the best domestic handler, with zero front scrub radius, a steering axis that coincided with the center of the tire contact patch. The Corvette's rear suspension was retuned with greater rebound travel and less camber change. As for the Corvette's ultimate in American braking systems, 1988 brought larger two piston front calipers, and larger disk brakes sized 12.9in front and 11.9in rearwards. Said rotors were also thicker now. An integral handbrake replaced the Corvette's previous auxiliary rear mini drums. Rather than the C3 Corvette-style between the buckets handbrake, the C4 Corvette's handbrake was like on a Porsche 928, living outboard of the driver's seat. The handle could fold down, once the handbrake was engaged, to aid ingress and egress. For 1988, said C4 Corvette handbrake lever was moved lower and back.

The Corvette's alloy rims changed for 1988, to a new Cuisinart design. These rims are colloquially referred to as 'Salad Shooters'. Standard 1988 Corvette rim and tire size involved four six-slot 16 x 8.5in Cuisinarts wrapped in P255/50ZR-16s of Goodyear Eagle GT variety. The 1988 Corvettes with

Z51 and Z52 handling packs sported 12-slot 17 x 9.5in Cuisinarts shod with new P275/40ZR-17s. The tire was the much respected Goodyear Eagle GT. A side specific choice, with unidirectional rims being a Corvette first! It was in the April 1988 issue of *Motor Trend* that Jack R Nerad provided lap times of the BMW M6, Porsche 928S4, and race trim SCCA Showroom Stock C4 Corvette, around Sears Point. The respective times were: 2:06.88, 2:04.88 and low 1:50s! The West Germans were obviously grand tourers, to the Corvette's sports car.

You can be too good at something – politicians sometimes say they care too much, for example. Corvette turned out to be too good for the SCCA's Showroom Stock production car racing. Yes, the Corvette went unbeaten during 1985-87. No losses in three years! So, obviously the SCCA banned the C4 Corvette! When that happens you just have to play by yourself. The answer being the 1988-89 Corvette Challenge, wherein 56 race-prepared, street legal Corvettes were constructed for this new SCCA series. Stock L98 350s made at GM's CPC engine plant in Flint, Michigan were sent to Bowling Green, Kentucky, in the usual Corvette manner.

The 35th Anniversary Corvette's theme color was Bright White. It looked almost as cool as the standard C68 climate control a/c. Cool tunes too, from the included UU8 Delco-Bose in-car audio.
(Courtesy Gulf Coast Motorworks)

The white hue was in keeping with the original '53 Corvette's Polo White exterior. Like that older Corvette, the latest 35th Anniversary Corvette also made a New York debut.
(Courtesy Orlando Classic Cars)

The completed coupes then traveled to Wixom, Michigan for a roll cage and safety equipment to be added. During 1988, Chevrolet replaced such V8s, with L98 350s of more even calibration for fair racing. Recall, back in 1971, Chevrolet engineers said there could be as much as a 15 gross horse, or more, variation in 350 2bbl V8s, built on the same day! After the Corvette Challenge Series, such coupes were sold to private owners. As always with a 'gentleman's racer', beware of ex-race cars, and look for signs of racing.

A 'Special Edition' option

1988 CORVETTES STARTED with a base coupe costing $29,489, with the convertible on $34,820. The latter had been well received, since returning to Corvette life in 1986. Enthusiasts had missed the Corvette roadster during 1976-85. After all, the Corvette started out as a ragtop! New to Corvette living from 1987 was an AC1 power passenger seat, joining the renamed AC3 power driver seat. Both costing $240 in 1987-88. The passenger option closed the popularity gap with the driver's side. That is, it was becoming normal to have both buckets powered. A D74 illuminated driver vanity mirror, had also become an RPO from 1987, for 58 bucks. Best known of the 1987 options was B2K.

This Callaway Twin-Turbo conversion carried on into 1988. It now cost $25,895, and involved 124 converted 1988 Corvettes.

In handling packages, Z51 was almost down for the count versus Z52. 1309 buyers went with Z51, but 16,017 for the Z52 compromise, which was cheaper. Bright Red still ruled as most popular color, with a 5340 '88 Corvette total, followed by white and black. The D84 two-tone paint option, that started in 1981 was history. There was a single two-tone choice, with 2050 '88 Corvette buyers going for code 40/41 black roof and white body. Five code 66 Dark Orange pilot Corvettes were built, but not included in the 1988 Corvette's production stats. Interior upholstery choices were simplified, Graphite and Bronze color choices were gone. However, there was something visually new, in the form of RPO Z01 Corvette 35th Anniversary Package, for coupes alone. RPO Z01 accounted for the aforementioned 2050 two-tone build, and added $4795 to the Corvette's base sticker.

The triple white 35th Anniversary Corvette, channeled the spirit of the original Corvette. That 1953 Polo White roadster made a New York City, Waldorf Astoria Hotel debut, so Chevrolet's executives paid homage to that first sports car by introducing the 1988 35th Anniversary Corvette on April 1 1988, at the New York Auto Show. And it was no fool that bought this coupe! The exterior was Bright White, contrasting with a black halo roof hoop, black acrylic transparent roof panel and black windshield framing. Bright White was also apparent on the door handles, mirrors, body side moldings and 17in Cuisinarts. White also featured for the interior's leather seats, center console cover, door trims and steering wheel. Even the graphite floor mats had a thin white band around the edge!

You would expect special badging with an Anniversary edition, and RPO Z01 provided same above the front fender body vents, as well as embroidered seat badging, and console plaque behind the shifter. Such special editions are usually heavy on the features, and the 1988 35th Anniversary Corvette proved no exception with: dual six-way power buckets, UU8 Delco-Bose audio, heated door mirrors and C68 climate control a/c. 1988 Corvettes had better stale air extraction, which was great for a/c performance. The original plan with RPO Z01 was to build 2000 cars, but the coupe went beyond! The 35th Anniversary Corvette was very well received, collectible, and today the best

examples can top 40 grand. However, there was an outlier of very special note. On January 18 2018, a Barrett-Jackson auction saw one 35th Anniversary Corvette attain $350,000! The reason was simple, the auctioned coupe was raising money for the American Heart Association's Charity.

1988 Corvette sales were 22,789, made up of 15,382 coupes and 7407 ragtops. You could say that Japanese competition in the sports car market was hotting up. That said, most blame for the Corvette's cooling sales could be attributed to the C4 Corvette being no longer new. Lack of newness was a quality that affected domestic car sales, more so than for Japanese models or upscale Europeans. The R107 Mercedes SL lasted 18 years, sans exterior or interior change! Then too, it was harder to update the more minimalist, clean styling of cars like the third gen F body or C4 Corvette. Back in the second gen F body days you did a nose/tail job every two to three years, played with the decals, and all was well. Sales aplenty. Now, buyers wanted new new, and Team Corvette was working on that, with some help from Hethel.

The almost all white get up would have pleased Miami Vice's Sonny Crockett! The 17in Cuisinart alloys, colloquially called 'Salad Shooters', were new to Corvette in 1988. *(Courtesy RMC Miami)*

C4 Corvette – Beyond L98 350

The other Corvette

TV'S *MOTOR WEEK* titled its look at the 1989 Corvette "The Other Corvette." That is, *MW* was testing the regular Corvette, as opposed to the Corvette ZR-1. In spite of the Geneva media teaser, the press launch to end all press launches, and more magazine cover appearances than Princess Diana, you couldn't actually buy a 1989 Corvette ZR-1, no sir! 84 1989 Corvette ZR-1s were built for evaluation purposes, with the final one being shipped on December 12 1988. However, not one was sold to the public. 1990 model year was the Corvette ZR-1's real moment of truth, and the official GM reason for the delay was, "… insufficient availability of engines caused by additional development."

Of course the forbidden fruit nature of the Corvette ZR-1 was unknown to *Motor Week* when it tried the 1989 Corvette. *MW*'s John Davis even said that no one seemed able to put a power figure on the new Corvette ZR-1's 5.7-liter LT5 V8 motor. Information was in short supply, but there was a hope that the Corvette ZR-1 was coming soon. Hence John Davis saying that putting some ZR-1 stuff on the regular Corvette was comforting, and "… makes not having the ZR-1 a little less painful." Oddly, Davis referred to the normal Corvette as RPO L98, which was the Corvette's standard and only factory powerplant during 1985-89. An engine designation, rather than a model name.

The ordinary 1989 Corvette had many worthwhile standard features and options, compared to even the 1988 Corvette. Such bounty was reflected in the base sticker price for a Corvette, climbing past the 30 grand mark for the first time ever! It cost more, but you got more. And all this would cost even more with an import. That starting price was $31,545 for coupe, and $36,785 with ragtop. The new NCO manual transmission was the much awaited six-speed jointly developed by ZF and Chevrolet. The six-speed was a cutting edge creature of contemporary '90s fashion. Its RPO MN6 code replacing the Doug Nash 4+3 box's MM4, a code which had been used since 1979 concerning Corvette four-on-the-floor. The post

Rising truck and SUV sales were the elephant in the sports car showroom. Nevertheless, Corvette sales were up for 1989, to 26,412 units. This figure included 9749 ragtops. *(Courtesy S Raizman Auto Sales)*

1982 Corvette Doug Nash 4+3 box was never much loved, as *MW*'s John Davis confided, "We won't miss the old transmission." Its long throws and clunky feel had pushed many C4 Corvette buyers to go slushbox. It did make the Corvette quicker accelerating.

The new six-speed was judged to shift smoothly, and with reasonably short throws. It had the gas guzzler avoiding CAFE benefits of not one, but two overdrive ratios! *Motor Week*'s '89 test coupe did 0-60mph in 6.1 seconds, with a 14.3 second ¼-mile pass at 97mph. Much the same as the show's previous Corvette test coupes, with Doug Nash 4+3 in 1985 and 1988. However, John Davis said, "Getting there is less work, and more fun." Then too, the six-speed changed the Corvette's nature, from a brutish, distinctly American sports car, to one you could handle with precision, common to German rivals, according to *Motor Week*. Less welcome was the six-speed's associated CAGS (Computer Aided Gear Selection). CAGS, or the dreaded 1-4 Skip Shift, that would be 'gifted' to the 4th gen GM F body from 1994 was an electronic Big Brother. It forcibly put one in direct top gear, on a light throttle. To be precise, under 35% throttle, or between 12 and 19mph, 2nd and 3rd gears were locked out.

The critics and public were not happy about CAGS. *Motor Week*'s John Davis noted that the latest Corvette six-speed's EPA City/Highway numbers were 16mpg/25mpg. *MW* got a real world 22mpg on test, but Davis added, "We'd gladly sacrifice an mpg or two if Chevrolet would lobotomize the transmission's economy computer." He also relayed, "We're told the feature can be defeated with a careful study of the Corvette's wiring diagram and some judicious snipping." According to Chevrolet engineers, clip one red wire. As observed by industry commentators then and now, the government, via the EPA, even had its fingers in Corvette's shifter! In the end, only 4113 of the 26,412 1989 Corvettes sold had the new six-speed stick. You can lead a guy to clover, but you can't make him shift!

There was a better chassis under the 1989 Corvette. The applauded Z52 suspension pack was now standard, with the coupe only Z51 Performance Handling Package costing $575, and

The lure and high value of a zero mile or low mile collector car is a distinctly North American phenomenon. This '89 Corvette convertible has only 1129 miles! *(Courtesy S Raizman Auto Sales)*

chosen by 2224 '89 Corvette customers. The 17in Cuisinarts were also standard for 1989, along with fast ratio steering and the formerly optional FG3 Delco-Bilstein shocks. The latter were optioned by most 1988 Corvette folk. What's more, the front end of the Uniframe was beefed up, as per Z52. If the six-speed was selected, the KC4 engine oil cooler, VO1 HD radiator and B4P radiator boost fan were included. Such items respectively cost: $110, $40 and $75, separately. Once again, more standard stuff explained the Corvette's rising price tag.

Aside from RPO ZR-1 and MN6, the other key hardware for 1989 were FX3 Selective Ride Control (SRC) and UJ6 low tire pressure warning indicator. FX3 retailed for $1695, and was optioned by 1573 Corvette faithful in 1989. FX3 SRC represented a joint development between GM Delco and Bilstein. Microprocessors activated mini electric motors, placed at the top of each shock absorber. The electric motors worked rotary valves that controlled the flow of fluid into the shock absorbers' pistons. A rotary console dial between the Corvette's buckets, allowed selection between the modes Touring, Sport and Competition. Touring was the softest, with Competition being the most aggressive. The system was arranged to firm up as the Corvette sped up, in six firmness levels rising with 25mph increments. Sport and Competition modes saw the firmness levels reached, 5mph sooner, to limit excessive adjustment. SRC adjusted

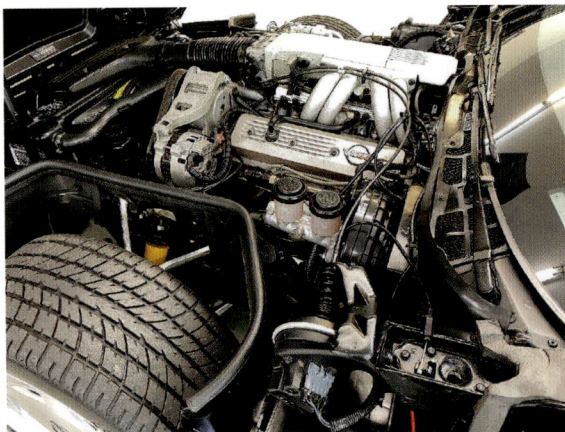

Come 1989, and there was talk of the Corvette's Lotus-developed 5.7-liter LT5 V8. However, many love the torquey and tough L98 350. In 1989, said L98 350 made 245 horse and 340lb/ft. *(Courtesy S Raizman Auto Sales)*

1989 saw Corvette convertibles optionable with the $1995 auxiliary hardtop. With very solid construction, and electric heated back glass, the option was desirable out East. It was chosen by 1573 '89 Corvette buyers. *(Courtesy S Raizman Auto Sales)*

10 times per second, and is another area of reliability concern with vehicle age.

Motor Week's '89 Corvette six-speed had both Z51 and FX3. *MW* took its Bright Red coupe to Savanna, Georgia's Roebling Road Raceway. There were positive comparisons made, against the 1988 Corvette with Doug Nash 4+3 box and Z51, tested earlier. For one, FX3 made Z51 easier to live with. *MW* rated its '89 Corvette as firm, but comfy. Secondly, *Motor Week* host John Davis said, "With the ride control set in the performance mode this was the stickiest Corvette we've ever had occasion to sling around a road course." There was also the observation that earlier Corvettes planted their front tires, and fought a turn. This led to eventual oversteer, corrected with the Corvette's quick steering. Now, the '89 Corvette was retuned to plow a little at the front, and combined with throttle induced oversteer, it became possible to throw the Corvette's entire weight evenly into a turn.

Also somewhat handling related were the Corvette's redesigned buckets for 1989. Stock seats implied leather, with cloth inserts. The pricy $1025 AQ9 sport seats were leather only, and came with six-way power adjustment as before. *MW*'s test coupe had RPO AQ9, with power adjustment for rake, side wings and lumbar pad. John Davis said that AQ9 may seem gimmicky, but such seats were

the most comfy buckets of any Corvette, and any sports car in the show's extensive experience for that matter. This was also *MW*'s first Corvette with the optional C68 climate control a/c. Once again, Davis said the system wasn't as pretentious as some of these systems could be, and you could even 'go manual', if that was your wont. The order rate for RPO C68 was almost universal in 1989, with 24,675 Corvettes so equipped. As for the Corvette's low tire pressure monitor, it had returned for 1989, now called UJ6, and costing $325. The option was more trustworthy now, with 6976 '89 Corvette buyers saying yes. As with any high end car, Corvette had the stuff that would be commonplace on average vehicles in the years to come.

Raising Corvette refinement had been a constant goal since 1953. For example, the $1995 RPO CC2 auxiliary hardtop convertible option. Best appreciated by Corvette owners out East, CC2 brought a hardtop with fiberglass reinforced polyester resin, over a rigid urethane molding that encased a steel/aluminum cage, coated with polyurethane. Plushness came courtesy of a cloth headliner, window weather stripping and an electrical heated element in the back glass, not plastic. Corvette convertibles had a special rear deck socket to plug in for the heated back glass of the optional CC2 hardtop.

A couple of further optioning aspects of the '89 Corvette were color and power. The RPO D84 two-tone paint option had been reintroduced on Corvettes for 1981, but wasn't available in 1989. A victim of fashion. One thing that never really goes out of fashion is performance. Yes, Corvette ZR-1 wasn't around for real in 1989, but that trip to the moon was still possible via RPO B2K. That is, the Callaway Twin-Turbo experience. However, you needed to have an extra $25,895 handy, and 69 1989 Corvette folks did! Also on the subject of performance, 60 additional production Corvette racers were built for the continuing SCCA Corvette Challenge series.

High performance was never in doubt, even with the regular '89 Corvette. In four days of continuous testing at Savanna, Georgia's Roebling Road Raceway, *Motor Week* failed to encounter brake fade, on its '89 Corvette L98 350 six-speed. And although staff purists leant towards analog gauges, *MW* still liked the C4 Corvette's instrument display, "We still call this the best electronic gauge package in the business." On the other hand, the C4 Corvette's 'Bread Loaf' passenger side crash pad was still present. What's more, *MW* added, concerning the 1984-89 Corvette dashboard molding, "The surrounding seam on the verge of engulfing you!" A Team Corvette mind game, no doubt!

There was no doubt the C4 Corvette Uniframe was better, now that the convertible strengthening elements had been incorporated on the Corvette coupe. That said, noise and vibration were still vocal on the inside, to a greater extent than in the unibody Porsche 944. At this price, the Corvette's groans and whines from the differential and driveshaft area were unwelcome and too frequent. However, park such concerns, due to the Corvette's traditional fun factor. As *Motor Week*'s John Davis said, "And you get a grin that lasts until you run out of gas!"

The V8's sound and fury drowned out much of the Corvette's unwanted audio. Then too, there was the new six-speed's shifter snap, not really present on the old Doug Nash 4+3 box. *MW* mentioned two '89 Corvette rivals, the Porsche 944 Turbo and in-house Camaro IROC Z. The former was a bit faster, and had greater body solidity, but cost a lot more for its superior refinement. The ultimate Camaro was half the Corvette's price, and the last IROC Z *MW* tested, even out-accelerated the Corvette. That said, the Camaro's handling was inferior, plus you couldn't have ABS, and the Corvette's suspension was a lot more sophisticated.

Concerning the '89 Corvette, *Motor Week* judged 'Hits' as being: the six-speed, new buckets, improved ride comfort and track performance. 'Misses' were: CAGS, body vibration and drivetrain noise. *MW* felt body vibration limited the Corvette's high handling potential. Even so, the '89 Corvette L98 350 still won the hearts of many a *MW* staffer, and that six-speed changed the Corvette's nature from a distinctly brutish US sports car, to one you could handle with the precision of a German rival. That said, code 81 Bright Red was still the C4 Corvette's most popular shade, contrasting with the silver of most Mercedes SLs!

Motor Week felt the '89 Corvette L98 350's biggest problem was getting overshadowed by its glamorous big brother, the Corvette ZR-1, which was faster and pricier. On this point *MW*'s John Davis concluded, "What a pity." The Corvette ZR-1 being present or not, GM's fastest accelerating car in 1989 wasn't a Corvette. It was the 20th Anniversary Trans Am, powered by the returning Buick 3.8 V6 Turbo of Buick Grand National fame. That said, Reeves Callaway would put you out in front with the B2K twin turbo conversion. At any rate, Corvette was America's only sports car in 1989, especially given the Pontiac Fiero's demise at the close of 1988.

GM & Lotus

THERE WAS A time, on both sides of the Atlantic, when it was thought that Japanese companies would only deal with economical family cars, leaving the special stuff to the established players. In America, the 1978 Toyota Cressida was a game changer. Setting aside Toyota's initial luxury foray with the 1957 Toyota Crown, which suffered durability problems Stateside, the Cressida was a luxo winner. At over seven grand the Toyota was compact in size, but priced equal to a fullsize Buick Electra 225 V8. An increasing buyer desire for smaller size, better fuel economy and higher build quality/reliability led buyers to Toyota's door.

Then, there was the sporty car story. The Mazda RX7, Datsun 280ZX and Toyota Supra amassed many sales. Come 1985, and Lloyd Reuss, GM VP since 1984 and GM of the newly formed CPC (Chevrolet-Pontiac Canada), identified a need for an ultimate image vehicle, to counteract the rising Japanese sports car threat, to GM's F body and Corvette. At the high end of the market, there was also concern. It was in 1985 that Porsche President Peter Schutz, the man who saved the Porsche 911, was asked why many Americans perceived German automobiles as having the highest quality in the world. The normally talkative Schutz, grinned and said, "There are three reasons for that, Mercedes. BMW. Porsche." Well, even Chevrolet bought a Porsche 924 as a benchmark coupe when developing the 1977 Camaro Z28. [112]

GM had a trick up its sleeve: respected British sports car maker Lotus. In mid 1986, GM got a controlling interest in Lotus, for brand image rub off, and for assistance with specialist projects that a mainstream family vehicle automaker lacks expertise in. The UK's Emtech did development engineering on the Pontiac Fiero. Cadillac GM John Grettenberger, for one, was happy about Lotus coming on board, "I am tremendously excited by the acquisition of Lotus by GM. We could put many of the company's ideas to good use at Cadillac."

Cadillac, America's one time luxury car pinnacle, had been losing sales since the late '60s to European opposition. The part Italian, Pininfarina assisted Allante was Cadillac's conquest sales attempt, that steered away from mainstream GM offerings. That is, the J car Cimarron. The Allante looked slinky, but apart from much computer tech, lacked adventure. A 1988 European launch was rumored. However, to compete with Mercedes, Porsche and Jaguar, mechanical changes were needed. John Grettenberger felt Lotus' Active Ride, etc, would be image boosters. Then too, the 32-valve Northstar V8, would help the Allante better target its true hoped for prey, the Mercedes SL. And yes, JR Ewing would eventually trade in his Three Pointed Starmobile, for an Allante! [113]

At first glance, you wouldn't think the Corvette needed help from Hethel. Surely the C4 Corvette, now with TPI and alloy heads, was sports car enough to slay all comers? Apparently not. It was

promised 18 months post Lotus acquisition that the Corvette would use Lotus' VARI (Vacuum Assisted Resin Injection) technique for Targa top panels and body panels. This represented a shift from SMC (Sheet Molded Compound), seen on the C4 Corvette and Pontiac Fiero. VARI promised lower tooling cost. Lotus displayed a C4 Corvette hood, created using VARI, at the National Exhibition Center (NEC) in Birmingham, England, the site of the nation's premier motor show in 1986.

Would VARI go into production concerning Corvette? Corvette's Chief Engineer since 1975, Dave McLellan said, "Sure, it is just a matter of figuring out a way of moving the manufacturing process from Lotus to Corvette volume." That is, from an annual Lotus output of 780 cars, to the Corvette's 20,000 plus unit per annum level. New resins, able to withstand high oven temperatures, came as part of the work with Lotus. [114] But of course, this wasn't the first time Lotus had been involved with an American automaker. Can you say DeLorean DMC-12?!

The DMC-12 brought together two major figures of the American and British car industries, John Z DeLorean and Colin Chapman. It was an era when such figures truly were larger than life. DeLorean had been a glittering star at General Motors. He took Pontiac to No 3 in the sales race, and then became boss of Chevrolet. John Z DeLorean raised Corvette prices, to take advantage of the nameplate's popularity. He also floated the idea of basing the Plastic Fantastic on the GM F body platform, to reduce engineering expense. Such business acumen saw DeLorean poised to take the reins of GM, but he left in 1973 to build his own car. Coinciding with DeLorean's corporate rise was a substantial change in his personal life. From being a fuddy duddy, pudgy engineer at GM in the '50s, he moved from square to mod, working out and hanging out with models. The term mid-life crisis wasn't in vogue yet. However, his departure from GM, and marriage to much younger model Christina Ferraro, marked John Z as a man in transition. Indeed, prior to leaving GM, he penned the book, *On A Clear Day You Can See General Motors*.

Colin Chapman, founder of Lotus and originator of the phrase 'for speed add lightness', needs no introduction to motoring enthusiasts. His sports car company popularized mid-engine racing cars in Formula One, rendering front-engine machines obsolete. Lotus was a respected sports car producer, and racing car constructor, famous for a superlative ride, handling compromise. In being a DeLorean DMC-12 development partner, the UK concern had a striking Giugiaro penned design to hone for production, and somewhat of a World Car at that. US and UK engineered, built in Northern Ireland, using British taxpayer funds on a greenfield site of poor employment prospects. The DMC-12's wedge shape was modern when unveiled in 1977, like a Bricklin SV-1 for the '80s. That is, a socially responsible gentleman's GT carriage, with gullwing doors. When DeLorean started his car project, a Chevrolet small block V8 was planned. However, like Malcolm's Bricklin, big power wasn't the goal. Indeed, the DMC-12's PRV V6 was intended to blend into the post fuel crisis 1980s.

Initially, DeLorean DMC-12 sales were good, helped by John Z's celebrity friendships, such as with Johnny Carson. However, a mixture of novelty wearing off, established European brands having a lock on the Gucci GT cruiser realm, and early '80s recession, put paid to the DMC-12. Apart from the Mercedes SL, BMW 6 series and Jag XJS, GM's new for '82 F body with Cross-Fire-Injection V8, offered sleek style, and even more performance, at a fraction of the DMC-12's price. It seemed that John Z DeLorean's former corporate masters, had the last laugh! Lotus said the DMC-12 came in overweight during development, which blunted performance and compromised handling. That said, the DMC-12 had the performance measure of the MB 380SL, a key target for conquest sales.

Allegations were made against Mr DeLorean concerning drug dealing, to keep the DMC-12 financially afloat. Meanwhile, it was contended that Colin Chapman had siphoned off $720,000 from the British taxpayer funded project into his Swiss bank account, prior to his sudden 1982 demise! DeLorean's defense attacked Chapman in the US District Court of Detroit, during October 1986. John Z DeLorean's lawyer Harold Weitzmann, said Colin Chapman was a "strange man" who "… didn't like paying taxes." Chapman also insisted on up front payment, prior to his company Lotus doing crucial R&D work on the DMC-12. Given government

actions, and DeLorean's shaky business practices, neither of Chapman's behaviors could be characterized as oddball. The DeLorean DMC-12 would go on to find fame, as a time traveling machine. However, Lotus played no part, in the creation of that coupe's flux capacitor! [115]

Honor the hyphen – Corvette ZR-1

IN CONTRAST TO the DeLorean DMC-12, Lotus' next US car project involved no horsepower shortfall. Rumors of a special Corvette being afoot started circulating. However, even earlier, 20 1986 Corvettes were shipped to the UK for prototype creation. A premium powerplant was necessary for such an ultra Corvette. Project leaders Lloyd Reuss and Dave McLellan, of the program internally called 'King of the Hill', spoke to GM Powertrain Engineering Director Russ Gee. Gee assigned GM's Chief Engineer of V-type engines, Roy Midgely, to the special motor task. Together, gents Gee and Midgely looked to firms outside GM for inspiration. It had to be something more than the L98 350 V8. A turbo V6 for the Corvette was considered, but

The Corvette ZR-1 made a 1990 model year debut. The 375 horse 'King of the Hill', represented a $27,016 RPO ZR1 surcharge over the $31,979 RPO 1YY07 base Corvette coupe! ZR-1 rims were 9.5in wide at the front, and 11in wide rearwards.
(Courtesy GM Archives)

rejected. The layout was considered too harsh, and Corvette buyers didn't fancy six-cylinder engines. This probably stemmed from the lackluster nature of the 1953-54 Corvette's Blue Flame Six.

Corvette Chief Engineer Dave McLellan was into the idea of a twin turbo V8. This factory avenue of performance was ruled out, in spite of a promising prototype, due to excessive gasoline thirst and pollution. That said, GM did greenlight the Callaway Twin Turbo RPO B2K package, from 1987. A pure factory option led to Lotus, and initial thoughts of a 16-valve DOHC conversion for the L98 350. However, by the close of 1987 model year, Lotus' engineering guru, Tony Rudd, told Team Corvette's head honcho, Dave McLellan, that converting the L98 350 wasn't possible. That is, an all alloy 32-valve DOHC layout would require a clean sheet design. It would become the LT5 5.7-liter V8, developed by Lotus and built by Mercury Marine in Stillwater, Oklahoma.

Getting into the 1990s contemporary automotive parlance, and considering the tremendous differences from the traditional 'Hot One' Chevrolet small block Mouse Motor, it seemed odd to call the LT5 a '350 V8'. It may have been 350 in size, 5727cc to be metric exact, but it wasn't one in nature, making 375 horses net, at 5800rpm and 370lb/ft at 4800rpm. Yes, the L48 was a 350, the LT5 was something else! That said, practical reality dictated that the LT5 share the same bore center spacing of 4.40in, with the regular Chevrolet small block V8. This necessitated a smaller bore, 3.90in rather than 4.00, plus a stroke increase from 3.48in to 3.66in. Then too, the LT5 V8 had to be a motor, that could be fitted at the Corvette Bowling Green, Kentucky plant, in the usual C4 Corvette manner. That is, installed in the engine bay from below, with the space between frame rails being 27 x 27in. It implied a LT5 V8 valve angle of 22 degrees. [116]

The LT5 V8 had the support of GM VP Lloyd Reuss, and the approval of GM CEO Roger Smith. It all implied meeting many requirements. For one, acceleration second to none, sound drivability and economy akin to the frugal L98 350. Yes, the Corvette ZR-1 would also avoid the dreaded gas guzzler tax, a technical feat in itself! Goals were 22.5mpg, being smog clean, durable and looking good underhood, the LT5 V8 had to do all that and

more! That last requirement was a distinctly Detroit thing. It wasn't a conscious goal of European companies until later. In fact, it was hard to even see the Porsche 911's engine, except for its oversize cooling fan! Reliability for the LT5 V8 was key, and all alloy construction was mandated for good heat dissipation. The LT5 V8 was a cool customer. The Corvette ZR-1's radiator was 15% larger, compared to a regular Corvette, with the thermostat relocated to the inlet side. There was a separate oil cooler, with thermostatic control. Indeed, versus the Corvette L98 350, the Corvette ZR-1 ran cooler, even if there was no practical distinction between idle and general running scenarios.

The LT5 V8's comp ratio was 11.25:1, with a redline of 7200rpm. However, the motor could drink 87 octane juice, at a pinch! These were some of the conflicting requirements that Lotus had to develop around. An engine of variable valve timing that could breathe through selected valves. It made modern ECU controlled fuel injection essential. Indeed, both the LT5 and later L98 350s, used Multec (Multiple Technology) fuel injectors, developed in-house by GM's Rochester Products Division. That said, whereas the L98 350 snuck by with a 5-quart sump, the LT5 V8 sported a 12-quart sump! Lubrication was key indeed for those expensive internals. There were integral four- and six-bolt cast iron main bearing caps, securing a forged steel crankshaft. Connecting rods were forged too. The five bearing crankshaft was supported by a one-piece aluminum cradle, attached to the block by 28 bolts. Said crankshaft bearings were sized 70mm for continuous 7000rpm usage. The crankshaft was cross drilled, with internal centrifugal oiling. Cast aluminum pistons were by Mahle, and aluminum wet cylinder liners and Nikasil coating were employed. The LT5 V8 had an externally ribbed and gusseted block, plus cast aluminum oil sump.

Roller chains were used to drive the LT5's cams. Gilmer belts were rejected because they would have made the V8 too wide, to 'bottom load' at the Corvette factory. The hydraulic lifter LT5 V8 had centrally located sparkplugs and dished pistons. The direct ignition system came with four coils and two sparkplugs per cylinder that fired simultaneously. The cue to fire was taken

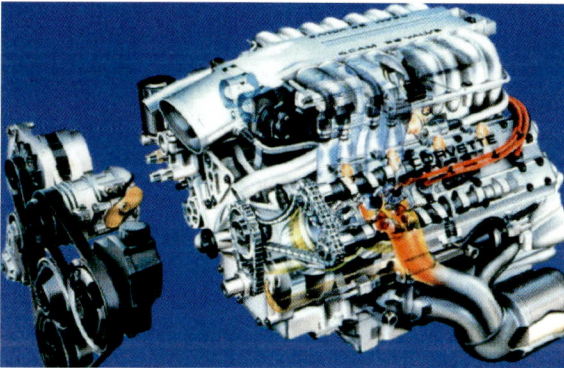

Lotus was unable to convert the L98 350 to a 32-valve DOHC configuration, so developed the clean sheet, all alloy LT5 5.7-liter V8. The LT5 V8 made 375bhp at 5800rpm and 370lb/ft at 4800rpm. The LT5 V8 was produced by Mercury Marine, in Stillwater Oklahoma. *(Courtesy GM Archives)*

from the crankshaft position sensor. The V8's ECU sensor read the position of machined notches on the crankshaft. Breathing came courtesy of an induction set up, with three-valve body. The small primary was for low speed running, with two large secondaries for the high end. That is, full throttle and or over 3500rpm. When called for, the ECU would bring the secondaries into play. Fuel and air went to the larger of the two intake valves, and cams with more radical timing lobes came into play! The LT5 V8's two phase throttle system was part of the motor's refinement.

To keep such a powerful road car safe, the Corvette ZR-1 had a Valet Mode. Entering the post-malaise era, fast cars really had some go again! In the words of GM CEO Roger Smith, "Some owners wouldn't want their spouses or sons in charge of the car's full potential." [117] The LT5 V8 had two fuel injectors per cylinder. In Valet Mode, activated via a console power key switch, the coupe flew on 80% power, using one injector per cylinder and only three of the four valves. The LT5 V8 was unquestionably one of the most advanced powerplants in the world. Mercury Marine sent completed LT5 V8s to Corvette's Bowling Green, Kentucky plant, for fitment. Mercury Marine also handled any major repairs that the LT5 V8 required. In worst case scenarios, Corvette ZR-1 owners could choose a new LT5 V8 over a repaired unit,

but, collectors note, the car would no longer be 'numbers matching'.

RPO ZR1 was a Special Performance Package, not just an engine. Chassis changes were abound. Rear tires became oversize units of P315/35ZR-17s, and the coupe's Goodyear Eagle Gatorbacks were specially made for the Corvette ZR-1. To fit such monster meats, this C4 Corvette's rear was 3in wider, with a new design soft polyurethane end cap. Compared to the regular C4 Corvette end cap, the new piece was convex rather than concave, with square taillamps in place of the Corvette's usual four round units. There was even a small, subtle red ZR-1 callout badge, gracing the lower right tail. Chevrolet 3 Studio Chief John Cafaro called the new look, one of a 'muscular physique'. There was also a high mount taillight above the backlight, for the Corvette ZR-1.

The regular Corvette kept P275/40ZR-17 rear rubber, so no need to push out its rear fenders. Indeed, both the LT5 and L98 350 powered Corvettes shared the same front wheels and tires. That said, the Corvette ZR-1 was 200lb heavier. In fact, the Corvette ZR-1's curb weight was 3461lb – at least that's what *Autocar* magazine listed. Beyond the Bosch ABS II system that the Corvette had been using since 1986, RPO ZR1 meant a hybridized Z51 Performance Handling Package. Z51 was for coupes only, and so too RPO ZR1. What's more, the Corvette ZR-1 was only available with a six-speed stick. RPO ZR1's Z51 pack combined standard Z51 with softer springs and swaybars for that 'just right' feel. Then too, the Corvette ZR-1 possessed a slower steering ratio, moving from 13.1:1 to 15.0:1. Therefore, this C4 Corvette was less darty. Even so, *Road & Track* picked up a 0.94g skid pad reading, with its Corvette ZR-1, and 65.7mph slalom speed. The latter figure, second only to a trick Mitsubishi Galant front driver with active suspension. That is, for the era, the Corvette ZR-1 was a civilized road racer, that stuck like glue! *R&T* recorded 60-0mph and 80-0mph, in a respective 132ft and 233ft. It was enough to best the Testarossa, Countach and Porsche 911 Turbo trio that the journal had tested. RPO ZR1 implied 13in twin caliper front disk brakes, derived from the 1988 RPO Z51 pack. The stronger front Uniframe was held in common with C4 Corvette ragtops.

For 1991, the Corvette ZR-1's convex rear end cap and square taillamps were bestowed upon the regular Corvette L98 350. Slowing sales due to high price and arrival of the 300 horse LT1 V8 saw the Corvette ZR-1 sadly discontinued at the close of '95 MY. *(Courtesy GM Archives)*

The Corvette ZR-1 implied standard fitment of the Corvette's usually optional RPO UJ6 low tire pressure warning system, which came with a center console warning light. Also standard was the Corvette's RPO FX3 selective ride control. FX3, seen since 1989, was the by now familiar Bilstein engineered system, like the Porsche 959's and Lotus own active ride system. That is, a gas over coil shock with hollow center shaft. An adjustable center orifice saw varying amounts of shock oil bled from around the piston. Six levels of damping, in three selectable modes (Touring, Sport, Performance), with the going from soft to firm in 25mph increments. Servo motor actuators lived on top of each shock, turning the shaft that regulated oil bypass. The ECU's microprocessor told the servos what to do, based on the inputs of road condition and vehicle speed. Whereas your regular '90 Corvette six-speed had a 3.33 rear axle, the Corvette ZR-1 went to a shorter 3.54:1, and RPO ZR1 implied an HD differential.

R&T's John Lamm said you had to be content with standard Corvette a/c, with a Corvette ZR-1. It was due to a physical conflict between RPO C68 climate control a/c, and the LT5 V8's right cylinder head. Exterior colors? Any of the Corvette's usual choices, except the '89 Geneva Show Car Corvette ZR-1's yellow. RPO UU8 Delco-Bose stereo was standard, so too leather-covered sport seats. However, the transparent, hard coated acrylic roof panel was optional. The official word was that the Corvette ZR-1 would be limited to 4000-5000 units per year. Limited by Mercury Marine's LT5 V8 supply. That said, the Corvette ZR-1 was built on the same Bowling Green line as your 'ordinary' Corvette L98 350.

The cost of all that RPO ZR1 goodness was $27,016, Corvette not included! Yes, in addition to the base 1990 Corvette price of $31,979. However, the B2K Callaway Twin-Turbo package was an extra $26,895 over base. No one ever said going quickly was cheap, but just how quick? Claims for 0-60mph in as little as 4.3 seconds, although *Autocar* magazine got 5.6 seconds in its April 1989 issue. Call it a safe five seconds flat. The best ¼-mile time for the Corvette ZR-1 was 12.8 seconds at 112mph. These best times came from TV show *Motor Week*'s testing of a Corvette ZR-1 prototype. The best Corvette L98 350 time was *MW*'s high 13s – figure mid 13s as an honest Corvette ZR-1 figure. Top speed? A claimed 180mph, and a verified 172mph in California's high desert, according to *Road & Track*'s John Lamm. Goodyear Gatorbacks were good for 193mph, by the by.

Autocar got 0-100mph in 13.5 seconds, with 0-100mph-0 in 19.3 seconds, along with 50-70mph in top gear in 6.9 seconds. The Corvette ZR-1 was tractable, with 300lb/ft from only 1500rpm, but did need a few revs to haul ale. A Corvette L98 350 would get the drop on a ZR-1 machine, up to 30mph. From then on, the Corvette ZR-1 would slingshot past. As *R&T*'s John Lamm said, drop a gear or two and blow past "... that slowpoke con brio!" In *Autocar*'s experience, the '84 Corvette automatic was only one second slower in 0-60mph, but 30mph slower on top speed. So yes, the LT5 V8 had the torque of a 350 V8, but enabled the Corvette ZR-1 to have mid range and top end delight that were plain out of sight! Available from 1990 model year, the Corvette ZR-1 could claim to be the world's fastest production car. The press certainly said it was one of the most useable. The proverbial iron fist in a velvet glove.

The international press response to Corvette ZR-1

FOR YEARS, THE Corvette was seen as America's most European car. Four-wheel disk brakes, IRS, smaller size two-seater, and a handbrake, all in one car! Corvette ZR-1, with the Lotus developed 32-valve V8 motor, pre-dated Cadillac's 32-valve Northstar V8. Now the most European of all Corvettes was imminent, what better place to have an international press debut than Europe itself?! So it was, that the world's automotive press congregated at Camargue, in the South of France. Try Corvette ZR-1 prototypes on European roads, but also the Goodyear proving ground near Montpellier. Earlier, as *Motor Week*'s host John Davis said, the Corvette ZR-1 could only be viewed at GM's Milford Proving Ground. Now journalists could drive the coupe to their hearts' content for hours on end. What's more, Davis added, "We're glad to say the automotive journalists wore out before the cars did!" Burnouts were performed for the *MW* camera, and 0-60mph in 4.3 seconds, along with a 12.8 second pass at 112mph concerning the

Reeves Callaway produced two 1990 Super Speedsters, with 750 horse Twin Turbo ZR-1 V8s. Callaway's aero enhancements, were in the style of the Callaway Corvette Sledgehammer. *(Courtesy National Corvette Museum)*

1320ft fandango, were forthcoming. The Michigan license plates of *MW*'s Bright Red Corvette ZR-1 test proto read '088REX'. It was a reference to the coupe's 1988 build date, and the Corvette ZR-1's 'King of the Hill' program code. It was a billing that Dave McLellan used to get his point across to GM brass. However, it was one that management shied away from as the Corvette ZR-1 came closer to availability. So said *Road & Track*'s John Lamm. Lamm even revealed that it had become a taboo title.

Corvette fan, owner and *CAR* magazine journalist Ian Fraser was on hand in France, and gave an explanation of GM's low key desire, "GM's people twitched nervously when power output figures were mentioned (Ralph Nader, people's friend and automotive Ayatollah is the specter on the shoulder of every horsepower ..." Then too, GM had been in a constant federal court battle, along with IBM, over monopolistic trade practices. Claiming to be number one, even in Latin, raised a regulator red flag. One can imagine a Paul Lynde voiced bureaucrat ready, willing and able to give the Corvette ZR-1 its marching orders! [118]

However, politics were far from journalistic thoughts during two very enjoyable days of high speed touring through the South of France. There were no fewer than 15 Corvette ZR-1s navigating their way through narrow village streets! As *Motor Week*'s John Davis said, like the standard Corvette L98 350, the ZR-1 version was very nimble. It got out of the way of startled oncoming traffic with aplomb. Performance wise, it felt like its plainer L98 350 powered cousin, up to four grand on the tach. It then lit up, and shot forth like a rocket!

CAR's Ian Fraser felt the LT5 V8 was good for 350 horses, by the seat of the pants, and was a good match for the Ferrari Daytona, Testarossa, Countach, and 911 Turbo crowd. The power wasn't meant to be apocalyptic, but part of a refined, controllable urge, free from excessive noise and brutal instincts. This the Corvette ZR-1 achieved, but Fraser met with severe detonation on repeated hot starts. The ZF six-speed gear change was judged very nice, with a smooth light clutch. However, a few revs were needed for a clean take up. Cruising in sixth on a light throttle was possible, even in Valet Mode. That said, Fraser didn't like the 1-4 skip shift, especially on the slow speed, tight parts of the route, "... which most folk find downright obnoxious." No one liked CAGS!

The outer exits of the quad pipe exhaust were bogus, a sign of things to come. However, the Corvette ZR-1's turn of speed was very real. *Autocar*'s resident racer Roger Bell, said the Corvette ZR-1 was as quick as anything from Europe, and cheaper, adding "... tough, durable and, compared to European exotics of roughly the same performance, relatively inexpensive." It had Titanic grip, good balance, quick steering and progressive breakaway. Brute force, but friendly with it. There was agility belying the Corvette ZR-1's size and weight, an excellent six-speed, roomy, comfy cabin, and bags of visual impact, to European eyes at any rate. Bell declared the Corvette ZR-1, "A performance classic," and, "... a shining example of US technology." The £35,000 UK sticker was considered very fair. [119]

CAR's May 1989 Corvette ZR-1 report saw Ian Fraser acknowledge that the 50 grand Corvette had arrived, "... but even then the ZR-1 could be the performance car bargain of them all." Initially, price gouging was in evidence. *Motor Week*'s John Davis noted big demands and offers for early serial number Corvette ZR-1s, of up to 100 grand! "That's a lot of money for any Corvette. But then, there has never been one like the ZR-1." Indeed, The Corvette ZR-1 took all Plastic Fantastic parameters to the next level. Chevrolet dealers selling Corvette ZR-1s had to have the GM-CAMS computer diagnostic

CAR's Ian Fraser felt the Corvette ZR-1 was closer to the R129 Mercedes SL, shown here with Hidemi Aoki, than mid-engine Italian exotica. *(Courtesy Capt John David Cranswick)*

system. Well, what would you expect from a car that *Road & Track*'s John Lamm said represented "... the best of the old and the new world."

Corvette Chief Engineer Dave McLellan offered some insight into the Corvette ZR-1's world. He didn't like the term exotic, for it implied a wildly styled, super expensive, highly temperamental limited production road racer. The Corvette ZR-1 was a civilized cross-continent Mercedes or BMW alternative in *R&T*'s John Lamm's opinion. *CAR*'s Ian Fraser also felt the Corvette ZR-1 was more akin to the new R129 Mercedes SL than the Ferrari and Lamborghini mid-engine jobs that GM offered for comparison. The new MB 500SL had 326bhp at 5500rpm and 332lb/ft at four grand, with top speed limited to 155mph, and zero to sixty in six seconds. Derestricted, the Mercedes would have been 10mph slower than the Corvette ZR-1, and a second slower in sprinting. However, it was also a refined, front-engine GT machine. So, perhaps this was the Corvette ZR-1's true crowd?

Dave McLellan warned, "There'll be a feeding frenzy for a while. After that we'll find out what the market will take." On '90 MY debut, 3049 Corvette ZR-1s found new homes. It was well within Mercury Marine's LT5 supply capability. One aspect that this special Corvette lived up to was superlative track handling. At the Goodyear Mireval test facility, *MW*'s John Davis noted the Corvette ZR-1 was totally civilized when pushed on the track. *CAR*'s Ian Fraser said that even on a wet track the Corvette ZR-1 and its Z rated 17in Goodyear Eagles, with 12.5in tire contact patches, were brilliant. In their natural home in fact. To use the Corvette ZR-1s out of Valet Mode, journalists had to be accompanied by an engineer, who would unlock the LT5 V8's full power with a key. Apparently, one proto had even left the road, with Lotus Engineering's Tony Rudd in the passenger seat! Plus, French goat paths were best tackled with the FX3 SRC in the softest Touring mode. *CAR*'s Ian Fraser found the Corvette ZR-1 wallowed in Touring. Sport mode brought a big change, and was used by Corvette Challenge racers. Fraser found Performance mode (as it was called at press launch) only made a small difference over Sport. However, as ever, the Corvette's handling prowess came at the expense of ride comfort.

Other problems with the Corvette ZR-1? General criticism centered on the Corvette ZR-1's styling similarity to the regular Corvette. *CAR* magazine felt the Corvette ZR-1 would benefit from an even stiffer chassis, bringing benefits to handling and ride comfort. That said, Corvette ZR-1 was still in a different league compared to its subsequent, quasi domestic rival, the Dodge Viper. The Viper wasn't subtle, and had engineering worthy of a blacksmith's forge! Its ingredients were a separate chassis, pushrod OHV 8-liter V10, stiff six-speed and heavy clutch, and unforgiving suspension.

Autocar magazine described the Dodge Viper as a show car that made it into production. Early versions lacked a/c and wind up windows! The Viper's brakes were easily overwhelmed in production car racing. Its limits weren't to be exceeded trackside, lest driver and vehicle leave the track, permanently! *Autocar*'s 1996/97 Viper GTS performance figures weren't exceptional versus the journal's Corvette ZR-1 test stats. For a straight line performer, the Viper GTS' 0-60mph in 5.3 seconds and 172mph were close to the *Autocar* Corvette ZR-1. The Corvette ZR-1 had a clear advantage in cornering and stopping. The Dodge Viper GTS was rated at a Corvette ZR-1 close 378bhp at 5100rpm, with 454lb/ft compensating for the Viper's heft. For all that, and the Dodge's outlandish looks, no V10 can ever match the aural qualities of a good V8, or any V8 for that matter, let alone a Corvette V8!

L98 Corvette 1990-91

IT WAS IN March 1990 that the Corvette ZR-1 set 12 FIA world records for speed and endurance, at Firestone's test track in Stockton, Texas. The Corvette ZR-1 was the headline maker of the day, and praised by many around the world. However, another fact was that the regular Corvette, the humble 1990 Corvette L98 350 was also a very impressive machine. An improved offering for '90 MY, good value and responsible for the majority of the Corvette's 23,646 1990 model year total. The Corvette coupe was now $31,979, with the ragtop $37,264. Respective sales were 16,016 and 7630 units.

Sales were down slightly for 1990, even with all the Corvette ZR-1 hullabaloo. This was mainly due to the 1990 world recession that would carry through the early '90s, affecting all automakers to varying degrees. To a smaller extent, lower Corvette sales were related to the all new Nissan 300ZX Twin Turbo, which made the greatest Z car impact on the sports car world, since the original 240Z. In any case, the regular Corvette continued with a revised version of the respected L98 350 V8, now with intake speed density control fuel injection, revised camshaft profile and higher comp ratio. The Corvette radiator was improved for 1990 too, so there was no longer a need for the 1986-89 B4P radiator boost fan.

The Corvette's Bosch ABS II system, first seen on Corvette in 1986, was upgraded for better yaw control input. The '90 MY Corvette changes were most noticeable in the cabin, with a new dashboard, influenced by a fighter jet; the slab like 1984-89 Corvette dashboard, with passenger side 'Breadloaf' molding was history. It meant the '90 MY Corvette had an honest to goodness glovebox! There was also curtailment of the dashboard LCD readouts, which was now limited to an amber backlit/black digit LCD speedo, complemented by a conventional tach and ¼ sweep analog gauges for gas, oil pressure and battery charge.

There was even a new engine oil light monitor lamp. An all leather interior was no longer restricted to the AQ9 super sport seat. Audio wise, another Corvette first, the RPO U1F Delco-Bose stereo compact disc system. The regular UU8 Delco-Bose audio option was $823, the new U1F cost $1219. However, option rates for the respective audio systems were 6401 versus 15,716 buyers. Folks obviously wanted the latest tech, which included U1F's anti theft lock out. A special code was needed to get the audio head unit working.

On the small and smaller Corvette scale, 58 folks ticked the B2K Callaway Twin-Turbo trick that cost $26,895. There were 23 '90 MY Corvettes with HD suspension, constructed for the new 1990 World Challenge race series. 1284 '90 MY Corvette ragtop buyers optioned the new $140 RPO V56 luggage rack. It was reminiscent of Corvettes from earlier times. 5446 Corvette enthusiasts selected RPO Z51Performance Handling Package, for coupes only, costing $460. The $1695 FX3 adjustable suspension was advisable with Z51, and 7576 '90 MY Corvette buyers chose FX3 SRC.

For exterior colors, code 25 Steel Blue Metallic, code 42 Turquoise Metallic, code 53 Competition Yellow, code 80 Quasar Blue Metallic, and code 91 Polo Green Metallic were all new for 1990! Yellow had been absent from Corvettes in 1989, and was the least popular color choice of 1990. Only 278 '90 Corvettes were yellow. Once again, as in all C4 Corvette years to date, code 81 Bright Red was the most popular Corvette hue. No less than 6956 '90 Corvettes were Bright Red.

1991 was a year of Corvette sharing. Although the Corvette ZR-1 kept its unique doors, and 3in wider rear fenders, the regular Corvette L98 350 got the ZR-1's convex end cap. That said, the regular Corvette lacked the ZR-1's rear callout badge. It was plain to see the more powerful model's oversize rear rims and tires were also absent. The supplemental brake light was placed just above the rear fascia Corvette script. Both L98 and LT5 V8 powered Corvettes got freshened frontal styling, for '91 MY. A slimmer front valence, and narrower integrated, wraparound parking/cornering/fog lights. Added to this new style, were 17in 'Saw Blade' rims, in place of the 1988-90 Cuisinarts. The result was an attractive, updated Corvette. Wider, color matched profile moldings and side strakes, underlined the low key sleeper look of the times. Only 5875 '91 Corvette buyers went with the NCO six-speed. A yellow 1991 Corvette was seen racing around to good effect in the 1994 Charlie Sheen movie *Terminal Velocity*.

Detail 1991 Corvette revisions saw a 15 minute delay timer, for audio/power window action, cancelled pronto by opening the door. A low oil level dashboard indicator was joined on ZR-1 coupes, by a Valet Mode off indicator lamp, now alongside the Valet Mode key slot. All '91 Corvettes were wired for cellular phone operation, or 12-volt accessory usage. Bigger mufflers added aural authority, as well as reducing back pressure. A finned power steering cooler boosted durability. The new Z07 Adjustable Suspension Package for coupes alone, replaced FX3 SRC and Z51, since Z07 incorporated both items, for $2155. It was optioned by 733 buyers in 1991.

A yellow exterior returned for 1991, code 35 Yellow, with the least popular color now being code 96 Charcoal Metallic, accounting for just 417 1991 Corvettes. Code 81 Bright Red was still the number one C4 Corvette color choice, seen on 5318 '91 Corvettes.

GM management was looking at what was selling, and what wasn't. 14,967 1991 Corvette coupes, starting from $32,455 and 5672 Corvette convertibles, retailing from $38,770. 62 folks optioned B2K Callaway Twin-Turbo, at an even 33 grand! The Callaway option was too slow selling by now, so '91 MY was its final outing. The Corvette ZR-1 was also selling well under the predicted 6000 per annum target. The new 400 horse Dodge Viper, with a specification more akin to a latter day C3 Corvette, seemed to have stolen the Corvette ZR-1's thunder. Plus, there was the long standing domestic performance car problem. Whether it was a Shelby Mustang, or '60s homologation special, once price rose above a certain level, sales dropped off the proverbial cliff. Cheap for an exotic, expensive for a Corvette. What's more, the Corvette L98 350 didn't require the same level of care as a Corvette ZR-1.

There was also the marketing reality that Chevrolet has always been a family vehicle and truck brand at heart. *Motor Week* tested the special 1990 Chevrolet C1500 454 SS. The truck edition entailed a limited run of 10,000 units, which sold out lickety split! Not a model, but an option named RPO B4U, and *MW*'s test truck cost $18,295. *Motor Week* host John Davis said trucks were selling like never before, and that in 1989 model year Chevrolet sold almost 1.4 million light trucks. The C1500

454 SS, in top level Silverado trim, represented a careful assemblage of mechanical and trim parts, but not the extent of work that produced the Corvette ZR-1! Then again, the C1500 454 SS didn't cost over 65 grand!

According to John Davis, buyers wanted big blocks, with cylinder bores the size of garbage cans, … if it was a truck. Trucks and commercial vehicles don't have to meet such exacting smog, safety and fuel economy laws as cars. This makes their appeal to the Big Three even greater. Don't trouble yourself about the gas guzzler tax, and 1-4 skip shift. Indeed, trucks could prove to be the Corvette's salvation. Where there are trucks, there has to be a V8, or turbo diesel inline six. Trucks and big SUVs will probably continue to be the Big Three's biggest sellers, forever fueling V8 development. In 2023, *Autoweek* revealed that Chevrolet was working on a new version of its classic small block V8, that went beyond current LS V8 motors, for truck application. Similarly, the Dodge Ram HD retains its Hemi V8, and no doubt Ford will follow suit, regardless of the Ford EV Lightning pickup's existence. And where there's a V8, there's a path into a domestic V8 performance car, even if it's a pure big buck, niche player.

A year earlier, *Motor Week* tested the $43,600 BMW 535i, which, like the Chevrolet C1500 454 SS, also did 0-60mph in 7.7 seconds, and a 15.9 second ¼-mile. Such respective automatic transmission vehicles came with city/highway EPA numbers of 15/19mpg and 10/11mpg. Although such modes of transport achieved their sales targets, the Corvette ZR-1 struggled. It seemed very big prices were only easily swallowed by import buyers.

The 1991 Corvette's modest 20,639 total was of concern to GM management, especially given recessionary times, when money was scarce at GM. Chevrolet GM Jim Perkins was brought before the GM brass. It was part of an assessment to see if the Plastic Fantastic was still viable, and should still continue in production? Fortunately, the decision was yes, the Corvette should carry on. That said, the long running, all new, mid-engine Corvette dream would have to wait. And wait it did, until the 2020 model year and the eighth generation C8 Corvette! For there would be no $$$ R&D mid-engine money for a startlingly new 1992 Corvette.

Then again, this kind of Corvette had been a long time coming.

Corvette plays 'Piggy in the middle'

THERE WERE A number of projects that the Corvette's spiritual father, Zora Arkus-Duntov, was working on within Team Corvette and Chevrolet Engineering in general. Many weren't intended to directly be the next Corvette, but oftentimes elements would wind up on future Corvettes, eventually. In terms of a sporty ride, the Astro I prototype featured a flip top engine cover and roof. It was rear-engined, and powered by a Corvair flat six. With Astro II, a pre C3 Corvette era machine, influenced by the Ford GT40 program and Henry's Mach sports car project, the engine was in the middle, and monocoque backbone frame construction was employed. As for proto parts, Pontiac supplied its OHC inline six, Tempest transaxle, and two-speed automatic. As Duntov would later say, Astro II was canned when Ford ended its Mach project.

Serious speed was suggested by the CERV type sports vehicles. CERV I was an open wheeler racer, whose full name was Chevrolet Experimental Racing Vehicle One. Speaking about this racer to John Lamm, in the June 1977 issue of *Road & Track*, Zora Arkus-Duntov said, "I did 167mph at the Daytona Speedway, and at that time stock cars did maybe 150mph. Then I went 206 something at our proving ground." CERV II was a more refined effort, whose technical significance was far greater than that of its 1850lb weight. This machine intended for Le Mans was mid-engine, all wheel drive, and had an automatic transmission. CERV II represented a world first combination. In this case, CERV II stood for Corporate Engineering Research Vehicle Two. With the Big Four automaker anti-racing pact, and Ralph Nader on the war path, having already laid low poor ol' Corvair, GM brass didn't wish to wave a red flag to the Wowser Brigade!

CERV II was also significant for a particular mid-engine arrangement of hardware that Zora Arkus-Duntov patented. That is, a transversely placed V8 with torque converter on the end, connected to a parallel placed automatic in front of the motor, by way of a chain drive. Bevel gear and shaft then turned matters 90 degrees towards the rear mounted differential. The driveshaft went through the V8's sump, and the diff was mounted on a crossmember, behind the transverse V8. This layout would feature on all post-CERV II Chevrolet prototypes.

Mid-engine proposals and projects abounded after CERV II, during Duntov's reign as Corvette Chief Engineer. However, one big obstacle was that the C3 Late Model Mako Shark II-inspired Corvette sold so well. The long running Plastic Fantastic generation defied commercial replacement by a more complex mid-engine design of lower production volume. That is, under 10,000 units per annum. The mid-engine machine required more investment funds. GM management desires and world events also worked against a mid-engine Corvette, even into Dave McLellan's Corvette

stewardship. One very near proposal was XP-882, rushed into view at the 1970 New York Auto Show, as well as the Chicago Auto Show. This mid-engine 'Next Corvette' had styling courtesy of GM's Chuck Jordan, who also penned the Opel Manta and Rekord.

GM wanted its machine to be at the New York show, because the Pantera and AMC AMX/3 were there. This was in spite of GM saying, "… there are no plans for its production." Even so, the corporation didn't fail to mention how much comfier and more practical its exponent of the mid-engine art was. XP-882 would indeed have been roomier than either the Pantera or AMX/3. Both DeTomaso and American Motors matched XP-882 by having a/c, but only the DM Design offered automatic transmission, thanks to Zora Arkus-Duntov. Otherwise it would have been the expected mid-engine exotica transaxle. In terms of XP-882, Duntov's design utilized an Olds

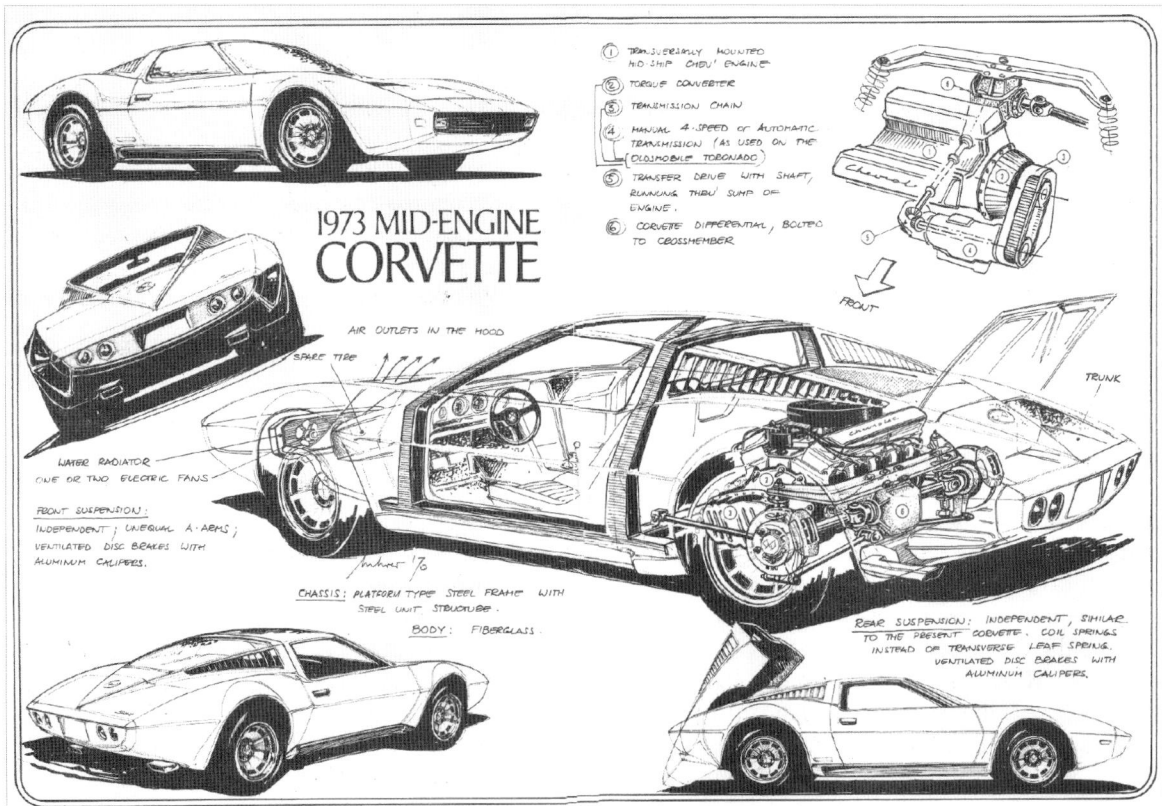

The XP-882 prototype embodied the mid-engine layout that Zora Arkus-Duntov patented from the CERV II racer. First seen at the 1970 New York Auto Show, XP-882 was believed to take on the Panter as the new Corvette from 1973. *(Courtesy Road & Track)*

GM CEO Ed Cole was behind the idea of a Wankel powered Corvette, hence the Two- and Four-Rotor Corvettes. They were also respectively known as the XP-987 GT and Aerovette. Fuel crisis thirst and rotor tip seal wear put paid to the Corvette rotary plan. *(Courtesy National Corvette Museum)*

Toronado automatic transmission, Morse Hy-Vo silent chain drive, and Corvette differential. The suspension layout was as per C3 Corvette, but with rear coil springs.

Predictably, outer panels were fiberglass, but the exact nature of the chassis was murky. It was suspected to be a variation on the separate chassis theme, with a welded tubular steel frame. Due to marketing, XP-882 would have to offer a stick shift. Due to market tastes, and those of Chevrolet Engineering, a big block 454 with aluminum heads was a given. A rear swaybar would feature as standard equipment, with all up big block weight of XP-882 coming in around 2900lb. Length, width and height were a respective 174.5in/74.8in/42.5in. Front and rear track were a respective 61.6in and 61.4in, with 15 x 8in rims at the front, and 15 x 9in rims rearwards, wearing E60-15 bias belted Firestone Wide Ovals. Four wheel disk brakes featured, naturally, with aluminum calipers, plus a Mercedes C111-like single windshield wiper! Wheelbase was 95.5in.

The XP-882 proto was completely functional, and built with a small block 400 cube V8. It was tested on the GM Milford Proving Ground; however, it wasn't put into production. At first the mid-engine Corvette was put on ice because Chevrolet GM John Z DeLorean wanted to place the Corvette on to a shared, truncated GM F body platform. With the Pantera assuming the mantle as America's best selling mid-engine exotic, XP-882 was thawed out as a 1973 model year production possibility. This time it was shelved due to GM CEO Ed Cole wanting the Corvette to go Wankel rotary. As things transpired, XP-882's alloy wheel design became a formal Corvette option from 1976 model year.

Next stop was GM's own design rotary powerplant, but not before 1973's XP-898. This prototype wasn't slated to be the next Corvette. That said, its styling and Uniframe construction would appear on the downsized 1984 C4 Corvette. A single unit of molded inner and outer fiberglass,

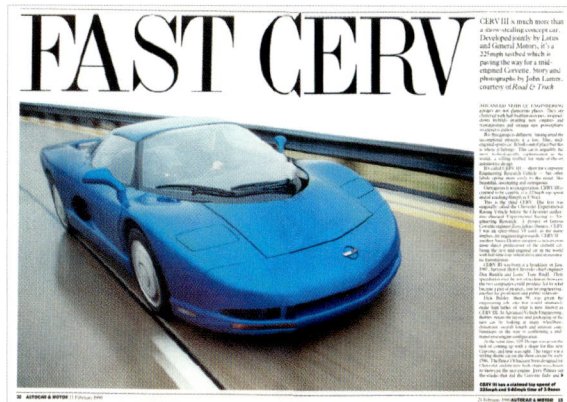

With engineering overseen by Dick Balsley, styling influence from Jerry Palmer, and technical assistance from Lotus, CERV III was a '90s successor to Zora Arkus-Duntov's CERV II. *(Courtesy Haymarket Magazines)*

with liquid polyurethane foam sandwich filling, which varied in thickness. XP-898 was good in a crash, had a quiet interior and sound performance using an inline four! Utilizing a Cosworth Vega 2.3-liter four-cylinder drivetrain, XP-898 could match the performance of the 1975 Corvette L48 350. A lowly performance target for sure, but it spoke to the recent world fuel crisis, where the same or better performance, combined with improved gas mileage, would come from physically smaller cars with reduced displacement engines. That said, fuel economy wasn't key when the '73 Corvette Two-Rotor XP-987 GT and Four-Rotor were considered. It was more the money saving of the rotary powerplant. That is, smoothness and better emissions, from a smaller engine with fewer parts, that could be cheaper to make.

Left: CERV III with its styling predecessor, the red Corvette Indy. Transforming the Indy into a genuine runner took four years. Below: CERV III is arguably the world's most technically advanced car with 4wd, 4ws and active suspension in an extremely aerodynamic body, Cd 0.277

Leather-clad interior features conventional analogue dials but sophisticated electronic displays for navigation and systems analysis. Below: Lotus-developed LT5 twin-turbocharged V8 engine develops a claimed 650bhp at 6000rpm and 655lb ft of torque at 4000rpm

'The thing that's most interesting is to have suspension, torque-split and steering actively controlled and integrated into something that's trying to do what the driver wants to do'

34 AUTOCAR & MOTOR 21 February 1990

21 February 1990 AUTOCAR & MOTOR 35

AWD CERV III was a possible new Corvette for 1995 too! *(Courtesy Haymarket Magazines)*

Featuring the 133ci GMRCE (GM Rotary Combustion Engine), this Two-Rotor machine had GM Experimental Studio style, and no pop ups! The rectangular headlamps may have influenced the later Bertone 1988 BMW Z1. XP-987 GT was built on a modified Porsche 914 chassis, with a body constructed by Pininfarina no less. GM had bought a Lamborghini Miura when doing its earlier XP-882. With XP-987 GT, unitary steel construction was combined with aluminum doors, hood and decklid panels. Pedals were adjustable, but the seats were not. The hatchback layout would appear on the 1982 Corvette Collector Edition. In XP-987 GT's case, horsepower was 180bhp, with the transverse engine layout driving through an automatic transmission. It was faithful to Zora Arkus-Duntov's CERV II. BY 1997, XP-987 GT wound up with UK car collector Tom Falconer in Kent. Its original GMRCE was replaced with a Mazda 13B rotary.

The next step was the Four-Rotor Aerovette, which came with two joined dual rotor RC2-195 GM Research Engineering units, displacing 195 cubes each. A real dream car, with the equivalent of 585 cubic inches, and over 500 net horses. Not only that, but a Bill Mitchell directed gullwing body. GM Styling boss Mitchell, until his 1977 retirement, wanted car guys working for him, "… with gasoline in their veins." Aerovette proved that desire, with a XP-882 matching 42.5in height, fixed gullwing glass, fiberglass skin, over structural members of steel and aluminum. There was an onboard computer, and digital readout. All far out elements on the 1973 car show circuit. The plan was for this rotary Corvette to cost no more than a piston Corvette.

The Four-Rotor got quietly mothballed for some key reasons. The fuel crisis made thirsty rotary power less than ideal. Then too, the Muskie Smog Bill was coming into effect for 1975, bringing super

Pop classical duo MARIERIKA with the 2024 model year mid-engine C8 Corvette! *(Courtesy MARIERIKA www.facebook.com/ marierika2006/)*

Zora Arkus-Duntov never lived to see a production mid-engine Corvette. The 2020 C8 Corvette made good on that dream. *(Courtesy MARIERIKA www. facebook.com/marierika2006/)*

stringent emissions targets. However, the biggest impediment was the specter of rotary powerplant unreliability. It was intended that the Vega related 1975 Monza coupe would debut with the GMRCE, so too the AMC Pacer. However, GM pulled the plug on GMRCE. The culprit was the infamous, rotor tip seal wear.

Going on the word of an ex GM Delco Moraine plant employee, said plant was tooled up to make the rotors for the GMRCE. Factory engine test cells had the GMRCE making a little over 300 horses SAE net. The problem was that the test engines couldn't make it to 30,000 miles, at best, before the rotor tip seals wore out. This necessitated an engine tear down, and rebuild with new seals. So, for durability reasons, the Chevrolet Monza came out with a 262ci version of the Chevrolet small block V8. The Four-Rotor prototype made a 1976 show circuit comeback, with a V8 in place of the rotary powerplant, and the sobriquet Aerovette. With the end of the GMRCE program, all rotary related Delco Moraine plant tooling was scrapped. GM wasn't the only one taken in by the rotary promise. Ford, Mercedes, and even Rolls-Royce paid NSU for rotary licenses to produce and develop the wondrous Wankel. So, rumors of an all new rotary powered Corvette for 1975 came to nothing.

The next magic date for the mid-engine Corvette was 1980. As ever with the Plastic Fantastic, designers and engineers mostly used what they had to hand. Given the fuel crisis, the hardware available was now different. Coming out of 1974, GM had the thirstiest fleet of the Big Four. This was no problem when gas was cheap, and big was King. Naturally, GM was biggest in size and sales.

However, with the fuel crisis and changing buyer tastes, MPG became the new BHP, and CAFE/gas guzzler tax were on the way for 1978. GM engaged in 15 billion bucks worth of downsizing, according to *Road & Track*'s Victor Appleton, in February 1977's issue.

GM had taken a look at weight saving in 1974, with an aluminum bodied Corvette prototype. Of unit construction, this mid-engine proposal with XP-882 powertrain layout, and a cast iron Chevrolet Mouse Motor V8, saved 40% in poundage versus an all steel design. Yet again, this aluminum proposal was thought to be the next Corvette, coming to a dealer near you soon. Styling was a development of the Two-Rotor XP-987 GT look, but with pop up headlamps and NACA hood ducts.

The project represented a feasibility study by Reynolds Metal Company, concerning its relatively new 2036-T4 alloy. GM worked with Reynolds to create a duplicate of a comparison steel prototype. With a view to a future mid-engine Corvette, the study observed the problems of mass production in aluminum. The necessity of increasing metal thickness, to combat aluminum's reduced resistance to beam loading, and spot welding challenges. In the end, weight saving at GM, and for the Corvette, took an even more comprehensive corporate approach.

GM's 1973-80 investment program of smaller and lighter, implied that the existing model lines the Corvette took hardware from were in the process of being superseded by a fuel efficient, frequently front drive, '80s line up. With the Chevrolet 305 becoming the entry level V8 for 1977 Camaro and Caprice, Dave McLellan considered a turbo 305 V8,

Apart from bringing the mid-engine layout to the Corvette nameplate, factory available export market right-hand drive spec was another C8 Corvette first. *(Courtesy MARIERIKA www.facebook.com/ marierika2006/)*

Well received by press and public alike, the C8 Corvette maintains Corvette tradition in its affordability for an exotic. 2022 MY sales of 34,510 make it a segment top seller too! *(Courtesy MARIERIKA www.facebook.com/marierika2006/)*

combined with Olds/Seville Bendix injection, in a 2200lb Corvette. That light, because the Chevrolet Nova's GM X car replacement, would offer up lighter, scaled down hardware than heretofore seen at GM. They were items that Team Corvette could arrange, in the CERV II layout manner of Zora Arkus-Duntov, to create the long awaited, mid-engine Plastic Fantastic. Unfortunately, this plan created something else.

Just as Ford's Mazda MX6/Probe plan produced a vehicle character not in keeping with the Mustang ethos, the mid-engine turbo V6 'Citation Corvette' would have been alien to traditional Plastic Fantastic devotees. Given the technology of the day, the blown V6 wouldn't have been capable of that instant, get up and low end go of even an L83 350 V8. Plus, a body shape covering a mid-engine layout would have once again fallen short of the forceful feel brought by a short deck, long hood leviathan that the Corvette faithful had grown accustomed to in post Mako Shark II times. Therefore, it came as little surprise that in late 1977 it was formally decided that the C4 Corvette would retain the nameplate's usual front-engine, rear drive layout. There was also a practical, commercial element to the decision. Powerful, mid-engine sports cars tended to be owned by very well heeled individuals. A plaything in their car collection, if you will. Corvette owners tended to be more down to earth. Their garage treasure might be an only

car, or a much used second car, that had to possess some modicum of utility; for example, the C4 Corvette's useful hatchback, and largely worry free conventional drivetrain. As Corvette Chief Engineer Dave McLellan would subsequently ask, where were the volume selling mid-engine cars?

Even so, the second gas crunch, CAFE, and perpetual fear of the gas guzzler tax kept the idea of a 2500lb mid-engine, turbo V6 Corvette alive, this time for 1988 model year. However, falling gas prices by the mid '80s, and relaxation of CAFE goals, plus perhaps even the letter writing campaign that prevented the Probe becoming the next Mustang, maintained the C4 Corvette's existing trajectory. That said, the new GM-Lotus liason revived Zora Arkus-Duntov CERV II thinking from 20 years earlier! It was at a June 1985 breakfast meeting between Chevrolet Chief Engineer Don Runkle and Lotus Engineering Chief Tony Rudd, that a successor to CERV II was conceived, called CERV III (Corporate Engineering Research Vehicle Three). CERV III was like a high-tech, road-going '90s update of Duntov's '60s Can Am racer-like CERV II, a response to the Jag XJ220. CERV II and CERV III were both mid-engine, AWD, automatic transmission two-seaters, with a transverse V8 layout, in keeping with Zora Arkus-Duntov's racing precedent.

At the aforementioned breakfast, proof of being the most important meal of the day, it was agreed to create a technical showcase, with one vehicle for engineering and one for PR. So it was, that a 39-year-old Dick Balsley of GM Advanced Vehicle Engineering oversaw and directed the engineering of CERV III. On the other side of the ledger, GM Design was in charge of producing a new mid-engine Corvette shape quickly, to hit the show circuit early in 1986. The new Ilmor V8 race engine would be showcased by this non-functional styling car, subsequently called the 'Pushmobile'. This Pushmobile or Corvette Indy, had its design overseen by Jerry Palmer, and was unveiled at the Detroit Auto Show in January 1986. The functional Corvette Indy version was worked on by Lotus in late 1986, and finished in January 1987. This running model was a test bed for CERV III technology. CERV III was, in effect, the 3rd Corvette Indy: a vehicle created with a view towards a produceable Corvette, for sale to the public.

The CERV III had a version of the LT5 V8, a motor that was being prepared for the 1990 Corvette ZR-1. Lotus engineers added not one but two Garrett T3 turbos, beefed up conrods, 8.5:1 Mahle pistons, with 12lb of boost to make 650bhp at six grand and 655lb/ft at 4000rpm. And, like Zora Arkus-Duntov had worked out on CERV II back in the '60s, power went through a torque converter, on the end of the crankshaft, to a parallel six-speed automatic, via a multilink chain. There was a differential splitting power to bevel gears, to front and rear Positraction lsd diffs.

CERV III was planned on paper with a manual transmission, just like XP-882 was intended to feature a compact three-speed manual box, but was built with an automatic. As Dick Balsley said, "I think that in the future the manual, or at least the clutch pedal, is going to disappear." [120] Just wait for the 2020 C8 Corvette!

CERV III was much bigger than the C4 Corvette, that is: 193.6in long, 80in wide and 45.2in high, on a 97.6in wheelbase. It was around the same length as the upcoming 4th gen GM F body. CERV III's body was carbon fiber, with Kevlar and Nomex, plus a thin veneer of fiberglass for perfect finish. The drag factor was a mere 0.277 Cd. Balsley and team identified maintenance to be a problem on exotics like the Countach and Testarossa – the solution? An easily removable body! Lotus liked a backbone

chassis, so that's what CERV III received, with carbon fiber construction, meaning the chassis weighed just 38lb.

Technology abounded on CERV III, like double braking with pad/rotor/pad/rotor/pad. It was all hidden by eight lug rims. The prototype's two steering racks had the smaller of the two permitting up to nine degrees of rear wheel steer. Inside, one console green screen had navigation mapping like James Bond's Aston Martin DB5 in Goldfinger! A second color console screen gave performance/ vehicle warning readouts. Steering, braking and handling were all computer integrated and coordinated, like steering assist for sidewinds. CERV III claimed top speed was 225mph, and it could scoot to sixty in just 3.9 seconds. Although not intended for production, it was designed to be makeable on an assembly line. What's more, a business case had been prepared, so yes, this was no rolling fantasy.

GM designers preferred realism to designing in abstract, it was more interesting. CERV III was done to provide ideas for the next Corvette. Design chief of GM at the time Chuck Jordan, and others, felt it was essential to do a mid-engine plan, with every Corvette proposal. It crucially provided perspective on proportions. Others at GM felt only one avenue should have been considered.

CERV III was a 4½ year project, and Chevrolet's Don Runkle said it was interesting that the car did what the driver wanted, and that it was essential to experiment with active driver aids, which Lotus did for suspension. In a perfect world, you would have been able to buy CERV III as the next Corvette. For 1995 model year, in fact. However, GM's precarious financial state in the early '90s world recession implied zero investment for a mid-engine Corvette at that moment. Pencil in one of those for 1998, but even then the coming of the all new front-engine layout 1997 C5 Corvette, which featured the new LS1 V8, dashed the mid-engine Corvette dream yet again!

New wine in the C4 Corvette bottle – LT1 V8

CORVETTE SALES FELL from 23,646 in 1990 to 20,639 in 1991, and were 20,479 in 1992. That last figure was composed of 14,604 coupes and 5875 ragtops. Respective starting prices for the 1992 Corvette coupe and convertible were $33,635 and $40,145. Yes, a base Corvette ragtop had cracked the 40 grand barrier! What's more, a white 1992 Corvette convertible would turn out to be (when it rolled off the Bowling Green, Kentucky assembly line on July 2 1992) the one millionth Corvette ever made! Zora Arkus-Duntov and other Chevrolet notables were on hand to greet the milestone machine. This Corvette convertible then made the less than one mile journey to the National Corvette Museum.

It had taken 24 years for the Corvette to reach the half million mark, 1953-77. Now, 15 years later, another half million. The greater sales speed of the later C3 Corvette and early C4 Corvette eras helped shorten the timeframe. In 1979 and 1984, Corvette sales had topped 50,000 units per annum, so what happened? The early '90s recession was a big part of the problem. As Ken Gross wrote in the September 1991 issue of *Automobile* magazine, 1991 had been a terrible year for the US auto industry. Sales were down 15.9% versus 1990. Luxury European makes were 23.8% lower in sales, with Porsche 52.5% down! New York Porsche dealers were discounting stock 30%, but Porsche was still profitable in America, due to the brand's high prices. The Corvette was also still turning a profit from lower sales numbers.

In North America, Porsche was never far from Corvette conversations, and it seemed Zuffenhausen's front-engine four pot family, a quasi Corvette rival, was in a world of sales pain. Porsche dealers wanted something like the Honda NSX. They wanted new, and the warmed over, slow selling leftovers that were the Porsche 944 S2 and 968 weren't cutting it. Compared to Porsche and others, the Corvette was still doing good business, with one exception, ... Corvette ZR-1.

Back in May 1989, *CAR*'s Ian Fraser said that Corvette "... is a valuable property that has earned huge respect around the world, mostly without any assistance from its makers." It's true that GM brass had long considered the Corvette to be a mere

trifle, while they concentrated on family cars and trucks. The skunkworks Corvette had made its own way, energizing Chevrolet and GM in the process. With the 1990 King of the Hill Corvette ZR-1, GM had finally given the hallowed Chevrolet nameplate its fair due, as Fraser wrote, "The Big Sleep Is Over," with the best Corvette yet, and probably the best value in the sporting car universe. However, 1992 Corvette ZR-1 sales fell to just 502 coupes, or one quarter of their 1991 level! The recession, Dodge Viper, and the RPO ZR1's high $31,683 price tag were all impediments. The last item especially so, in light of the new for '92 Corvette LT1 V8.

As shown with *Motor Week*'s 1989 Corvette L98 coupe report, the Plastic Fantastic's engine code had become the car's model name too. *Road & Track* said the same when testing the newly powered 1992 Corvette LT1, which the journal called "A new traditionalist". What exactly was Corvette LT1? In a sentiment relayed by *Performance Car*'s John Barker in April 1992, the brand new Corvette LT1 was, effectively, 'Son of

The 1990 Nissan 300ZX Twin Turbo is reputed to have pushed Corvette on to 300 horse, with its new standard 1992 LT1 5.7-liter V8. *(Courtesy The Motor Company)*

the King of the Hill Corvette ZR-1' and, "… raises a doubt over the future of the much more expensive ZR-1 which, although it has close on 400bhp, isn't much quicker in real terms." *Motor Week*'s host John Davis concurred with this viewpoint, when the TV show tried the '92 Corvette LT1 V8. With 0-60mph in a scant 5.4 seconds, it was a mere half second slower than the exalted Corvette ZR-1. A 1991 *MW* test of the outgoing Corvette L98 350 six-speed produced 0-60mph in six seconds flat. The older car was 0.5 seconds tardier, with a trap speed 7mph slower than the 13.8 second pass at 104mph, managed by *Motor Week*'s '92 Corvette LT1 six-speed. *Road & Track* said when last testing a '91 Corvette L98 350, said coupe was beaten by a Dodge Stealth R/T Turbo in both 0-60mph and the ¼-mile. However, the latest LT1 V8 powered Corvette had the measure of the opposition, regardless of price. And you got all that performance as standard equipment.

Performance Car **April 1992**

The 1992 Corvette LT1 V8, with 300bhp at five grand and 330lb/ft at four grand, was dubbed 'Son of King of the Hill' by some. So close was its performance to the exalted Corvette ZR-1. *(Courtesy Jabaay Motors)*

	Corvette LT1 Auto	Jaguar XJR-S	Porsche 928 GT
Weight (lb)	3307	3925	3572
0-60mph (sec)	5.8	6.1	5.5
0-100mph (sec)	14.6	14.7	13
Top speed (mph)	162	159	165
¼-mile (sec)/ trap speed (mph)	14.3/100	14.4/100	14.0/105
mpg	17.8	15.1	16.1

It explained the King of the Hill getting dethroned, as it were. The new LT1 5.7-liter V8, or 5733cc, from a 4.00in bore and 3.48in stroke, is sometimes also referred to as the Gen II. This was because it was a major reworking of the Chevrolet small block V8 Mouse Motor that the Bow Tie brand introduced way back in 1955 model year.

The Corvette LT1 produced 300 SAE net bhp at five grand, and 330lb/ft at four grand. The motor also sported a 10.5:1 CR. It was the kind of compression ratio a regular Corvette mill hadn't witnessed since before 1971! Back to the good ol' premium fuel era. The outgoing L98 350 made 245bhp at 4000rpm and 340lb/ft at 3200rpm, using a 10.0:1 CR. Obviously, the new motor was more hi po in nature. It enjoyed a good rev! Aluminum heads for a small block OHV V8, and four-bolt mains, useful for a 5700rpm redline. The LT1 V8 was happy to reach that limit on a 100 degree day, according to *Road & Track*.

Yes, the modern day LT1 V8 was smoother, revved more freely, and had a wider power band than ye olde L98 350, which fell flat by 4500rpm. *Performance Car* magazine in April 1992, said that although basic in design, the LT1 V8 was undeniably effective. It offered storming performance allied to a super sound. It was a better sound, in fact, than the Porsche 928 GT's V8, according to *Performance Car*'s John Barker. The Corvette LT1 V8 was the fastest accelerating automatic car, that the journal had ever tested. However, there was a distinct lull in the Corvette's fire-power at 100mph.

Versus L98 350, the LT1 V8 had a less restrictive air filter, and one piece intake plenum with short, large diameter runners. The TPI intake had long, thin runners to maximize torque. The LT1 V8 also had better porting, and a less restrictive exhaust side. A cast iron exhaust manifold replaced the L98 350's stainless steel headers. Not just inhaling and exhaling, the camshaft had a sportier profile too. Revised computer controlled ignition timing, the coil pack era had started, along with dual exhaust oxygen sensors and dual cats for more efficiency. The icing on the cake was reverse flow cooling.

The LT1 5.7-liter V8 implied radiator coolant going to the head first, not the block. Post head, the coolant went to the block, then back to the radiator. There was a gear driven water pump, and the thermostat lived on the inlet side. The motor's higher comp ratio was helped by cooler coolant visiting the area nearer the sparkplugs and valves first. This led to a hotter cast iron block, with higher cylinder bore temperature that implied reduced ring bore friction. Therefore, Chevrolet could switch to synthetic 5W-30 motor oil, Mobil 1 recommended. There was no need for the Corvette's previous HD oil cooler. So, no extra lines, and leak sources.

Car and Driver June 1992

	Corvette LT1 Convertible 6sp	Porsche 968 Convertible 6sp	Nissan 300ZX Convertible 5sp
0-60mph (sec)	5.3	6.1	6.8
0-130mph (sec)	29.2	37.6	63.4
¼-mile (sec)/ trap speed (mph)	13.9/100	14.7/95	15.4/91
Top speed (mph)	157	148	137
Lateral (g)	0.87	0.87	0.87
70mph-0 (ft)	173	172	171
EPA City/Hwy (mpg)	17/25	17/26	18/24
Test mpg	16	19	18
Weight (lb)	3480	3280	3580
Test price ($)	41,765	54,745	39,500 (est)

The 1992 Corvette LT1 brought power and control, with a standard traction control system, co-developed with Bosch. Called ASR (Acceleration Slip Regulation), the Corvette's traction control utilized the ABS wheel speed sensors, to cut torque by retarding the ignition spark/reducing the throttle, while at the same time applying the rear brakes independently of each other. *Road & Track* called the latest Plastic Fantastic, "... the first all-weather Corvette." The driver would feel ASR working, via a pulsating gas pedal, and see ASR's operation via a warning light on the center console's warning screen. In dry conditions, *Road & Track* found 0-60mph to worsen by 0.5 seconds with the traction control on. ASR automatically turned on every time the Corvette was started. However, you could turn it off using a switch above the headlight control. In any case, *R&T* said the Corvette's ASR was a lot less Big Brother like than the equivalent system on the Nissan 300ZX Turbo.

You had more grip all the time, thanks to the Goodyear Eagle GS-C tire design, which Corvette had an exclusive on for '92 MY. These GS-Cs were a replacement for the Goodyear Gatorbacks seen since 1983. GS-C implied a wider inner groove that channeled water away. Fitted to 17 x 9.5in Saw Blade alloys, the GS-Cs were sized 275/40ZR-17. Subjectively, they felt better than Gatorbacks, but *R&T*'s 0.89g lateral grip '92 Corvette LT1 result was inferior to the last Corvette L98 350's 0.91g skid pad reading it obtained in 1991. Corvette's FX3 SRC active suspension system cost $1695 in 1992, and was optioned by 5840 buyers. Its software was revised for more ride comfort, while maintaining handling prowess in 1992 model year.

Measures had been taken to beef up the C4 Corvette's Uniframe rigidity over time. Like incorporating the C4 Corvette convertible's strengthening tricks, on the coupe. *Motor Week* acknowledged Team Corvette's success in reducing squeaks and rattles. *Road & Track* said the revised FX3 placed overall ride quality in the grand tourer

The Corvette got a jet fighter style cockpit for 1990. Come 1992 and faceplates and buttons were all black, plus the digital speedo was above the gas gauge. Night illumination was orange. *(Courtesy Jabaay Motors)*

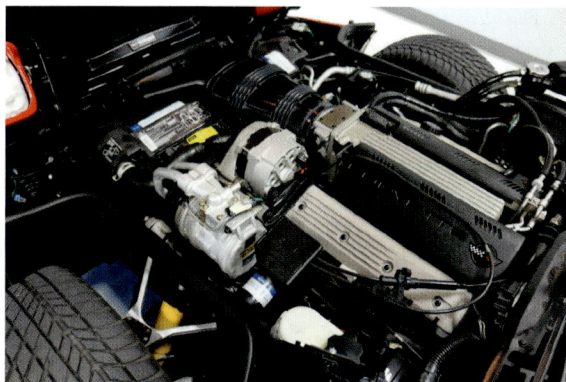

For '92 MY you got the 300bhp reverse coolant flow LT1 V8, and standard ASR (Anti Slip Regulation). However, you also got Optispark electronic ignition. The latter was positioned under the water pump, and was often associated with engine timing gremlins. *(Courtesy Jabaay Motors)*

class, albeit with a floaty, wallowing feel in Touring mode. However, others still wished for more chassis rigidity. *Performance Car*'s John Barker said in April 1992, "The Corvette has more grip than a Velcro factory, but the chassis isn't rigid enough to exploit it." At the same time, the Corvette still didn't like bumps in the road. The test coupe didn't have FX3, and Barker said they would like to try it, to avoid the body panel shakes. As ever, on smooth surfaces, the Corvette provided fast, flat handling. *Car and Driver*'s Dom Schroeder, mentioned the Corvette's Uniframe improvements for 1992. However, the magazine's test Corvette ragtop six-speed, still exhibited shake, rattle and roll. There was a flexing of the turn signal lever, and a rumbling gearbox, in the June '92 issue's report.

The Corvette had been on an evolutionary refinement path since 1953. For 1992, that trip brought improved weather sealing strips, and better insulation for the doors and the transmission tunnel area. The Corvette's electrical system power delay function was extended to the passenger door for 1992. *Road & Track* said improvements in sound deadening and weather strip sealing caused the Corvette's horn to be nigh on inaudible inside the two-seater! Among small alterations during 1990-91, the Corvette's instrument faces and buttons, had been a respective gray and black. Now they were all black, and *Road & Track* favored this all business approach, compared to the previous two-tone affair. That said, *R&T* noticed that the Corvette's right flank gauges, showed an increase in values as the needles went down. What's more, such readouts were non linear. The journal felt that a serious sports car required serious gauges. For 1992, the Corvette's digital speedo now lived above the gas gauge. 1992 Corvette ZR-1s also featured newly added front fender ZR-1 callout badges. For all '92 Corvettes, there were two squared off exhaust outlets. L83 and L98 350 Corvettes had four round openings. And a six-way power passenger seat was

At $33,635 base list, the '92 Corvette was a value for money standout. The color is the C4 perennial No 1 choice, code 81 Bright Red, the rims are 17in Saw Blades, seen from '91 MY. *(Courtesy Jabaay Motors)*

optional on '92 Corvettes. It had been four-way.

Unfortunately the CAGS (Computer Aided Gear Selection), or 1-4 skip shift, still annoyed every magazine tester and owner that wielded the Corvette's six-speed stick. When the coolant was hot enough, and the vehicle speed low enough, using under 35% throttle invited a Big Brother gear change, from first to fourth! As compensation, the Corvette still avoided the gas guzzler tax. Concerning the 1988 BMW M6 and Porsche 928S4, respective EPA city/highway ratings of 10mpg/19mpg and 15mpg/23mpg, brought gas guzzler surcharges of $2250 and $650. Since Chevrolet GM John Z DeLorean's decision to raise Corvette prices, and the inflationary 1970s, the ever rising Corvette price has been a constant bone of contention. Raising the Corvette's price higher with a gas guzzler tax would have shaken sales which had been in decline since 1984.

Something also to consider had been the Corvette's drive to frugality. The 1988 BMW M6 five-speed had a range of just 166 miles. In September 1970, *Road & Track*'s big block Corvette LS5 454 automatic got close, with a range of 162 miles. In comparison, the 1992 Corvette LT1 six-speed, with two overdrive ratios (first 2.68, second 1.80, third 1.31, fourth 1.00, fifth 0.75, sixth 0.50 & 3.45 axle) was practically an econobox!

For '92 MY, code 103 White Leather interior was optionable, something only available previously during 1976-77 and in 1988. Indeed, RPO AR9 White Leather base seats costing $555, and RPO AQ9 White Leather sports seats retailing for $1180, carried a price premium over non white leather equivalents. AR9 and AQ9 were selected by a respective 752 and 709 Corvette fanciers in 1992. 3416 buyers went for the $325 UJ6 low tire pressure warning indicator, and 738 Corvette fans chose the $2045 Z07 Adjustable Suspension Package, available for coupes alone. With exterior colors, Charcoal Metallic, Steel Blue Metallic and Turquoise Metallic ended at the close of '91 MY. However, code 43 Bright Aqua Metallic and code 73 Black Rose Metallic were new hues for 1992. Code 35 Yellow was the least popular color, just 678 '92 Corvettes were so painted. Code 81 Bright Red Metallic was still No 1 in Corvette land, chosen on 4466 1992 Corvettes.

Inside, Saddle was replaced by code 643 Light Beige Leather. Saddle was an interesting Corvette interior shade. It was introduced with the new Mid-Year Corvette of 1963, and remained available through 1974 model year, with the exception of 1968. Saddle then returned with the 1984 C4 Corvette, and, for the first time, with cloth insert possible. As ever, changing fashions covered clothes, cars and home interiors. By '92 MY, climate control a/c, Delco-Bose stereo and power driver's seat, were all part of Preferred Equipment Group #1.

In praise (mostly) of the C4 Corvette LT1

IN GENERAL, PRESS and owner conclusion concerning the 1992 Corvette LT1 was that it was a good car worth owning. Then too, with

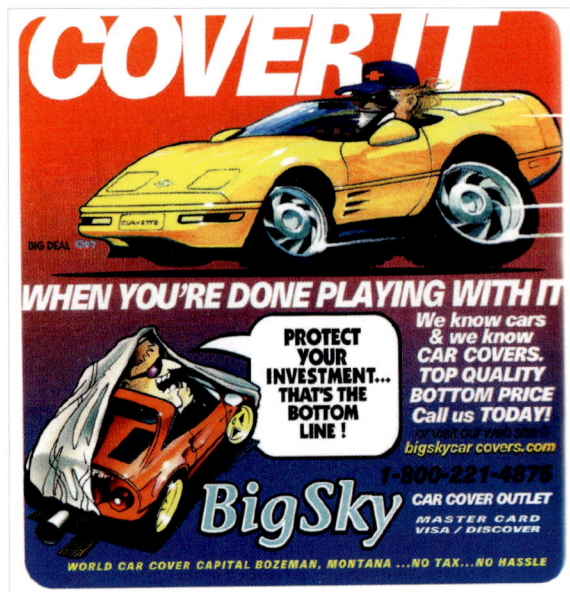

Artist Dave 'Big' Deal depicts a late C4 Corvette with somewhat nemesis the Ferrari 308 GTS. Not everyone wanted to be Magnum PI, eh Enzo?! *(Courtesy Big Sky)*

reference to country & western music, *Road & Track* characterized the latest Corvette as a New Traditionalist. The New Traditionalists, or 'Men in Hats' like Garth Brooks, were considered the perfect antidote to the over-produced, synthetic pop C&W that seemed to have infected Nashville. This modern revival brought back feelings of the good ol' days, like Merle Haggard and Waylon Jennings, while still bringing something new to the table.

In recent years the Japanese automakers had introduced high tech, high powered sports coupes. The 1990 Nissan 300ZX Twin Turbo, Mitsubishi 3000GT, FC Mazda RX7 Turbo II, and Toyota Supra were long on innovation, short on feeling. Possibly akin to driving a four wheeled computer! Keeping it real, the latest C4 Corvette LT1 5.7L V8 brought back some old school rough housing, blended with useful electronic driver aids. It worked, and the value for money was plain to see. *Performance Car* magazine could see smiles per mile, with John Barker noting that the '92 Corvette LT1 V8 was fantastic value for money, £15,000 less than a Jag XJR-S, and £30,000 below the Porsche 928 GT. True, the Corvette didn't have the suspension refinement or slushbox smoothness of the Jaguar. The Corvette's 4L60 four-speed auto thumped, where the Jag's GM THM 400 slurred, but, "... you could have two Corvettes for the price of the Porsche."

In the April '92 issue of *Performance Car*, John Barker said no one would guess that the Corvette was half the Porsche's price. He noted that in early evening traffic out of Manchester, England, most folks were rubber necking at the aubergine Corvette. Plus, given the traffic congestion, the Corvette's automatic was a blessing. The Corvette's dashboard was considered a little wacky, in such restrained company at least. This was pretty much the first time that the UK press had experienced the Corvette's post-1989 dashboard. Previously, when the Corvette ZR-1 was tried at the European press launch, such 1988 build date prototypes still had the old slab style, Breadloaf type dashboard, with Atari 2600 look instruments. The current Corvette's dashboard, with its blend of futuristic curves, bizarre instruments, and flight deck interior with orange lighting, was considered far out!

Performance Car noted that the C4 Corvette LT1 had a lot going for it: fine driving position, lots of toys, looks, performance, economy at a neat price. Even at the imported £34,000, instead of the home market $34,000, the Corvette was judged a good deal and, "... we'd have to say that the Corvette is most handsome, being the only one that looks great from all angles." At home, *Motor Week* said the Corvette was one of its perennial favorites, with a blend of power, handling and style "... and by sportscar standards a reasonable price." The improvements for 1992 took *MW* by surprise, as host John Davis said, "After all the great things Chevy added for '91 we thought there was no room for improvement, but we were wrong!" Its conclusion to the report "A Quick Look", was that the Corvette improved upon its reputation, "... as one of the best balanced and most forgiving sports cars ever built." Were more improvements up its sleeve? 1978 Corvette owner John Davis said, "We can't wait to find out!"

Road & Track said its test red coupe, picked up from Phoenix, Arizona for a jaunt to *R&T*'s Newport Beach California office, was well put together. *Car and Driver* found its '92 Corvette LT1 ragtop came

with spotty build quality. However, the convertible aspect was a snap to use. It was a manual system that could be put up or down, in less than one hot minute! The top fitted under a sleek fiberglass cover, and the Corvette looked a million bucks, with the top up or down. The Nissan 300ZX cabrio came with an awkward looking rollbar, and the top wasn't so easy to use, but the Nissan had a stouter structure than the Corvette. The 300ZX was, "Smooth, relaxed, friendly: the Dick Clark of sports cabrios." *C/D*'s Porsche 968 cabrio on test, although, like Corvette, using ASC for the convertible conversion, didn't have such an easy top to work with.

You needed wrenches to unfasten the top from the Porsche's windshield header. The Corvette's virtues, in *C/D*'s opinion, were: almighty power, Adonis looks, convenient top. However, quality and Uniframe shake, rattle and roll were questionable. As a sports car, the Porsche was tops in the Vallecito Mountains, light and nimble. The chassis was flex free, but the four cylinder engine according to *C/D* sounded like a hopped up '74 Corolla, with a Super Trapp muffler! For 20 grand over a comparable Corvette convertible with automatic, *C/D*'s December 1992 test of a Porsche 968 Cabrio Tiptronic left something to be desired, according to John Phillips.

With slowing Porsche 944 sales, Porsche moved four pot production to Zuffenhausen, and the 968 ragtop came from ASC's Heilbronn werks in Germany. Even so, *C/D*'s test Tiptronic 968, saw its right side reversing mirror fall out of its housing. The collar holding the turn signal/wiper stalks shifted a lot, the rubber molding around the wheelwell fell off, and the trunk remote release cable just dangled in the door jamb hole. It even tore flesh! The cabrio's 0-60mph in eight seconds flat, and 16.1 seconds ¼-mile at 90mph, were also slow at a price that *Car and Driver* called reckless.

If you go back to the pre 3-liter Porsche 911 era, Zuffenhausen's North American wares had a reputation for great handling, high price and no better than adequate acceleration. So, perhaps the Porsche 968 was a true Porsche after all?! As for the Corvette LT1, *Car and Driver* said only the Dodge Viper offered a quicker ragtop. Perhaps recollections are what legends are all about? *CAR*

'It reminds me of American cars of another era. And the pizza I just ate'

magazine's 1990s US correspondent was New York attorney Jamie Kitman. In his column "Lost In America", he sampled the new, or reborn, '95 Impala SS. This Impala had a detuned Corvette LT1 mill. Kitman was in Manhattan, after a pizza from V&T's Italian Restaurant. The whole experience made him think back to his childhood in mid '70s Leonia, where a local pizzeria's pie twirler had a blue '66 Corvette 396 roadster, with factory hardtop. Said pie twirler did two 360s on the street to entertain the neighborhood brogadacio! An expensive car for a pie twirler, underworld connections were suspected. Wasn't the Corvette L78 396 V8, 1965½ only? You remember what you remember … [121]

1993-94

WHEN *ROAD & Track* tested a 1957 Fuelie Corvette and a 1992 C4 Corvette LT1, it got 0-60mph in 5.7 seconds from both cars. However, the progress in 35 years with comfort, passive safety, handling,

CAR's US correspondent, New York attorney Jamie Kitman, tried Corvette's detuned LT1 V8, in a '95 Impala SS. He also recalled a pie twirler who owned a big block Mid-Year Corvette, in mid '70s Leonia. *(Courtesy CAR)*

braking, etc, was tremendous for all cars, including the Corvette. For 1993, the Corvette's standard rims were machined differently, and there were some rolling stock revisions. The front of regular coupes, and ragtops, changed from 17 x 9.5in to 17 x 8.5in rims, and from 275/40ZR-17s to 255/45ZR-17s. The rear rims remained at 17 x 9.5in, but tires were upsized from 275/40ZR-17s to 285/40ZR-17s. Little chance of oversteer in normal driving! The Z07 Adjustable Suspension Package, still solely for coupes, had taken over from Z51 as the standard export Corvette default already. In 1993 North America, Z07 still cost $2045, with its order rate lifting to 824 coupes, and implied 17 x 9.5in Saw Blades wearing 275/40ZR-17s all around. The Goodyear Eagle GS-Cs, now shared with the GM F body, were redesigned to cope with cornering stresses on inner and outer edges, concerning '93 Corvettes. And on a Corvette, expect some cornering stresses!

For '93 MY, the LT1 V8's heatshield went from a one piece to a two piece stamping of sandwich construction, for quieter living. Torque was up from 330 to 340lb/ft, at a lower 3600rpm. This was achieved through a modified camshaft exhaust lobe profile. It produced shorter inlet stroke duration, longer exhaust stroke, with no increase in valve overlap. As Ford would find on new 1994 4.6-liter Modular Mustangs, buyers liked V8 torque and weren't used to pokey power delivery. In Corvette's case, buyers had gotten used to the L98 350's immediate 'on cam' feel. A further '93 MY refinement was the new thermo-polyester valve cover material, replacing magnesium covers used from 1984 Corvettes. There were also extra gaskets under the head's mounting hardware.

To make life easier, 1993 Corvettes also had PKE (Passive Keyless Entry). The Corvette recognized its driver when the owner drew near. A code was then sent to one of two antennas, in the driver side door and rear deck of coupes, driver door and convertible boot cover of ragtops. The driver

Chevrolet celebrated the Corvette's 40th birthday, with the RPO Z25 40th Anniversary Package, costing $1455 for coupe and convertible. *(Courtesy GM Archives)*

and passenger doors would unlock, interior lights turned on, and, most importantly, the car alarm was switched off! PKE could be programmed to turn it all off, or to unlock just the driver's door, or driver and passenger door. Corvette coupes received an extra button on the plipper, to unlock the rear hatch.

There were no 10th, 20th or even 30th Anniversary Corvettes. However, there was an RPO Z25 40th Anniversary Package retailing for $1455 extra, optioned by 6749 '93 Corvette faithful. It was available for Corvette coupe and convertible. Outside it was code 68 Ruby Red paint, inside code 793 Ruby Red Leather. Badges and insignia informed all parties of the Corvette's birthday! Rarer was the Corvette ZR-1. RPO ZR1 involved a $31,683 surcharge that 448 '93 Corvette patrons paid, and yet the model had been improved for 1993. Power rose from 385 to 405 horses, with torque now towering at 385lb/ft, up from 370lb/ft. The heads had been ported, and valvetrain modified. Electrical EGR made the LT5 V8 motor cleaner, with platinum tipped sparkplugs boosting efficiency. Like LT5, even the Corvette's standard LT1 V8, had four-bolt mains. 220 '93 Corvette ZR-1s carried the 40th Anniversary package, making such coupes even more collectible!

Corvette sales improved for 1993, to 21,590 cars. The total was made up of 15,898 coupes, starting from $34,595 and 5692 ragtops priced from $41,195. Code 10 Arctic White paint, new in '92 MY, continued. Code 53 Competition Yellow was new for '93 MY, but the least popular with just 517 Corvettes. The C4 Corvette's previous popularity champ since 1984, Bright Red, was gone! Second most popular color after the 40th Anniversary ensemble's Ruby Red, was code 70 Torch Red, with 3172 '93 Corvettes so decorated. Your cloth insert interior choice for '93 MY was limited to code 19C Black Cloth, and only 426 Corvettes were so upholstered. Therefore, no cloth after 1993!

The '93 Corvette ZR-1 may have lacked sales power, but didn't want for star power. It won *Car*

220 of the 6749 Corvette 40th Anniversary cars were also Corvette ZR-1s. With Corvette ZR-1 costing $31,683 over base coupe in 1993, and only 448 RPO ZR1 boxes ticked that year, such as this coupe with both options … Holy Collector Car, Batman! *(Courtesy Mecum)*

and Driver magazine's top speed contest, and was included in the journal's January 1994 'Ten Best' issue selection. Electrical linear EGR, plus exclusive Mobil 1 oil usage, boosted top speed from 175 to 179mph. Take that Viper! The Corvette ZR-1 was marginally cheaper for 1994, RPO ZR1 was now $31,258. The package came with new non directional five-spoke style rims. Sales of the Corvette ZR-1 stuck on 448 units, way less than ever planned. Therefore, the decision was taken that 1995 would be the Corvette ZR-1's final model year.

Like with the 1979 Pontiac Trans Am W72 400, the LT5 V8 motors in the '95 Corvette ZR-1, represented held over stock from the previous year. That is, Mercury Marine had made enough 405 horse LT5 V8s, for 1994 and 1995. The Corvette ZR-1 was still the one to get, according to the *Daily Express* Guide to World Cars 1994. For starters, this introduction: "Chevrolet's Corvette has ruled the roost as America's only true sports car since it was launched in 1953. Today, it still retains its muscle car image." Yes, by now those fine distinctions of sport compact, hot intermediate, personal car and banker's hot rod were lost in the mists of time. Now, if it had a thumping V8, by golly it was a muscle car! Fortunately, the Corvette was still considered as possessing superb handling, "... even if the suspension is a little on the firm side." And, "Huge performance on the LT-1, even more on the ZR-1." Yes indeed. "But for sheer performance, the limited production ZR-1 is the only way to go." Official stats were given as 3503lb and 19.1mpg for the 405bhp Corvette ZR-1. But what of the Dodge Viper? According to the *Daily Express*, that Viper was a limited production model, whereas almost 20,000 Corvettes issued forth from Bowling Green, Kentucky in 1992. [122] 20,479 to be precise, and 23,330 in 1994, an increase on 1993! *CAR* magazine was more dismissive of the Viper. The Dodge's dreary exhaust note was mentioned, and a chassis upset by bumpy roads. [123] As for the decision to end the Corvette ZR-1 in 1995, a decade hence historian Graham Robson said profit had won out over image. [124]

The 1994 Corvette LT1 had a more powerful ignition system, and newly sequential fuel injection. For 1993 the LT1 V8 was shared with the new 4th gen GM F body, and for '94 MY it would find its way under the hood of GM B bodies the Chevrolet Impala SS, Buick Roadmaster and Cadillac Fleetwood Brougham. However, not exactly in Corvette spec. Only Corvette had four-bolt mains, the others just two-bolt. The GM F body came with alloy heads, but used mineral oil, not synthetic. B body cars had cast iron heads. Those B body machines sported 260bhp and 330lb/ft, but in the case of the Fleetwood, the official figures were of 115mph top speed, and 0-60mph in 8.5 seconds. That said, swapping in the LT1 resulted in greased lightning, versus using the Olds 307 V8. The Impala SS LT1 V8 *Motor Week* tried in 1994 was only $21,920, and did 0-60mph in 7.3 seconds, with a 15.6 second ¼-mile at 90mph. Apart from the Corvette and F body, the GM B body cars were column shift automatic only. So yes, the Corvette had its sporting distinctions within the GM family.

By now the Corvette Chief Engineer was John Heinricy, and the Corvette's testbed platform status at GM continued apace. For example, the newly optional WY5 Extended Mobility Runflat tires. They cost 70 bucks extra, and were chosen by 2781 '94 Corvette buyers. As a prerequisite, you needed the $325 RPO UJ6 low tire pressure warning indicator, chosen by 5097 buyers. However, you couldn't run deflated for more than 50 miles, lest the tire and or rims sustained damage. That was GM's official warning.

Federal law directed that new cars have two airbags standard, and a knee bolster. So, for '94 MY the Corvette lost its glovebox (again!), stowage now being reliant on door armrest locations alone. There was also a new two-spoke style steering wheel, and the interior dash light changed from white to tangerine. 1994 Corvettes, like most cars, switched to CFC free R134a a/c refrigerant. Some cars, like the Volvo 240, made the change from R12 gas a year earlier. It was to do with a coming mandate, to stop the hole in the ozone layer getting larger. All '94 Corvette interiors featured full leather seating surfaces, albeit with less side bolstering for standard seats. Indeed, interior color schemes were now the fab four of code 143 Light Gray, code 193 Black, code 643 Light Beige or code 703 Red Leather.

Power seat controls for the $305 AC3 driver seat and like-priced AC1 passenger seat were moved from the front of said seats to the console area. Then too, you could adjust the lumbar support and side bolster. A one-touch, express down, driver-side power window button also made for easy living. The 1994 Corvette ragtop's backlight was glass, no longer plastic, and a rear defogger was standard. The 4L60E automatic, in deference to the *60 Minutes* TV runaway Audi 5000 scandal, came with a new lockout switch. That is, depress or hold the brake pedal before shifting out of park position. The price for all these improvements? The 1994 Corvette commenced from $36,185, with 17,984 coupe sales forthcoming, and $42,960 for the ragtop, bringing 5346 sales.

Two new exterior colors were Admiral Blue and the limited availability Copper Metallic. Just 116 '94 Corvettes featured the latter, whereas code 66 Copper Metallic was the rarest, and code 70 Torch Red was the most popular 1994 Corvette hue, seen on 5073 cars. Plus, the 1994 Corvette did pace car duty, with 12 black convertibles and 13 red convertibles at the inaugural NASCAR Brickyard 400. All official pace cars got a power boost, so that they could run hot laps. However, if you wanted a C4 Corvette that really ran hot, in a good way, then John Greenwood and Reeves Callaway could help.

Greenwood & Callaway – C4 Corvette tuning unlimited

CORVETTE LEGEND JOHN Greenwood had some definite views concerning the C4 Corvette: "Although the car was quite well designed, the engineering flaws simply meant that the car would never stay in total alignment." Greenwood even had thoughts on the Corvette ZR-1, saying that without the engineering flaws the C4 Corvette came with, there was no way the Dodge Viper could have beaten the Corvette ZR-1. Greenwood felt the C4 Corvette's potential was never achieved. Now, that's not to say the C3 Corvette was perfect. Greenwood confessed the C3 Corvette needed improvement too, in suspension, aerodynamics and sound dampening. With both C3 and C4 Corvettes, Greenwood's company went from production car to racer, and then street version of the racer.

John Greenwood wanted to revive the ragtop in his work, and this he did, applying bodykits, suspension upgrades, aftermarket rims and in-car audio, along with necessary improvement to braking hardware. Sound deadening and custom trim pieces on the C4 Corvette helped to cure rattles. With Greenwood chassis stiffening, the C4 became better than a stock C5 Corvette, and the tuner's tubeframe experience helped in this area. However, there was the frustration of fixing one area only to find another problem surface. Like a powerful front driver, where torque steer doesn't permit the power at hand to be used.

Greenwood found that the various C4 Corvette Uniframe on-the-line fixes, or band-aids as he put it, had to be removed and the chassis re-engineered. He said that the C5 Corvette, even with its double wishbone rear suspension, shared C4 Corvette problems, better though it was. So, Greenwood concluded that Corvette tuners didn't achieve radical power increases, in light of the big

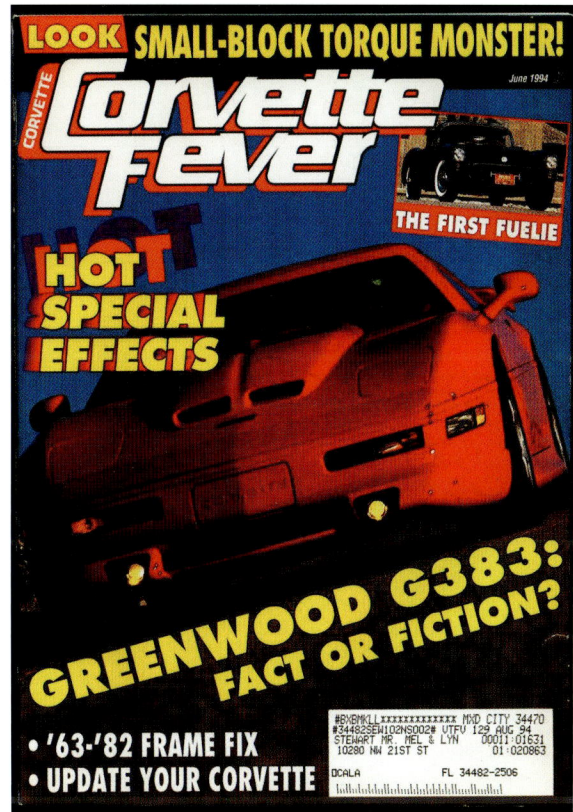

John Greenwood said some G-350 and G-383s were indeed sold. However, the Greenwood G-572 monster sadly went unrealized. *(Courtesy Corvette Fever)*

$$$ they were charging, due to the abovementioned design limitations. Greenwood cited the Callaway Twin Turbo package as a case in point. Amazing torque yes, but the chassis didn't work. Ditto Lingenfelter's C5 Corvette. It cost big money, but ETs and track lap times were inconsistent.

To solve the problem, John Greenwood created a whole new car, in his 'G-series' of supercars. A few were sold, in terms of the G-350 and G-383, but the G-572 went unrealized. In the end, the challenge was Corvette improvement at a reasonable price. Greenwood felt that not even the big surcharge he and others wanted was enough to pay for the C4 Corvette's re-engineering work, and make some kind of profit. So, the cars lost money. Ultimately, John Greenwood also considered big block power to be essential with his G-series, saying, "You have ample proof that this is the right answer, since even

The Greenwood G-383 moniker signified a
Lingenfelter Performance Engineering stroker
Corvette LT1 V8. With John Greenwood's
re-engineered C4 Corvette Uniframe
and Burt Greenwood's functional aero
addendum, the G-383 was a whole new car.
(Courtesy www.corvetteforum.com)

GM has bumped the displacement of the LS-1 to
427 cubic inches on the C5-R." The result with the
G-series was 0-60mph in three seconds and low
11s in the ¼-mile. Greenwood's annoyances also
involved the stock C4 Corvette V8's ignition system
woes, when he tried to extract more horsepower.

It has to be understood, that when the C4
Corvette was being developed in the wake of the
fuel crisis, a 200 horse 300lb/ft machine was big
stuff. A need to cut vehicle weight for CAFE and
smog restrictions meant designing the C4 Corvette's
Uniframe to cope with 1000bhp wasn't a high
priority. Back in the late '70s, even the stock 1992
Corvette's 300 horse LT1 V8 was fantasy *I Dream of
Jeannie* stuff, let alone the Corvette ZR-1's 400 plus
ponies! Limitations and problems aside, John and
Burt Greenwood still pursued their Corvette G-series

This is a genuine Greenwood G-383 Corvette. There
were some orders for the G-350 and G-383 coupes,
in spite of the latter's approximate $130,000 price tag!
(Courtesy www.corvetteforum.com)

dream cars. A gentleman's racer that went beyond
Countach, and Corvette ZR-1 even!

The Greenwood G-series coupes hailed from
the 1991-94 era. All came with race prepared
THM automatics. The G-350sc, had a Vortech
supercharged 350 LT1 V8, and cost over 100 grand.
It was the entry level Greenwood C4 Corvette! Next
up was the $130,000 G-383, with a Lingenfelter
Performance Engineering (LPE) stroker LT1 motor.
There were some orders for such small block
V8 coupes, but none for Greenwood's big block
editions. The Greenwood G-572, featured an all
alloy Keith Black 572 cube big block Rat Motor,
making 575 horse. A prototype G-572, with cross
ram fuel injection, produced 700bhp!

Engines aside, the Greenwood G-series featured
Burt Greenwood's functional aerodynamic
addendum. This included a rear spoiler that
attached to the frame, plus body. The cars had a
super rigid frame, four-wheel coil over suspension,
and anti dive/squat five-link rear suspension.
Oversize racing wheels, better tires and brakes
complemented the G-series' bountiful power.
Greenwood cars were also about quality, and a
plush leather and suede interior, and woodgrain,
along with bright colors. The worth of Burt
Greenwood's aero work can be judged from the
1991 Greenwood G4R.

The Greenwood G4R's bodykit, ground effects,
along with integrated lights on the front valence,
all worked. In driving, the aero and attendant
grip were perceivable, at even reasonable speeds.
Optional carbon fiber windshield fairings, mirrors
that reduced air turbulence, and more sound
deadening for refinement. Burt Greenwood's
aerodynamic work also improved radiator cooling,
with heat escaping via venting. Hard rubber skids
were under the front spoiler, and the rear quarter
panels, with protective paint to ward off scrapes.

Sean Roe's Greenwood bodied Corvette
dominated racing and set records in the
Bridgestone Supercar Series. All Greenwood G4Rs
were serial numbered. The plan was to have C4

If you look up the definition of 'desirable' you would probably find a picture of this car, the 1996 Callaway Grand Sport Super Natural Corvette Convertible! *(Courtesy RK Motors)*

Corvettes sent to Greenwood Performance in Sanford, Florida, for conversion work to G-series nature. The 9.4-liter G-572 V8 came with a price tag of $179,333, for which one got 0-60mph in 3.4 seconds, and an 11.51 second ¼-mile at 135mph, along with a 218mph top speed. Sadly, there were no takers for this four-speed automatic machine, featuring a reinforced chassis, and functional aero panels. Afterwards, Greenwood bodykits were offered for the C5 and C6 Corvettes, in the style of the C4 G-series Corvettes.

Greater commercial success in modified C4 Corvettes came from Reeves Callaway, but the story of the twin turbo C4 Corvette started with SVIC (Specialized Vehicles Incorporated), a Troy, Michigan outfit contracted by Chevrolet. The contract occurred because Team Corvette, Corvette Chief Engineer Dave McLellan and his crew, weren't happy with turbo V6 experiments. More was needed, and Chevrolet worked out that a twin turbo V8 would fit in the C4 Corvette. In the wake of the 1970 Muskie Smog Bill and 1975 Energy Conservation Act, which led to tight 1975 emissions and 1978's CAFE respectively, GM and Chevrolet were researching high performance avenues that would fit in with the new legislative framework. Before and during the Lotus LT5 V8 program, fuel injection, turbocharging and multivalve setups were all under consideration, hence the SVI hook up.

In May 1983, SVI was contracted to produce 16 twin turbo V8s, supplied to Chevrolet early in 1985, with the contract completed August 1985. The exercise was to observe production feasibility concerning C4 Corvette fitment of said blown V8, and the effect of the powerplant on the C4 Corvette's Uniframe. This was where Reeves Callaway's concern came in. The company's job was to come up with a complete package, meeting GM requirements without affecting the Corvette's smog equipment. So, the accumulated SVI knowledge, plus one C4 Corvette fitted with the SVI blown V8, was given to Callaway in June 1985. Reeves Callaway knew how to get a turbo package low volume certifiable, and commercially saleable.

Reeves Callaway completed a distinguished apprenticeship with Autodynamics Corporation and Bob Sharp Racing. He gained initial fame for a bolt-on turbo kit for the late '70s BMW 320i with Bosch K-Jetronic that truly was a bolt-on kit. The kit showcased his ingenuity, and was sold by BMW tuner Miller & Norburn. This start led to respected turbo kits for four- and six-cylinder BMWs through 1982. Such kits were single turbo affairs. However,

Not the usual Callaway twin turbo V8 mill, but an uprated and up-liveried Grand Sport LT4 5.7-liter V8, bored and stroked to a good ol' fashioned 383 cubes, 450bhp and 450lb/ft. Who doesn't enjoy a good old fashioned?! *(Courtesy RK Motors)*

Callaway had covered the C4 Corvette's 1990-96 jet fighter style dashboard with teal colored leather. However, this Super Natural ragtop has contemporary fashionable Alcantara suede. *(Courtesy RK Motors)*

in 1983 Callaway sold a low volume, smog legal twin turbo system for the admired Alfa Romeo GTV6 coupe. Then, it was on to twin turbo C4 Corvettes!

Engineering challenges were fuel injection and space, so Callaway bypassed Chevrolet's planned integrated, scaled fuel injection. Boost enrichment was tackled by a couple of Bosch injectors placed ahead of the throttle body. Independent of the stock Bosch L-Jetronic ECU was a separate Callaway proprietary Micro fueler II control system. Off boost, it was stock Bosch L-jet/Rochester injection. Compact Japanese IHI RHB52 turbos were mounted either side of the engine, low down, with two air to air intercoolers on top of the V8. Cooling air was admitted by two oversize NACA hood ducts. Under EPA rules, small shops like Callaway could pass smog without a complete 50,000 mile certification, since an existing engine was utilized. The Callaway deal was set up by Chevrolet Marketing Planning Chief at the time, Don Runkle. GM provided technological, logistical and financial support to Callaway Cars of Old Lyme, Connecticut.

After moving from the first four cars, with HD four-bolt main bearing Chevrolet LF5 truck blocks, much reworked L98 350 blocks were employed by Callaway for the $19,995 1987 RPO B2K package, chosen by 184 buyers. The option would live on through '91 MY. Callaway had done its GM job

within a year, producing 345bhp and 465lb/ft. Boost started from 1100rpm, with a full 10psi by two grand! Low comp forged aluminum Cosworth or Mahle pistons were fitted, plus a forged, gas nitride treated steel crankshaft. A high output Melling brand oil pump and dry sump lubrication kept things safe.

Stock aluminum heads were re-machined, with stainless steel intake and exhaust valves, plus stronger valve springs. Each and every twin turbo motor's reciprocating assembly was carefully balanced, with cooling system and transmission upgrades incorporated. Regular Corvettes left Bowling Green, Kentucky, going to Callaway in Connecticut for conversion, and then on to a participating Chevrolet dealer. There was a media meet at the GM Milford Proving Ground, as part of the Chevrolet '87 MY press preview, held in June 1986. Official stats were 0-60mph in 4.6 seconds, a 13-second flat ¼-mile at 108mph, 178mph top speed, and it was all backed by a full Chevrolet warranty. 1987's RPO B2K, offered aftermarket 17in Dymag rims, which became standard for 1988.

Not taking anyone's word for it, *Motor Week* tested a Callaway Twin Turbo Corvette against a normal production Corvette ZR-1 in 1990 at Pocono International Raceway. Previously, *MW* had only tested a proto Corvette ZR-1, at the European press launch. So, this was its first experience of a ZR-1 coupe, with the new Corvette jet fighter cockpit. First off, the Corvette ZR-1, and its standard Z51 13in front brake rotors, plus FX3 SRC. *Motor Week*'s John Davis said the 5800rpm peak power level was, "A bit high compared to what we're used to in V8s." On the ZR-1's sump capacity, "... and 12, yes 12 quarts of oil ..." The Corvette ZR-1 managed 0-60mph in 4.5 seconds, and a 12.9 second ¼-mile pass at 111mph. True, Chevrolet claimed better performance. However, Davis said, "But either way the result is enough force to nearly cure driver myopia." Rain in Pennsylvania meant top speed couldn't be verified, but wet weather traction was impressive. *MW*'s only Corvette ZR-1 problem? Only around 3000 copies to be made for '90 MY!

Next up, the Callaway Twin Turbo Corvette. *Motor Week* thought that if your Bow Tie dealership was fresh out of Corvette ZR-1s, and you fancied something a little out of left field, then the Callaway coupe could be your bag. More aggressive bodywork, with some styling touches like the 'Bubble Flush' pairs of round taillights, that polarized popular opinion. However, this car was an individual!

It was nice to see a tricked out L98 350 with Callaway Twin Turbo plenum script, and, as *MW*

said, it got 0-60mph in 4.5 seconds and a 12.7 second pass at 114mph. Therefore, the Callaway coupe would be gaining on a Corvette ZR-1! *Motor Week* made the understatement of the 20th Century, the Callaway Twin Turbo Corvette made power at low rpm, "Perhaps the best thing about the Callaway is that it comes with the blessing of Chevrolet!" Plus, said *MW*, unlike a Corvette ZR-1, you could order the Callaway B2K pack on a Corvette ragtop. *Motor Week* was mightily impressed with both special Corvettes. Every bit as competent and exciting as European exotica, that the show had taken to Pocono earlier. That included Ferrari's Testarossa, and *Motor Week* host John Davis added one more thing, "But here's what impresses us most about the two Corvettes. For the price of one Testarossa you can buy them both."

To help fulfill unfulfilled dreams, order the 1990 Callaway Super Speedster. Callaway built two of these fresh air fiends, with 750 horse twin turbo Corvette-Lotus 32-valve LT5 ZR-1 motors. They were different from what came to be known as Series 1 Callaway Corvettes, by the two intercoolers now being mounted at the front of the engine compartment. Air entered the front valence, and underhood heat was exhaled through the hood

Complete with Callaway Aero Body, those Bubble Flush round taillights polarized popular opinion. At $67,703.60, Callaway's Super Natural was a Grand Sport in both name and price, no question! *(Courtesy RK Motors)*

vents. The early '90s Callaway look involved bigger front aero, and the Speedster part implied a cut down windshield. The body was influenced by the Callaway Sledgehammer Corvette, and came with a new, and necessary, rear quarter panel come fender flare. Callaway wound up building ten 1991 C4 Corvette Speedsters, with the twin turbo L98 350 V8. For 1991, such Speedsters had 450bhp, 600lb/ft, OZ rims, Connolly leather, and a starting price of 107 grand!

The factory RPO B2K's popularity went down as the option's price went up, and the Corvette ZR-1 became more readily available. RPO B2K 1988: 124 cars $25,895, 1989: 69 cars $25,895, 1990: 58 cars $26,895, 1991: 62 cars $33,000. Eventually, the LT1, and even more hi po LT4 5.7-liter V8s, made the Corvette ZR-1 and Callaway Twin Turbo Corvettes kind of redundant for many buyers. When you have a starting point as righteous as the 1996 Corvette Grand Sport, well, why not go with that? And Reeves Callaway did just that! In came the Callaway GS Super Natural Corvette coupe and convertible. The latter being $67,703.60, which provided Corvette fans with a '96 Corvette Grand Sport LT4, with Callaway benefits.

The Callaway Aero body had an accessory hardtop, plus those signature Bubble Flush round taillights. Extended Callaway Aero Body nose clip, with Callaway crossed flags, Callaway branded hood, extended valence, and Callaway branded fuel door, between Callaway style quarter louvers. On the subject of wheels and tires: 19in powder coated CCW rims had 275/30ZR-19s on the front and 305/30ZR-19s out back. A Callaway coil over suspension upgrade, helped one keep it between the ditches.

Inside, it was a tale of soft Alcantara Ultrasuede trimmed dashboard, decorated with Callaway insignia. Callaway door cards and floor mats, customized pillars, accessory gauges and shifter knob, all carried the Callaway mark. The convertible's roll bar improved chassis stiffness, and passive safety. For a Callaway car, what lay underhood came as a surprise ... look Mom, no turbo! Yes, the Callaway GS Super Natural, featured an upgraded Corvette Grand Sport LT4 V8 motor, with 450bhp and 450lb/ft. It all came courtesy of a bored and stroked 383 cube displacement.

The sounds from the Callaway GS Super Natural exhaust were sporting, and the Corvette's ZF six-speed allied to lsd 3.45 ratio differential made for a cohesive package, as all Callaways were intended to be.

When you can practically count the number of cars on your hand, like the Greenwood G-series, it's bespoke. However, Callaway made way more than that. On September 26 1991, the 500th C4 Corvette Callaway was produced! To celebrate, add 600 bucks, for some special badges denoting the 'Callaway 500'.

1995-96, C4 Corvette endgame

1995 MODEL YEAR was a time for hellos and goodbyes in Corvette World. For starters, the opening of the new National Corvette Museum, on September 2, 1994. The museum's creation had been funded by Chevrolet along with private donations. The Corvette's first two chief engineers, Zora Arkus-Duntov and Dave McLellan were on hand for the opening ceremony. Goodbye came in the form of the Corvette ZR-1's final model year. Price and annual sales of this milestone Corvette were a repeat of 1994's result, that is, $31,258 and 448 coupes sold.

The Corvette ZR-1 was the recipient of a special send off. The Bowling Green, Kentucky line was halted at 1.12pm on Friday April 28, 1995. The last Corvette ZR-1 had been produced on Monday, with the ceremony involving the Corvette plant manager Wil Cooksey, UAW's Billy Jackson and Chevrolet GM Jim Perkins. The special coupe rolled off the Corvette production line, with Jim Perkins driving the code 70 Torch Red Corvette ZR-1, and checkered flag and retired Corvette Chief Engineer Dave McLellan in tow, to the National Corvette Museum across the street. The Corvette ZR-1 was the gift that kept on giving, in the sense that all '95 Corvettes got the ZR-1's bigger brakes, along with the new Bosch V ABS traction control system.

Ever since '92 MY, the regular 'Son of King of The Hill' had seemed like such good value, and now even more so. For 1995, the LT1 V8 came with stronger connecting rods of more uniform weight, a hushed engine fan, new injector solenoids that didn't drip when the engine was shut down, not to

The Corvette LT1 convertible paced the 1995
Indy 500. You could buy a replica of the pace car,
as shown. RPO Z4Z cost $2816 with 527 replicas
featuring an exclusive code 05/10 Dark Purple
Metallic over Arctic White exterior.
(Courtesy Smoky Mountain Traders)

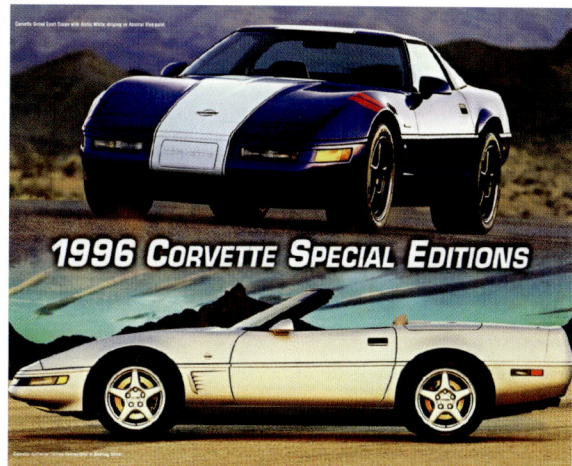

The C4 Corvette's final outing, '96 MY, saw not one
but two special editions! The Corvette Grand Sport
(RPO Z16) and Corvette Collector Edition (RPO Z15).
(Courtesy GM Archives)

mention a fuel injection system compatible with
Gasohol. Transmission wise, the 1995 story was
one of a smoother shifting 4L60E, with a lighter,
stronger torque converter. The ZF six-speed stick
now had a high detent in place of the previous
reverse lock out. Base suspension had lower,
softer spring rates. They brought better handling
on rough roads. Perhaps less need for FX3 SRC,
costing $1695, and chosen by 3421 Corvette fans in
1995?

For in-car audio, the RPO UU8 Delco-Bose stereo,
which was the big news on the 1984 Corvette,
became standard for 1994. For 1995, the 396 buck
RPO U1F Delco-Bose stereo with compact disc
facility was optioned by 15,528 Corvette fans. The
unit had a stronger mounting bracket now. Plus,
the C4 Corvette for '95 MY itself, utilized adhesive
fabric strips to reduce the Corvette's long time
bugbear of cabin rattles. French seam stitching
stepped in to solve the Corvette's leather interior
surface tearing problem. A new code 05 Dark
Purple Metallic arrived for 1995. Copper and Black
Rose Metallics had ended in 1994. Admiral Blue
commenced in '94 MY. Outside of code 43 Bright
Aqua Metallic (909 '95 Corvettes), two-tone code
05/10 Dark Purple Metallic over Arctic White was
the least popular exterior. Torch Red came tops
with 4531 1995 Corvettes adopting this shade.

Given the RPO WY5 extended mobility tires,
a RPO N84 spare tire delete was introduced to
take advantage of WY5. 418 '95 Corvette buyers
saved 100 bucks via N84. That was the cost of RPO
YF5 California Emissions Requirements and NG1
New York Emissions Requirements. The former
mandatory RPO started in 1972, the latter in 1994,
if you purchased a new Corvette in such locations.
On the rise of the Corvette LT1, against Corvette
ZR-1, Chevrolet GM Jim Perkins acknowledged that
there was too much inhouse competition between
the two. However, he added that the latter was
always intended to be a short run special. In any
case, 1995 was the C4 Corvette's penultimate year.
Corvette was still profitable, even if dealers were
discounting 'em in 1995. This was partly from the
impact of rampant SUV/pickup sales, and the LT1
V8's presence in the newish GM 4th gen F body,
plus the fact the C4 Corvette was no longer the
new kid in town. As for the low 527 buyer tally, that
went for Dark Purple Metallic over Arctic White
for a 1995 Corvette exterior, that was because this
was an exclusive combination, for 1995's RPO Z4Z
Indianapolis 500 Pace Car Replica, costing $2816!

RPO Z4Z was ragtop only, with the nearly stock
Corvette LT1 convertible good enough to pace
that year's Brickyard 500 miler. The convertible's
top was all white, headrests were embroidered,

You couldn't obtain a new Corvette ZR-1 in 1996, but this Corvette Grand Sport in exclusive code 28 Admiral Blue came awfully close. Corvette Grand Sport coupe and convertible, were limited to a 1000 unit joint total build. *(Courtesy Roger's Corvette Center)*

unique graphics and trim, added to A-mold tires introduced by the 1990 Corvette ZR-1. The code 194 Black Pace Car Replica interior was new for 1995, and a Corvette pace car exclusive, naturally. Of the 527 1995 Corvette Indy 500 Pace Car replicas made, 87 were sent to the Indy 500, 415 went to Chevrolet's top selling dealers, and 20 were exported. The Corvette's 1995 total was down from its 1994 equivalent. The figure was now 20,742, made up of 15,771 '95 Corvette coupes priced from $36,785, and convertibles accounting for 4971 units retailing from $43,665 base sticker. As for the Corvette ZR-1's all time 1990-95 total, figure on 6939 coupes. Commercial reality carries less weight at the track. Here, 1995's Le Mans 24 Hour race saw a #3 Callaway Corvette come 11th, and a #001 factory C4 Corvette finish 9th. It affirmed the C4 Corvette's reputation as an excellent production racer. Very much in the Corvette tradition!

1996, the C4 Corvette's final model year, witnessed an almost new V8 motor, and not one but two special editions! If you were sad about the demise of the GM-Lotus LT5 V8 mill, then the new 330 horse Gen II LT4 5.7-liter V8 might have put a smile on your dial. As Homer Simpson was won't to say about free chocolate chip cookies, the price was right, just $1450 for RPO LT4. You could have this motor in any 1996 Corvette, but had to be prepared for manual labor. The LT4 V8 implied mandatory NCO RPO MN6, aka Corvette six-speed stick shift. It was a lot less than the departed LT5 V8, and even the Corvette ZR-1 was stick shift only. Of course, LT4 maintenance requirements were much less than for those concerning LT5 V8. After all, the OHV LT4 was really just a souped up LT1 V8.

While LT1 and LT4 mills had equal displacement, the hi po LT4 had a higher compression ratio of 10.8:1, not 10.4:1. There were new aluminum heads, with taller ports and bigger valves. For intake and exhaust valves, a respective 2.00in and 1.55in, and to save weight, hollow valve stems were in evidence. Oval wire springs, and Crane Cam's higher 1.6:1 ratio roller rocker arms were part of the action. Versus the LT1 V8, the LT4 cam sported a more radical profile. Intake duration rose from 200 to 203 degrees, exhaust side from 207 to 210 degrees. Intake valve lift was now 0.476in, and exhaust side was 0.479in. The crankshaft, cam, water pump, drive gear, main bearing gaskets, and premium head gaskets all represented upgrades over the regular LT1 V8. Even the throttle body got redesigned. Performance testing showed a discernible, if modest, improvement in acceleration and top speed, with the LT4 V8 aboard. However, sustained top speed usage invited overheating, due to the shared LT1 oil cooler absence. Redline was bumped up from the LT1's 5600rpm to 6300rpm. Therefore, the regular 6000rpm tach, gave way to an 8000rpm unit. A freer flowing intake manifold, and roller type timing chain, underlined the LT4's seriousness and sound. It was a pushrod hi po V8 that took one back to the good ol' days. Helping with such nostalgia was an underhood dress up kit, with bright red paint and matching red ignition wires!

Continuing with the Corvette's hardware evolution, the former FX3 SRC became the improved, new RPO F45 Real Time Damping (RTD). This electronic system adjusted once every 10-15 milliseconds. Also concerning suspension, the Z07 Adjustable Suspension Package for coupes only, costing $2045 in 1995, was replaced by the returning RPO Z51 Performance Handling Package costing 350 bucks, and chosen by 1869 '96 Corvette buyers. The hardcore, infamous Z51 pack was last seen in 1990, and as ever was for coupes only. And, as in past times, the critics said Z51 made for a bad ride on rough roads. However, for track use, it was the right horse for the autocross course. As before, Z51 implied Bilstein shocks, special front and rear springing, beefy swaybars, harder bushings and now 17 x 9.5in Saw Blade rims with 275/40ZR-17s. If your '96 Corvette had automatic transmission and Z51, a 3.07 rear axle was supplied.

As for the C4 Corvette's swansong packages, there was the RPO Z16 Grand Sport Package, concerning 1000 Corvettes in an exclusive code 28 Admiral Blue, a color first seen in 1994. The package retailed for $3250 for coupes, $2880 concerning convertibles. It was the first time something Corvette convertible related was

Corvette Grand Sports could have a code 195 Black or code 705 Red/Black interior, but always a six-speed stick connected to the hi po LT4 5.7L V8. *(Courtesy Roger's Corvette Center)*

cheaper since 1975! Interiors for the Grand Sport, a tribute model to the '60s Mid-Year Corvette racers, were either code 195 Black or code 705 Red/Black. A single white stripe ran down the middle from nose to tail, with two red Sebring stripes placed on the driver side front fender. All '96 Grand Sports came with the LT4 V8 six-speed stick power team, and black 17in five spoke alloys wearing 275/40ZR-17s at the front and 315/35ZR-17s at the rear. That is, former Corvette ZR-1 tire sizes. The now departed Corvette ZR-1 had wider rear fenders and tail to accommodate such monster meats. To get around the problem the '96 Corvette Grand Sport simply used rear fender flares. C4 Corvette Grand Sport convertibles toned down to 255/45ZR-17s at the front, and 285/40ZR-17s rearwards, and no rear flares.

For those wishing for something more low key, there was RPO Z15 Collector Edition to tick. The asking price was $1250, and 5412 '96 Corvette patrons bought this Collector Edition in one exterior color: code 13 Sebring Silver Metallic. Interiors could be code 144 Light Gray, code 194 Black or code 704 Red. Coupe or convertible, it was

The 330 horse LT4 V8 was related to the regular Corvette LT1 V8, but with detail improvements like higher 10.8:1 CR and better breathing aluminum heads. The LT4 V8 could be specified on any 1996 Corvette for 450 bucks. *(Courtesy Roger's Corvette Center)*

Motor Week farewells the C4 Corvette!

MOTOR WEEK WAS there from the start, introducing the C4 Corvette to viewers in 1983. The show also performed a farewell road test, involving the 1996 C4 Corvette Grand Sport six-speed. Host John Davis noted that it was official, 1997 would witness the all new C5 Corvette, "But what about the 1996 Corvette?" "Well clearly Chevy wanted the current Vette to exit like a winner!" And objectively speaking, Davis was right, given consensus opinion concerning the C4 Corvette Grand Sport. It was a fine ride, inspired by the lightweight Mid-Year Corvette racers of the early '60s. Corvettes that took on the likes of the AC Cobra, and Ferrari coupes. *MW*'s John Davis mentioned gentlemen Roger Penske, Dick Guldstrand and Dick Thompson, and lack of development that prevented the original Grand Sport's potential from being realized. After all, Zora Arkus-Duntov had to deal with GM and Big Four anti-racing pact sentiment that threw cold water on manufacturer support for motorsport.

In the case of 1996's Corvette Grand Sport, John Davis said extra wide 17in rims, and same size rubber as the "... late lamented ZR-1" implied rear fender flares. The LT4 V8's 330bhp and 340lb/ft helped the *MW* '96 Corvette Grand Sport hit sixty in 5.2 seconds, and do a 13.7 second ¼-mile at 104mph. However, those oversize rear meats and the LT4's somewhat pokey power, led some to experience bogging off the line. That said, this coupe really shone at Georgia's Roebling Road Raceway, on the curves, where the C4 Grand Sport's SLA front and five-link transverse leaf spring rear was "at its forgiving best." Early on *MW* found C4 Corvettes oversteered when pushed, then from 1989 they understeered a mite, but now it was Swiss neutral all the way. Those Goodyear Eagles, Bilsteins, and ABS four-wheel disk brakes all added up to Corvette control. John Davis said the Grand Sport's brakes were some of the most track ready brakes found on a street car. Inside, snappy leather sports seats, with GS logo writ on the headrests, complemented the coupe's sporting nature.

Ride comfort wasn't Caddy smooth, but still wouldn't beat you up like many performance cars. Precise rack and pinion steering allied to a

a case of five-spoke alloys with Collector Edition wheel cap centers, plus black calipers bearing Corvette lettering. Chrome Collector Edition badging abounded. Perforated sports seats had Collector Edition embroidery. The Grand Sport also possessed special GS emblem embroidery on head restraints, and such Grand Sports were sequentially numbered.

As in 1993, code 70 Torch Red was pushed into second most popular exterior color spot, by a special edition color scheme. However, this time that color scheme didn't involve a shade of red, but the new code 13 Sebring Silver Metallic. The new least popular color for Corvettes in 1996 was a dubious honor that befell code 05 Dark Purple Metallic. Only 320 '96 Corvettes carried this shade. Corvette sales were slightly up for 1996, to a 21,536 total composed of 17,167 coupes and 4369 ragtops. The former started from $37,225, the latter involved folding stuff to the tune of $45,060. It was yet another milestone reached, the 45 grand Corvette roadster! Pricey for a domestic, cheap for an import, that seemed to be the Corvette's story. Plus, as ever, the Corvette was profitable. No loss leader, this halo car earned its keep!

Corvette's second Chief Engineer Dave McLellan
oversaw the C4 Corvette's development and
introduction, plus Corvette ZR-1 genesis.
So, it's fitting that he literally left his mark
on this '96 Corvette Grand Sport motor!
(Courtesy Roger's Corvette Center)

nimbleness belying the coupe's 3300lb girth was discernible. The six-speed was firm but positive. And perhaps *Motor Week*'s only complaint? That 1-4 skip shift of course. "Delete it!" exclaimed Davis. *Motor Week* said the new C5 Corvette would have to go some to beat the '96 C4 Corvette Grand Sport. Even the test coupe's $44,894 price was judged sound value and, "Nothing else this fast even comes close." In *MW*'s opinion, this was the best C4 Corvette, "This Grand Sport is clearly a nod to a proud past, but the promise of an even better future." Davis said a steel spaceframe would be the Corvette's next C5 move, but before then, a time for C4 Corvette reflection.

C4 Corvette qualities

IN SELECTING A C4 Corvette today, some factors are to be considered. The L83 350 powered C4 Corvette of 1984 had GM's widely used and oftentimes reliable TBI system, times two. However, with sheer age, the GM proprietary Rochester setup ECU governing fuel mixture and ignition timing can experience electronic gremlins that are hard to diagnose, given the lack of OBD. Then too, such

ECUs are getting harder to find, given the TBI Cross Fire era was 1982-84.

The post-1984 cars took one into the TPI era with a largely Bosch L-Jetronic ECU basis. However, even these cars are heavily electronic, running reference voltage from one system to another. For example, from wiper motor to a/c compressor, with voltage feed to the a/c. This may have been done to reduce wiring. However, the C4 Corvette wiring loom is still thick and daunting to many. 1989 Corvettes were the first Plastic Fantastics to get the ZF six-speed. The gearbox was considered good at the time, clunky now, with a heavy feel. It is expensive to repair. A CAGS eliminator kit runs 15 bucks, banishing the dreaded 1-4 skip shift! 1989 was also the first year for a factory C4 Corvette convertible hardtop. It's desirable in colder climes, but getting harder to find in good shape. 1989 Corvette six-speeds are getting harder to locate too.

1990 model year, like 1968, saw a number of one year only Corvette items, which are therefore hard to find today. This includes the instrument cluster, and driver side airbag hardware. This includes the derm to fire said airbag via impact sensors. 1992-93 LT1 Optispark Corvettes have a commonly troublesome ECU, which ends in 278 concerning the ECU part number. The ECU unit is infamous for age related, intermittent problems. Four huge plugs go into the ECU, and there is limited diagnostic feedback in this era. The connector pins pullout with age, causing a bad connection.

The Corvette's interior got slightly refined for 1994, and the nameplate received early OBD II. This was superior to the 1992-93 OBD I, concerning problem diagnosis. 1994-96 Corvettes had a different ECU that was better made. Some say Optispark is a deal breaker concerning 1992-96 Corvettes, since the ignition hardware is just under the water pump, making it vulnerable. However, others say Optispark isn't as bad as it is made out to be. 1996 Corvettes had full OBD II, a good thing for troubleshooting. Plus, the LT1 and LT4 V8s switched from bank fire to sequential fire ignition. This made for a smoother, better revving V8. That said, with any classic, condition is king. The condition of a particular car, oftentimes carries more weight than a certain year or specification level.

The next Corvette, and beyond …

BY 1992, CHEVROLET III Studio's main focus was the upcoming 4th gen Camaro. However, there was also a concept car called Sting Ray III that made its debut at the January 1992 North American International Auto Show. Sting Ray III hinted at the next generation Corvette, and the GM Design Chief wasn't too happy with how the C5 Corvette proposal was going. Therefore, he contracted Advanced Concepts Center (ACC) and John Schinella concerning a C5 Corvette plan. The result was the 'Purple Car' prototype, which provided insight concerning the future C5 and C6 Corvettes.

Like the coming C5 Corvette convertible, the Purple Car had a trunk and rear mounted gearbox, plus exposed headlights like a C6 Corvette. The Purple Car received a mixed reception, and many in GM management, and Chevrolet III Studio for that matter, didn't think much of Sting Ray III. However, the public attending the Detroit Auto Show loved Sting Ray III! The idea of a more affordable 20-25 grand Corvette really resonated. In the end, Sting Ray III wasn't carried forward, and Chevrolet III Studio boss John Cafaro finalized the C5 Corvette's look.

By the start of 1995 model year, Team Corvette's main focus was the C5 Corvette. What's more, GM announced the C5 Plastic Fantastic was on its way for 1997 model year, and it was! When the C5 Corvette did arrive, *CAR* magazine judged it a more complete global package. It rode comfy! The new all alloy LS1 V8 was prodigiously powerful. Value for money was also beyond question, "… nothing else gets close for the money." As far as looks went, *CAR*'s Jason Barlow called the C5 Corvette the maddest, baddest looking Corvette since the mid-60s Sting Ray. [125]

The stats for the new Corvette and, new water cooled Porsche 911 (996), looked like a replay of 1970. Corvette: 344bhp 356lb/ft 5.7L V8, 0-60mph 4.7 seconds, 175mph, 21.2mpg, £36,525; Porsche: 296bhp 251lb/ft 3.4L F6, 0-60mph 5.1 seconds, 174mph, 23.7mpg, £64,650. In subsequent times the 996 911 generation has been judged lacking in looks and engine durability. The latter quality not apparent when new.

CAR felt the C5 Corvette lacked sharp, nimbleness and firm control, although the gearchange was precise. Other critics at the time, and since, have judged the C5 Corvette to look a little bland, even though it was undoubtedly attractive, in a conventional way. The mood contrasted with the 1984 Corvette Z51's no compromise approach. That car was the closest a volume selling sports car got to a single seat open wheeler racer in nature! The C4 Corvette's look and style made an immediate deep impact on many: it was a classic in its own time.

Appendix A:
GM Y, F & P body

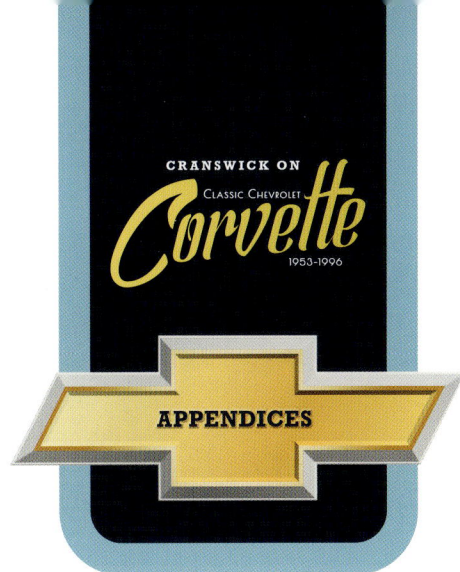

Another one bites the dust ...

ONCE THE CORVETTE had seen off '50s rivals, the Kaiser Darrin and Ford Thunderbird, they just kept on coming. In the '60s it was the Studebaker Avanti and AMC AMX. The '70s brought the Bricklin SV-1 and Pantera. The Bricklin was a Canuck coupe, and although some called the Pantera a Ford, as Bing Crosby once sang, "You're stretching it kid." No, even the '80s DeLorean DMC-12 was a touch Irish. The Corvette was the true domestic sports car, you understand? The Avanti continued in very small numbers, as Altman & Newman's Avanti II with a Chevrolet V8! This 2+2 machine was based on the Studebaker Lark platform, and AMX was a truncated Javelin unibody. Corvette was the specialist in the midst of grand tourers.

Cometh the hour, cometh the Camaro

DOMESTICALLY, THE MUSTANG was no Corvette, never was. However, the home grown sporty cars that came closest to the Plastic Fantastic did hail from the GM family, and one was even a two-seater sports car! That last car came much later. For '67 MY, the world started to get acquainted with Corvette's 'little brother', in a spiritual sense: the Chevrolet Camaro. From the outset, the relationship was carefully complimentary, and beneficial in a way impossible with the Mustang and GT40. The GT40 was too remote, esoteric, exotic even! However, with Camaro, design, hardware and image could and were, Corvette linked. As part of

Outside the National Corvette Museum, with the (from left to right) 1953 Corvette, half millionth Corvette (1977), one millionth Corvette (1992), and one and a half millionth Corvette (2009). *(Courtesy National Corvette Museum)*

Ford's Thunderbird gave Harley Earl, Chevrolet's Ed Cole, and soon to arrive Zora Arkus-Duntov, the GM brass mandate to put some fire in the Corvette's belly! *(Courtesy Marc Cranswick)*

Camaro PR came the blurb of styling that originated in the Corvette studio, and it did, Chevrolet II Studio to be precise. The new C3 Corvette's Coke bottle look made its debut on the Camaro, but was developed for Corvette first. What's more, the PR folks said the long hood, short deck style was popularized in America by the Corvette.

1962 was the final year for the Straight Axle C1 Corvette, but not for this '62 Corvette. The National Corvette Museum sinkhole incident happened February 12 2014. *(Courtesy National Corvette Museum)*

The Corvette has long been a survivor. When a sinkhole opened under the National Corvette Museum, this '62 Corvette and seven other Corvettes plunged into it! *(Courtesy National Corvette Museum)*

This '62 Corvette received only minimal damage, when falling into the NCM sinkhole. Starting price of the '62 Corvette was $4038, with 14,531 roadsters sold that year. This Corvette is Tuxedo Black. *(Courtesy National Corvette Museum)*

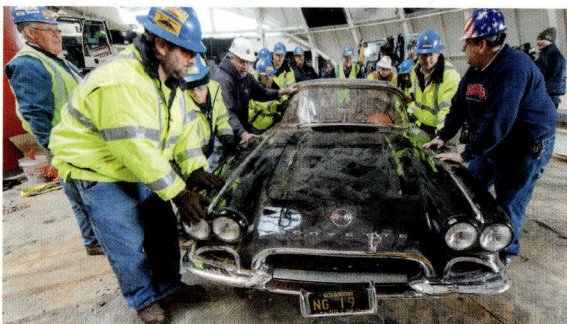

The ads said it all: Camaro was an encore to Corvette, and 1968's Camaro Z28: "It's the closest thing to a 'Vette yet." And they weren't just blowing smoke up your derriere! That Penske Sunoco Camaro Z28 had a Corvette aluminum radiator, and homologation parts for the brake kits used Corvette rotors, calipers and pads. The rear brake line adjustable proportioning valve was an HD Corvette item. Then too, Camaro's new for '69 MY 79 buck ZL-2 Cowl Induction Hood was like the system on the C3 Corvette.

The Camaro handled; it was known as 'The Hugger'. However, there were problems. *Road & Track*'s March 1967 assessment of Camaro vs Mustang vs Barracuda ponies, said these weren't sports cars, but American sedans in fancy dress. *Consumer Reports*' June 1969 report concurred, saying Camaro rode like a bouncing brick, on all but smooth roads. So, with more time to design a better mousetrap, came 'Super Hugger', and a genuine alternative to the fabled European GT machines costing so much more. Once again, the TV ad said it all, "You expect it from Corvette, but this Camaro is really a pleasant surprise." The Canyon carving in a red 70½ Camaro with faux wires, and Jag XJ6 inspired RS nosecone, promised

a reliable V8 road car that Browns Lane had yet to deliver.

Then, there was product placement. In the 1970-71 season 7 of TV's *Bewitched*, good witch (Elizabeth Montgomery) Samantha's ad-man husband Darrin parked their blue '71 Camaro in the driveway. Darrin was followed by boss Larry in his Sunflower Yellow '71 Corvette convertible. That roadster would be seen pulling up in the Stephen's family driveway in several episodes. Chevrolet had been a sponsor from the show's start. Unfortunately, a legislative smog haze ruled out a planned 70½ Camaro LS6 454 option. One had to be merely content with the 396 big block V8, really 402 cubes by now.

Road & Track called the Camaro SS 396 the best car made in America, and the Vega the best handling. The 1970 Corvette made a belated debut, but Zora Arkus-Duntov was at the press launch, with no less than a 70½ Corvette LS7 454 coupe! As *Car and Track*'s Bud Lindemann said when testing a '69 Impala 396, "From the Corvette to the Caprice, Chevy tries to be all things to all people. Maybe that's why they're number one." The Camaro Z28 continued as the closest thing to a Corvette through '74 MY. It shared a 'detuned' LT1 350, then L82 350

The '63 Mid-Year Corvette seemed dominant, but that didn't stop domestic challengers from appearing.
(Courtesy Autocar)

The Studebaker Avanti (foreground), and AMC AMX (background), didn't commercially challenge Corvette. However, the latter did pose more of a threat in SCCA production car racing.
(Courtesy Marc Cranswick)

on route. However, when safety, smog law and CAFE hit the Bow Tie Boys, a certain tin Indian called Pontiac came to the fore.

Firebird – Friend or foe?

THE FIREBIRD WAS initially GM's move to placate John Z DeLorean, for not getting his Banshee sports car. That said, from being an upscale Mercury Cougar rival, the Firebird and subsequent Trans Am carved out a performance image that was hard to ignore. The Firebird had the Big Inch 400 mill, not some measly K-code 289 or lame ass FE 390 snooze motor. And although the Firebird Trans Am never really made it big in the race series it was named after, and paid the SCCA five bucks per car sold to

use that name, it gradually became the hot car to have. Especially post-1974, when everyone else had given up. After all, it was the car that inspired the Camaro Z28's return for 1977!

The real contention started in 1973. Pontiac had a special engine, and the Corvette didn't. The Great Ones somehow brought out their Holy Grail Super Duty 455 LS2 V8 flame thrower, 310 net horses strong, probably more. The Corvette folks had the LS4 454, with a meek 275 ponies. It was the equivalent of Pontiac's L75 455 V8. How did this happen?! The coup de grace occurred, when the Trans Am SD 455 stomped on the Pantera, in the June '73 issue of *Hot Rod*. Pontiac practically put the Pantera back on the boat to Italy by the end of 1974 model year. Gone on the gondola indeed.

The closest domestic to the Plastic Fantastic? That would be the new '67 Chevrolet Camaro!
(Courtesy Exidy)

Chevrolet played on the Corvette association in Camaro ads. There truly were hardware connections between the Corvette and Camaro Z28.
(Courtesy GM Archives)

Two fantabulous sports cars from Chevrolet in the psychedelic era. How was that? Like WOW! *(Courtesy GM Archives)*

Hidemi Aoki with Dave 'Big' Deal's '70½ Camaro ZZZZZ28! *(Courtesy www.nepoeht.com)*

Leeroy Carzero cruised Rev Street, Midtown USA at 6000rpm in his Camaro ZZZZZ28. Leeroy represented a younger, less affluent Camaro buyer demographic, versus the oftentimes professional Corvette owner. *(Courtesy Marc Cranswick)*

Even once the Muskie Smog Bill had taken effect, the Trans Am was troubling the Corvette's position as the Ultra Go Fast American automobile. With Honeycomb rims, spoilers and Buccaneer Red paint, the '75 Firebird Trans Am looked just as mean and planted as it had in 1974. In Super Duty guise the Trans Am held the mantle as the last of the truly fast cars for many a year. The 1975 Trans Am's tepid L78 400, with 185 net Naderized horses, still exceeded the Corvette's base L48 350, with 165bhp! Okay, the Formula and Trans Am weighed 300lb more, but you could get a four-speed, and in the public's mind, the Corvette and Trans Am were getting equivalent.

Corvette and Firebird seemed to be jousting, amid a domestic performance sector in marked decline, or 1975½ Corvette L82 350 (205bhp) vs 1975½ Trans Am 455 HO (200bhp). Were those extra five horses the start of GM's hierarchy plan? In any case, the '75½ Trans Am 455 HO was four-speed only, and a 455 shaker decal still implied street cred unlimited. This was in spite of the humble by now, L75 455 Catalina wagon smog motor, lying under said shaker. For 1976, the Corvette L82 350 was re-rated to 210 horses at 400rpm higher, possibly to gain marketing breathing space over the renamed 200 horse '76 Trans Am 455. Don't call it HO, because it really

wasn't. With the Pontiac 455 V8 gone after 1976, it seemed Corvette would go unrivaled again, but no.

Pontiac developed a W72 400 V8 that matched the 200 ponies of its outgoing 455 V8. For an extra 50 bucks, your Trans Am had chrome valve covers, in an equivalent to the Corvette's special L82 350 option. When the Poncho W72 400 moved on to 220bhp for 1978, it was only natural that the Corvette's L82 350 would now make 225bhp, and it did! Even so, in the CB radio, *Smokey and the Bandit* era, there was nothing cooler than Bandit's Black & Gold Chariot, nor bigger than that shaker's T/A 6.6 callout decal on Trans Am W72 400 coupes. Magazines had the Trans Am W72 400 and Corvette L82 350 four-speeds running low 15s with 0-60mph in 6.5 seconds, at best. Which was greased lightning at the time, or more than Jimmy Carter thought was seemly. However, fear not tree huggers, 1978's CAFE would soon make good citizens out of one and all!

Come 1980 and things got cloudy, performance wise, but in image the Trans Am was still holding court, with Burt Reynolds in Son of Trigger aka Black & Gold Turbo Trans Am SE. The Trans Am had been GM's most profitable car of the late '70s. Not as expensive as Corvette you understand, but more sales volume. Half of '76 Fire Chickens were Trans Ams, and as written by *Road & Track*'s Victor Appleton in February 1977, buyer studies showed

That non stock GM 6/71 blower helped Leeroy avoid retired hermit Jed Cluffer's shotgun buckshot! *(Courtesy Marc Cranswick)*

The Camaro Z28 shared its engine, 1970-72 LT1 350 and 1973-74 L82 350, with Corvette. However, Zora Arkus-Duntov was always miffed at the association, saying the LT1 350 originated with Corvette. *(Courtesy Marc Cranswick)*

DKM sold two Corvette L-82S coupes. Only seven of its '79 Camaro Macho Zs ever got beyond this one '78 prototype. Amazing coupe, but only Corvette could charge big money. DKM had planned 200 Camaro Macho Zs! *(Courtesy Hot Rod)*

that the Trans Am was eroding Corvette sales by 1976, with the latter defaulting to hardcore Plastic Fantastic fanciers.

The Trans Am's big inch image and great handling, in an American auto era that now valued the latter quality, was pushing the Fire Chicken as the nation's premier performance car. In 1979, the WS6 Formula and Trans Am joined the Corvette in being some of the few domestics with four-wheel disk brakes. The Turbo Trans Am was a tad doggy in 0-30mph, but matched a 1980 Corvette L48 350 in acceleration, the L82 350 optioned '80 Corvette was a rare sight. 1981 was the start of times when Corvette gave up being the fastest car in a particular model year, because something big was looming. It would happen again in 1987 and 1989, with these years, along with 1981, all being related to the Buick's turbo system. In 1981, the Turbo Trans Am with electronic Q-jet had a definite edge on the 1981 Corvette L81 350. The Corvette's mile high CAFE gearing that year produced a one whole second deficit in 0-60mph and ¼-mile acceleration times, versus the Turbo Trans Am, in some magazine reports.

Corvette rules OK?

WAS THE CORVETTE ever really commercially challenged by the GM F body? The answer seems to be no, different cars for different crowds was the answer. Car buying, when it came to hot rides,

was a little more practical back in the day. A lot of fellas needed a back seat, and a real trunk. Those qualities alone ruled out the Corvette, regardless of how road car effective it was. American Motors officially said it canned its two-seater AMX because showroom visitors requested a back seat. Hence the '71 Javelin AMX.

In demographic studies, the Camaro owner was oftentimes younger, not so flushed with funds, nor as educated as the Corvette crowd. Think of TV's *Bewitched*, with ad agency boss Larry owning that '71 Sunflower Yellow Corvette ragtop. For Camaro Z28, think more *Fast Times at Ridgemont High*. Did the Trans Am really steal Corvette sales? If it did, you wouldn't have noticed, because it's an accepted fact Corvette's St Louis plant production could never keep up with demand, even or especially in the 1977-81 Bandit era. Plus, Corvette, Camaro

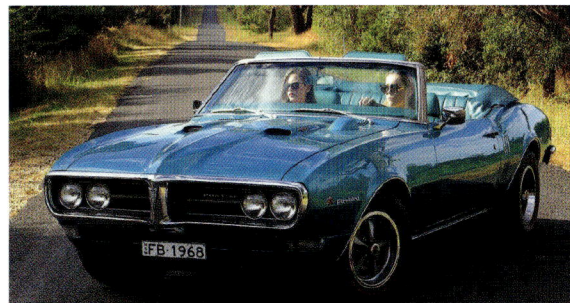

The Pontiac Firebird started as an upscale Mercury Cougar rival, but it didn't stop there. That big inch Poncho V8 allowed this little birdy to fly its own course! *(Courtesy Larry McGrath & band Chicanery)*

Junior borrowed Pappy's Tirebird, so Pappy was late for the Trans-Um race! *(Courtesy Marc Cranswick)*

Z28 and Trans Am all set sales records in 1979, with respective totals of: 53,807 units, 84,877 units and 117,108 units. In truth, each of these cars was running its own race.

The commercial difference between a Y body Corvette and the F body 2+2s was also shown by their response to tough times. Between August 1978 and August 1979, domestic auto sales fell 20%. Chrysler Corp had nearly gone bankrupt in 1978. There was a prediction that 25% of new car dealers, would be out of business by the end of 1979. The Corvette and F bodies seemed to weather this storm. However, the 1979-80 fuel crisis, economic downturn, and imports taking 30% market share for the first time in 1980, seemed to affect the Camaros and Firebirds more. Certainly the gas crunch was part of the reason for the imports flying high in 1980.

At a time when a 50 day surplus stock was normal, the GM X body cars were on 60 days, and the Foxstang/Capri siblings had 70 days excess,

according to *Motor Week*'s 1980 TV pilot episode. For 1980, Corvette sales fell to 40,614 units, but Camaro Z28 and Firebird Trans Am sank to a respective 41,825 and 50,898 units. This calls into question management's hierarchical power plan for GM's sporty cars, but maybe there was some reason to do this post-1981? For 1982, the new downsized GM F body would join the C3 Late Model Corvette, the latter now in its final year. For the rationalized 1980s, there would be no Chevrolet, Pontiac, Olds, etc, V8s – just GM family engines. The new F bodies were sized only slightly larger than the current Corvette. The '82 Firebird even sported a super sleek shape, with pop up headlamps. Both F bodies were now hatchbacks, just like the 1982 Corvette Collector Edition.

The F bodies, once again matching Corvette, featured an automatic transmission only Cross Fire Injection V8, but in 305 cube LU5 form. The bigger L83 350 was reserved for the Corvette. Pontiac had planned to offer turbo and non turbo versions of its 301 V8, for 1982. The blown 301 V8 in the new lighter Firebird, would have produced performance equal to the 1984 Corvette. The '82 Firebird featured an asymmetric hood bulge to clear the 301 turbo's air cleaner. Publicity photos of the 1982 Turbo Trans Am V8 were taken. However, the GM corporate gods decided that only Chevrolet, Oldsmobile and Cadillac could retain their own design V8s for 1982.

Junior had to get the Tirebird free from Ma's elm tree! As a great handling street car, with punch, the Fire Chicken had a medium block V8, 100lb lighter than Chevrolet's big block. *(Courtesy Marc Cranswick)*

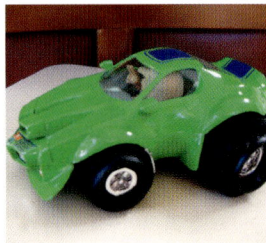

From 1971 through 1974, Firebird Formula and Trans Am offered hot and really hot V8s. The Tin Indian went Super Duty in 1973-74, to which Team Corvette had no answer. *(Courtesy Marc Cranswick)*

Corvette lost the big block LS4 454 V8 at the close of '74 MY. Pontiac retained its mild L75 455 through 1976. Buyer studies showed Trans Am was purloining Corvette sales in 1976. *(Courtesy Marc Cranswick)*

GM's Corvette and Trans Am had an image, and possibly sales, drag race during 1975-81. *(Courtesy CAR)*

This was when the GM hierarchical plan hurt the F body. The new Camaros and Firebirds needed more motor to compete toe-to-toe with the lighter, cheaper and faster, but cruder, Foxstang. No stick shift for the LU5 305 CFI V8 either. The '82 Camaros and Firebirds really needed a detuned L8 3 350, but no dice. Once again, the F body and Corvette received TPI (Tuned Port Injection) for 1985, but the ponies were limited to automatic 305 cube LB9 V8s. The F bodies also got a detuned version of the Corvette's L98 350, for 1987 model year, but only with a slushbox. It's true that the F body's BW T5 manual transmission couldn't handle the L98 350's torque. Plus, the Doug Nash 4+3 box used in the Corvette, that could cope with the torque, was a real pig to shift, even if GM allowed its usage, which it didn't.

GM's '80s plan was on show in *Motor Week*'s TV comparison from 1985, concerning the Mustang GT 5.0 hatchback, versus the Firebird Trans Am HO L69 305/5 speed, versus Camaro IROC-Z LB9 305 four-speed automatic. Testing took place at the Maryland 75-80 Dragway and at Pocono International Raceway. That is, ¼-mile and road circuit evaluation for coupes with respective weights around 3200lb, 3400lb and 3600lb. Prices were in the same relative order, Mustang cheapest, Camaro priciest and Trans Am piggy in the middle, oink! At the drag strip *MW*'s John Davis said the IROC-Z's TPI motor carried a torque advantage, but the lighter, stick shift Trans Am won out in a 14.7 seconds versus 14.8 seconds Chrondek encounter. Henry smoked 'em both, with the Foxstang's 14.3 second pass.

At Pocono the Mustang handled so badly it was comical. The Trans Am showed a lot more composure and control. The Camaro IROC-Z was like the Trans Am, only more so, with an even better lap time. John Davis summed up the result, saying the Trans Am was fast like the Mustang, but had more sophisticated handling like the IROC-Z. The expensive Camaro IROC-Z was considered a suave stepping stone to its big brother ... the Corvette! And that was the entire American performance scene in 1985. Chrysler was only represented by its fast, but front drive turbo fours. 1987 saw Pontiac go upscale with its GTA (Gran Turismo Americano). In *Road & Track*'s view it was

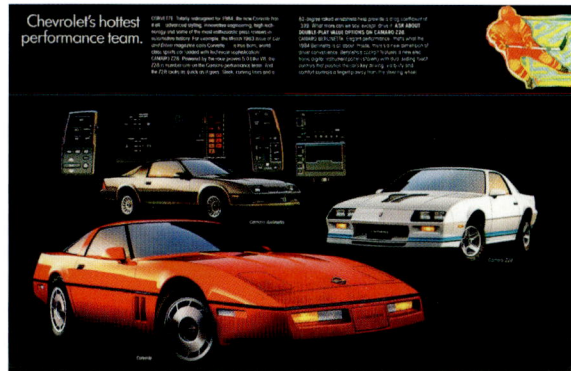

Camaro Berlinetta, Z28, then Corvette, in that order. That was Chevrolet and GM's performance hierarchy for the downsized '80s. *(Courtesy GM Archives)*

a budget Ferrari 412i, with automatic only L98 350 V8 motorvation.

America's only Fiat X1/9 ← Fiero

ONE OCCASION WHEN a sports car challenge to Corvette came from within GM was Pontiac's Fiero or P car. The project made it through GM's sports car sieve, by calling itself a commuter car project, that could in the right version, hit 50mpg! In the wake of the fuel crisis, and with 1978's CAFE showing the importance of domestically earned gas mileage credits, management gave the P car the green light. Despite two temporary cutbacks in project funding, Hulki Aldikacti's team brought Fiero to fruition as a 1984 model year debutant.

Corporate planning was for the Corvette to be GM's key image maker. However, the third gen F body really needed the Chevy 350 V8 pre-1987 to combat the smaller, lighter Foxstang. *(Courtesy GM Archives)*

The Corvette's performance pre-eminence in the GM clan, stymied Pontiac's progress with its Fiero and Firebird. *(Courtesy GM Archives)*

Mid-September 1983 to be precise, therefore post-late '83 MY (read 1984) Corvette's arrival. Fiero was a mid-engine two-seater sports car: indeed, the first American volume-produced car of this configuration. Sheet molded compound (SMC), and reaction injection molded urethane (RIM) panels, were attached to a steel spaceframe. Similar to the C4 Corvette and its Uniframe/plastic panels, with one key difference: Fiero's precision mill and drill production process, economic for a 100,000 to 150,000 unit production per annum run. Fiero's first year total was 136,840 units.

In the finest tradition of the MG T-series and Porsche 356, the Fiero utilized humble GM parts.

The rear-driven Chapman struts/lower A arm ensemble, came from the front drive GM X car, the Fiero's front suspension was the SLA set up, from the Pontiac T-1000. There were some slight modifications to these existing parts systems, but the upshot of using 'two fronts', was four-wheel independent suspension and four-wheel disk brakes, like a Corvette! Price was half that of the Corvette's, with this smaller TBI Iron Duke four pot powered car, aimed at the Fiat X1/9 and Mazda RX7 crowd.

The Fiero's early discourse involved two words: potential and conflict. Potential, since here was a versatile platform that could have taken on Porsche, Corvette et al, with more power. There was initial talk of a Chevrolet V6, and subsequent plans for a turbo V6. As *Road & Track*'s Tony Hogg said in May 1981's "Pontiac P-Car" article, "Chevrolet may be more than a little reticent to release such an engine to Pontiac because it would give the P-car Corvette performance at half the price." The Fiero paced the Indy 500, got a Citation V6 for 1985, and better suspension along with a fastback bodystyle by its final 1988 model year. In the end, nigh on 300,000 Fieros had been sold.

So, what went wrong with Fiero? There was some initial bad press from engine fires, related to substandard connecting rods produced at the GM Saginaw foundry for the Iron Duke I4. Then too, America remembered it didn't normally buy two-seater sports cars in big numbers, at least not domestic ones. The Fiero's development was also undoubtedly stymied by Team Corvette's

Pace the 1993 Indy 500? Yeah, why not?! The new Camaro Z28 with detuned Corvette LT1 V8 and standard six-speed stick, from just $16,779, was good looking value next to the $34,595 '93 Corvette LT1 V8 coupe. *(Courtesy Smoky Mountain Traders)*

By the time of this 40th Anniversary Corvette convertible it was likely sales of the Plastic Fantastic were being reduced by the all new 4th gen GM F body. *(Courtesy GM Archives)*

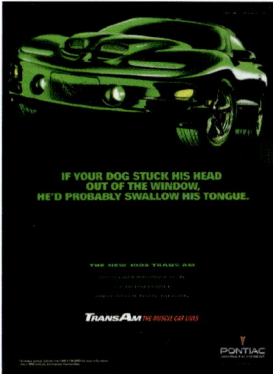

The Camaro Z28 and Firebird Trans Ams with LS1 V8s were state of the art pony cars. Streets ahead of the contemporary Mustang. However, with a shrinking passenger car market favoring truck and SUV sales, the GM F bodies and Corvette increasingly became interchangeable V8 playthings. *(Courtesy GM Archives)*

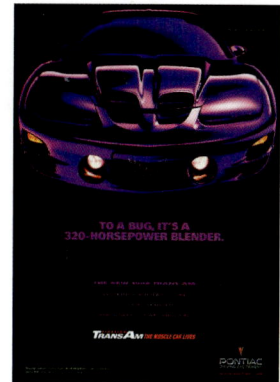

From 1987, the Corvette had been bestowing a detuned version of the Chevy 350 upon Camaros and Firebirds. By 1998, that meant the C5 Corvette's LS1 V8 exclusive was over. Time to share! *(Courtesy GM Archives)*

resistance to having an in-house rival. This was proven by the subsequent popularity of aftermarket Caddy V8 swaps into Fiero, showing the potential demand for a Fiero V8. More than this, there was also GM's habit of canceling a car once the bugs had been ironed out and it started showing promise. There were plans for a restyled 1990 Fiero that utilized the Olds 'Quad 4' motor, but unfortunately this came to nothing, partly due to GM's economic woes of the early '90s. The fact that Fiero stopped just as the Mazda Miata/MX5 was about to start showed yet another missed opportunity.

The self fulfilling prophecy ➡ GM 4th gen F body

GM MANAGEMENT HAD long had a paranoia over threats to Corvette sales, both from outside and within GM. With the arrival of the 4th gen F body, it seemed the Fire Chickens had come home to roost! The use of Fiero style SMC and RIM plastic panels on an underlying steel structure, detuned Corvette Gen II LT1 V8 mill, and, in the Firebird's case, styling influence from the exciting 1988 Banshee show car, seemed to point to a true in-house Corvette rival. A 1993 Formula LT1 V8 six-speed was $17,995, at a time when a Corvette coupe retailed from $34,595. Such 4th gen F body value for money was leagues ahead of the, by now, even more antiquated Foxstang, or even Ford's modular V8 powered successor.

With the rise of truck and SUV sales, and falling passenger car sales, the 1990s auto environment saw, for the first time, the GM F body and Corvette as interchangeable V8 playthings. Perhaps no

longer the distinctly different sporty cars. Value for money 4th gen Camaros and Firebirds may have contributed to the Corvette's soft sales numbers post-1992. Although the Plastic Fantastic remained in the black, all its year-to-year upgrades seemed to have promised better sales than eventuated. There was also a changed public perception from earlier times, with statements like: they put the big Corvette V8 in the 4th gen Firebirds, and oddly, how did they squeeze the Corvette's engine under the hood of the 2004 GTO?! In the modern world, it's all just one muscle car.

It also seems the case that the arrival of the all new, LS1 V8 powered C5 Corvette for 1997 model year contributed to the GM 4th gen F body's 2002 model year demise, even though Camaro did return for 2010 post hiatus. Once again, in the late '90s auto scene, where neither the 4th gen F body nor C5 Corvette served as practical transport, the newer and more powerful would win out. That would be Chevrolet Corvette, America's only sports car!

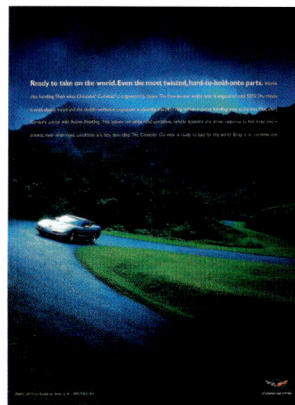

Strong, peak C5 Corvette sales of 35,627 in 2001 and 35,767 in 2002, probably contributed to the 4th Gen GM F body's demise in 2002 model year. *(Courtesy GM Archives)*

Appendix B:
Corvette Sales, Service & Groups

C&S CORVETTES – Bee Ridge, Florida
www.corvettepartscenter.com
Est 1974 – Corvette parts center. A big inventory of new and used parts.

ROGER'S CORVETTE CENTER, INC – Orlando, Florida
www.rogerscorvette.com
Est 1965 – Florida's biggest Corvette dealer, started by Roger Judski.

X FIRE PERFORMANCE – Gilbert, Arizona
www.xfireperformance.com
Catering to the 1982-84 Cross Fire Injection system, for Corvette, Camaro and Firebird. Run by Datalink engineer Tom. Apart from providing CFI products, also involved in the development and handling of the Renegade Performance intake manifold, for Cross Fire Injection cars.

BATEE.COM – Rolla, Missouri
Est 1999 by Bryan A Thompson – specialist in the repair of parts and information concerning the C4 Corvette digital instrument cluster, plus 1986-2004 HVAC controls.

CLAREMONT MOTORSPORT LTD – Kent UK
corvette.co.uk
Est 1977 – Formerly called Claremont Corvette. Started by Tom Falconer, now run by Matt Davison. Specializing in service, repair, restoration and parts. Used to sell Corvettes too.

CORVETTE CORNER – Point Cook, Victoria, Australia
corvettecorner.com.au
Parts and restoration specialist.

CORVETTE KINGDOM – Felmingham UK
www.corvettekingdom.co.uk
Est 1964 – Britain's biggest Corvette specialist, started by the Groves family. Car sales, restoration and spare parts.

WWW.CORVETTEFORUM.COM
Est 1999. Nearly 600,000 members – the biggest Corvette forum in the world!

Appendix C:
Corvette Big Block Quartet – Performance Tables

1967 Corvette Sting Ray L71 427 four-speed convertible

Price (base convertible)	$4240; L71 427 V8: $437
Motor/gearbox	OHV cast iron block and heads, solid lifter L71 427 V8, 11.0:1 CR, 3 x 2bbl Holleys/M21 close ratio Muncie four-speed, 3.55 final drive ratio
Dimensions/curb weight	175.1in length, 69in width, 49.8in height, 98in wheelbase/3340lb
Horsepower/torque	435bhp @ 5800rpm/460lb/ft @ 4000rpm (gross ratings)
Chassis	Body on frame
Suspension	Front: SLA, coils, tube shocks, 0.875in swaybar. Rear: IRS, lower lateral links, halfshafts (upper links), trailing arms, transverse multileaf spring, tube shocks
Brakes	11.75in power assisted, ventilated disk x 4
Wheels and tires	15 x 6in Rally rims and 7.75-15in rayon bias ply tires
0-60mph	5.5 seconds
¼-mile @ trap speed	13.8 seconds @ 104mph
Top speed	143mph
Gas mileage	9-12mpg (range on premium fuel)

Source: Motor Trend April 1967

You could order a Mid-Year Corvette with a mild 250 horse 327 Mouse Motor, and a 'Glide', a/c plus 3.08 axle ... this was NOT that car!

1969 Corvette Stingray L71 427 four-speed coupe

Price (as tested)	$6573.30 (includes $147.45 N14 side mount exhaust system)
Motor/gearbox	OHV cast iron block and heads, solid lifter L71 427 V8, 11.0:1 CR, 3 x 2bbl Holleys/M21 close ratio Muncie four-speed, 3.70 final drive ratio
Dimensions/curb weight	182.5in length, 69in width, 47.8in height, 98in wheelbase/3450lb
Horsepower/torque	435bhp @ 5800rpm/460lb/ft @ 4000rpm (gross ratings)
Chassis	Body on frame
Suspension	Front: SLA, coils, tube shocks, 0.9375in swaybar Rear: IRS, lower lateral links, halfshafts (upper links), trailing arms, transverse multileaf spring, tube shocks, 0.562in swaybar
Brakes	11.75in power assisted, ventilated disk x 4
Wheels and tires	15 x 8in Rally rims and Goodyear Redstripe F70-15 bias ply tires, N44 nylon cord
0-60mph	5.3 seconds
¼-mile @ trap speed	13.8 seconds @ 106.8mph
Top speed	138mph (estimate)
Gas mileage	9.5-14mpg (premium fuel)

Source: Car and Driver September 1969

In January 1968, *Road & Track* pronounced the Mako Shark II inspired C3 Corvette "A Psychedelic Car." Hit the loud pedal in this bolide, and in less than one hot minute, you would be like … FAR OUT MAN! You dig it?!

1971½ Corvette Stingray LS6 454 four-speed coupe

Price (as tested)	$7619.35 (includes $1220.70 LS6 454 and $100.35 M22 Rock Crusher HD four-speed)
Motor/gearbox	OHV cast iron block/aluminum heads, solid lifter LS6 454 V8, 9.0:1 CR, 4bbl Holley/M22 close ratio HD four-speed, 3.36 final drive ratio
Dimensions/curb weight	182.5in length, 69in width, 47.8in height, 98in wheelbase/3475lb
Horsepower/torque	425bhp @ 5600rpm/475lb/ft @ 4000rpm (gross ratings)
Chassis	Body on frame
Suspension	Front: SLA, coils, tube shocks, 0.9375in swaybar Rear: IRS, lower lateral links, halfshafts (upper links), trailing arms, transverse multileaf spring, tube shocks, 0.562in swaybar
Brakes	11.75in power assisted, ventilated disk x 4
Wheels and tires	15 x 8in Rally rims and Goodyear Redstripe F70-15 bias ply tires, N44 nylon cord
0-60mph	5.3 seconds
¼-mile @ trap speed	13.8 seconds @ 104.65mph
Top speed	152mph (at redline)
Gas mileage	9-14mpg (premium fuel)

Source: Car and Driver June 1971

The promised land of the showroom available LS7 454 V8 with 460 horse, didn't happen. However, for half a model year, the smogged equivalent LS6 454 was around. Effectively four-speed only, and no a/c, but 188 buyers ticked that RPO LS6 option box!

1973 Corvette Stingray LS4 454 automatic coupe

Price (as tested)	$7,097.50 (includes: $250 LS4 454; $452 C60 a/c; $113 N40 power steering; and $173 U69 AM-FM (non stereo) radio)
Motor/gearbox	OHV cast iron block and heads, hydraulic lifter LS4 454 V8, 8.25:1 CR, 4bbl Rochester Quadrajet/M40 THM 400 three-speed automatic, 3.08 final drive ratio
Dimensions/curb weight	184.7in length, 69in width, 47.7in height, 98in wheelbase/3742lb (with a/c)
Horsepower/torque	275bhp @ 4400rpm/395lb/ft @ 2800rpm (net ratings)
Chassis	Body on frame
Suspension	Front: SLA, coils, tube shocks, 0.875in swaybar Rear: IRS, lower lateral links, halfshafts (upper links), trailing arms, transverse multileaf spring, tube shocks, 0.562in swaybar
Brakes	11.75in power assisted, ventilated disk x 4
Wheels and tires	15 x 8in YJ8 alloys and Firestone GR70-15 radials
0-60mph	6.4 seconds
¼-mile @ trap speed	14.7 seconds @ 97.2mph
Top speed	135mph (estimate)
Gas mileage	13mpg overall – '73 Corvette LS4 454 four-speed with no a/c – Road Test June 1973 (regular/low lead gas)

Source: Car and Driver December 1972

The fabled Big Block 'Rat Motor' featured in Corvettes during 1965 to 1974. The final 1973-74 LS4 454 was a good natured, smogged LS5 motor. *Car and Driver* tested Corvette LS4 454s with both slushbox and stick shift. The former was quicker in 0-100mph, by a whole second! A precedent had been set, think C4 Corvette L83 & L98 350.

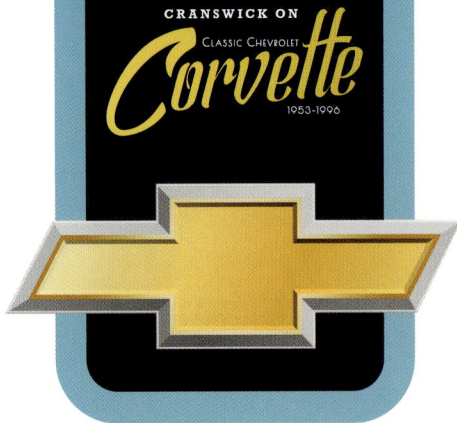

Bibliography

Adcock, Ian. "Design Switch" *Autocar* February 6 1985.

Barlow, Jason. "Newcomers Chevrolet Corvette Overpaid, oversexed, oversteer" *CAR* August 1998.

Barnett, Bernard (ed). "Sport: GM's New Target In Racing" *Autocar* August 10 1984.

Bell, Roger. "100 Greatest Sports Cars" *Autocar* June 2 1999.

Bentley, John (ed). *All The World's Cars 1954*. New York: Cornell Publishing Corp, 1954.

CAR August 1998.

Carter, Matthew (ed). "Cadillacs to feature Lotus tech" *Autocar* October 1 1986.

Chapman, Giles (ed). *The Car Book – The Definitive Visual History*. London: Dorling Kindersley Ltd, 2011.

Chapman, Giles (ed). *The Classic Car Book – The Definitive Visual History*. London: Dorling Kindersley Ltd, 2016.

Consumer Reports. "5 Specialty Cars" June 1969.

Consumer Reports. "Specialty Cars" May 1970.

Cranswick, Marc. *Cranswick On Camaro 1967-1981*. Dorchester: Veloce Publishing, 2021.

Dinkel, John (ed). "1985 Chevrolet Corvette" *Road & Track* December 1984.

Dunne, Jim. "Detroit Report – Being Brief" *Popular Science* August 1985.

Dunne, Jim. "Detroit Report – New Corvette" *Popular Science* August 1985.

Dunne, Jim. "Detroit Report – Skylark name stays" *Popular Science* August 1985.

Dunne, Jim. "GM for '86 GM's all-new luxury sedans" *Popular Science* August 1985.

Frater, Peter (ed). "Newsweek DeLorean Defence Attacks Chapman" *Motor* November 1 1986.

Garnier, Peter (ed). "World Wide Comment – Major Confrontation" *Autocar* August 31 1974.

Gillies, Mark. "Last Of The Big Spenders" *Autocar* October 1 1986.

Grove, Noel. "Swing Low, Sweet Chariot!" *National Geographic* July 1983.

Hall, Jim. "2002 Acura 3.2TL Type-S The sports-sedan value play" *Road & Track* September 2001.

Holloway, Hilton & Buckley, Martin. *The A-Z Of Classic Cars - The Greatest Automobiles Ever Made*. Victoria: Hardie Grant Books, 2015.

Holmes, Mark. *Ultimate Convertibles Roofless Beauty*. London: Kandour Ltd, 2007.

Hope, Anne. "Towards 2000" *Autocar* October 1 1986.

Huntington, Roger. "Detroit Notebook" *Autocar* August 31 1974.

Jefferis, David (ed). *Daily Express Guide to World Cars 1994*. London: Pedigree Books, 1993.

Kelly, Steve. "Road Test: Shelby GT500 & 427 Sting Ray" *Motor Trend* April 1967.

Kelly, Steve. "Sports Car Tournament: Cobra vs. Corvette" *Motor Trend* March 1968.

Kitman, Jamie. "Lost In America" *CAR* January 1995.

Lamm, John. "Ahead Of The Game" *Autocar* January 7 1987.

Lamm, John. "Fast CERV" *Autocar & Motor* February 21 1990.

Lamm, John. "Seasonal Changes" *Autocar* October 1 1986.

Lamm, John. "The converter route to a cleaner and healthier environment" *Autocar* October 10 1984.

Lamm, Michael. "Popular Mechanics Owners Report: BMW" *Popular Mechanics* July 1975.

Ludvigsen, Karl. "Fuel Injection: One Answer To Smog?" *Motor Trend* March 1968.

MacDonald, Donald (ed). "As Rumor Has It" *Motor Trend* April 1967.

Mandel, Leon (ed). "Chevrolet Corvette Coupe" *Car and Driver* September 1969.

Mandel, Leon (ed). "Opel GT 1.9" *Car and Driver* September 1969.

McDowell, Bart. "Those Successful Japanese" *National Geographic* March 1974.

Mueller, Mike & David, Dennis. *Classic Fifties Cars.* Wisconsin: MBI, 2006.

Murray, Bob (ed). "How Fast, How Good" *Autocar & Motor* February 21 1990.

Oliver, Ben (ed). *The Best of CAR: The '70s and '80s.* London: Portico Books Ltd, 2008.

Parker, Frank (ed). *Daily Express Guide To 1987 World Cars.* London: Express Newspapers P.L.C., 1987.

Radley, Kevin. "Nissan Restyle 300ZX" *Motor* November 1 1986.

Robson, Graham. *The Illustrated Directory of Classic Cars.* London: Greenwich Editions, 2004.

Rettie, John. "Sport A Corvette at Le Mans … 25 years ago" *Road & Track* September 2001.

Scott, Jason. "Project XP-833 Banshee" *Pontiac Enthusiast* July/August 2008.

St Antoine, Arthur. "Life with Corvette" *Car and Driver* February 1987.

Wakefield, Ron (ed). "1965 Fuel Injection Corvette" *Road & Track* February 1975.

Wakefield, Ron (ed). "Letters to the Editor Beyond the 55-mph Limit" *Road & Track* February 1975.

Wakefield, Ron (ed). "Used Car Classic Corvette Sting Ray 1963-67" *Road & Track* February 1975.

Ward, Daniel. "Corvette To Use Lotus Technology" *Motor* November 1 1986.

Westwood, Ashley. "Corvette C1 Authentic 50's Americana" *The Garage Journal* Volume .003 June 2017.

Wheeler, Mark. "Upwardly Mobile" *Autocar* December 17/24 1986.

Whipple, Jim (ed). *All The 1964 Models Popular Mechanics CAR FACTS.* New York: Popular Mechanics Company, 1963.

Willson, Quentin. *Great Car.* New York: Dorling Kindersley Publishing Inc, 2001.

Yunick, Smokey. "Readers Talk Back Smokey's engine update" *Popular Science* August 1985.

Endnotes

[1] Giles Chapman (ed), *The Car Book: The Definitive Visual History*. (London: Dorling Kindersley Ltd, 2011): p78

[2] Giles Chapman (ed), Ibid. p78

[3] John Bentley (ed), *All The World's Cars 1954*. (New York: Cornell Publishing Corp, 1954): p105

[4] Hilton Holloway & Martin Buckley, *The A-Z Of Classic Cars - The Greatest Automobiles Ever Made*. (Victoria: Hardie Grant Books, 2015): p81

[5] Ron Wakefield (ed), "Used Car Classic Corvette Sting Ray 1963-67" *Road & Track* (February 1975): p53

[6] Bentley (ed), op cit. p49

[7] Bentley (ed), Ibid. p35

[8] Graham Robson, *The Illustrated Directory of Classic Cars*. (London: Greenwich Editions, 2004): p118

[9] Ashley Westwood, "Corvette C1 Authentic 50's Americana" *The Garage Journal* Volume 003. (June 2017): p76

[10] Quentin Willson, *Great Car*. (New York: Dorling Kindersley Publishing Inc, 2001): p116

[11] Graham Robson, *The Illustrated Directory of Classic Cars*. (London: Greenwich Editions, 2004): p123

[12] Bentley (ed), op cit. p106

[13] Bentley (ed), Ibid. p106

[14] Giles Chapman (ed), *The Car Book – The Definitive Visual History*. (London: Dorling Kindersley Ltd, 2011): p150

[15] Bentley (ed), op cit. p106

[16] Giles Chapman (ed), *The Car Book: The Definitive Visual History*. (London: Dorling Kindersley Ltd, 2011): p79

[17] Giles Chapman (ed), Ibid. p154

[18] Mike Mueller & Dennis David, *Classic Fifties Cars*. (Wisconsin: MBI, 2006): p52

[19] Willson, op cit. p121

[20] Roger Bell, "100 Greatest Sports Cars" *Autocar* (June 2 1999): p84

[21] Ron Wakefield (ed), "Used Car Classic Corvette Sting Ray 1963-67" *Road & Track* (February 1975): p52

[22] Mueller & David, op cit. p62

[23] Mark Holmes, *Ultimate Convertibles Roofless Beauty*. (London: Kandour Ltd, 2007): p53

[24] Karl Ludvigsen, "Fuel Injection: One Answer To Smog?" *Motor Trend* (March 1968): p41

[25] Ludvigsen, Ibid. p70

[26] Holloway & Buckley, op cit. p82

[27] Ludvigsen, op cit. p41

[28] Ron Wakefield (ed), "Used Car Classic Corvette Sting Ray 1963-67" *Road & Track* (February 1975): p57

[29] Willson, op cit. p127

[30] Willson, Ibid. p126

[31] Ron Wakefield (ed), "Used Car Classic Corvette Sting Ray 1963-67" *Road & Track* (February 1975): p52

[32] Willson, op cit. p118

[33] Giles Chapman (ed), *The Classic Car Book – The Definitive Visual History*. (London: Dorling Kindersley Ltd, 2016): p33

[34] Giles Chapman (ed), *The Car Book – The Definitive Visual History*. (London: Dorling Kindersley Ltd, 2011): p152

[35] Holloway & Buckley, op cit. p84

[36] Willson, op cit. p128

[37] Giles Chapman (ed), *The Classic Car Book – The Definitive Visual History*. (London: Dorling Kindersley Ltd, 2016): p32

[38] Ron Wakefield (ed), "Used Car Classic Corvette Sting Ray 1963-67" *Road & Track* (February 1975): p52

[39] Michael Lamm, "Popular Mechanics Owners Report: BMW" *Popular Mechanics* (July 1975): p94

[40] Giles Chapman (ed), *The Car Book - The Definitive Visual History.* (London: Dorling Kindersley Ltd, 2011): p151

[41] Ron Wakefield (ed), "Used Car Classic Corvette Sting Ray 1963-67" *Road & Track* (February 1975): p53

[42] Robson, op cit. p119

[43] Willson, op cit. p144

[44] Willson, Ibid. p131

[45] Ron Wakefield (ed), "Used Car Classic Corvette Sting Ray 1963-67" *Road & Track* (February 1975): p55

[46] Jim Whipple (ed), *All The 1964 Models Popular Mechanics CAR FACTS.* (New York: Popular Mechanics Company, 1963): p96

[47] Ron Wakefield (ed), "1965 Fuel Injection Corvette" *Road & Track* (February 1975): p58

[48] Whipple (ed), op cit. p93

[49] Ron Wakefield (ed), "1965 Fuel Injection Corvette" *Road & Track* (February 1975): p57

[50] Ron Wakefield (ed), "Used Car Classic Corvette Sting Ray 1963-67" *Road & Track* (February 1975): p53

[51] Ron Wakefield (ed), Ibid. p54

[52] Steve Kelly, "Road Test: Shelby GT500 & 427 Sting Ray" *Motor Trend* (April 1967): p24

[53] Kelly, Ibid. p25

[54] Donald MacDonald (ed), "As Rumor Has It" *Motor Trend* (April 1967): p21

[55] Steve Kelly, "Road Test: Shelby GT500 & 427 Sting Ray" *Motor Trend* (April 1967): p28

[56] Marc Cranswick, *Cranswick On Camaro 1967-1981.* (Dorchester: Veloce Publishing, 2021): p6

[57] Robson, op cit. p119

[58] Ron Wakefield (ed), "Used Car Classic Corvette Sting Ray 1963-67" *Road & Track* (February 1975): p55

[59] Ron Wakefield (ed), Ibid. p54

[60] Bell, op cit. p84

[61] Jason Scott, "Project XP-833 Banshee" *Pontiac Enthusiast* (July/August 2008): p50

[62] Leon Mandel (ed), "Chevrolet Corvette Coupe" *Car and Driver* (September 1969): p44

[63] Hilton Holloway & Martin Buckley, op cit. p88

[64] Willson, op cit. p142

[65] Steve Kelly, "Sports Car Tournament: Cobra vs. Corvette" *Motor Trend* (March 1968): p56

[66] Kelly, Ibid. p55

[67] Leon Mandel (ed), "Chevrolet Corvette Coupe" *Car and Driver* (September 1969): p39

[68] *Consumer Reports.* "5 Specialty Cars" (June 1969): p318

[69] *Consumer Reports.* "Specialty Cars" (May 1970): p294

[70] *Consumer Reports.* "5 Specialty Cars" (June 1969): p317

[71] *Consumer Reports.* "Specialty Cars" (May 1970): p298

[72] Leon Mandel (ed), "Chevrolet Corvette Coupe" *Car and Driver* (September 1969): p39

[73] Leon Mandel (ed), Ibid. p41

[74] Leon Mandel (ed), Ibid. p41

[75] Leon Mandel (ed), Ibid. p39

[76] Willson, op cit. p137

[77] Willson, Ibid. p146

[78] Willson, Ibid. p150

[79] Bart McDowell, "Those Successful Japanese" *National Geographic* (March 1974): p342

[80] Noel Grove, "Swing Low, Sweet Chariot!" *National Geographic* (July 1983): p13

[81] Ron Wakefield (ed), "Letters to the Editor Beyond the 55-mph Limit" *Road & Track* (February 1975): p6

[82] Roger Huntington, "Detroit Notebook" *Autocar* (August 31 1974): p44

[83] Leon Mandel (ed), "Opel GT 1.9" *Car and Driver* (September 1969): p66

[84] Peter Garnier (ed), "World Wide Comment – Major Confrontation" *Autocar* (August 31 1974): p17

[85] Huntington, op cit. p44

[86] Mike Knepper, "SCCA Annual Run Offs" *Road & Track* (February 1975): p98

[87] Willson, op cit. p106

[88] Ron Wakefield (ed), "Used Car Classic Corvette Sting Ray 1963-67" *Road & Track* (February 1975): p53

[89] John Rettie, "Sport A Corvette at Le Mans…25 years ago" *Road & Track* (September 2001): p127

[90] Smokey Yunick, "Readers Talk Back Smokey's engine update" *Popular Science* (August 1985): p6

[91] Jim Hall, "2002 Acura 3.2TL Type-S The sports-sedan value play" *Road & Track* (September 2001): p79

[92] Bernard Barnett (ed), "Sport: GM's New Target In Racing" *Autocar* (October 10 1984): p16

[93] Jim Dunne, "Detroit Report – New Corvette" *Popular Science* (August 1985): p11

[94] Grove, op cit. p28

[95] John Lamm, "The converter route to a cleaner and healthier environment" *Autocar* (October 10 1984): p20

[96] John Dinkel (ed), "1985 Chevrolet Corvette" *Road & Track* (December 1984): p143

[97] John Dinkel (ed), Ibid. p142

[98] Arthur St. Antoine, "Life with Corvette" *Car and Driver* (February 1987): p75

[99] Arthur St Antoine, Ibid. p77

[100] Jim Dunne, "Detroit Report – Skylark name stays" *Popular Science* (August 1985): p11

[101] Jim Dunne, "GM for '86 GM's all-new luxury sedans" *Popular Science* (August 1985): p83

[102] John Lamm, "Ahead Of The Game" *Autocar* (January 7 1987): p25

[103] Frank Parker (ed), *Daily Express Guide To 1987 World Cars.* (London: Express Newspapers P.L.C., 1987): p12

[104] Ian Adcock, "Design Switch" *Autocar* (February 6 1985): p8

[105] Bob Murray (ed), "How Fast, How Good" *Autocar & Motor* (February 21 1990): p78

[106] Frank Parker (ed), op cit. p9

[107] John Lamm, "Seasonal Changes" *Autocar* (October 1 1986): p38

[108] Mark Gillies, "Last Of The Big Spenders" *Autocar* (October 1 1986): p48

[109] Anne Hope, "Towards 2000" *Autocar* (October 1 1986): p37

[110] Mark Wheeler, "Upwardly Mobile" *Autocar* (December 17/24 1986): p18

[111] Kevin Radley, "Nissan Restyle 300ZX" *Motor* (November 1 1986): p6

[112] Jim Dunne, "Detroit Report – Being Brief"

Popular Science (August 1985): p11

[113] Matthew Carter (ed), "Cadillacs to feature Lotus Tech" *Autocar* (October 1 1986): p9

[114] Daniel Ward, "Corvette To Use Lotus Technology" *Motor* (November 1 1986): p4

[115] Peter Frater (ed), "Newsweek DeLorean Defence Attacks Chapman" *Motor* (November 1 1986): p5

[116] Hilton Holloway & Martin Buckley, op cit. p90

[117] Hilton Holloway & Martin Buckley, Ibid. p90

[118] Ben Oliver (ed), *The Best of CAR: The '70s and '80s.* (London: Portico Books Ltd, 2008): p145

[119] Bell, op cit. p85

[120] John Lamm, "Fast CERV" *Autocar & Motor* (February 21 1990): p34

[121] Jamie Kitman, "Lost In America" *CAR* (January 1995): p57

[122] David Jefferis (ed), *Daily Express Guide to World Cars 1994.* (London: Pedigree Books, 1993): p21

[123] *CAR*, "The Good The Bad And The Ugly" (August 1998): p168

[124] Robson, op cit. p121

[125] Jason Barlow, "Newcomers Chevrolet Corvette Overpaid, oversexed, oversteer" *CAR* (August 1998): p35

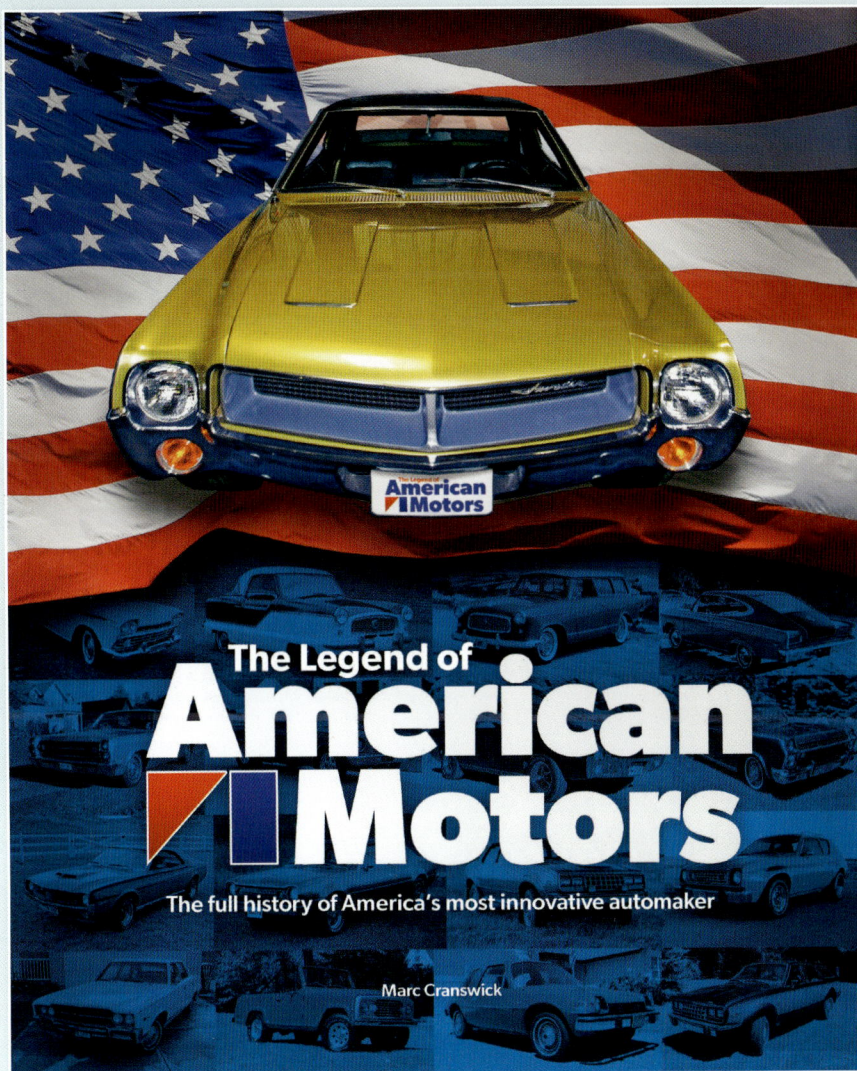

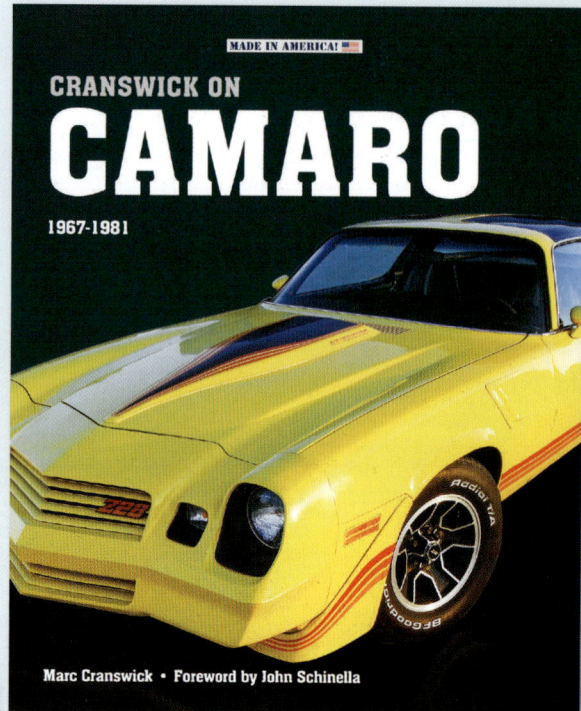

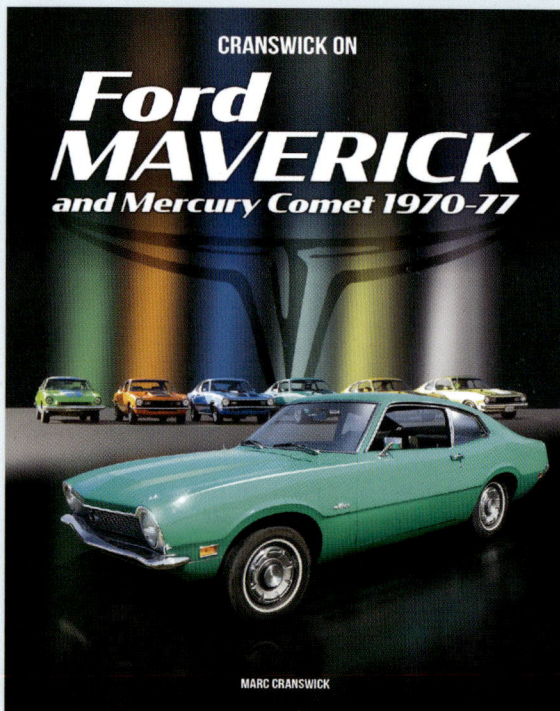

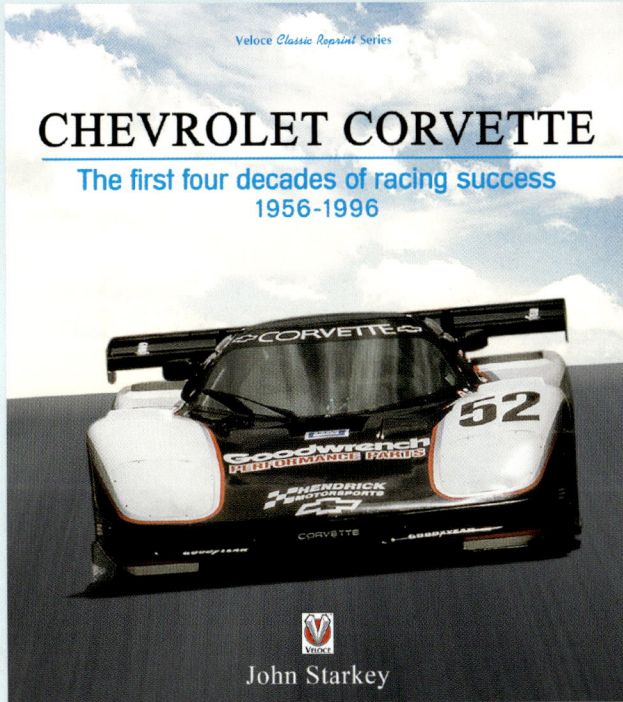

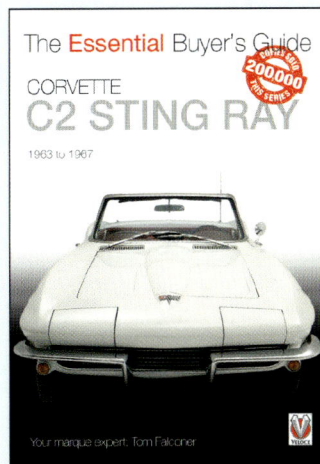

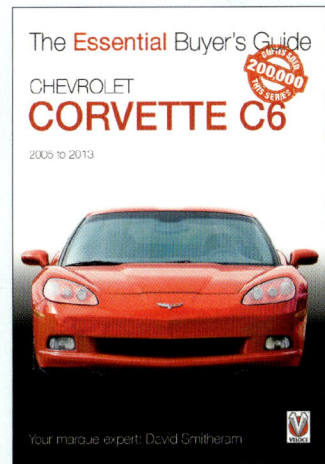

Index